A Pearson Custom Publication

BTEC Level 4/5 HNC in Computing and Systems Development

Compiled from:

Management Information Systems: Managing the Digital Firm
Eleventh Edition
by Kenneth C. Laudon and Jane P. Laudon

Business Information Systems: Analysis, Design and Practice
Sixth Edition
by Graham Curtis and David Cobham

The Complete A+ Guide to PC Repair
Fifth Edition
by Cheryl A. Schmidt

Managing Careers: Theory and Practice
by Yehuda Baruch

Pearson Education Limited
Edinburgh Gate
Harlow
Essex CM20 2JE

And associated companies throughout the world

Visit us on the World Wide Web at:
www.pearsoned.co.uk

First published 2011

Compiled from:

Management Information Systems: Managing the Digital Firm Eleventh Edition
by Kenneth C. Laudon and Jane P. Laudon
ISBN 978 0 13 607846 3

Business Information Systems: Analysis, Design and Practice Sixth Edition
by Graham Curtis and David Cobham
ISBN 978 0 273 71382 1

The Complete A+ Guide to PC Repair
Fifth Edition
by Cheryl A. Schmidt
ISBN 978 0 13 212954 1

Managing Careers: Theory and Practice
by Yehuda Baruch
ISBN 978 0 273 67800 7

ISBN 978 0 85776 001 2

Printed and bound in Great Britain by Henry Ling Limited at the Dorset Press,
Dorchester DT1 1HD

Contents

CHAPTER 1

Business Skills for e-Commerce

Unit 1: Business Skills for e-Commerce

Unit code: Y/601/1244
QCF Level 4: BTEC Higher National
Credit value: 15

Aim

To enable learners to apply the business skills needed to design an e-Commerce solution for an organisation.

Unit abstract

Organisations of all sizes, structures and aims can benefit from the opportunities made available by the intelligent application of communication based technologies and there will always be a need for practitioners who have a good understanding of those technologies. E-Commerce has become a vital part of an organisation's ability to reach out to the marketplace and position itself to maximise commercial returns on investment.

Poor choices of technology and processes will result in poorly managed opportunities which could lose business, market position and profitability. Learners will investigate the values of business skills by exploring current, topical examples of e-Commerce practices. Learners will consider how to design an e-Commerce solution to the best advantage of the organisation and its stakeholders (for example employees, suppliers and customers). Learners will explore current legislation concerning e-Commerce based trading, organisational responsibilities and finance/payment systems.

The first part of the unit considers the structure and aims of organisations to better understand how they could benefit from an e-Commerce structure. Then follows an opportunity to investigate and evaluate the impact of e-Commerce systems on organisations and their stakeholders. Once these areas have been studied the learner will be in a position to examine the process of the development of an e-Commerce presence followed by the opportunity to design an e-Commerce system.

Learning outcomes

On successful completion of this unit a learner will:

1. Understand the structure and aims of business organisations
2. Understand the impact of e-Commerce
3. Be able to design e-Commerce solutions

Unit content

1 Understand the structure and aims of business organisations

Organisations: type eg private, public, voluntary, charitable business organisations; aims eg profit, market share, Return on Capital Employed (ROCE), sales; growth, customer service; Political, Economic, Social and Technological (PEST) analysis

Stakeholders: identification of stakeholders; satisfying stakeholder objectives; pluralist perspectives; the concept of corporate mission objectives and policies

Business functions: key internal business functions eg marketing, sales, accounting, administration; Management Information Systems (MIS), operations

2 Understand the impact of e-Commerce

Consumer impact: empowered customers eg online sales, direct communication with customers, greater choice, lower prices, availability of new products; global markets; new marketing models; on-line advertising

Business impact: global business and consumer markets; issues eg challenge of new technology, security issues, impact and implications of dealing with customers on-line, creating new distribution channels, greater competition, challenge to monopoly power, re-training of staff, lower overheads, new selling chains; legislation

3 Be able to design e-Commerce solutions

Objectives: business idea eg unique selling proposition, business-to-business opportunities, business to consumer markets; domain name

Market research: purpose of research eg identifying information sources, online and offline competition; types of research eg primary, secondary

Target markets: market analysis eg size, characteristics, dynamics, competitors, historical background, emerging trends, market share, market segmentation

Key processes: technology requirements eg hardware, software, security, maintenance, back end systems; supply sources; distribution channels

e-Commerce: payment systems eg electronic cheque, PayPal, NoChex, credit or debit cards; start-up capital; working capital; funding sources

Security: key areas eg prevention of hacking, viruses, identity theft, firewall, impact on site performance, Secure Sockets Layer (SSL), Secure HTTP (HTTPS), digital certificates, strong passwords, alternative authentication methods

Legislation: relevant legislation eg Data Protection Act 1998, Computer Misuse Act 1990, Consumer Credit Act 1974, Trading Standards, Freedom of Information Act 2000, copyright legislation

Learning outcomes and assessment criteria

Learning outcomes **On successful completion of this unit a learner will:**	**Assessment criteria for pass** **The learner can:**
LO1 Understand the structure and aims of business organisations	1.1 assess an organisation's core business functions 1.2 evaluate an organisation's business aims and show how they relate to stakeholders
LO2 Understand the impact of e-Commerce	2.1 analyse the impact, including the risks, of introducing an e-Commerce system to an organisation 2.2 discuss the global impact of e-Commerce on society
LO3 Be able to design e-Commerce solutions	3.1 investigate market potential for an e-Commerce opportunity 3.2 evaluate current e-Commerce systems in use by organisations 3.3 discuss the financial implications of an e-Commerce solution 3.4 design an e-Commerce solution 3.5 evaluate the suitability of an e-Commerce solution

Guidance

Links to National Occupational Standards, other BTEC units, other BTEC qualifications and other relevant units and qualifications

The learning outcomes associated with this unit are closely linked with:

Level 3	Level 4	Level 5
Unit 3: Information Systems	Unit 16: e-Commerce Technologies	Unit 29: e-Commerce Strategy
Unit 8: e-Commerce		Unit 30: Information Systems in Organisations
Unit 33: Exploring Business Activity		
Unit 34: Business Resources		

This unit has links to the Level 4 and Level 5 National Occupational Standards for IT and Telecoms Professionals, particularly the areas of competence of:

- Systems Analysis
- Systems Design
- Systems Development
- Change and Release Management
- Supplier Management

Essential requirements

Learners must have access to a wide range of material covering current and proposed e-Commerce implementations encompassing a number of organisations from small start-ups to large multi-nationals. The material can be sourced from online for example organisations' websites, journals, newspapers, broadcast material and visiting speakers who are experts in their subject area.

Resources

Books

Chaffey D—*E-business and E-Commerce Management, Fourth Edition* (FT Prentice Hall, 2009) ISBN 0273719602

Courtland B, Thill J—*Business in Action* (Pearson, 2010) ISBN 0132546884

Hall D, Jones R, Raffo C, Anderton A, Chambers I, Gray D—*Business Studies* (Causeway Press, 2008) ISBN 1405892315

Laudon K, Guercio Traver C—*E-Commerce 2010: International Version: Business, Technology, Society* (Pearson, 2009) ISBN 0135090784

Malmsten E, Leander K, Portanger E and Drazin C—*Boo Hoo: A Dot.com Story from Concept to Catastrophe* (Arrow Books Ltd, 2002) ISBN 0099418371

Rich J—*Design and Launch an eCommerce Business in a Week* (Entrepreneur Magazine's Click Starts) (Entrepreneur Press, 2008) ISBN 1599181835

Ridderstrale J and Nordstrom K—*Funky Business Forever* (Prentice Hall, 2007) ISBN 0273714139

Stanwick P, Stanwick S—*Understanding Business Ethics* (Prentice Hall, 2008) ISBN 013173542X

Vise D—*The Google Story* (Pan, 2008) ISBN 0330508121

Wood G and Mellahi K—*The Ethical Business: Possibilities, Challenges and Controversies* (Palgrave Macmillan, 2002) ISBN 0333949935

Journals

Business Review Magazine (Phillip Allan Publishers—see www.phillipallan.co.uk)

The Economist (The Economist Newspaper Group, Inc)

Employer engagement and vocational contexts

Any opportunity to study an existing e-Commerce implementation, either developing or mature would be advantageous.

Information Systems in Global Business Today

THE ROLE OF INFORMATION SYSTEMS IN BUSINESS TODAY

It's not business as usual in America anymore, or the rest of the global economy. In 2008, American businesses will spend about $840 billion on information systems hardware, software and telecommunications equipment. In addition, they will spend another $900 billion on business and management consulting and services—much of which involves redesigning firms' business operations to take advantage of these new technologies. Figure 1.1 shows that between 1980 and 2007, private business investment in information technology consisting of hardware, software, and communications equipment grew from 32 percent to 51 percent of all invested capital.

As managers, most of you will work for firms that are intensively using information systems and making large investments in information technology. You will certainly want to know how to invest this money wisely. If you make wise choices, your firm can outperform competitors. If you make poor choices, you will be wasting valuable capital. This chapter is dedicated to helping you make wise decisions about information technology and information systems.

How Information Systems are Transforming Business

You can see the results of this massive spending around you every day by observing how people conduct business. More wireless cell phone accounts were opened in 2008 than telephone land lines installed. Cell phones, BlackBerrys, iPhones, e-mail, and online conferencing over the Internet have all become essential tools of business. Fifty-eight percent of adult Americans have used a cell phone or mobile handheld device for activities other than voice communication, such as texting, emailing, taking a picture, looking for maps or directions, or recording video (Horrigan, 2008).

By June, 2008, more than 80 million businesses worldwide had dot-com Internet sites registered (60 million in the U.S. alone) (Versign, 2008). Today 138 million Americans shop online, and 117 million have purchased on line. Every day about 34 million Americans go online to research a product or service.

In 2007, FedEx moved over 100 million packages in the United States, mostly overnight, and the United Parcel Service (UPS) moved 3.7 billion packages worldwide. Businesses sought to sense and respond to rapidly changing customer demand, reduce inventories to the lowest possible levels, and achieve higher levels of operational efficiency. Supply chains have become more fast-paced, with companies of all sizes depending on just-in-time inventory to reduce their overhead costs and get to market faster.

As newspaper readership continues to decline, more than 64 million people receive their news online. About 67 million Americans now read blogs, and 21 million write blogs, creating an explosion of new writers and new forms of customer feedback that did not exist five years ago (Pew, 2008). Social networking sites like MySpace and Facebook attract over 70 and 30 million visitors a month, respectively, and businesses are starting to use social networking tools to connect their employees, customers, and managers worldwide.

E-commerce and Internet advertising are booming: Google's online ad revenues surpassed $16.5 billion in 2007, and Internet advertising continues to grow at more than 25 percent a year, reaching more than $28 billion in revenues in 2008.

New federal security and accounting laws, requiring many businesses to keep e-mail messages for five years, coupled with existing occupational and health laws requiring firms to

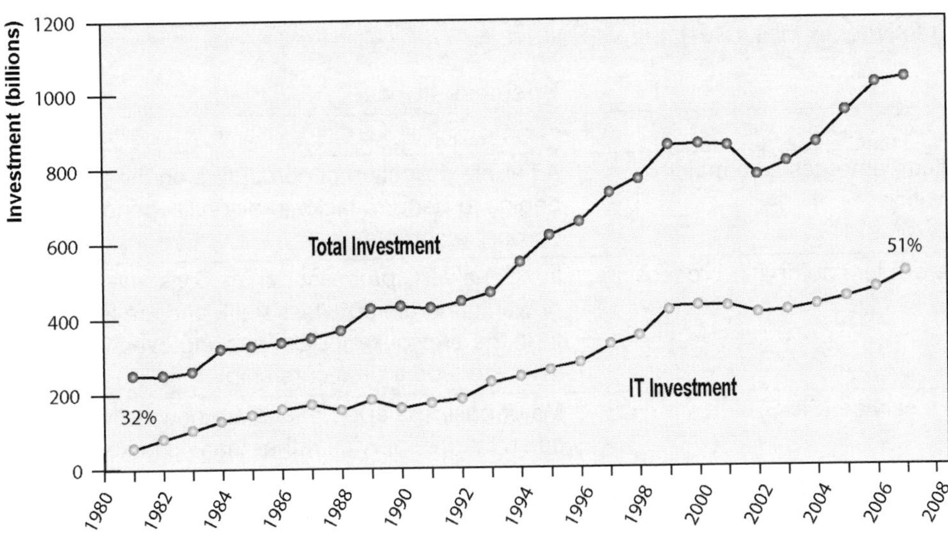

Information technology capital investment, defined as hardware, software, and communications equipment, grew from 32 percent to 51 percent of all invested capital between 1980 and 2008.

Source: Based on data in U.S. Department of Commerce, Bureau of Economic Analysis, *National Income and Product Accounts*, 2008.

Figure 1.1 **Information technology capital investment**

store employee chemical exposure data for up to 60 years, are spurring the growth of digital information now estimated to be 5 exabytes annually, equivalent to 37,000 new Libraries of Congress.

What's New in Management Information Systems?

Lots! What makes management information systems the most exciting topic in business is the continual change in technology, management use of the technology, and the impact on business success. Old systems are being creatively destroyed, and entirely new systems are taking their place. New industries appear, old ones decline, and successful firms are those who learn how to use the new technologies. Table 1.1 summarizes the major new themes in business uses of information systems. These themes will appear throughout the book in all the chapters, so it might be a good idea to take some time now and discuss these with your professor and other students. You may want to even add to the list.

In the technology area there are three interrelated changes: (1) the emerging mobile digital platform (think iPhones, BlackBerrys, and tiny Web-surfing netbooks), (2) the growth of online software as a service, and (3) the growth in "cloud computing" where more and more business software runs over the Internet. Of course these changes depend on other building-block technologies described in Table 1.1, such as faster processor chips that use much less power.

YouTube, iPhones and Blackberrys, and Facebook are not just gadgets or entertainment outlets. They represent new emerging computing platforms based on an array of new hardware and software technologies and business investments. Besides being successful products in their own right, these emerging technologies are being adopted by corporations as business tools to improve management and achieve competitive advantages. We call these developments the "emerging mobile platform."

Managers routinely use so-called "Web 2.0" technologies like social networking, collaboration tools, and wikis in order to make better, faster decisions. Millions of managers rely heavily on the mobile digital platform to coordinate vendors, satisfy customers, and manage their employees. For many if not most U.S. managers, a business day without their cell phones or Internet access is unthinkable.

Table 1.1 What's New in MIS

Change	Business Impact
Technology	
Cloud computing platform emerges as a major business area of innovation	A flexible collection of computers on the Internet begins to perform tasks traditionally performed on corporate computers.
More powerful, energy efficient computer processing and storage devices	Intel's new PC processor chips consume 50% less power, generate 30% less heat, and are 20% faster than the previous models, packing over 400 million transistors on a dual-core chip.
Growth in software as a service (SaaS)	Major business applications are now delivered online as an Internet service rather than as boxed software or custom systems.
Netbooks emerge as a growing presence in the PC marketplace, often using open source software	Small, lightweight, low-cost, energy-efficient, net-centric sub-notebooks use Linux, Google Docs, open source tools, flash memory, and the Internet for their applications, storage, and communications.
A mobile digital platform emerges to compete with the PC as a business system	Apple opens its iPhone software to developers, and then opens an Applications Store on iTunes where business users can download hundreds of applications to support collaboration, location-based services, and communication with colleagues.
Management	
Managers adopt online collaboration and social networking software to improve coordination, collaboration, and knowledge sharing	Google Apps, Google Sites, Microsoft's Office Sharepoint and IBM's Lotus Connections are used by over 100 million business decision makers worldwide to support blogs, project management, online meetings, personal profiles, social bookmarks, and online communities.
Business intelligence applications accelerate	More powerful data analytics and interactive dashboards provide real-time performance information to managers to enhance management control and decision making.
Managers adopt millions of mobile tools such as smartphones and mobile Internet devices to accelerate decision making and improve performance	The emerging mobile platform greatly enhances the accuracy, speed, and richness of decision making as well as responsiveness to customers.
Virtual meetings proliferate	Managers adopt telepresence video conferencing and Web conferencing technologies to reduce travel time and cost while improving collaboration and decision making.
Organizations	
Web 2.0 applications are widely adopted by firms	Web-based services enable employees to interact as online communities using blogs, wikis e-mail, and instant messaging services. Facebook and MySpace create new opportunities for business to collaborate with customers and vendors.
Telework gains momentum in the workplace	The Internet, wireless laptops, iPhones, and BlackBerrys make it possible for growing numbers of people to work away from the traditional office. 55 percent of U.S. businesses have some form of remote work program.

Table 1.1 What's New in MIS (continued)

Change	Business Impact
Organizations	
Outsourcing production	Firms learn to use the new technologies to outsource production work to low wage countries.
Co-creation of business value	Sources of business value shift from products to solutions and experiences and from internal sources to networks of suppliers and collaboration with customers. Supply chains and product development become more global and collaborative; customer interactions help firms define new products and services.

As management behavior changes, how work gets organized, coordinated, and measured also changes. By connecting employees working on teams and projects, the social network is where works gets done, where plans are executed, and where managers manage. Collaboration spaces are where employees meet one another—even when they are separated by continents and time zones. The strength of cloud computing, and the growth of the mobile digital platform means that organizations can rely more on telework, remote work, and distributed decision making. Think decentralization. This same platform means firms can outsource more work, and rely on markets (rather than employees) to build value. It also means that firms can collaborate with suppliers and customers to create new products, or make existing products more efficiently.

All of these changes contribute to a dynamic new global business economy. In fact, without the changes in management information systems just described, the global economy would not succeed.

Globalization Challenges and Opportunities: A Flattened World

In 1492 Columbus reaffirmed what astronomers were long saying: the world was round and the seas could be safely sailed. As it turned out, the world was populated by peoples and languages living in near total isolation from one another, with great disparities in economic and scientific development. The world trade that ensued after Columbus's voyages has brought these peoples and cultures closer. The "industrial revolution" was really a world-wide phenomenon energized by expansion of trade among nations.

By 2005, journalist Thomas Friedman wrote an influential book declaring the world was now "flat," by which he meant that the Internet and global communications had greatly reduced the economic and cultural advantages of developed countries. U.S. and European countries were in a fight for their economic lives, competing for jobs, markets, resources, and even ideas with highly educated, motivated populations in low-wage areas in the less developed world (Friedman, 2006). This "globalization" presents both challenges and opportunities.

A growing percentage of the economy of the United States and other advanced industrial countries in Europe and Asia depends on imports and exports. In 2009, more than 33 percent of the U.S. economy results from foreign trade, both imports and exports. In Europe and Asia, the number exceeds 50 percent. Many Fortune 500 U.S. firms derive half their revenues from foreign operations. For instance, more than half of Intel's revenues in 2006 came from overseas sales of its microprocessors. Toys for chips: 80 percent of the toys sold in the U.S. are manufactured in China, while about 90 percent of the PCs manufactured in China use American-made Intel or Advanced Micro Design (AMD) chips.

It's not just goods that move across borders. So too do jobs, some of them high-level jobs that pay well and require a college degree. In the past decade the U.S. lost several million manufacturing jobs to offshore, low-wage producers. But manufacturing is now a very small part of U.S. employment (less than 12 percent). In a normal year, about 300,000 service jobs move offshore to lower wage countries, many of them in less-skilled information system occupations, but also including "tradable service" jobs in architecture, financial services, customer call centers, consulting, engineering, and even radiology.

On the plus side, the U.S. economy creates over 3.5 million new jobs a year, and employment in information systems, and the other service occupations listed above, has expanded in sheer numbers, wages, productivity, and quality of work. Outsourcing has actually accelerated the development of new systems in the United States and worldwide.

The challenge for you as a business student is to develop high-level skills through education and on-the-job experience that cannot be outsourced. The challenge for your business is to avoid markets for goods and services that can be produced offshore much less expensively. The opportunities are equally immense. You will find throughout this book examples of companies and individuals who either failed or succeeded in using information systems to adapt to this new global environment.

What does globalization have to do with management information systems? That's simple: everything. The emergence of the Internet into a full-blown international communications system has drastically reduced the costs of operating and transacting on a global scale. Communication between a factory floor in Shanghai and a distribution center in Rapid Falls, South Dakota, is now instant and virtually free. Customers now can shop in a worldwide marketplace, obtaining price and quality information reliably 24 hours a day. Firms producing goods and services on a global scale achieve extraordinary cost reductions by finding low-cost suppliers and managing production facilities in other countries. Internet service firms, such as Google and eBay, are able to replicate their business models and services in multiple countries without having to redesign their expensive fixed-cost information systems infrastructure. Half of the revenue of eBay (as well as General Motors) in 2009 originates outside the United States. Briefly, information systems enable globalization.

The Emerging Digital Firm

All of the changes we have just described, coupled with equally significant organizational redesign, have created the conditions for a fully digital firm. A digital firm can be defined along several dimensions. A **digital firm** is one in which nearly all of the organization's *significant business relationships* with customers, suppliers, and employees are digitally enabled and mediated. *Core business processes* are accomplished through digital networks spanning the entire organization or linking multiple organizations.

Business processes refer to the set of logically related tasks and behaviors that organizations develop over time to produce specific business results and the unique manner in which these activities are organized and coordinated. Developing a new product, generating and fulfilling an order, creating a marketing plan, and hiring an employee are examples of business processes, and the ways organizations accomplish their business processes can be a source of competitive strength.

Key corporate assets—intellectual property, core competencies, and financial and human assets—are managed through digital means. In a digital firm, any piece of information required to support key business decisions is available at any time and anywhere in the firm.

Digital firms sense and respond to their environments far more rapidly than traditional firms, giving them more flexibility to survive in turbulent times. Digital firms offer extraordinary opportunities for more flexible global organization and management. In digital firms, both time shifting and space shifting are the norm. *Time shifting* refers to business being conducted continuously, 24/7, rather than in narrow "work day" time bands of 9 A.M. to 5 P.M. *Space shifting* means that work takes place in a global workshop, as well as within national boundaries. Work is accomplished physically wherever in the world it is best accomplished.

A few firms, such as Cisco Systems and Dell Computers, are close to becoming digital firms, using the Internet to drive every aspect of their business. Most other companies are not fully digital, but they are moving toward close digital integration with suppliers, customers, and employees. Many firms, for example, are replacing traditional face-to-face meetings with "virtual" meetings using videoconferencing and Web conferencing technology. The Interactive Session on Management provides more detail on this topic.

INTERACTIVE SESSION: MANAGEMENT

VIRTUAL MEETINGS: SMART MANAGEMENT

For many businesses, including investment banking, accounting, law, technology services, and management consulting, extensive travel is a fact of life. The expenses incurred by business travel have been steadily rising in recent years, primarily due to increasing energy costs. In an effort to reduce travel expenses, many companies, both large and small, are using videoconferencing and Web conferencing technologies.

A June 2008 report issued by the Global e-Sustainability Initiative and the Climate Group estimated that up to 20 percent of business travel could be replaced by virtual meeting technology.

A videoconference allows individuals at two or more locations to communicate through two-way video and audio transmissions at the same time. The critical feature of videoconferencing is the digital compression of audio and video streams by a device called a codec. Those streams are then divided into packets and transmitted over a network or the Internet. The technology has been plagued by poor audio and video performance in the past, usually related to the speed at which the streams were transmitted, and its cost was prohibitively high for all but the largest and most powerful corporations. Most companies deemed videoconferencing as a poor substitute for face-to-face meetings.

However, vast improvements in videoconferencing and associated technologies have renewed interest in this way of working. Videoconferencing is now growing at an annual rate of 30 percent. Proponents of the technology claim that it does more than simply reduce costs. It allows for 'better' meetings as well: it's easier to meet with partners, suppliers, subsidiaries, and colleagues from within the office or around the world on a more frequent basis, which in most cases simply cannot be reasonably accomplished through travel. You can also meet with contacts that you wouldn't be able to meet at all without videoconferencing technology.

The top-of-the-line videoconferencing technology is known as telepresence. Telepresence strives to make users feel as if they are actually present in a location different from their own. Telepresence products provide the highest-quality videoconferencing available on the market to date. Only a handful of companies, such as Cisco, HP, and Polycom, supply these products. Prices for fully equipped telepresence rooms can run to $500,000.

Companies able to afford this technology report large savings. For example, technology consulting firm Accenture reports that it eliminated expenditures for 240 international trips and 120 domestic flights in a single month. The ability to reach customers and partners is also dramatically increased. Other business travelers report tenfold increases in the number of customers and partners they are able to reach for a fraction of the previous price per person. Cisco has over 200 telepresence rooms and predicts that it saves $100 million in travel costs each year.

Videoconferencing products have not traditionally been feasible for small businesses, but another company, LifeSize, has introduced an affordable line of products as low as $5,000. Reviews of the LifeSize product indicate that when a great deal of movement occurs in a frame, the screen blurs and distorts somewhat. But overall, the product is easy to use and will allow many smaller companies to use a high-quality videoconferencing product.

There are even some free Internet-based options like Skype videoconferencing and ooVoo. These products are of lower quality than traditional videoconferencing products, and they are proprietary, meaning they can only talk to others using that very same system. Most videoconferencing and telepresence products are able to interact with a variety of other devices. Higher-end systems include features like multi-party conferencing, video mail with unlimited storage, no long-distance fees, and a detailed call history.

Companies of all sizes are finding Web-based online meeting tools such as WebEx, Microsoft Office Live Meeting, and Adobe Acrobat Connect especially helpful for training and sales presentations. These products enable participants to share documents and presentations in conjunction with audioconferencing and live video via Webcam. Cornerstone Information Systems, a Bloomington, Indiana business software company with 60 employees, cut its travel costs by 60 percent and the average time to close a new sale by 30 percent by performing many product demonstrations online.

Before setting up videoconferencing or telepresence, it's important for a company to make sure it really needs the technology to ensure that it will be a profitable venture. Companies should determine how their employees conduct meetings, how they communicate and with what technologies, how much travel they do, and their network's capabilities. There are still plenty of times when face-to-face interaction is more desirable, and often traveling to meet a client is essential for cultivating clients and closing sales.

Videoconferencing figures to have an impact on the business world in other ways, as well. More employees may be able to work closer to home and balance their work and personal lives more efficiently; traditional office environments and corporate headquarters may shrink or disappear; and freelancers, contractors, and workers from other countries will become a larger portion of the global economy.

Sources: Steve Lohr, "As Travel Costs Rise, More Meetings Go Virtual," *The New York Times*, July 22, 2008; Karen D. Schwartz, "Videoconferencing on a Budget," *eWeek*, May 29, 2008; and Jim Rapoza, "Videoconferencing Redux," *eWeek*, July 21, 2008; Mike Fratto, "High-Def Conferencing At a Low Price," *Information Week*, July 14, 2008; Marianne Kolbasuk McGee, "Looking Into The Work-Trend Crystal Ball," *Information Week*, June 24, 2008; Eric Krapf, "What's Video Good For?", *Information Week*, July 1, 2008.

CASE STUDY QUESTIONS

1. One consulting firm has predicted that video and Web conferencing will make business travel extinct. Do you agree? Why or why not?
2. What is the distinction between videoconferencing and telepresence?
3. What are the ways in which videoconferencing provides value to a business? Would you consider it smart management? Explain your answer.
4. If you were in charge of a small business, would you choose to implement videoconferencing? What factors would you consider in your decision?

MIS IN ACTION

Explore the WebEx Web site (www.webex.com) and note all of its capabilities for both small and large businesses, then answer the following questions:

1. List and describe its capabilities for small-medium and large businesses. How useful is WebEx? How can it help companies save time and money?
2. Compare WebEx video capabilities with the video-conferencing capabilities described in this case.
3. Describe the steps you would take to prepare for a Web conference as opposed to a face-to-face conference.

Strategic Business Objectives of Information Systems

What makes information systems so essential today? Why are businesses investing so much in information systems and technologies? In the United States, more than 23 million managers and 113 million workers in the labor force rely on information systems to conduct business. Information systems are essential for conducting day-to-day business in the United States and most other advanced countries, as well as achieving strategic business objectives.

Entire sectors of the economy are nearly inconceivable without substantial investments in information systems. E-commerce firms such as Amazon, eBay, Google, and E*Trade simply would not exist. Today's service industries—finance, insurance, and real estate, as well as personal services such as travel, medicine, and education—could not operate without information systems. Similarly, retail firms such as Wal-Mart and Sears and manufacturing firms such as General Motors and General Electric require information systems to survive and prosper. Just like offices, telephones, filing cabinets, and efficient tall buildings with elevators were once the foundations of business in the twentieth century, information technology is a foundation for business in the twenty-first century.

There is a growing interdependence between a firm's ability to use information technology and its ability to implement corporate strategies and achieve corporate goals (see Figure 1.2). What a business would like to do in five years often depends on what its systems will be able to do. Increasing market share, becoming the high-quality or low-cost producer, developing new products, and increasing employee productivity depend more and more on the kinds and quality of information systems in the organization. The more you understand about this relationship, the more valuable you will be as a manager.

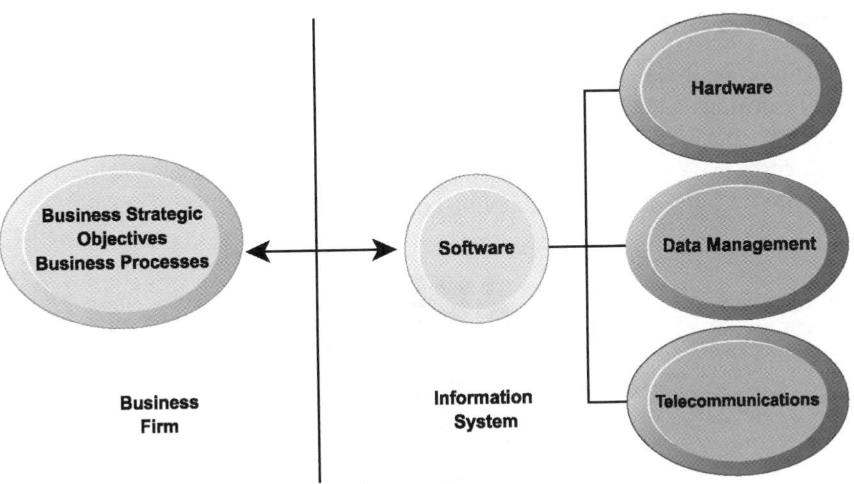

In contemporary systems there is a growing interdependence between a firm's information systems and its business capabilities. Changes in strategy, rules, and business processes increasingly require changes in hardware, software, databases, and telecommunications. Often, what the organization would like to do depends on what its systems will permit it to do.

Figure 1.2 **The interdependence between organizations and information systems**

Specifically, business firms invest heavily in information systems to achieve six strategic business objectives: operational excellence; new products, services, and business models; customer and supplier intimacy; improved decision making; competitive advantage; and survival.

Operational Excellence

Businesses continuously seek to improve the efficiency of their operations in order to achieve higher profitability. Information systems and technologies are some of the most important tools available to managers for achieving higher levels of efficiency and productivity in business operations, especially when coupled with changes in business practices and management behavior.

Wal-Mart, the largest retailer on Earth, exemplifies the power of information systems coupled with brilliant business practices and supportive management to achieve world-class operational efficiency. In 2007, Wal-Mart achieved close to $379 billion in sales—nearly one-tenth of retail sales in the United States—in large part because of its RetailLink system, which digitally links its suppliers to every one of Wal-Mart's stores. As soon as a customer purchases an item, the supplier monitoring the item knows to ship a replacement to the shelf. Wal-Mart is the most efficient retail store in the industry, achieving sales of more than $28 per square foot, compared to its closest competitor, Target, at $23 a square foot, with other retail firms producing less than $12 a square foot.

New Products, Services, and Business Models

Information systems and technologies are a major enabling tool for firms to create new products and services, as well as entirely new business models. A **business model** describes how a company produces, delivers, and sells a product or service to create wealth.

Today's music industry is vastly different from the industry in 2000. Apple Inc. transformed an old business model of music distribution based on vinyl records, tapes, and CDs into an online, legal distribution model based on its own iPod technology platform. Apple has prospered from a continuing stream of iPod innovations, including the iPod, the iTunes music service, and the iPhone.

Customer and Supplier Intimacy

When a business really knows its customers, and serves them well, the customers generally respond by returning and purchasing more. This raises revenues and profits. Likewise with suppliers: the more a business engages its suppliers, the better the suppliers can provide vital inputs. This lowers costs. How to really know your customers, or suppliers, is a central problem for businesses with millions of offline and online customers.

With its stunning multi-touch display, full Internet browsing, digital camera, and portable music player, Apple's iPhone set a new standard for mobile phones. Other Apple products have transformed the music and entertainment industries.

The Mandarin Oriental in Manhattan and other high-end hotels exemplify the use of information systems and technologies to achieve customer intimacy. These hotels use computers to keep track of guests' preferences, such as their preferred room temperature, check-in time, frequently dialed telephone numbers, and television programs, and store these data in a giant data repository. Individual rooms in the hotels are networked to a central network server computer so that they can be remotely monitored or controlled. When a customer arrives at one of these hotels, the system automatically changes the room conditions, such as dimming the lights, setting the room temperature, or selecting appropriate music, based on the customer's digital profile. The hotels also analyze their customer data to identify their best customers and to develop individualized marketing campaigns based on customers' preferences.

JC Penney exemplifies the benefits of information systems-enabled supplier intimacy. Every time a dress shirt is bought at a Penney store in the United States, the record of the sale appears immediately on computers in Hong Kong at the TAL Apparel Ltd. supplier, a giant contract manufacturer that produces one in eight dress shirts sold in the United States. TAL runs the numbers through a computer model it developed and then decides how many replacement shirts to make, and in what styles, colors, and sizes. TAL then sends the shirts to each Penney store, bypassing completely the retailer's warehouses. In other words, Penney's shirt inventory is near zero, as is the cost of storing it.

Improved Decision Making

Many business managers operate in an information fog bank, never really having the right information at the right time to make an informed decision. Instead, managers rely on forecasts, best guesses, and luck. The result is over- or underproduction of goods and services, misallocation of resources, and poor response times. These poor outcomes raise costs and lose customers. In the past decade, information systems and technologies have made it possible for managers to use real-time data from the marketplace when making decisions.

For instance, Verizon Corporation, one of the largest regional Bell operating companies in the United States, uses a Web-based digital dashboard to provide managers with precise real-time information on customer complaints, network performance for each locality served, and line outages or storm-damaged lines. Using this information, managers can immediately allocate repair resources to affected areas, inform consumers of repair efforts, and restore service fast.

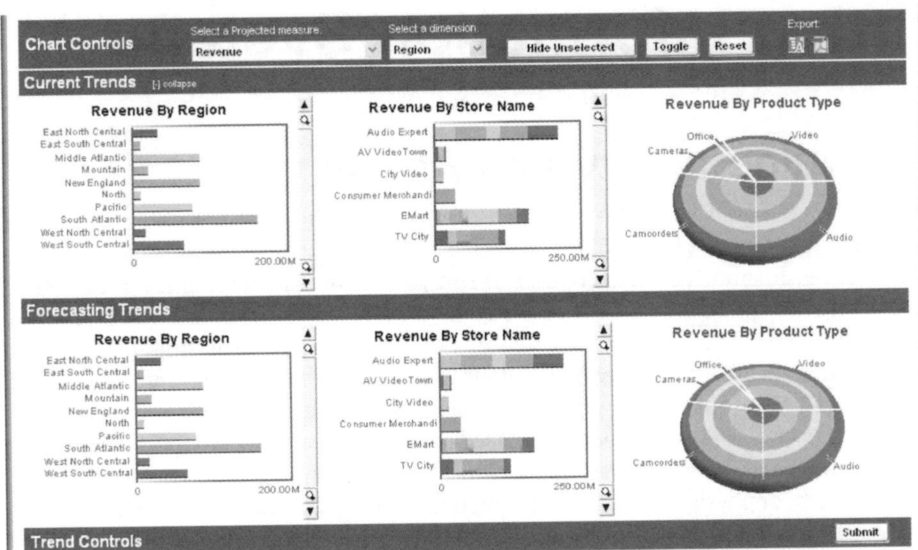

Information Builders' digital dashboard delivers comprehensive and accurate information for decision making. The graphical overview of key performance indicators helps managers quickly spot areas that need attention.

Competitive Advantage

When firms achieve one or more of these business objectives—operational excellence; new products, services, and business models; customer/supplier intimacy; and improved decision making—chances are they have already achieved a competitive advantage. Doing things better than your competitors, charging less for superior products, and responding to customers and suppliers in real time all add up to higher sales and higher profits that your competitors cannot match.

Perhaps no other company exemplifies all of these attributes leading to competitive advantage more than Toyota Motor Company. Toyota has become the world's largest auto maker because of its high level of efficiency and quality. Competitors struggle to keep up. Toyota's legendary Toyota Production System (TPS) focuses on organizing work to eliminate waste, making continuous improvements, and optimizing customer value. Information systems help Toyota implement the TPS and produce vehicles based on what customers have actually ordered.

Survival

Business firms also invest in information systems and technologies because they are necessities of doing business. Sometimes these "necessities" are driven by industry-level changes. For instance, after Citibank introduced the first automatic teller machines (ATMs) in the New York region in 1977 to attract customers through higher service levels, its competitors rushed to provide ATMs to their customers to keep up with Citibank. Today, virtually all banks in the United States have regional ATMs and link to national and international ATM networks, such as CIRRUS. Providing ATM services to retail banking customers is simply a requirement of being in and surviving in the retail banking business.

There are many federal and state statutes and regulations that create a legal duty for companies and their employees to retain records, including digital records. For instance, the Toxic Substances Control Act (1976), which regulates the exposure of U.S. workers to more than 75,000 toxic chemicals, requires firms to retain records on employee exposure for 30 years. The Sarbanes—Oxley Act (2002), which was intended to improve the accountability of public firms and their auditors, requires certified public accounting firms that audit public companies to retain audit working papers and records, including all e-mails, for five years. Many other pieces of federal and state legislation in healthcare, financial services, education, and privacy protection impose significant information retention and reporting requirements on U.S. businesses. Firms turn to information systems and technologies to provide the capability to respond to these.

Securing Information Systems

System Vulnerability and Abuse

Can you imagine what would happen if you tried to link to the Internet without a firewall or antivirus software? Your computer would be disabled in a few seconds, and it might take you many days to recover. If you used the computer to run your business, you might not be able to sell to your customers or place orders with your suppliers while it was down. And you might find that your computer system had been penetrated by outsiders, who perhaps stole or destroyed valuable data, including confidential payment data from your customers. If too much data were destroyed or divulged, your business might never be able to operate!

In short, if you operate a business today, you need to make security and control a top priority. **Security** refers to the policies, procedures, and technical measures used to prevent unauthorized access, alteration, theft, or physical damage to information systems. **Controls** are methods, policies, and organizational procedures that ensure the safety of the organization's assets; the accuracy and reliability of its records; and operational adherence to management standards.

Why Systems Are Vulnerable

When large amounts of data are stored in electronic form, they are vulnerable to many more kinds of threats than when they existed in manual form. Through communications networks, information systems in different locations are interconnected. The potential for unauthorized access, abuse, or fraud is not limited to a single location but can occur at any access point in the network. Figure 1.3 illustrates the most common threats against contemporary information systems. They can stem from technical, organizational, and environmental factors compounded by poor management decisions. In the multi-tier client/server computing environment illustrated here, vulnerabilities exist at each layer and in the communications between the layers. Users at the client layer can cause harm by introducing errors or by accessing systems without authorization. It is possible to access data flowing over networks, steal valuable data during transmission, or alter messages without authorization. Radiation may disrupt a network at

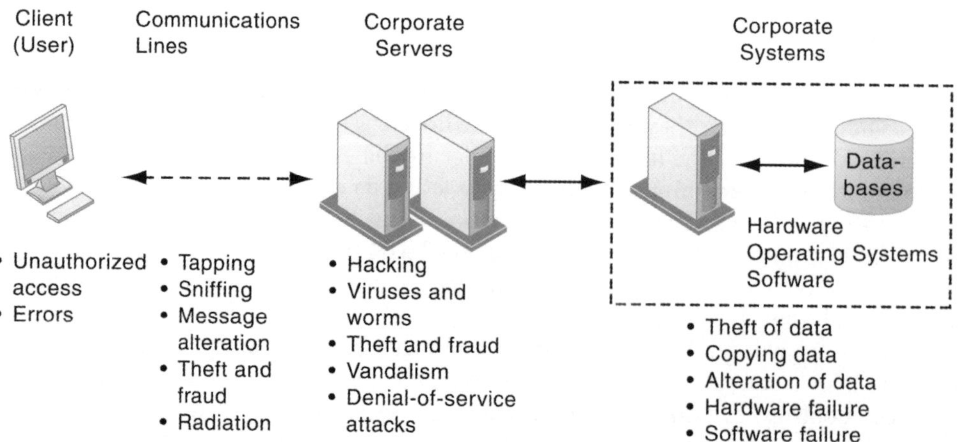

The architecture of a Web-based application typically includes a Web client, a server, and corporate information systems linked to databases. Each of these components presents security challenges and vulnerabilities. Floods, fires, power failures, and other electrical problems can cause disruptions at any point in the network.

Figure 1.3 **Contemporary Security Challenges and Vulnerabilities**

various points as well. Intruders can launch denial-of-service attacks or malicious software to disrupt the operation of Web sites. Those capable of penetrating corporate systems can destroy or alter corporate data stored in databases or files.

Systems malfunction if computer hardware breaks down, is not configured properly, or is damaged by improper use or criminal acts. Errors in programming, improper installation, or unauthorized changes cause computer software to fail. Power failures, floods, fires, or other natural disasters can also disrupt computer systems.

Domestic or offshore partnering with another company adds to system vulnerability if valuable information resides on networks and computers outside the organization's control. Without strong safeguards, valuable data could be lost, destroyed, or could fall into the wrong hands, revealing important trade secrets or information that violates personal privacy.

The growing use of mobile devices for business computing adds to these woes. Portability makes cell phones and smartphones easy to lose or steal, and their networks are vulnerable to access by outsiders. Smartphones used by corporate executives may contain sensitive data such as sales figures, customer names, phone numbers, and e-mail addresses. Intruders may be able to access internal corporate networks through these devices. Unauthorized downloads may introduce disabling software.

Internet Vulnerabilities

Large public networks, such as the Internet, are more vulnerable than internal networks because they are virtually open to anyone. The Internet is so huge that when abuses do occur, they can have an enormously widespread impact. When the Internet becomes part of the corporate network, the organization's information systems are even more vulnerable to actions from outsiders.

Computers that are constantly connected to the Internet by cable modems or digital subscriber line (DSL) lines are more open to penetration by outsiders because they use fixed Internet addresses where they can be easily identified. (With dial-up service, a temporary Internet address is assigned for each session.) A fixed Internet address creates a fixed target for hackers.

Telephone service based on Internet technology is more vulnerable than the switched voice network if it does not run over a secure private network. Most voice over IP (VoIP) traffic over the public Internet is not encrypted, so anyone with a network can listen in on conversations. Hackers can intercept conversations or shut down voice service by flooding servers supporting VoIP with bogus traffic.

Vulnerability has also increased from widespread use of e-mail, instant messaging (IM), and peer-to-peer file-sharing programs. E-mail may contain attachments that serve as springboards for malicious software or unauthorized access to internal corporate systems. Employees may use e-mail messages to transmit valuable trade secrets, financial data, or confidential customer information to unauthorized recipients. Popular instant messaging applications for consumers do not use a secure layer for text messages, so they can be intercepted and read by outsiders during transmission over the public Internet. IM activity over the Internet can in some cases be used as a back door to an otherwise secure network. Sharing files over peer-to-peer (P2P) networks, such as those for illegal music sharing, may also transmit malicious software or expose information on either individual or corporate computers to outsiders.

Wireless Security Challenges

Is it safe to log onto a wireless network at an airport, library, or other public location? It depends on how vigilant you are. Even the wireless network in your home is vulnerable because radio frequency bands are easy to scan. Both Bluetooth and Wi-Fi networks are susceptible to hacking by eavesdroppers. Although the range of Wi-Fi networks is only several hundred feet, it can be extended up to one-fourth of a mile using external antennae. Local-area networks (LANs) using the 802.11 standard can be easily penetrated by outsiders armed with laptops, wireless cards, external antennae, and hacking software. Hackers use these tools to detect unprotected networks, monitor network traffic, and, in some cases, gain access to the Internet or to corporate networks. The Interactive Session on Organizations describes how poor wireless security may

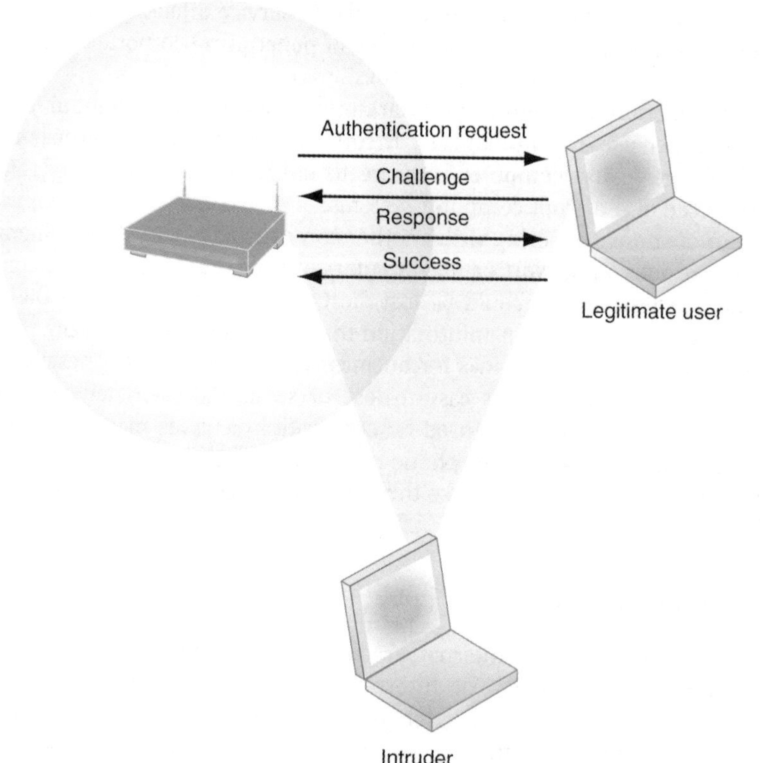

Many Wi-Fi networks can be penetrated easily by intruders using sniffer programs to obtain an address to access the resources of a network without authorization.

Figure 1.4 **Wi-Fi Security Challenges**

have enabled criminals to break into the corporate systems of TJX Companies and other major retailers and steal credit card and personal data on over 41 million people.

Wi-Fi transmission technology was designed to make it easy for stations to find and hear one another. The *service set identifiers (SSIDs)* identifying the access points in a Wi-Fi network are broadcast multiple times and can be picked up fairly easily by intruders' sniffer programs (see Figure 1.4). Wireless networks in many locations do not have basic protections against **war driving**, in which eavesdroppers drive by buildings or park outside and try to intercept wireless network traffic.

A hacker can employ an 802.11 analysis tool to identify the SSID. (Windows XP and Vista have capabilities for detecting the SSID used in a network and automatically configuring the radio NIC within the user's device.) An intruder that has associated with an access point by using the correct SSID is capable of accessing other resources on the network, using the Windows operating system to determine which other users are connected to the network, access their computer hard drives, and open or copy their files.

Intruders also use the information they have gleaned to set up rogue access points on a different radio channel in physical locations close to users to force a user's radio NIC to associate with the rogue access point. Once this association occurs, hackers using the rogue access point can capture the names and passwords of unsuspecting users.

The initial security standard developed for Wi-Fi, called *Wired Equivalent Privacy (WEP)*, is not very effective. WEP is built into all standard 802.11 products, but its use is optional. Many users neglect to use WEP security features, leaving them unprotected. The basic WEP specification calls for an access point and all of its users to share the same 40-bit encrypted password, which can be easily decrypted by hackers from a small amount of traffic. Stronger encryption and authentication systems are now available, but users must be willing to install them.

INTERACTIVE SESSION: ORGANIZATIONS

THE WORST DATA THEFT EVER?

In early August 2008, U.S. federal prosecutors charged 11 men in five countries, including the United States, Ukraine, and China, with stealing more than 41 million credit and debit card numbers. This is now the biggest known theft of credit card numbers in history. The thieves focused on major retail chains such as OfficeMax, Barnes & Noble, BJ's Wholesale Club, the Sports Authority, and T.J. Maxx.

The thieves drove around and scanned the wireless networks of these retailers to identify network vulnerabilities and then installed sniffer programs obtained from overseas collaborators. The sniffer programs tapped into the retailers' networks for processing credit cards, intercepting customers' debit and credit card numbers and PINs (personal identification numbers). The thieves then sent that information to computers in the Ukraine, Latvia, and the United States. They sold the credit card numbers online and imprinted other stolen numbers on the magnetic stripes of blank cards so they could withdraw thousands of dollars from ATM machines. Albert Gonzalez of Miami was identified as a principal organizer of the ring.

The conspirators began their largest theft in July 2005, when they identified a vulnerable network at a Marshall's department store in Miami and used it to install a sniffer program on the computers of the chain's parent company, TJX. They were able to access the central TJX database, which stored customer transactions for T.J. Maxx, Marshalls, HomeGoods, and A.J. Wright stores in the United States and Puerto Rico, and for Winners and HomeSense stores in Canada. Fifteen months later, TJX reported that the intruders had stolen records with up to 45 million credit and debit card numbers.

TJX was still using the old Wired Equivalent Privacy (WEP) encryption system, which is relatively easy for hackers to crack. Other companies had switched to the more secure Wi-Fi Protected Access (WPA) standard with more complex encryption, but TJX did not make the change. An auditor later found that TJX had also neglected to install firewalls and data encryption on many of the computers using the wireless network, and did not properly install another layer of security software it had purchased. TJX acknowledged in a Securities and Exchange Commission filing that it transmitted credit card data to banks without encryption, violating credit card company guidelines.

Incidents of credit card fraud tied to TJX stores started surfacing in the United States and abroad. Customers at Fidelity Homestead, the Louisiana savings bank, began seeing strange transactions on their credit card bills in November 2005—unauthorized purchases in Wal-Mart stores in Mexico and in supermarkets and other stores in southern California.

In March 2007, the Gainesville Police Department and the Florida Department of Law Enforcement arrested six people using fake credit cards with the stolen TJX data. They had purchased $8 million in gift cards from Wal-Mart and Sam's Club stores in 50 Florida counties, and used them to buy flat-screen TVs, computers, and other electronics.

The following July, the U.S. Secret Service arrested four more people in south Florida who had been using the stolen TJX customer data. The arrests recovered about 200,000 stolen credit card numbers used in fraud losses calculated to be more than $75 million.

In question was whether TJX was adhering to the security rules established by Visa and MasterCard for storing such data, known as the Payment Card Industry (PCI) Data Security Standard. According to these rules, merchants are not supposed to maintain certain types of cardholder data in their systems because the data facilitate the creation of fraudulent card accounts. Communications between Visa and card-issuing financial institutions revealed that TJX did violate this principle by holding onto data for years, rather than for the short amount of time they are actually needed.

On paper, PCI standards are rigorous. It requires merchants to implement twelve account-protection mechanisms, including encryption, vulnerability scans, and the use of firewalls and antivirus software. However, the PCI standards are not well enforced. Merchants who fail to abide by them remain eligible to process electronic payments, and only a fraction of them are thoroughly audited.

In March 2008, TJX management agreed to strengthen the company's information system security. It also agreed to have third-party auditors review security measures every 2 years for the next 20 years.

A few months earlier, TJX had reached an agreement with Visa U.S.A. to establish a $40.9 million fund to compensate banks that were affected by its security breach. Banks that issued the credit and debit cards might have to spend $300 million just to replace the stolen cards, in addition to covering fraudulent purchases.

TJX reported having already spent $202 million to deal with its data theft, including legal settlements, and that it expected to spend $23 million more in fiscal 2009. Forrester Research estimates that the cost to TJX for the data breach could surpass $1 billion over five years, including costs for consultants, security upgrades, attorney fees, and additional marketing to reassure customers. TJX declined to comment on those numbers.

A report from Javelin Strategy & Research revealed that more than 75% of the consumers it surveyed would not continue to shop at stores that had been victimized by data theft. The same study showed that consumers trust credit card companies to protect their data far more than retailers.

Sources: Brad Stone, "11 Charged in Theft of 41 Million Card Numbers," *The New York Times*, August 6, 2008; Andrew Conry-Murray, "PCI and the Circle of Blame," *Information Week*, February 25, 2008; Dan Berthiaume, "Data Breaches Cause Concern," *eWeek*, April 7, 2008; Joseph Pereira, Jennifer Levitz, and Jeremy Singer-Vine, "Some Stores Quiet Over Card Breach," *The Wall Street Journal*, August 11, 2008; Robin Sidel, "Giant Retailer Reveals Customer Data Breach," *The Wall Street Journal*, January 18, 2007; "Hack Attack Means Headaches for TJ Maxx," *Information Week*, February 3, 2007, and T.J. Maxx Probe Reveals Data Breach Worse Than Originally Thought," *Information Week*, February 21, 2007.

CASE STUDY QUESTIONS

1. List and describe the security control weaknesses at TJX Companies.
2. What management, organization, and technology factors contributed to these weaknesses?
3. What was the business impact of TJX's data loss on TJX, consumers, and banks?
4. How effectively did TJX deal with these problems?
5. Who should be held liable for the losses caused by the use of fraudulent credit cards in this case? TJX? The banks issuing the credit cards? The consumers? Justify your answer.
6. What solutions would you suggest to prevent the problems?

MIS IN ACTION

Explore the Web site of the PCI Security Standards Council (www.pcisecuritystandards.org) and review the PCI Data Security Standard (PCI DSS).

1. Based on the details in this case study, how well was TJX complying with the PCI DSS. What requirements did it fail to meet?
2. Would complying with this standard have prevented the theft of credit card data from TJX?

Malicious Software: Viruses, Worms, Trojan Horses, and Spyware

Malicious software programs are referred to as **malware** and include a variety of threats, such as computer viruses, worms, and Trojan horses. A **computer virus** is a rogue software program that attaches itself to other software programs or data files in order to be executed, usually without user knowledge or permission. Most computer viruses deliver a "payload." The payload may be relatively benign, such as the instructions to display a message or image, or it may be highly destructive—destroying programs or data, clogging computer memory, reformatting a computer's hard drive, or causing programs to run improperly. Viruses typically spread from computer to computer when humans take an action, such as sending an e-mail attachment or copying an infected file.

Most recent attacks have come from **worms**, which are independent computer programs that copy themselves from one computer to other computers over a network. (Unlike viruses, they can operate on their own without attaching to other computer program files and rely less on human behavior in order to spread from computer to computer. This explains why computer worms spread much more rapidly than computer viruses.) Worms destroy data and programs as well as disrupt or even halt the operation of computer networks.

Worms and viruses are often spread over the Internet from files of downloaded software, from files attached to e-mail transmissions, or from compromised e-mail messages or instant messaging. Viruses have also invaded computerized information systems from "infected" disks or infected machines. E-mail worms are currently the most problematic.

There are now more than 200 viruses and worms targeting mobile phones, such as CABIR, Comwarrior, and Frontal A. Frontal A, for example, installs a corrupted file that causes phone failure and prevents the user from rebooting. Mobile device viruses could pose serious threats to enterprise computing because so many wireless devices are now linked to corporate information systems.

Web 2.0 applications, such as blogs, wikis, and social networking sites such as Facebook and MySpace, have emerged as new conduits for malware or spyware. These applications allow users to post software code as part of the permissible content, and such code can be launched automatically as soon as a Web page is viewed. For example, in August 2008, malicious hackers targeted unsuspecting Facebook users via postings on the site's Wall feature, which is used by members to leave each other messages. Impersonating members' friends, malicious hackers posted messages urging users to click on a link to view a video that transported them to a rogue Web page where they were told to download a new version of Adobe's Flash player in order to view the video. If users authorized the download, the site would install a Trojan horse, Troj/Dloadr-BPL, that funneled other malicious code to their PCs (Perez, 2008).

Table 1.2 describes the characteristics of some of the most harmful worms and viruses that have appeared to date.

Over the past decade, worms and viruses have cause billions of dollars of damage to corporate networks, e-mail systems, and data. According to Consumer Reports' State of the Net 2008 survey, U.S. consumers lost $8.5 billion because of malware and online scams, and the majority of these losses came from malware (Consumer Reports, 2008).

A **Trojan horse** is a software program that appears to be benign but then does something other than expected. The Trojan horse is not itself a virus because it does not replicate but is

Table 1.2 Examples of Malicious Code

Name	Type	Description
Storm	Worm/ Trojan horse	First identified in January 2007. Spreads via e-mail spam with a fake attachment. Infected up to 10 million computers, causing them to join its zombie network of computers engaged in criminal activity.
Sasser.ftp	Worm	First appeared in May 2004. Spread over the Internet by attacking random IP addresses. Causes computers to continually crash and reboot, and infected computers to search for more victims. Affected millions of computers worldwide, disrupting British Airways flight check-ins, operations of British coast guard stations, Hong Kong hospitals, Taiwan post office branches, and Australia's Westpac Bank. Sasser and its variants caused an estimated $14.8 billion to $18.6 billion in damages worldwide.
MyDoom.A	Worm	First appeared on January 26, 2004. Spreads as an e-mail attachment. Sends e-mail to addresses harvested from infected machines, forging the sender's address. At its peak this worm lowered global Internet performance by 10 percent and Web page loading times by as much as 50 percent. Was programmed to stop spreading after February 12, 2004.
Sobig.F	Worm	First detected on August 19, 2003. Spreads via e-mail attachments and sends massive amounts of mail with forged sender information. Deactivated itself on September 10, 2003, after infecting more than 1 million PCs and doing $5 to $10 billion in damage.
ILOVEYOU	Virus	First detected on May 3, 2000. Script virus written in Visual Basic script and transmitted as an attachment to e-mail with the subject line ILOVEYOU. Overwrites music, image, and other files with a copy of itself and did an estimated $10 billion to $15 billion in damage.
Melissa	Macro virus/ worm	First appeared in March 1999. Word macro script mailing infected Word file to first 50 entries in user's Microsoft Outlook address book. Infected 15 to 29 percent of all business PCs, causing $300 million to $600 million in damage.

often a way for viruses or other malicious code to be introduced into a computer system. The term *Trojan horse* is based on the huge wooden horse used by the Greeks to trick the Trojans into opening the gates to their fortified city during the Trojan War. Once inside the city walls, Greek soldiers hidden in the horse revealed themselves and captured the city.

An example of a modern-day Trojan horse is Pushdo Trojan, which uses electronic greeting-card lures in e-mail to trick Windows users into launching an executable program. Once the Trojan is executed, it pretends to be an Apache Web server and tries to deliver executable malware programs to the infected Windows machines.

Some types of **spyware** also act as malicious software. These small programs install themselves surreptitiously on computers to monitor user Web surfing activity and serve up advertising. Thousands of forms of spyware have been documented. Harris Interactive found that 92 percent of the companies surveyed in its Web@Work study reported detecting spyware on their networks (Mitchell, 2006).

Many users find such spyware annoying and some critics worry about its infringement on computer users' privacy. Some forms of spyware are especially nefarious. **Keyloggers** record every keystroke made on a computer to steal serial numbers for software, to launch Internet attacks, to gain access to e-mail accounts, to obtain passwords to protected computer systems, or to pick up personal information such as credit card numbers. Other spyware programs reset Web browser home pages, redirect search requests, or slow computer performance by taking up too much memory.

Hackers and Computer Crime

A **hacker** is an individual who intends to gain unauthorized access to a computer system. Within the hacking community, the term *cracker* is typically used to denote a hacker with criminal intent, although in the public press, the terms hacker and cracker are used interchangeably. Hackers and crackers gain unauthorized access by finding weaknesses in the security protections employed by Web sites and computer systems, often taking advantage of various features of the Internet that make it an open system that is easy to use.

Hacker activities have broadened beyond mere system intrusion to include theft of goods and information, as well as system damage and **cybervandalism**, the intentional disruption, defacement, or even destruction of a Web site or corporate information system. For example, cybervandals have turned many of the MySpace "group" sites, which are dedicated to interests such as home beer brewing or animal welfare, into cyber-graffiti walls, filled with offensive comments and photographs (Kirk, 2008).

Spoofing and Sniffing

Hackers attempting to hide their true identities often spoof, or misrepresent, themselves by using fake e-mail addresses or masquerading as someone else. **Spoofing** also may involve redirecting a Web link to an address different from the intended one, with the site masquerading as the intended destination. For example, if hackers redirect customers to a fake Web site that looks almost exactly like the true site, they can then collect and process orders, effectively stealing business as well as sensitive customer information from the true site. We provide more detail on other forms of spoofing in our discussion of computer crime.

A **sniffer** is a type of eavesdropping program that monitors information traveling over a network. When used legitimately, sniffers help identify potential network trouble spots or criminal activity on networks, but when used for criminal purposes, they can be damaging and very difficult to detect. Sniffers enable hackers to steal proprietary information from anywhere on a network, including e-mail messages, company files, and confidential reports.

Denial-of-Service Attacks

In a **denial-of-service (DoS) attack**, hackers flood a network server or Web server with many thousands of false communications or requests for services to crash the network. The network receives so many queries that it cannot keep up with them and is thus unavailable to service legitimate requests. A **distributed denial-of-service (DDoS)** attack uses numerous computers to inundate and overwhelm the network from numerous launch points. For example, Bill O'Reilly's official Web site was bombarded by data that overloaded the system's firewalls for two days in early March 2007, forcing the site to be taken down to protect it (Schmidt, 2007).

Although DoS attacks do not destroy information or access restricted areas of a company's information systems, they often cause a Web site to shut down, making it impossible for legitimate users to access the site. For busy e-commerce sites, these attacks are costly; while the site is shut down, customers cannot make purchases. Especially vulnerable are small and midsize businesses whose networks tend to be less protected than those of large corporations.

Perpetrators of DoS attacks often use thousands of "zombie" PCs infected with malicious software without their owners' knowledge and organized into a **botnet**. Hackers create these botnets by infecting other people's computers with bot malware that opens a back door through which an attacker can give instructions. The infected computer then becomes a slave, or zombie, serving a master computer belonging to someone else. Once a hacker infects enough computers, her or she can use the amassed resources of the botnet to launch DDos attacks, phishing campaigns, or unsolicited "spam" e-mail.

In the first six months of 2007, security product provider Symantec observed over 5 million distinct bot-infected computers. Bots and botnets are an extremely serious threat because they can be used to launch very large attacks using many different techniques. For example, the Storm worm, which was responsible for one of the largest e-mail attacks in the past few years, was propagated via a massive botnet of nearly 2 million computers. Botnet attacks thought to have originated in Russia were responsible for crippling the Web sites of the Estonian government in April 2007 and the Georgian government in July 2008.

Computer Crime

Most hacker activities are criminal offenses, and the vulnerabilities of systems we have just described make them targets for other types of computer crime as well. For example, Yung-Sun Lin was charged in January 2007 with installing a "logic bomb" program on the computers of his employer, Medco Health Solutions of Franklin Lakes, New Jersey. Lin's program could have erased critical prescription information for 60 million Americans (Gaudin, 2007). **Computer crime** is defined by the U.S. Department of Justice as "any violations of criminal law that involve a knowledge of computer technology for their perpetration, investigation, or prosecution." Table 1.3 provides examples of the computer as a target of crime and as an instrument of crime.

No one knows the magnitude of the computer crime problem—how many systems are invaded, how many people engage in the practice, or the total economic damage. According to the 2007 CSI Computer Crime and Security Survey of nearly 500 companies, participants' average annual loss from computer crime and security attacks was $350,424 (Richardson, 2007). Many companies are reluctant to report computer crimes because the crimes may involve employees, or the company fears that publicizing its vulnerability will hurt its reputation. The most economically damaging kinds of computer crime are DoS attacks, introducing viruses, theft of services, and disruption of computer systems.

Identity Theft

With the growth of the Internet and electronic commerce, identity theft has become especially troubling. **Identity theft** is a crime in which an imposter obtains key pieces of personal information, such as Social Security identification numbers, driver's license numbers, or credit card numbers, to impersonate someone else. The information may be used to obtain credit, merchandise, or services in the name of the victim or to provide the thief with false credentials. According to Javelin Strategy and Research, 8.4 million Americans were victims of identity theft in 2007 and they suffered losses totaling $49.3 billion (Stempel, 2007).

Identify theft has flourished on the Internet, with credit card files a major target of Web site hackers. Moreover, e-commerce sites are wonderful sources of customer personal information—

Table 1.3 Examples of Computer Crime

Computers as Targets of Crime
Breaching the confidentiality of protected computerized data
Accessing a computer system without authority
Knowingly accessing a protected computer to commit fraud
Intentionally accessing a protected computer and causing damage, negligently or deliberately
Knowingly transmitting a program, program code, or command that intentionally causes damage to a protected computer
Threatening to cause damage to a protected computer

Computers as Instruments of Crime
Theft of trade secrets
Unauthorized copying of software or copyrighted intellectual property, such as articles, books, music, and video
Schemes to defraud
Using e-mail for threats or harassment
Intentionally attempting to intercept electronic communication
Illegally accessing stored electronic communications, including e-mail and voice mail
Transmitting or possessing child pornography using a computer

name, address, and phone number. Armed with this information, criminals are able to assume new identities and establish new credit for their own purposes.

One increasingly popular tactic is a form of spoofing called **phishing**. Phishing involves setting up fake Web sites or sending e-mail messages that look like those of legitimate businesses to ask users for confidential personal data. The e-mail message instructs recipients to update or confirm records by providing social security numbers, bank and credit card information, and other confidential data either by responding to the e-mail message, by entering the information at a bogus Web site, or by calling a telephone number. EBay, PayPal, Amazon.com, Wal-Mart, and a variety of banks, are among the top spoofed companies.

New phishing techniques called evil twins and pharming are harder to detect. **Evil twins** are wireless networks that pretend to offer trustworthy Wi-Fi connections to the Internet, such as those in airport lounges, hotels, or coffee shops. The bogus network looks identical to a legitimate public network. Fraudsters try to capture passwords or credit card numbers of unwitting users who log on to the network.

Pharming redirects users to a bogus Web page, even when the individual types the correct Web page address into his or her browser. This is possible if pharming perpetrators gain access to the Internet address information stored by Internet service providers to speed up Web browsing and the ISP companies have flawed software on their servers that allows the fraudsters to hack in and change those addresses.

The U.S. Congress addressed the threat of computer crime in 1986 with the Computer Fraud and Abuse Act. This act makes it illegal to access a computer system without authorization. Most states have similar laws, and nations in Europe have comparable legislation. Congress also passed the National Information Infrastructure Protection Act in 1996 to make virus distribution and hacker attacks to disable Web sites federal crimes. U.S. legislation, such as the Wiretap Act, Wire Fraud Act, Economic Espionage Act, Electronic Communications Privacy Act, E-Mail Threats and Harassment Act, and Child Pornography Act, covers computer crimes involving intercepting electronic communication, using electronic communication to defraud, stealing trade secrets, illegally accessing stored electronic communications, using e-mail for threats or harassment, and transmitting or possessing child pornography.

Click Fraud

When you click on an ad displayed by a search engine, the advertiser typically pays a fee for each click, which is supposed to direct potential buyers to its products. **Click fraud** occurs when an individual or computer program fraudulently clicks on an online ad without any intention of learning more about the advertiser or making a purchase. Click fraud has become a serious problem at Google and other Web sites that feature pay-per-click online advertising.

Some companies hire third parties (typically from low-wage countries) to fraudulently click on a competitor's ads to weaken them by driving up their marketing costs. Click fraud can also be perpetrated with software programs doing the clicking, and botnets are often used for this purpose. Search engines such as Google attempt to monitor click fraud but have been reluctant to publicize their efforts to deal with the problem.

Global Threats: Cyberterrorism and Cyberwarfare

The cybercriminal activities we have described—launching malware, denial-of- service attacks, and phishing probes—are borderless. Computer security firm Sophos reported that 42 percent of the malware it identified in early 2008 originated in the United States, while 30.1 percent came from China, and 10.3 percent from Russia (Sophos, 2008). The global nature of the Internet makes it possible for cybercriminals to operate—and to do harm—anywhere in the world.

Concern is mounting that the vulnerabilities of the Internet or other networks make digital networks easy targets for digital attacks by terrorists, foreign intelligence services, or other groups seeking to create widespread disruption and harm. Such cyberattacks might target the software that runs electrical power grids, air traffic control systems, or networks of major banks and financial institutions. At least 20 countries, including China, are believed to be developing offensive and defensive cyberwarfare capabilities. In 2007, there were 12,986 reported attacks on U.S. government agencies, with incursions on U.S. military networks up 55 percent from a year earlier. Companies that are defense department contractors have also come under siege (Grow et al., 2008).

To deal with this threat, President George W. Bush signed a Cyber Initiative directive on January 8, 2008, authorizing the National Security Agency to monitor the computer networks of all federal agencies and identify the source of cyber-attacks. The U.S. Department of Homeland

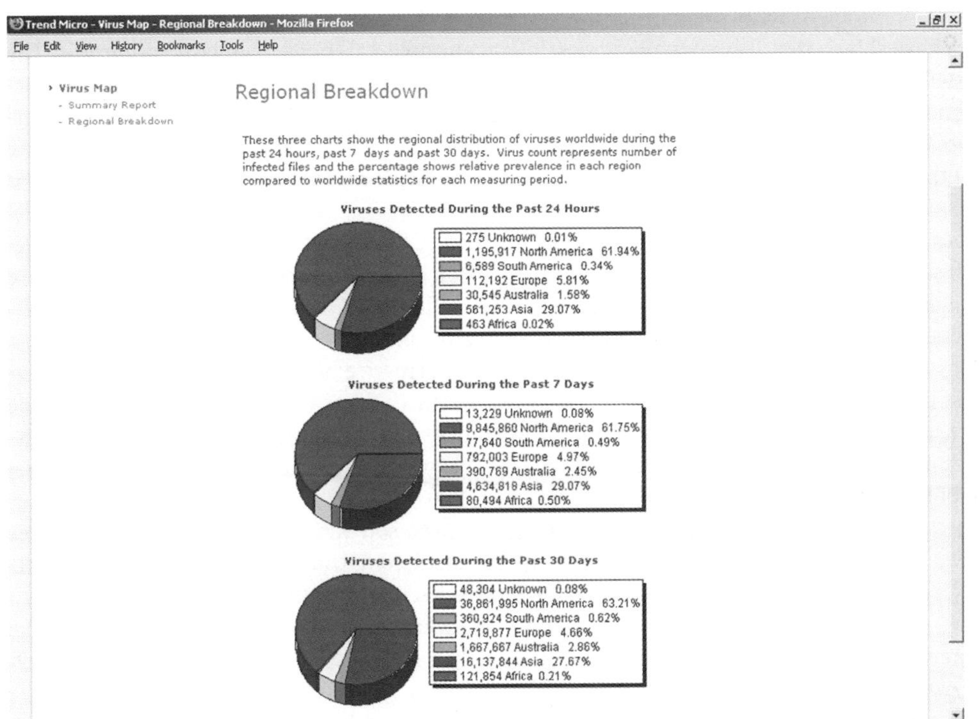

Malware is active throughout the globe. These three charts show the regional distribution of worms and computer viruses worldwide reported by online security provider Trend Micro over periods of 24 hours, 7 days, and 30 days. The virus count represents the number of infected files, and the percentage shows the relative prevalence in each region compared to worldwide statistics for each measuring period.

Security will work to protect the systems, and the Pentagon will devise strategies for counterattacks against intruders. All government agencies were ordered to cut the number of ports, or communication channels, through which their networks connect to the Internet from more than 4,000 to less than 100.

Internal Threats: Employees

We tend to think the security threats to a business originate outside the organization. In fact, company insiders pose serious security problems. Employees have access to privileged information, and in the presence of sloppy internal security procedures, they are often able to roam throughout an organization's systems without leaving a trace.

Studies have found that user lack of knowledge is the single greatest cause of network security breaches. Many employees forget their passwords to access computer systems or allow co-workers to use them, which compromises the system. Malicious intruders seeking system access sometimes trick employees into revealing their passwords by pretending to be legitimate members of the company in need of information. This practice is called **social engineering**.

Both end users and information systems specialists are also a major source of errors introduced into information systems. End users introduce errors by entering faulty data or by not following the proper instructions for processing data and using computer equipment. Information systems specialists may create software errors as they design and develop new software or maintain existing programs.

Software Vulnerability

Software errors pose a constant threat to information systems, causing untold losses in productivity. Growing complexity and size of software programs, coupled with demands for timely delivery to markets, have contributed to an increase in software flaws or vulnerabilities For example, a flawed software upgrade shut down the BlackBerry e-mail service throughout North America for about 12 hours between April 17 and April 18, 2007. Millions of business users who depended on BlackBerry were unable to work, and BlackBerry's reputation for reliability was tarnished (Martin, 2007). The U.S. Department of Commerce National Institute of Standards and Technology (NIST) reported that software flaws (including vulnerabilities to hackers and malware) cost the U.S. economy $59.6 billion each year (NIST, 2005).

A major problem with software is the presence of hidden **bugs** or program code defects. Studies have shown that it is virtually impossible to eliminate all bugs from large programs. The main source of bugs is the complexity of decision-making code. A relatively small program of several hundred lines will contain tens of decisions leading to hundreds or even thousands of different paths. Important programs within most corporations are usually much larger, containing tens of thousands or even millions of lines of code, each with many times the choices and paths of the smaller programs.

Zero defects cannot be achieved in larger programs. Complete testing simply is not possible. Fully testing programs that contain thousands of choices and millions of paths would require thousands of years. Even with rigorous testing, you would not know for sure that a piece of software was dependable until the product proved itself after much operational use.

Flaws in commercial software not only impede performance but also create security vulnerabilities that open networks to intruders. Each year security firms identify about 5,000 software vulnerabilities in Internet and PC software. For instance, in 2007 Symantec identified 39 vulnerabilities in Microsoft Internet Explorer, 34 in Mozilla browsers, 25 in Apple Safari, and 7 in Opera. Some of these vulnerabilities are critical (Symantec, 2007).

To correct software flaws once they are identified, the software vendor creates small pieces of software called **patches** to repair the flaws without disturbing the proper operation of the software. An example is Microsoft's Windows Vista Service Pack 1, released in February 2008, which includes some security enhancements to counter malware and hackers. It is up to users of the software to track these vulnerabilities, test, and apply all patches. This process is called *patch management*.

Because a company's IT infrastructure is typically laden with multiple business applications, operating system installations, and other system services, maintaining patches on all devices and services used by a company is often time-consuming and costly. Malware is being created so rapidly that companies have very little time to respond between the time a vulnerability and a patch are announced and the time malicious software appears to exploit the vulnerability.

BUSINESS VALUE OF SECURITY AND CONTROL

Many firms are reluctant to spend heavily on security because it is not directly related to sales revenue. However, protecting information systems is so critical to the operation of the business that it deserves a second look.

Companies have very valuable information assets to protect. Systems often house confidential information about individuals' taxes, financial assets, medical records, and job performance reviews. They also can contain information on corporate operations, including trade secrets, new product development plans, and marketing strategies. Government systems may store information on weapons systems, intelligence operations, and military targets. These information assets have tremendous value, and the repercussions can be devastating if they are lost, destroyed, or placed in the wrong hands. One study estimated that when the security of a large firm is compromised, the company loses approximately 2.1 percent of its market value within two days of the security breach, which translates into an average loss of $1.65 billion in stock market value per incident (Cavusoglu, Mishra, and Raghunathan, 2004).

Inadequate security and control may result in serious legal liability. Businesses must protect not only their own information assets but also those of customers, employees, and business partners. Failure to do so may open the firm to costly litigation for data exposure or theft. An organization can be held liable for needless risk and harm created if the organization fails to take appropriate protective action to prevent loss of confidential information, data corruption, or breach of privacy (see the Interactive Session on Organizations). For example, BJ's Wholesale Club was sued by the U.S. Federal Trade Commission for allowing hackers to access its systems and steal credit and debit card data for fraudulent purchases. Banks that issued the cards with the stolen data sought $13 million from BJ's to compensate them for reimbursing card holders for the fraudulent purchases (McDougall, 2006). A sound security and control framework that protects business information assets can thus produce a high return on investment.

Strong security and control also increase employee productivity and lower operational costs. For example, Axia NextMedia Corp., a Calgary, Alberta firm that builds and manages open-access broadband networks, saw employee productivity go up and costs go down after it installed an information systems configuration and control system in 2004. Before then, Axia had lost valuable employee work time because of security or other network incidents that caused system outages. Between 2004 and 2007, the new configuration and control system saved the company $590,000 by minimizing system outages (Bartholomew, 2007).

Legal and Regulatory Requirements for Electronic Records Management

Recent U.S. government regulations are forcing companies to take security and control more seriously by mandating the protection of data from abuse, exposure, and unauthorized access. Firms face new legal obligations for the retention and storage of electronic records as well as for privacy protection.

If you work in the healthcare industry, your firm will need to comply with the Health Insurance Portability and Accountability Act (HIPAA) of 1996. **HIPAA** outlines medical security and privacy rules and procedures for simplifying the administration of healthcare billing and automating the transfer of healthcare data between healthcare providers, payers, and plans. It requires members of the healthcare industry to retain patient information for six years and ensure the confidentiality of those records. It specifies privacy, security, and electronic transaction standards for healthcare providers handling patient information, providing penalties for breaches of medical privacy, disclosure of patient records by e-mail, or unauthorized network access.

If you work in a firm providing financial services, your firm will need to comply with the Financial Services Modernization Act of 1999, better known as the **Gramm-Leach-Bliley Act** after its congressional sponsors. This act requires financial institutions to ensure the security and confidentiality of customer data. Data must be stored on a secure medium, and special security measures must be enforced to protect such data on storage media and during transmittal.

If you work in a publicly traded company, your company will need to comply with the Public Company Accounting Reform and Investor Protection Act of 2002, better known as the **Sarbanes-Oxley Act** after its sponsors Senator Paul Sarbanes of Maryland and Representative Michael Oxley of Ohio. This Act was designed to protect investors after the financial scandals at Enron, WorldCom, and other public companies. It imposes responsibility on companies and their management to safeguard the accuracy and integrity of financial information that is used internally and released externally. One of the Learning Tracks for this chapter discusses Sarbanes-Oxley in detail.

Sarbanes-Oxley is fundamentally about ensuring that internal controls are in place to govern the creation and documentation of information in financial statements. Because information systems are used to generate, store, and transport such data, the legislation requires firms to consider information systems security and other controls required to ensure the integrity, confidentiality, and accuracy of their data. Each system application that deals with critical financial reporting data requires controls to make sure the data are accurate. Controls to secure the corporate network, prevent unauthorized access to systems and data, and ensure data integrity and availability in the event of disaster or other disruption of service are essential as well.

Electronic Evidence and Computer Forensics

Security, control, and electronic records management have become essential for responding to legal actions. Much of the evidence today for stock fraud, embezzlement, theft of company trade secrets, computer crime, and many civil cases is in digital form. In addition to information from printed or typewritten pages, legal cases today increasingly rely on evidence represented as digital data stored on portable floppy disks, CDs, and computer hard disk drives, as well as in e-mail, instant messages, and e-commerce transactions over the Internet. E-mail is currently the most common type of electronic evidence.

In a legal action, a firm is obligated to respond to a discovery request for access to information that may be used as evidence, and the company is required by law to produce those data. The cost of responding to a discovery request can be enormous if the company has trouble assembling the required data or the data have been corrupted or destroyed. Courts now impose severe financial and even criminal penalties for improper destruction of electronic documents.

An effective electronic document retention policy ensures that electronic documents, e-mail, and other records are well organized, accessible, and neither retained too long nor discarded too soon. It also reflects an awareness of how to preserve potential evidence for computer forensics. **Computer forensics** is the scientific collection, examination, authentication, preservation, and analysis of data held on or retrieved from computer storage media in such a way that the information can be used as evidence in a court of law. It deals with the following problems:

- Recovering data from computers while preserving evidential integrity
- Securely storing and handling recovered electronic data
- Finding significant information in a large volume of electronic data
- Presenting the information to a court of law

Electronic evidence may reside on computer storage media in the form of computer files and as *ambient data*, which are not visible to the average user. An example might be a file that has been deleted on a PC hard drive. Data that a computer user may have deleted on computer storage media can be recovered through various techniques. Computer forensics experts try to recover such hidden data for presentation as evidence.

An awareness of computer forensics should be incorporated into a firm's contingency planning process. The CIO, security specialists, information systems staff, and corporate legal counsel should all work together to have a plan in place that can be executed if a legal need arises.

ESTABLISHING A FRAMEWORK FOR SECURITY AND CONTROL

Even with the best security tools, your information systems won't be reliable and secure unless you know how and where to deploy them. You'll need to know where your company is at risk and what controls you must have in place to protect your information systems. You'll also need to develop a security policy and plans for keeping your business running if your information systems aren't operational.

Information Systems Controls

Information systems controls are both manual and automated and consist of both general controls and application controls. **General controls** govern the design, security, and use of computer programs and the security of data files in general throughout the organization's information technology infrastructure. On the whole, general controls apply to all computerized applications and consist of a combination of hardware, software, and manual procedures that create an overall control environment.

General controls include software controls, physical hardware controls, computer operations controls, data security controls, controls over implementation of system processes, and administrative controls. Table 1.4 describes the functions of each of these controls.

Application controls are specific controls unique to each computerized application, such as payroll or order processing. They include both automated and manual procedures that ensure that only authorized data are completely and accurately processed by that application. Application controls can be classified as (1) input controls, (2) processing controls, and (3) output controls.

Input controls check data for accuracy and completeness when they enter the system. There are specific input controls for input authorization, data conversion, data editing, and error handling. *Processing controls* establish that data are complete and accurate during updating. *Output controls* ensure that the results of computer processing are accurate, complete, and properly distributed. You can find more detail about application and general controls in our Learning Tracks.

Table 1.4 General Controls

Type of General Control	Description
Software controls	Monitor the use of system software and prevent unauthorized access of software programs, system software, and computer programs.
Hardware controls	Ensure that computer hardware is physically secure, and check for equipment malfunction. Organizations that are critically dependent on their computers also must make provisions for backup or continued operation to maintain constant service.
Computer operations controls	Oversee the work of the computer department to ensure that programmed procedures are consistently and correctly applied to the storage and processing of data. They include controls over the setup of computer processing jobs and backup and recovery procedures for processing that ends abnormally.
Data security controls	Ensure that valuable business data files on either disk or tape are not subject to unauthorized access, change, or destruction while they are in use or in storage.
Implementation controls	Audit the systems development process at various points to ensure that the process is properly controlled and managed.
Administrative controls	Formalize standards, rules, procedures, and control disciplines to ensure that the organization's general and application controls are properly executed and enforced.

Risk Assessment

Before your company commits resources to security and information systems controls, it must know which assets require protection and the extent to which these assets are vulnerable. A risk assessment helps answer these questions and determine the most cost-effective set of controls for protecting assets.

A **risk assessment** determines the level of risk to the firm if a specific activity or process is not properly controlled. Not all risks can be anticipated and measured, but most businesses will be able to acquire some understanding of the risks they face. Business managers working with information systems specialists should try to determine the value of information assets, points of vulnerability, the likely frequency of a problem, and the potential for damage. For example, if an event is likely to occur no more than once a year, with a maximum of a $1,000 loss to the organization, it is not be wise to spend $20,000 on the design and maintenance of a control to protect against that event. However, if that same event could occur at least once a day, with a potential loss of more than $300,000 a year, $100,000 spent on a control might be entirely appropriate.

Table 1.5 illustrates sample results of a risk assessment for an online order processing system that processes 30,000 orders per day. The likelihood of each exposure occurring over a one-year period is expressed as a percentage. The next column shows the highest and lowest possible loss that could be expected each time the exposure occurred and an average loss calculated by adding the highest and lowest figures together and dividing by two. The expected annual loss for each exposure can be determined by multiplying the average loss by its probability of occurrence.

Table 1.5 Online Order Processing Risk Assessment

Exposure	Probability of Occurrence (%)	Loss Range/ Average ($)	Expected Annual Loss ($)
Power failure	30%	$5,000–$200,000 ($102,500)	$30,750
Embezzlement	5%	$1,000–$50,000 ($25,500)	$1,275
User error	98%	$200–$40,000 ($20,100)	$19,698

This risk assessment shows that the probability of a power failure occurring in a one-year period is 30 percent. Loss of order transactions while power is down could range from $5,000 to $200,000 (averaging $102,500) for each occurrence, depending on how long processing is halted. The probability of embezzlement occurring over a yearly period is about 5 percent, with potential losses ranging from $1,000 to $50,000 (and averaging $25,500) for each occurrence. User errors have a 98 percent chance of occurring over a yearly period, with losses ranging from $200 to $40,000 (and averaging $20,100) for each occurrence.

Once the risks have been assessed, system builders will concentrate on the control points with the greatest vulnerability and potential for loss. In this case, controls should focus on ways to minimize the risk of power failures and user errors because anticipated annual losses are highest for these areas.

Security Policy

Once you've identified the main risks to your systems, your company will need to develop a security policy for protecting the company's assets. A **security policy** consists of statements ranking information risks, identifying acceptable security goals, and identifying the mechanisms for achieving these goals. What are the firm's most important information assets? Who generates and controls this information in the firm? What existing security policies are in place to protect the information? What level of risk is management willing to accept for each of these assets? Is it willing, for instance, to lose customer credit data once every 10 years? Or will it build a security system for credit card data that can withstand the once-in-a-hundred-year disaster? Management must estimate how much it will cost to achieve this level of acceptable risk.

The security policy drives policies determining acceptable use of the firm's information resources and which members of the company have access to its information assets. An **acceptable use policy (AUP)** defines acceptable uses of the firm's information resources and computing equipment, including desktop and laptop computers, wireless devices, telephones, and the Internet. The policy should clarify company policy regarding privacy, user responsibility, and personal use of company equipment and networks. A good AUP defines unacceptable and acceptable actions for every user and specifies consequences for noncompliance. For example, security policy at Unilever, the giant multinational consumer goods company, requires every employee equipped with a laptop mobile handheld device to use a company-specified device and employ a password or other method of identification when logging onto the corporate network.

Authorization policies determine differing levels of access to information assets for different levels of users. **Authorization management systems** establish where and when a user is permitted to access certain parts of a Web site or a corporate database. Such systems allow each user access only to those portions of a system that person is permitted to enter, based on information established by a set of access rules.

The authorization management system knows exactly what information each user is permitted to access as shown in Figure 1.5. This figure illustrates the security allowed for two sets of users of an online personnel database containing sensitive information, such as employees' salaries, benefits, and medical histories. One set of users consists of all employees who perform clerical functions, such as inputting employee data into the system. All individuals with this type of profile can update the system but can neither read nor update sensitive fields, such as salary, medical history, or earnings data. Another profile applies to a divisional manager, who cannot update the system but who can read all employee data fields for his or her division, including medical history and salary. These profiles are based on access rules supplied by business groups.

SECURITY PROFILE 1

User: Personnel Dept. Clerk

Location: Division 1

Employee Identification Codes with This Profile: 00753, 27834, 37665, 44116

Data Field Restrictions	Type of Access
All employee data for Division 1 only	Read and Update
• Medical history data	None
• Salary	None
• Pensionable earnings	None

SECURITY PROFILE 2

User: Divisional Personnel Manager

Location: Division 1

Employee Identification Codes with This Profile: 27321

Data Field Restrictions	Type of Access
All employee data for Division 1 only	Read Only

These two examples represent two security profiles or data security patterns that might be found in a personnel system. Depending on the security profile, a user would have certain restrictions on access to various systems, locations, or data in an organization.

Figure 1.5 **Security Profiles for a Personnel System**

The system illustrated in Figure 1.5 provides very fine-grained security restrictions, such as allowing authorized personnel users to inquire about all employee information except that in confidential fields, such as salary or medical history.

Disaster Recovery Planning and Business Continuity Planning

If you run a business, you need to plan for events, such as power outages, floods, earthquakes, or terrorist attacks that will prevent your information systems and your business from operating. **Disaster recovery planning** devises plans for the restoration of computing and communications services after they have been disrupted. Disaster recovery plans focus primarily on the technical issues involved in keeping systems up and running, such as which files to back up and the maintenance of backup computer systems or disaster recovery services.

For example, MasterCard maintains a duplicate computer center in Kansas City, Missouri, to serve as an emergency backup to its primary computer center in St. Louis. Rather than build their own backup facilities, many firms contract with disaster recovery firms, such as Comdisco Disaster Recovery Services in Rosemont, Illinois, and SunGard Availability Services, headquartered in Wayne, Pennsylvania. These disaster recovery firms provide hot sites housing spare computers at locations around the country where subscribing firms can run their critical applications in an emergency. For example, Champion Technologies, which supplies chemicals used in oil and gas operations, is able to switch its enterprise systems from Houston to a SunGard hot site in Scottsdale, Arizona in two hours (Duvall, 2007).

Business continuity planning focuses on how the company can restore business operations after a disaster strikes. The business continuity plan identifies critical business processes and determines action plans for handling mission-critical functions if systems go down. For example, Deutsche Bank, which provides investment banking and asset management services in 74 different countries, has a well-developed business continuity plan that it continually updates and refines. It maintains full-time teams in Singapore, Hong Kong, Japan, India, and Australia to coordinate plans addressing loss of facilities, personnel, or critical systems so that the company can continue to operate when a catastrophic event occurs. Deutsche Bank's plan distinguishes between processes critical for business survival and those critical to crisis support and is coordinated with the company's disaster recovery planning for its computer centers.

Business managers and information technology specialists need to work together on both types of plans to determine which systems and business processes are most critical to the company. They must conduct a business impact analysis to identify the firm's most critical systems and the impact a systems outage would have on the business. Management must determine the maximum amount of time the business can survive with its systems down and which parts of the business must be restored first.

The Role of Auditing

How does management know that information systems security and controls are effective? To answer this question, organizations must conduct comprehensive and systematic audits. An **MIS audit** examines the firm's overall security environment as well as controls governing individual information systems. The auditor should trace the flow of sample transactions through the system and perform tests, using, if appropriate, automated audit software. The MIS audit may also examine data quality.

Security audits review technologies, procedures, documentation, training, and personnel. A thorough audit will even simulate an attack or disaster to test the response of the technology, information systems staff, and business employees.

The audit lists and ranks all control weaknesses and estimates the probability of their occurrence. It then assesses the financial and organizational impact of each threat. Figure 1.6 is a sample auditor's listing of control weaknesses for a loan system. It includes a section for notifying management of such weaknesses and for management's response. Management is expected to devise a plan for countering significant weaknesses in controls.

Function: Loans Location: Peoria, IL	Prepared by: J. Ericson Date: June 16, 2009		Received by: T. Benson Review date: June 28, 2009	
Nature of Weakness and Impact	Chance for Error/Abuse		Notification to Management	
	Yes/No	Justification	Report date	Management response
User accounts with missing passwords	Yes	Leaves system open to unauthorized outsiders or attackers	5/10/09	Eliminate accounts without passwords
Network configured to allow some sharing of system files	Yes	Exposes critical system files to hostile parties connected to the network	5/10/09	Ensure only required directories are shared and that they are protected with strong passwords
Software patches can update production programs without final approval from Standards and Controls group	No	All production programs require management approval; Standards and Controls group assigns such cases to a temporary production status		

This chart is a sample page from a list of control weaknesses that an auditor might find in a loan system in a local commercial bank. This form helps auditors record and evaluate control weaknesses and shows the results of discussing those weaknesses with management, as well as any corrective actions taken by management.

Figure 1.6 **Sample Auditor's List of Control Weaknesses**

TECHNOLOGIES AND TOOLS FOR PROTECTING INFORMATION RESOURCES

Businesses have an array of tools and technologies for protecting their information resources. They include tools and technologies for securing systems and data, ensuring system availability, and ensuring software quality.

Access Control

Access control consists of all the policies and procedures a company uses to prevent improper access to systems by unauthorized insiders and outsiders. To gain access a user must be authorized and authenticated. **Authentication** refers to the ability to know that a person is who he or she claims to be. Access control software is designed to allow only authorized users to use systems or to access data using some method for authentication.

Authentication is often established by using passwords known only to authorized users. An end user uses a password to log on to a computer system and may also use passwords for accessing specific systems and files. However, users often forget passwords, share them, or choose poor passwords that are easy to guess, which compromises security. Password systems that are too rigorous hinder employee productivity. When employees must change complex passwords frequently, they often take shortcuts, such as choosing passwords that are easy to guess or writing down their passwords at their workstations in plain view. Passwords can also be "sniffed" if transmitted over a network or stolen through social engineering.

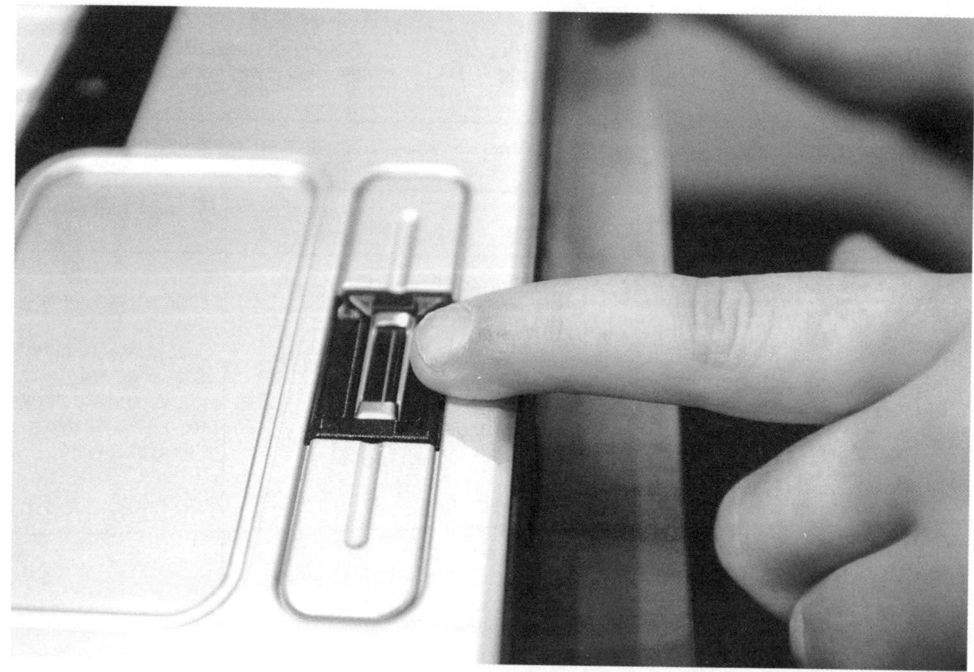

This NEC PC has a biometric fingerprint reader for fast yet secure access to files and networks. New models of PCs are starting to use biometric identification to authenticate users.

New authentication technologies, such as tokens, smart cards, and biometric authentication, overcome some of these problems. A **token** is a physical device, similar to an identification card, that is designed to prove the identity of a single user. Tokens are small gadgets that typically fit on key rings and display passcodes that change frequently. A **smart card** is a device about the size of a credit card that contains a chip formatted with access permission and other data. (Smart cards are also used in electronic payment systems.) A reader device interprets the data on the smart card and allows or denies access.

Biometric authentication uses systems that read and interpret individual human traits, such as fingerprints, irises, and voices, in order to grant or deny access. Biometric authentication is based on the measurement of a physical or behavioral trait that makes each individual unique. It compares a person's unique characteristics, such as the fingerprints, face, or retinal image, against a stored profile of these characteristics to determine whether there are any differences between these characteristics and the stored profile. If the two profiles match, access is granted. Fingerprint and facial recognition technologies are just beginning to be used for security applications. PC laptops are starting to be equipped with fingerprint identification devices.

Firewalls, Intrusion Detection Systems, and Antivirus Software

Without protection against malware and intruders, connecting to the Internet would be very dangerous. Firewalls, intrusion detection systems, and antivirus software have become essential business tools.

Firewalls

A firewall is a combination of hardware and software that controls the flow of incoming and outgoing network traffic and prevents unauthorized users from accessing private networks. It is generally placed between the organization's private internal networks and distrusted external networks, such as the Internet, although firewalls can also be used to protect one part of a company's network from the rest of the network (see Figure 1.7).

The firewall acts like a gatekeeper who examines each user's credentials before access is granted to a network. The firewall identifies names, IP addresses, applications, and other characteristics of incoming traffic. It checks this information against the access rules that have been

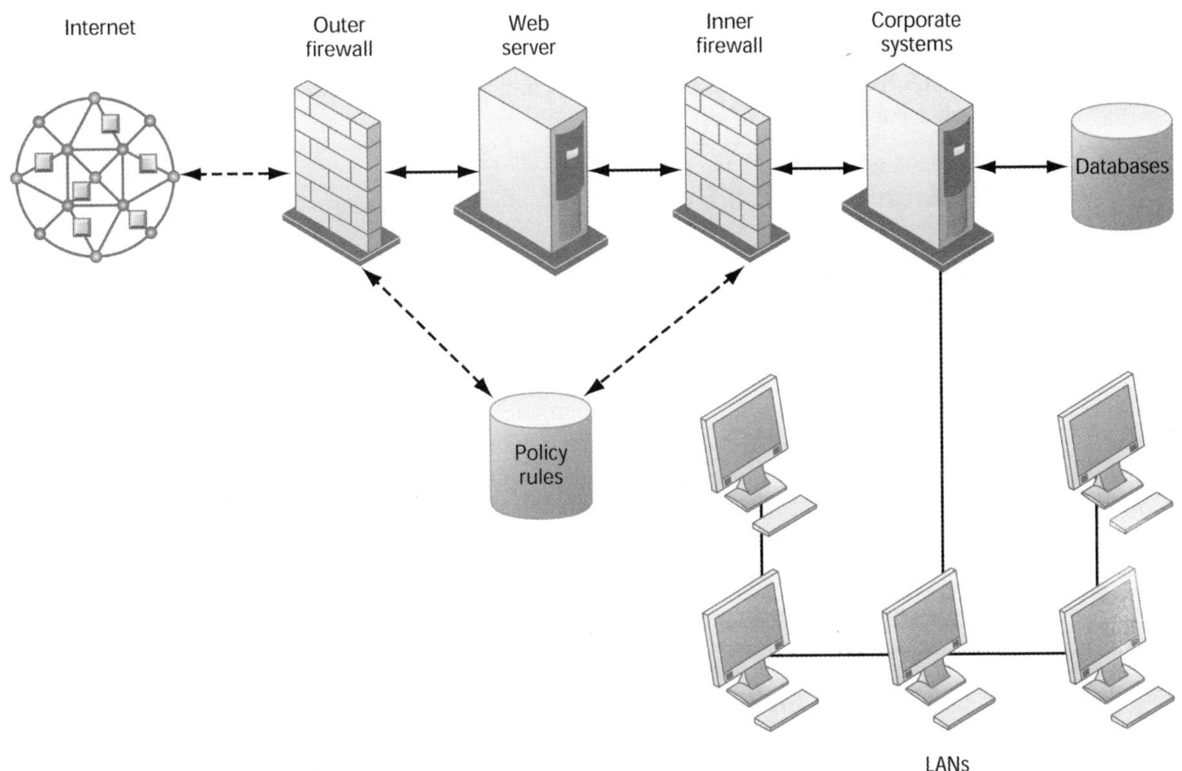

The firewall is placed between the firm's private network and the public Internet or another distrusted network to protect against unauthorized traffic.

Figure 1.7 **A Corporate Firewall**

programmed into the system by the network administrator. The firewall prevents unauthorized communication into and out of the network.

In large organizations, the firewall often resides on a specially designated computer separate from the rest of the network, so no incoming request directly accesses private network resources. There are a number of firewall screening technologies, including static packet filtering, stateful inspection, Network Address Translation, and application proxy filtering. They are frequently used in combination to provide firewall protection.

Packet filtering examines selected fields in the headers of data packets flowing back and forth between the trusted network and the Internet, examining individual packets in isolation. This filtering technology can miss many types of attacks. *Stateful inspection* provides additional security by determining whether packets are part of an ongoing dialogue between a sender and a receiver. It sets up state tables to track information over multiple packets. Packets are accepted or rejected based on whether they are part of an approved conversation or whether they are attempting to establish a legitimate connection.

Network Address Translation (NAT) can provide another layer of protection when static packet filtering and stateful inspection are employed. NAT conceals the IP addresses of the organization's internal host computer(s) to prevent sniffer programs outside the firewall from ascertaining them and using that information to penetrate internal systems.

Application proxy filtering examines the application content of packets. A proxy server stops data packets originating outside the organization, inspects them, and passes a proxy to the other side of the firewall. If a user outside the company wants to communicate with a user inside the organization, the outside user first "talks" to the proxy application and the proxy application communicates with the firm's internal computer. Likewise, a computer user inside the organization goes through the proxy to talk with computers on the outside.

To create a good firewall, an administrator must maintain detailed internal rules identifying the people, applications, or addresses that are allowed or rejected. Firewalls can deter, but not completely prevent, network penetration by outsiders and should be viewed as one element in an overall security plan.

Intrusion Detection Systems

In addition to firewalls, commercial security vendors now provide intrusion detection tools and services to protect against suspicious network traffic and attempts to access files and databases. **Intrusion detection systems** feature full-time monitoring tools placed at the most vulnerable points or "hot spots" of corporate networks to detect and deter intruders continually. The system generates an alarm if it finds a suspicious or anomalous event. Scanning software looks for patterns indicative of known methods of computer attacks, such as bad passwords, checks to see if important files have been removed or modified, and sends warnings of vandalism or system administration errors. Monitoring software examines events as they are happening to discover security attacks in progress. The intrusion detection tool can also be customized to shut down a particularly sensitive part of a network if it receives unauthorized traffic.

Antivirus and Antispyware Software

Defensive technology plans for both individuals and businesses must include antivirus protection for every computer. **Antivirus software** is designed to check computer systems and drives for the presence of computer viruses. Often the software eliminates the virus from the infected area. However, most antivirus software is effective only against viruses already known when the software was written. To remain effective, the antivirus software must be continually updated. Antivirus products are available for many different types of mobile and handheld devices in addition to servers, workstations, and desktop PCs.

Leading antivirus software vendors, such as McAfee, Symantec, and Trend Micro, have enhanced their products to include protection against spyware. Antispyware software tools such as Ad-Aware, Spybot S&D, and Spyware Doctor are also very helpful.

Unified Threat Management Systems

To help businesses reduce costs and improve manageability, security vendors have combined into a single appliance various security tools, including firewalls, virtual private networks, intrusion detection systems, and Web content filtering and antispam software. These comprehensive security management products are called **unified threat management (UTM)** systems. Although initially aimed at small and medium-sized businesss, UTM products are available for all sizes of networks. Leading UTM vendors include Crossbeam, Fortinent, and Secure Computing, and networking vendors such as Cisco Systems and Juniper Networks provide some UTM capabilities in their equipment.

Securing Wireless Networks

Despite its flaws, WEP provides some margin of security if Wi-Fi users remember to activate it. A simple first step to thwart hackers is to assign a unique name to your network's SSID and instruct your router not to broadcast it. Corporations can further improve Wi-Fi security by using it in conjunction with virtual private network (VPN) technology when accessing internal corporate data.

In June 2004 the Wi-Fi Alliance industry trade group finalized the 802.11i specification (also referred to as Wi-Fi Protected Access 2 or WPA2) that replaces WEP with stronger security standards. Instead of the static encryption keys used in WEP, the new standard uses much longer keys that continually change, making them harder to crack. It also employs an encrypted authentication system with a central authentication server to ensure that only authorized users access the network.

Encryption and Public Key Infrastructure

Many businesses use encryption to protect digital information that they store, physically transfer, or send over the Internet. **Encryption** is the process of transforming plain text or data into cipher text that cannot be read by anyone other than the sender and the intended receiver. Data are encrypted by using a secret numerical code, called an encryption key, that transforms plain data into cipher text. The message must be decrypted by the receiver.

Two methods for encrypting network traffic on the Web are SSL and S-HTTP. **Secure Sockets Layer (SSL)** and its successor Transport Layer Security (TLS) enable client and server computers to manage encryption and decryption activities as they communicate with each other during a secure Web session. **Secure Hypertext Transfer Protocol (S-HTTP)** is another protocol used for encrypting data flowing over the Internet, but it is limited to individual messages, whereas SSL and TLS are designed to establish a secure connection between two computers.

The capability to generate secure sessions is built into Internet client browser software and servers. The client and the server negotiate what key and what level of security to use. Once a secure session is established between the client and the server, all messages in that session are encrypted.

There are two alternative methods of encryption: symmetric key encryption and public key encryption. In symmetric key encryption, the sender and receiver establish a secure Internet session by creating a single encryption key and sending it to the receiver so both the sender and receiver share the same key. The strength of the encryption key is measured by its bit length. Today, a typical key will be 128 bits long (a string of 128 binary digits).

The problem with all symmetric encryption schemes is that the key itself must be shared somehow among the senders and receivers, which exposes the key to outsiders who might just be able to intercept and decrypt the key. A more secure form of encryption called **public key encryption** uses two keys: one shared (or public) and one totally private as shown in Figure 1.8. The keys are mathematically related so that data encrypted with one key can be decrypted using only the other key. To send and receive messages, communicators first create separate pairs of private and public keys. The public key is kept in a directory and the private key must be kept secret. The sender encrypts a message with the recipient's public key. On receiving the message, the recipient uses his or her private key to decrypt it.

Digital certificates are data files used to establish the identity of users and electronic assets for protection of online transactions (see Figure 1.9). A digital certificate system uses a trusted third party, known as a certificate authority (CA), to validate a user's identity. There are many CAs in the United States and around the world, including VeriSign, IdenTrust, and Australia's KeyPost.

The CA verifies a digital certificate user's identity offline. This information is put into a CA server, which generates an encrypted digital certificate containing owner identification information and a copy of the owner's public key. The certificate authenticates that the public key

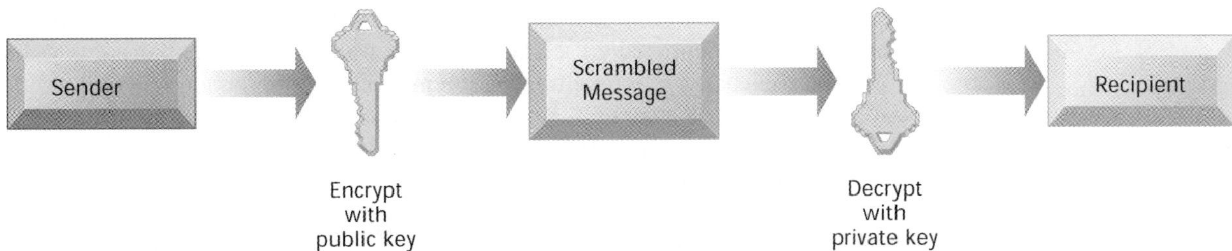

A public key encryption system can be viewed as a series of public and private keys that lock data when they are transmitted and unlock the data when they are received. The sender locates the recipient's public key in a directory and uses it to encrypt a message. The message is sent in encrypted form over the Internet or a private network. When the encrypted message arrives, the recipient uses his or her private key to decrypt the data and read the message.

Figure 1.8 **Public Key Encryption**

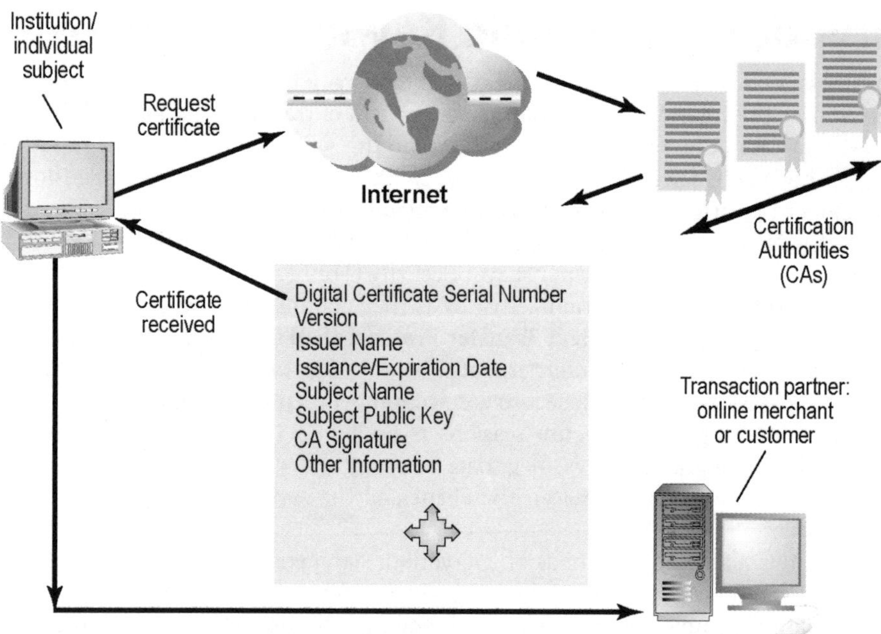

Digital certificates help establish the identity of people or electronic assets. They protect online transactions by providing secure, encrypted, online communication.

Figure 1.9 **Digital Certificates**

belongs to the designated owner. The CA makes its own public key available publicly either in print or perhaps on the Internet. The recipient of an encrypted message uses the CA's public key to decode the digital certificate attached to the message, verifies it was issued by the CA, and then obtains the sender's public key and identification information contained in the certificate. Using this information, the recipient can send an encrypted reply. The digital certificate system would enable, for example, a credit card user and a merchant to validate that their digital certificates were issued by an authorized and trusted third party before they exchange data. **Public key infrastructure (PKI)**, the use of public key cryptography working with a certificate authority, is now widely used in e-commerce.

Ensuring System Availability

As companies increasingly rely on digital networks for revenue and operations, they need to take additional steps to ensure that their systems and applications are always available. Firms such as those in the airline and financial services industries with critical applications requiring online transaction processing have traditionally used fault-tolerant computer systems for many years to ensure 100-percent availability. In **online transaction processing**, transactions entered online are immediately processed by the computer. Multitudinous changes to databases, reporting, and requests for information occur each instant.

Fault-tolerant computer systems contain redundant hardware, software, and power supply components that create an environment that provides continuous, uninterrupted service. Fault-tolerant computers use special software routines or self-checking logic built into their circuitry to detect hardware failures and automatically switch to a backup device. Parts from these computers can be removed and repaired without disruption to the computer system.

Fault tolerance should be distinguished from **high-availability computing**. Both fault tolerance and high-availability computing try to minimize downtime. **Downtime** refers to periods of time in which a system is not operational. However, high-availability computing helps firms recover quickly from a system crash, whereas fault tolerance promises continuous availability and the elimination of recovery time altogether.

High-availability computing environments are a minimum requirement for firms with heavy e-commerce processing or for firms that depend on digital networks for their internal operations. High-availability computing requires backup servers, distribution of processing across multiple servers, high-capacity storage, and good disaster recovery and business continuity plans. The firm's computing platform must be extremely robust with scalable processing power, storage, and bandwidth.

Researchers are exploring ways to make computing systems recover even more rapidly when mishaps occur, an approach called **recovery-oriented computing**. This work includes designing systems that recover quickly, and implementing capabilities and tools to help operators pinpoint the sources of faults in multi-component systems and easily correct their mistakes.

Controlling Network Traffic: Deep Packet Inspection

Have you ever tried to use your campus network and found it was very slow?

It may be because your fellow students are using the network to download music or watch YouTube. Bandwith-consuming applications such as file-sharing programs, Internet phone service, and online video are able to clog and slow down corporate networks, degrading performance. For example, Ball Sate University in Muncie, Indiana, found its network had slowed because a small minority of students were using peer-to-peer file sharing programs to download movies and music.

A technology called **deep packet inspection (DPI)** helps solve this problem. DPI examines data files and sorts out low-priority online material while assigning higher priority to business-critical files. Based on the priorities established by a network's operators, it decides whether a specific data packet can continue to its destination or should be blocked or delayed while more important traffic proceeds. Using a DPI system from Allot Communications, Ball State was able to cap the amount of file-sharing traffic and assign it a much lower priority. Ball State's preferred network traffic speeded up (White, 2007).

Security Outsourcing

Many companies, especially small businesses, lack the resources or expertise to provide a secure high-availability computing environment on their own. They can outsource many security functions to **managed security service providers (MSSPs)** that monitor network activity and perform vulnerability testing and intrusion detection. Guardent (acquired by VeriSign), BT Counterpane, VeriSign, and Symantec are leading providers of MSSP services.

Ensuring Software Quality

In addition to implementing effective security and controls, organizations can improve system quality and reliability by employing software metrics and rigorous software testing. Software metrics are objective assessments of the system in the form of quantified measurements. Ongoing use of metrics allows the information systems department and end users to jointly measure the performance of the system and identify problems as they occur. Examples of software metrics include the number of transactions that can be processed in a specified unit of time, online response time, the number of payroll checks printed per hour, and the number of known bugs per hundred lines of program code. For metrics to be successful, they must be carefully designed, formal, objective, and used consistently.

Early, regular, and thorough testing will contribute significantly to system quality. Many view testing as a way to prove the correctness of work they have done. In fact, we know that all sizable software is riddled with errors, and we must test to uncover these errors.

Good testing begins before a software program is even written by using a *walkthrough*—a review of a specification or design document by a small group of people carefully selected based on the skills needed for the particular objectives being tested. Once developers start writing software programs, coding walkthroughs also can be used to review program code. However, code must be tested by computer runs. When errors are discovered, the source is found and eliminated through a process called *debugging*.

INTERACTIVE SESSION: TECHNOLOGY

SECURITY AT ICICI BANK

ICICI Bank Limited (ICICI Bank) is India's second largest bank, with total assets of U.S. $ 79.00 billion at March 31, 2007. It provides a wide range of products and services related to consumer/retail banking, and corporate banking. It has a network of about 950 branches, 3,300 ATMs in India and presence in 17 countries.

Started in 1994, ICICI Bank's systems were built up from a point at which nothing had been done, as there was no old legacy system in place. It adopted a flexible IT structure instead of a traditional mainframe-based system. It had centralized its back office operations, leaving branches to focus on the customers for better service. Information security was also managed with central control.

By June 2003, the bank already had a security infrastructure in place. To perfect its security strategies, it hired Murli Nambiar as Head of the Information Security Group in 2005. The first thing on Nambiar's agenda was to identify the vulnerable areas to determine security gaps. For example, perimeter security, internal networks and wireless networks were some of the areas that were identified. Securing these different domains, one at a time, coupled with the stress on security awareness for users and regular policy compliance audits, helped the bank to have a well-rounded security strategy.

In 2007, a risk management framework was developed to assess every application for risk before it was deployed at the bank's datacenter. To avoid internal risk, the bank developed stringent policies to lock down devices, and facilities were provided on a need-to-use basis. Only a few employees were allowed to use external storage devices such as pen drives and CD-Rs.

A security operations center for monitoring the security 24/7 was also set up. The group normally resolved the issues and escalated matters to the security officers—comprising domain experts for LAN, WAN, Web and database security—for second level support. The security officers further escalated the issues to the management for any corporate decisions.

An alternate disaster-recovery site, with the equipment identical at both the primary and secondary site, was also created. The BCP plan included the recovery time objective for each system.

Several security systems were used to protect the assets from internal and external threats. Firewalls, intrusion detection systems, anti-virus, as well as routers, were use to secure the perimeter. Encryption software was loaded on desktops, servers and laptops. The bank also developed in-house messenger software to provide secure instant messaging for users. The wireless LAN was secured with encryption and unnecessary protocols were disabled on the network printers.

In order to make sure that each device on the network was always updated with the latest patches, the bank's Information Security team decided to centralize and automate the process of updating and rolling out patches. This was accomplished by customizing LANDesk Manager from Allied Digital, in order to inhibit selected applications from launching and protect data leakages through centralized port control.

The bank also conducted training programs for the IT administrators, system and application owners and Web developers. While the Web developers were trained annually on secure coding practices, code reviews were done to determine the efficacy of the process. E-mails were sent regularly to end users and administrators to make them aware of the security threats.

In May 2008, the bank developed the Logical Access Management (LAM) system as a centralized control application for users accessing the bank's Web site. In the past, the bank had used paper/mail based approval for identity and access management, which involved retaining the record for audit and compliance. The centralized repository of user database across applications was not available and manual review of user access rights in various applications was time-consuming. LAM had helped the bank in reducing turnaround time for requests, strengthening access controls and reducing cost in servicing customers.

In September 2008, the bank was awarded the Symantec Visionary Award for innovative use of Symantec's products for secure and better management of systems and information. The bank implemented an array of new systems including Symantec Endpoint Protection for endpoint security; Symantec Security Information Manager for centralized security management; and Symantec DeepSight Threat management System for real-time threat reports.

Sources: Anil Patrick R., "Step by Step," networkmagazineindia.com, accessed November 2008; Vinita Gupta, "ICICI Bank," networkmagazineindia.com, accessed November 2008; "ICICI Bank—Security and Patch Management," www.ciol.com, accessed November 2008; Fakir Balaji, "ICICI Bank, TVS Motor Bag Symantec Awards," sify.com, September 2008; "ICICI Bank: Logical Access Management," pcquest.ciol.com, May 2008.

CASE STUDY QUESTIONS

1. List and describe the security measures at ICICI bank.
2. For each security measure, describe the threats that it is effective for.
3. Do you think these measures are adequate? What should the bank do to safeguard its systems in future?
4. How do the measures at ICICI bank compare with those mentioned earlier in the chapter? Are there any gaps?

MIS IN ACTION

Visit the ICICI Web site at www.icicibank.com and then answer the following questions related to Internet security:

1. What assurances, if any, does the bank provide on its Web site to indicate to its customers that its banking systems are safe and secure? For example, look under Internet Banking (and customer care).
2. Look at the information present at the link below. http://www.icicibank.com/Pfsuser/temp/onlinesecurity.htm
3. What types of IT breaches are mentioned and what recommendations does the bank have for its customers? Compare them with the guidelines mentioned in the chapter.

- Case contributed by Neerja Sethi and Vijay Sethi, Nanyang Technological University

Electronic Commerce and Business

A BRIEF INTRODUCTION TO E-COMMERCE

E-commerce is certainly not a new phenomenon. Electronic data interchange has been available for over 25 years and has had a number of very successful applications in that time. The range of EDI applications includes such diverse activities as the issuing of student examination results from central examining boards to schools and the registering of investors who are interested in purchasing new issues of shares in companies. However, the major concentration of EDI activity has been in heavy manufacturing industries and in high-volume and routine restocking.

In the last 10 years there has been explosive growth in e-commerce developments. The reducing cost and complexity involved in establishing electronic connectivity is clearly a prime factor in this growth. In addition, the Internet has opened the door to different ways of trading; it supports the traditional system-to-system trading seen in EDI but also allows for computer-mediated trading between otherwise unconnected companies, and between companies and individuals.

The development of websites

There are many advantages to an organization in developing a website. These include:

- **Reduction in cost of advertising:** Organizations, particularly those selling products or services, rely on providing information and advertising to a marketplace in order to attract new customers and retain existing ones. The cost of this is considerable, especially if achieved through the media—newspapers, magazines, television, radio, advertising hoardings. Alternatively, mailshots may also be used. These are also very expensive unless target mail groups are tightly defined. However, running a website is comparatively cheap. Computer hardware, the design of the site and maintenance seldom take a start-up cost of more than a few thousand pounds or dollars. Once running, the website provides 24-hour access daily across the world. Nowadays, the content of advertising on the web is sophisticated in relation to that provided a few years ago. The move towards regarding the design of website material to be the province of the creative rather than the computing media has ensured that the approaches towards advertising commonly seen on television are now becoming more prevalent on the Web.
- **Cheaper and easier provision of information:** Some organizations, particularly public services, provide information. These traditionally have been by way of paper-based publications or through recorded telephone messages. Putting such reports on a website to provide electronic access offers a cheaper way to disperse information for the host organization and a faster and more convenient method of access for the public (at least the public with access to the Internet). Governments, and non-government organizations that are not commercial, now provide extensive information services on the Web.
- **Ease of update:** An organization can easily update its product range, list of services, list of prices or any other information if provided on a web page. This compares with the costly resending of catalogues and other paper-based information through the postal system.
- **Lack of need to maintain a shop front:** When viewing an organization's supply of information, or list of products and services, the web user does not need to enter the organization's premises—there is no need therefore for the organization to maintain a costly shop front. Indeed, the view of the organization is largely determined by the impression given by its web pages, unless the organization is a household name. For a business this is important as it can overcome the limitations of capital investment in the provision of expensive buildings to impress clients. Importantly for the business, the web user has little idea whether they are dealing with a large multinational or a small business. In this way, the small business can compete with the large. From the perspective of the customer,

however, it is difficult to make judgements about the status of the business behind the web page.

- **The ease of crossing geographical boundaries:** Because the Internet provides global access the business has a worldwide audience through its web pages. If the business is selling a product, provided that postal or shipping services are reliable, even a small business is able to market and sell its products globally. If the product is information, this can easily be dispensed electronically.
- **The absence of the middleman:** A business that needs a distributor and a retailer to ensure its goods are sold and delivered to a customer can now dispense with these middlemen. Direct marketing to the customer is possible. It should, however, be pointed out that in many cases retailers provide a service over and above that of merely being point of sale. Advice and other services may also be provided. But if the customer is in need of no such help, then the shop front becomes superfluous.

Multi-channel commerce

For most existing businesses the issue is not about e-commerce being a new or alternative way of conducting business but about providing an additional complementary avenue for trade. The challenge here is to align the electronic business with existing channels, such as the traditional so-called bricks and mortar business, tele-sales, catalogue business, and so on. This requires a strategic approach that looks holistically at the business and fits e-commerce into the overall structure of the organization. Recent evidence suggests that the most successful e-commerce ventures are those with a traditional business background or infrastructure; these multi-channel organizations are sometimes called 'clicks and mortar' businesses.

E-COMMERCE—KEY FEATURES

E-commerce can be defined as

> *any exchange of information or business transaction that is facilitated by the use of information and communications technologies.*

Although the popular perception of e-commerce is that of individuals buying goods and services over the Internet, the parties involved are more likely to be small and large companies and public authorities or other not-for-profit organizations rather than home computer users. The variety of systems used to facilitate e-commerce is huge, and it is helpful to attempt to categorize them. Whiteley (2000) classifies e-commerce systems as falling into one of three categories:

1. **Electronic markets:** These are information sources that can be used to search for a particular service or product. Rail travel operators might provide timetables of services, details about seat types and other services, and various ticket options. In such an electronic market, customers can examine the alternatives and make comparisons between the services and prices offered before making a purchasing decision. In addition, the Internet allows for the provision of other information services, such as after-sales service, technical support and the sharing of expertise.
2. **Electronic data interchange:** Companies, in their regular dealings with other trading partners, such as suppliers and retail outlets, might establish electronic communications to process the volume of transactions carried out. These lines of communication might be permanent, using leased telephone connections, or established temporarily for the duration of the transactions, using the Internet to establish the connection. EDI provides a standard protocol for encoding this data exchange.
3. **Internet commerce:** This category of e-commerce incorporates the popular image of home computer users making purchases over the Internet. In fact it includes a much broader range of trading. In Internet commerce, goods and services are advertised and individual transactions are executed. The participants might both be businesses, leading to a business-to-business (B2B) transaction, or might involve a private individual, in which case the transaction is described as business-to-customer (B2C).

CONDUCTING BUSINESS OVER THE INTERNET

Trading over the Internet creates challenges and opportunities. As has already been stated, business can be conducted at any time of the day. Markets become globally accessible, whether on the opposite side of the world or, possibly just as important, in the locality of the company itself. Small operators discover new-found access to large companies, and vice versa. In addition, e-commerce pays no attention to time differences between countries.

In many market sectors, the introduction of e-commerce has changed the nature of the business itself. In the music distribution and software industries, the medium adopted for creating and storing the product has evolved progressively using advances in the hardware (from tapes through CDs to DVDs). Now the distribution of the product is being revolutionized with Internet releases and online product updates.

The features that make a product more likely to be able to be sold over the Internet are:

- browsing over a range of products where touch prior to purchase is not needed;
- no advice is needed from the seller;
- the desired choice is known unambiguously by a title or specification;
- the range of products is large (and difficult to accommodate under one shop front);
- the products can be dispatched easily (ideally non-bulky, high-price products);
- there would not be differences in the quality of the product between one seller and another.

The economic comparison of retailing through a shop front and through the Internet is given for a typical outlet in Figure 1.10.

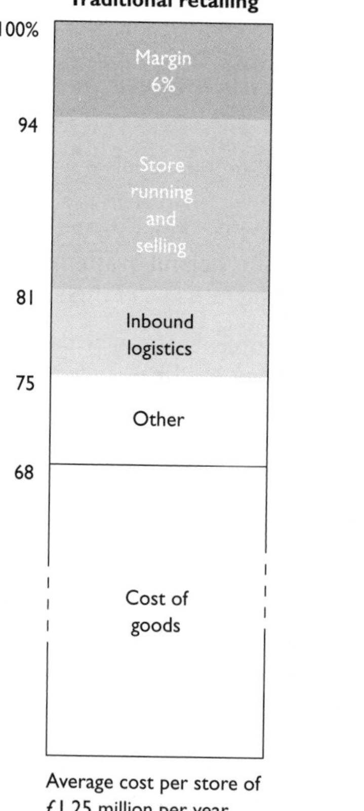

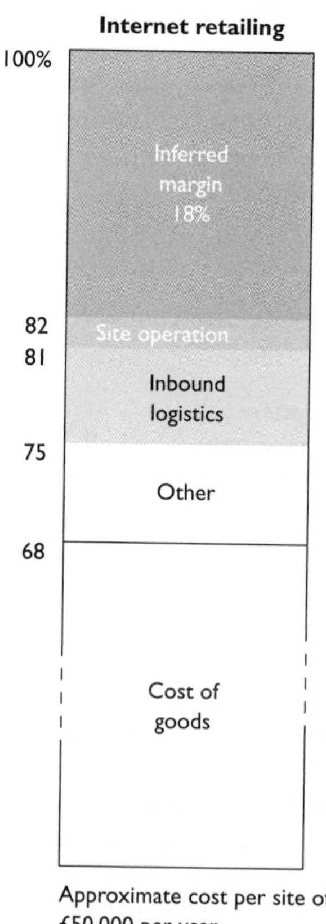

Source: Authors' own work based on figures presented by Hoskyns Gemini

Figure 1.10 **A comparison of Internet and traditional retailing margins**

The expansion of e-commerce brings about associated benefits. The participants become members of virtual communities in ways that are not possible through traditional trading. Marketplaces have become more open and trading activities more diverse. In addition, e-commerce allows businesses to gain competitive advantage in a number of ways:

- **Price competitiveness:** Reduced transaction costs in automated ordering and invoicing systems can lead to lower prices.
- **Timeliness:** Faster ordering, delivery and invoicing can reduce the time to market for suppliers.
- **Knowledge of market:** Trading electronically provides additional methods for companies to acquire knowledge of the market in which they operate. Customer information and profiling can improve the trading relationship and lead to new marketing opportunities.

MINI CASE 1.1

LEGAL SERVICES

The provision of legal services over the Internet is becoming increasingly widespread. Examples include the writing of wills, support for the purchase and sale of property, and online quotations.

Traditionally, in the UK, the buyer of a property instructs a solicitor to act on their behalf. If the client also has a property to sell the same solicitor will often take on this additional role. The solicitor acts on behalf of their client by liaising with the solicitor of the vendor of the desired property, with local authorities, with the land registry and other interested parties. They also collect and hold the deposit paid on the property and ensure that the exchange of contracts occurs smoothly and moves through to the completion of a sale.

Fidler and Pepper are a UK-based partnership of solicitors comprising six partners and fifty staff distributed over three offices in the Nottinghamshire area. They have been operating a website (www.fidler.co.uk) since 1995 that offers a range of services to clients, including an online matter progress report to inform their clients about the latest developments in the sale and purchase of their properties. The system also preserves confidentiality by assigning a unique case number to each property purchase or sale and by using a system of passwords to prevent unauthorized access.

'The system has made a huge difference', says Mat Slade, the partner responsible for conveyancing. 'From the client's viewpoint there is up-to-the-minute notification about all issues. The system cuts out those frustrating switchboard delays and telephone transfers. More importantly, it gives 24-hours-a-day access to information that previously could only be obtained by speaking to a solicitor and thereby incurring additional expense. It also makes us accountable to the client in that if any piece of work hasn't been done the client will see that it hasn't been done on the online reports.'

'From a company perspective', said Slade, 'it provides an internal tracking system across our intranet whereby we can trace and monitor work flow and, if necessary, share work loads between us. Another useful advantage is the reduction in low-priority phone calls from clients which, although well intentioned, could slow down progress.'

The latest improvements to the system include a facility to communicate case matters on the website to clients using the mobile phone short message service (SMS). Slade says: 'With over 50% of the population having mobile phones we believe that this is a huge step forward in providing clients with up-to-date information at what is a very stressful time. As soon as an important step is progressed on a file, for example exchange of contracts or the local search is received, a short text message is automatically sent to the client's mobile phone telling them what has happened.'

'We definitely believe we have gained a competitive advantage from using the system', added Slade. 'Solicitors are notoriously slow at adopting new technology. Our client base has opened up, taking us from being essentially a regional service to becoming an international operation.'

QUESTIONS

1. Outline the advantages of web-based support for legal services.
2. In a customer-focused environment such as this, could the Internet eventually replace the personal contact traditionally offered by solicitors?

The drivers for using the Internet for business

A number of factors are promoting the adoption of e-commerce:

- **Cost:** For a business, the entry costs for participating in e-commerce are relatively low. Systems can be designed and implemented and a web presence can be established relatively cheaply. The systems therefore offer a potentially fast return on the investment.
- **Flexibility:** Organizations can select the appropriate level of participation from simple access to the Internet through the creation of a Web presence to full-blown transaction-handling systems. The systems can be developed incrementally to add this additional functionality.
- **Protecting investment:** In the Internet world, many common and open standards are employed. The switching costs incurred when a business selects an alternative system are, as a result, relatively low.
- **Connectivity and communications opportunities:** Buying into Internet technology brings an accompanying range of opportunities, such as creating a local intranet or establishing video-conferencing links.
- **Low risk:** A critical mass of e-commerce participants already exists, and the technology, although constantly developing, is well understood. In addition, there are many government initiatives aimed at promoting e-commerce, and there is a significant level of activity in educational institutions to provide additional backup.
- **Improved customer service:** Although essentially a medium that promotes relationships at a distance, the Internet does also provide opportunities for businesses to work more closely with customers. For example, many techniques of directed, or focused, marketing are made easier when trading over the Internet.
- **Globalization:** The competitive pressures on businesses are increasingly of an international dimension. The Internet provides an easier and lower cost route for companies to participate in global business activity.

MINI CASE 1.2

E-COMMERCE AND GLOBALIZATION

Blue Nile, an online seller of diamonds and jewellery, is to become one of the first 'pure play'* US retailers to cross the Atlantic, in a move that reflects the growing interest of such companies in international expansion.

The potential of international sales for US retailers has been demonstrated by Amazon, the world's largest retailing website. Amazon's sites in the UK, Japan, Germany, China and France accounted for 46% of the company's $3bn sales in its first quarter, and rose faster than North American sales.

Scott Silverman, executive director of Shop.org, an association whose membership is made up of US e-commerce retailers, said he had seen evidence of growing interest in international markets as his members became more confident. 'Companies such as Blue Nile that have been around for six or seven years are pretty big. They are seeing some signs that 50% per year growth cannot continue, so international expansions seem to be an increasingly attractive option for them', he said.

At the same time, UK underwear retailer Figleaves.com and the Italian fashion site Yoox have established US offshoots. Jim Okamura, partner at JC Williams retail consultancy, noted that online-led international expansion is being explored by US chains that have started to reach the limits of market growth at home. 'It's not for everyone, but we've definitely seen a growing interest in international expansion strategies that use an e-commerce platform as an initial entry point', he said, citing efforts by JC Penney and Victoria's Secret to develop online sales in Canada.

Blue Nile says its operation will be in Ireland and involve 'only a handful of employees', with site technology handled from the US. So far, it has sold goods worth about $3.3m to UK customers using a trial site with products priced in dollars.

Adapted from: **Blue Nile uses website to extend across the Atlantic**
Jonathan Birchall in New York, 14 May 2007

QUESTIONS

1. What motivates businesses to expand into new international markets?
2. To what extent does e-commerce make international expansion a more realistic proposition?

* 'pure play' is where a company specializes in one particular product or service area to obtain a brand identity and large market share in that area.

Barriers to entry

Despite the many drivers persuading businesses to venture into e-commerce activities, there are nonetheless several concerns that might induce caution.

- **Uncertainty over business models:** The technology has developed at such a pace that businesses have had little time to reflect on the most appropriate structures to facilitate e-commerce. This concern could lead to a reluctance of some businesses to commit themselves to e-commerce solutions. Business models are discussed further in the section on e-commerce business models (p. 50).
- **Telecommunications costs:** In many geographical areas, particularly outside the USA, the cost of telephone communications is a significant factor. This situation is changing rapidly, as local calls in particular are becoming much cheaper, if not completely free, in many countries. The cost of leased lines, while an expensive option for smaller enterprises, is also becoming less prohibitive.
- **Bandwidth:** The multimedia content of the traffic on the Internet can create bottlenecks and slow down other forms of Internet access. The managers of many organizations fear that providing a facility for employees to access online sports updates and events, radio and TV broadcasts on their PCs might interfere with the normal running of the business. Continuing improvements in hardware, software and network infrastructure, along with the increasing uptake of broadband connectivity, are helping to alleviate the effects of increasing volumes of data transfer requests.
- **Security:** Several notable breaches of security have caused organizations to be cautious about implementing e-commerce solutions. Major problems have been caused by recent violations of confidentiality such as the customers of Internet banks being shown the account details of other customers, by virus attacks, and by unauthorized intrusion (e.g. Microsoft source code being stolen).
- **Lack of clear standards:** Although the Internet operates on largely open standards some tensions remain, for example the battle between Netscape and Microsoft to produce the de facto web browser.
- **Law and legal frameworks:** The global Internet environment poses many questions over legal issues, particularly when disputes occur. Trading may cross national boundaries, and the appropriate contract law must be employed. This can be difficult to establish where customer, vendor and web server are all located in different countries.
- **Preparedness:** Many businesses foresee the 'crest of the wave' effect of participating in e-commerce and are cautious about entering this global marketplace until completely prepared (for example, Fedex competitors).

TRADE CYCLES AND E-COMMERCE

This section considers the three modes of e-commerce identified earlier in the chapter and investigates how they map on to more traditional business trade cycles.

E-commerce and traditional trade cycles

Business transactions have traditionally fallen into one of three so-called trade cycles. These cycles reflect the participants, the frequency of the transactions and the nature of the transactions involved.

Repeat trade cycles

This pattern of trading is characterized by companies that are closely linked in the supply chain. A typical example might be a manufacturer selling components to an assembly plant, or a regional warehouse supplying stocks to a supermarket. Often the restocking follows the just-in-time approach of maintaining minimal stock levels. In repeat trade cycles, orders are placed at regular intervals, invoicing is carried out periodically, and settlement is often automated.

Transactions that feature in repeat trade cycles are most suited to an EDI e-commerce solution. The placing of orders, raising and issuing of invoices and transfer of funds electronically (represented by the shaded area in Figure 1.11) can all be carried out using EDI technology. Once the initial negotiations have established the specification of product or service and price, the trading cycle iterates around the execution and settlement phases. Changes to the initial contract are shown by the feedback loop to the pre-sale phase. Once renegotiated, the business falls back into a new iteration of execution and settlement.

Irregular invoiced transactions

This form of trade is normally characterized by business-to-business transactions. One company might search for the best price or trading arrangements from a number of competing suppliers before placing an order. Settlement is often achieved through an invoice relating to the particular order placed, and payment is made at a later date. An example of this sort of trade is an estate agent locating a property on behalf of a customer, based on a set of criteria.

The search described above reflects the category of e-commerce that was classified as electronic markets. An estate agent might use a property management system to compare details such as location, number of bedrooms and price. The focus of the interaction is usually only on the investigation (highlighted in Figure 1.12), although in other situations, such as a travel agent locating a particular journey, it may follow the transaction through to payment. The e-commerce trade cycle in the former case is unlikely to cover all stages of the transaction, as the estate agent is acting only as an intermediary. The settlement and after-sales components are more likely to be dealt with by traditional business methods.

Irregular cash transactions

The third type of trade cycle is that of irregular cash transactions. This equates to a one-off purchase of a service or product by an individual or a company. The settlement is normally made

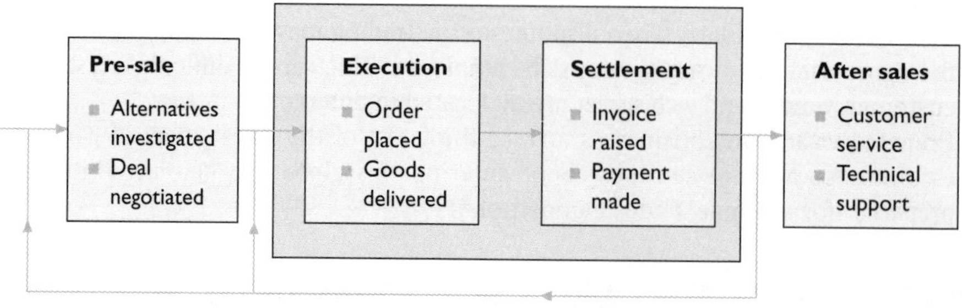

Source: FT.com

Figure 1.11 Repeat trade cycles

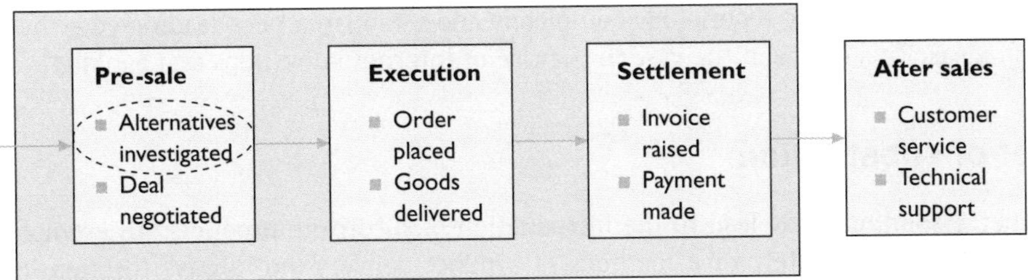

Figure 1.12 Irregular invoiced transactions

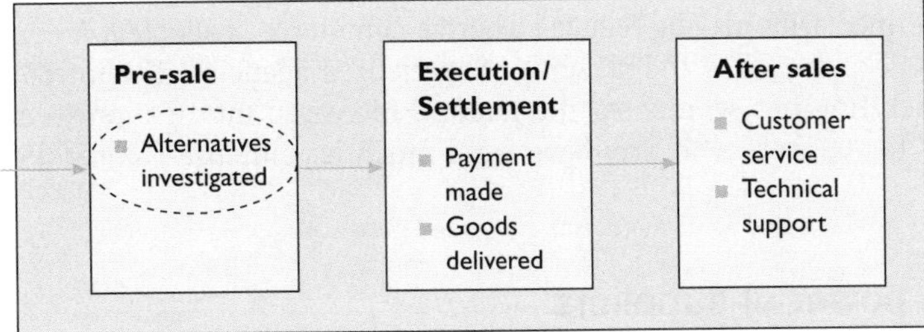

Figure 1.13 Irregular cash transactions

at the point of sale. The term 'cash' is therefore misleading, as payment may be by a variety of methods, such as a credit card. However, the principle is that mechanics of payment are established and commenced.

The best-understood aspect of e-commerce is that of individual 'home shoppers' purchasing goods and services over the Internet. However, the model does also apply to business-to-business transactions. As with the previous example, the Internet-based component may only comprise the search for and investigation of alternative products (highlighted in Figure 1.13). This again is characteristic of the electronic market classification of e-commerce. More often, however, the search leads to an online purchase with settlement and execution being combined into one phase and, in the case of software and music, delivery may be instantaneous. After-sales service may also be provided through access to a website with e-mail contact. In this case, the full activity of Internet commerce occurs with the entire transaction from pre-sale through to after-sales being conducted electronically.

New variants on the trade cycles

An e-commerce solution provides additional business opportunities and creates variations on the traditional trade cycles described above. Customers participating in irregular transactions may undertake only a pre-sales enquiry or use only the after-sales facilities such as 'frequently asked questions'.

Once the lines of communication between participants in e-commerce have been established, it is possible to distribute a company newsletter or marketing mailshot. In other situations, it may be desirable to implement an order and delivery tracking service.

Porter's five forces model and e-commerce

This model of competitive forces can usefully be applied to the e-commerce marketplace.

Threat of new entrants

Competitors considering adopting e-commerce may not need to match the IT infrastructure of the existing players. Indeed, because of the rapid development of new technology, it may be possible to bypass existing technology completely and establish a new 'leading edge' by employing fresh ideas. This has been the case in the rise of Internet bookshops and banking.

Threat of substitution

E-commerce solutions may lead to the introduction of substitute products. An example is seen in the introduction of alternative methods of product delivery, not always through legitimate channels, such as in the software, books and recorded music businesses.

Bargaining power of buyers

The role of intermediaries may be reduced where e-commerce is adopted. An example of this is seen in airline ticketing, once the preserve of specialized agencies. The introduction of cheap online flight ticketing has segmented the market. Increased information to customers poses similar threats to suppliers who may have faced much less intense competition in traditional markets.

Bargaining power of suppliers

As has been stated previously, the adoption of e-commerce may be a requirement of the suppliers. This is the case in some industries where EDI is a precondition to engaging in trade.

Competition with rivals

E-commerce solutions can reduce transaction costs, reduce stockholding, increase the reliability of supply and help to differentiate the company's product or service.

E-COMMERCE BUSINESS MODELS

There are many different models for conducting business. The introduction of e-commerce has brought a revolution in some markets, with accompanying new business models being introduced. Traditional business models coexist alongside these new models for e-commerce. In other cases, the traditional model for business has been modified but not overhauled by the introduction of new electronic trading relationships.

Business models

A business model is the theoretical design for an organization that describes how it makes money on a sustainable basis and grows. Business models take on many forms, including:

- straightforward industry classifications, such as heavy industry, service sector;
- methods of trading, such as shop, supermarket, auction;
- structural definitions, such as functional responsibilities, 'everyone does everything'.

The following section introduces a number of business models for conducting e-commerce. These models are summarized in Table 1.6.

E-shops

An e-shop is a virtual store front that sells products and services online. Orders are placed and payments made. The logistics of delivery are usually accomplished by traditional methods,

Table 1.6 Business models for electronic commerce

Type	Features	Examples
E-shop	Business-to-business	www.cisco.com
	Business-to-customer	www.amazon.com
E-mall	Diverse range of products and services	www.emall.com
E-procurement	Supply chain operations on the Internet	www.sap.com
E-auction	Electronic bidding for goods and services	www.ebay.co.uk
Specialist services	Online provision of goods and services	www.mcafee.com
Market segmenters	Differentiated markets	www.comet.co.uk
Content providers	Information services	www.ft.com
Internet infrastructure	Trust services, electronic payments	www.verisign.com

although some electronic products can be downloaded directly. Examples of electronic delivery can be seen at the site for recorded music company SonicNet (www.sonicnet.com), and the image and photographic services provider Photodisc (www.photodisc.com). An example of a business-to-consumer e-shop is shown in Figure 1.14. Toys'Я'Us, the children's toy retailer, offer a range of items which customers can order and have delivered to their home. An example of a business-to-business e-shop is shown in Figure 1.15. Ladybird is a brand label for children's clothing and distributes its products via a network of franchised retail businesses.

E-shops are a convenient way of effecting direct sales to customers; they allow manufacturers to bypass intermediate operators and thereby reduce costs and delivery times. This is referred to as disintermediation.

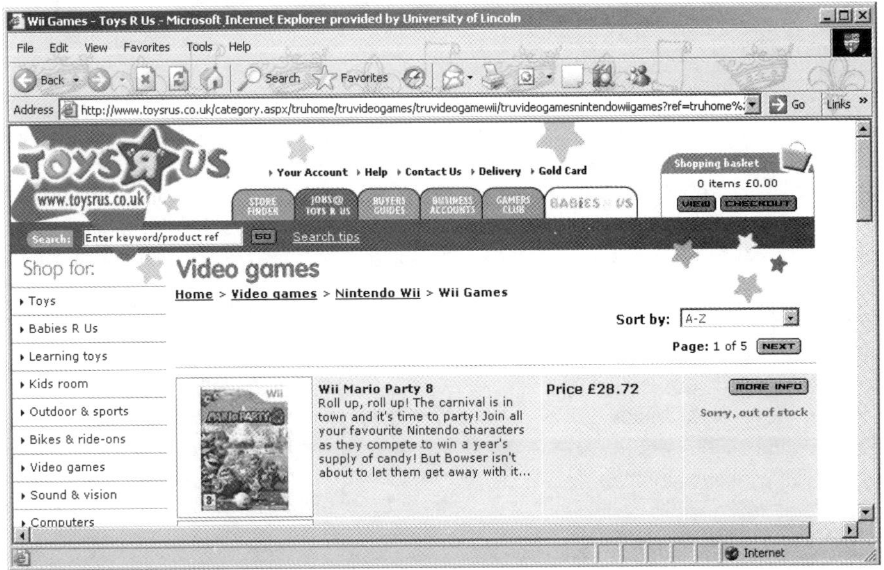

Figure 1.14 A business-to-consumer website

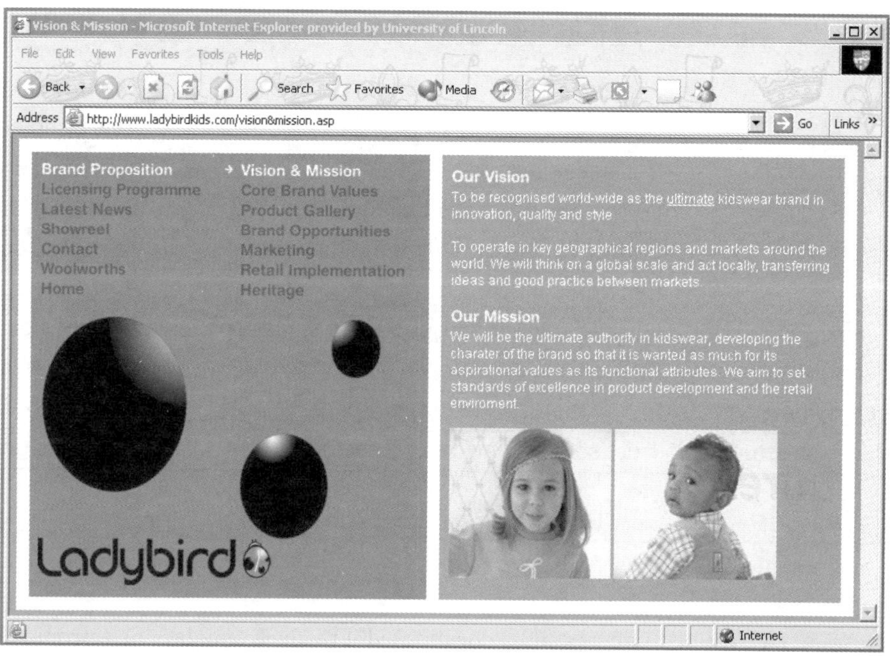

Source: with permission from Woolworths

Figure 1.15 A business-to-business website

MINI CASE 1.3

INTERNET SHOPPING

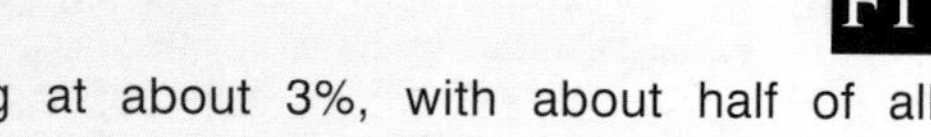

With a couple of clicks, fashion consumers can snap up a pair of Chloé 'as seen on the catwalk' three-strap cream heels for £335 from Net-a-Porter, or a belted trench coat 'in the style of Kate Moss' for £50 from Asos.

A decade after Internet shopping began to transform the retail experience, selling clothing online is finally becoming big business as new technology makes it easier for consumers to see what they are buying without recourse to a changing room.

Retailers have been using new web tricks to make buying clothing easier. Exclusive brands such as Gucci and Burberry, as well as more mainstream stores such as Marks & Spencer, have been using zoom and rotate tools on their websites to make it easier for shoppers to get a good look at what they are buying.

However, the US research showed that the conversion rates from browse to buy were still low, remaining at about 3%, with about half of all customers abandoning their transactions before they were complete. Natalie Massenet, the founder and chairman of upmarket online boutique Net-a-porter.com, said: 'More and more next-generation fashion consumers are growing up on the internet.'

Adapted from: **Online tricks turn browsers to sales clicks**
Elizabeth Rigby, *Financial Times*, 18 May 2007

QUESTIONS

1. If many Internet transactions are abandoned before they are completed why do companies persist with developing e-commerce shop fronts?
2. What are the challenges for clothing and shoe retailers in developing e-commerce sites? How do web designers improve the on-line shopping experience?

E-malls

The retailing model of a shopping mall, a conglomeration of different shops situated in a convenient location, is mirrored in e-commerce by the development of electronic malls or e-malls. The e-mall provides a common interface to the range of participants. This amalgamation of different businesses produces a virtual community with associated benefits such as shared costs and mutual advertising.

The iMegaMall e-mall, shown in Figure 1.16, is an electronic marketplace offering a wide range of products and services.

Another type of e-mall development comes about where an individual e-business diversifies to the extent that it presents itself as a virtual shopping arcade. E-companies such as Lastminute.com present customers with a wide range of products and services, all hosted from a single website providing a common interface.

E-procurement

Procurement is the whole process of obtaining services, supplies and equipment from identifying a business need through to fulfilment of contract. With the continuing trend in globalization of business the management of the supply chain has become an increasingly complex activity. An operation that has traditionally been controlled by specialists has now been largely automated. The ease of establishing connections using the Internet and web browsers rather than a costly infrastructure of dedicated private networks enables suppliers to open up their catalogues and product ranges at significantly reduced costs. The provision of information to customers thereby improves, and alternative methods of tender specification become possible. In addition, delivery times are reduced, leading to lower stockholding and further cost savings.

Source: www.imegamall.com, with permission

Figure 1.16 An e-mall website

MINI CASE 1.4

E-PROCUREMENT

FT

The predominant message from the history of e-procurement is that there has to be something in it for both buyers and suppliers. Too often, suppliers have been put off by initiatives they perceive to be 'buyer-led', and vice versa.

Recent developments are well illustrated at the St Mary's National Health Service Trust in London, one of a group of hospital trusts introducing the Zanzibar e-procurement system. Andrew Holden, its finance director, says improved flows of information about prices should now prevent any individual health trust being 'picked off' by suppliers. On the other hand, he notes, a fully electronic system in which an online order is 'flipped over' to become an invoice means suppliers can be paid much more quickly. And while suppliers may, within a year or two, have to use Zanzibar to sell to St Mary's, those with catalogues adopted by the system can look forward to bigger markets as Zanzibar develops critical mass within buying organizations.

Until recently, progress has been stymied by a mismatch in technology. It could be either side's technological immaturity to blame, but in the UK health service, at least, the problems have been on the buyers' side.

Janice Kite, UK e-business manager at Johnson & Johnson Medical Devices, part of the US healthcare company, visited an NHS customer in 2001 who did not even have an e-mail account or a personal computer. She says J&J still receives a high volume of NHS orders by fax or e-mail. 'For us, that isn't electronic—it still has to be pulled out and keyed into our system', she says. But things have improved significantly, and last year J&J saw its NHS-related transactions double in number, albeit from a small base, on Global Healthcare Exchange (GHX), one of the few surviving dotcoms offering e-procurement and marketplace services to the NHS. Another crucial issue, says Ms Kite, is ensuring that catalogue information within a system such as GHX is kept up to date and consistent: 'You can have all the technology in place, but if the data are not aligned and up to date, then you will get failures.'

Adapted from: **E-procurement: History proves the greatest teacher**
Andrew Baxter, *Financial Times*, 11 July 2007

QUESTIONS

1. Using the models of the supply chain described in Chapter 2 analyse the effect of e-procurement on both the purchasers and the suppliers of healthcare products and services.
2. To what extent might e-procurement address the issues raised in the article of purchasers getting 'picked off', or suppliers dealing with inconsistencies in data and systems?

E-auctions

The e-auction business model is based on the traditional auction concept of a bidding mechanism where the customer making the highest offer secures the purchase. The multimedia nature of e-auctions allows the supplier to make a more attractive presentation of the product offered. Figure 1.17 shows the popular eBay auction website. This is the longest running and most successful of the web-based electronic auction sites.

Highly interactive e-auctions can operate like clearing houses, where the prices of goods fluctuate in real time as the stocks vary. Revenue for the auctioneer is derived from transaction fees and from associated advertising. The potential global audience for an e-auction makes the sale of low-cost, small-margin items a more viable proposition. Business-to-business auctions may offer additional services, for example guaranteed payment for the seller or a warranty for the buyer. As described before, membership of an e-auction leads to the development of a virtual community, with accompanying benefits for all participants.

An alternative model for the e-auction is for a number of buyers to make a communal bid for an item. As more buyers are persuaded to participate in the purchase, the web company can strike a better deal and thereby reduce the price. An example of an e-auctioneer is LetsBuyIt.com.

A novel twist to the concept of an auction is the **reverse auction**, where buyers submit their proposed price to multiple suppliers in an attempt to secure the best deal. An example of a reverse

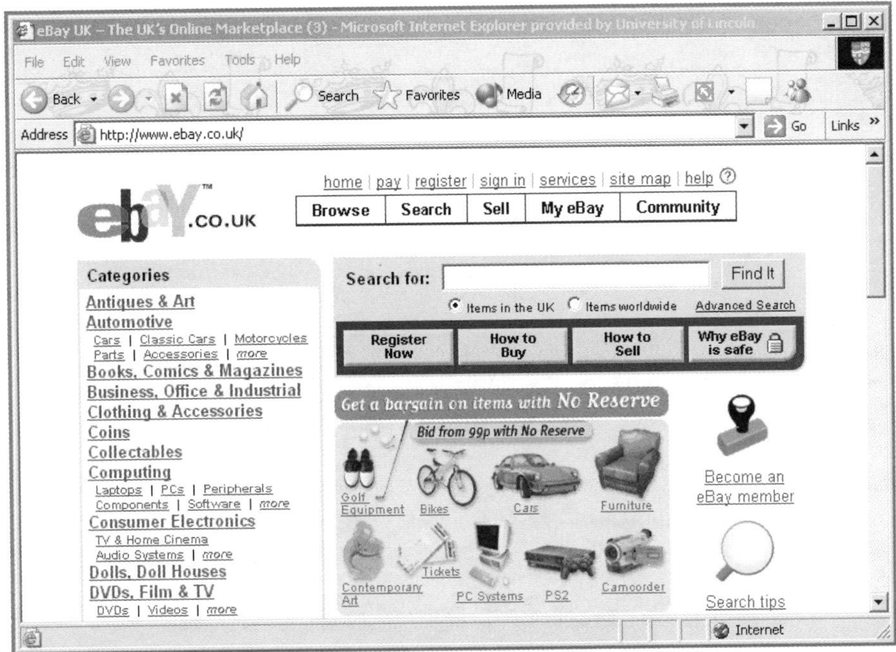

Source: eBay

Figure 1.17 **A web auction site**

auction specialist is Priceline.com, which offers a range of products such as airline tickets, cars and hotel rooms. The customer supplies key information (in the case of airline tickets the dates, cities and desired price), along with a credit card number. Priceline locates possible matches from a range of suppliers and, if successful, books the ticket at up to the price desired and charges the credit card automatically. The customer has to be flexible and is not allowed to be too prescriptive about times of travel or particular hotels in a given city.

In addition to the models above, there are an increasing number of more innovative business models for e-commerce.

Specialist service providers

Many companies engaged in e-commerce specialize in a particular market function. An example is the provision of logistics support, where Federal Express is a leading player (www.fedex.com), and in postal services, where the UK Royal Mail offers a range of delivery and tracking facilities. Another example of specialist services is the online computer support offered by companies such as NortonWeb (www.nortonweb.com). This service provides software updates, technical support and tools to tune and enhance the performance of a personal computer.

MINI CASE 1.5

PARCEL-TRACKING SERVICES

The parcel-tracking sector of the commercial World Wide Web was the first sector to reach maturity. The largest courier services in the world provide tracking facilities for their customers at no customer cost. Each of the companies claims to be saving money as it cuts down the staff needed to answer telephone enquiries on the location of packages. In order to use the facilities, customers enter their parcel reference number through a form on the company's web page as viewed through a standard web browser. The carrier's computer system is then searched and the latest information on the parcel retrieved—when and where it was

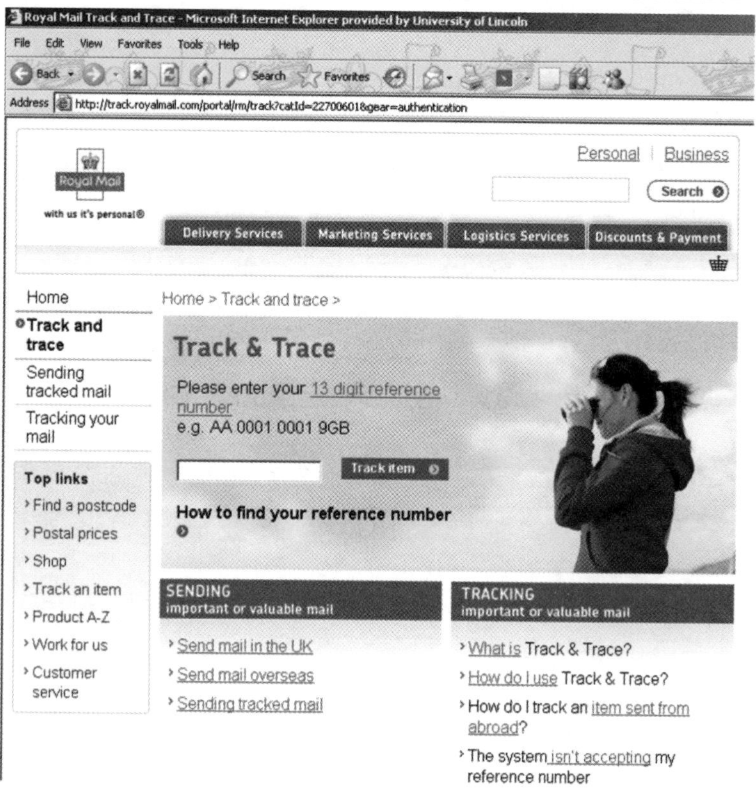

Figure 1.18 An example of a shipment tracking page

picked up, its current location, or, if it has already been delivered, the time of delivery and the receiver's name will be displayed. The main courier companies register hundreds of thousands of 'hits' on their web tracking pages each week. The service is expanding.

Companies are placing foreign-language interfaces on their sites. It is now possible to arrange pickup of parcels over the Internet with each of these carriers.

The stimulus has come from the pre-emptive introduction of the first tracking service. Once one provider had offered this service it became imperative for all others to follow suit. An example tracking interface can be seen in Figure 1.18.

QUESTION

What advantages do you think have accrued to these companies by offering tracking services to their customers?

Market segmenters

The immediate and accessible nature of electronic business has enabled some large companies to engage in market fragmentation in ways that would not otherwise have been possible. Recently, the major airlines identified electronic markets as a way of offering the same product, an airline ticket, at a lower price to certain sectors of the market. By creating e-businesses to handle these cut-price sales they successfully separated these alternative markets from traditional business customers, who continued to purchase tickets at a higher price through more conventional channels. Similarly, retailers of consumer durables and electronic goods have had great success in creating online stores as an alternative to the conventional high street or retail park store.

Content providers

The developments in digital storage media, particularly optical media, have led to the creation of e-businesses whose function is purely to maintain electronic archives. Newspapers have traditionally been archived in paper and microfiche formats. Now dedicated websites such as FT.com maintain archives of news reports and press releases and provide search facilities to extract the desired content. Other content providers are creating a niche as information specialists. Search engines such as Altavista provide an increasing range of search facilities and post-search links and services to enrich the information provided.

Internet infrastructure providers

Electronic commerce requires its own infrastructure. E-businesses are being created to fulfil those facilitating roles. Examples can be seen in companies that offer trust services, which provide facilities to enable secure transactions and communications. These companies provide certified authority that the service provided is reliable and secure. One such company is Verisign (www.verisign.com), which offers facilities to make secure a website, intranet or extranet to enable secure payments and to protect program code from being tampered with or corrupted.

Push and pull marketing strategies

A number of the business models above feature highly interactive participation. A key marketing decision for an e-business is to decide whether a proactive strategy to marketing will be adopted. The passive activity of customers or clients accessing and downloading pages from the Internet is termed **pull marketing**. The information is made available by suppliers, and customers search for and request, or pull, the pages from the server. Once a supplier has stored details about its customers, it could then develop a more active strategy of distributing information. This is known as **push marketing**. Particular benefits can be gained when push marketing is targeted at selected users. However, much of the activity in push technology is of a broadcast nature, with suppliers sending streams of information relating to recent developments such as price changes or new products. The information can be broadcast globally or sent to a select group of interested individuals. The recipients can receive the information in many different ways:

- For general release of product information, e-mails can be composed and distributed to those identified.
- Details of software upgrades, such as the latest version of a web browser, can be transmitted when the user logs on for a new session.
- If the user runs special software in the background on their computer it becomes possible for the information to be transmitted in real time, for example across a scrolling banner or as an update on a screen saver.

Often a mixed approach is employed where there is an initial (customer) pull followed by subsequent (supplier) push of information. An example of this mixed marketing approach can be seen in the use of **RSS** (Really Simple Syndications) feeds. Once a user has subscribed to an RSS feed, the content provider will publish material to the feed; typically this will be material that is updated frequently. The user must be running a feed reader (sometimes called an aggregator). The reader performs regular checks to see if new material is available and, if updates are detected, the material is transmitted from the host server.

CHAPTER 2

Computer Systems

Unit 2: Computer Systems

Unit code: L/601/0446
QCF Level 4: BTEC Higher National
Credit value: 15

Aim

To enable learners to understand computer systems and apply theoretical knowledge to practical application when building, configuring and maintaining computer systems.

Unit abstract

Most IT professionals will at some stage have to set up, use, customise and maintain computer systems. In order to do so effectively they will need to understand how computer systems work. Learners will understand the theoretical aspects of computer systems, and how information is processed. This unit explores the hardware, software and peripheral components that make up a computer system.

There are many different manufacturers of computer systems and each manufacturer will produce a wide range of models with different specifications. Deciding which particular model is appropriate for a given situation depends on a variety of factors. Custom-built computer systems are also an advantage when meeting specialised requirements, whilst maintaining performance and keeping costs low. These aspects are explored in this unit so that learners can make informed choices when designing a computer system for a given purpose.

Learners will be able to apply their theoretical knowledge to practical application by building, configuring and testing a functional computer system which will meet a given specification.

Computer users also need the skills required to set up and carry out routine maintenance of computer systems. Although this unit does not extensively cover fault finding and repair, it includes the basic maintenance skills that would normally be expected of most computer users.

Learning outcomes

On successful completion of this unit a learner will:

1. Understand the function of computer systems
2. Be able to design computer systems
3. Be able to build and configure computer systems
4. Be able to undertake routine maintenance on computer systems.

Unit content

1. Understand the function of computer systems

Computer systems: microcomputers eg personal computers; mobile computers; minicomputers eg mid-range servers, workstations; mainframes eg large scale network systems; supercomputers eg high performance systems; models; multiprocessing

Environments: home, business, computer gaming, networking, real-time, communication

Function: main components (Arithmetic Logic Unit (ALU), control unit, memory and input/output devices), connection eg busses; Central Processing Unit (CPU) (control unit, arithmetic logic unit, registers, input/output); memory (Random Access Memory (RAM), Read Only Memory (ROM), registers, programmable, cache), auxiliary storage; computer architecture

Hardware: central processing unit; motherboard, power supply unit, cooling units, backing storage eg hard disc drive; controllers, ports, main memory, memory types, battery, specialised cards eg Peripheral Component Interconnect (PCI), Accelerated Graphics Port (AGP), network, graphics, modem, sound, optical drives; performance factors

Software: systems software eg operating systems, utility programs, library programs, translator programs; applications software eg special purpose software, bespoke software; performance factors

Peripherals: printers, plotters, cameras, scanners; keyboard and mouse; monitors, display adapters; multimedia devices; storage media; networking; portable drives; plug and play components; performance factors

2. Be able to design computer systems

Needs analysis: client and system requirements, problems/limitations with current/new system, functionality, costs, timescales, resources, investigation/analytical techniques eg interviews, questionnaires

Selection: costs, client requirements, maintenance contracts, outputs required, compatibility; system integration eg home entertainment; storage capacity; accessibility; performance eg speed, time, power, efficiency, effectiveness, usability, alternative solutions

System specification: client requirements, system requirements, system components, configuration, time, tools and resources, alternatives eg processor types, backup options; security measures; documentation

3. Be able to build and configure computer systems

Health and safety: health and safety practices; electrostatic precautions eg antistatic mats, antistatic wrist straps

System installation: hardware: assemble and disassemble a computer system; install motherboard, processor, heat-sink and fan, memory, power supply unit and connect to internal components; install hard disc drive, optical drive; install specialised cards eg graphics, network, modem, audio; install and configure software eg operating system, application software, utility software; install peripheral devices eg printer, scanner, camera; install communication devices eg modem, router

System configuration: configure Basic Input Output System (BIOS) eg date/time, power management, security; install latest antivirus/security updates; update user profiles; configure desktop, icon size, font size, colour, background, customise menu; file management, files and folders, setting file/folder sharing permissions; peripheral devices, printer, scanner, camera; communication devices

System testing: fault detection, Power On Self Test (POST), diagnostic faults, troubleshoot devices; technical support documentation eg reference manuals, online manufacturer support; test hardware eg input/output devices, peripheral devices; test software; documentation eg test plan

4. Be able to undertake routine maintenance on computer systems

Software maintenance: upgrade software eg virus definition files; patches/updates; scheduling maintenance tasks; utility software eg defragmentation, clean-up, back-up, system profilers; other third party utility software eg compression utilities, spyware/malware removal

Hardware maintenance: upgrade hardware; install and configure new peripherals eg printers, scanners; install and configure additional or replacement devices eg hard drive, memory, graphics, sound, optical media, network; cleaning equipment

File management: manage files/folders; back-up procedures

Learning outcomes and assessment criteria

Learning outcomes **On successful completion of this unit a learner will:**	**Assessment criteria for pass** **The learner can:**
LO1 Understand the function of computer systems	1.1 explain the role of computer systems in different environments 1.2 explain the hardware, software and peripheral components of a computer system 1.3 compare different types of computer systems
LO2 Be able to design computer systems	2.1 produce a system design specification to meet a client's needs 2.2 evaluate the suitability of a system design specification
LO3 Be able to build and configure computer systems	3.1 build and configure a computer system to meet a design specification 3.2 test and document a computer system
LO4 Be able to undertake routine maintenance on computer systems	4.1 perform routine maintenance tasks on a computer system 4.2 upgrade the hardware and software on a computer system

Guidance

Links to National Occupational Standards, other BTEC units, other BTEC qualifications and other relevant units and qualifications

The learning outcomes associated with this unit are closely linked with:

Level 3	Level 4	Level 5
Unit 2: Computer Systems	Unit 24: Networking Technologies	Unit 47: IT Virtualisation
Unit 5: Managing Networks	Unit 28: IT Support for End Users	Unit 48: IT Security Management
Unit 9: Computer Networks		
Unit 12: IT Technical Support		
Unit 13: IT Systems Troubleshooting and Repair		
Unit 25: Maintaining Computer Systems		
Unit 29: Installing and Upgrading Software		

This unit has links to the Level 4 and Level 5 National Occupational Standards for IT and Telecoms Professionals, particularly the areas of competence of:

- Systems Architecture
- Systems Design
- IT/Technology Infrastructure Design and Planning
- Systems Development
- IT/Technology Solution Testing
- IT/Technology Service Operations and Event Management
- IT Application Management/Support
- IT/Technology Management and Support
- Technical Evaluation

Essential requirements

Learners must have access to computer systems that they can disassemble, assemble and configure. They will also need a range of components and peripherals that they can install and configure.

Learners must understand the functions of computer systems before they can begin the practical aspects of this unit. It is important that the underpinning knowledge of computer systems supports the practical approach to building and configuring computer systems.

Centres must begin this unit by giving an overview of the topics that will be covered, and what benefits the unit will bring to those who aspire to get involved with IT support and networking. Centres must give a brief history of computer systems, and how they have evolved. The different generations of computer systems will be useful at this point. There are different types of computer systems, and this must be covered in detail in terms of their functionality, performance and where they are typically used (environments). The benefits and drawbacks of computer systems must also be discussed, particularly IT security. Centres must keep abreast of modern developments in computer systems, and must also present mobile computing technologies as well. The future of computer systems must also be covered in respect of emerging technologies.

Learners must explore the full range of hardware, software and peripheral components. Centres must demonstrate and explain the role of common components, including the central processing unit, memory, motherboard, power supply unit, optical drives, storage devices and specialised cards.

Centres must present a range of typical client and system requirements, and discuss the range of components needed to fulfil those requirements. The range of hardware, software and peripheral components covered in this unit is at the centre's discretion. However, these components must be available for practical activities to ensure that fully functional computer systems can be built.

Centres must cover health and safety guidelines before commencing any practical work, and ensure that the working environment is safe and hazard free. Learners must also practise using electrostatic equipment to prevent any damage to components. Centres must demonstrate (in stages) the processes involved with building, configuring and testing a functional computer system.

Computer systems at some stage will need to be monitored and maintained to ensure consistency, reliability and performance. Learners must be equipped with the skills to maintain computer systems and follow a recommended schedule of activities. Learners must also be able to upgrade a computer system.

Resources

Books

Anfinsin, D—*IT Essentials: PC Hardware and Software Companion Guide* (Cisco Press, 2010) ISBN 158713263X

Dick, D—*The PC Support Handbook: The Configuration and Systems Guide* (Dumbreck Publishing, 2009) ISBN 9780954171131

MacRae K—*The Computer Manual: The Step-by-step Guide to Upgrading and Repairing a PC* (Haynes Group, 2002) ISBN 1859608884

MacRae K and Marshall G—*Computer Troubleshooting: The Complete Step-by-step Guide to Diagnosing and Fixing Common PC Problems* (2nd Edition, Haynes Group, 2008) ISBN: 9781844255177

White R and Downs T—*How Computers Work* (Que, 2003) ISBN 0789730332

Journals

Which? Computer
Computer Weekly

Websites

http://www.computerweekly.com
http://www.bized.co.uk

Employer engagement and vocational contexts

Working with a live system will present many risks that the centre, employer and learner must be aware of. Using a current vocational context to deploy an additional or alternate solution will enhance the learner's experience and enable understanding of wider technical application.

Introduction to Computer Repair

Basic Computer Parts

Computer systems include hardware, software, and firmware. **Hardware** is something you can touch and feel—the physical computer and the parts inside the computer are examples of hardware. The monitor, keyboard, and mouse are hardware components. **Software** interacts with the hardware. Windows, Linux, OS X, Microsoft Office, Solitaire, Google Chrome, Adobe Acrobat Reader, and WordPerfect are examples of software.

Without software that allows the hardware to accomplish something, a computer is nothing more than a doorstop. Every computer needs an important piece of software called an **operating system**, which coordinates the interaction between hardware and software applications. The operating system also handles the interaction between a user and the computer. Examples of operating systems include DOS, Windows XP, Windows Vista, Windows 7, OS X, and various types of Unix, such as Red Hat and Mandrake.

A **device driver** is a special piece of software designed to enable a hardware component. The device driver enables the operating system to recognize, control, and use the hardware component. Device drivers are hardware and operating system specific. For example, a printer requires a specific device driver when connected to a computer loaded with Windows 98. The same printer requires a different device driver when using Windows XP. Each piece of installed hardware requires a device driver for the operating system being used. Figure 2.1 shows how hardware and software must work together.

Software applications are normally loaded onto the hard drive. When a user selects an application, the operating system controls the loading of the application. The operating system also

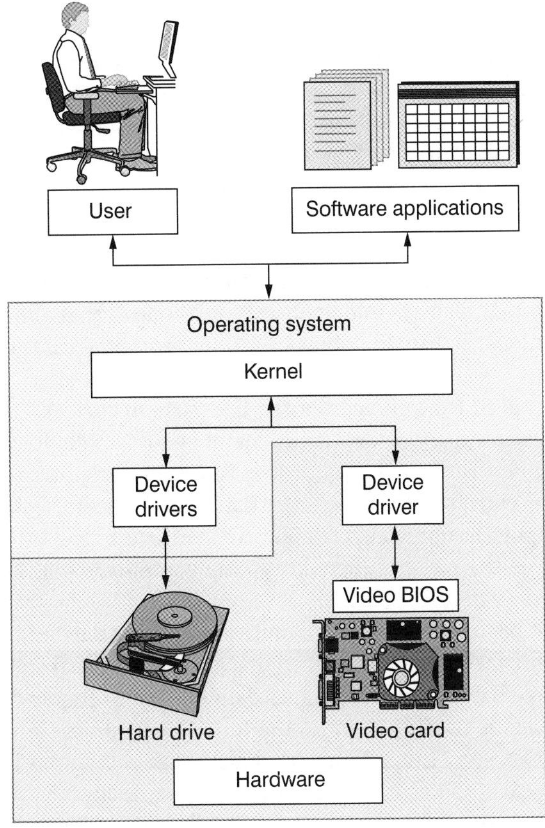

Figure 2.1 Hardware and software

Figure 2.2 Apple iPhones

controls any hardware devices (such as the mouse, keyboard, monitor through the video adapter, and printer) that must be accessed by the application.

Firmware combines hardware and software into important chips inside the computer. It is called firmware because it is a chip, which is hardware, and it has software built into the chip. An example of firmware is the **BIOS** (basic input/output system) chip. BIOS chips always have software inside them. The BIOS has startup software that must be present for a computer to operate. This startup software locates and loads the operating system. The BIOS also contains software instructions for communication with input/output devices, as well as important hardware parameters that determine to some extent what hardware can be installed. For example, the system BIOS has the ability to allow other BIOS chips that are located on adapters (such as the video card) to load software that is loaded in the card's BIOS.

The simplest place to start to learn about computer repair is with the hardware components and their common names. A **computer**, sometimes called a microcomputer or a PC, is a unit that performs tasks using software applications. Computers come in three basic models: (1) a **desktop** model that normally sits on top of a desk; (2) a **tower** model that sits under a desk; and (3) a **laptop** model, which is portable. Laptops are sometimes called notebooks; smaller versions are called netbooks or nettops. A fourth type of computer is a handheld computer or palmtop computer. These replaced the **PDA** (personal digital assistant). The palmtype computer is normally incorporated into a cell phone. Figure 2.2 shows Apple's iPhone, which has the ability to send and receive phone calls and emails, view and listen to movies and songs, and take pictures.

A computer consists of a case (chassis), a **keyboard** that allows users to provide input into the computer, a **monitor** that displays information, and a **mouse** that allows data input or is used to select menus and options. Figure 2.3 shows a tower computer case, monitor, keyboard, and mouse.

Once the case is removed from the computer, the parts inside can be identified. The easiest part to identify is the **power supply**, which is the metal box normally located in a back corner of the case. A power cord goes from the power supply to a wall outlet or surge strip. One purpose of the power supply is to convert the AC voltage that comes out of the outlet to DC voltage the computer can use. The power supply also supplies DC voltage to the internal parts of the computer. A fan located inside the power supply keeps the computer cool, which avoids damage to the components.

A computer usually has a device to store software applications and files. Two examples of storage devices are the floppy drive and the hard drive. A slot in the front of the computer easily identifies the floppy drive. The **floppy drive** allows data storage to **floppy disks** (sometimes called diskettes or disks) that can be used in other computers. Floppy disks store less information than hard drives. The **hard drive**, sometimes called hard disk, is a rectangular box normally inside the computer's case that is sealed to keep out dust and dirt. In a desktop computer, the hard drive is normally mounted below or beside the floppy drive. A **CD drive** holds disks (CDs) that have data, music, or software applications on them. A popular alternative to a CD drive is a **DVD drive** (digital versatile disk drive), which supports CDs as well as music and video DVDs.

Figure 2.3 **Tower computer**

The **motherboard** is the main circuit board located inside a PC and contains the most electronics. It is normally located on the bottom of a desktop or laptop computer and mounted on the side of a tower computer. Other names for the motherboard include mainboard, planar, or systemboard. The motherboard is the largest electronic circuit board in the computer. The keyboard frequently connects directly to the back of the motherboard, although some computers have a keyboard connection in the front of the case. Figure 2.4 shows a different view of a tower computer with a hard drive, floppy drive, power supply, motherboard, and DVD drive. Notice that the floppy drive has a slot in the front of the computer, whereas the hard drive does not.

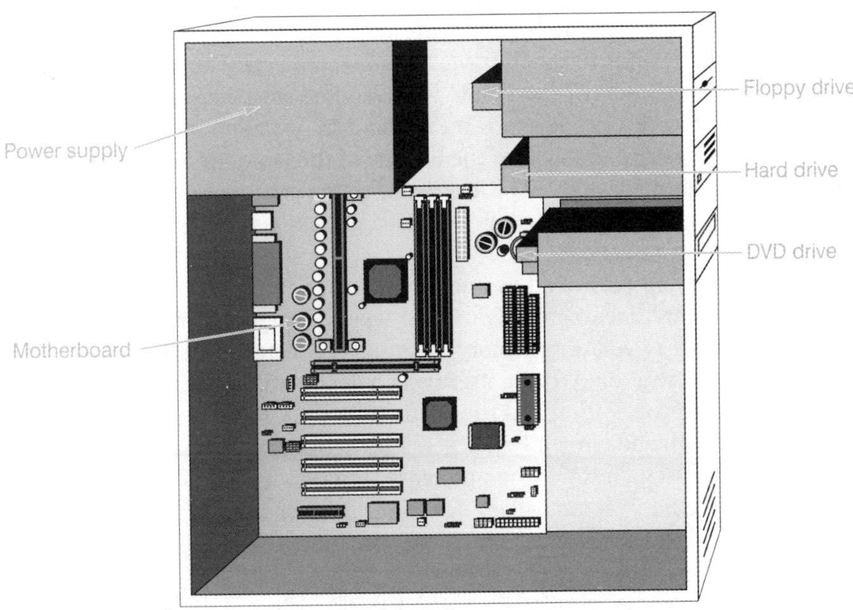

Figure 2.4 **Tower computer with hard drive, floppy drive, power supply, motherboard, and DVD drive**

Some devices have a cable that connects the device to the motherboard. Other devices require an adapter. **Adapters** are electronic circuit cards that normally plug into an **expansion slot** on the motherboard. Other names for an adapter are controller, card, controller card, circuit card, circuit board, and adapter board. The number of available expansion slots on the motherboard depends on the manufacturer.

How to identify an adapter's function

Tracing the cable(s) attached to the adapter or looking at the device connected to the adapter can usually help with identifying an adapter's function. For example, typically a monitor has a cable going between it and a video adapter or motherboard.

An adapter may control multiple devices such as the DVD drive and speakers. An alternative to an adapter plugging directly into the motherboard is the use of a riser board. A **riser board** plugs into the motherboard and has its own expansion slots. Adapters can plug into these expansion slots instead of directly into the motherboard. Figure 2.5 is an illustration of a riser board and one adapter.

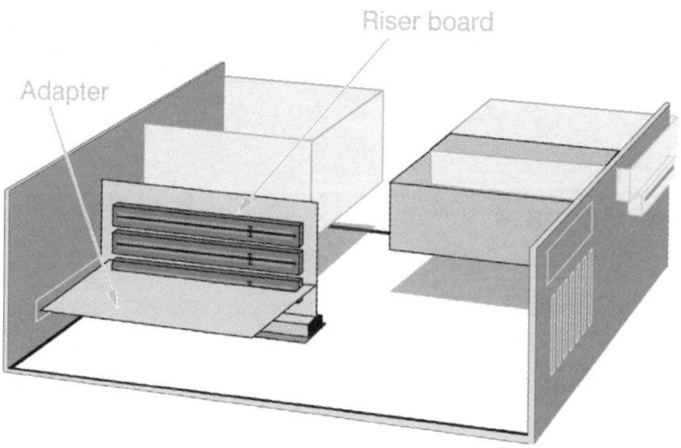

Figure 2.5 Microcomputer with a riser board and one adapter

A laptop has similar parts to a tower or desktop computer, but they are smaller. Portable computers (laptops) normally use a battery as their power source, but they can have an AC connection. Laptop batteries are normally modules that have one or two release latches that are used to remove the module. Figure 2.6 shows common laptop parts.

When the laptop has the AC adapter attached, the battery is being recharged on most models. The laptop AC adapter converts the AC from the wall outlet to DC, which the laptop needs. Figure 2.7 shows the laptop port to which the AC adapter connects. The port sometimes has a DC voltage symbol below or beside it. This symbol is a solid line with a dashed line below it (⎓).

Laptops frequently have one or more media bays to install removable drives such as a CD/DVD drive or a floppy drive. A latch on the bottom of the laptop normally releases the drive. The bays allow hot swapping (device can be inserted with the power applied), but it is always safer to shut down the computer before installing a device unless you are sure it is hot swappable. Figure 2.8 shows a laptop media bay.

Memory is an important part of any computer. Memory chips hold applications, part of the operating system, and user documents. Two basic types of memory are RAM and ROM. **RAM** (random access memory) is volatile memory meaning the data inside the chips is lost when power to the computer is shut off. When a user types a document in a word processing program, both the word processing application and the document are in RAM. If the user turns the computer off without saving the document to a disk or the hard drive, the document is lost because the information does not stay in RAM when power is shut off.

ROM (read-only memory) is nonvolatile memory because data stays inside the chip even when the computer is turned off. ROM chips are sometimes installed on adapters such as a network or video card.

RAM and ROM chips come in different styles: DIP (Dual In-line Package), DIMM (Dual In-line Memory Module), and RIMM (a memory module developed by Rambus). RAM chips can be any of the types, but they are usually DIMMs. Some ROM chips are DIP chips. They are usually distinguishable by a sticker that shows the manufacturer, version, and date produced. Memory

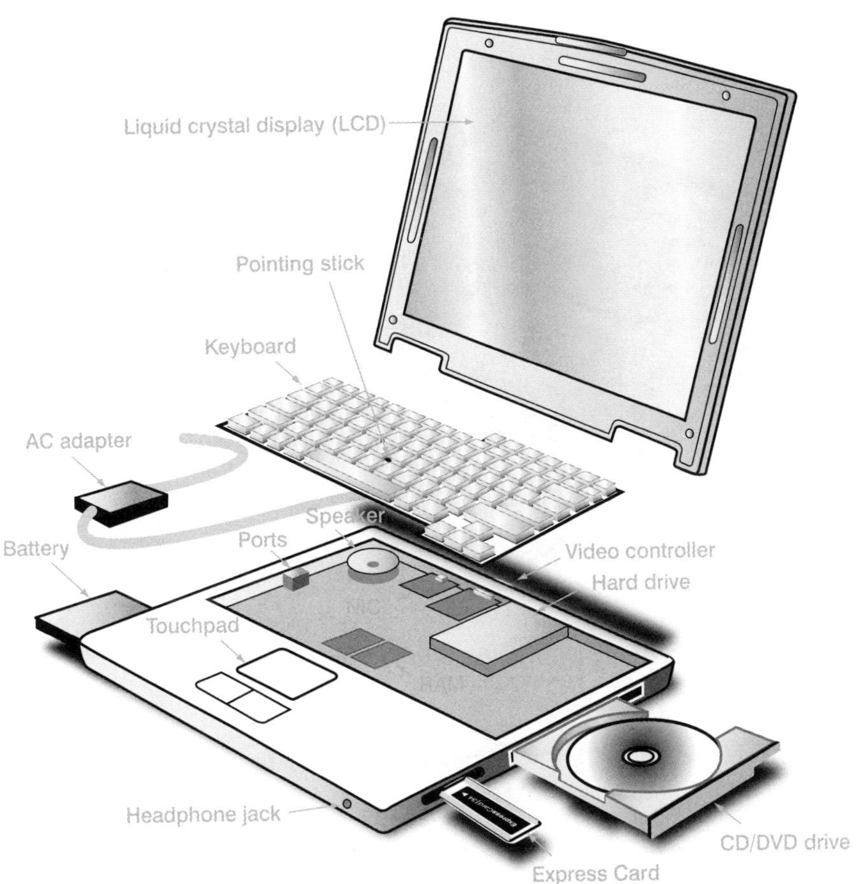

Figure 2.6 Laptop battery

Figure 2.7 Laptop AC adapter and power port

Figure 2.8 Laptop media bay

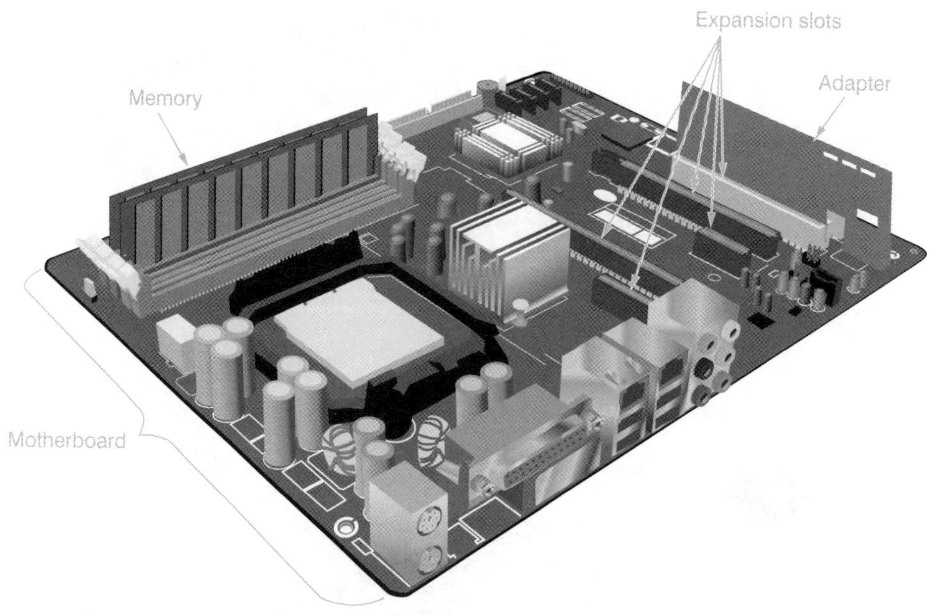

Figure 2.9 Motherboard with expansion slots and adapter

chips are covered in great detail in the section on memory later in the chapter. See Figure 2.9 for an illustration of a motherboard, various expansion slots, memory, and an adapter in an expansion slot.

Part of the startup software the motherboard BIOS contains is **POST** (power on self test). POST performs a basic test of the individual hardware components such as the motherboard, RAM memory chips, keyboard, floppy drive, and hard drive. When a computer is turned on with the power switch, BIOS executes POST. Numbers appearing in the upper-left corner of the monitor indicate that POST is checking RAM. Turning the computer on with the power switch is known as a **cold boot**. Users perform a cold boot every time they power on their computers. A technician performs a cold boot when he or she is troubleshooting a computer and needs POST to execute.

You can restart a Windows XP computer with a warm boot by clicking the *Start* button, clicking *Shut Down*, selecting *Restart* from the drop-down menu, and clicking the *OK* button. It can also be performed by holding down the Ctrl key, the Alt key, and the Del key at the same time, selecting *Task Manager*, selecting the *Shut Down* option, selecting *Restart* from the drop-down menu, and clicking the *OK* button. Warm booting causes any changes that have been made to take effect without putting as much strain on the computer as a cold boot does. In Vista, click on the right arrow adjacent to the lock button and select *Restart* or press Ctrl+Alt+Del, select the up arrow in bottom right corner, and choose *Restart* from the menu.

External Connectivity

A **port** is a connector on the motherboard or on a separate adapter that allows a device to connect to the computer. Sometimes a motherboard has ports built directly into the motherboard. Motherboards that have ports built into them are called **integrated motherboards**. A technician must be able to identify these common ports readily to ensure that (1) the correct cable plugs into the port; and (2) the technician can troubleshoot problems in the right area.

Many port connections are referred to as male or female. **Male ports** have metal pins that protrude from the connector. A male port requires a cable with a female connector. **Female ports** have holes in the connector into which the male cable pins are inserted.

Many connectors on integrated motherboards are either D-shell connectors or DIN connectors. A **D-shell connector** has more pins or holes on top than on the bottom, so a cable connected to the D-shell connector can only be inserted in one direction and not accidentally flipped upside down. Parallel, serial, and video ports are examples of D-shell connectors. Many documents represent a D-shell connector by using the letters DB, a hyphen, and the number of pins—for example, DB-9, DB-15, or DB-25.

A **DIN connector** is round with small holes and is normally keyed. When a connector is **keyed** it has an extra metal piece or notch that matches with an extra metal piece or notch on the cable, and the cable can only be inserted into the DIN connector one way. Older keyboard and mouse connectors are examples of DIN connectors. Today, keyboard and mouse connectors can also be USB connectors. These are covered later in the chapter. Figure 2.10 shows the back of a computer with an integrated motherboard. There are various DIN and D-shell connectors on the motherboard.

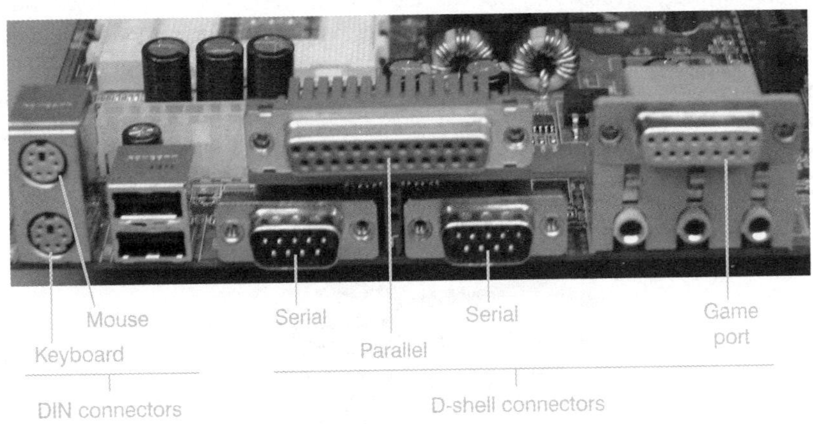

Figure 2.10 DIN and D-Shell connectors

Video Port

A **video port** is used to connect a monitor. Today, there are two types normally seen and they both have three rows. The older one is a three-row, 15-pin female D-shell. The 15-pin female connector is used to attach VGA, SVGA, XGA, SXGA, or UXGA monitors. These monitors have a CRT (cathode ray tube) and are heavier and bulkier than a flat panel monitor. Even though it can have different types of monitors attached, it is normally referred to as a **VGA port**. The newer port is called a **DVI port** (Digital Visual Interface) and it has three rows of square holes. This is the newer video port and is used to connect flat panel digital monitors. Flat panel monitors can also use the older VGA port. There are actually different types of DVI ports. Some video adapters also allow you to connect a video device (such as a television) that has an S-Video port. Figure 2.11 shows

Figure 2.11 Video ports

a video adapter with all three ports. The top port is the DVI connector, the center port is for S-video, and the bottom port is a VGA port.

USB Port

USB stands for Universal Serial Bus. A **USB port** allows up to 127 devices to transmit at speeds up to 5Gbps (5 billion bits per second) with version 3.0. Compare these speeds to parallel port transfers of 1Mbps (1 million bits per second). Devices that can connect to the USB port include printers, scanners, mice, keyboards, joysticks, CD drives, DVD drives, tape drives, floppy drives, flight yokes, cameras, modems, speakers, telephones, video phones, data gloves, and digitizers. In order for the computer to use the USB port, it must have a Pentium or higher CPU; an operating system that supports USB, such as Windows 9x or higher, Apple OS X, or *nix (any flavor of Unix) and a chipset that acts as a host controller. Additional ports can sometimes be found on the front of computer cases. Figure 2.12 shows a close-up view of two USB ports. Figure 2.13 is a photograph of computer USB ports.

Figure 2.12 USB ports

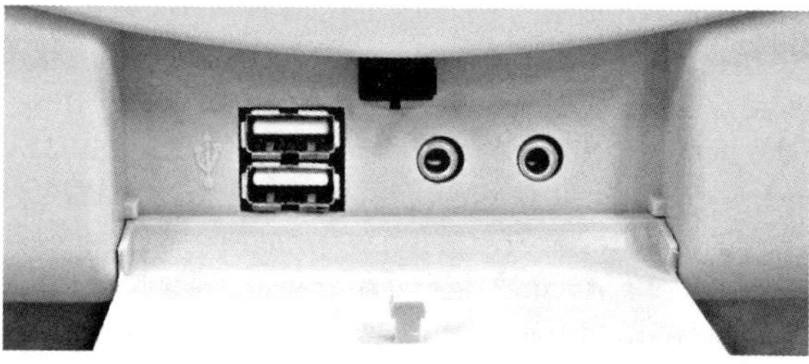

Figure 2.13 USB ports on the front of a computer

USB ports and devices come in three versions—1.0, 2.0, and 3.0. Version 1.0 supported speeds of 1.5Mbps and 12Mbps. Version 2.0 increased the supported speed to 480Mbps; and Version 3.0 supports speeds up to 5Gbps. A symbol that looks like a trident is sometimes seen on the USB port or on the USB cable. A plus sign above one prong identifies a Version 2.0 port, but not all manufacturers use this symbol. Version 3.0 is sometimes referred to as SuperSpeed USB, and the logo has two S's on it. Figure 2.14 shows the USB symbols.

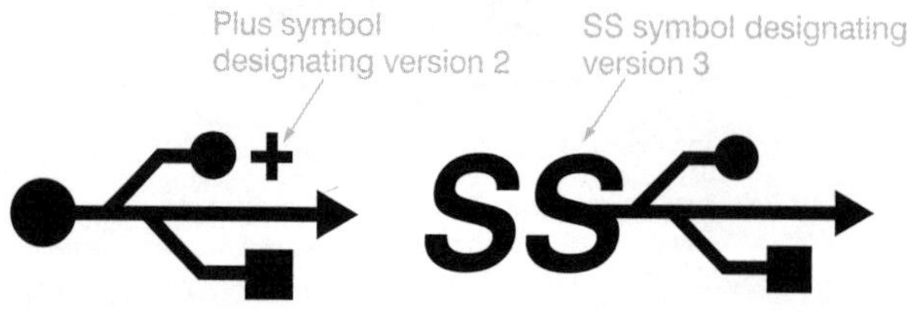

Figure 2.14 USB symbols

Converters are available to convert a USB port to a different type of connector (or vice versa), such as serial, parallel, PS/2 mouse/keyboard, or mini-DIN. Figure 2.15 shows a converter that inserts into a PS/2 mini-DIN connector and allows a USB mouse or keyboard to be connected.

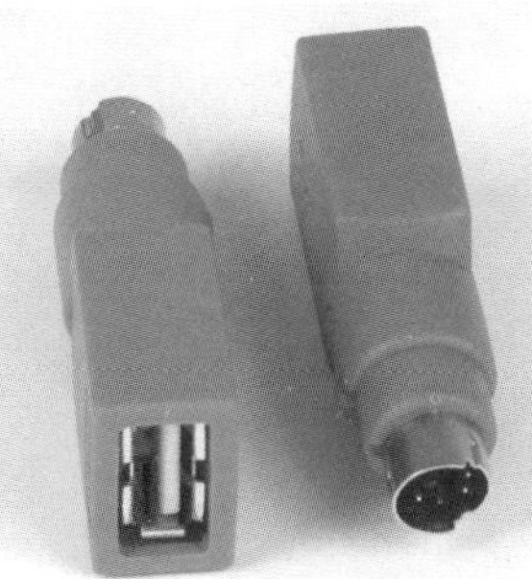

Figure 2.15 **Mini-DIN to USB converter**

A smaller USB port used on small devices such as a USB hub, PDA, digital camera, and phones is known as a mini-USB port. There are three types of mini-USB ports: mini-A, mini-B, and mini-AB. The mini-AB port accepts either a mini-A or a mini-B cable end. The two leftmost connectors shown in Figure 2.16 are mini-B and standard A USB connectors. (The three connectors shown on the right are 6-, 4-, and 9-pin IEEE 1394 connectors, which are discussed later in this section.)

Figure 2.16 **Mini-B and a standard A USB connectors (as well as IEEE 1394 connectors)**

Parallel Port

The **parallel port** is a 25-pin female D-shell connector used to connect a printer to the computer. Some motherboards have a small picture of a printer etched over the connector. Parallel ports transfer eight bits of data at a time to the printer or any other parallel device connected to the parallel port. Other parallel devices include tape drives, Iomega's Zip drive, scanners, and external hard drives. Parallel ports are becoming obsolete due to USB ports. Refer to Figure 2.10 for a photo of a parallel port.

Serial Port

A **serial port** (also known as a COM port or an asynchronous (async) port) can be a 9-pin male D-shell connector or a 25-pin male D-shell connector (on very old computers). Serial ports are used for a variety of devices including mice, external modems, digitizers, printers, PDAs, and digital cameras. Serial ports are becoming obsolete for the same reason that parallel ports are—USB ports. The most common reason to have a serial port would be for an external modem.

The serial port transmits one bit at a time and is much slower than the parallel port that transmits eight bits at a time. Serial ports sometimes have a small picture of two rows of square blocks (two digital square waves) tied together etched over the connector. The other type of picture sometimes shown above a serial port is a series of 1s and 0s. Figure 2.17 shows both types of markings. Figure 2.18 shows a USB to serial port converter if a serial port is needed and only USB ports are available. A converter may be purchased to convert a USB port to almost any other type of port.

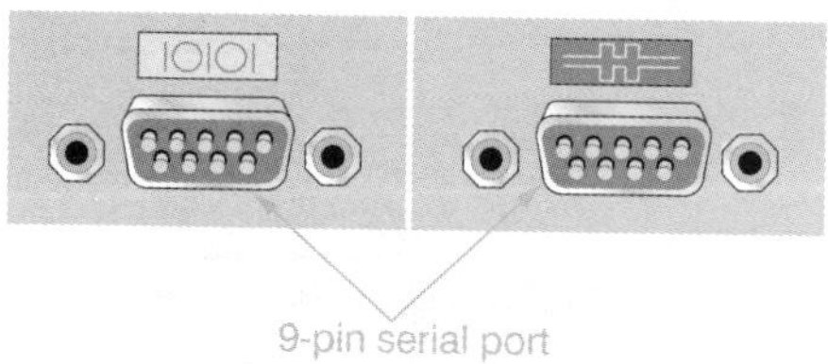

Figure 2.17 Serial port markings

Figure 2.18 USB to serial port converter

Serial and parallel ports are typically bidirectional, which means that data transfers to/from the port to the motherboard/adapter in both directions. Video, keyboard, and mouse ports are typically unidirectional. The mouse and keyboard are normally input-only devices, so data flows from the device to the computer. The monitor is normally an output device, and data flows from the computer to the monitor.

Mouse and Keyboard Ports

Mouse and **keyboard ports** have traditionally been 6-pin mini-DIN connectors, but some computer manufacturers are using USB ports to connect mice or keyboards. The mini-DIN port is sometimes called a PS/2 port. Refer to Figure 2.10 to see the mouse and keyboard ports. Most manufacturers color code the mouse and keyboard ports and/or put a small diagram of a keyboard and a mouse on the connectors.

Normal mouse use typically causes its internal parts to become dirty. Before explaining how to clean a mouse, understanding the basic internal mouse workings is important because the topics are interrelated. There are two basic types of mice—mechanical and optical. A **mechanical mouse** uses a rubber ball inserted into the bottom of the mouse. The rubber ball turns small metal, rubber, or plastic rollers mounted on the sides. The rollers relay the mouse movement to the computer. On the other hand, an **optical mouse** has optical sensors that detect the direction in which the mouse ball moves. It uses reflections from LEDs using a grid pattern mouse pad or almost any surface to detect mouse location.

A trackball is a replacement for the mouse. It sits in one location and does not move around on a mouse pad or desk. Instead, a person uses his or her palm to move the mouse pointer by means of a ball that rolls on bearings located inside the device.

Keyboards are input devices that connect to the keyboard port. There are two main types of keyboards: mechanical and capacitive. **Mechanical keyboards** are the cheapest and most common type. They use a switch that closes when a key is depressed. When the switch

Don't confuse the mouse and keyboard ports

On most motherboards, the mouse and keyboard ports are not interchangeable even though they are of the same pin configuration. The keyboard cable must plug into the keyboard port connector. The mouse cable must plug into the mouse port connector.

gets dirty, it sticks. Mechanical keyboards require more cleaning and are more error-prone than their capacitive counterparts. A **capacitive keyboard** is more reliable and more expensive than a mechanical keyboard because of the electronics involved in the design.

Wireless Input Devices

Many input devices have cordless connectivity. Two common devices are the keyboard and mouse. There are two types of technologies used with wireless input devices: infrared and radio. Whichever one is used, a transceiver is connected to a serial, PS/2 mouse/keyboard, or USB port. Infrared is used for shorter distances and is cheaper than the radio method. However, infrared devices must be kept within the line of sight of the transceiver (the device that picks up the wireless signal that attaches to the computer) and this can be cumbersome. Radio controlled wireless devices can have interference from other devices in the home or office such as microwave ovens, cordless phones, and other wireless devices (see Figure 2.19).

Figure 2.19 Wireless devices

If a wireless device is not operating properly, check to see if it has a battery and if the battery is losing its charge. Check for blocked line of sight if the device uses infrared. Move the device closer to the transceiver to see if performance is improved. Verify that the transceiver connects to the appropriate port. If the wireless device uses a radio frequency to communicate with the transceiver, ensure that no other device is causing interference by moving the wireless input device, hanging up the telephone, or shutting off other devices that could be causing the interference.

Mouse and Keyboard Preventive Maintenance

Mouse cleaning kits are available in computer stores, but normal household supplies also work. For an optical mouse, simply wipe the bottom of the mouse with a damp, lint-free cloth. For a mechanical mouse, the ball inside the mouse gets dirty and clogged with lint and dirt. Turn the mechanical mouse over and rotate the ball's retainer ring or access cover counterclockwise to remove it. Sometimes a mouse has screws that secure the ball's access cover. After removing the mouse cover, turn the mouse over while cupping your hand over the mouse ball. Catch the mouse ball as it falls into your hand. To clean the mouse ball, use a mild detergent, soapy water, contact cleaner, or alcohol. Rinse the mouse ball and dry completely with a lint-free cloth. With compressed air or your breath, blow out where the rubber ball sits in the mouse. A trackball's rollers are similar to a mouse ball's rollers and can be cleaned the same way.

The rollers inside a mechanical mouse also get dirty, which causes erratic mouse behavior. Use a cotton swab or lint-free cloth with alcohol to clean the rollers. If you are at a customer site with no supplies, use water to clean the mouse ball. Use a fingernail, small screwdriver, or unfolded paperclip to scrape the rollers. Occasionally, threads or hair get wrapped around the rollers. Unwrap the obstructions for better mouse performance. With an optical mouse, use a lint-free cloth or compressed air to clean the optical sensors. Any small piece of dirt or lint blocking the sensors causes poor mouse behavior and reaction.

Keyboards also need periodic cleaning, especially because most are mechanical. Keyboard cleaning kits and wipes are available at computer stores. Simply turn the keyboard upside down and shake it to remove the paper bits and paper clips. Compressed air also helps with keyboard cleaning. Obtain compressed air that has a plastic straw that attaches to the nozzle. If the keys are dirty from finger oils, turn the computer off before cleaning the keys. Then, using keyboard cleaning wipes or a cloth and all-purpose cleaner, wipe the keyboard keys. A cotton or lint-free swab can be used between the keys. The lint-free swab works best. Make sure the keyboard is completely dry before re-energizing.

Keyboard Troubleshooting

If a particular key is not working properly, remove the key cap. The chip removal tool included with PC tool kits is great for this. They are not great for removing chips, but they are good for removing key caps. A tweaker (small, flat-tipped) screwdriver also does a good job. After removing the key cap, use compressed air around the sticky or malfunctioning key.

If coffee or another liquid spills into the keyboard, all is not lost. Many people have cleaned their keyboard by soaking it in a bathtub, a flat pan of water, or the top rack of a dishwasher. If you use a dishwasher, run it through one rinse cycle only and do not use detergent. Distilled or boiled water cooled to room temperature works best. Afterward, the keyboard can be disassembled and/or scrubbed with lint-free swabs or cloths.

Keyboards and mice are normally considered throw-away technology. The customer's cost to pay a technician to keep cleaning a keyboard over and over again would pay for many new capacitive keyboards. Keep this in mind when troubleshooting the cheaper devices.

Other Input Devices

A variety of input devices are available. Most connect to the serial, PS/2, USB, or IEEE 1394 port. Installation and troubleshooting of these devices follows the same procedure as the common devices that attach to these ports. Table 2.1 lists a description of some of the common input devices. Figure 2.20 shows a digital tablet with a mouse and pen.

Table 2.1 Common input devices

Device	Description
digital pen	Translates words written with the pen for input into the computer. The pen can also be used to control the cursor or mouse. The pen is frequently a wireless device and is sometimes used with a digital tablet.
digital tablet	Allows graphical or desktop publishing information to be input. The tablet can be wireless or connected to a USB or serial port. A tablet can come with an integrated mouse and/or digital pen. This is sometimes called a drawing tablet.
signature pad	Allows someone to sign and digitally store his or her name.
touch screen	Allows a finger or a pen-like device to control a special monitor. The screens are popular with bank ATMs and with kiosks such as those found in schools, hotels, and shopping malls.
trackball	Allows a user to use the palm or fingertip to move the pointer on the screen. This is achieved by manipulating a device that has a ball mounted in the center.
track pad	Allows the pointer to be manipulated with fingertip movement by means of an integrated window or a place located on a laptop. Flat buttons that are similar to mouse control buttons are mounted above or below the track pad.
TrackPoint (by IBM) or **track stick**	Controls pointer operations as an alternative to a mouse by means of a rubber nipple that is normally situated between keys in the center of the laptop keyboard.

Figure 2.20 Digital tablet

Sound Card Ports

A **sound card** converts digital computer signals to sound and sound to digital computer signals. A sound card is sometimes called an audio card and can be integrated into the motherboard or an adapter that contains several ports. The most common ports include a port for a microphone, one or more ports for speakers, and an input port for a joystick or MIDI (musical instrument digital interface) device. Examples of MIDI devices include electronic keyboards and external sound modules. The joystick port is sometimes known as a **game port**. Game ports are 15-pin female D-shell connectors, and are sometimes confused with older Ethernet connectors. Game ports are becoming extinct because of the popularity of USB ports. Another type of digital sound port that is gaining popularity is **S/PDIF** (Sony/Philips Digital Interface). There are two main types of S/PDIF connectors: an RCA jack used to connect a coaxial cable and a fiber-optic port for a TOSLINK cable connection. Sound cards, however, are still popular because people want better sound than what is available integrated into a motherboard. See Figure 2.21 for an illustration of a sound card. Figure 2.29 later in the section shows the S/PDIF ports.

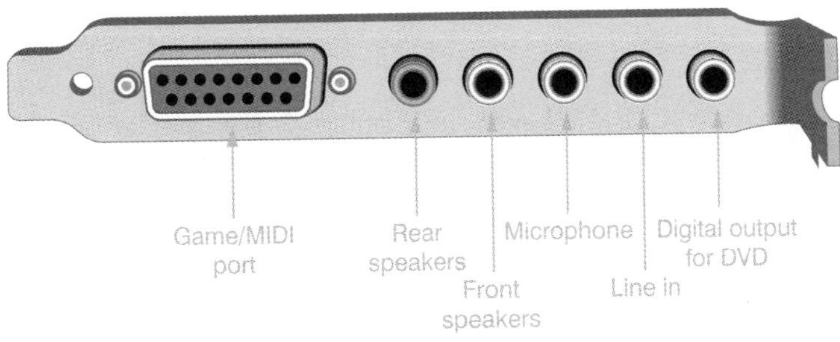

Figure 2.21 Sound card ports

IEEE 1394 Port

The IEEE 1394 standard is a serial technology developed by Apple Computer. Sometimes it is known as FireWire or i.Link, which is a Sony trademark. **IEEE 1394 ports** have been more predominant on Apple computers, but are now becoming a standard port on PCs. Windows and Apple operating systems support the IEEE 1394 standard. Many digital products now have an integrated IEEE 1394 port for connecting to a computer. IEEE 1394 devices include camcorders, cameras, printers, storage devices, DVD players, CD-R drives, CD-RW drives, tape drives, film readers, speakers, and scanners.

Speeds supported are 100, 200, 400, 800, and 1200Mbps. As many as 63 devices (using cable lengths up to 14 feet) can be connected with FireWire. The IEEE 1394 standard supports hot swapping (plugging and unplugging devices with the power on), plug and play, and powering low-power devices. The cable has six wires—four for data and two for power. Newer IEEE 1394 standards support the use of RJ-45 and fiber connectors. Figure 2.22 shows FireWire ports. Figure 2.23 shows three IEEE 1394 adapter ports.

Figure 2.22 FireWire ports

Figure 2.23 IEEE 1394 adapter ports

Figure 2.24 shows an IEEE 1394 port on a laptop. This is similar to a port found on a camera or video device. Other common laptop ports are also shown.

Figure 2.24 IEEE 1394 laptop port

Network Ports

Network ports are used to connect a computer to other computers, including a network server. Two different network adapters, Ethernet and Token Ring, are available, but most networks use Ethernet ports. The ports on these adapters can be quite confusing because the connectors are sometimes the same. A network cable inserts into the network port.

Ethernet adapters are the most common type of **NIC** (network interface card/controller). They can have a BNC, an RJ-45, a 15-pin female D-shell connector, or a combination of these on the same adapter. The BNC connector attaches to thin coax cable. The 15-pin D-shell connector connects to thick coax cable. The RJ-45 connector connects to UTP (unshielded twisted-pair) cable and is the most common Ethernet port used. The 15-pin female D-shell connector is confusing because this connector is also used with game ports. The RJ-45 connector (the most common one) looks like a phone jack, but it uses eight wires instead of four. Figure 2.25 shows examples of different Ethernet adapter ports.

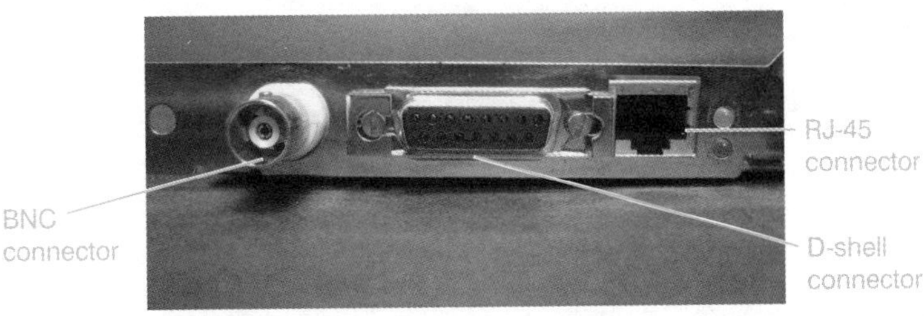

Figure 2.25 Ethernet ports

Today's Ethernet adapters have a single RJ-45 jack (port), as shown in Figure 2.26.

Figure 2.26 RJ-45 Ethernet port

Token Ring adapters are not as popular as Ethernet, and they can have two different connectors: RJ-45 and/or 9-pin female D-shell connectors. Some adapters have a little green sticker with the numbers 4/16 on it, which indicates the two speeds, 4Mbps and 16Mbps, at which Token Ring adapters can run. The 4/16 sticker is a helpful indicator that the port is a Token Ring port. Figure 2.27 shows examples of Token Ring ports.

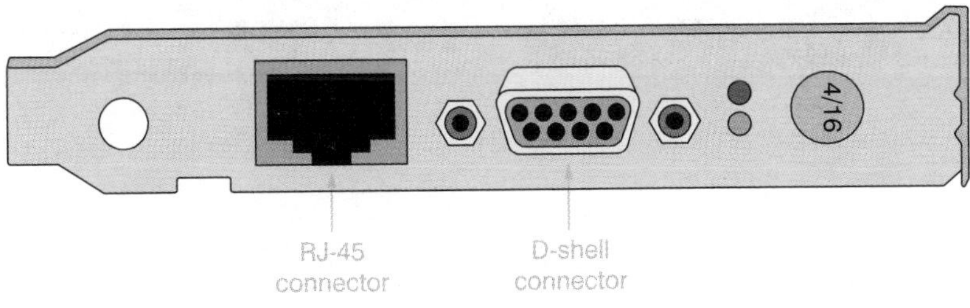

Figure 2.27 Token Ring ports

Modem Ports

A **modem** connects a computer to a phone line. A modem can be internal or external. An internal modem is an adapter that has one or two RJ-11 connectors. An external modem is a separate device that sits outside the computer and connects to a 9-pin or 25-pin serial port. The external modem can also have one or two RJ-11 connectors. The RJ-11 connectors look like typical phone jacks. With two RJ-11 connectors, one can be used for a telephone and the other has a cable that connects to the wall jack. The RJ-11 connector labeled *Line* is for the connection to the wall jack. The RJ-11 connector labeled *Phone* is for the connection to the phone. An internal modem with only one RJ-11 connector connects to the wall jack. Figure 2.28 shows an internal modem with two ports.

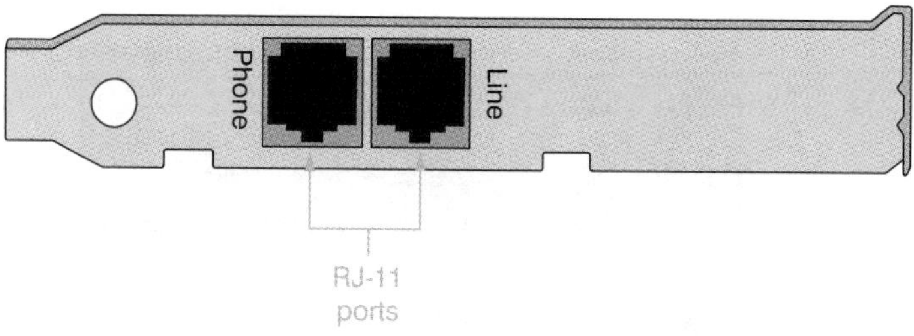

Figure 2.28 Internal modem with two ports

Pros and Cons of Integrated Motherboards

An integrated motherboard provides expandability because ports are built in and do not require separate adapters. If the motherboard includes the serial, parallel, and video ports, there is more space available for other adapters such as network or sound cards. Some motherboards include the network connection and the ports normally found on sound cards. The number of available expansion slots in a system depends on the motherboard manufacturer. Figure 2.29 shows integrated motherboard ports.

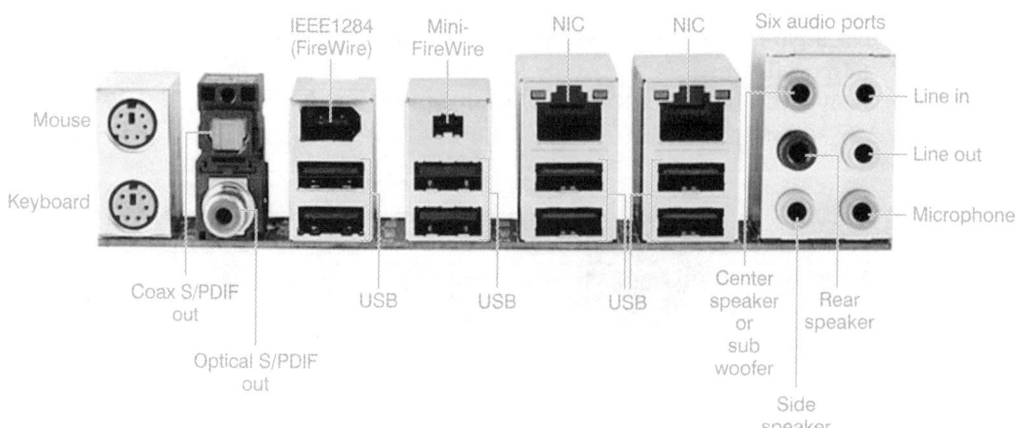

Figure 2.29 Integrated motherboard ports

Ports built into a motherboard are faster than those on an expansion board. All adapters in expansion slots run slower than the motherboard components. Computers with integrated motherboards are easier to set up because you do not have to install an adapter or configure the ports. Normally, systems with integrated motherboards are easier to troubleshoot because the components are on one board. The drawback is that when one port goes bad, you have to add an adapter that has the same type of port as the one that went bad.

Ports have different parameters set to keep one port from interfering with another. The ability to alter the configuration is important to a technician. Of course, having good documentation about the features and abilities of an integrated motherboard is crucial. Without documentation, you cannot disable a port or change a port's settings. In addition, proper documentation allows you to determine the features of the individual ports or of the other motherboard components. The Internet is a great resource for documentation when the original documentation is unavailable.

Docking Station and Port Replicator

Docking stations and port replicators add connectivity and expansion capability to laptop computers. A **docking station** allows a laptop computer to be more like a desktop system. A docking station can have connections for a full-size monitor, printer, keyboard, mouse, and printer. In addition, a docking station can have expansion slots or cards and storage bays.

To install a laptop into a docking station, close the laptop and slide the laptop into the docking station. Optionally (depending on the model), secure the laptop with locking tabs. Figure 2.30 shows a Toshiba 660CDT laptop computer installed in a docking station. The docking station shows the cover removed and you can see where the Ethernet network adapter is installed.

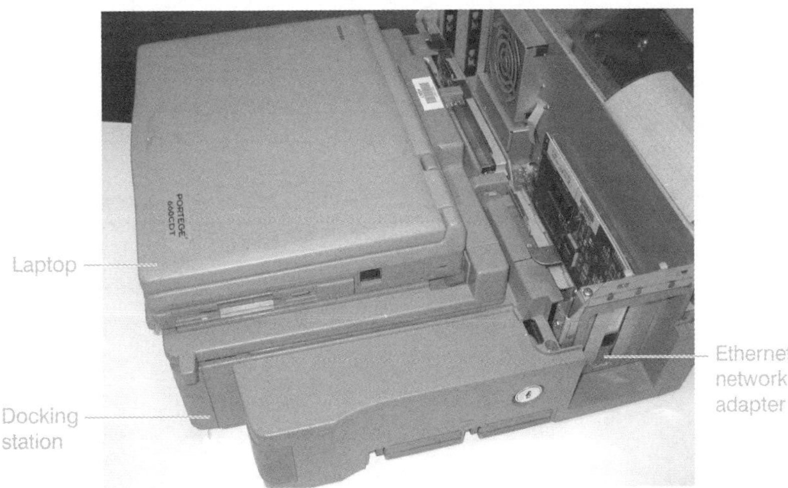

Figure 2.30 **Toshiba laptop installed in a docking station**

The **port replicator** is similar to a docking station, but does not normally include an expansion slot or drive storage bays. The port replicator attaches to the laptop and allows more devices to be connected, such as an external monitor, keyboard, mouse, joystick, and printer. To use a port replicator, normally the external devices are connected first. Align the laptop connector with the port replication connector. Attach the port replicator to the laptop. Today, most laptops come with many integrated ports; therefore, docking stations and port replicators are not as popular. Also, port replicators and docking stations are normally proprietary, which means that if you have a particular brand of laptop, you must use the same brand docking station or port replicator.

Being able to identify ports quickly and accurately is a critical skill in computer repair. Table 2.2 lists the most common computer ports.

Table 2.2 Common computer ports

Port	Usage	Port color code	Common connector
PS/2 mouse	Mouse	Green	6-pin mini-DIN
PS/2 keyboard	Keyboard	Purple	6-pin mini-DIN
IEEE 1394	Camcorder, video recorder, camera, printer, CD/DVD drive, scanner, speaker	Gray	6-pin IEEE 1394
USB	Printer, mouse, keyboard, digital camera, scanner, digitizer, plotter, external hard drive, CD/DVD drive	Black	USB Type A
Parallel	Printer, tape backup	Burgundy (dark pink)	25-pin female D-shell
Serial	External modem, digitizer, plotter	Teal or turquoise	9-pin male D-shell
Video	Analog monitor (VGA or higher)	Blue	3-row 15-pin female
Video	DVI digital or analog monitor	White	3-row DVI
S-Video	Composite video device	Yellow	7-pin mini-DIN
Audio	Analog audio input	Light pink	3.5mm jack
Audio	Analog line level audio input	Light blue	3.5mm jack
Audio	Analog line level audio output from main stereo signal	Light (lime) green	3.5mm jack
Audio	Analog line level audio for right to left speaker	Brown	3.5mm jack
S/PDIF	Digital audio output (sometimes used as an analog line output for a speaker instead)	Orange	3.5mm jack
Game port/MIDI	Joystick or MIDI device	Gold	15-pin female D-shell
Ethernet	UTP network	N/A	8-conductor RJ-45
Modem	Internal modem or phone	N/A	4-conductor RJ-11

On the Motherboard

Processor Overview

At the heart of every computer is a special motherboard chip called the **processor** that determines, to a great extent, the power of the computer. The processor is also called the CPU (central processing unit) or microprocessor. The CPU executes instructions, performs math calculations, and coordinates input/output operations. Each motherboard has electronic chips that work with the CPU and are designed to exact specifications. Whether or not these other components can keep up with the processor depends on the individual component's specifications. The major processor manufacturers today are Intel, Motorola, VIA, and AMD (Advanced Micro Devices, Inc.). The processors designed by Motorola have been used in Apple computers for years.

Intel designed the processors IBM used in their first computers. IBM put microcomputers in the workplace and the home. Those early computers influenced much of what happened in the computer industry. The machines sold by companies who copied IBM's first computers were known as clones or IBM-compatibles. These two terms are still used in the computer industry. Another name for the computer is **PC** (personal computer). This chapter focuses on compatibles (non-Apple computers) because they are the majority used in businesses today. Intel and AMD processors are covered extensively because they are the most common in the computer industry.

Processor Basics

All processors use 1s and 0s. One 1 or one 0 is a **bit**. Eight bits grouped together are a **byte**. The letter A looks like 01000001 to the processor. Each character on a keyboard appears as one byte or eight bits to the processor. Approximately 1,000 bytes is a **kilobyte** (kB). (1,024 bytes to be exact, but the computer industry rounds off the number to the nearest thousand for ease of calculation.) Ten kilobytes is shown as 10K or 10kB. Approximately one million bytes is a **megabyte** (MB). 540 megabytes is shown as 540MB or 540M. A true megabyte is 1,048,576 bytes. Approximately one billion bytes (1,073,741,824 bytes) is a **gigabyte** and is shown as 1GB or 1G. Table 2.3 shows the different terms associated with computer storage and capacity.

When information needs to be expressed exactly, binary prefixes are used. For example, when describing a value of 2^{10} (1024), instead of saying that it is 1 kilobyte, which people tend to think of as approximately 1,000 bytes, the term **kibibyte** (KiB) is used. When describing a value of 2^{20} or 1,048,576, the term **mebibyte** (MiB) is used. Table 2.4 shows the terms used with binary prefixes or when exact measurements are needed.

Microprocessors come in a variety of speeds. The speed of processors is measured in **gigahertz** (GHz). Hertz is a measurement of cycles per second. One hertz equals one cycle per

Table 2.3 Byte table

Term	Abbreviation	Description
Kilobyte	kB	~1 thousand bytes
Megabyte	MB	~1 million bytes
Gigabyte	GB	~1 billion bytes
Terabyte	TB	~1 trillion bytes
Petabyte	PB	~1,000 trillion bytes
Exabyte	EB	~1 quintillion bytes
Zetabyte	ZB	~1,000 exabytes
Yottabyte	YB	~1 million exabytes

Table 2.4 Binary prefixes

Term	Abbreviation	Description
Kibibyte	KiB	2^{10} and closely associated with kilobyte
Mebibyte	MiB	2^{20} and closely associated with megabyte
Gibibyte	GiB	2^{30} and closely associated with gigabyte
Tebibyte	TiB	2^{40} and closely associated with terabyte
Pebibyte	PiB	2^{50} and closely associated with petabyte
Exbibyte	EiB	2^{60} and closely associated with exabyte
Zebibyte	ZiB	2^{70} and closely associated with zettabyte
Yobibyte	YiB	2^{80} and closely associated with yottabyte

second. One gigahertz is one billion cycles per second or 1GHz. Older CPUs used megahertz (MHz) as the standard measurement. One megahertz is one million cycles per second or 1MHz. The original PC CPU, the 8088 microprocessor, ran at 4.77MHz. Today's microprocessors run at speeds over 3GHz.

The number of bits processed at one time is the microprocessor's **register size** (**word size**). Register size is in multiples of 8 bits (i.e., 8-, 16-, 32-, 64-, or 128-bit). Intel's 8086 processor's register size was 16 bits or two bytes. Today's CPUs have register sizes of 64 or 128 bits.

The 1s and 0s must travel from one place to another inside the processor as well as outside to other chips. To move the 1s and 0s around, electronic lines called a **bus** are used. The electronic lines inside the CPU are known as the **internal data bus** or system bus. In the 8086 the internal data bus comprises 16 separate lines with each line carrying one 1 or one 0. The word size and the number of lines for the internal data bus are equal. The 8086, for example, had a 16-bit word size, and 16 lines carried 16 bits on the internal data bus. In today's microprocessors, 64 or 128 internal data bus lines operate concurrently.

For the CPU to communicate with devices in the outside world, such as a printer, the 1s and 0s travel on the **external data bus**. The external data bus connects the processor to adapters, the keyboard, the mouse, the floppy drive, the hard drive, and other devices. The external data bus is also known as the external data path. One can see the external data lines by looking between the expansion slots on the motherboard. Some solder lines between the expansion slots are used to send data out along the external data bus to the expansion slots. The Intel 8088 had an 8-bit external data bus. Today's processors have 64- and 128-bit external data paths. Figure 2.31 shows the internal and external data buses.

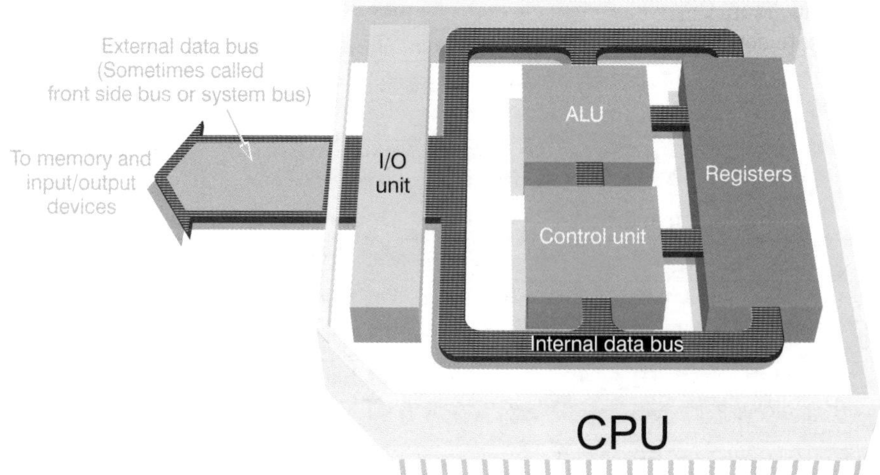

Figure 2.31 Internal and external data buses

Processors have a special component called the **ALU** (arithmetic logic unit), which does all the calculations and comparison logic needed by the computer. Refer to Figure 2.31 and see how the ALU connects to the registers, control unit, and internal bus. Today's processors actually have two ALUs, but Figure 2.31 simply shows how the buses connect. The control unit coordinates activities inside the processor. The I/O unit manages data entering and leaving the processor. The registers within the CPU are a very high speed storage area for 1s and 0s before the bits are processed.

To make sense of all of this, take a look at a letter typed on a computer that starts out: *Dear Mom*. To the computer, the letters of the alphabet are different combinations of eight 1s and 0s. For example, the letter *D* is 01000100; the letter *e* is 01000101. The 8086 microprocessor has a word size of 16-bits and an external data path of 16-bits. Therefore, the letters *D* and *e* travel together down the bus; the letters *a* and *r*, then the letters (space) and *M*, and finally the letters *o* and *m* travel as 1s and 0s. Each bit travels along a single data path line. Intel's 80386DX CPU has 32-bit internal and external data buses. In the same *Dear Mom* letter, the letters *D*, *e*, *a*, and *r* are processed at the same time, followed by (space), *M*, *o*, and *m*. An AMD 64-bit processor would allow the words *Dear Mom* to be sent all at one time. You can see that the size of the bus greatly increases performance on a computer.

Processors have multiple **pipelines** (separate internal buses) that operate simultaneously. To understand pipelining, take the example of a fast-food restaurant. In the restaurant, say there are five steps (and one employee per step) to making a burger and giving it to the customer: (1) take the order and input it into the computer system; (2) brown the buns and cook the burgers; (3) take the bun and burger and add the condiments; (4) wrap the burger, add fries, and insert it into the bag; (5) take the customer's money and give the bag to the customer. Keep in mind that the person taking the customer's order and inputting the order can serve another customer once he or she has completed this task for the first customer. The same is true for each person along the line. To make this burger process go faster, you could: (1) make your employees work faster; (2) break the tasks into smaller tasks (such as seven steps instead of five and have seven people); or (3) have more lines of people doing the exact same process tasks.

To relate this to processors, making the employees work faster is the same as increasing the CPU clock speed. Breaking the tasks into smaller tasks is the same as changing the structure of the CPU pipeline. Instead of the standard five tasks the CPU performs, 6, 7, 14, 20, or even more steps are created. This allows each step to be acted upon quicker, the task to be smaller, and production to be faster. Having more lines of people doing the same complete process is having multiple pipelines.

A 32- or 64-bit CPU can have separate paths, each of which handles 32 or 64 bits. For example, the Pentium has two pipelines. In the *Dear Mom* scenario, the letters *D*, *e*, *a*, and *r* can be in one pipeline, while (space), *M*, *o*, and *m* can be in the other pipeline.

AMD's Athlon has 9 execution pipelines and the Opteron has 12 pipelines (for integers and 17 pipelines for floating point numbers (numbers that can have a decimal point in it). Intel Pentium 4 and Xeon CPUs have various models that contain anywhere from 20- to 31-stage pipelines. Debate continues about whether a longer pipeline improves performance.

Intel Processors

Traditionally, Intel has rated its processors by GHz and people have compared processors based on speed alone. Now, Intel arranges its products by family numbers. Within a family of microprocessors, you can compare things such as speed and the amount of cache memory and other technologies within the family. Table 2.5 shows Intel's processor families.

Intel also makes processors for more powerful computers such as network servers. The processors used by these computers include the Itaniums, Xeons, Pentium Ds, and Pentium 4s. The 64-bit Itanium Intel processors are based on the EPIC (Explicitly Parallel Instruction Computing) architecture that has been developed jointly by Hewlett-Packard and Intel. This type of technology is known as IA-64. The Itanium family of processors is best suited for network servers. With this architecture, up to 18EBs (exabytes) of memory can be accessed. This is 18,446,744,073,709,551,616 bytes. The 64-bit architecture is also backward compatible with 32-bit instructions. However, in Itanium 2 processors, the 32-bit instructions are done in an emulation mode, which could make them run slower. Figure 2.32 shows an Intel quad-core CPU.

Table 2.5 **Intel processor families**

Processor family*	Comments
Core i7	Multi-core (2 packages with 2 cores in each package) with 8MB L2 cache shared between cores Desktop processor for virtualization, graphic/multimedia design and creation, gaming On-board memory controller
Core2	Multi-core (single- and dual-core models in a single package; quad core has 2 processors in 2 packages for a total of 4 cores) with 6MB to 12MB L2 cache shared between cores Desktop/laptop processor for gaming and multimedia
Pentium	Single- or dual-core desktop/laptop processor for general computing
Celeron	Entry-level desktop processor for general computing
Centrino	Laptop processor for general computing that has extended battery life
Atom	Nettop/netbook/mobile Internet device** processor

*Intel is constantly upgrading processors. More information is available at www.intel.com.
**A nettop is smaller than a laptop used to extend Internet access at home. Mobile Internet devices are small enough to fit in a pocket. Netbooks are a portable version of your desktop used for Internet research, email, or streaming audio/video.

Figure 2.32 Intel quad-core processor

AMD Processors

AMD rivals Intel in processors. Anyone buying a processor should research all vendors, including Intel and AMD. Table 2.6 lists the characteristics of AMD processor families. The AMD Opteron processor is shown in Figure 2.33. The 64 indicates that it supports a 64-bit operating system and applications.

Table 2.6 **AMD processor families**

Processor family*	Comments
Phenom	Multi-core (3 or 4 in a single package) high-end desktop for HD support, megamedia creation and editing, and virtualization Supports 32- and 64-bit computing, 3DNow!, SSE, SSE2, SSE3, SSE4a, HyperTransport, and DirectConnect technologies*
Athlon	Single- or dual-core desktop/notebook processor
Sempron	Lower-cost desktop/notebook processor for basic productivity, email, and web browsing
Turion	Dual-core notebook processor

*These technologies are covered later in the section.

Figure 2.33 AMD Opteron

Speeding Up Processor Operations Overview

The processor speed can be determined by looking at the model number on the chip, but processors frequently have fans or heat sinks attached to them for cooling, which makes it difficult to see the writing on the chip.

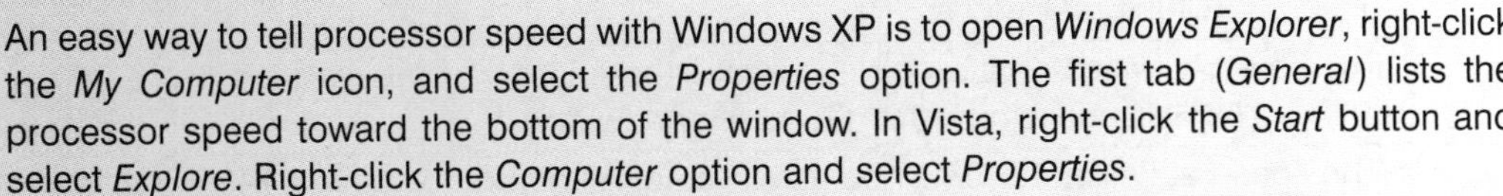

Locating your processor speed

An easy way to tell processor speed with Windows XP is to open *Windows Explorer*, right-click the *My Computer* icon, and select the *Properties* option. The first tab (*General*) lists the processor speed toward the bottom of the window. In Vista, right-click the *Start* button and select *Explore*. Right-click the *Computer* option and select *Properties*.

We have already taken a look at how increasing the CPU pipeline to some extent can improve processor operations, but other technologies also exist. Some of the hardest concepts to understand about the motherboard revolve around understanding the computer's timing and interaction with the CPU with other components such as memory and expansion slots. We will start by defining some of the terms that relate to this area and associating those terms to concepts and the various technologies used. Table 2.7 lists the terms related to speed.

Cache

An important concept related to CPU speed is keeping data flowing into the processor. Registers are a type of high speed memory storage inside the CPU and is an integral part of CPU processing. The data or instruction the CPU needs to operate on is usually found in one of three places: the cache, the motherboard memory (main memory), or the hard drive.

Cache memory is a very fast type of memory designed to increase the speed of CPU operations. When cache memory is integrated as part of the CPU, it is called **L1 cache**. Included in the processor packaging, but not part of the CPU is **L2 cache**, which some refer to as **on-die cache**. Finally, there is a third level of memory found when using higher end server processors called **L3 cache**, which can be located in the CPU housing or on the motherboard. CPU efficiency is increased when data continuously flows into the CPU. Cache gives the fastest access. If the information is not in cache, the microprocessor looks for it in the motherboard memory. If the information is not there, it is retrieved from the hard drive and placed into the motherboard memory or the cache. Hard drive access is the slowest of the three.

An analogy best explains this. Consider a glass of cold lemonade, a pitcher of lemonade, and a can of frozen lemonade concentrate. If you were thirsty, you would drink from the glass because it is the fastest and easily accessible. If the glass is empty, you would pour lemonade from the pitcher to refill the glass. If the pitcher is empty, you would go to the freezer to get the frozen concentrate to make more. The glass of lemonade is like cache memory. It is easily accessible. The pitcher of lemonade is like the motherboard memory. If the glass is empty, you have to get more lemonade from the pitcher. Likewise, if the 1s and 0s are not in cache,

Table 2.7 PC speed terms

Term	Explanation
clock or **clock speed**	The speed of the processor's internal clock, measured in gigahertz.
bus speed	The speed in which data is delivered when a particular bus on the motherboard is being used.
FSB (front side bus)	The speed between the CPU and some of the motherboard components. This is what most people would term the motherboard speed. Sometimes the speed is listed in megatransfers per second, or MT/s. With MT/s, not only is the speed of the FSB considered but how many processor transfers occur each clock cycle. A 266 MHz FSB that can do four transfers per second could list as 1064MT/s. The FSB is being upgraded with technologies such as AMD's HyperTransport and Intel's QPI (QuickPath Interconnect).
back side bus	The speed between the CPU and the L2 cache located outside the main CPU, but on the same chip.
PCI bus speed	The speed in which data is delivered when the PCI bus is being used. The PCI bus is the main bus used on the motherboard. Common speeds for the PCI bus are 33 and 66MHz allowing bandwidths up to 533MBps.
PCI-E bus speed	The speed in which data is delivered when the PCI-E bus is being used. This bus is used for PCI-Express cards.
AGP bus speed	The speed in which data is delivered when the AGP bus is being used. The AGP bus is a 66MHz bus allowing 2.1GBps of bandwidth.
CPU speed	The speed at which the CPU operates. Some motherboards have a BIOS option to change the speed. Other motherboards either use motherboard jumpers or cannot be changed.
CPU throttling	Reducing the clock frequency in order to reduce power consumption. This is especially useful in laptops.

they are retrieved from the motherboard memory chips. The pitcher holds more lemonade than the glass, just like motherboard memory holds more information than cache memory. The lemonade concentrate is like the hard drive—the lemonade concentrate takes longer to make and get to than the glass or the pitcher. In a computer, it takes roughly a million times longer to access information from the hard drive than it does from the memory on the motherboard or cache.

Usually the more cache memory a system has, the better that system performs, but this is not always true. System performance also depends on the efficiency of the cache controller (the chip that manages the cache memory), the system design, the amount of available hard drive space, and the speed of the microprocessor. When determining a computer's memory requirements, you must consider the operating system used, applications used, and hardware installed. The Windows 98 operating system takes a lot less memory than Windows 7. High-end games and desktop publishing take more RAM than word processing. Free hard drive space and video memory are often as important as RAM in improving a computer's performance. Memory is only one piece of the puzzle. All of the computer's parts must work together to provide good system performance. Figure 2.34 shows this hierarchy of data access for the CPU.

Clocking

The motherboard generates a clock signal that is used to control the transfer of 1s and 0s to the CPU. Processor clock timing signals go as fast as 100, 133, 166, 200, 266, or 333 MHz (millions of cycles per second). A clock signal can be illustrated as a sine wave. One clock cycle is from one point on the sine wave to the next point that is located on the same point on the sine wave later in time, as shown in Figure 2.35.

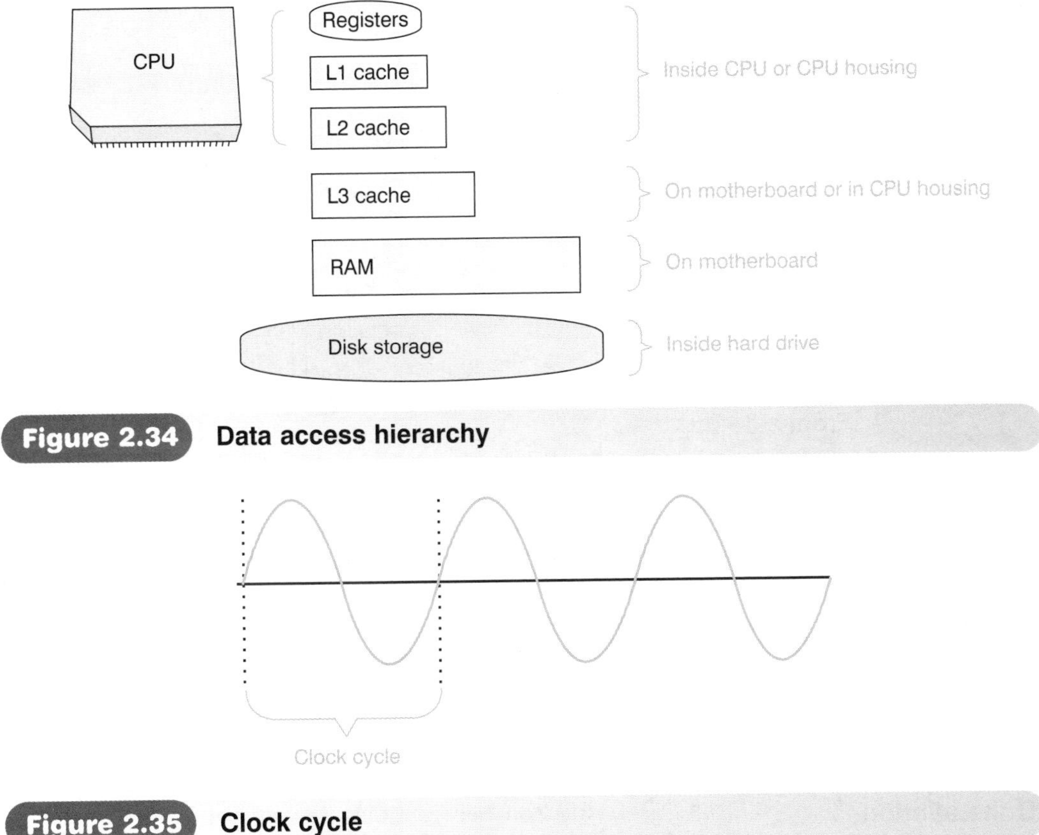

Figure 2.34 Data access hierarchy

Figure 2.35 Clock cycle

In older computers, data was sent to the CPU only once during a clock cycle. Then, newer memory technologies evolved that allow data to be sent twice during every clock cycle. Today, data is sent four times during a single clock cycle, as shown in Figure 2.36.

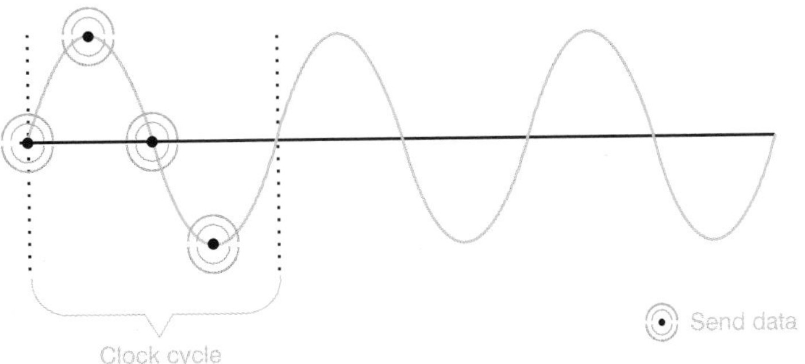

Figure 2.36 Clock cycle that clocks data four times per cycle

We have considered various ways to speed up processor operations, including having more stages in the processor, increasing the speed of the clock, and sending more data in the same amount of time. Accessing L2 cache and motherboard components was a bottleneck in older systems because the CPU used the same bus to communicate with RAM and other motherboard components as it did with L2 and motherboard cache. Intel's Pentium Pro and AMD's Athlon/Duron CPUs take a different approach called DIB. With DIB (dual independent bus), two buses are used: a back side bus and a front side bus. The back side bus connects the CPU to the L2 cache. The FSB (front side bus) connects the CPU to the motherboard components. The FSB is considered the speed of the motherboard. Figure 2.37 illustrates the concept of a front side bus. Remember that the front side bus is more detailed than what is shown; the figure simply illustrates the difference between the back side bus and the front side bus.

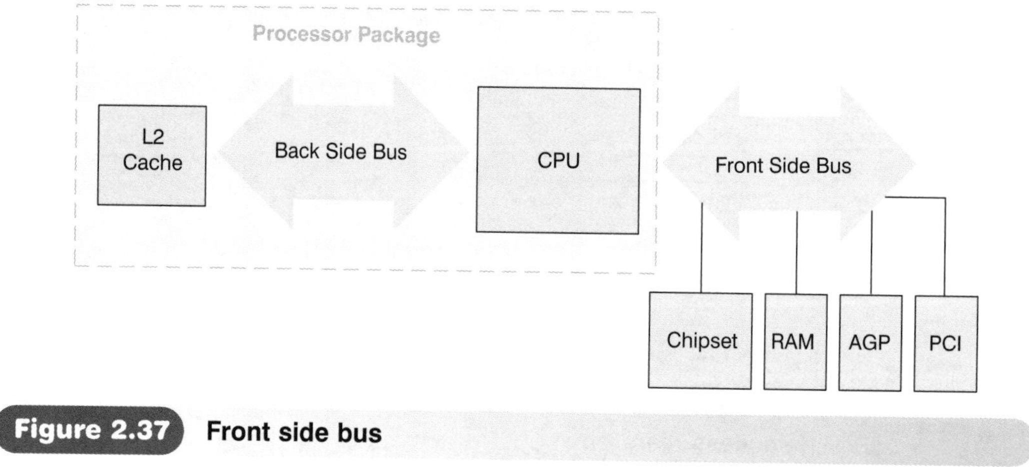

Figure 2.37 Front side bus

Many people think that the higher the CPU speed, the faster the computer. This is seldom true. Several factors contribute to computer speed. One factor is bus speed. Bus speed describes how fast the CPU can communicate with motherboard components, such as memory, chipset, or PCI bus. The first Pentium CPUs ran at the same speed as the bus—60Mhz; however CPUs got faster and buses stayed the same. Advances in technology have not reached the rest of the motherboard components (and it would cost too much to try to have them keep up).

Intel and AMD have new technologies to replace the front side bus in some parts. **AMD's** solution is DirectConnect. Intel has **QPI** (QuickPath Interconnect), a full-duplex (traffic can flow in both directions simultaneously) point-to-point connection between the processor and one or more motherboard components.

Settings for CPU installations

When upgrading a processor or installing a new one, frequently there are two sets of motherboard jumpers or BIOS settings that are very important: CPU bus frequency and bus frequency multiple. The CPU bus frequency setting allows the motherboard to run at a specific speed, such as 200 or 266 MHz. This speed is the external rate data travels *outside* the processor. The bus frequency multiple enables the motherboard to recognize the *internal* processor speed.

A multiplier is a number that, when multiplied by the bus speed, gives the CPU speed. Other names for the multiplier include CPU clock ratio, bus frequency multiple, and bus frequency ratio. The motherboard speed is increased to a faster rate for the CPU that can operate at the increased level of speed. For example, if the motherboard is using a 200Mhz clock speed and the CPU multiplier is set to 12, then the speed of the CPU is 2.4Ghz. Multipliers can be from 1.5 to 23 or higher. The available multiplier and the bus speed are determined by the motherboard manufacturer.

Knowing the CPU's speed is no longer an issue unless you are upgrading the computer to a faster microprocessor or configuring the motherboard. Many motherboards accept processors with different speeds. The microprocessor settings can be configured through system BIOS or by **jumpers** (pins on the motherboard). The software in the BIOS requires a specific key to be pressed during startup to access the software. The processor settings are normally in the *Advanced Settings* section, which is covered in more detail in the next section of the chapter.

A motherboard manufacturer determines how the motherboard is configured and the number of jumpers (if any) on the motherboard. Jumpers are also found on devices and older adapters. Each jumper can have more than one setting. For example, consider a motherboard with a jumper block and three pins labeled 1, 2, and 3. The jumper can be placed over pins 1 and 2 for one setting or pins 2 and 3 for a different setting. For example, jumper pins 1 and 2 may need to be jumpered together to erase the password that has been forgotten. In that case, the jumper is placed over pins 1 and 2; pin 3 is left uncovered. Refer to Figure 2.38 for an illustration of JP1 pins 1 and 2 jumpered together.

Figure 2.38 shows an enlarged jumper; the jumper blocks and jumpers on a motherboard are much smaller. When a jumper is not in use, instead of putting it in a drawer somewhere, place the jumper over a single pin in the jumper block. This action does not enable anything and it keeps the jumper safe and convenient for when it is needed later.

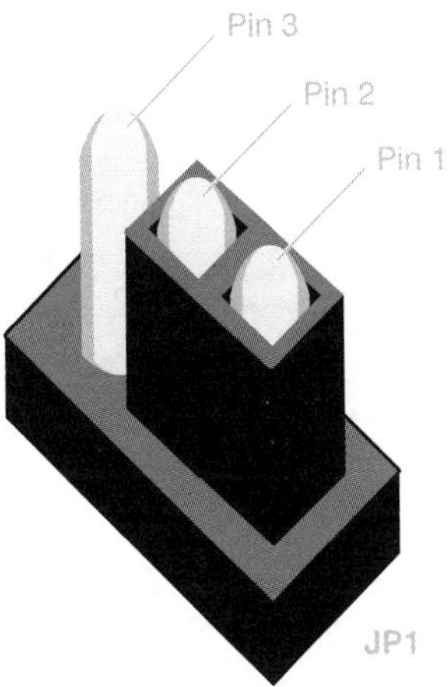

Figure 2.38 JP1 jumper block with pins 1 and 2 jumpered together

Multi-core Processors

Another way to speed up operations is to have two or more processors. Intel developed **HT** (hyperthreading technology), which is an alternative to using two processors. HT allows a single processor to handle two separate sets of instructions simultaneously. To the operating system, HT makes the system appear as if it has multiple processors. Even before HT, software was written so that instructions could be split and acted upon by multiple processors. In order to take advantage of Intel's technology the following requirements must be met:

- The CPU must support HT
- The chipset (covered later in the chapter) must support HT
- The BIOS must support HT
- The operating system must support HT

Intel claims that the system can have up to a 30 percent increase in performance, but studies have shown that this is application-dependent. In some instances it has actually slowed down performance. If the applications being used cannot take advantage of the multiple threading, then HT can be disabled in the BIOS.

In the past when two processors were installed, software had to be specifically written to support it. That is no longer true. A **dual-core CPU** combines two CPUs in a single unit. Both Intel and AMD offer dual-core processors. AMD offers a **tri-core CPU**, which has three processors in a single unit. Both Intel and AMD have **quad-core CPU** technologies, which is either two dual-core CPUs installed on the same motherboard (Intel's solution) or two dual-core CPUs installed in a single socket (AMD and Intel solution). Intel and AMD's dual and quad core technologies are different, especially in regard to how the CPU accesses L2 cache memory and motherboard RAM.

AMD core processors directly access RAM on the motherboard, and each core has its own L2 cache and, optionally, L3 cache. An advertisement that shows a 2x2MB cache means the computer has two sets of 2MB of cache memory, 2MB for each CPU. Intel processors share L2 cache and access RAM via an external memory controller or have an integrated memory controller within the CPU packaging. An Intel advertisement would just show the amount of shared L2 cache. Figures 2.39 and 2.40 show how the AMD and some of the Intel multi-processors can have integrated memory controllers.

In the past, dual processors were most beneficial in servers and gaming PCs where software could take advantage and was written for two-processor technology. Today, dual-core CPUs are useful to almost anyone who has multiple applications open at the same time. All applications can take advantage of the dual-core technology as well as the background processes that are associated with the operating system as well as the applications. This improves operations when multitasking or when running powerful applications that require many instructions to be executed, such as drawing applications and games.

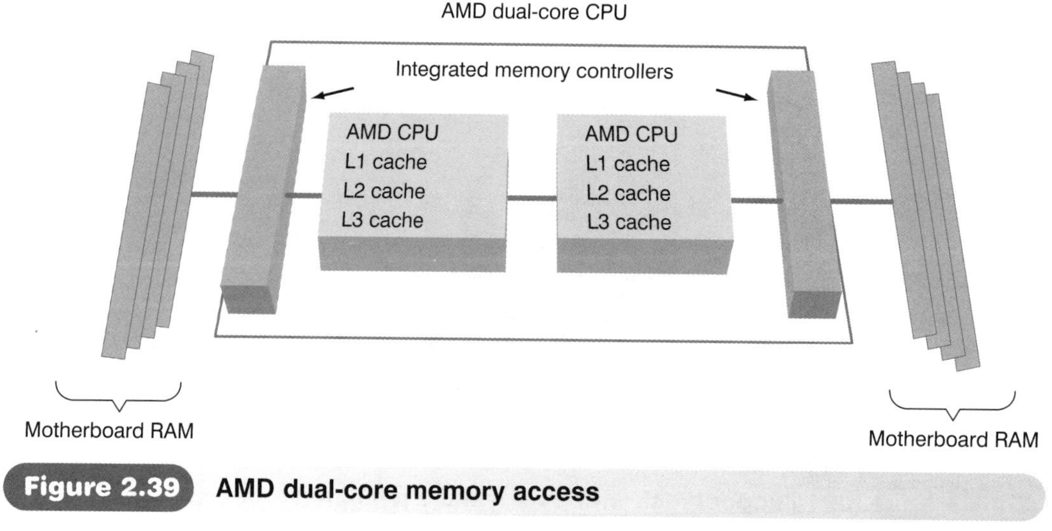

Figure 2.39 AMD dual-core memory access

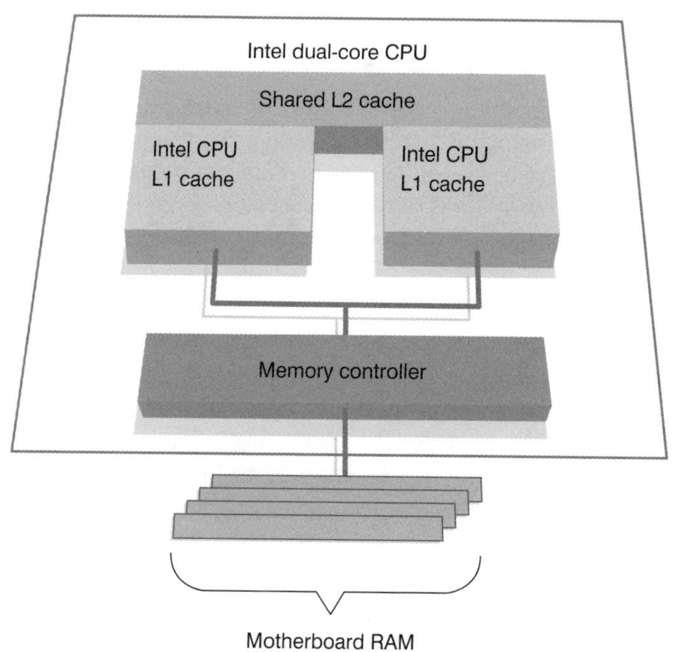

Figure 2.40 Intel dual-core memory access

Sockets and Slots

A processor inserts into a socket or slot depending on the model. Most processors today insert into a socket. There are different types of sockets: PGA (pin grid array), which has even rows of holes around the square socket; SPGA (staggered pin array), which has staggered holes so more pins can be inserted; PPGA (plastic pin grid array) used on Intel Celerons and Pentium 4s; µPGA (micro pin grid array) used by AMD; and LGA (land grid array) used with AMD and Intel processors. Figure 2.41 shows a LGA775 socket (also called a Socket T).

The processor sockets used today are called **ZIF sockets** (zero insertion force); even though people call all sockets with a lever a ZIF socket, they come in different sizes, depending on the processor installed. They have a small lever to the side of the socket that, when lifted, brings the processor slightly up out of the socket holes. When installing a processor, the CPU is aligned over the holes and the lever is depressed to bring the processor pins into the slot with equal force on all the pins. Refer to Figure 2.41 and notice the lever beside the socket.

Figure 2.41 LGA775 socket

Buy the right CPU

If you buy a motherboard and processor separately, it is important to ensure that the motherboard CPU socket is the correct type for the processor.

Table 2.8 lists the commonly used Intel CPU sockets and slots. Table 2.9 shows some of the AMD CPU sockets and slots that can be found.

Table 2.8 Intel desktop CPU sockets and slots

Socket or slot	Description
Slot 1	242-pin 2.8V and 3.3V connector for Pentium IIs, IIIs, and Celerons
Slot 2	330-pin 1.5V to 3.5V connector for Pentium II and III Xeons
Socket 423	423-pin 1.7V and 1.75V for Pentium 4s
Socket 478	478-pin 1.7V and 1.75V for Pentium 4s and Celerons
Socket 603	603-pin 1.5V and 1.7V for Pentium 4 Xeons, and Xeon MPs
Socket 604	604-pin for Pentium 4 Xeons
Socket 611	611-pin 3.3V for Itanium 2s
Socket 755	755-pin for Pentium 4s and Celerons
Socket 775	775-pin for Pentium 4s, Celerons, Core 2 Duo, Core 2 Extreme, and Core 2 Quads
Socket B or Socket 1366	1366-pin for Core i7s

Table 2.9 AMD desktop CPU sockets and slots

Socket or slot	Description
Socket A or Socket 462	462-pin 1.1V to 1.85V for Duron and Athlons
Socket AM2	940-pin for Athlon, Athlon X2, and Semprons
Socket AM2+	940-pin for Athlon X2, Phenom X3, and Phenom X4s
Socket AM3	940-pin for Phenom II X3 and Phenom II X4s
Socket 754	754-pin for Athlon and Semprons
Socket 939	939-pin for Athlon and Athlon X2s 1207-pin

Processor Cooling

In today's systems the fans and heat sinks are very large. A heat sink looks like metal bars protruding from the processor. The largest chip or cartridge on or inserted into the motherboard with a fan or a heat sink attached is easily recognized as the processor. Some systems have multiple fans to keep the CPU cool. Figure 2.42 shows a fan and a heat sink.

Additional motherboard components can also have heat sinks attached. These are normally the chipset and/or the I/O (Input/Output) controller chips. Figure 2.43 shows a motherboard with these cooling elements.

Heat sinks and fans attach to the processor using different methods. The most common methods are screws, thermal compound, or clips. Clips can use retaining screws, pressure release (press down on them and they release), or a retaining slot. Small screwdrivers can be used to release the clips that attach using the retaining slot. Clips for fans or heat sinks can be difficult to install.

Figure 2.42 CPU fan and heat sink

Figure 2.43 Motherboard heat sinks

When installing a heat sink, a thermal pad or thermal compound may be used. A thermal pad provides uniform heat dispersion for the CPU. If thermal compound is used, only apply the prescribed amount. Spread the compound evenly in a fine layer over the portion of the CPU that comes in contact with the heat sink. Always follow the heat sink installation procedures.

Some heat sinks are known as active heat sinks. These have power provided by a motherboard connection or through one of the power supply drive connectors. Some motherboards come with sensors that monitor CPU temperatures, motherboard temperatures, and fan speed. The BIOS (covered further later in the chapter) can be used to configure the CPU. Additional fans can be installed to provide additional cooling for the PC.

Tech Tip

Watch out for screwdrivers

Screwdrivers can cause damage to a motherboard. They can slip when trying to remove a retaining clip for a heat sink or fan and can gouge the motherboard. Be careful not to scratch the surface of the motherboard with a screwdriver.

Expansion Slots

If the computer is going to be useful, the CPU must communicate with the outside world, including other motherboard components and adapters plugged into the motherboard. An expansion slot is used to add an adapter to the motherboard, and it has rules that control how many bits can be transferred at a time to the adapter, what signals are sent over the adapter's gold connectors, as well as how the adapter is configured. Figure 2.44 shows expansion slots on a motherboard.

Figure 2.44 **Motherboard expansion slots**

Expansion slots used in PCs are usually some form of PCI (peripheral component interconnect) or AGP (accelerated graphics port). Other types of expansion slots that have been included with older PCs are **ISA** (industry standard architecture), EISA (extended industry standard architecture), MCA (micro channel architecture), and VL-bus (sometimes called VESA [video electronics standards association] bus). A technician must be able to distinguish among adapters and expansion slots and be able to identify the adapters/devices that use an expansion slot. The technician must also realize the abilities and limitations of each type of expansion slot when installing upgrades, replacing parts, or making recommendations.

ISA (Industry Standard Architecture)

ISA is the oldest expansion slot. ISA allows 16-bit transfers to adapters installed in ISA slots. The number of expansion slots available depends on the motherboard manufacturer. ISA is also referred to as the AT bus. Because computer manufacturers want customers to be able to use their old adapters in an upgraded motherboard or a new computer, ISA is still available on the market.

ISA operates at 8MHz, although some vendors reliably achieve 10MHz throughput. Some vendors have achieved 12MHz, but the industry pronounced 10MHz the maximum speed for ISA. With today's microprocessor speeds, it's easy to see how the ISA architecture can be a detriment. Adapters that require high-speed transfers, such as network memory and video, are hampered by the slowness of the ISA standard.

ISA was designed to be backward compatible with IBM's first two computer models, the PC and the XT, which had an 8-bit external data bus. The only adapters that worked in the PC and the XT computers were 8-bit adapters. The ISA architecture allows an 8-bit adapter to fit and operate in the 16-bit ISA slot. Today, motherboards normally do not come with ISA slots.

PCI (Peripheral Component Interconnect)

A previously popular expansion slot is **PCI** (peripheral component interconnect) bus. PCI comes in four varieties: 32-bit 33MHz, 32-bit 66MHz, 64-bit 33MHz, and 64-bit 66MHz. Figure 2.45 shows the most common type of PCI expansion slot.

Figure 2.45 PCI expansion slots

There are several different types of PCI slots, as shown in Figure 2.46. One type of PCI expansion slot used by some vendors is called a combo slot; it is a connector that combines ISA and PCI. The connector is one molded piece, but the piece contains both an ISA expansion slot and a PCI expansion slot for maximum flexibility.

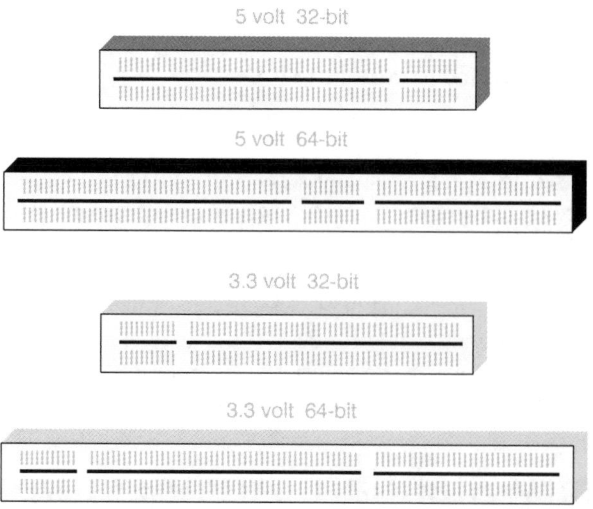

Figure 2.46 3.3 volt and 5 volt PCI expansion slots

An upgrade to the PCI bus is called **PCI-X**. PCI-X can operate at 66, 133, 266, 533, and 1066MHz. The PCI-X bus is backward compatible with the previous versions of the bus, but it allows faster speeds. A chip called the PCI bridge controls the PCI devices and PCI bus. With the PCI-X bus, a separate bridge controller chip is added. Figure 2.47 shows how the PCI-X bus integrates into the system board.

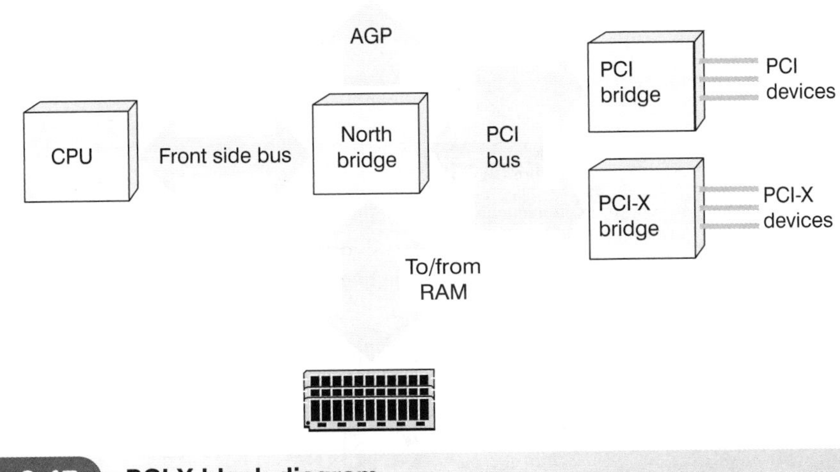

Figure 2.47 PCI-X block diagram

PCI-X adapters are more often found in network servers or high-end gaming workstations to control video, network adapters (such as gigabit Ethernet), and SCSI adapters (that control hard drives, tape drives, CD/DVD drives, scanners, and other internal and external peripherals). Today's motherboards have a limited number of PCI or PCI-X expansion slots because of a newer standard called PCI-Express or PCI-E, which is covered later in the chapter.

PCI cards in PCI-X slots

Remember that older PCI cards can fit in a PCI-X expansion slot, but a PCI-X adapter *requires* a PCI-X expansion slot.

AGP (Accelerated Graphics Port)

AGP (accelerated graphics port) is a bus interface for graphics adapters developed from the PCI bus. Intel does the majority of the development for AGP and the specification was originally designed around the Pentium II processor. AGP speeds up 3-D graphics, 3-D acceleration, and full-motion playback.

With AGP, the processor on the video adapter can directly access RAM on the motherboard when needed. This helps with video-intensive applications. 3-D graphics, for example, are resource-intensive and use a lot of memory. Software developers can produce better and faster 3-D graphics using AGP technology. The best performance is achieved when applications use the RAM on the AGP adapter. However, because more memory than the amount on the adapter is needed, motherboard RAM is the next best option. Previous video adapters have been limited by the bottleneck caused by going through an adapter and a bus shared with other devices. With AGP, the video subsystem is isolated from the rest of the computer. The different versions of AGP are known as 1X, 2X, 4X, and 8X. All versions transfer 32-bits at a time. Table 2.10 summarizes the differences between the AGP versions.

Figure 2.48 shows an illustration of an AGP slot compared with PCI and ISA expansion slots. All of the expansion slots previously covered are being replaced by PCI-E (covered next). Figure 2.49 shows various expansion slots.

Table 2.10 AGP versions

AGP version	1X	2X	4X	8X
Bus Speed	66MHz	133MHz	266MHz	533MHz
Transfer Rate	266MBps	512MBps	>1GBps	>2GBps
Data Path	32 bits	32 bits	32 bits	32 bits
Connector Voltage	3.3V	3.3V	1.5V	1.5V

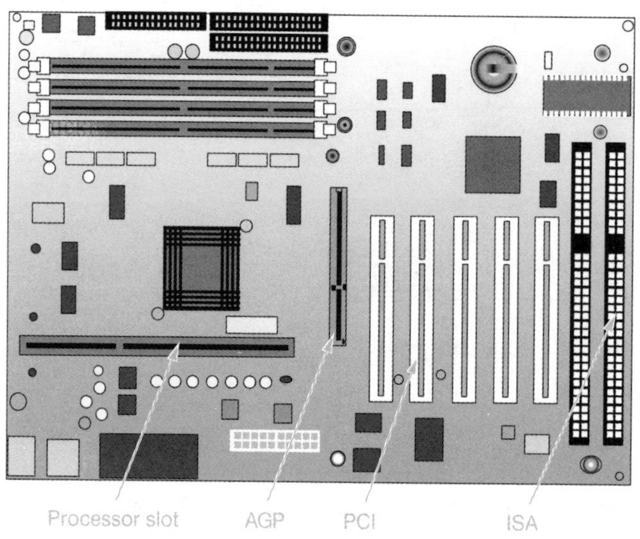

Figure 2.48 AGP expansion slot

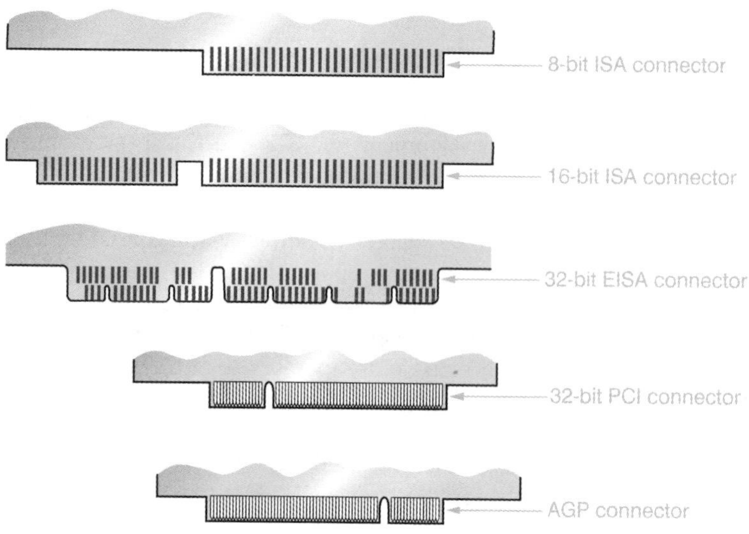

Figure 2.49 A comparison of expansion slots

PCI-E (Peripheral Component Interconnect-Express)

The PCI bus has almost reached its limit in terms of speed. PCI, PCI-X, and AGP are being replaced with **PCI-E** (PCI-Express), which is also seen as PCIe. PCI-E is better than the other types of PCI expansion slots. PCI-E 3.0 allows transfers up to 1GBps per lane in one direction with a maximum of 32 lanes. PCI-E 2.0 increases the transfer rate from 2.5GT/s (gigatransfers per second) to 5.0 GT/s, and version 3.0 increases it to 8GT/s. This allows a 16-lane PCI-E link to transfer data at a rate up to 32GBps. Competing technologies to PCI-E include Rapid IO, HyperTransport, InfiniBand, and StarFabric. These are great types of technologies to research if you are interested in hardware development.

PCI cards in PCI-E slots

Older PCI, PCI-X, and AGP adapters will *not* work in any type of PCI-E slots.

The older PCI standard is half-duplex bidirectional, which means that data is sent to and from the PCI or PCI-X card, but in only one direction at a time. PCI-E sends data full-duplex bidirectionally; in other words, it can send and receive at the same time. Figure 2.50 shows this concept.

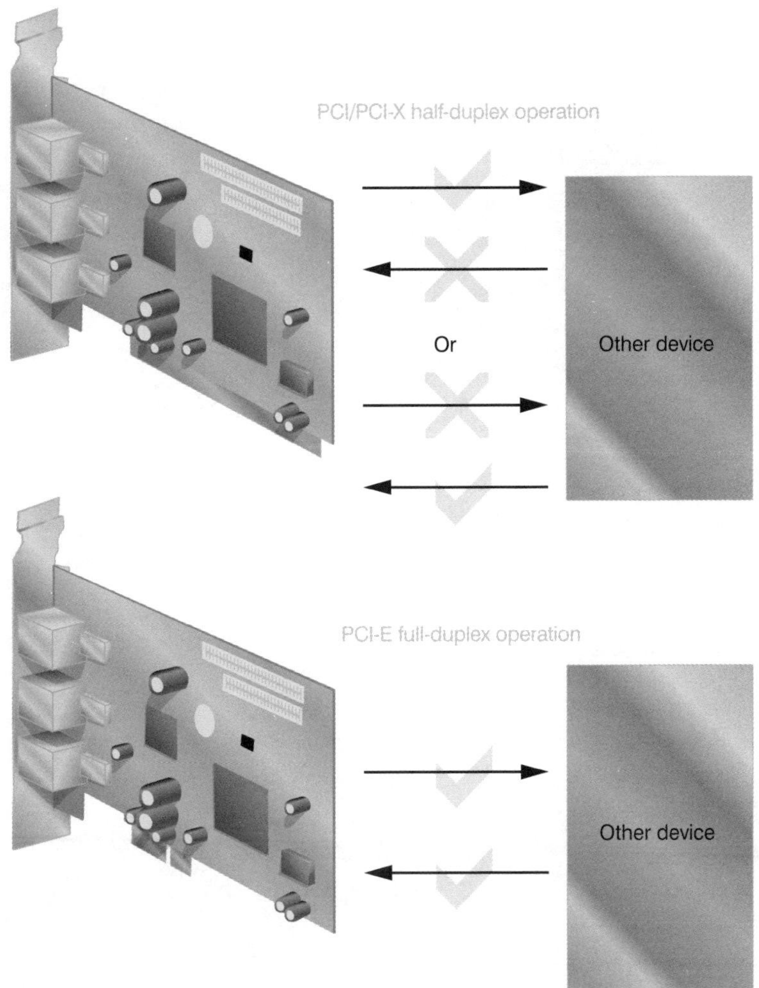

Figure 2.50 A comparison of PCI/PCI-X and PCI-E transfers

Beware of the PCI-E fine print

Some motherboard manufacturers offer a larger slot size (such as x8), but the slot runs at a slower speed (x1, for example). This keeps cost down. The manual would show such a slot as x8 (x1 mode) in the PCI-E slot description.

The older PCI standard including PCI-X uses a parallel bus where data is sent with multiple 1s and 0s simultaneously. PCI-E is a serial bus and data is sent one bit at a time. Another difference is that PCI-E slots come in different versions depending on the maximum number of lanes that can be assigned to the card inserted into the slot. For example, an x1 slot can have only one transfer lane used by the x1 card inserted into the slot—x4, x8, and x16 slots are also available. An x16 slot accepts up to 16 lanes, but fewer lanes can be assigned. An x16 slot accepts x1, x4, x8, and x16 PCI-E adapters. Figure 2.51 shows the concepts of PCI-E lanes. Figure 2.52 shows some sample PCI-E slots.

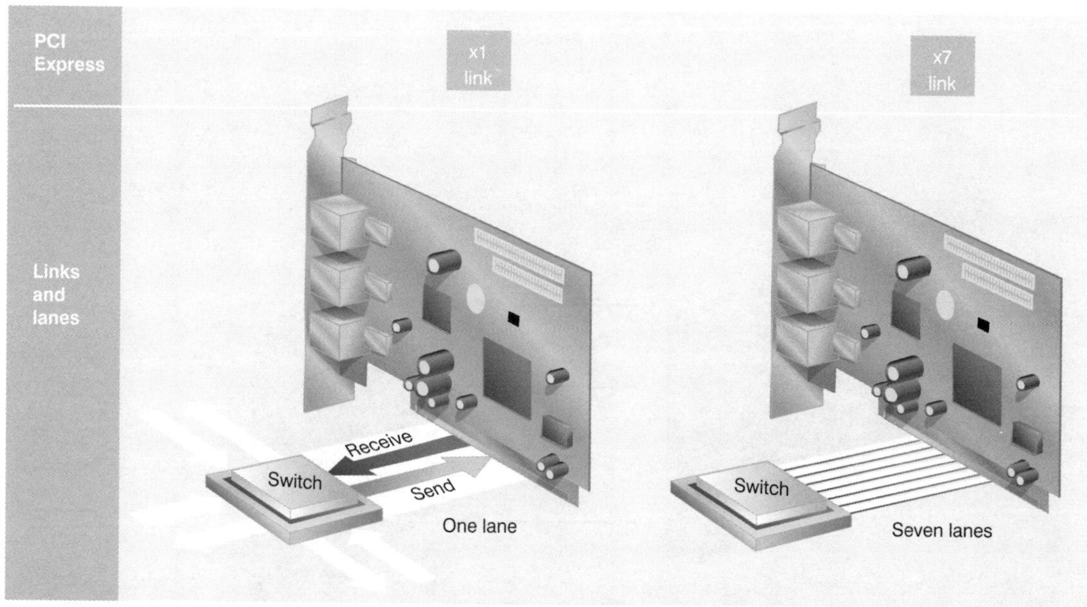

Figure 2.51 **PCI-E lanes**

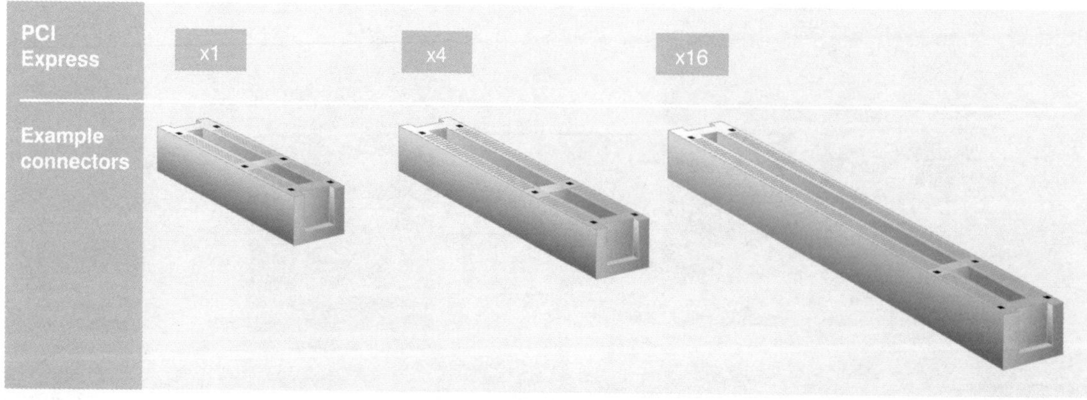

Figure 2.52 **A comparison of PCI-E and PCI expansion slots**

AMD has a different method of interfacing with PCI and PCI-E interfaces than the traditional FSB. AMD uses a technology called **HyperTransport**, which is a high-speed bus used to connect multiple CPUs, interface an AMD CPU with input/output devices, interface the CPU with PCI, PCI-X, and PCI-E slots, and interface the CPU with RAM. Figure 2.53 shows how the HyperTransport bus connects various technologies.

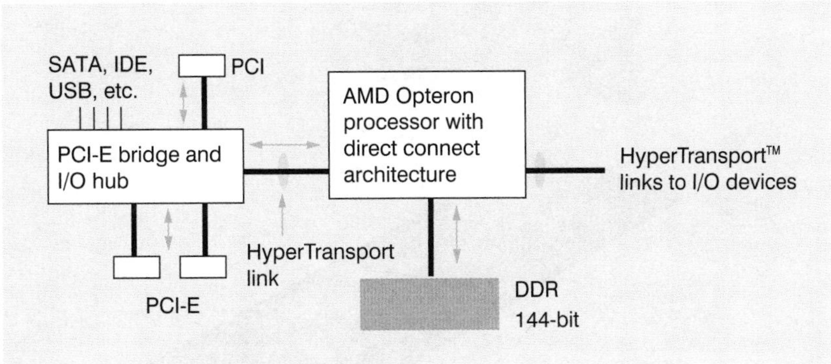

Figure 2.53 HyperTransport used with AMD processors

HyperTransport is a feature of AMD's Direct Connect architecture. With Direct Connect, there are no front side buses. Instead, the CPUs, memory controller, and input/output functions directly connect to the CPU at CPU speed. When removing an ISA, PCI, PCI-X, or AGP adapter, normally it is just a matter of removing a retaining screw or plate and lifting the adapter out of the slot. Some PCI-E expansion slots have a retention lever attached.

Figure 2.54 shows an example of the PCI-E adapter removal process. Figure 2.55 shows a motherboard with one x16 and two x1 PCI-E slots. There are also four PCI slots.

Removing PCI-E adapters

You must use the release lever to remove a PCI-E adapter that has such a lever installed, or the board (and possibly the motherboard) could be damaged.

Installing PCI-E adapters

A PCI-E x1 slot accepts only x1 PCI-E adapters. A PCI-E x8 slot accepts x1, x4, and x8 adapters. A PCI-E x16 slot accepts x1, x4, x8, and x16 adapters.

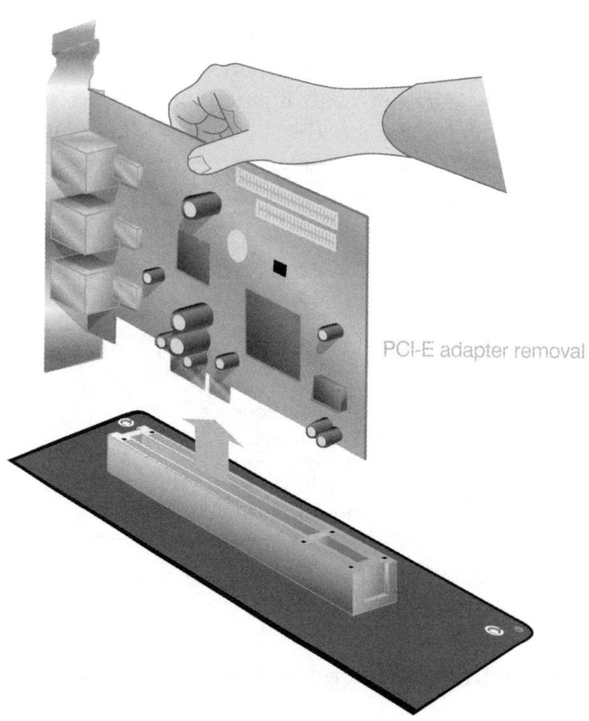

Figure 2.54 PCI-E adapter removal

Figure 2.55 Motherboard with PCI-E slots

System Configuration

The Setup Program

Most computers require Setup software to access the Setup program. This software is built into the system BIOS chip on the motherboard and accessed by specific keystrokes determined by the BIOS manufacturer. During the boot process, most computers will display a message stating which keystrokes will launch the Setup program. The keystroke can be one key pressed during startup such as the Esc, Ins (or Insert), Del (or Delete), F1, F2, or F10 keys. Other BIOS manufacturers use a combination of keystrokes where two or more keys are held down simultaneously during the boot process: Ctrl+Alt+Enter, Ctrl+Alt+Esc, Ctrl+Alt+Ins, Ctrl+Alt+Shift, Ctrl+Alt+F1, Ctrl+Esc, or Ctrl+Alt+F11.

How to access setup

The key(s) to press to access Setup are normally displayed briefly during the boot process. Otherwise, look in the motherboard or computer documentation.

Flash BIOS

Flash BIOS is the most common type of BIOS that allows changing the BIOS without installing a new chip or chips. Common computer BIOS manufactures include AMI (American Megatrends, Inc.), Phoenix, and Insyde Software. Many computer companies produce their own BIOS chips or subcontract with AMI or Phoenix to customize the BIOS. The following procedure is one example of "flashing the BIOS":

1. Once the system BIOS upgrade is downloaded from the Internet, execute the update.
2. Follow the directions on the screen or from the manufacturer.
3. Reboot the computer.

There are various reasons why a computer may need a BIOS upgrade: to provide support for new or upgraded hardware, support for higher capacity hard drives, virus protection, password protection, or to solve problems with the current BIOS.

Some motherboards have a utility that allows recovery if a BIOS becomes corrupted or the BIOS update fails. Other motherboards come with a Flash recovery jumper or switch used for BIOS recovery. Another motherboard manufacturer option includes a backup BIOS in case a BIOS upgrade fails or stalls during the upgrade process. Also, an alternative is a portion of the BIOS that cannot be changed so that the computer can still boot even if a BIOS update fails. A computer without an operational BIOS cannot boot. See the motherboard manual or documentation for specific BIOS details and the method that is being used to protect the BIOS.

How to flash the BIOS

Updating the system BIOS involves downloading an updated file from the Internet and executing that file according to the instructions.

How to remove the BIOS write protection

Because the Flash BIOS is frequently write-protected, a motherboard jumper, switch, or BIOS setting may need to be changed to allow the update. Refer to the computer or motherboard documentation to find the exact procedure for removing the write-protection and updating the Flash BIOS.

Protect the Flash BIOS

Viruses can infect the Flash BIOS. Keep the BIOS write-protected until you need to update it.

CMOS Memory

Settings changed in system BIOS are recorded and stored in **CMOS** (complementary metal oxide semiconductor) found in the motherboard chipset (south bridge or I/O controller hub). CMOS is low-powered memory powered by a small coin-sized lithium battery when the system is powered off. The memory holds the settings configured through BIOS. Part of the BIOS software routine that runs after the computer is turned on checks CMOS for information about what components are supposed to be installed. These components are then tested.

Incorrect Setup information causes POST errors

The wrong configuration information causes POST error codes or error messages that would normally indicate a hardware problem.

The information inside CMOS memory can be kept there for several years using a small coin-sized lithium battery. When the battery dies, all configuration information in CMOS is lost and must be re-entered.

Recall from earlier in the chapter that POST (power on self test) runs whenever the computer cold boots and it performs a hardware check on installed components. POST knows what hardware is *supposed* to be in the computer by obtaining the settings from CMOS.

When working on a computer with a POST error code, ensure that the user or another technician (1) has not changed the configuration through the Setup program or (2) removed or installed any hardware without changing the Setup program or updating the operating system. Correct Setup information is crucial for proper PC operation.

Keep a record of current Setup settings

Technicians should keep a record of the current settings for all the computers they service. If the wrong information is entered into the Setup program and saved in CMOS, a computer can operate improperly and may not boot.

BIOS Configuration Settings

BIOS options vary according to manufacturer, but many options are similar. Table 2.11 shows some common BIOS settings and a brief explanation of each. Most Setup programs have help that can be accessed from within the Setup program to explain the purpose of each option.

Table 2.11 Common Setup options

Setup option	Description
System Information	Displays general information such as the processor, processor speed, amount of RAM, BIOS manufacturer, and BIOS date
Boot Sequence or Boot Menu	Prioritizes from what device the computer looks for an operating system
CPU Configuration or Advanced CPU Settings	Contains settings such as CPU TM function, which affects CPU throttle management (slows the CPU when overheated); Execute Disable Bit, which helps with virus protection; PECI, which affects how the thermal sensors report the core temperature of your CPU; Max CPUID, which is used to be compatible with older operating systems; CPU Ratio control, which sets the CPU multipliers; and Vanderpool Technology, which is used with Intel virtualization.
Video Options	Allows configuration such as DVMT (dynamic video memory technology) to control video memory, aperture size (the amount of system RAM dedicated for the AGP adapter use), and which video controller is primary or secondary.
Onboard Device Configuration	Allows modification of devices built into the motherboard such as any serial, network, USB, or video ports

Table 2.11 Common Setup options (continued)

Setup option	Description
Power on Password, Password Options, Supervisor Password, or User Password	Allows configuration of a password to enter the Setup program, to allow the computer to boot, or to distinguish between someone who can make minor changes such as boot options or date and time (user password) and someone who can view and change all Setup options (supervisor password)
Virus Protection	A small virus scanning application located in BIOS. Some operating systems and software updates require disabling this option for the upgrade
Numlock On/Off	Allows default setting (enabled or disabled) of the number lock key option after booting
USB Configuration	Allows modification of parameters such as support for legacy devices, USB speed options, and the number of ports to enable
HyperThreading	Allows enable/disable of HyperThreading technology
Integrated Peripherals	Allows enabling/disabling and configuration of motherboard-controlled devices such as PATA/SATA drives, integrated ports including USB, audio, and network. Sets the amount of RAM dedicated for the AGP adapter's use. If the computer has an ample amount of RAM, increasing this setting can increase performance, especially in applications (such as games) that use high definition graphics.
HD Audio Controller	Enables/disables high definition audio controller
Advanced BIOS Options	Allows configuration of options such as CPU and memory frequencies, CPU, front side bus, Northbridge, Southbridge, chipset, and memory voltage levels
IDE Configuration	Allows manual configuration of IDE devices such as IDE, hard drives, and CD/DVD drives
SATA Configuration	Allows viewing Serial ATA values assigned by BIOS and changing some of the related options
PCI/PnP Configuration	Allows viewing and changing PCI slot configuration including IRQ and DMA assignments
ACPI (advanced configuration and power interface)	Determines what happens if power is lost, power options if a call comes into a modem, power options when directed by a PCI or PCI-E device or by mouse/keyboard action
Hardware Monitor	Allows viewing CPU and motherboard temperature as well as the status of CPU, chassis, and power supply fans

For a new system, use default BIOS settings in the beginning

When installing a new system, use the default BIOS settings until all components are tested.

Some motherboards have pins that, when jumpered together, remove the power-on password. Look at the computer or motherboard documentation for the exact procedure to remove the power-on password. Some motherboards distinguish between supervisor and user passwords. Another security option of some BIOSs is whether a password is needed every time the computer boots or only when someone tries to enter the Setup program. The options available in Setup and Advanced Setup are machine dependent due to the different BIOS chips and the different chipsets installed on the motherboard. Always refer to the computer or motherboard documentation for the meaning of each option.

What to do for a forgotten BIOS password

When a power-on password is set and forgotten, some motherboards have pins that, when jumpered together, remove the power-on password. With other motherboards, the only way to remove the password is by jumpering pins together to clear all the CMOS settings. Refer to Figure 2.38 for a graphic of a jumper.

You must save your changes whenever you make configuration changes. Incorrectly saving the changes is a common mistake made by a new technician. The options available when exiting BIOS depend on the model of BIOS being used. Sample BIOS exit options are shown in Table 2.12.

Table 2.12 Sample configuration change options

Option	Description
Save & Exit Setup	A commonly used option that saves all changes and leaves the Setup program
Exit without Saving	Used when changes have been made in error or more research is needed
Load Fail-Safe Defaults	Sets the default settings programmed by the manufacturer. Used when getting unpredictable results after changing an option
Load Optimized Defaults	An option programmed by the manufacturer. It has more aggressive settings than the *Load Fail-Safe Defaults* option

Motherboard Batteries

Computer batteries come in various shapes and sizes. The most common battery used today is a lithium battery about the size of a nickel. Figure 2.56 shows a photo of a lithium battery installed on a motherboard. If you cannot find the motherboard battery, refer to the motherboard or computer documentation for the exact location.

Figure 2.56 Computer motherboard battery

No battery lasts forever. Higher temperatures and powering devices that use batteries to power up and power down shorten a battery lifespan. Computer motherboard batteries last 3 to 8 years. Today, batteries last longer and people replace their computers more frequently; therefore, replacing batteries is not the issue it once was.

Battery replacement hints

Before replacing a battery, write down or print the settings in Setup. Also, check the motherboard for any evidence of battery corrosion and verify that no battery acid has come in contact with the motherboard. If the motherboard is contaminated with battery acid, it will probably need to be replaced. A first indication that a battery is failing is the loss of the date or time on the computer. The battery should be replaced before more configuration information is lost.

When batteries fail, several options are available to the technician, depending on which type of battery is installed. Table 2.13 shows various battery options.

Table 2.13 Battery options

Option	Replacement description
Lithium	Replace with the same kind normally obtained at a local electronics or computer store or from the computer manufacturer. If on a motherboard, gently lift the clip that holds the battery in place and slide the battery out of the holder.
Battery pack	Note which way the battery wires connect to the motherboard. Replace with an approved part number. Some laptop batteries that are *not* from the original manufacturer may not have the Li-ion safety features in place or the "intelligence" used to monitor power levels.
AA or AAA	Replace the batteries the same as any electronic portable device by making note of polarity (positive and negative).

Refer to documentation for battery replacement procedures

Always refer to the motherboard documentation for the exact battery replacement procedure. Replace the battery with one of the proper voltage and check on any recharging procedures.

Plug and Play

Plug and play (PnP) allows automatic software configuration of an adapter. A PnP adapter plugs into an expansion slot without the technician having to configure the board or worry about the adapter conflicting with other adapters already installed in the system. The motherboard BIOS must be the type that supports plug and play. ISA, PCI, PCI-E, and AGP adapters support plug and play. More information on configuring adapters that support plug and play is available later in the chapter and in the various hardware and operating system chapters.

Use a battery recycling program

Many states have environmental regulations regarding battery disposal. Many companies also have battery recycling programs. The earth911.com Web site has information regarding recycling and disposing of batteries and computer components by zip code or city/state.

Configuration through Switches

A **switch** (sometimes called a DIP switch) can be used to configure motherboard and adapter options. Switches can be found on older adapters and still can be found on motherboards and devices. There are two basic models of switches: slide and rocker. With the slide switch, a sliding tab sticks up from each switch in the switch bank. A switch bank is a group of switches. Each switch is normally numbered starting with 1. Each side of the switch bank is normally labeled with either On/Off, 1/0, or Closed/Open. On, 1, and Closed mean the same thing; Off, 0, and Open mean the same thing. The manufacturer determines how a switch bank is labeled.

To change a switch in the slide DIP switch bank, move the tab with an ink pen or small tweaker (flat-tipped) screwdriver to one of the two positions. For example, say that a switch needs positions 5 and 8 turned *on*. A technician turns the computer off, removes the computer cover, and moves the tabs in switch positions 5 and 8 to *on*. Figure 2.57 shows an example of a slide type DIP switch with the sliding tabs in positions 5 and 8 in the *on* position. Notice that the switch bank has eight individual switch positions.

Use updated device drivers

Just because an adapter is PnP does not mean that an updated device driver does not have to be obtained and installed loaded. A device driver is a small piece of software designed to allow a specific operating system to detect, configure, and control a hardware device. A best practice is to let the operating system detect the device if possible and then obtain an updated driver. Even if an adapter is automatically recognized by the operating system, an updated driver may be available and should be used.

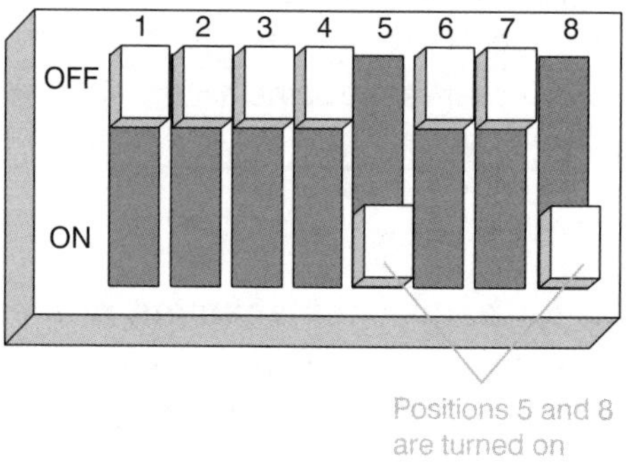

Figure 2.57 **Slide type switch**

A rocker switch does not have sliding tabs. Instead, each switch position has a rocker switch that presses down to either the On or Off position. To change a rocker switch position, use an ink pen or small tweaker screwdriver to push *down* on one side of the rocker switch. One end of the switch will be pushed down into the switch bank and the other end will extend up from the switch bank. The side of the rocker switch that is pushed down determines whether the switch is On or Off, 1 or 0, or Open or Closed. For example, Figure 2.58 shows a rocker type switch with switch positions 1, 4, and 5 Closed (which also means On or 1). Positions 2, 3, and 6 are Open (which also means Off or 0).

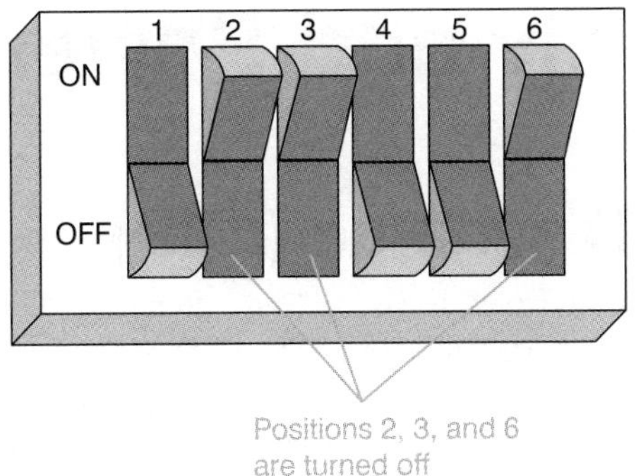

Figure 2.58 Rocker type switch

Use an ink pen or small tweaker screwdriver to change a switch

Never use a pencil to change a DIP switch because the pencil lead may break off into the switch. The lead is conductive. If it breaks off into the switch, the switch may be ruined. Instead, use an ink pen or small tweaker screwdriver to change the switch position.

Disassembly and Power

Electrostatic Discharge (ESD)

Many precautions must be taken when disassembling a computer. The electronic circuits located on the motherboard and adapters are subject to ESD. **ESD** (electrostatic discharge) is a difference of potential between two items that causes static electricity. Static electricity can damage electronic equipment without the technician's knowledge. The average person requires a static discharge of 3,000 volts before he or she feels it. An electronic component can be damaged with as little as 30 volts. Some electronic components may not be damaged the first time static electricity occurs. However, the effects of static electricity can be cumulative, weakening or eventually destroying a component. An ESD event is not recoverable—nothing can be done about the damage it induces. Electronic chips and memory modules are most susceptible to ESD strikes.

Atmospheric conditions affect static electricity. When humidity is low, the potential for ESD is greater than at any other time. Keep humidity above 50 percent to reduce the threat of ESD.

A technician can prevent ESD by using a variety of methods. The most common tactic is to use an **antistatic wrist strap**. One end encircles the technician's wrist. At the other end, an alligator clip attaches to the computer. The clip attaches to a grounding post or a metal part such as the power supply. The electronic symbol for ground follows:

An antistatic wrist strap allows the technician and the computer to be at the same voltage potential. As long as the technician and the computer or electronic part are at the same potential, static electricity does not occur. An exercise at the end of the chapter demonstrates how to attach an antistatic wrist strap and how to perform maintenance on it. Technicians should use an ESD wrist strap whenever possible.

When *not* to wear an antistatic wrist strap

Technicians should not wear an ESD wrist strap when working inside a CRT monitor because of the high voltages there.

A resistor inside the wrist strap protects the technician in case something accidentally touches the ground to which the strap attaches while he or she is working inside a computer. This resistor cannot protect the technician against the possible voltages inside a monitor. Refer to Figure 2.59 for an illustration of an antistatic wrist strap.

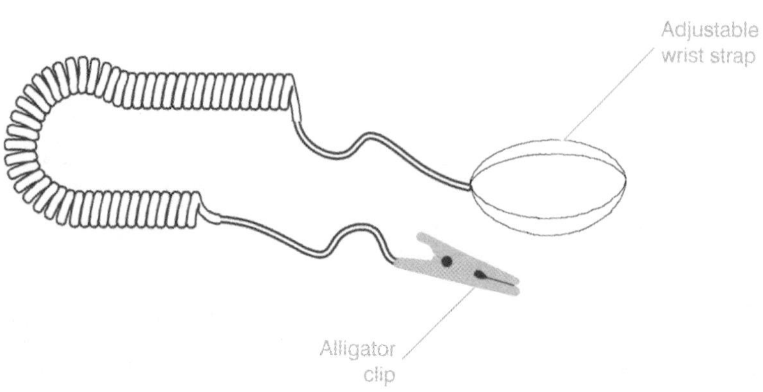

Figure 2.59 Antistatic wrist strap

Antistatic bags are good for storing spare adapters and motherboards when the parts are not in use. However, antistatic bags are not as effective after a few years. Antistatic mats are available to place underneath a computer being repaired; many of the mats have a snap for connecting the antistatic wrist strap. Antistatic heel straps are also available.

If an antistatic wrist strap is not available, you can still reduce the chance of ESD damage. After removing the computer case, if you are right-handed, place your bare left arm on the power supply. Remove the computer parts one by one, always keeping your left elbow (or some bare part of your arm) connected to the power supply. If you are left-handed, place your right arm on the power supply. By placing your elbow on the power supply, both hands are free to remove computer parts. This method is an effective way of keeping the technician and the computer at the same voltage potential, thus reducing the chance of ESD damage. It is not as safe as using an antistatic wrist strap. Also, removing the power cable from the back of the computer is a good idea. Power supplies provide a small amount of power to the motherboard even when the computer is powered off. Always unplug the computer and use an antistatic wrist strap when removing or replacing parts inside the computer!

EMI (Electromagnetic Interference)

EMI (electromagnetic interference, sometimes called EMR for electromagnetic radiation) is noise caused by electrical devices. Many devices can cause EMI, such as a computer, pencil sharpener, motor, vacuum cleaner, air conditioner, and fluorescent lighting. The electrical devices around the computer case, including the CRT-type monitor and speakers, cause more problems than the computer.

A specific type of electromagnetic interference that affects computers is **RFI** (radio frequency interference). RFI is simply those noises that occur in the radio frequency range. Anytime a computer has an intermittent problem, check the surrounding devices for the source of that problem. For example, if the computer only goes down when the pencil sharpener operates or when using the CD/DVD player, then EMI could be to blame. EMI problems are very hard to track to the source. Any electronic device including computers and printers can be a source of EMI/RFI. EMI/RFI can affect any electronic circuit. EMI can also come through power lines. Move the computer to a different wall outlet or to a totally different circuit to determine if the power outlet is the problem source. EMI can also affect files on a hard drive.

Replace empty slot covers

To help with EMI and RFI problems, replace slot covers for expansion slots that are no longer being used. Slot covers also keep out dust and improve the airflow within the case.

Disassembly

Before a technician disassembles a computer, several steps should be performed or considered. The following list is helpful:

1. Do not disconnect the battery from the motherboard or the configuration information in CMOS will be lost.
2. Use proper grounding procedures to prevent ESD damage.
3. Keep paper and pen nearby for note taking and diagramming. Even if you have taken computers apart for years, you might find something unique or different inside.
4. Have ample workspace.
5. When removing adapters, do not stack the adapters on top of one another.
6. If possible, place removed adapters inside a special ESD protective bag.

7. Handle each adapter or motherboard on the side edges. Avoid touching the gold contacts on the bottom of adapters. Sweat, oil, and dirt cause problems.
8. Hard disk drives require careful handling. A very small jolt can cause damage to stored data.
9. You can remove a power supply, but do not disassemble a CRT-style monitor or power supply without proper training and tools.

Tools

No chapter on disassembly and reassembly is complete without mentioning tools. Tools can be divided into two categories: (1) do not leave the office without and (2) nice to have in the office, home, or car.

Many technicians do not go on a repair call with a full tool case. Ninety-five percent of all repairs are completed with the following basic tools:

- Medium flat-tipped screwdriver
- Small flat-tipped tweaker screwdriver
- #1 Phillips screwdriver
- #2 Phillips screwdriver
- 1/4-inch nut driver
- 3/16-inch nut driver
- Pair of small diagonal cutters
- Pair of needlenose pliers

Screwdrivers take care of most disassemblies and reassemblies. Sometimes manufacturers place tie wraps on new parts, new cables, or the cables inside the computer case. The diagonal cutters are great for removing the tie wraps without cutting cables or damaging parts. Needlenose pliers are good for getting disks or disk parts out of disk drives, straightening bent pins on cables or connectors, and doing a million other things. Small tweaker screwdrivers and needlenose pliers are indispensable.

Many technicians start with a basic $15 microcomputer repair kit and build from there. A bargain table 6-in-1 or 4-in-1 combination screwdriver that has two sizes of flat blade and two sizes of Phillips is a common tool used by new technicians. A specialized Swiss army knife with screwdrivers is the favorite of some technicians. Other technicians prefer the all-in-one tool carried in a pouch that connects to their belt.

Do not use magnetized screwdrivers

Avoid using a magnetic screwdriver. It can cause permanent loss of data on hard or floppy disks. Magnetism can also induce currents into components and damage them. Sometimes, technicians are tempted to use a magnetic screwdriver when they drop a small part such as a screw into a hard-to-reach place or when something rolls under the motherboard. It is best to avoid using a magnetic screwdriver when working inside a computer.

Alternatives to the magnetic screwdriver include a screw pick-up tool and common sense. The screw pick-up tool is used in the hard-to-reach places and sometimes under the motherboard. If a screw rolls under the motherboard and cannot be reached, tilt the computer so that the screw rolls out. Sometimes the case must be tilted in different directions until the screw becomes dislodged.

There are tools that no one thinks of as tools, but which should be taken on a service call every time. They include: a pen or pencil with which to take notes and fill out the repair slip and a bootable disc containing the technician's favorite repair utilities. Usually a technician has several bootable disks or CDs for different operating systems and utilities. Often a flashlight comes in handy because some rooms and offices are dimly lit. Finally, do not forget to bring a smile and a sense of humor.

Tools that are nice to have, but not used daily, include the following:

- Multimeter
- Screw pick-up tool
- Screwdriver extension tool
- Soldering iron, solder, and flux
- Screw-starter tool
- Medium-size diagonal cutters
- Metric nut drivers
- Cable-making tools
- AC circuit tester
- Right-angled, flat-tipped, and Phillips screwdrivers
- Hemostats
- Pliers
- CD/DVD cleaning kit
- Network cable tester
- Nonstatic vacuum
- Disposable gloves

You could get some nice muscle tone from carrying all of these nice to have, but normally unnecessary tools. When starting out in computer repair, get the basics. As your career path and skill level grow, so will your toolkit. Nothing is worse than getting to a job site and not having the right tool. However, because there are no standards or limitations on what manufacturers can use in their product line, always having the right tool on hand is impossible. Always remember that no toolkit is complete without an antistatic wrist strap.

Reassembly

Reassembling a microcomputer is easy if the technician is careful and properly diagrams during the disassembly. Simple tasks such as inserting the CD/DVD drive in the correct drive bay become confusing after many parts have been removed. Writing down reminders takes less time than having to troubleshoot the computer because of poor reassembly. Reinsert all components into their proper place; be careful to replace all screws and parts. Install missing slot covers if possible.

Three major reassembly components are motherboards, cables, and connectors. Motherboards sometimes have plastic connectors called **standoffs** on the bottom. The standoffs slide into slots on the computer case. Do not remove the standoffs from the motherboard. Take the motherboard out of the case with the standoffs attached. The first step in removing a motherboard involves removing the screws that attach the motherboard to the case. Then, the motherboard (including the standoffs) slides to one side and lifts up. Some motherboards have retaining clips that must be lifted. Others have one or more retaining tabs that you must push while sliding the motherboard out of the case.

When reinstalling the motherboard, reverse the procedure used during disassembly. Ensure that the motherboard is securely seated into the case and that all retaining clips and/or screws are replaced. This procedure requires practice but eventually a technician will be able to tell when a motherboard is seated properly into the case. Visual inspection can also help. As a final step, ensure that the drives and cover are aligned properly when the case is reinstalled.

Logical Troubleshooting

Troubleshooting Overview

When a computer does not work properly, technicians must exhibit one essential trait—the will to succeed. The main objective is to return the computer or peripheral to service as quickly and economically as possible. When a computer is down a business loses revenue and productivity. Therefore, a technician must have a good attitude and a large amount of perseverance and drive to resolve the problem at hand quickly and efficiently in a professional, helpful manner.

Technicians must also use all available resources. Resources can be documentation for a particular peripheral, motherboard, or computer; the Internet; another technician; corporate documentation; textbooks; experience with similar problems; training materials; previous service history on a particular customer/computer; or an online database provided by a company or partner. Technicians can be stubborn, but they must always remember that time is money and solving the problem quickly and with the least amount of downtime to the customer is a critical component of a computer support job.

Solving a computer problem is easier if a technician uses reasoning and takes logical steps. Logical troubleshooting can be broken down into the following six simple steps:

1. Identify the problem
2. Establish a theory
3. Divide and conquer: separate the problem into logical areas to isolate it
4. Repair the problem or go back to test another theory
5. Test the solution
6. Provide feedback to the user

Back up data if possible

Before any changes are made to the system, ensure data is backed up if possible.

Identify the Problem

Computer problems come in all shapes and sizes. Many problems relate to the people who operate computers—the users. They may fail to choose the correct printer, push the wrong key for a specific function, or issue an incorrect command.

Have the user demonstrate or re-create the problem. Because the user is often the problem, you can save a great deal of time with this step. Do not assume anything! A user may complain that "my hard drive does not work" when in fact, there is no power to the computer. Often users repeat computer terms they have heard or read, but they do not use them correctly or in the right syntax. By asking a user to re-create a problem, a technician creates the chance to see the problem as the client sees it. Even during a phone consultation, the same rules apply:

- Do not assume anything; ask the user to re-create the problem step-by-step.
- Ask the user if anything has been changed, but do not be threatening. Otherwise, they will not be forthright and honest.
- Verify obvious things such as power to the monitor or speakers muted through the control panel.
- Do not assume that there is not a problem if it cannot be re-created by the user. Some problems are intermittent.
- Back up data, if possible, before making changes.

Establish a Theory

In order to establish a theory, you have to have heard or seen the problem as explained by the user. A lot of times, you establish a theory based on analyzing the problem and determining if the problem is hardware or software related (or both) by using your senses: sight, hearing, and smell can reveal a great deal. Smell for burning components. Watch the computer boot, look for lights, listen for beeps, and take notes. Frequently, a hardware problem is detected during POST (power on self-test) executed by the BIOS when the computer is first powered on. POST checks out the hardware in a sequential order and if it finds an error, the BIOS issues a beep and/or displays a numerical error code. Make note of any error codes or beeps. The number or duration of beeps and the numerical error codes that appear are different for different computers. The secret is knowing the BIOS chip manufacturer. Major manufacturers of motherboard BIOS chips include Award (now merged with Phoenix Technologies), AMI, IBM, and Phoenix. The computer or motherboard documentation sometimes contains a list of codes or beeps used for troubleshooting. A single beep is a common tone heard on a successful completion of POST because no hardware errors were detected. Table 2.14 lists the audio beeps heard on a computer with an AMI BIOS chip installed Table 2.15 lists the POST error messages seen on a computer with an Award/Phoenix BIOS installed.

Table 2.14 AMI BIOS audio beeps

Beeps	Description of problem
1	OK if screen appears. If not, DRAM refresh (memory)
2	Parity circuit (memory)
3	1st 64KM of RAM or CMOS
4	System timer/memory
5	Microprocessor (memory/motherboard)
6	Keyboard controller or A20 line
7	Virtual mode exception error (CPU)
8	Video memory (read/write test)
9	BIOS
10	CMOS shutdown (read/write test)
11	Cache memory
1 long, 3 short	RAM
1 long, 8 short	Video

Table 2.15 Award (now Phoenix Technologies) BIOS POST error messages

Message	Description
BIOS ROM checksum error—System halted	The BIOS has a problem and needs to be replaced.
CMOS battery failed	Replace the motherboard battery.
CMOS checksum error—Defaults loaded	CMOS has detected a problem. Check the motherboard battery.
Floppy disk(s) failed	The system has been configured to have a floppy disk installed and the drive has not responded. Check the drive connectivity and power. If no drive is installed, change the setting in BIOS Setup.
Hard disk install failure	The BIOS could not find or initialize the hard drive. Check the hard drive connectivity and power.
Keyboard error or no keyboard present	The keyboard could not be found. Check the cabling.
Keyboard is locked out—Unlock the key	Ensure nothing rests on the keys during POST.
Memory test fail	A RAM error occurred. Swap the memory modules.
Override enabled—Defaults loaded	The current settings in CMOS could not be loaded and the BIOS defaults are used. Check the battery and CMOS settings.

Table 2.15 Award (now Phoenix Technologies) BIOS POST error messages (continued)

Message	Description
Primary master hard disk fail	The PATA hard drive attached to the primary IDE connector and configured as master could not be detected. If a new installation, check the cabling, power, and master/slave/cable select settings. See p.000 for more details.
Primary slave hard disk fail	The PATA hard drive attached to the primary IDE connector and configured as slave could not be detected. If a new installation, check the cabling, power, and master/slave/cable select settings. See p.000 for more details.
Secondary master hard disk fail	The PATA hard drive attached to the secondary IDE connector and configured as master could not be detected. If a new installation, check the cabling, power, and master/slave/cable select settings. See p.000 for more details.
Secondary slave hard disk fail	The PATA hard drive attached to the secondary IDE connector and configured as slave could not be detected. If a new installation, check the cabling, power, and master/slave/cable select settings. See p.000 for more details.

Phoenix BIOS is sold to various computer manufacturers, who are allowed to create their own error codes and messages. Other BIOS manufacturers do the same. Look in the motherboard/computer manual or on the manufacturer's Web site for a listing of exact error messages. Table 2.16 lists the audio beeps heard on a computer with a Phoenix BIOS chip installed.

Table 2.16 Phoenix audio beep codes

Beeps	Description
1-2-2-3	BIOS ROM (flash the BIOS/motherboard)
1-3-1-1	Memory refresh (RAM contacts/RAM)
1-3-1-3	8742 keyboard controller (keyboard/motherboard)
1-3-4-1	Memory address line error (RAM contacts/RAM/power supply/motherboard)
1-3-4-3	Memory error (RAM contacts/RAM/motherboard)
1-4-1-1	Memory error (RAM contacts/RAM/motherboard)
2-2-3-1	Unexpected interrupt (adapter/motherboard)
1-2	Adapter ROM error (video card memory/video adapter/adapter/motherboard)

In addition to hearing audio tones, a technician might see numerical error codes or a series of colored indicators displayed during POST. Some motherboards also have a numeric display that helps with hardware troubleshooting. The numeric codes can be found in the motherboard or computer manual. Like audio clues, the numerical error codes are BIOS dependent. Table 2.17 lists IBM POST codes. These codes are somewhat generic and similar to those found on other systems.

POST error codes direct a technician to the correct general area only. Sometimes multiple POST errors occur. If this is the case, start the troubleshooting process with the first error code detected

Hardware errors might also occur. For example, the monitor might suddenly go black, the CD/DVD drive's access light might not go on when it attempts to access the CD disc, or the printer might repeatedly flash an error code. Hardware errors are usually obvious because of POST error codes or errors that occur when accessing a particular device. Also, some peripherals such as hard drives and printers include diagnostics as part of the software loaded when the device is installed. These diagnostics are frequently accessed through the device's Properties window or from the Windows All Programs software list.

Motherboard manual or Web site lists latest error codes

Because manufacturers constantly produce BIOS upgrades, use the Internet to verify POST errors that occur and the recommended actions to take.

Table 2.17 IBM POST error codes

Error	Description
01x	Undetermined problem
02x	Power supply
1xx	Motherboard error
2xx	RAM error
3xx	Keyboard error
6xx	Floppy drive error
9xx	Parallel port error
11xx	Serial COM1 error
12xx	Serial COM2, 3, or 4 error
104xx	IDE error
112xx	SCSI adapter error
113xx	Motherboard SCSI error
208xx	SCSI device error
209xx	SCSI removable disk error
210xx	SCSI hard drive error
215xx	SCSI CD drive error

Software errors, on the other hand, occur when the computer user accesses a particular application or file, or when the system boots. Files that affect the booting process, such as files in the Startup folder, are dependent on the operating system. If in doubt as to whether a problem is hardware or software related, use Windows Device Manager to test the hardware to eliminate that possibility. Every software program has problems (bugs). Software manufacturers offer a software **patch** or a **service release** that fixes known problems. Patches or service releases are usually available on the Internet from the software manufacturer. A **service pack** usually contains multiple patches and installs them at the same time rather than in multiple downloads.

Divide and Conquer

Divide the problem into logical areas and continue subdividing the problem until it is isolated. For example, if an error appears each time the computer user tries to write data to a CD, then the logical place to look is the CD/DVD drive system. The CD/DVD drive system includes the user's disc, the CD/DVD drive, electronics that tell the drive what to do, a cable that connects the drive to the controlling electronics, and the software program currently being used. Any of these may be the cause of the problem.

Ernie Friend, a technician of many years, advises students to divide a problem in half; then divide it in half again; then continue to divide until the problem is manageable. This way of thinking carries a technician a long way. Also, always keep in mind that you will beat the problem at hand! You are smarter than any problem!

Use Ernie's philosophy with the CD problem: divide the problem in half and determine if the problem is hardware or software related. To determine if the software application is causing the CD problem, try accessing the disc from another application. If the second application works, then the problem is in the first application. If both applications have problems, the problem is most likely in the disc or in the drive hardware system. The next easiest thing to eliminate as a suspect is the CD. Try a different disc. If a different disc works, then the first disc was the problem. If neither disc accepts data, the problem is the CD/DVD drive, cable, or electronics.

Swap parts one at a time until you locate the problem. Always reinstall the original part if the symptoms did not change and continue troubleshooting.

If a hardware problem is evident once a POST error or peripheral access/usage error occurs, consider the problem a subunit of the entire computer. For example, if a POST error occurs for the CD/DVD drive, the subunit is the CD/DVD drive subsystem. The subsystem consists of the drive, the cable, and the controlling circuits that may be on an adapter or the motherboard.

Change or check the easy stuff first

When isolating the problem to a specific area, be practical; change or check the easy stuff first. Time is money—to the company or person whose computer is down and to the company that employs the technician.

If the problem is software related, narrow it to a specific area. For example, determine if the problem is related to printing, saving, or retrieving a file. This may give you a clue as to what section of the application is having a problem or even lead you back to considering other hardware components as the cause of the problem.

When multiple things could cause the problem, make a list of possibilities and eliminate the potential problems one by one. If a monitor is down, swap the monitor with another before opening the computer and swapping the video adapter. Also, check with the computer user to see if anything about the computer has changed recently. For example, ask if anyone installed or removed something from the computer or if new software was loaded before or since the problem started. If the problem is hardware related, Device Manager and Windows troubleshooting wizards can narrow it down to a subunit. Isolating a problem frequently requires part swapping, but try not to replace good parts. If a replacement part does not solve the problem, put the old part back in.

Ethics are an important part of any job, including the job of being a technician. When a replacement part does not fix the job, do not leave it in the machine and charge the customer. Good technicians, like good automobile mechanics, take pride in doing an honest day's work. Start practicing these good habits in the classroom.

If you do not hear any unusual audio beeps or see any POST error codes and you suspect a software error, reboot the computer. In Windows, press the F8 key to bring up a startup menu. Select a menu option, such as Step-by-Step Confirmation or Last Known Good Configuration.

Repair the Problem or Go Back to Test Another Theory

Swapping a part, checking hardware settings, and referring to documentation are necessary steps when troubleshooting. Noting error or beep codes is just one element in the diagnostic routine. Determining what the problem is usually takes longer than fixing it. Software problems frequently involve reloading software applications, software drivers, or getting software updates and patches from the appropriate vendor. The Internet is an excellent resource for these files and vendor recommendations. Hardware problem resolution simply involves swapping the damaged part. Sometimes it is necessary to remove or disable unnecessary components and peripherals. This is especially true with notebook computers.

If swapping a part or reloading the software does not solve the problem, go back to logical troubleshooting. Step 2 reminds you to divide the problem into hardware and software related issues. Go back to this step if necessary. Step 3 advises you to divide and conquer. This step is the most likely place to resume your troubleshooting. Eliminating what could be the problem is important. Take notes during these steps so that you know what you have tried. People who troubleshoot randomly—repairing parts or replacing files without a plan—are known as "gunslingers." Gunslingers are the most dangerous technicians to have on staff. Sometimes gunslingers get lucky and fix a problem faster than a logical technician would, but gunslingers frequently cause more problems than they solve. Consistent, logical troubleshooting is a better path to follow. If you are methodical there is no problem you cannot solve.

Test the Solution and Document

Never assume that the hardware component or the replaced software repairs the computer. The computer can have multiple problems, or the repair may not offer a complete solution. Test the computer yourself and have the user test the computer in normal conditions to prove that the problem is indeed solved. Document the solution.

Figure 2.60 shows a simple troubleshooting flowchart, but keep in mind that each chapter has one or more troubleshooting sections to help with problems. Also, the chapters toward the end of the book address problems related to the operating system.

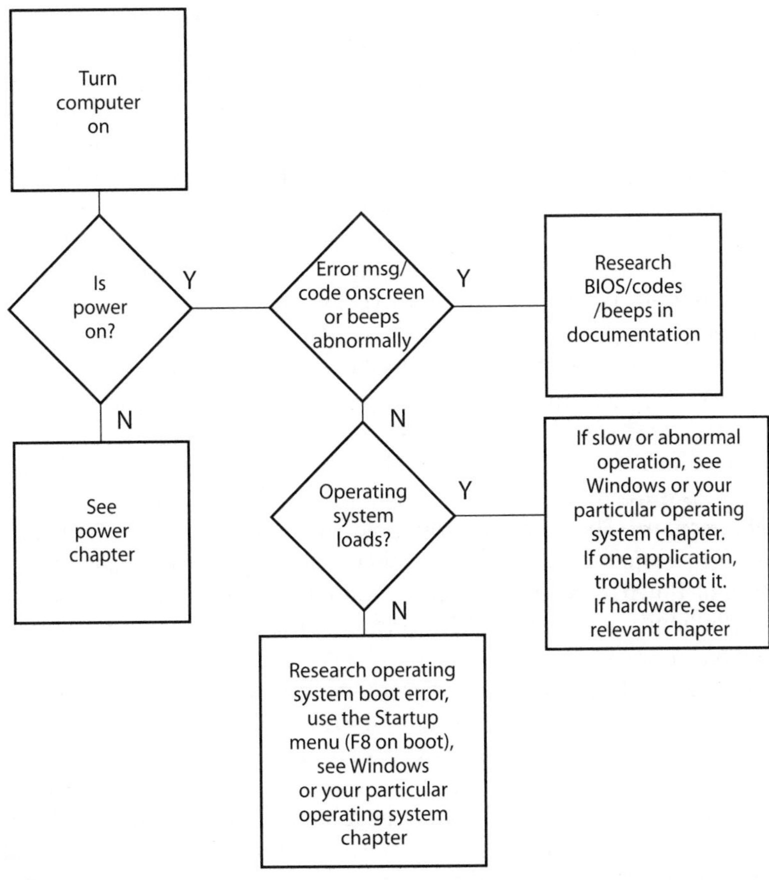

Figure 2.60

Memory

Memory Overview

Computer systems need software to operate; the computer is an expensive doorstop without software. For the computer to operate, the software must reside in computer memory. Memory is simple to upgrade, but a technician must understand memory terminology, determine the optimum amount of memory for a system, install the memory, fine-tune it for the best performance, and finally, troubleshoot and solve any memory problems.

The two main types of memory are RAM (random access memory) and ROM (read only memory). RAM is found on the motherboard and stores the operating system, the software applications, and the data being used by all of the software. RAM is also found on adapters such as video cards. RAM is volatile memory; the information in RAM is lost when you power off the computer. ROM is nonvolatile memory; the information is in ROM even when the computer is powered off. ROM chips can also be found on adapters including SCSI, network, and video cards. The software contained inside the ROM chip is allowed to execute during the boot process and initialize the adapter and possibly detect devices attached to the adapter.

RAM is divided into two major types: **DRAM** (dynamic RAM) and **SRAM** (static RAM). DRAM is less expensive, but slower than SRAM. With DRAM, the 1s and 0s inside the chip must be refreshed. Over time, the charge, which represents information inside a DRAM chip, leaks out. The information, stored in 1s and 0s, is periodically rewritten to the memory chip through the **refreshing** process. The refreshing is accomplished inside the DRAM while other processing occurs. Refreshing is one reason DRAM chips are slower than SRAM.

Most memory on the motherboard is DRAM, but a small amount of SRAM can be found on a motherboard or, as is the norm for today's computers, inside the microprocessor. SRAM is also known as **cache memory**. The cache memory holds the most frequently used data so the CPU does not return to the slower DRAM chips to obtain the data. For example, on a motherboard with a bus speed of 100MHz, accessing DRAM could take as long as 180 nanoseconds. (A nanosecond (ns) is a billionth of a second.) Accessing the same information in cache could take as little as 45 nanoseconds.

The CPU fetches a software instruction from memory and then the processor sits idle. In a fast food restaurant, this is the same as not allowing waiting customers to be served until the first customer has his or her food. Most restaurants serve the next customer while the food is being prepared and open more registers when lots of customers are waiting. With pipelining, the processor is allowed to obtain more software instructions without waiting for the first instruction to be executed. Opening more registers is similar to how manufacturers use processor models with more pipelines. Using cache memory and using pipelining are popular technologies used today.

The CPU should never have to wait to receive an instruction

Using pipelined burst cache speeds up processing for software applications.

The data or instruction that the microprocessor needs is usually found in one of three places: cache, DRAM, or the hard drive. Cache gives the fastest access. If the information is not in cache, the microprocessor looks for it in DRAM. If the information is not in DRAM, it is retrieved from the hard drive and placed into DRAM or the cache. Hard drive access is the slowest of the three. In a computer, it takes roughly a million times longer to access information from the hard drive than it does from DRAM or cache.

When determining a computer's memory requirements, you must take into consideration the operating system used, applications used, and hardware installed. The Windows 98 operating system takes a lot less memory than the Windows XP or Vista. High-end games and desktop publishing take more RAM than word processing.

Free hard drive space and video memory are often as important as RAM in improving a computer's performance

RAM is only one piece of the puzzle. All of the computer's parts must work together to provide good system performance.

Memory Physical Packaging

A DIP (Dual In-line Package) chip has a row of legs running down each side. The oldest motherboards use DIP chips for the DRAM. SIMMs (Single In-line Memory Modules) came along next. Two types of SIMMs were used: 30-pin and 72-pin. The memory chip used today is a **DIMM** (Dual In-line Memory Module), which has 168, 184, or 240 pins. Figure 2.61 shows the progression of memory packaging.

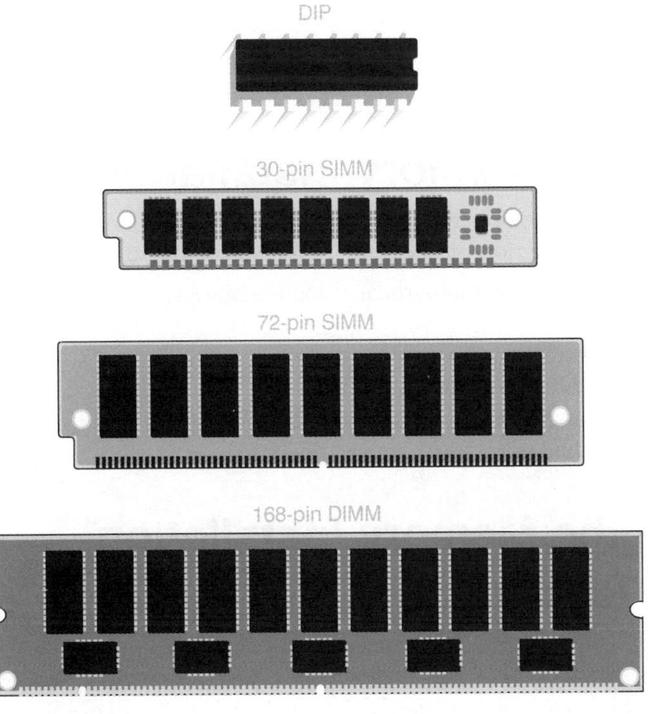

Figure 2.61 Memory chips

Memory chips are also called memory sticks, or a technician might call one memory module a stick of memory or RAM. RIMMs are used in older Intel Pentium 4 computers. Figure 2.62 illustrates these types. Notice the single notch at the bottom of the 184-pin DDR DIMM. This distinguishes it from the other dual-notched DIMMs. The RIMM has two notches in the center.

Use tin or gold memory modules

Memory module contacts are either tin or gold (although most are gold). If the computer is designed to accept tin memory modules and you install gold ones, over time a chemical reaction between the metals can damage the connector. Memory errors also occur. Be certain to purchase the appropriate memory module for the computer by referring to the documentation or by examining other chips already installed.

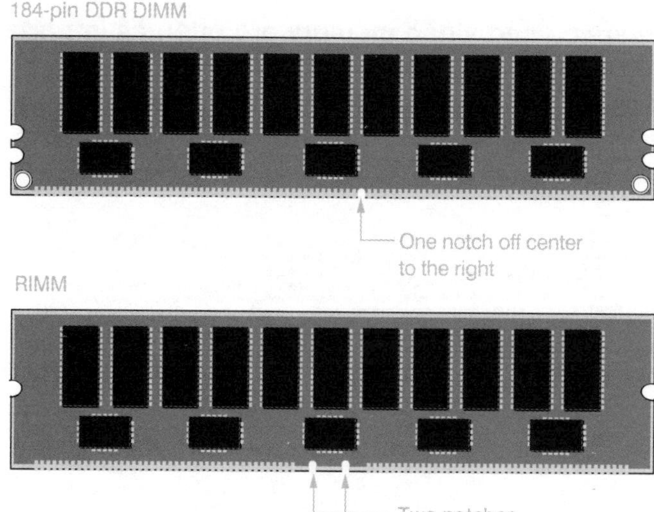

Figure 2.62 184-pin DDR DIMM and RIMM

Planning the Memory Installation

Now that you know a little more about memory types, let us look at the practical side—how do you go about planning a memory installation. Some key points to discuss follow:

- Refer to the system or motherboard documentation to see what type of memory is supported
- Determine what features are supported
- Determine how much memory is needed
- Determine how many of each memory module is needed
- Research prices and purchase memory module(s)

Planning the Memory Installation—Memory Technologies

Technology has provided faster DRAM speeds without increasing the cost too greatly. These DRAM technologies include FPM (fast page mode) RAM, EDO (extended data out) RAM, BEDO (burst EDO) RAM, **SDRAM** (synchronous DRAM), DDR RAM, and **RDRAM** (Rambus DRAM). The motherboard must be designed to use one of these technologies or the faster memory *will not* speed up the computer. Table 2.18 explains some of the memory technologies.

Whether a motherboard supports faster memory chips is determined by the chipset, which performs most functions in conjunction with the microprocessor. A chipset is one to five electronic chips on the motherboard. The chipset contains the circuitry to control the local bus, memory, DMA, interrupts, and cache memory. The motherboard manufacturer determines which chipset to use.

Keep in mind that a DIMM could use EDO, be a DDR module, or be a DDR2 module. In other words, once you determine that you need a DIMM or a RIMM (or if it is really old, a SIMM), then you have to determine what type of DIMM you need.

Use the type of memory chips recommended by the motherboard manufacturer

It is best to use the manufacturer-specified type of memory chips. The chipset and motherboard design are very specific as to what type, speed, and features the memory chips can have.

Table 2.18 Memory technologies

Technology	Explanation
FPM (fast page mode)	FPM, EDO, and Burst EDO speed up DRAM on sequential accesses to the memory chip. For example, if you have a 50ns DRAM and a 50ns FPM memory module, both types take 50 ns to access the chip the first time. On the second try, the FPM SIMM is accessed in 40ns. Used with SIMMs.
EDO (extended data out)	See explanation for FPM. A 50ns EDO memory module would take 50ns to access the chip, but on the second access, only 25ns are needed. Used with 72-pin SIMMs and 168-pin DIMMs.
BEDO (burst EDO)	See explanation for FPM. A 50ns BEDO memory module would take 50ns to access the chip, but on the second access, only 15ns are needed. Used with SIMMs.
SDRAM (synchronous DRAM)	Performs very fast burst memory access similar to BEDO. New memory addresses are placed on the address bus before the prior memory address retrieval and execution is complete. SDRAM synchronizes its operation with the CPU's clock signal to speed up memory access. Used with DIMMs.
PC100 SDRAM	Designed for the 100MHz front side bus.
PC133 SDRAM	Designed for the 133MHz front side bus, but will work with 100MHz motherboards (at 100MHz, not 133MHz). If you mix PC100 and PC133 DIMMs on the same motherboard, the memory and the bus will run at the lower speed (100MHz).
DDR (double data rate)	Sometimes called DDR SDRAM or DDR RAM and developed from SDRAM technology. With previous SDRAM, data was only sent on the rising clock signal. DDR RAM can send twice as much data as PC133 SDRAM because with DDR RAM, data is transmitted on both sides of the clock signal (rising and falling edges). A DDR DIMM uses 184 pins, and cannot be inserted into a DDR2 or DDR3 memory slot.
DDR2	An upgrade to the DDR SDRAM standard and sometimes is called DDR2 RAM. It includes the following modules DDR2-400, DDR2-533, DDR2-667, DDR2-800, and DDR2-1000. DDR2 uses 240-pin DIMMs and is not compatible with DDR; however, the higher end (faster) DDR2 modules are backwards compatible with the slower DDR2 modules.
DDR3	The latest in DDR SDRAM technology that is an upgrade from DDR2 for speeds up to 1600MHz. The technology better supports multi-core processor-based systems.
RDRAM (Rambus DRAM)	Developed by Rambus, Inc. and is packaged in RIMMs (which is not an acronym, but a trademark of Rambus, Inc.). The BIOS and chipset must both support the technology to use it. Examples of RIMMs include PC600, PC700, PC800, PC1066, PC1200, RIMM1600, RIMM3200, RIMM4200, RIMM6400, RIMM8500, and RIMM9600. When RIMMs are used, all memory slots must be filled even if the slot is not needed because the memory banks are tied together. Put a C-RIMM (Continuity RIMM), which is a blank module, in any empty (unfilled) slot.

Most people cannot tell the difference between a DDR, DDR2, or DDR3 memory module. Even though DDR uses 184 pins and DDR2 uses 240 pins, they are the same physical size. DDR3 modules also have 240 pins but will not fit in a DDR2 slot. Figure 2.63 shows DDR2 and DDR3 DIMMs and Table 2.19 lists many of the DIMM models.

Because a DIMM can be shown with either the PCx- or DDRx- designation, it can be confusing as to what you are buying. A brief explanation might help. DDR2-800 is a type of DDR2 memory that can run on a 400Hz front side bus (the number after DDR2 divided in half). Another way

Figure 2.63 DDR2 and DDR3 DIMMs

Table 2.19 DIMMs

Memory type	Other name	Clock speed	Data transfer rate (per second)
PC100	N/A	100MHz	100M
PC133	N/A	133MHz	133M
PC1600	DDR-200	100MHz	200M
PC2100	DDR-266	133MHz	266M
PC2700	DDR-333	166MHz	333M
PC3200	DDR-400	200MHz	400M
PC2-3200	DDR2-400	200MHz	400M
PC2-4200	DDR2-533	266MHz	533M
PC2-5300	DDR2-667	333MHz	667M
PC2-6400	DDR2-800	400MHz	800M
PC2-8000	DDR2-1000	500MHz	1G
PC2-8500	DDR2-1066	533MHz	1.07G
PC2-9200	DDR2-1150	575MHz	1.15G
PC2-9600	DDR2-1200	600MHz	1.2G
PC3-6400	DDR3-800	400MHz	800M
PC3-12800	DDR3-1600	800MHz	1.6G
PC3-16000	DDR3-2000	1000MHz	2G

of showing the same chip would be to use the designation PC2-6400, which is the theoretical bandwidth of the memory chip in MBps.

Planning the Memory Installation—Memory Features

In addition to having to determine what type of memory chips are going to be used, you must determine what features the memory chip might have. The computer system or motherboard

How parity works

If a system uses even parity and the data bits 10000001 go into memory, the ninth bit or parity bit is a 0 because an even number of bits (2) are 1s. The parity changes to a 1 only when the number of bits in the data is an odd number of 1s. If the system uses even parity and the data bits 10000011 go into memory, the parity bit is a 1. There are only three 1s in the data bits. The parity bit adjusts the 1s to an even number. When checking data for accuracy, the parity method detects if one bit is incorrect. However, if two bits are in error, parity does not catch the error.

documentation is going to delineate what features are supported. Table 2.20 helps characterize memory features.

Keep in mind that some motherboards may support both non-parity and ECC or may require a certain feature such as SPD. It is important that you research this *before* you look to purchase memory.

A memory module may use more than one of the categories listed in the two previous tables. For example, a DIMM could be a DDR2 module, be registered, and support ECC for error detection. Most registered memory also uses the ECC technology. DDR memory modules can support either ECC or non-ECC as well as be registered or unbuffered as the type of technology.

Memory technology is moving quite quickly today. Chipsets also change constantly. Technicians are continually challenged to keep up with the features and abilities of the technology so that they can make recommendations to their customers. Trade magazines and the Internet are excellent resources for updates. Never forget to check the motherboard's documentation when dealing with memory. Information is a technician's best friend.

Table 2.20 Memory features

Feature	Explanation
parity	A method for checking the accuracy of data going in or out of the memory chips.
non-parity	Non-parity memory chips are chips that do not use any error checking. Most memory modules today are non-parity because the memory controller circuitry provides error correction.
ECC (error correcting code)	An alternative to parity checking that uses a mathematical algorithm to verify data accuracy. ECC can detect up to four-bit memory errors and correct one-bit memory errors. ECC is used in higher-end computers such as network servers.
registered memory	Registered memory modules have extra chips (registers) near the bottom of the chip that, unlike unbuffered DDR or DDR2 modules, delay all data transfers by one clock tick to ensure accuracy. They are used in servers and high-end computers. If you install a registered memory module into a system that allows both registered and unbuffered memory, all installed memory must be registered modules.
unbuffered memory	The opposite of registered memory and is used in low- to medium-powered computers. Unbuffered memory is faster than registered or fully buffered memory.
fully buffered memory	A technology used in network server memory that requires a special memory controller. Fully buffered memory buffers the data pins from the channel and uses point-to-point serial signaling connections similar to PCI-E. You sometimes see these chips advertised as FBDIMMs.
SPD (serial presence detect)	The memory modules have an extra EEPROM that holds information about the DIMM such as capacity, voltage, refresh rates, and so on. The BIOS can read and use this data to adjust motherboard timing for the best performance.

Storage Devices

Hard Drive Overview

Hard drives are one of the most popular devices for storing data. They store more data than floppy drives and move data faster than tape drives. Today's hard drive capacities extend into the terabytes. Hard drives are frequently upgraded in a computer, so it is important for you to understand all the technical issues. These issues include knowing the parts of the hard drive subsystem, how the operating system and the BIOS work with a hard drive, how to configure a hard drive, and how to troubleshoot it. The hard drive subsystem can have up to three parts: (1) the hard drive; (2) a cable that attaches to an adapter or the motherboard; and (3) control circuits located on an adapter or the motherboard.

Hard Drive Geometry

Hard drives have multiple hard metal surfaces called **platters**. Each platter typically holds data on both sides and has two read/write heads, one for the top and one for the bottom. The read/write heads float on a cushion of air without touching the platter surface. If a read/write head touches the platter, a **head crash** occurs. This is sometimes called HDI (head to disk interference), and it can damage the platters or the read/write head, causing corrupt data. See Figure 2.64 for an illustration of a hard drive's arms, heads, and platters. Figure 2.65 shows the inside of a Seagate Barracuda hard drive. You can see the top read/write head and the top platter. Keep in mind that hard drives should not have their cover removed.

Each hard drive surface is metallic and has concentric circles, each of which is called a **track**. Tracks are numbered starting with the outermost track, which is called track 0. One corresponding track on all surfaces of a hard drive is a **cylinder**. For example, cylinder 0 consists of all track 0s; all of the track 1s comprise cylinder 1, and so on. A track is a single circle on one platter. A cylinder is the same track on all platters. Figure 2.66 shows the difference between tracks and cylinders. Notice in Figure 2.66 how a concentric circle makes an individual track. A single track on all the surfaces makes an individual cylinder.

Each track is separated into **sectors** by dividing the circle into smaller pieces. 512 bytes are normally stored in each sector, as shown in Figure 2.67.

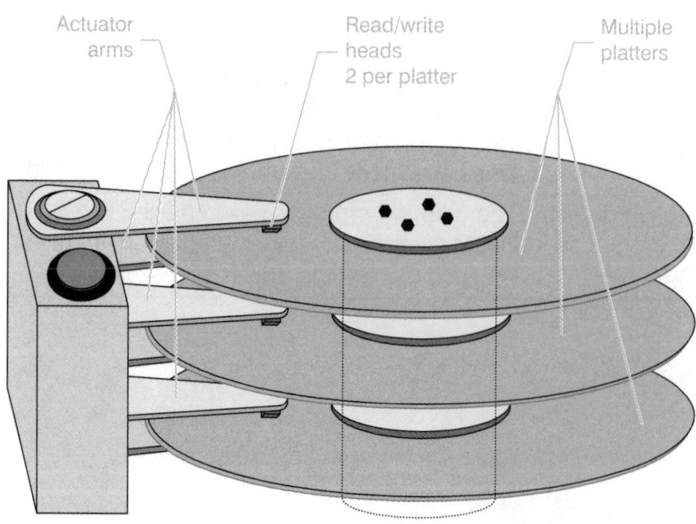

Figure 2.64 Hard drive geometry

Figure 2.65 Seagate Barracuda hard drive

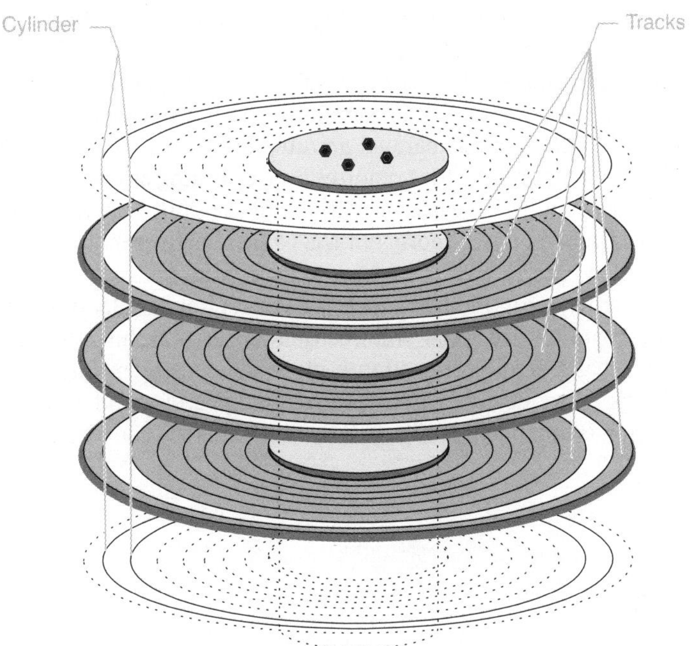

Figure 2.66 Cylinders versus tracks

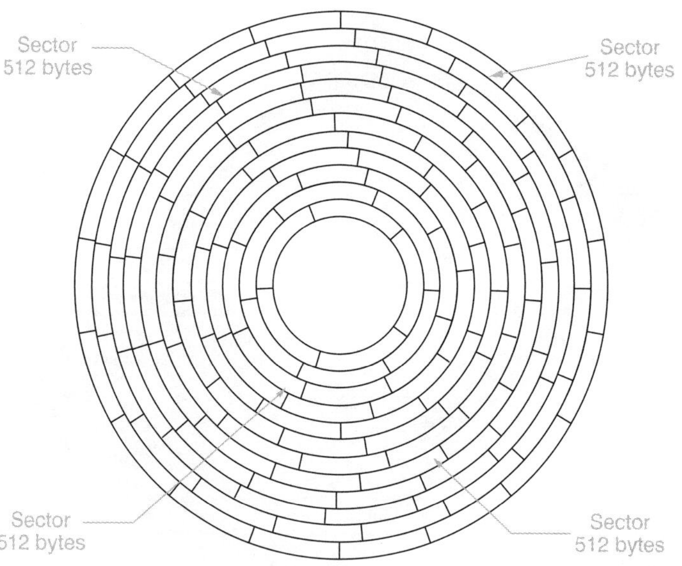

Figure 2.67 Hard drive sectors

Hard Drive Interfaces Overview

A hard drive system must have a set of rules to operate. These rules specify the number of heads on the drive, what commands the drive responds to, the cables used with the drive, the number of devices supported, the number of data bits transferred at one time, and so on. These rules make up a standard called an interface that governs communication with the hard drive. There are two major hard drive interfaces: **IDE** (integrated drive electronics), also known as the ATA (AT Attachment) standard, and **SCSI** (small computer system interface). IDE is the most common in home and office computers. SCSI is commonly found in network servers.

Both IDE and SCSI started out as parallel architectures. This means that multiple bits are sent over multiple paths. This architecture requires precise timing as transfer rates increase. Also with both types of devices, multiple devices can attach to the same bus. With parallel IDE, it was only two devices and with SCSI it was more, but the concept is the same. When multiple devices share the same bus, they have to wait their turn to access the bus and there are configuration issues with which to contend. Figure 2.68 shows the concept of parallel transfer.

Today, there is a trend toward serial architectures. A serial architecture is a point-to-point bus where each device has a single connection back to the controller. Bits are sent one bit at a time over a single link. More devices can attach to this type of architecture because it scales easier and configuration is much easier. Figure 2.69 illustrates the concept of serial data transfer.

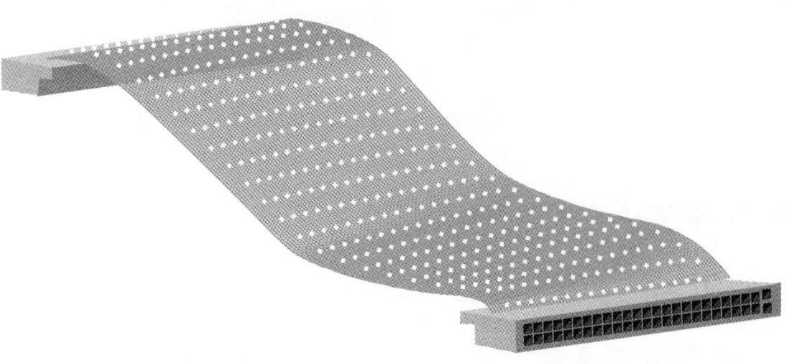

Figure 2.68 Parallel transfer

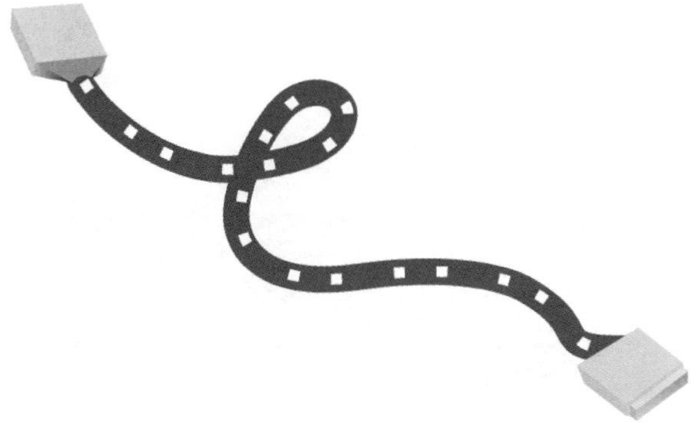

Figure 2.69 Serial transfer

IDE (Integrated Drive Electronics)

IDE (integrated drive electronics) is not only for hard drives, but for other internal devices such as tape, Zip, CD, and DVD drives. The original IDE standard was developed only for hard drives and is officially known as ATA (AT attachment). Later other devices were supported by the standard and the standard evolved to ATA/ATAPI (AT attachment packet interface). ATAPI increased support of devices such as CD/DVD and tape drives. There are two types of IDE—PATA (Parallel ATA) and **SATA** (Serial ATA).

PATA (parallel ATA) is the older IDE type, which uses a 40-pin cable that connects the IDE hard drive to an adapter or the motherboard and transfers 16 bits of data at a time. Each cable normally has either two or three connectors. Many motherboards have both SATA and PATA IDE connectors. Figure 2.70 shows the difference between a PATA and a SATA IDE motherboard connection.

Figure 2.70 PATA and SATA motherboard connectors

A motherboard that has two IDE connectors can have up to four PATA devices, two per motherboard connection. Figure 2.71 shows a PATA IDE hard drive. Notice the 40-pin connector on the left and the power connector on the right.

Figure 2.71 PATA IDE hard drive

If a PATA cable has two connectors and two devices are needed, buy another cable

One 40-pin motherboard PATA connector can support up to two PATA devices. However, some cables only have two connectors—one that connects to the motherboard and one that attaches to the PATA device. If a second device is added, a new cable must be purchased.

The original IDE interface supported up to two drives and is also known as the ATA-1 Standard (AT attachment standard). ATA-2 has faster transfer rates (8.3MBps, then later 16.6MBps) than the original ATA-1 standard of 3.3MBps. The ATA-2 standard also improves drive compatibility through an Identify Drive command that allows the BIOS to better determine the drive's properties. ATA-2 supports DMA transfers. **DMA mode** (direct memory access mode) allows data transfer between the hard drive and RAM without going through the CPU. The older method is known as PIO (programmed input/output) mode that was slower than DMA mode because data had to pass through the CPU. PIO is defined in different modes according to the transfer speed and will probably be removed in future ATA standards.

The latest type of DMA transfers is called **UDMA** (ultra DMA) or bus-master DMA. With UDMA the interface gains control of the PCI bus under the direction of the motherboard chipset. UDMA comes in different modes, which represent different transfer speeds. Table 2.21 shows the Ultra DMA modes for ATA hard drives.

Table 2.21 Ultra DMA modes for IDE hard drives

Ultra-DMA mode	Transfer rate (MBps)
UDMA0	16.7
UDMA1	25
UDMA2	33.3
UDMA3	44.4
UDMA4	66.6
UDMA5	100
UDMA6	133

ATA-3 includes power management and a technology called S.M.A.R.T (Self-Monitoring Analysis & Report Technology) that lets the drive send messages about possible data loss. The ATA-4 standard includes faster transfer modes (up to 33MBps) and is called Ultra ATA or Ultra DMA/33. It implements bus mastering and uses CRC for data integrity. **CRC** (cyclic redundancy checking) is a method of checking data for errors. The drive and controller (host) calculate a value based on an algorithm. If the value is different, the controller (host) drops to a slower transfer mode and requests a retransmission.

80-conductor PATA IDE cable is required with newer drives

The 80-conductor cable works with older IDE devices. UDMA modes 3 and higher require the 80-conductor (40-pin) cable.

The ATA-5 standard is also known as Ultra ATA/66 or simply ATA/66. A 40-pin cable is used with this standard as with the other standards, but the cable is different—it has 80 conductors. The 40 extra conductors are ground lines, which are situated between the existing 40 wires. These ground lines reduce crosstalk, improves the accuracy of data transfers, and allows faster speed. Crosstalk is when signals from one wire interfere with the signals on an adjacent wire. Figure 2.72 shows the older 40-pin cable and the newer 80-conductor cable. Table 2.22 shows the ATA standards.

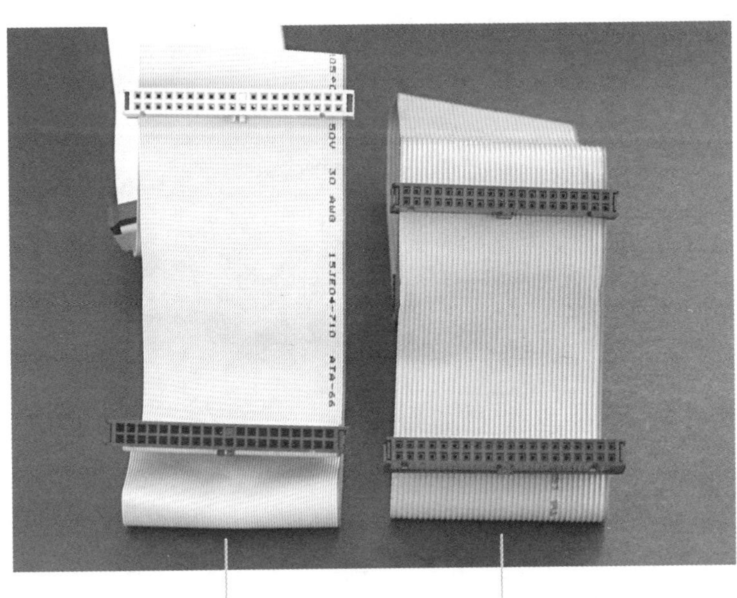

Figure 2.72 80- and 40-conductor cable

Table 2.22 IDE PATA standards

ATA standard	Speed (Mbps)	Cable	Notes
ATA-1	3.3	40-pin	IDE hard drives
ATA-2	8.3 & 16.6	40-pin	Supports other devices besides hard drives; sometimes called EIDE
ATA-3	8.3 & 16.6	40-pin	Includes SMART
ATA-4	33	40-pin	Also called Ultra DMA/33 or Ultra ATA/33
ATA-5	66	40-pin (80 conductor)	Also called Ultra DMA/66 or Ultra ATA/66
ATA-6	100	40-pin	Also called Ultra DMA/100 or (80 conductor) Ultra ATA/100
ATA-7	133	40-pin (80 conductor)	Also called Ultra DMA/133 or Ultra ATA/133

The newer IDE standard is **SATA** (serial ATA). The original specification transfers data at 1.5Gbps (sometimes seen as 1.5Gb/s) with the latest release at 6Gbps. The SATA specification was released as three different sections: SATA 1.5Gbps, SATA 1.5Gbps with extensions, and SATA 3.0Gbps. SATA 1.5Gbps uses the same commands as PATA and the same operating system drivers.

Serial ATA is a point-to-point interface, which means that (1) each device connects to the host through a dedicated link (unlike the traditional parallel IDE where two devices share the host link), and (2) each device has the entire interface bandwidth. Serial ATA uses a smaller cable that is more like a network cable than the traditional IDE ribbon cable. SATA supports both internal and external devices. Figure 2.73 shows a SATA drive. Figure 2.74 shows a SATA internal 7-pin device cable.

Figure 2.73 SATA hard drive

Figure 2.74 SATA cable

eSATA (external SATA) provides external device connectivity using the SATA standard. eSATA allows shielded cable lengths up to 2 meters (~6.56 feet), with faster connections than USB 2.0 or most IEEE 1394 types. However, the eSATA connection does not provide power to external devices. Furthermore, a single eSATA connector can attach to a **SATA-PM** (SATA port multiplier), which is similar to a USB hub. A SATA-PM can support up to 15 devices. Figure 2.75 shows an eSATA cable and eSATA port. An eSATA cable can be rated for 1.5Gbps or 3GBps. eSATA cables are limited to 1 meter (~3.3 feet) for 1.5Gbps devices and 2 meters (~6.6 feet) for 3.0Gbps transfers. The eSATA connector may be integrated (especially in a laptop) as a combination USB/eSATA port.

eSATA 3.0Gbps cable

eSATA port

Figure 2.75 **eSATA cable and port.**

A SATA-PM requires that controllers support either command-based switching or FIS. With **command-based switching**, the host adapter/port can issue commands to only one drive at a time. This means that access is limited to one drive at a time. This technology is best suited for situations in which storage capacity is more important than performance. **FIS** (Frame Information Structure), in contrast, is a faster technology than command-based switching because the host to port multiplier link is used more efficiently, and multiple drives can be performing operations simultaneously.

SSDs (solid state drives) are storage devices that use nonvolatile Flash memory technologies instead of hard drive technologies. SSDs eliminate the number-one cause of hard drive failure: moving parts. SSDs use Flash memory and can therefore be low heat producing, reliable, quiet, secure, long-lasting, and fast. SSDs are being installed in laptops and desktop models as internal and external units. They are being used to replace hard drives as a faster alternative and used in arenas where hard drive storage was not always possible or feasible. SSDs are used in the following industries:

- Medical—CRT/MRI image storage, monitoring equipment, portable devices
- IT—Video surveillance, wireless base stations, security appliances
- Industrial—Robotic systems, test equipment, manufacturing devices
- Automotive—Diagnostics, store safety information, store travel statistics

Another difference between hard drives and SSDs is how data is actually written. Write amplification and wear leveling are two terms used with SSDs that technicians should understand. To write data, an SSD may have to do an erase operation, move data to another location, and then write the information to memory. Still, overall performance is increased. **Write amplification** is the minimum amount of memory storage space affected by a write request. For example, if there is 4KB of information to be written and the SSD has a 128KB erase block, 128KB must be erased before the 4KB of information can be written. Writing takes longer than reading with SSDs.

Wear leveling is a technique used to erase and write data using all of the memory blocks instead of the same memory blocks repeatedly. SSD manufacturers are using various technologies: (1) software to track usage and direct write operations, (2) a certain amount of reserved memory blocks to use when a memory block does fail, and (3) a combination of the two techniques.

Two types of technologies used with SSDs are SLC and MLC. **SLCs** (single-level memory cells) store 1 bit in each memory cell and last longer than MLCs, but they are more expensive. **MLCs** (multi-level memory cells) store more than 1 bit in each memory cell and are cheaper to manufacturer, but they have slower transfer speeds.

The main drawback to SSDs is cost. SSDs are expensive compared to hard drives. As with Flash drives, each memory block of an SSD has a finite number of reads and writes. An SSD that writes data across the entire memory capacity will last longer. Some companies are including software with the drive that tracks or estimates end of life. Figure 2.76 shows the insides of an SSD.

Figure 2.76 SanDisk solid state drive

SCSI (Small Computer System Interface)

SCSI (Small Computer System Interface) can control many different types of devices such as scanners, tape drives, hard drives, optical drives, printers, disk array subsystems, and CD/DVD drives. The SCSI standard allows connection of multiple internal and external devices to the same adapter. All devices that connect to the same SCSI controller share a common data bus called the **SCSI bus** (or SCSI chain). With features such as increased speed and multiple device support comes added cost. SCSI is more expensive than any other interface used with hard drives.

SCSI hard drives have the "intelligence" built into the drive, similar to IDE hard drives. The SCSI host adapter (usually a separate card, but it can be built into the motherboard) connects the SCSI device to the motherboard and coordinates the activities of the other devices connected. Three basic standards of SCSI are called SCSI-1, SCSI-2, and SCSI-3. The original SCSI standard is a parallel architecture. Figure 2.77 shows an SCSI hard drive.

Figure 2.77 SCSI hard drive

The original SCSI standard is a parallel architecture. SCSI-1, left a lot of room for vendor specifications on the wide range of supported devices. Technicians had to cope with the fact that not all SCSI adapters handled all SCSI devices. SCSI-1 was primarily for hard drives; however, other device manufacturers such as those making tape drives, made do with SCSI-1 and adapted their devices as they saw fit. SCSI-1 supports up to eight devices (one host adapter and seven devices) on one SCSI 8-bit bus at a transfer rate of up to 5MBps. SCSI-2 supports 16 devices and speeds up to 20MBps. SCSI-2 hardware is compatible with SCSI-1 devices. SCSI-3 improves on data transfer rates and includes fiber optical cable standards. Figure 2.77 shows a SCSI hard drive.

Fast SCSI is a term associated with the SCSI-2 interface. It transfers data at 10MBps, eight bits at a time. 32-bit SCSI was defined in SCSI-2, but never adopted by the industry, so the 32-bit standard was dropped in SCSI-3, which is an improvement on the SCSI-2 interface. The various SCSI-3 standards all start with the word "Ultra." Ultra-Wide SCSI transfers 16 bits of data at 40MBps, Ultra2 SCSI transfers eight bits of data at 40MBps, and Ultra2-Wide SCSI transfers 16 bits of data at 80MBps.

SCSI-3 comprises different SPI (SCSI parallel interface) standards that include SPI, SPI-2, SPI-3, SPI-4, SPI-5, and SPI-6. SPI is commonly called Ultra SCSI; SPI-2 is called Ultra2 or Fast-40 SCSI; SPI-3 is called Ultra3, Ultra 160 SCSI, or Fast 80 DT; SPI-4 is known as Ultra4 or Fast-160DT SCSI; SPI-5 is known as Fast 320, transferring data at 640MBps; and SPI-6 is known as Fast 640. Table 2.23 shows a breakdown of the common parallel SCSI standards.

Table 2.23 SCSI standards

SCSI standard	SCSI term	Speed (MBps)
SCSI-1	N/A	5
SCSI-2	N/A	5
	Fast	10
	Wide	20
	Fast-Wide	20
SCSI-3	Ultra	20
	Ultra	40
	Ultra-Wide	40
	Ultra2-Wide	80
	Ultra3	160
	Ultra 160	160
	Ultra 160+	160
	Ultra 320	320
	Ultra 640	640

The latest SCSI devices that might be found in a PC are known as **SAS** (serial attached SCSI). SAS devices connect through a serial architecture which means they attach in a point-to-point bus. SAS devices are said to be more expensive than SATA IDE devices because they target the enterprise environment where high reliability and high MTBF (mean time between failures) is important.

SCSI storage devices are more frequently found in a network environment. Other types of SCSI used with networking include FC-AL (Fibre Channel Arbitration Loop), SSA (Serial Storage Architecture), and iSCSI.

Storage Device Configuration Overview

Drive configuration sometimes includes setting jumpers on the drive and sometimes on the associated adapter and proper termination. Termination is a method used to prevent signals from reflecting back up the cable. Each drive type has a normal configuration method. However, individual drive manufacturers may develop their own configuration steps. Always refer to the documentation included with the drive, adapter, or motherboard for configuration and installation information.

PATA Physical Installation

PATA IDE devices (including hard drives) are simpler to configure than parallel SCSI devices. The overall steps for installing a PATA device are as follows:

- Keep the drive in the protective antistatic container until you are ready to install
- Use proper antistatic handling procedures when installing the drive and handle the drive by the edges; avoid touching the drive electronics and connectors
- Turn off and remove the power cord when installing the drive
- Determine how many devices will attach to the same cable and configure their jumpers accordingly
- Physically mount and secure the device in the computer and attach the proper cable
- Configure the BIOS if necessary
- If a hard drive, prepare the drive for data as described later in the chapter

Actually, these steps apply to SATA and SCSI as well except for configuring jumpers and for SATA, determining how many devices attach to the same cable because SATA is a point-to-point architecture and only one device attaches to the connector.

Motherboards frequently have two PATA IDE connectors (although a few have three or four). The IDE connectors are known as the primary or primary IDE channel, secondary or secondary IDE channel, and if there are third or fourth connectors, they are known as the tertiary channel and quaternary channel respectively. Figure 2.78 shows a motherboard with four integrated IDE connectors.

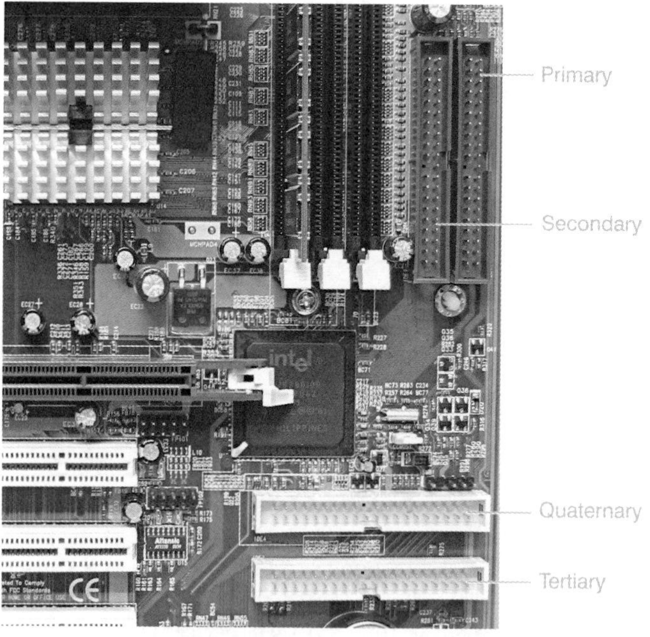

Figure 2.78 PATA motherboard connectors

Each channel (connector) can have a master and a slave device. To distinguish between the devices, use the channel name followed by the words **master** or **slave**. The two settings are simply used to distinguish between the two devices because only one of the two devices (master or slave) can transmit data when connected to the same IDE channel (cable). For example, if two hard drives are installed on the primary channel, they are called primary master and primary slave. Table 2.24 shows the common IRQs and I/O addresses used by the IDE channels.

Table 2.24 PATA IDE system resources

IDE channel	IRQ(s)	I/O addresses
Primary	14	1F0-1F7h and 3F6-3F7h
Secondary	15 or 10	170-177h and 376-377h
Tertiary	11 or 12	1E8-1EF and 3EE-3EF
Quaternary	10 or 11	168-16F and 36E-36F

PATA IDE devices are normally configured using jumpers. The four options commonly found are single, master, slave, and cable select. The **single** IDE setting is used when only one device connects to the cable. The master IDE setting is used in conjunction with the slave setting and both are used when two IDE devices connect to the same cable. One device is set to the master setting while the other device uses the slave setting. The **cable select** IDE option replaces the master/slave setting. The device automatically configures itself to either the master setting or the slave setting depending on the specific cable connector to which the device attaches. To use the cable select option, a special 80-conductor, 40-pin cable is needed. This cable has pin 28 disabled. Figure 2.79 shows the connections for the 80-conductor cable.

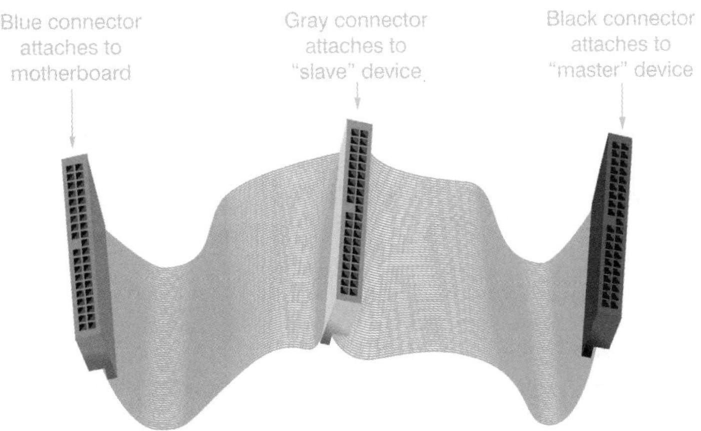

Figure 2.79 80-conductor PATA IDE cable connections

Check your PATA IDE default setting

Most hard drives come preset to master or single whereas most other devices such as tape drives, CD/DVD drives, and Zip drives come preset to the slave setting. Devices that are set to slave and installed as the only device on the IDE cable still function properly. However, it is always best to check the settings of installed devices and of any new devices being installed.

All 80-conductor (40-pin) cables that meet the ATA specifications automatically support cable select, and the connectors, are color-coded according to the specifications. The 80-conductor (40-pin) cable must be used in Ultra DMA Mode 3 and higher, but can be used in lower modes as well.

Determining which cable select connector to use

When the cable select became a standard with ATA-5, the master connector (the black connector) is at the end of the cable. The slave connector (the gray one) is in the middle of the connector, and the blue connector attaches to the motherboard.

The following criteria must be met to use the cable select option:

1. A special IDE cable select cable or the 80-conductor (40-pin) cable must be used.
2. The host interface (controlling circuits) must support the cable select option.
3. The one or two attached devices must be set to the cable select option.

Do not use the 40-conductor 40-pin IDE cable with the cable select option

Do not set an IDE device to the cable select option unless the special cable is installed and the host interface supports this option. If two devices are set to the cable select option and a regular IDE cable is used, both devices are configured as master and will not work properly.

There are two methods of configuring PATA IDE devices: (1) configure one device as master and the other device as slave, or (2) configure both devices to the cable select option. By doing this, the device that connects to the black connector becomes the "master" and the device that connects to the gray connector becomes the "slave." Whichever method is used, the following are recommendations:

- When two IDE devices connect to the same cable, the faster or larger capacity device should be configured as master. Hard drives are normally the fastest IDE devices.
- When only one device (the master) connects to an older 40-conductor IDE cable, connect the device to the end connector (the one farthest from the motherboard) for best performance. Some devices show errors when there is only one IDE device and it connects to the center cable connector.
- If there are two IDE devices installed in the computer, a hard drive and a CD/DVD drive, install the hard drive on one IDE channel (primary) and the CD/DVD drive on the secondary IDE channel.
- Avoid putting a hard drive and an optical (CD or DVD) drive on the same channel. The optical device uses a more complicated command set than the hard drive and it can slow down the hard drive.
- If you have a CD-RW or DVD/RW drive and a CD-ROM or DVD drive and you transfer data frequently between the two, it is best to put them on separate channels. However, putting one of these devices with a hard drive is not a good idea either.
- For optimum performance, connect the hard drive that you boot from to the primary IDE motherboard connector and configure it as master.

Figure 2.80 illustrates how multiple PATA devices connect to the motherboard.

Watch out for PATA cable lengths

IDE devices connect to a 40-pin, 80-conductor ribbon cable. The maximum IDE cable length is 18 inches, which presents a problem with tower computers. Some companies sell 24- or 36-inch IDE cables. These do not meet specifications. If IDE problems or intermittent problems occur, replace the cable with one that meets specifications.

Almost all PATA IDE devices ship with cable select option selected. Figure 2.81 shows an illustration of two PATA IDE hard drives configured with the cable select option. Some drives can be limited to 2.1, 32, or 128GB. (The 128GB limitation is not supported on the drives shown.)

The table in Figure 2.81 shows several possible configurations. A similar table is found either on top of the hard drive or in the documentation included with the hard drive. The third alternative is to use the manufacturer's Internet site. If only one IDE hard drive is to be installed, the drive is to be configured as the master. Either leave the jumper set to cable select and simply attach to the black 80-conductor cable *or* move the jumper from pins 5 and 6 to pins 7 and 8 to configure the drive manually as master.

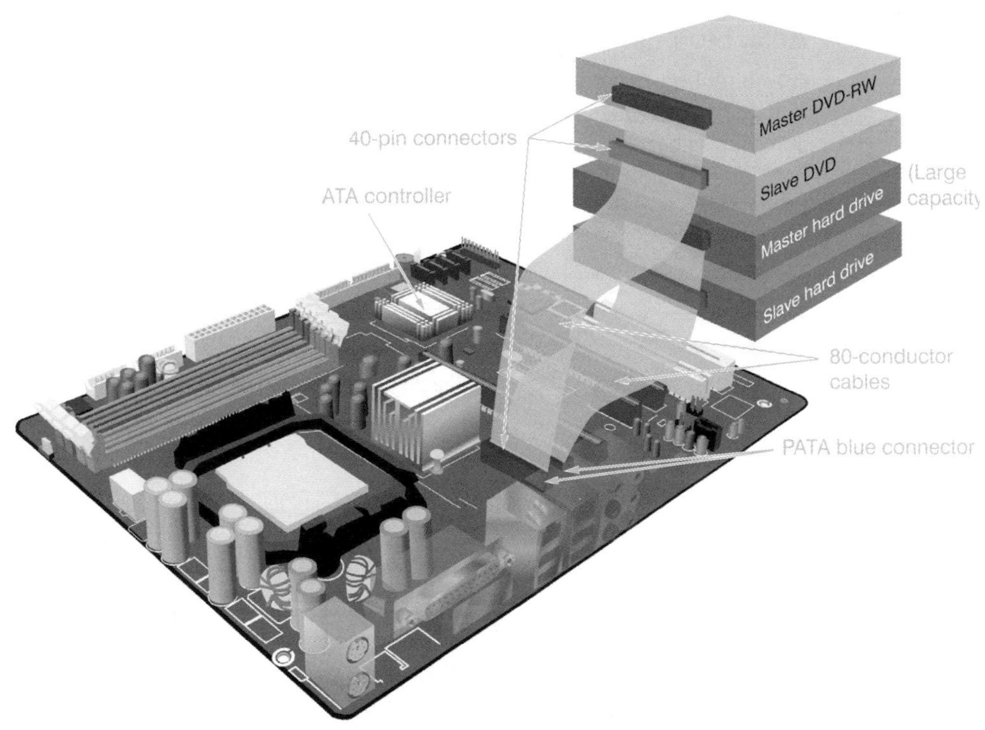

Figure 2.80 PATA device connectivity

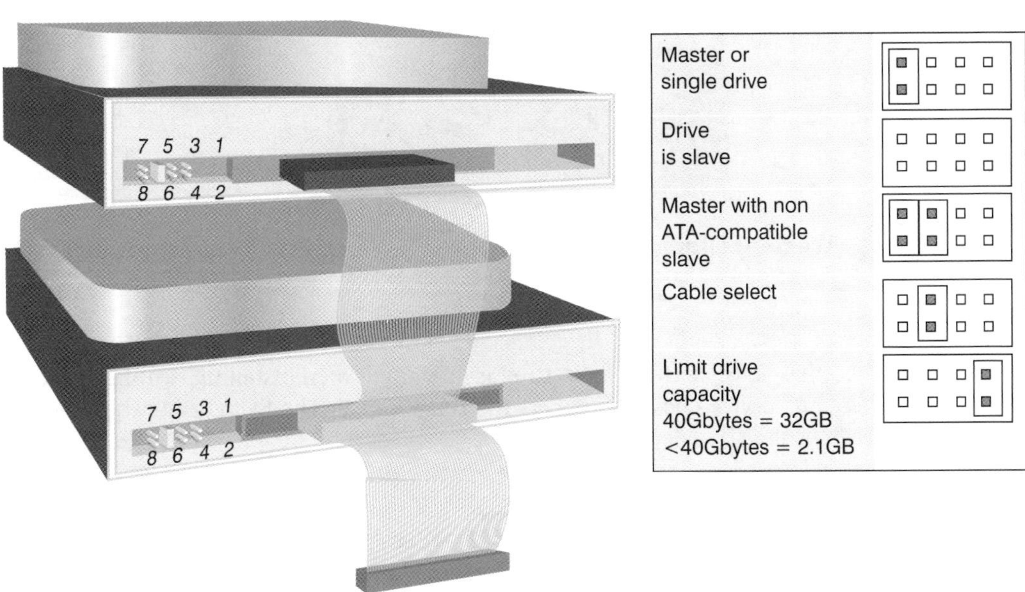

Figure 2.81 Two PATA devices configured as cable select

Closed means jumpered or enabled

Storage device documentation varies in how these are shown. When documentation shows an option as closed, jumpered, or enabled, this means to put a jumper over the two pins to configure the option.

Adjust to poorly written documentation

How a manufacturer uses the terms and configures a storage device is up to the manufacturer. The technician must learn to adjust to poorly written and sometimes confusing documentation. Jumpers other than the master/slave jumpers may be present, but you must refer to the hard drive's documentation for the proper settings. If documentation is unavailable, use the Internet; most manufacturers place their jumper setting documentation online and/or on top of the drive.

Figure 2.82 shows Western Digital's IDE hard drive with the documentation stenciled on top of the drive.

Figure 2.82 **Western Digital IDE hard drive**

If an IDE device has an SP setting, the setting is only used when installing two IDE devices on one cable where one device does not support the DASP signal. The SP setting, when set on the master device, tells it a slave device is present.

SATA Physical Installation

SATA drives are easy to install. Most internal drives require a special host adapter that supports one to four drives or an integrated motherboard connection. Each drive is seen as a point-to-point connection with the host controller.

SATA drives do not have any master/slave, cable select, or termination jumpers or settings. A serial 7-pin connector attaches from the SATA controller to the internal SATA drive. A longer cable connects power to the drive. The internal SATA power connector is not a Molex or Berg connector; it is a different type of connector. A cable converter can be obtained if a Molex connector is the only one available from the power supply. Figure 2.83 shows a Serial ATA hard drive with associated cabling. Notice the Molex-to-internal SATA cable converter in the photo.

There are also products available that allow a serial ATA hard drive to connect to a standard IDE controller. Figure 2.84 shows how two SATA drives attach to a motherboard that has two SATA connectors.

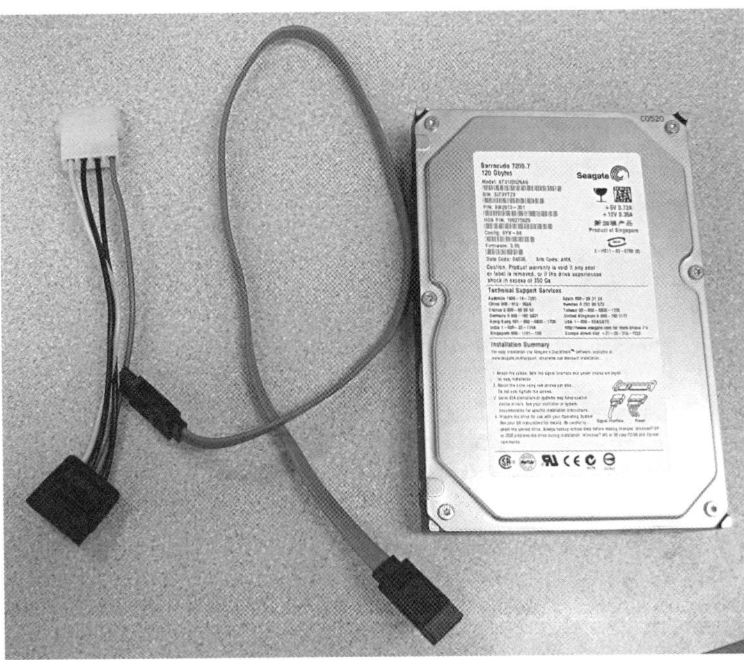

Figure 2.83 SATA hard drive and cables

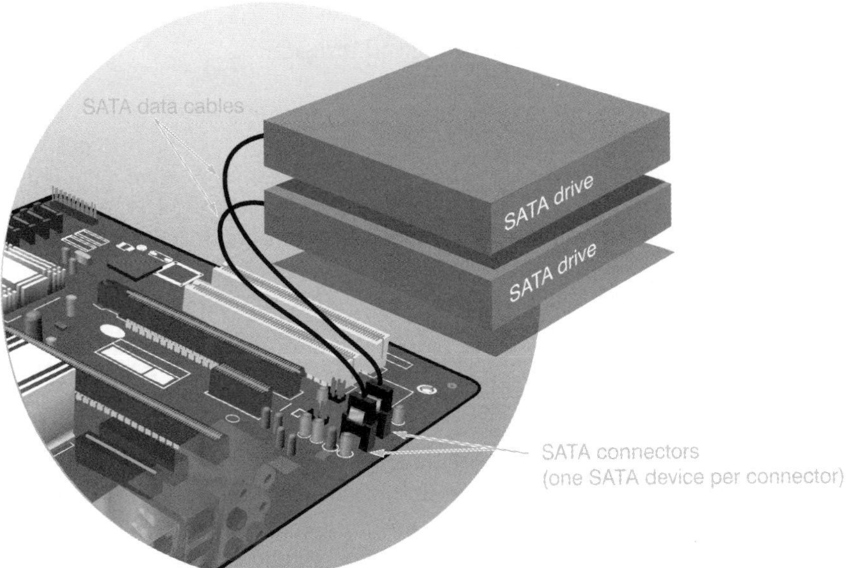

Figure 2.84 SATA connectivity

To install a SATA host adapter, power off the computer and remove the computer power cord. Remove the computer cover and locate an open expansion slot. Some adapters have jumpers for configurable options. Some common options include 16- and 32-bit PCI operations, adapter BIOS enabled/disabled, and Mode 0 enabled/disabled. Some adapters may provide master/slave emulation options. Most adapters' default settings will work, but always refer to the adapter's documentation for details.

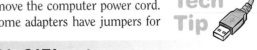

Enable SATA port

Many manufacturers require that you enable the motherboard port through the system BIOS before any device connected to the port is recognized.

To install an internal SATA hard drive, power off the computer, and remove the computer's power cord. Physically mount the drive into a drive bay. Connect the SATA signal cable between the drive and the host controller. Connect the SATA power cord to the drive and an available Molex connector from the power supply. Figure 2.85 shows an installed SATA hard drive attached to a host adapter.

Figure 2.85 **Installed SATA hard drive and adapter**

An external (eSATA) drive normally has no jumpers, terminators, or switches to be configured. However, when installing a faster drive to a slower port—such as when installing a 3.0Gbps drive to a 1.5Gbps port—a jumper may need to be configured so the drive is compatible with the port. Always refer to the drive manufacturer's documentation when installing a drive. Attach the power cord to the drive, if applicable, and insert the other end of the power cord into a wall outlet. Attach one end of the eSATA cable to the drive. Plug the other end of the cable into an eSATA port on the computer. Note that some systems use the original SATA 1.5Gbps (sometimes called SATA I) port, and the drive may be a 3.0Gbps (sometimes called SATA II) drive. A cable converter may be necessary. Laptops sometimes have combination USB/SATA ports. eSATA ports are commonly disabled in BIOS and sometimes require BIOS changes, updates, and/or device drivers.

Before switching on eSATA drive power, ensure that the drive is positioned where it will stay during operation and that all data and power cords are attached securely. Switch on the drive power. The drive mounts. When a drive is mounted, a communications channel is opened between the drive and the operating system. Whenever the drive is to be disconnected, it is to be unmounted. Some drive manufacturers provide software for backing up data or configuring the drive in a RAID configuration. Use the Disk Management Windows tool to ensure that the drive is recognized.

Unmounting an eSATA drive

To unmount an eSATA drive, click on the Safely Remove Hardware icon in the systray. Select the appropriate drive letter. Remove the drive when prompted by the operating system.

SSD Physical Installation

For a desktop computer, an SSD can be internally mounted and connected to a SATA/PATA motherboard or an adapter port. An SSD can also attach as an external device to a SATA, USB, or FireWire port. An SSD can be mounted as a replacement part for a laptop hard drive. SSDs do not normally require special drivers. Always refer to the SSD mounting directions provided by the manufacturer. The following steps are generic ones.

If installing an SSD internally into a desktop computer, power off the computer and locate an empty drive bay, a power connector of the appropriate type (or buy a converter), and an available SATA/PATA port or free PATA connector on a PATA cable. Attach mounting brackets to the SSD. Mounting brackets may have to be purchased separately, be provided with the drive, or be provided as spares that came with the computer. Slide the SSD into the drive bay and secure it, if necessary. Connect the data cable from the motherboard or adapter to the drive. Attach a power cable to the SSD. Reinstall the computer cover and power on the computer.

Beware of static electricity

SSDs are Flash memory and are susceptible to static electricity. Use proper ESD handling procedures when installing an SSD.

If installing an SSD internally into a laptop, power off the computer, disconnect the AC adapter, and remove the battery. Remove the drive bay access cover and install the SSD. Reattach the access cover, battery, and AC adapter, if necessary. Power on the laptop.

The BIOS should recognize an internally installed SSD. If it does not, go into the system BIOS setup and ensure that the connector to which the SSD attaches is enabled. Be especially careful with SATA ports and port numbering. Configure the system to automatically detect the new drive, save the settings, and reboot the system.

If installing an external SSD, attach the appropriate USB, SATA, or IEEE 1394 (FireWire) cable from the drive to the computer. Power on the SSD. The system should recognize the new drive.

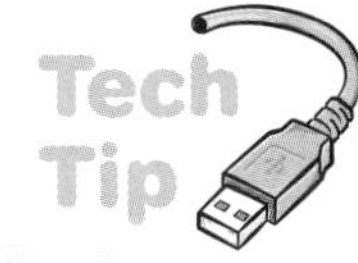

Use only one technology

If an external drive supports more than one technology, such as eSATA, FireWire, and USB, attach only one type of cable from the drive to the computer.

Parallel SCSI Configuration

Configure a parallel SCSI device by doing the following:

1. Setting the proper SCSI ID
2. Terminating both ends of the SCSI chain
3. Connecting the proper cable(s)

The parallel SCSI chain consists of several SCSI devices cabled together. The SCSI chain includes SCSI devices and a single controller, sometimes called a **host adapter**. The SCSI controller is usually a separate adapter, but it may be built into the motherboard. The SCSI chain includes internal SCSI devices that connect to the SCSI host adapter and any external SCSI devices that connect to an adapter's external port. Multiple SCSI chains can exist in a system, and a computer can contain up to four SCSI host adapters. A SCSI-1 host adapter supports up to seven internal or external devices. SCSI-2 or higher adapters support up to 15 internal or external devices.

SCSI ID Configuration and Termination

Each device on a SCSI chain, including the SCSI host adapter, is assigned a **SCSI ID**. (Some SCSI hard drive manufacturers refer to this setting as the drive select ID.) The SCSI ID allows each device to share the same SCSI bus, and it assigns a priority for each device. The SCSI interface allows a SCSI device to communicate directly with another SCSI device connected on the same SCSI chain. The higher the SCSI number, the higher the priority of the device on the SCSI chain. SCSI IDs are normally set using switches, jumpers, SCSI BIOS software, or manufacturer-provided software.

Standard SCSI devices (8-bit devices) recognize SCSI IDs 0 through 7. Wide SCSI devices (16-bit devices) recognize SCSI IDs 0 through 15. The SCSI ID priority values are as follows from highest priority value to lowest. Figure 2.86 shows the SCSI priority numbers from highest to lowest.

Power on all external SCSI devices *before* turning on the computer

The host adapter detects all SCSI devices along the SCSI chain during the boot process. However, if a SCSI device is not used frequently the device can be powered off. The rest of the SCSI devices operate even if a SCSI device is powered off. If two devices have the same SCSI ID, a SCSI ID conflict occurs and the devices will not work properly. Setting an improper SCSI ID (priority) setting results in slower SCSI device performance.

Highest — Lowest

7 6 5 4 3 2 1 0 15 14 13 12 11 10 9 8

Figure 2.86 SCSI ID priority levels

The SCSI host adapter is normally preset to SCSI ID 7, the highest priority, and should not be changed. Slower devices such as scanners, CD/DVD drives, or video encoders should be assigned a higher SCSI ID such as 6 or 5 for a standard SCSI device and 15 or 14 for a Wide SCSI device, so they receive ample time to move data onto the SCSI bus. SCSI ID 0 is the default for most SCSI hard drives. A development that is helpful in setting SCSI IDs is **SCAM** (SCSI Configured AutoMatically).

Termination of SCSI devices is very important. Proper termination of SCSI devices keeps the signals from bouncing back up the cable and provides the proper electrical current level for the SCSI chain. The SCSI bus cannot operate properly without terminating both ends of the SCSI bus. Improper termination can make one, many, or all SCSI devices not work properly. Over time, improper termination can damage a SCSI adapter or a SCSI device. SCSI termination is performed in several ways: (1) by installing a SIPP; (2) by installing a jumper; (3) by setting a switch; (4) by installing a terminator plug; (5) by installing a pass through terminator; or (6) with software.

When setting or removing termination, refer to the documentation included with the adapter or device. If the terminator to an external SCSI device is not provided with the device, it must be purchased separately. Some internal SCSI cables do not have a terminator built into them.

Figure 2.87 shows a Seagate Cheetah SCSI hard drive. The SCSI ID configuration is shown with the diagram on the right side that has four pins for the SCSI ID and these pins are labeled ADDR with the numbers 8, 4, 2, and 1 above ADDR. To the left of the SCSI ID jumpers is a jumper that is reserved, and it is labeled RES. The jumper to the far left that has a funny symbol under it is for a remote LED connection. This drive is a SCSI Fast-20 16-bit SCSI drive. Termination is set with a jumper shown to the left labeled TERM ENABLE.

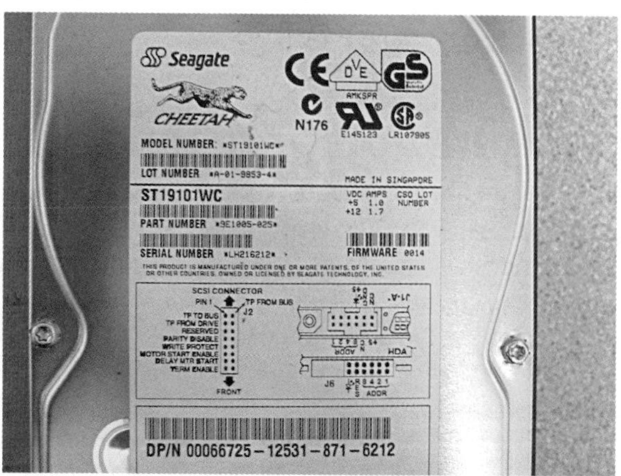

Figure 2.87 Seagate Cheetah SCSI hard drive

There are several types of SCSI electrical signals and terminators. The three major categories are SE, HVD, and LVD. Table 2.25 explains these. The majority of terminators in use are either active or the FPT active terminator.

Table 2.25 SCSI electrical signals/terminator technologies

Technology/term	Explanation
SE (Single Ended) terminator	Terminators used by most SCSI devices. It can use passive and active terminators. It has a maximum bus length of 9 feet (2.7 meters).
Passive terminator	Terminators used on SCSI-1 devices. They are not good for long cable distances because they are susceptible to noise interference.
Active terminator	Terminators that can be used on SCSI-1, -2, and -3 devices. They allow for longer cable distances and provide the correct voltage for SCSI signals. This type must be used with Fast, Wide or Fast-Wide SCSI devices. A passive and an active terminator can be used on the same chain. SCSI-3 requires active termination.
FPT (Forced Perfect Termination)	A special type of active terminator that can be used with SE devices.
HVD (High Voltage Differential)	A technology that was used in a few SCSI-2 devices that allowed a longer SCSI bus length. HVD devices must use HVD terminators (sometimes called differential terminators).
LVD (Low Voltage Differential)	A technology that is backward compatible with SE and required on all devices that adhere to the Ultra SCSI standard. LVD bus length can be up to 39 feet (11.88 meters) depending on the number of devices. LVD devices use either LVD terminators or LVD/SE terminators.
Pass through terminator	A terminator used by most internal hard drives. It has an extra connector and allows a device that does not have terminators to be terminated through the connector that attaches to the cable.

Being able to distinguish among various SCSI devices is very difficult because there are many SCSI flavors. Special icons are placed on SCSI devices to differentiate them. Figure 2.88 shows these icons.

If only internal devices connect to the SCSI host adapter, terminate the adapter and the last internal device connected to the cable. Remove the termination from all other devices.

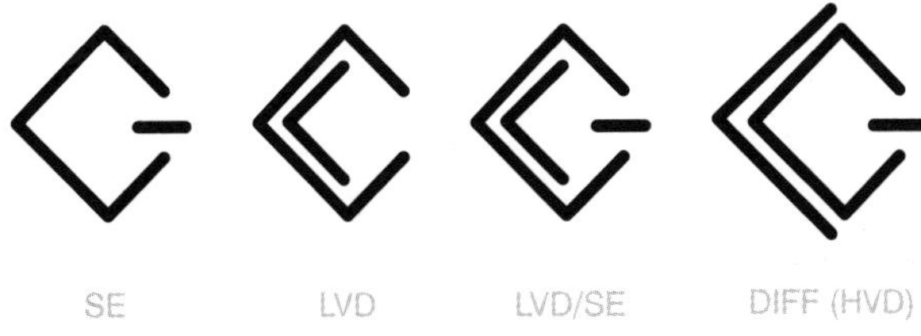

Figure 2.88 SCSI symbols

Never connect an HVD device or terminator to SE, LVD, or LVD/SE bus

Never connect an HVD device/terminator to a SCSI bus/adapter that uses an SE, LVD, or LVD/SE bus. Equipment can be damaged!

When connecting only external devices to the SCSI host adapter or motherboard, terminate the adapter and the last external device. Remove the terminations from all other external devices.

Figure 2.89 shows SCSI IDs and termination for an internal and external device scenario. If both internal and external devices attach to the SCSI host adapter, the last internal device connected to the SCSI cable is terminated as well as the last external device. All other devices and the SCSI host adapter must have their terminators removed. The SCSI chain in Figure 2.89 consists of two internal SCSI devices (a CD drive and a hard drive) and two external SCSI devices (a tape drive and a scanner). The two ends of the SCSI chain that must be terminated are the CD drive and the scanner. All other devices are not terminated.

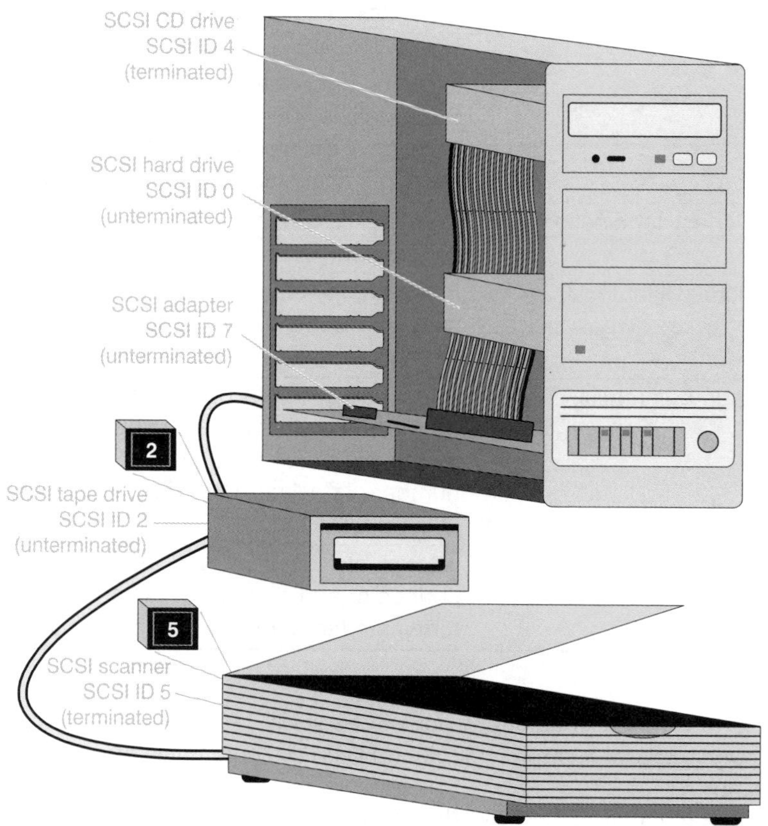

Figure 2.89 Internal and external SCSI devices—termination

Use software that comes with the SCSI adapter for configuration

Newer SCSI cards have either a software utility that ships with the adapter or a software program built into the adapter's ROM chip that allows configuration through software instead of jumpers and switches. Refer to the adapter's documentation for configuration instructions.

A smart technician plans the configuration of the drive before installing the drive in the system. A good plan of attack is the best strategy to avoid problems during installation. Draw the configuration on a piece of paper to help get the installation straight in your mind. To help new technicians with different configurations, the exercises at the end of the chapter contain sample practice configurations.

SCSI Cables

Parallel SCSI cabling allows multiple devices to be connected to one SCSI host adapter and share the same SCSI bus; this is called daisy chaining. Daisy chaining is like connecting multiple Christmas light sets together. If multiple internal SCSI devices attach to the SCSI adapter, then use an internal SCSI cable with multiple connectors. Most internal SCSI-1 and SCSI-2 cables are 50-pin ribbon cables. Internal SCSI-3 cables are 68-pin ribbon cables.

To connect external SCSI-1 devices, a 50-pin Centronics to 50-pin Centronics cable is used. The SCSI-1 cable is also known as an A Cable. The SCSI-2 standard has a different cable for connecting to the first external SCSI device. This cable has a 50-pin D-shell connector that connects to the SCSI host adapter, and a Centronics connector that connects to the external device. For 16-bit SCSI devices, a second 68-pin cable, called the B Cable, must be used in addition to the A Cable. This B Cable is not in the SCSI-3 specifications because industry did not fully support it. SCSI-3 has a 68-pin cable called the P Cable. Figure 2.90 illustrates some SCSI cables.

Buy quality SCSI cables

Not all SCSI cables are created equal. Do not recommend or buy the cheaper, thinner SCSI cables available for external devices. These cheaper cables are susceptible to outside noise. The section on Configuration and Setup Procedures covers more cabling issues.

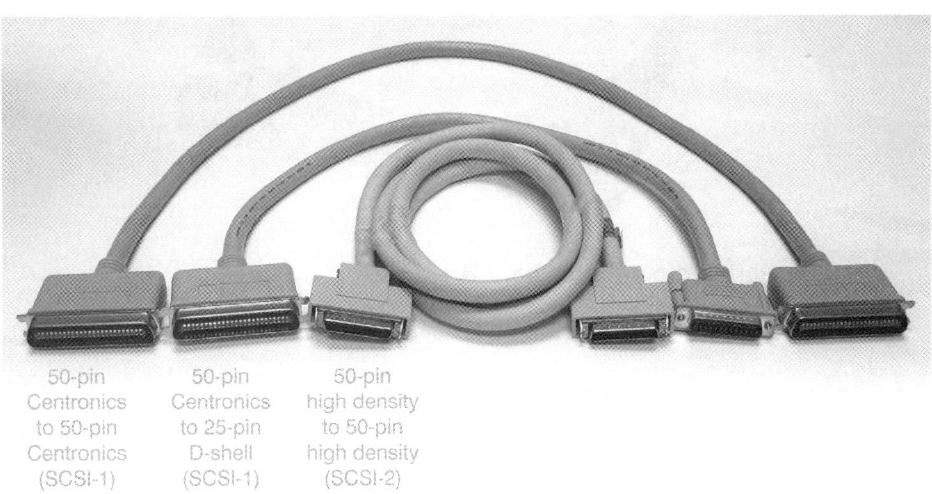

Figure 2.90 External SCSI cables

Install one SCSI device at a time and test

When installing multiple SCSI devices, install them one at a time and test each one before installing the next one.

Laptop Storage Devices

A laptop normally has a PATA or SATA hard drive installed but could have an SSD instead of or in addition to the hard drive. A mini PCI adapter can be used to connect the drive to the system, or the drive can be directly attached to the motherboard. Additional storage can be provided by devices that connect to USB, eSATA, or IEEE 1394 ports. PC Cards or ExpressBus hard drives can also be used to provide storage expansion.

Two methods are used with hard drives installed in portable computers: proprietary or removable. With the proprietary installation, the hard drive is installed in a location where it cannot be changed, configured, or moved very easily. Proprietary cables and connectors are used. With removable hard drives, the laptop has a hard drive bay that allows installation/removal through a 44-pin connector. This connector provides power as well as data signaling. The drive is usually mounted in a carrier that attaches to the 44-pin connector and is the primary master device. If a CD or DVD drive is installed, it is normally configured as the secondary master.

Many laptops use some type of hard drive casing or brackets to hold the drive. Upgrading a drive may include installing the new drive into the old drive's brackets or case and attaching it or sliding it into the laptop. Some vendors sell the drive with the drive casing, but it is usually more expensive than just buying the drive. Figure 2.91 shows a hard drive that is used in a portable computer.

Figure 2.91 Portable computer hard drive

What to do if you want more storage space for a laptop

Laptops do not normally allow a second IDE hard drive. Instead, add an additional hard drive to the USB or eSATA port.

System BIOS Configuration for Hard Drives

The hard drive is configured through the system BIOS Setup program. As mentioned previously, Setup is accessed through keystrokes during the boot process. In the past, a drive type number was entered and the drive geometry information appeared to the right of the drive type number. In today's computers, the setting is Auto and the BIOS automatically detects the hard drive type. The drive type information is saved in CMOS.

IDE hard drives are normally configured using the Auto-Detect feature included with BIOS. The Auto-Detect feature automatically determines the drive type for the system. For SCSI hard drive installations, the most common CMOS setting for the hard drive type is type 0 or None. Once the system boots, the SCSI controller's BIOS initializes and the SCSI hard drive takes over and boots the system. Even though the drive type number is set to 0 or None, if this step is omitted, the hard drive will not operate.

Table 2.26 shows the most commonly used hard drive settings. Note that the BIOS is also where you select the drive that you want to boot the system.

Configure BIOS according to drive manufacturer's instructions

Drive manufacturers normally include documentation describing how to configure the drive in BIOS Setup. Also, they provide software for any system that does not recognize the drive.

Table 2.26 Common hard drive setup settings

Hard drive type	Common setting
IDE PATA/SATA	AUTO
SCSI	TYPE 0

Hard Drive Preparation Overview

Once a hard drive is installed and configured properly, and the hard drive type is entered into the Setup program, the drive must be prepared to accept data. The two steps of hard drive preparation are as follows:

1. Partition
2. High-level format

Partitioning the hard drive allows a drive letter to be assigned to one or more parts of the hard drive. **High-level formatting** prepares the drive for use for a particular operating system. This allows the drive to accept data from the operating system. For today's computers, a drive cannot be used until it has been partitioned and high-level formatted; thus technicians should be very familiar with these steps.

Partitioning

The first step in preparing a hard drive for use is partitioning. Partitioning a hard drive divides the drive so the computer system sees the hard drive as more than one drive. DOS and Windows 9x have a software program called `FDISK` that partitions hard drives. Windows NT and higher versions partitions can be set up during the operating system installation process, by using the **Disk Administrator** program that is available after the operating system is installed, or by using the `diskpart` utility from the command line. Disk Administrator is normally used to partition additional hard drives and to manage all of them. The first hard drive in the system is normally partitioned as part of the Windows installation process. Additional partitions can be created using Disk Administrator once the operating system is installed.

Partitioning provides advantages that include the following:

- Dividing a hard drive into separate subunits that are then assigned drive letters such as `C:` or `D:` by the operating system
- Organizing the hard drive to separate multiple operating systems, applications, and data
- Providing data security by placing data in a different partition to allow ease of backup as well as protection
- Using the hard drive to its fullest capacity

How to determine what file system is being used

From the desktop, right-click the *My Computer* desktop icon and select the *Properties* option. The *General* tab shows the type of file system being used.

The original purpose of partitioning was to allow for loading multiple operating systems. This is still a good reason today because placing each operating system in its own partition eliminates the crashes and headaches caused by multiple operating systems and multiple applications co-existing in the same partition. The type of partition and how big the partition can be depends on the file system being used. A **file system** defines how data is stored on a drive. The most common file systems are FAT16, FAT32, and NTFS. The file system that can be used depends on what operating system is installed. Table 2.27 lists file systems and explains a little about each one.

When `FDISK` is used to partition the hard drive and you select the option to create a partition, a message appears that asks if you wish to enable large disk support. This option is what allows FAT32 to be installed. If you select *N* (No) when this question is asked, FAT32 will not be installed.

An even better reason for partitioning than loading multiple operating systems or separating the operating system from data is to partition the hard drive for more efficient use of space. The

Table 2.27 File systems

File system type	Explanation
FAT12	Pre-DOS 3.x. Used on floppy disks smaller than16MB
FAT16	Also called **FAT**. Used with DOS 3.x+ and all versions of Windows including Vista and 7. 2GB partition limitation with DOS and Windows 9x. 4GB partition limitation with all versions of Windows higher than NT.
FAT32	Used with all versions of Windows 9x and higher. Supports drives up to 2TB. Can recognize volumes greater than 32GB, but cannot create them that big.
NTFS	Used with Windows NT, 2000, XP, Vista, and 7. Supports drives up to 16EB (16 exabytes that equals 16 billion gigabytes), but in practice is only 2TB (2 terabytes that equals 2 thousand gigabytes). Supports file compression and file security. NTFS allows faster file access and uses hard drive space more efficiently. Supports individual file compression and has the best file security.

How to convert partitions in NT, 2000, or XP

Use the **CONVERT**.EXE program in NT, to convert a FAT16 partition to NTFS, or in Windows 2000 or XP to convert a FAT16/FAT32 partition to NTFS. Access a command prompt window. Type the following command:

CONVERT *x*: /FS:NTFS (where ***x*** is the drive letter of the partition being converted to NTFS).

Press [Enter] and then press [Y] (Yes) and press [Enter]. Close the command prompt window and restart the computer. You can add a /V switch to the end of the command for a more verbose operation mode. Any type of partition conversion requires free hard drive space. The amount depends on the size of the partition.

operating system sets aside one cluster as a minimum for every file. A **cluster** is the smallest amount of space reserved for one file and is made up of a specific number of sectors. Figure 2.92 illustrates the concept of a cluster. Keep in mind that the number of hard drive sectors per track varies. The outer tracks hold more information (have more sectors) than the inner tracks.

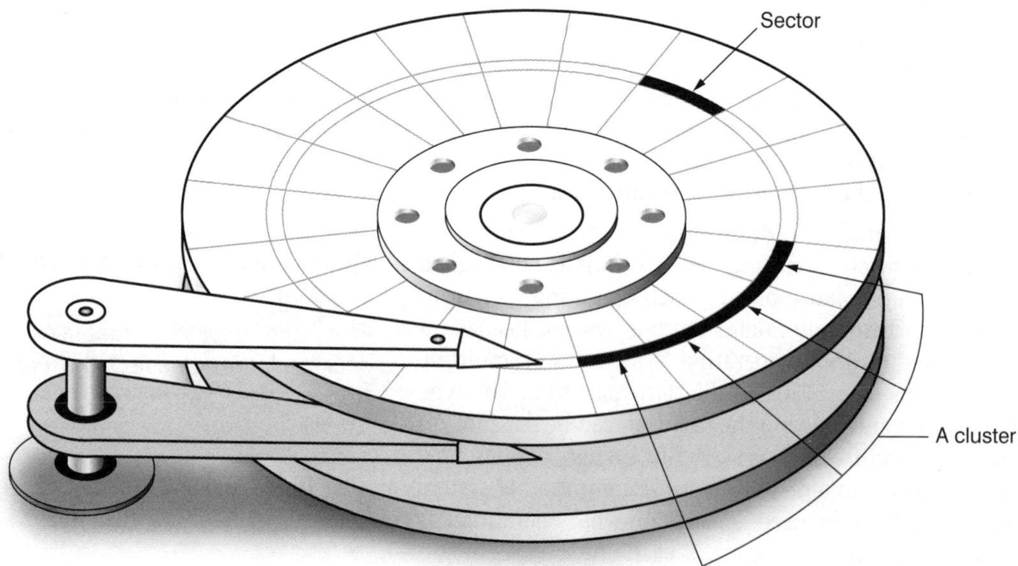

One cluster is the minimum amount of space for a file.

Figure 2.92 Clusters

You can see in Table 2.28 that partitioning large drives into one FAT partition wastes hard drive space. Most people do not have big files. An efficiently partitioned hard drive allows more files to be saved because less of the hard drive is wasted. Computer users with CAD (Computer-Aided Design) software would naturally have bigger files and need larger partitions.

Table 2.28 FAT16 partitions and cluster size

Partition size	Number of sectors	Cluster size
0–15MB	8	4K
16MB–127MB	4	2K
128MB–255MB	8	4K
256MB–511MB	16	8K
512MB–1GB	32	16K
>1GB–2GB	64	32K
>2GB–4GB	128	64K

Things to note about NTFS partitions

Windows 2000 and higher automatically convert older NTFS partitions to the newer type of NTFS.

Applications should be in a separate partition from data files. The following are some good reasons for partitioning the hard drive and separating data files from application files:

- Multiple partitions on the same hard drive divide the drive into smaller subunits, which makes it easier and faster to back up the data (which should be backed up more often than applications).
- The data is protected from operating system failures, unstable software applications, and any unusual software problems that occur between the application and the operating system.
- The data is in one location, which makes the files easier and faster to back up, organize, and locate.

Windows 9x, and higher systems can use FAT32 partitions. The FAT32 file system makes more efficient use of the hard drive than FAT16. Table 2.29 shows the cluster size for FAT32 partitions.

Table 2.29 FAT32 partitions and cluster size

Partition size	Number of sectors	Cluster size
0–511MB	N/A	N/A
512MB–8GB	8	4K
>8GB–16GB	16	8K
>16GB–32GB	32	16K
>32GB	64	32K

The NTFS file system is a very efficient one. NTFS can use cluster sizes as small as 512 bytes per cluster. Table 2.30 lists the default cluster sizes for all versions of Windows since NT including Windows Vista and 7.

Table 2.30 NTFS partitions and cluster size

Partition size	Number of sectors	Cluster size
0–16TB	8	4KB
16TB–32TB	16	8KB
>32TB–64TB	32	16KB
>64TB–128TB	64	32KB
>128TB–256TB	128	64KB

The Windows Setup installation program can be used to create a partition, and the Disk Management tool or `diskpart` utility can be used once the operating system is installed. Use the Disk Management tool to partition and manage any drive that is installed after the first hard drive. The first hard drive is partitioned initially through the Windows XP installation process. Figure 2.93 shows a screen capture from Windows XP.

Benefits of NTFS

NTFS supports disk quotas, which means that individual users can be limited on the amount of hard drive space. It can also automatically repair disk problems. For example, when a hard drive sector is going bad, the entire cluster is moved to another cluster.

Partitions are defined as primary and extended. If there is only one hard drive installed in a system and the entire hard drive is one partition, it is the **primary partition**. The primary partition on the first detected hard drive is assigned the drive letter `C:`.

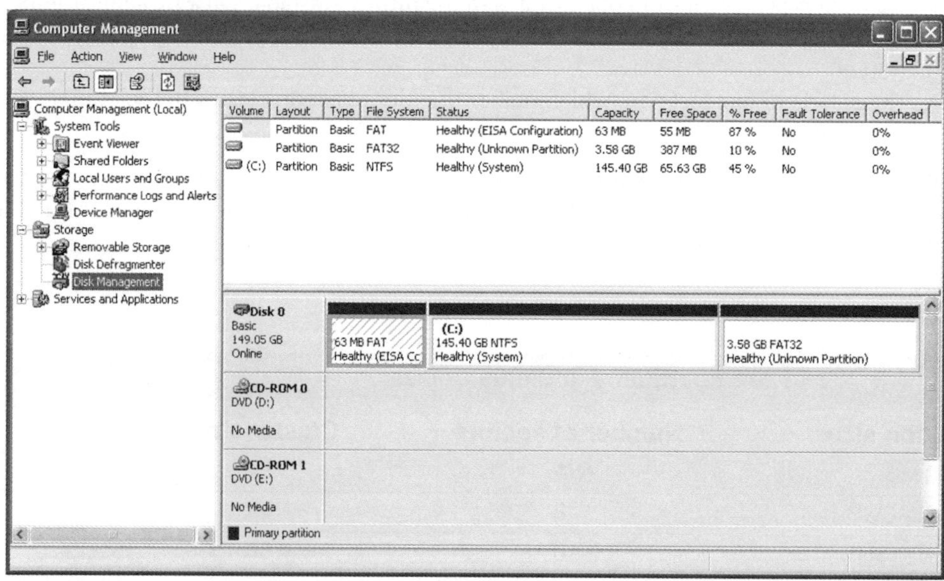

Figure 2.93 Windows XP's disk management

eSATAs might already be partitioned

Some eSATA drives are already partitioned and formatted. Others have software that runs when the drive is connected for the first time. All of them should allow repartitioning and reformatting.

If the drive is divided so only part of the drive is the primary partition, the rest of the cylinders can be designated as the **extended partition**. An extended partition allows a drive to be further divided into **logical drives**. A logical drive is sometimes called a **volume**. A volume is assigned a drive letter and can include a logical drive as well as removable media such as a CD, diskette, DVD, or Flash drive. There can only be one extended partition per drive. A single hard drive can be divided into a maximum of four primary partitions. Remember that a partition is a contiguous section of storage space that functions as if it is a separate drive. See Figure 2.94 for an illustration of how one hard drive can be divided into partitions.

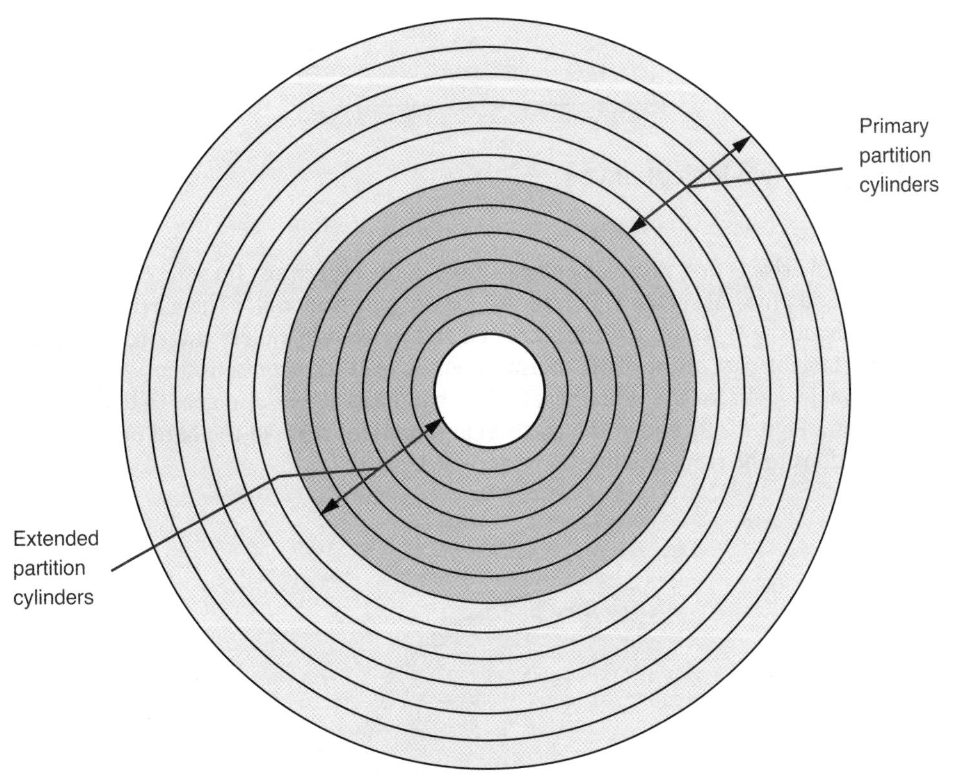

Figure 2.94 **Hard drive partitioning**

The first hard drive in a computer system must have a primary partition, but it does not require an extended partition. If the drive has an extended partition, it can be further subdivided into logical drives that appear as separate hard drives to the computer system. Logical drives created in the extended partition are assigned drive letters such as `D:`, `E:`, or others. The only limit for logical drives is the number of drive letters. An extended partition can have a maximum of 23 logical drives with the drive letters `D:` through `Z:`. A second operating system can reside in a logical drive. Figure 2.95 shows an illustration of a hard drive divided into a primary partition and an extended partition further subdivided into two logical drives.

If two hard drives are installed in a computer, the first hard drive *must* have a primary partition. The second hard drive is not required to have a primary partition and may simply have a single extended partition. If the second hard drive does have a primary partition, it can have an extended partition too.

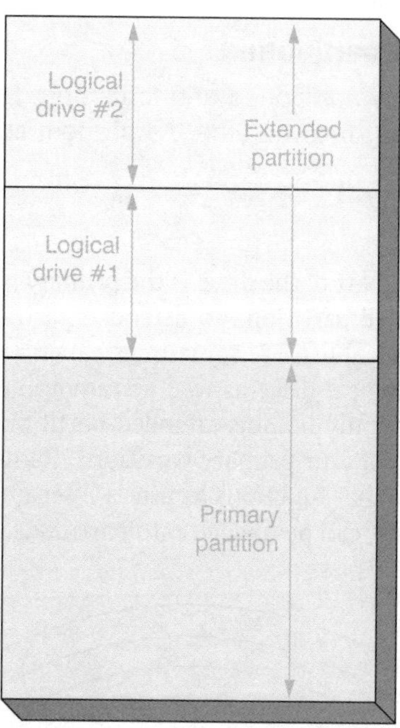

Figure 2.95 Two logical drives

When a hard drive is first installed and partitioned, the outermost track on the platter (cylinder 0, head 0, and physical sector 1) is reserved for the partition table. The partition table holds information about the types of partitions created and in what cylinders these partitions reside. The partition table is part of the **MBR** (master boot record) that contains a program that reads the partition table, looks for the primary partition marked as active, and goes to that partition to boot the system. Figure 2.96 shows the location of important parts of the hard drive that allows booting, partitions to be read, and files to be accessed.

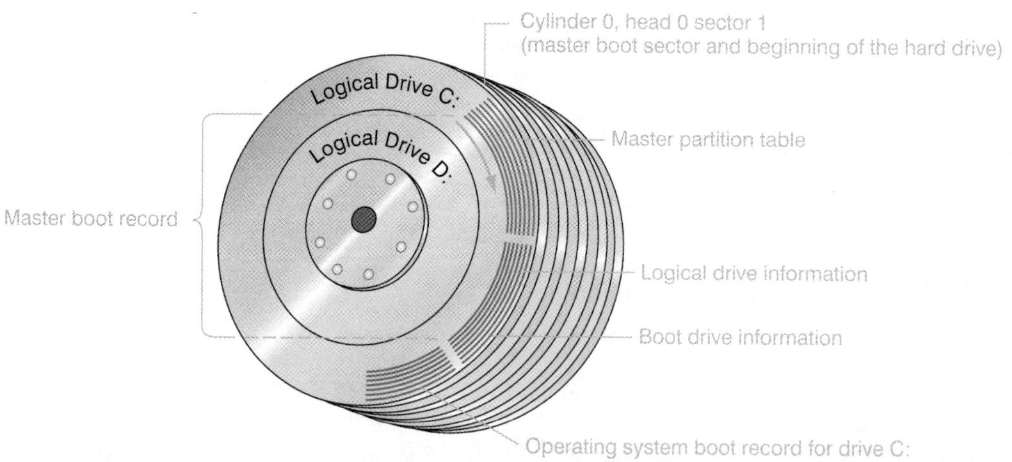

Figure 2.96 Hard drive structure

NTFS has two additional terms that you need to be aware of as a technician: system partition and boot partition. A Windows **system partition** is the partition on the hard drive that holds the hardware-specific files needed to load the operating system. A Windows **boot partition** is the partition on the hard drive that contains the operating system. The boot partition and the system partition can be on the same partition with Windows.

What happens when different types of partitions are deleted?

When a partition is deleted, all information in the partition is lost. A partition can be resized by deleting the partition and re-creating it, but the Disk Administrator program removes all information in the deleted partition. When logical drives in an extended partition are deleted, all data is lost. The other logical drives within the extended partition retain their information.

The ATA-4 standard included support for an HPA that has become quite popular with new computers. The **HPA** (Host Protected Area) is a hidden area of the hard drive used to hold a copy of the operating system; sometimes installed applications use the HPA when the operating system becomes so corrupted that a re-installation is necessary. Many manufacturers provide a BIOS setting or a keystroke that can be used when the system boots in order to access this area. The HPA is commonly found on the hard drive beyond the normal data storage locations; it reduces the amount of storage space available for data.

New partition type with Windows x64

A partition type known as GPT is available with Windows 64-bit operating systems. **GPT** (GUID, or globally unique identifier, partition table) allows up to 128 partitions and volumes up to 18EB. GPT partitioning is done through the Disk Management tool or the `diskpart` command-line utility. MBR-based partitions can be converted to GPT and vice versa, but data is not preserved.

How Drive Letters Are Assigned

Any operating system assigns drive letters to hard drives during the partitioning step. The order in which the partitions are assigned drive letters depends on three factors: (1) the number of hard drives; (2) the type of partitions on the hard drives (primary or extended); and (3) the operating system.

Note that if a new drive is installed, drive letters for these devices, volumes, partitions, or logical drives are added afterward. Drive letters can be changed through the Disk Management tool (right-click on the drive letter) or by using the `diskpart` command-line utility. Be careful, though, because some applications have pointers to specific files on a specific drive letter. Special products can be used that partition the hard drive and allow repartitioning without any data loss. Examples include Acronis Partition Manager, Power-Quest Corporation's Partition Magic, Avanquest's Partition Commander, and Symantec's Norton Partition Magic.

Determining what type of partition you have

To determine the type of partition on a computer, double-click the *My Computer* icon. Right-click a drive letter and select *Properties*. The *General* tab shows the type of file system used in the partition.

Windows Logical Disk Management

In the Windows environment, manage storage devices with a snap-in (an installable module) called Logical Disk Management. With Windows 2000 and higher, there are two types of storage: basic storage and dynamic storage. Table 2.31 explains these and other associated terms.

Table 2.31 Logical disk management terms

Term	Description
Basic storage	One of the two types of storage. This is what traditionally has been known as a partition. It is the default method because it is used by all operating systems.
Basic disk	Any drive that has been partitioned and setup for writing files. A basic disk has primary partitions, extended partitions, and logical drives contained within the extended partitions.
Dynamic storage	The second type of storage; contrast with basic storage. Allows you to create primary partitions, logical drives, and dynamic volumes on removable storage devices. More powerful than basic storage. Uses a dynamic disk (see this term for more information).
Dynamic disk	A disk made up of volumes. A volume can be the entire hard disk, parts of the hard disk combined into one unit, and other specific types of volumes, such as single, spanned, or striped volumes.
Simple volume	Disk space allocated from one hard drive. The space does not have to be contiguous.
Spanned volume	Disk space created from multiple hard drives. Windows writes data to a spanned volume in such a way that the first hard drive is used until the space is filled. Then, the second hard drive's space is used for writing. This continues until all hard drives in the spanned volume are utilized.
Striped volume	Data is written across 2 to 32 hard drives. It is different from a spanned volume in that each drive is used alternately. Another name for this is striping or RAID 0 (covered in the next section).
System volume	Holds the files needed to boot the operating system.
Boot volume	Holds the remaining operating system files. Can be the same volume as the system volume.
RAW volume	A volume that has never been high-level formatted and does not contain a file system.

Managing dynamic disks

Use the Disk Management tool (found in the Computer Management console) to work with dynamic disks or to convert a basic disk to a dynamic one. Once accomplished, the conversion process cannot be reversed.

Figure 2.97 shows some of these concepts.

Fault Tolerance

RAID (redundant array of independent, formerly inexpensive, disks) allows writing to multiple hard drives for larger storage areas, better performance, and fault tolerance. **Fault tolerance** is the ability to continue functioning after a hardware or software failure. RAID can be implemented with hardware or software on IDE or SCSI hard drives. RAID comes in many different levels, but the ones implemented in the Windows environment are 0, 1, and 5. Some motherboards supported "nested"

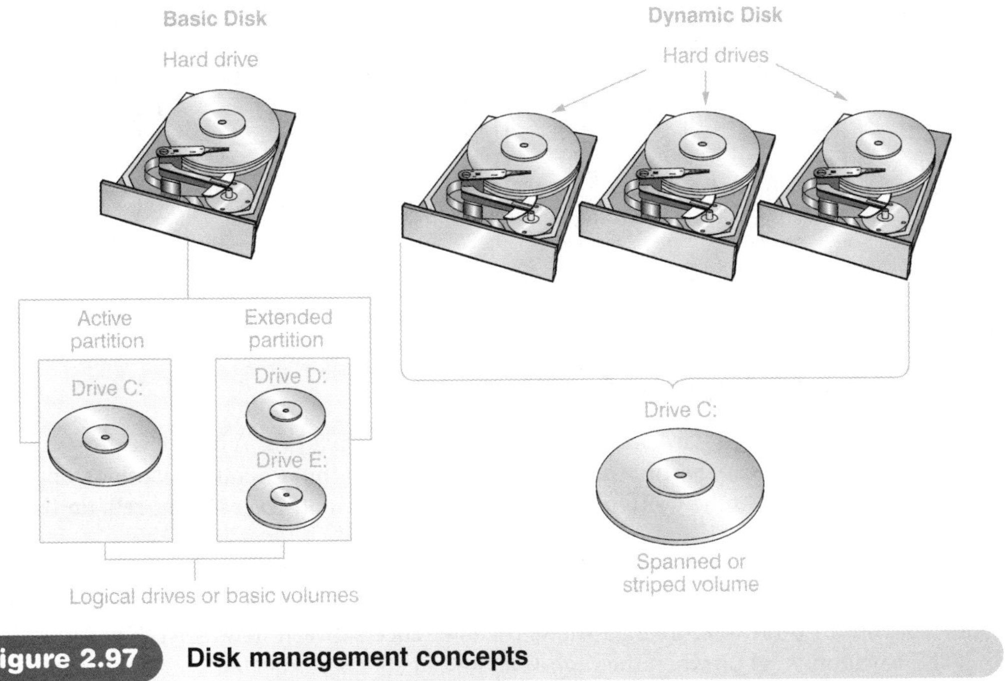

Figure 2.97 Disk management concepts

RAID which means RAID levels are combined. This method also increases the complexity of the hard drive setup. Table 2.32 explains these levels.

Table 2.32 RAID

RAID level	Description
0	Also called disk striping without parity. Data is alternately written on two or more hard drives, which increases system performance. These drives are seen by the system as one logical drive. **RAID 0** does not protect data when a hard drive fails.
1	Also called disk mirroring or disk duplexing. **RAID 1** protects against hard drive failure. **Disk mirroring** uses two or more hard drives and one disk controller. The same data is written to two drives. If one drive should fail, the system continues to function. With **disk duplexing**, a similar concept is used except that two disk controllers are used. Disk duplexing allows the system to continue functioning if one hard drive and one controller fail because of the redundancy.
0+1	A striped set and a mirrored set combined. Four hard drives minimum are required with an even number of disks. It creates a second striped set to mirror a primary striped set of disks. Also called RAID 01.
1+0	A mirrored set and a striped set combined with four hard drives as a minimum. Difference between 1+0 and 0+1 is that 1+0 has a striped set from a set of mirrored drives. Also called RAID 10.
5	Also called disk striping with parity. **RAID 5** writes data to three or more hard drives. Included with the data is parity information. If a drive fails, the data can be rebuilt from the other two drives' information.

Figure 2.98 shows the different types of RAID. With RAID 0, blocks of data (B1, B2, B3, etc.) are placed on alternating drives. With RAID 1, the same block of data is written to two drives. RAID 5 has one drive that contains parity information (P) for particular blocks of data such as B1 and B2.

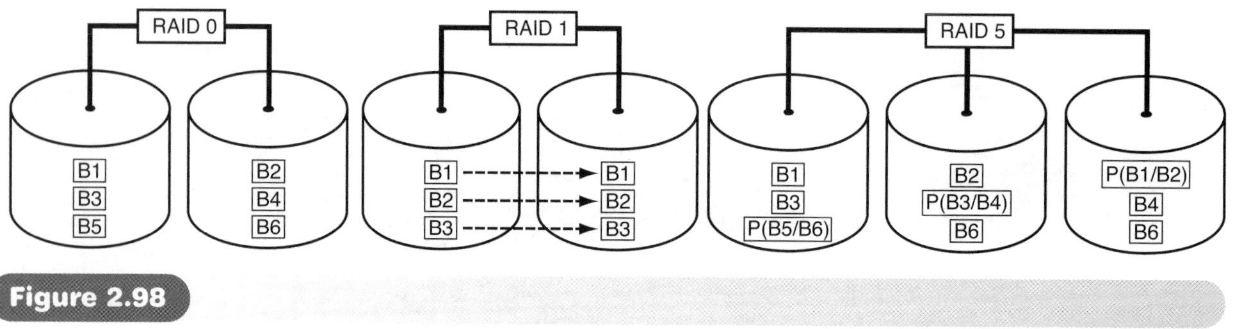

Figure 2.98

High-Level Format

The last step in preparing a hard drive for use is high-level formatting. A high-level format must be performed on all primary partitions, logical drives located within extended partitions, and GPT partitions before data can be written to the hard drive. The high-level format sets up the file system so it can accept data.

NTFS allows support for multiple data streams and support for every character in the world. NTFS also automatically remaps bad clusters to other sections of the hard drive without any additional time or utility. Figure 2.99 shows the difference between how a FAT16 partition and an NTFS partition is set up when the high-level format step is completed.

FAT16 Volume Structure

Partition boot sector | FAT #1 | FAT #2 (backup) | Root directory | Directories and files

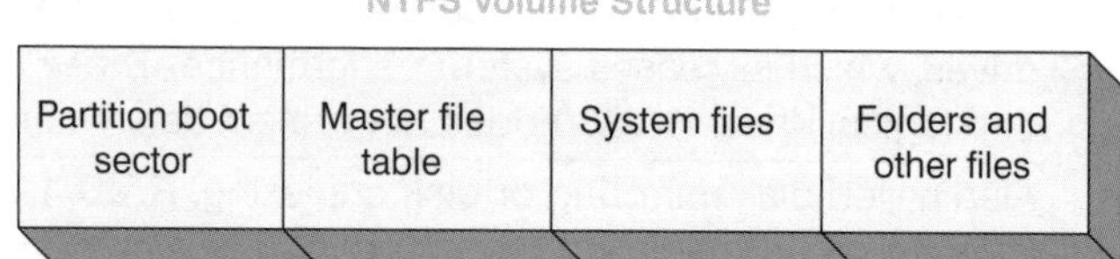

Figure 2.99 FAT16 and NTFS volume structure

The high-level format creates two **FATs** (file allocation tables), one primary and one secondary. It also creates the root directory that renumbers the sectors. The FAT keeps track of the hard disk's file locations. It is similar to a table of contents in a book as it lists where the files are located in the partition. Table 2.33 shows the differences between the file systems.

Table 2.33 Comparing file systems

	FAT16	FAT32	NTFS
Maximum file size	4GB	4GB	~16TB
Maximum volume (partition) size	4GB (2GB if files are shared with DOS or Windows 95 computer)	32GB (max format) 2TB (max size can read)	2TB (or greater)*
Maximum files per volume	64KB	4MB	4GB

*Higher capacities are possible—up to 16EB (exabytes).

High-level formatting can be performed using the `FORMAT` command or by using Windows Disk Management tool. The area of the disk that contains information about the system files is the **DBR** (DOS boot record) and is located on the hard drive's cylinder 0, head 1, sector 1. The more common term for this today (since DOS is no longer a major operating system) is **boot sector** or volume boot record.

Additional drive partitions and drives installed after the first hard drive partition is created use the Windows Disk Management tool to high-level format the drive. The first hard drive partition is normally high-level formatted as part of the operating system installation process.

How to change the cluster size

If you want to adjust the cluster size on a partition, you can do it during the high-level format step using the `FORMAT` command. The syntax for the command is **`FORMAT`** ***`driveletter:`*** **`/FS:NTFS /A:`*****`clustersize`*** where ***`driveletter`*** is the letter of the partition and ***`clustersize`*** is the size you want each cluster in the partition to be.

Troubleshooting Devices

Most problems with new drive installation stem from improper configuration of jumpers, SCSI ID settings, termination, or problems with cabling. The following steps assist with checking possible problems.

- Check the physical settings, if necessary.
- Check cabling. Pin 1 of the cable should be attached to pin 1 of the adapter connector.
- Check drive type setting in BIOS Setup. Refer to the documentation, contact the manufacturer of the drive for the correct setting, or use the Internet to obtain the setting.
- If after you have configured the drive, installed it, and powered it on, the BIOS shows the drive type as "None, Not installed," or displays all 0s in the drive parameters even though you set it to automatically detect the drive, then the BIOS is not able to detect it. Check all jumper settings, check cable connection(s), and check the power connection. If two PATA drives connect to the same cable, disconnect the slave drive. If the drives can be detected individually, but not together, they are incompatible on the same cable. In Setup, reduce any advanced features such as block mode, multi-sector transfer, PIO mode, 32-bit transfers, and so forth to their lowest values or disable them. Increase the amount of time the computer takes to initialize the hard drive by going into Setup and modifying such features as hard drive boot delay or set the boot speed to the lowest value. This gives the hard drive more time to spin up and reach its appropriate RPM before data is read from it. Make sure the motherboard port is enabled.
- Has the drive been partitioned and one partition marked as the active partition?
- Has the drive been high-level formatted?
- Verify that the mounting screw to hold the drive in the case is not too tight. Loosen the screw and power up the computer. Figure 2.100 shows the mounting screws for a hard drive installed in a tower case.

Stop 0x00000077 Kernel_Stack_Inpage error

If your computer has a boot sector virus or data cannot be read from the paging file, run antivirus software for the potential virus. If there is a paging file error, search for this error code on the Internet. Depending on the output shown, take the appropriate steps.

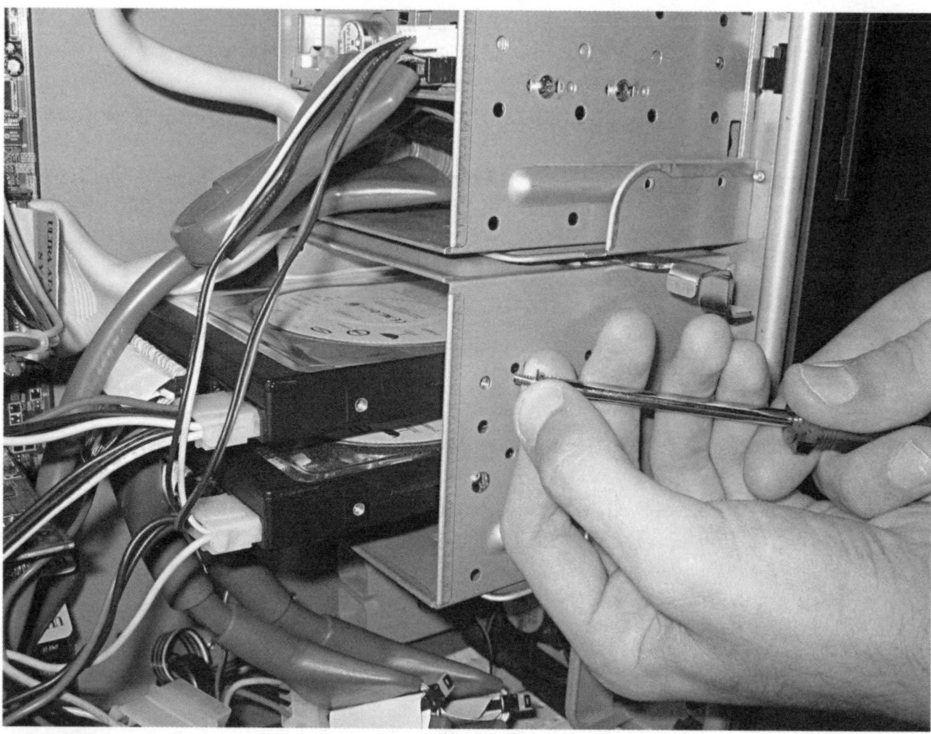

Figure 2.100 Hard drive mounting screws

- If during partitioning the "No fixed disks present" error appears, check the hard drive cabling, power connection, configuration jumpers (cable select, master/slave, SCSI ID), termination, and BIOS configuration.
- If the hard drive does not format to full capacity: (a) the drive parameters may be set incorrectly in Setup; (b) the BIOS does not support large hard drives; or (c) translation is not set up for the hard drive in the Setup program. Confirm the drive's parameters reported by the Disk Management tool with the drive's actual parameters and capacity.
- If the error message "Disk Boot failure" appears, check to see that the primary partition is marked active.
- If on initial boot after setting up a hard drive in BIOS Setup, you see the message "HDD Controller Failure, Press F1 to continue," then the system is not partitioned or high-level formatted. Press the necessary key and boot from a CD, then partition and high-level format the hard drive. If the message still continues, check the cabling and jumper configuration(s) on the hard drive.

Stop 0x0000007B Inaccessible_Boot_Device error

Your computer most likely has a boot sector virus. Run antivirus software.

- If during power-on the hard drive does not spin up or the hard drive spins down after a few seconds, check the power connector, the pin 1 orientation on the interface cable, the drive type in BIOS Setup, master/slave/cable select settings, energy management jumpers or settings in Setup, and any software that came with the drive that enables power management. Disable power management in BIOS Setup. Try installing the drive in another system.
- Run a virus checker on the system.

Stop 0x00000024 NTFS_File System error

The NTFS file system may be corrupt. Boot to Windows XP recovery console, back up data files, reinstall operating system.

- Try a warm boot (Ctrl+Alt+Del). If the drive is recognized after the warm boot, the Setup program may be running too fast for the drive to initialize. Refer to the hard drive documentation to see if the hard drive has a setting to help with this problem.
- Is the correct cable used?

The following are generic guidelines for hard drives that did work, but are now having problems.

- Run a virus-checking program after booting from a virus-free boot disk. Many viruses are specifically designed to attack the hard drive.
- Has there been a recent cleaning of the computer or has someone recently removed the top from the computer? If so, check all cables and verify that they correctly connect pin 1 to pin 1 of the adapter or motherboard. Check the power connection to the hard drive.
- If the hard drive flashes quickly on boot up, the controller is trying to read the partition table in the Master Boot Record. If this information is not found, various symptoms can be shown, such as the error messages "Invalid boot disk," "Inaccessible boot device," "Invalid partition table," "Error loading operating system," "Missing operating system," or "No operating system found." Use the **`DISKPART`** command from recovery console to see if the hard drive partition table is OK. Try running `FDISK/MBR` from Recovery Console or use a hard drive utility to repair the partition table.

Does your hard drive stick?

Place a hand on top of the drive as you turn on the computer. Does the drive spin at all? If not, the problem is probably a "sticky" drive or a bad drive. A hard drive must spin at a certain rpm before the heads move over the surface of the hard drive. To check if the drive is sticking, remove the drive and try spinning the spindle motor by hand. Otherwise, remove the drive, hold the drive in your hand, and give a quick jerk with your wrist. Another trick that works is to remove the hard drive from the case, place the drive in a plastic bag, and put in the freezer for a couple of hours. Then, remove the drive and allow it to warm up to room temperature. Reinstall the drive into the system and try it.

- Do you receive a message such as "Disk Boot Failure," "Non-System Disk," or "Disk Error"? These errors may indicate a boot record problem. The solution is to boot from a bootable disk or CD to see if drive `C:` is available. The operating system may have to be reloaded. Also, verify that the primary partition is marked as active.
- If you receive a message "Hard drive not found," "No boot device available," "Fixed disk error," or "Disk boot failure," the BIOS cannot find the hard drive. Check cabling.
- When Windows has startup problems, Recovery Console and the *Advanced Options* menu are used. Many times startup problems are due to a virus. Other utilities that help with MBR, boot sector, and system files are `FIXBOOT`, `FIXMBR`, System File Checker, and the *Advanced Options* menu. To use `FIXBOOT`, type `FIXBOOT` *`x`*`:` command where *`x`*`:` is the drive letter of the volume that has the problem. To use `FIXMBR`, type `FIXMBR` from a command prompt.

Use System File Checker

The System File Checker program can be run from the *Run* dialog box by typing **`x:\Windows\System32\SFC.EXE /scannow`** where **`x:`** is the drive letter of the drive on which Windows is installed.

- Indications that there is a problem with the Master Boot Record or the system files are as follows: "Invalid partition table," "Error loading operating system," "Missing operating system," "A disk read error has occurred," "NTLDR is missing," or "NTLDR is corrupt."
- When Windows has startup problems due to incompatible hardware or software, or a corrupted installation process, the *Advanced Options* menu can help. This option can be selected by pressing the F8 key during the boot process.
- If an insufficient disk space error appears, delete unnecessary files, including .tmp files, from the hard drive, empty the Recycle Bin, and save files to a CD/DVD, a Flash drive, or an external hard drive and remove the moved files from the hard drive. Use the Disk Cleanup and Defragmenter tool. Another option is to add another hard drive and move some (or all) data files to it.
- For eSATA drives, check the power cabling and data cabling. Ensure that the data cable is the correct type for the port and device being used. Partition and format the drive before data is written to it. Ensure that the port is enabled through BIOS. The BIOS may require an update, or a device driver may be required (especially if the drive is listed under "other devices" in Device Manager). BIOS incompatibilities are the most common issue with deployments. Note that some operating systems report SATA drives as SCSI drives.
- If the computer reports that the hard drive may have a defective area, use the hard drive error checking tool (right-click) on the hard drive volume, select *Properties*, select the *Tools* tab, and click the *Check now* button.
- A ticking sound is sometimes called by a failed or failing hard drive.

Table 2.34 shows some of the normal and problem drive status messages seen in the Windows Disk Management tool. These status messages can help with drive management, troubleshooting, and recovery.

Table 2.34 Disk management status states

Disk Management Status	Description
Active	The bootable partition, usually on the first hard drive, is ready for use.
Dynamic	An alternative to the basic disk the dynamic disk has volumes instead of partitions. Types of volumes include simple volumes, volumes that span more than one drive, and RAID volumes.
Failed	The basic disk or dynamic volume cannot be started; the disk or volume could be damaged; the file system could be corrupted; or there may be a problem with the underlying physical disk (turned on, cabled correctly) or with an associated RAID drive. Right-click the disk and select *Reactivate disk*. Right-click the dynamic volume and select *Reactivate volume*.
Foreign	A dynamic disk from another computer has just been installed. Right-click the disk and select *Import Foreign Disks*.
Healthy	The drive is ready to be used.
Not Initialized	A basic disk is not ready to be used. Right-click the disk and select *Initialize Disk*.
Invalid	Vista Home (any version) cannot access the dynamic disk. Convert the disk to a basic disk (right-click the disk number and select *Convert to basic disk*).
Offline	Ensure that the physical disk is turned on and cabled correctly. Right-click it and select *Reactivate Disk* or *Activate*.
Online (errors)	Use the hard drive error checking tool (in Explorer, right-click the hard drive partition and then select *Properties*, the *Tools* tab, and *Check now button*).
Unallocated	Space on a hard drive has not been partitioned or put into a volume.
Unknown	A new drive has not been initialized properly. Right-click it and select *Initialize disk*. The volume boot sector may be corrupted or infected by a virus.
Unreadable	The drive has not had time to spin up. Restart the computer and rescan the disk (use the *Action* menu item).

Preventive Maintenance for Hard Drives

Keeping the computer system in a clean and cool operating environment extends the life of a hard drive. The most common hard drive failures are due to moving parts (heads and motors) and power fluctuations and/or failures. Performing preventive maintenance on the entire computer is good for all components found inside the computer, including the hard drive subsystem.

A program called **CHKDSK** can be executed from within the GUI or from Recovery Console and the program locates clusters disassociated from data files. These disk clusters occupy disk space. When CHKDSK executes and reports that there are **lost clusters**, it means that the FAT cannot determine to which file or directory these clusters belong.

Tech Tip

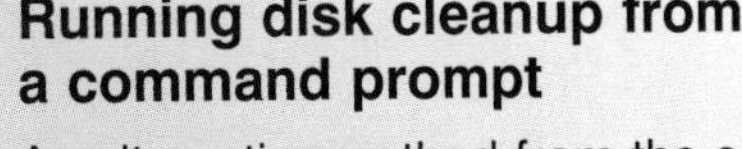

Running disk cleanup from a command prompt

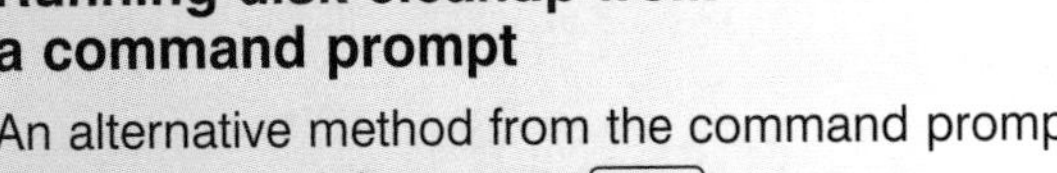

An alternative method from the command prompt is `CLEANMGR` and then press Enter.

In Windows you can perform this function by locating the drive partition in Explorer, right-click the drive letter and select *Properties* → *Tool* tab → *Check Now* button. Windows also has a program called **Disk Cleanup** that removes temporary files, removes offline Internet files, empties the Recycle Bin, compresses unused files, removes unused programs, and prompts you before doing any of this. To access Disk Cleanup use the following procedures:

1. Click the *Start* button → *All Programs* → *Accessories* → *System Tools* → *Disk Cleanup*.
2. Select the drive letter, and click *OK*.
3. On the *Disk Cleanup* tab, click in the checkboxes for the options desired and click *OK*.

Data Security

Another preventive maintenance procedure for a hard drive is performing a backup of the data and operating system. Most people do not realize that the most important part of any computer is the data that resides within it. Data cannot be replaced like hardware can be. Traditionally, backups have been saved to magnetic tape (quarter-inch cartridge, LTO (linear tape-open) or DLT (digital linear tape) being the most common types), but CDs, DVDs, and external drives are viable alternatives today. Some people use CDs or DVDs to back up the data and periodically do a full backup to an external drive.

A second hard drive makes an excellent backup device

Hard drives are inexpensive and easy to install. Install a second one to backup your data. Backups should be done routinely. Have a routine maintenance plan that you recommend to users. Important data should be backed up daily or frequently, but routine data is usually handled by a monthly backup. The sensitivity and importance of the data determines how frequent backups are performed.

Windows comes with a backup utility, but many of the external hard drives come with their own software that is easier to use, has more features, and allows easy and selective data backup scheduling. No matter what method of backup you use, test your backup for restoration. Install to a different drive if necessary.

Laptops sometimes have an additional password for their hard drive. That way if the laptop hard drive is stolen, it cannot be inserted into another device and used without knowing the hard

For critical data, keep backups in a different location

Offsite storage for critical data is important even for home users in case of disaster such as flooding, fire, or theft. A safe deposit box can be used for important data records such as textbooks, income taxes, personal records (insurance policy numbers and financial data) and student tests (just kidding).

Don't use the same hard drive as a backup device

Backing up data to a different partition on the hard drive is *not* a good idea. Even though there is some chance that your data might be saved, it is more likely the drive will fail. The drive is a physical device with moving parts—motor, heads, and so on. Mechanical failure is always a possibility.

drive password. It is a password in addition to the power on password or Windows password. This option is configured through the BIOS if it is available.

Even though much data is stored locally for most users, many companies are favoring centralized storage even for individual users. One, this protects the company's interest and two it ensures backups are done on a regular and reliable basis. Some companies are moving toward a **thin-client** environment in which no hard drives are included with the system. Storage is provided across the network. This reduces hardware and software costs, PC maintenance staffing costs, and makes data security easier to manage.

Store data on remote servers

Many folks who travel frequently use data storage servers at their company or use the services of an Internet storage site. Part of their services includes backing up the data stored on their drives and having redundant hard drives in their servers.

When replacing a hard drive, destroy the drive so that data can never be retrieved. Open the drive and physically damage the platters. Scratch the platters with a screwdriver or other implement.

There are utilities that allow the entire drive to be rewritten with all ones or all zeros. Removing all partitions and re-partitioning and re-formatting the drive also helps.

Erase data from old drive

When upgrading (and removing) a hard drive, install the new drive, re-install data and/or applications, but ensure the data and remnants of data are no longer on the drive.

Removable Drive Storage

IDE and SCSI are the two most common types of hard drives, but these interfaces are also used for internal and external storage devices such as CD/DVD drives and tape drives. IDE PATA has traditionally only been internal devices, but now with SATA, external devices are available. SCSI has always supported internal and external devices. These external devices can also attach to the parallel port (not common today) or the USB port (a very popular option).

Tape drives can be attached using SCSI or IDE (SATA only) or attach to parallel, USB, eSATA, or IEEE 1394 ports if they are external devices. Tape drives are installed using similar methods of like devices that use these ports. When tapes are used, the most common types of tapes used for backups are DAT (digital audio tape) and Traven. The most common type of removable storage is optical (CD/DVD).

SSD defragmentation kills

Do not defragment an SSD as you would a magnetic hard drive. Defragmentation causes more reads and writes, which reduces the life span of the SSD.

Hard Drive Fragmentation

Over time, as files are added to a hard drive, the files become fragmented, which means that the clusters that make up the file are not adjacent to one another. Fragmentation slows down the hard drive in two ways: (1) the FAT has to keep track of scattered clusters, and (2) the hard drive read/write head assembly must move to different locations on the drive's surface to access a single file. Figure 2.101 illustrates fragmentation of

How to defragment in Windows

To access the defragmentation tool in Windows, open *Explorer*, locate a hard drive letter, right-click it, and select *Properties* → *Tools* tab → *Defragment Now* button.

Three fragmented files

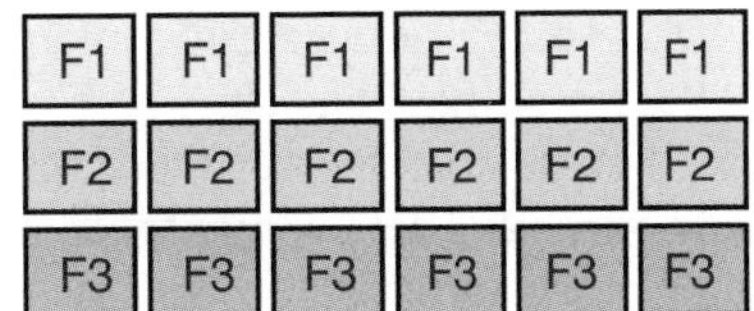

Three contiguous files

Figure 2.101 Fragmented hard drive

three files (F1, F2, and F3) and the results after defragmentation has been executed on the hard drive. **Defragmentation** is the process of placing files in contiguous sectors. Notice the results in Figure 2.101 of the defragmentation process.

Windows includes a program that defragments the hard drive. This program places the file clusters in adjacent sectors. Defragmenting the hard drive makes for faster hard disk access. These measures also extend the life of the hard drive because the drive's mechanical movements are reduced.

The DEFRAG command or the Defragment Windows XP tool come with some advanced options. Table 2.35 shows the XP defragmentation options.

Table 2.35 Windows XP or DEFRAG command options

Option	Description
Full Defragmentation	Takes the longest but is the best choice.
Defragment Files Only	Faster than Full Defragmentation but does not consolidate space on the hard drive.
Consolidate Free Space Only	Locates the largest amount of free space to place smaller clusters. Files could be more fragmented as a result.
Check Drive for Errors checkbox	Looks for and corrects lost clusters. Enabled by default.

How often should you defragment a hard drive?

Periodically defragment files on a hard drive. Users who delete files often and have large files that are constantly revised should run these utilities more often. You can use the *Analyze* button in XP in Disk Defragmenter to check if a drive partition needs to be defragmented. Once the analysis is complete, click *View Report* to determine whether or not the drive partition needs to be defragmented.

Disk Caching/Virtual Memory

An easy way to speed up the hard drive is to create a **disk cache**. This puts data into RAM where it can be retrieved much faster than if the data is still on the hard drive. When data is read from the hard drive, the next requested data is frequently located in the adjacent clusters. Disk caching reads more data from the hard drive than requested. The data is placed in a reserved portion of RAM called the cache. Cache on a hard drive controller, sometimes called a data buffer, allows the read/write heads to read more than just one sector at a time. A hard drive can read up to an entire track of information and hold this data until needed without returning to the hard drive for each sector.

Both IDE and SCSI drives can contain 2MB to 16MB or more of RAM. Because drives are mechanical devices, they take time to reorder write data to the platters. With cache memory installed, information can be prefetched from the computer's system RAM and stored in the hard drive's cache memory. This frees up the system RAM for other tasks and improves the system and hard drive's performance.

A different way of using a hard drive is with virtual memory. Virtual memory is a method of using hard disk space as if it were RAM. The amount of RAM installed in a system is not normally enough to handle all of the operating system and the multiple applications that are opened and being used. Only the program and data of the application that is currently being used is what is in RAM. The rest of the opened applications and data are stored in what is called a swap file or a page file on the hard drive. When you click over to a different application that is held in the swap/page file, data is moved from RAM into the swap file and the data you need to look at is moved into RAM for faster access and data manipulation.

Windows uses **VMM** (Virtual Memory Manager). The disk cache is dynamic—it increases or decreases the cache size as needed. If the system begins to page (constantly swapping data from RAM to the hard drive), the cache size automatically shrinks. In Windows NT and higher, the virtual memory swap file (sometimes called the page file) is called `PAGEFILE.SYS`.

Where should you keep the swap file?

If multiple hard drives are available, a technician might want to move the swap file to a different drive. Always put the swap file on the fastest hard drive unless that hard drive lacks space. NT, 2000, and XP allow the swap file to reside on multiple hard drives. It is best to keep the swap file on a hard drive that does not contain the operating system.

How to adjust virtual memory in XP

1. If using category view, select *Performance and Maintenance* control panel followed by *System*. If using classic view, double-click the *System* control panel.
2. Click the *Advanced* tab.
3. In the Performance section, click the *Settings* button.
4. Click the *Advanced* tab, locate the Virtual Memory section, and click the *Change* button.
5. Change the size parameters and click the *OK* button until you return to the *Performance and Maintenance* window.

32-bit Windows versions use 32-bit demand-paged virtual memory, and each process gets 4GB of address space divided into two 2GB sections. One 2GB section is shared with the rest of the system while the other 2GB section is reserved for the one application. All the memory space is divided into 4KB blocks of memory called "pages." The operating system allocates as much available RAM as possible to an application. Then, the operating system swaps or pages the application to and from the temporary swap file as needed. The operating system determines the optimum setting for this swap file; however, the swap file size can be changed.

Adding more physical RAM to the motherboard helps with caching

One of the most effective ways to speed up a computer is to reduce the amount of data that has to be swapped from the hard drive to RAM. This is done by increasing the amount of RAM on the motherboard. Accessing RAM is much faster than accessing a mechanical drive that rotates and has heads that have to move and find the data.

Multimedia Devices

Multimedia Overview

The term *multimedia* has different meanings for people because there are many types of multimedia devices. This chapter focuses on the most popular areas—CD and DVD technologies, sound cards, cameras, and speakers. A CD/DVD drive can be internally mounted and attached to a PATA or SATA interface, or it can be an external unit like some of the other multimedia devices that attach to USB, IEEE 1394 (FireWire), or eSATA ports. Internal CD/DVD drives usually cost less than external ones. The following sections on multimedia are not intended to be a buyer's guide or an electronics "how it works" book; instead, they are a guide for technicians with an emphasis on installation and troubleshooting. Multimedia devices can be a lot of fun once they are installed. However, they can also cause headaches during installation.

CD Drive Overview

A CD drive (compact disc) is sometimes called a CD-ROM (CD read-only memory) and it uses discs that store large amounts of information (628MB and higher). The disc for the CD drive is known as a **CD**, CD-ROM disc, or simply disc. Figure 2.102 shows a BenQ U.S.A. Corp.'s CD drive and its various front panel controls.

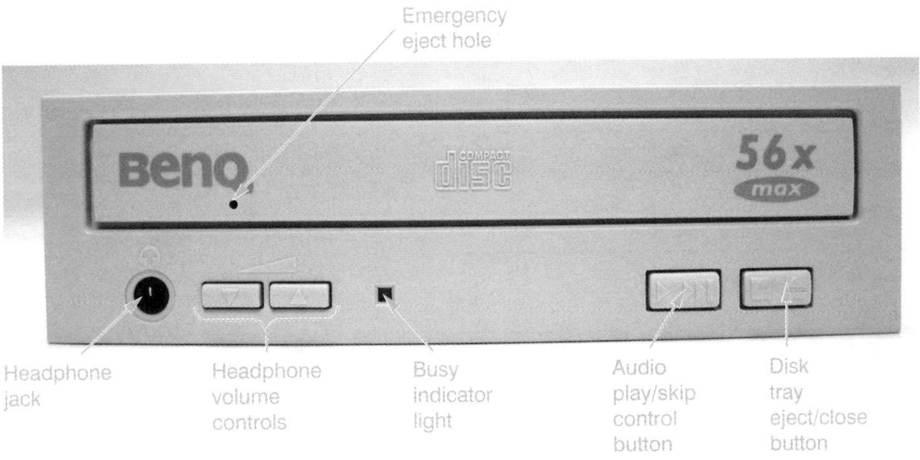

Figure 2.102 **BenQ CD drive front panel controls**

A CD has pits or indentations along the track. Flats, sometimes called lands, separate the pits. Reading information from a CD involves using a laser diode or similar device. The laser beam shines through the protective coating to an aluminum alloy layer, where data is stored. The laser beam reflects back through the optics to a photo diode detector that converts the reflected beam of light into 1s and 0s. The transitions between the pits and lands create the variation of light intensity. Figure 2.103 shows an inside view of a CD drive.

CD Drive Speeds

CD drives come in a variety of types classified by the X factor: 1X (single speed), 2X (double speed), 32X, 48X, 52X, and higher. Table 2.36 shows the transfer rates for several drive types. There are drives being advertised as 100X that use hard drive space to cache the CD contents and provide faster speeds (1.5MBps). See the next section, *CD Drive Buffers/Cache*, for information on how this works.

Take, for example, a 48X CD drive installed in two different computers. One computer has a 2GHz computer, 512MB of RAM, and an AGP video adapter with 64MB of video memory. Another

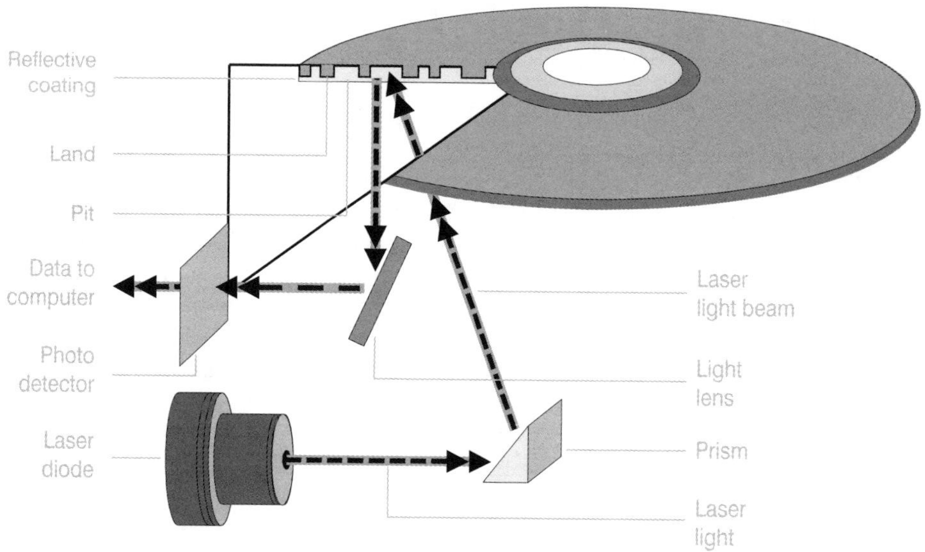

Figure 2.103 Inside a CD drive

Table 2.36 CD drive transfer speeds

Type of CD-ROM drive	Typical transfer rate (in kilobytes per second)
1X	150
2X	300
16X	2,400
24X	3,600
32X	4,800
36X	5,400
40X	6,000
48X	7,200
52X	7,800

2GHz computer has 1GB of RAM and a PCI-E video adapter with 128MB of video memory. The CD drive in the second example can put graphics on the screen or play audio files much faster than the first drive. The increased amount of system RAM, increased amount of video adapter RAM, and the use of a video card that is PCI-E or AGP, not ISA, all contribute to the performance increase. Buying a faster CD drive does not necessarily mean the drive performs to expectations. As with all computer devices, components in the computer must work together to provide the fastest data transfer. Many people do not realize buying the latest and greatest X factor CD drive does not provide faster access. The drawback to CD drives is that they operate much slower than hard drives.

What affects CD drive performance?

The particular CD drive performance depends on several factors—the microprocessor installed, how much RAM is in the system, what video card is used (PCI-E, PCI, AGP, ISA), and how much video memory is on the video card. Note that DVD drives have the same dependency factors and also use X factors.

Two confusing specifications of these drives are average seek time and average access time. The **average seek time** is the amount of time the drive requires to move randomly around the disc. The **average access time** is the amount of time the drive requires to find the appropriate place on the disc and retrieve information. Another comparison point is **MTBF** (mean time between failures), which is the average number of hours before a device is likely to fail. Keep in mind that the lower the access time number, the better the performance.

CD drive access times are much slower than hard drives and CD drive manufacturers usually quote access times using only optimum test conditions. When buying or recommending a CD drive to a computer user or customer, check magazines or online data for the latest test performance results.

CD Drive Buffers/Cache

One way to reduce CD data transfer time is through buffer memory located on the CD drive. When requesting data, the drive looks ahead on the CD for more data than requested and places the data in the buffers. The buffer memory ensures data is constantly sent to the microprocessor instead of the microprocessor waiting for the drive's slow access time. Buffer sizes typically range from 64KB to 2MB and higher. A drive should not be installed or purchased unless it has a minimum of 500KB buffer.

CD-R and CD-RW

Being able to create CDs is important in today's home and business environments. Two CD technologies, CD-R (compact disc recordable) and CD-RW (CD rewritable) allow this to become a reality. The two technologies have many similarities and CD-RW is the most popular. Technicians should understand the differences between the two. Table 2.37 lists the different CD technologies.

Table 2.37 CD technologies

Technology	Description
CD-ROM	Drive that can play pre-recorded discs
CD-R	Drive that can play pre-recorded discs and record on media during one session
CD-RW	Drive that can play pre-recorded discs and record, erase, and re-record on media during one session or multiple sessions
MultiRead	The OSTA (Optical Storage Technology Association)–defined term that describes drives that can read audio CD, CD-ROM, CD-R, and CD-RW discs

How to read the CD-RW numbers

CD-RW drives are frequently shown with three consecutive numbers such as 52×32×52. The first number is the CD-R write speed, the second number the CD-RW speed, and the last number is the read speed used when reading a pre-recorded disc.

Most CD-R blank discs hold 650MB (sometimes labeled as 74min). However, some manufacturers distribute 700MB discs. Not all CD-Rs can write or read CDs of this capacity. There are software packages that allow writing to 700MB discs such as Roxio, Inc.'s Easy CD Creator. Another type of disc used in CD-Rs is the mini-disc. Many CD drives can accept both the common 5-inch and the mini 3-inch CDs. Look at the drive tray to see if there is a 3-inch diameter depression in the center of the tray. If so, the depression is for the 3-inch CDs. Place the mini CD in the depression, close the tray, and most CD drives will be able to read the disc. Figure 2.104 shows a mini CD disc.

Some CD-RW drives are backward compatible

MultiRead or MultiRead2 is an OSTA (optical storage technology association) specification that states the CD-RW drive is backward compatible with CD-ROM and CD-R discs.

Keep the data coming to the writable CD

One problem with CD-R drives occurs when data is written to the CD-R disc. If the CD-R drive does not receive data in a steady stream, a buffer underrun error occurs and the CD-R disc is ruined. To avoid this problem, do not perform other tasks while creating a disc.

Some older CD drives cannot read the discs created by a CD-R drive

On the problem CD drives, the laser is not calibrated to read recordable discs that have a surface different from that on regular CDs. An indication of this problem is if a disc created by a CD-R drive is readable by some CD drives, but not others. There is no solution to this problem except to replace the drive.

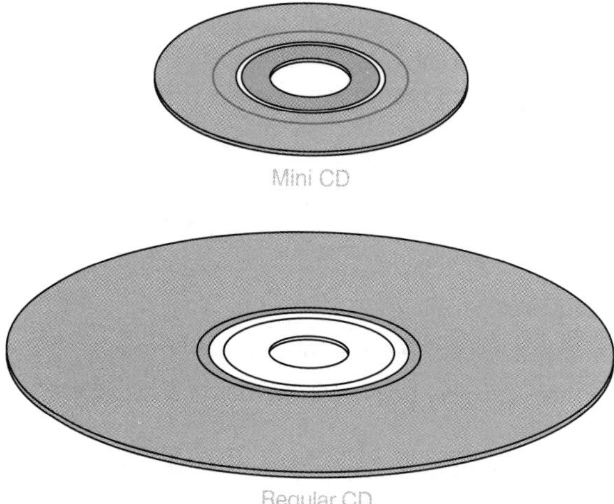

Figure 2.104 A mini CD compared to a regular CD

When creating a CD, the computer must transmit a steady stream of data that is written in a continuous format on the CD. The memory buffers included with the CD-R drive help with this task, but a computer that does not have enough free hard drive space or RAM can still slow down or abort the recording process.

Creating a CD takes time

You should not perform other tasks such as playing games or working in another application when recording a CD. This takes away from CPU time, available RAM, and available hard drive space.

Most CD creation software packages allow you to select the hard drive partition where the data is cached before it is written to the CD. Make sure you select a partition that has twice the amount of free space as the data being written. For example, if 100MB of data is going onto a CD, make sure 200MB of hard drive space is available. If the computer continuously displays errors when writing a CD, most CD recording software allows you to reduce the recording speed. This will take longer, but increases chances of success. Turn off power management and screen savers when creating a CD (or DVD).

Some people like creating an emergency boot CD that allows the computer to start in case of hard drive failure. Many computer manufacturers supply a CD for restoring a system back to factory defaults. However, all applications and operating system environment settings are lost. There are software programs that help create a bootable CD such as Roxio, Inc.'s Easy CD Creator; there are freeware programs available too. The software used to create the bootable CD is loaded and the CD is created. Always test a bootable CD *before* a hard drive failure occurs.

Consider the specifications for a CD-RW drive found in Table 2.38. The cache size is how much buffer memory the drive has installed. The speeds that follow in the left column are what is normally seen in the first line of the advertisement—CD-RW 52×24×52 USB/FireWire Drive. The load type is a tray that comes out when the eject button is pushed. The top item in the right column tells us this drive has both USB and IEEE 1394 ports. What it does not mention anywhere is whether or not cables are shipped with the drive. The specifications tell us that the drive is external and can read and write to CD-R and CD-RW discs.

The writing modes shown in Table 2.38 are Disk-at-Once, Multisession, and Track-at-Once. A **multisession** drive has the ability to store data on a disc and, later, add more data to the disc. **Disc-at-Once** (sometimes called DAO) means that the disc is created in one pass rather than the alternative of **Track-at-Once** (sometimes called TAO) which the laser stops writing normal data after a track is finished. Track-at-Once supports the disc having both audio and data. A writing mode that is not shown in Table 2.38, **Session-at-Once**, allows multiple sessions to be recorded on a single disc. These discs can normally be read by computer-based CD drives, but not audio CD drives such as ones found in a vehicle. The supported formats section are the standards supported by this drive.

Also mentioned in the specification are the supported formats. Commonly called CD Book standards, they are associated with a specific color. For example, CD-DA is the Red Book standard for digital audio, and CD-i/FMV is the Green Book standard for full motion video.

Table 2.38 CD-RW sample advertisement specifications

Specification	Specification
Cache Size: 2MB	Interface Types: USB 2.0 and IEEE 1394
CD Write Speed: 52×	Enclosure Type: External
CD Rewrite Speed: 24×	Compatible Writable Media: CD-R and CD-RW
CD Read Speed: 52×	Writing Modes: Disc-at-Once, Multisession, and Track-at-Once
Load Type: Tray	Supported Formats: CD-DA, CD-i/FMV, CD-ROM XA, CD-RW, and Enhanced CD

Magneto-Optical Drives

A similar technology used for reading and writing compact discs is magneto-optical (MO). Magneto-optical discs cannot be used in regular CD drives; they require a magneto-optical drive. Magneto-optical drives are great for data backups and archiving. They use a laser beam to heat the surface of the disc, and then a magnet applies a charge to the surface. They can be erased by reheating the disc and using the magnet to erase the data. Magneto-optical discs are read using the laser similar to CD drive technology.

DVD Drives

The DVD drive has made the CD drive obsolete. **DVD-ROM** originally stood for digital video disc, then digital versatile disc. Some people confuse DVD-Video with DVD-ROM. DVD-Video holds a video DVD and the DVD-Video player connects to a TV. DVD drives can be both internal and external devices connected to PATA IDE (internal), SATA IDE, SCSI, IEEE 1394 or USB. There are other DVD technologies covered later in the chapter.

Transfer rate is different between CD and DVD drives

When you see a DVD × factor, do not use the same numbers as used with CD drives. A 1× DVD has a 1.32MBps transfer rate compared to a 150KBps transfer rate for a CD drive.

DVD discs provide more storage capacity than a CD disc, but can still play CDs. The discs used with DVD drives are the same diameter and thickness as traditional CDs and like CDs, the DVD discs tolerate dust, dirt, and fingerprints. The data on the DVD disc has pits that are smaller and more closely spaced than CD discs. Because of this, DVDs cannot be read by CD drives. DVD discs provide high video resolution and high quality sound unmatched in the computer industry.

The DVD-ROM drives currently come in two different configurations, 4.7GB and 8.5GB. The 4.7GB format (sometimes known as DVD-5) has a single layer of data on one side of the disc. The 8.5GB capacity (known as DVD-9) uses two layers on the same side to increase storage capacity.

Two other capacities are 9.4GB and 17.1GB. The 9.4GB disc (also referred to as DVD-10) uses a single layer on both sides of the disc. The 17.1GB disc (also known as DVD-18) has two layers on both sides of the disc. This capacity disc is difficult to manufacture.

A software development that helps with DVD technology is Microsoft's **DirectX**. DirectX allows people who write software such as games and Web design not to have to write code to access specific hardware directly. DirectX translates generic hardware commands into special commands for the hardware, which speeds up development time for hardware manufacturers and software developers. DirectX is available in Windows.

Verifying DVD decoder in Windows

When you insert a DVD disc into the drive, a window appears asking you what you want Windows to do with the disc. If you click *Play DVD*, you should see the contents of the DVD and you have an encoder installed. If you get a message saying that a DVD decoder is not installed, contact the PC manufacturer (if the DVD shipped with the PC) or contact the DVD drive manufacturer (if the DVD drive was purchased separately).

Decoders

MPEG (Moving Picture Experts Group) created a compression technique called MPEG2, which is used by DVDs. The computer must decompress the video and audio from the DVD. This is called decoding. There are two methods for decoding: hardware and software. A hardware decoder requires a PCI adapter and less work is put on the computer's CPU because the adapter does the decoding. The adapter decodes both video and audio. This solution is good for slower computers. Figure 2.105 shows how a hardware decoder connects to a DVD drive.

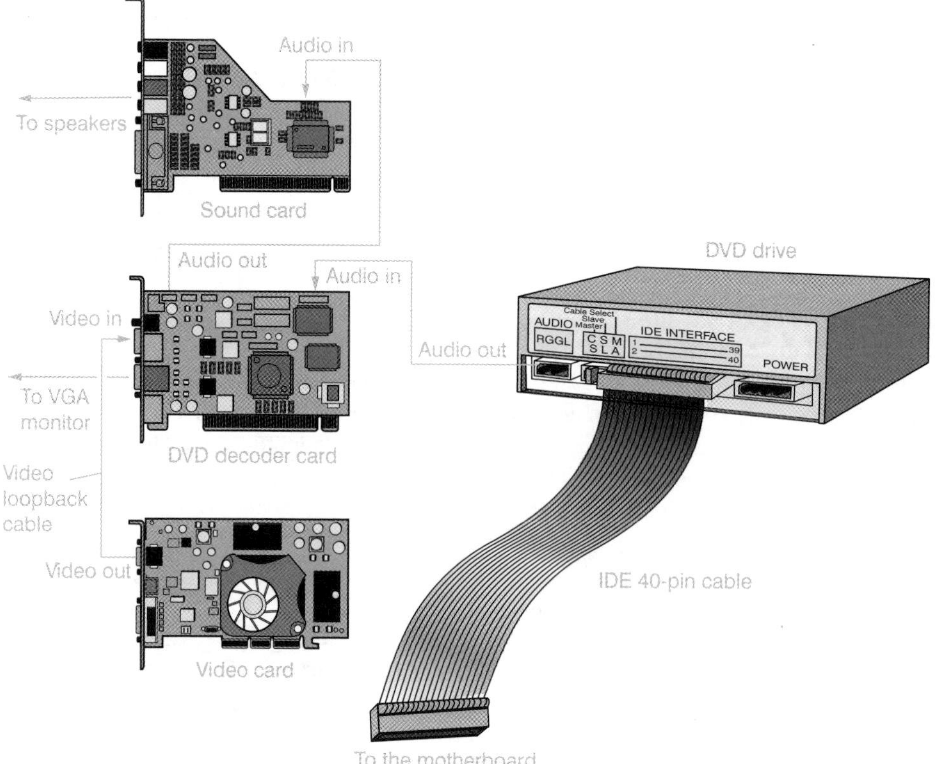

Figure 2.105 DVD data flow

A **software decoder** does not need a PCI adapter, but CPU power is needed. A 400MHz processor is the minimum to use. Software decoders provide varying playback quality. The installed video adapter must support DirectX's overlay mixers in order to do software decoding. Most video cards now include this feature but not all do.

Some software decoders require an AGP or PCI-E video card, or their performance is weak. Software decoding also requires a PCI/PCI-E or integrated sound card that supports 48KHz decoding for DVDs.

DVD Region Codes

To protect DVD software, movies, and audio, a DVD drive has a **region code**. The world is divided into six regions and the DVD drive must be set for the correct region code or else the DVDs made for that area do not work. When a DVD is inserted, the decoder checks what region it is configured for (or in the case of software decoding, what region the drive is configured for) and then checks the DVD region code. If the two match, then the movie plays. Table 2.39 shows the region codes.

Table 2.39 DVD region codes

DVD region code	Geographic area
1	United States and Canada
2	Europe, Near East, Japan, and South Africa
3	Southeast Asia
4	Australia, Middle America, and South America
5	Africa, Asia, and Eastern Europe
6	China

Some DVD drives do not require this setting (it is region free). The current standards allow five region changes before the drive is locked. If you have a hardware decoder, make sure that you configure it for the appropriate region. If you are using software decoding, the program must be configured for the correct region and it too normally allows five changes. There are freeware programs on the Internet to check the drive for its region requirements without incrementing the number of times the region code has been changed.

Other DVD Technologies

In addition to DVD-ROM, there are other types of DVD technologies currently in the marketplace: DVD-RAM, DVD-R, DVD+R, DVD-RW, DVD+RW, DVD±RW, DVD-R DL, and DVD+R DL. DVD-ROM is the most common, but that is changing. Compatibility with the various CDs and DVDs are issues to be aware of today.

Several technologies have been developed to write on the disk to label it without having to apply a paper label. LightScribe by Hewlett-Packard, DiscT@2 by Yamaha, and LabelFlash (introduced by NEC using DiscT@2 improvements) are three such technologies. Table 2.40 shows these technologies.

DVD Book Types

At the beginning of every DVD is a field where four bits define the type of DVD format the disc will use. A DVD drive reads this field to determine whether or not the drive can read the disc. The book type field values are as follows: DVD-ROM 0000, DVD-RAM 0001, DVD-R and DVD-R DL 0010, DVD-RW 0011, DVD+RW 1001, DVD+R 1010, DVD+RW DL 1101, and DVD+R DL 1110.

Table 2.40 DVD technologies*

Technology	Explanation
DVD-RAM	These discs are incompatible with older DVD-ROM drives, but look for the MultiRead2 capability. Discs include the following: 2.6 and 4.7GB (one side) and 5.2 and 9.4GB (two sides). Can usually write to a DVD-RW disc and can read them.
DVD-R	Uses WORM technology. Can record one time and uses one or two sided discs. Has capacities of 3.95, 4.7, and 9.4GB. Sometimes two different types are shown: DVD-R(A) and DVD-R(G). The DVD-R(A) targets the authoring business for professional development of DVDs. The DVD-R(G) is more for home users and lay people.
DVD+R	Can record (one time per disc) up to 4.7 or 9.4GB on single-sided DVD+R discs.
DVD-RW (DVD-Rewritable)	Similar to DVD-R except you can erase and rewrite data. Uses 4.7 or 9.4GB discs and most DVD-ROM drives and DVD-Video players support this format. Sometimes known as DVD-R/W or DVD-ER.
DVD+RW	Backward compatible with DVD-ROM drives and DVD video players. Discs hold 4.7 or 9.4GB per side. Reads most CD, DVD, DVD-R, DVD-RW, and DVD+R DL discs. Writes to CD-R, CD-RW, DVD+R, and DVD+RW discs.
DVD±RW	Reads most CD, DVD, and DVD+R DL discs. Writes to CD-R, CD-RW, DVD+R, DVD-R, DVD-RW, and DVD+RW discs.
DVD-R DL (dual layer)	Similar to DVD-R except it uses double-layered discs to store up to 8.5GB.
DVD+R DL	Similar to DVD+R except it uses double-layered discs to store up to 8.5GB.

*The formats shown with a + (plus sign) are supported by the DVD+RW Alliance. The formats shown with a – (minus sign) are supported by the DVD Forum.

Blu-ray Drives

Blu-ray is a development in optical disc technology that uses blue-violet laser technology rather than the red laser technology currently used by CD/DVD drives. Blue-violet laser technology has a shorter wavelength, which means that smaller data pit sizes can be used to create higher disk capacities. This laser technology is also more expensive than red laser.

Blu-ray has a higher data transfer rate (36Mbps) compared to DVD (10Mbps) and stores 25GB on a single-sided disc and 50GB on a dual-side disc. Blu-ray drives frequently have the Blu-ray symbol on them, as shown in Figure 2.106.

Figure 2.106 Blu-ray logo

Blu-ray was developed by industry leaders—Apple, Dell, Hitachi, HP, JVC, LG, Mitsubishi, Panasonic, Pioneer, Philips, Samsung, Sharp, Sony, TDK, and Thomson. The target marked is for high-definition video and data storage. Blu-ray discs that can be written to once are known as BD-Rs and discs that are rewritable are known as BD-REs. Both have a 25GB capacity for single-layer discs and 50GB for dual-layer discs. Blu-ray discs have region codes. The A/1 code is used for North and South America, but most Blu-ray discs are region-free. Figure 2.107 shows a Blu-ray drive.

CD/DVD drives cannot read Blu-ray discs

Currently installed CD/DVD drives cannot read Blu-ray discs because CD/DVD drives use a red laser and Blu-ray drives use a blue-violet laser. Drives that have both lasers installed are available.

Figure 2.107 Blu-ray drive

CD/DVD Drive Interfaces and Connections

CD and DVD drives can use PATA IDE, SATA IDE, eSATA, USB, and IEEE 1384. In both desktop and portable computers, the IDE interface is the most common for internal devices and USB for external devices. The differences between these are great. The particular interface the technician recommends to the customer depends on several factors. The following questions will help customers decide what interface to use:

- Is the drive going to be an external device? If so, SATA, USB, and IEEE 1394 are the choices, and USB is one of the most popular.
- Is the drive going to be an internal device? If so, is price an issue? Internal drives can be PATA IDE, SATA IDE, or SCSI. Either of the IDE options is cheaper than SCSI.
- Does the customer plan to add more devices such as a scanner or tape backup unit in the near future? If so, SCSI, USB, eSATA, and IEEE 1394 have more expandability than IDE.

PATA IDE connectivity

When connecting a drive to a PATA IDE connector with a hard drive connected, verify that the CD/DVD device is configured as the slave or connected to the gray (middle) slave connector and cable select is configured. For the best performance, connect the CD/DVD drive as secondary master by putting it on a separate PATA interface from any installed hard drive(s) or use SATA.

CD/DVD Drive Upgrades

If the customer wants to upgrade a drive, find out why. Many times, slow access is due to other components in the computer, not the drive. Use the same questions listed previously for a new drive. If it is a slow CD drive, such as a 1x, 2x, 4x, or 8x drive, upgrade the drive but be sure the other parts of the computer complement the CD/DVD drive's performance. The following questions help when upgrading drives:

- Does the customer want sound (speakers)? If so, a CD/DVD kit that includes speakers might be the best solution. If the customer is an audiophile, then special speakers may be needed.
- Is there an available slot in the computer for a sound card? Also, check if there are sound connections built into the motherboard. If so, a sound card may not be needed. The sound card should use PCI or PCI-E and support 48KHz decoding if software decoding is being used.
- Is the customer going to be using discs that are video intensive? If so, what type of interface is the video adapter? AGP and PCI-E provide the best throughput and performance for video. How much memory is on the video adapter? If DVDs are being used, 8MB of memory should be the minimum amount installed on the video card. DVDs require that the video adapter support DirectX's overlay mixers if software decoding is being used.
- Does the customer have enough RAM on the motherboard for the type of disc used?
- In order to achieve the best DVD effects, connect a sound system that accepts digital audio input and supports Dolby Digital surround sound.

Preventive Maintenance for CD/DVD Drives and Discs

Handling CDs and DVDs

Always handle a disc by the edges and keep the disc in a sleeve or case. Proper handling of the disc aids in good performance. As with audio CDs, handle the disc on the outside edge of the disc. Never touch the surface of the disc, and store the disc in a cool location.

When LP records were used, handling of the records was quite a problem. Fingerprints, dust, and dirt negatively affected the performance of the record. CDs and DVDs are less prone to these problems because they have a protective coating over the aluminum alloy-based data layer.

When reading information, the laser beam ignores the protective coating and shines through to the data layer. Even if the disc has dirt on the protective coating, the laser beam can still operate because the beam is directed at the data layer rather than the disc surface. An exception to this is surface material with reflective properties. The reflection could reflect and distort the laser beam, thus causing distortion or data corruption. Another exception is if the dust or dirt completely blocks the laser beam. A heavy accumulation of dust and dirt can reduce the quality of the data retrieved from the disc. Special cleaning discs, cloths, and kits are available for cleaning CD/DVD disks.

Cleaning CDs and DVDs

When using the cleaning cloth, wipe the disc from the inside (near the center hole) to the outside of the disc (*not* in a circular motion) on the side of the disc that has data. (If you cannot tell, wipe both sides.)

If a disc is scratched, mild abrasives or special disc repair kits are available. Examples of mild abrasives include plastic, furniture, or brass polish. When applying the abrasive, do not rub in circles. Instead, use the same technique as cleaning: start from the innermost portion of the disc and rub outward. The abrasive can remove the scratch if it is not too deep. A wax such as furniture or car wax can be used to fill the scratch if it is not removed by the abrasive.

A special component of the CD/DVD drive, the **laser lens** (also known as the objective lens), is responsible for reading information from the disc. If the laser lens gets dust, dirt, or moisture on it, the drive may report data or read errors. Some drives have the lens encased in an airtight enclosure and others have a self-cleaning laser lens. If the drive does not have this feature, laser lens cleaning kits are available at computer and music stores. Also, the laser lens can be cleaned with an air blower like ones used on a camera lens. Cleaning the laser lens should be a preventive maintenance routine. Some drive manufacturers include a special plate to keep dust away from the internal components. In any case, keep the disc compartment closed to prevent dust and dirt from accumulating on the laser lens and other drive parts.

CD/DVD Drive Installation

The following steps for installing an internal drive are similar to installing any drive:

1. Install any necessary mounting brackets onto the drive.
2. Check what interface (PATA IDE, SATA IDE, or SCSI) the drive uses. Set the appropriate master/slave, SCSI ID, or termination according to the drive interface type, if necessary. Refer to the documentation included with the drive for the proper configuration of these settings.
3. Turn off computer power and optionally install the appropriate adapter into the system if necessary.
4. Install the drive into the computer.
5. Attach the power cable from the power supply and interface cable from the drive to an adapter or motherboard.
6. (Optional) Attach the audio cable from the drive to the motherboard or sound card.

Some PATA IDE drives are pre-configured as the slave device

Always check the drive's master/slave/cable select setting and refer to the drive documentation for configuration issues.

The drive is now installed, but is not operational until software drivers are installed properly and the drive is tested by reading from it or writing to it. Refer to the manufacturer's installation instructions.

External drives can be USB, IEEE 1394, eSATA, or a combination of any or all of these three technologies. For external USB or eSATA CD/DVD drives, attach the drive to external power if necessary. Some USB devices require external power; others take two USB ports. Attach the USB cable from the drive to the USB port or hub. Many manufacturers also include software tools that can be installed once the drive is operational. Some manufacturers may require you to install provided software before attaching the drive. Once installed, use Device Manager to ensure the drive is recognized by the operating system. Test the drive.

For external FireWire connectivity, attach external power to the drive if necessary. Install the manufacturer provided software, which frequently includes the driver. Attach the FireWire cable between the FireWire port and CD/DVD drive. Once installed, use Device Manager to ensure the drive is recognized by the operating system. The drive may appear under the IEEE 1394 Devices section. Test the drive.

Always test the installation

As with any hardware installation, test the installation by using the device. Ensure the customer tries the device and is comfortable with the changes caused by the installation.

Laptop CD/DVD Drive

Many laptop computers have drive bays that allow storage devices to be exchanged. PATA or SATA IDE interfaces are commonly used for internally mounted drives including CD/DVD drives. Usually these drive bays have a lock on them that prevents the drive from sliding out. Slide the lever to one side and the drive can be removed. Different laptop models use different part numbers and models for removable CD/DVD drives. Laptops sometimes have removable CD/DVD internal

Minimum requirements to play video on a laptop

In order to play video DVDs on a laptop, your computer must be faster than 400MHz and have at least an MPEG-2 decoder. This can be integrated into your computer as hardware or software that comes with your DVD player application.

drives, and some of them are hot swappable. Always refer to the laptop manufacturer's documentation before removing the drive with power applied. Laptops sometimes have slot-loaded CD/DVD drives. Such a drive does not have a tray that holds the disc. Instead, the disc inserts into a slot, similar to that in an automobile CD player. Figure 2.108 shows a laptop with a removable drive bay.

Figure 2.108 Laptop CD/DVD removable drive bay

To access an internally mounted drive, the keyboard is frequently removed to access the drive. Always refer to the laptop manual for instructions on replacing a drive.

For external notebook connectivity, use a USB or IEEE 1394 connection. USB is the most common. The external device can be attached with power applied and can be used with other portable computers.

Troubleshooting CD/DVD Drive Problems

Windows XP and Vista have troubleshooting tools in the Help and Support Center:

1. Click *Start* and select *Help and Support*
2. Select the *Fixing a problem* Help topic (XP) or *CDs* and *DVDs* (Vista)
3. Select the *Games, Sound, and Video Problems* link (XP) or an appropriate topic (Vista)
4. In the right panel, use the *Games and Multimedia Troubleshooter* link (XP)

Check the easy stuff first

Verify a CD/DVD disc is inserted in the drive. Ensure the disc is inserted correctly (label-side up). Test the disk in another drive. Verify that the drive has a drive letter assigned by using the *My Computer* desktop or *Explorer* icon. If no drive letter is present for the device, check power and cabling and configuration settings. If a drive letter is available, use Device Manager to see if any resource conflicts exist. Update the driver if a new service pack has been installed.

The following is a list of problems with possible solutions or troubleshooting recommendations:

- If a drive tray cannot be opened, make sure there is power attached to the drive. Some drives have an emergency eject button or a hole that you can insert a paper clip to eject the disc.
- If a CD or DVD drive is not recognized by the operating system, check cables, power cords, and configuration (master/slave, cable select, port enabled in BIOS).
- If a CD or DVD drive busy indicator light flashes slower than normal, the disc or the laser lens may be dirty. Refer to the manufacturer's Web site for their recommendations on cleaning the laser lens. See the Preventive Maintenance section for details on how to clean a disc.

- If a CD/DVD drive cannot read a disc, refer to the drive manual to see what discs are supported. Not all disc formats are supported by all drives. Ensure the disc label is facing up. You may need to install a software application for the particular disc being used. Ensure the disc is clean and without scratches.
- If a CD-R or CD-RW drive is not recognized as a recordable device (if you view the properties and you don't have a *Recording* tab), a registry edit is required. Locate the Microsoft resolution.
- If a DVD sound track works, but the video is missing or distorted, check the cabling between the video adapter and DVD decoder. Verify the video drivers and that the video adapter supports DVD playback. Set the display resolution to a lower resolution and number of colors using the *Display* control panel.

If a CD or DVD doesn't work properly

Try the disc in another machine or try a different disc.

- If a DVD movie suddenly stops playing, the DVD may be double-sided and needs to be flipped over. Also, make sure that you have not paused the movie and check the video resolution settings.
- If you receive an illegal DVD region error or region code error, change the region.
- If a DVD drive only reads CDs, then the most likely problem is with bus mastering or the DVD drivers. Go to the manufacturer Web site for the latest drivers.
- Many DVD problems are solved by (1) reinstalling DirectX or obtaining the latest version of DirectX, (2) installing the latest drivers for the DVD drive, video adapter, and sound card, or (3) changing the screen resolution if it's too high. A computer should have approximately 80 percent free system resources when playing DVDs. For optimum performance, do not multitask (have other applications loaded).
- If you add DVD to a system, be careful that the video adapter can handle DVD playback. Sometimes a DVD player error occurs stating that you have low video memory. Make sure the latest video card drivers are loaded. If playback is still a problem, adjust the video card refresh rate to a lower value.
- When troubleshooting Windows XP multimedia applications and devices, two tools are handy—Sounds & Multimedia or Sounds and *Audio Devices* control panel and the DirectX Diagnostic tool. The *Hardware* tab contains a *Properties* button and a *Troubleshoot* button. Under the device section, click (right or double) on the device you want to check. The *Properties* button shows the version of driver being used. Windows XP allows the driver to be rolled back to a previous version with this option. The *Troubleshoot* button helps when diagnosing a specific multimedia device.
- A misapplied label on the disc can cause problems with the disc being read. Peeling labels can also cause insertion/ejection problems.
- If you cannot hear sound when playing a DVD, but you can when playing a CD. If your computer meets hardware and software requirements for DVD playback, obtain the latest DVD driver from your PC manufacturer (if the drive shipped with the computer) or from the DVD drive manufacturer.
- If your computer meets hardware and software requirements for DVD playback, your video driver may need updating. Also, if your video disappears or turns a different color, turn off video overlays. In Windows Media Player, select *Options* from the *Tools* menu. Select *Performance* tab, *Advanced* button, and in the Video Acceleration area, uncheck the *Use overlays* checkbox.

The DirectX Diagnostic Tool is used in troubleshooting multimedia devices and DirectX drivers. You can view the driver, view system information, and test multimedia devices with this tool. Access the DirectX Diagnostic tool by clicking *Start*, accessing *Run*, typing *dxdiag* and pressing Enter in XP. In Vista, select *Start*, select *Help and Support*, type **dxdiag**, and press Enter. Select the *DirectX Diagnostic Tool* link.

You can see video, but you can't hear sound or vice versa

Verify that your computer has the hardware and software requirements for DVD playback.

Other Peripherals

Video Overview

Video quality is very important to computer users. The monitor, which displays the data, is one of the most expensive computer components. Users usually derive the most gratification from their monitor, although sound quality is now becoming as important. Technicians must look at video as a subsystem that consists of the monitor, the electronic circuits that send the monitor instructions, and the cable that connects them. The electronic video circuits are on a separate video adapter or built into the motherboard. Figure 2.109 illustrates a computer's video subsystem.

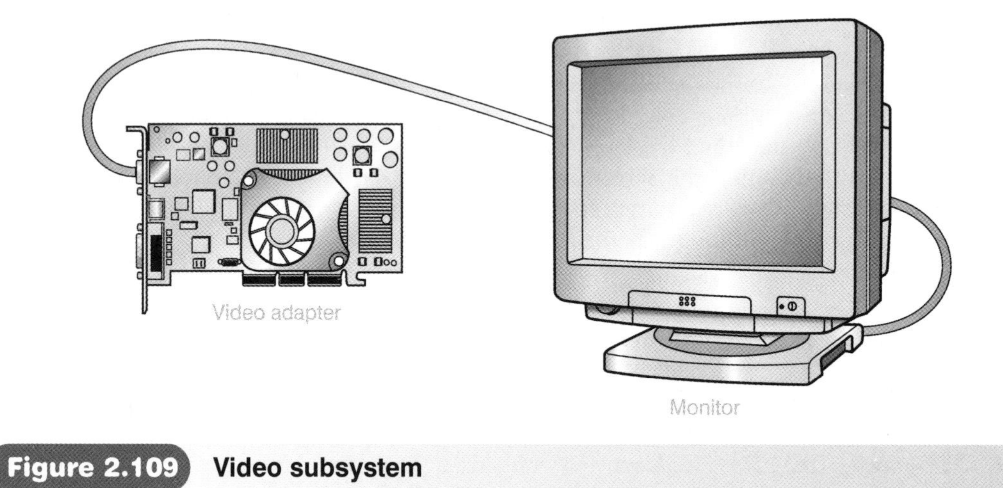

Figure 2.109 Video subsystem

Types of Video Output Devices

Video output devices such as monitors and projectors are commonly used with desktop and laptop computers. Monitors can be classified several ways—color or non-color, analog or digital signals used to produce colors, and the type of video adapter used. The easiest way to classify video output is by the way in which the output is created—the technology. Table 2.41 lists some of the most popular display output technologies.

Other technologies used in video output include LCoS, SED, FED, OLED, and plasma. LCoS (liquid crystal on silicon) is similar to DLP except that it uses liquid crystals instead of mirrors for higher resolutions. SED (surface-conduction electron-emitter display) and FED (field emission display) technologies are similar: both use electron emitters to energize color phosphor dots to produce an image. The electron emitter used is what makes them different. An OLED (organic light-emitting diode) display does not require a backlight, like LCDs. An OLED has a film of organic compounds placed in rows and columns that can emit light.

Recycle CRTs

CRTs contain toxic substances that can cause health risks to humans if CRTs are disposed of improperly. Consider donating a CRT or using a Web site such as www.crtusedmonitors.com instead of throwing it away.

Plasma displays work very similarly to LCDs, except that they have plasma gas in little chambers. When electricity is applied inside the chambers, excited electrons hit red, green, and

Table 2.41 Video output technology

Technology	Description
CRT	CRT (cathode ray tube) monitors are the traditional-looking monitors. They are bulky and resemble TVs. A CRT monitor has three color beams (red, green, and blue) directed at a phosphorous dot on the back of the monitor tube. The phosphorous dot is a **dot triad** (three colored dots grouped together). The result is a single image on the screen called a **pixel**, or picture element. Figure 2.110 shows how that dot triad makes a pixel. Dot pitch is the distance between like-colored phosphorous dots on adjacent dot triads. **Dot pitch** is measured in millimeters. The lower a monitor's dot pitch, the smaller the distance between the dot triads and the sharper the image. CRTs have been replaced with flat panel monitors or LCDs.
LCD	LCD (liquid crystal display) technology is used in laptops, flat panel monitors, TVs, and projectors. Two glass substrates have a thin layer of liquid crystal between them. One glass substrate is the color filter, with three main colors—red, green, and blue—that allow more than 16 million colors to be displayed on a screen. The other glass substrate is the **TFT** (thin film transistor) array, which has the technology to direct the liquid crystal to block the light. A **backlight** (that used to be a fluorescent lamp but now can be LED technology) extends behind the combined glass assembly, and the light is always on. This is why an LCD monitor appears to sometimes glow even when it's off and why crystals are needed to block some of the light to create the intensities of light. Liquid crystals are sensitive to temperature changes. Laptop displays may appear distorted in cold or hot temperatures due to the liquid crystals. Figure 2.111 shows the inside parts of an LCD monitor.
DLP	DLP (Digital Light Processing) is a technology used in projectors and rear projection televisions. It is also a trademark owned by Texas Instruments. DLP has an array of mounted miniature mirrors, one of which is smaller than the width of a human hair and represents one or more pixels. The mirrors are used to create a light or dark pixel on a projection surface by being repositioned to different angles to reflect light. A color wheel or LEDs are used for the primary colors red, green, and blue. Figure 2.112 illustrates the concepts of DLP technology.

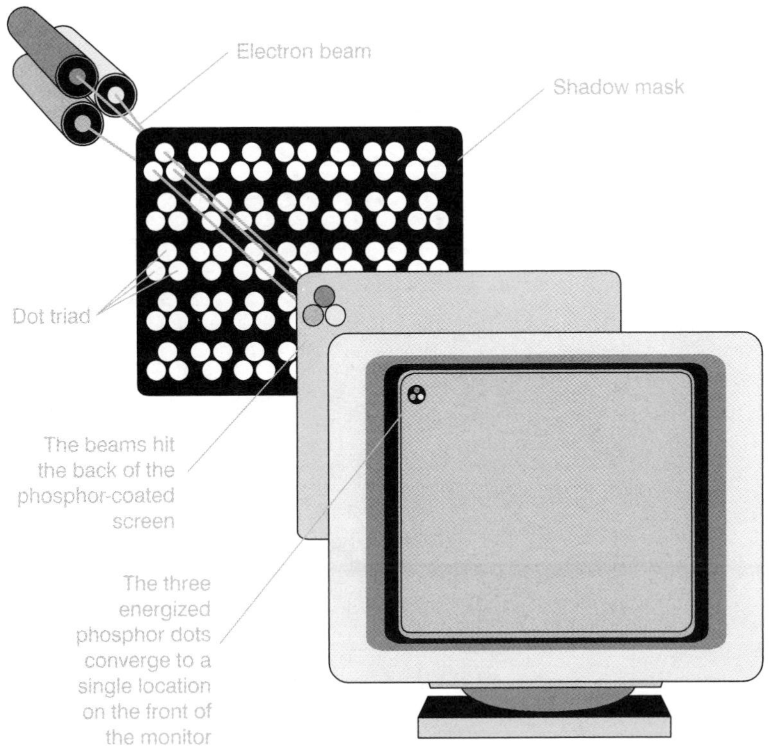

Figure 2.110 Video theory of operation

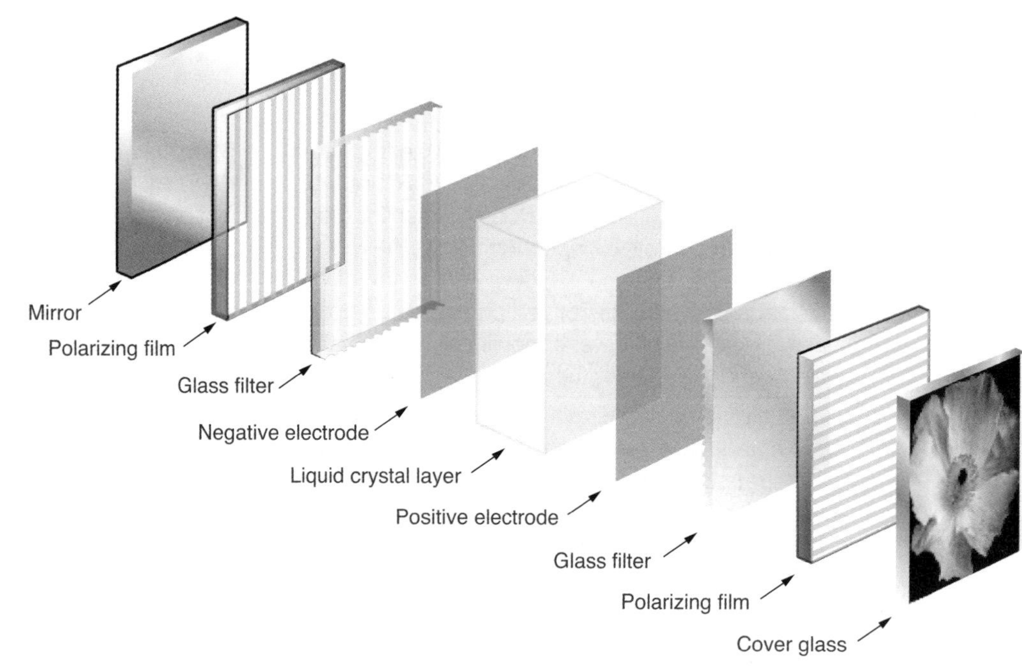

Figure 2.111 LCD technology

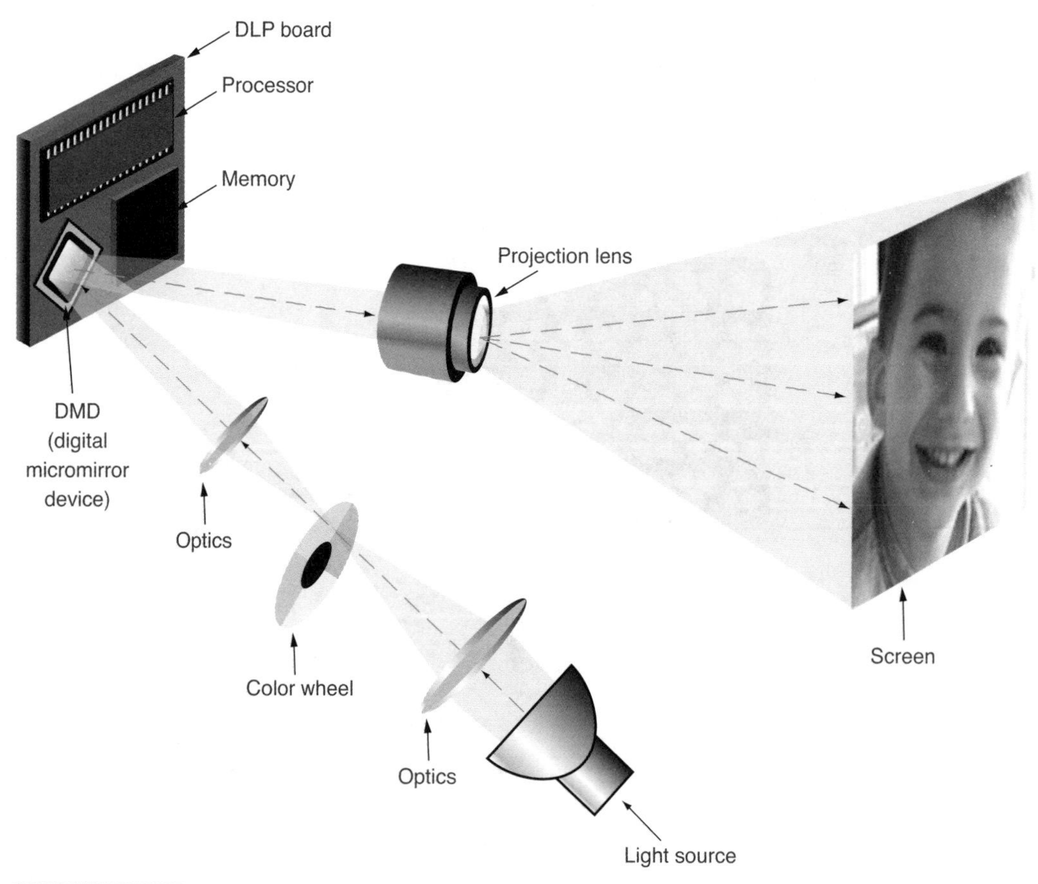

Figure 2.112 DLP technology

blue phosphorous dots that glow. Many believe that plasma displays require less energy than CRTs. This is not necessarily true. However, LCDs do take less energy than CRTs. Figure 2.113 shows the size difference when using CRT and LCD technologies.

Touch screen monitors connect to PCs and respond to contact on the screen rather than keyboard or mouse input. They are both an input and output device and are used in situations where information is to be controlled and in public areas such as kiosks in airports, malls, and entrance areas of schools or businesses. Touch screen monitors normally attach to a USB, IEEE 1394, VGA port, DVI port, a combination of these ports, or wirelessly. Special drivers and software are used to control the monitor.

The video adapter must match the monitor

One of the most important things to remember about video is that the video adapter must match the type of monitor. Video adapters that allow two or more video output devices to be connected can be purchased.

Figure 2.113 **Flat panel versus regular-sized monitor**

There are several technologies used to manufacture a touch screen monitor. The two most common ones are resistive and capacitive. Resistive touch screen monitors have a flexible membrane stretched over the face of the monitor. The membrane contains a special metal oxide coating and has spacers that are used to locate the touched spot on the screen. Resistive touch screen monitors are good in manufacturing or medical areas where the personnel wear gloves. A stylus pen can also be used with these types of monitors.

Capacitive touch screen monitors are more durable than resistive monitors. They respond to a touch on the screen and easily detect contact. Most touch screen monitors are the capacitive type. There are also some companies that make a touch screen that attaches to a regular monitor.

To install a touch screen monitor, attach the cable(s) to the appropriate port(s), install the software driver, and install the software that comes with the monitor. Always follow the manufacturer's instructions and, if possible, test the monitor using a variety of applications.

Video Terminology and Theory

Video has unique terminology associated with it. It is important for a technician to be familiar with video terminology. Let's start with an important term—resolution. A monitor's **resolution** is the maximum number of pixels on the monitor. Two numbers separated by an *x* (meaning *by*) describe a monitor's resolution, such as 640×480 (640 "by" 480). The first number, 640, is the number of pixels that fit horizontally across the screen. The second number, 480, describes the number of pixels that fit vertically on the screen. The possible monitor resolutions depend on the monitor and the video adapter. Table 2.42 shows terms used with resolution and the different modes that can be chosen for the display output. Table 2.43 lists important video features with which technicians need to be familiar.

Determining the number of pixels

To determine the number of pixels a display has, look at the resolution such as 1920×1200. Multiply the horizontal pixel number (the first number or 1920 in the example), by the vertical number of pixels, (the second number shown or 1200 in the example). The result is the total number of pixels or 2,304,000 (approximately 2.3 million pixels).

The monitor refresh rate is for a specific resolution. If the electron beam has to handle more pixels, it will naturally take longer. Video card capabilities are the main factor in determining what refresh rate the monitor uses, provided the monitor can perform it.

To set the refresh rate for the monitor on an XP computer, use the *Display* control panel. Select the *Settings* tab and click the *Advanced* button. Select the *Adapter* tab and click the *Refresh rate* down arrow. A listing of possible settings is displayed. The Optimal setting is the default. If you select another setting, click the *Apply* button and a warning message normally appears. Click the *OK* button and the monitor changes. A dialog box asks if you want to keep this setting. Selecting *No* will reset back to the default. If the mouse does not work or the mouse pointer does not appear on this screen, just press Enter and the *No* selection will be accepted.

Table 2.42 Video adapters/monitor types

Video adapter	Description
VGA (Video Graphics Array)	Connects to a 15-pin, three-row, female D-shell connector. Resolutions are up to 640×480. (Resolution is how many dots go across the screen and how many rows of dots there are. This is explained in greater technical detail later in the chapter.)
SVGA (Super VGA)	Not really a standard, but some monitor manufacturers advertise that they provide higher resolution than VGA. VESA (Video Electronics Standards Association) came up with a standard for this that covers resolutions up to 1280×1024.
UVGA (Ultra VGA)	Not really a standard, but usually refers to the 1024×768 resolution.
XGA (eXtended Graphics Array)	Developed by IBM to describe resolutions of 1024×768 and up to 64K of colors.
SXGA (Super XGA)	Describes resolutions up to 1280×1024 and over 16 million colors.
SXGA+	An improvement over SXGA to support resolutions up to 1400×1050.
UXGA (Ultra XGA)	Describes resolutions up to 1600×1200 and over 16 million colors. Sometimes used on powerful laptops and using applications that more of the screen needs to be seen (such as with a spreadsheet).
WXGA (Wide XGA)	Describes resolutions up to 1366×768 and over 16 million colors. There are variations called WSXGA or WUXGA. This is for those who like viewing wide screen DVDs on a computer monitor.
WUXGA (Wide UXGA)	Describes resolutions up to 1920×1200.
QXGA (quad XGA)	Describes resolutions up to 2048×1536.
QSXGA	Describes resolutions up to 2560×2048.
WQSXGA	Describes resolutions up to 3200×2048.
WQUXGA (wide quad ultra XGA)	Describes resolutions up to 3840×2400.
HXGA (hex XGA)	Describes resolutions up to 4096×3072.
HUXGA (hex ultra XGA)	Describes resolutions up to 6400×4800.
WHUXGA (wide hex ultra XGA)	Describes resolutions up to 7680×4800.

Table 2.43 **Video features**

Feature	Explanation
Refresh rate	In CRTs, the maximum times a screen is scanned or redrawn in one second. Measured in Hertz (Hz). An electron beam continuously sweeps left to right, scanning every row of pixels.
Horizontal scanning frequency	The speed that the beam traverses the screen to refresh the pixels. The rate for one line to be drawn. Determined by the video adapter and ranges from 35 to 90kHz.
Vertical scan rate	The number of times the electron beam draws from the top-left corner to the bottom-right corner and back again to the top left. A slow rate can cause a monitor to appear to flicker.
Multi-scan monitor	A monitor that can lock onto different vertical and horizontal scanning frequencies. Also called multi-synch or multiple-frequency.
Interlacing	A monitor that scans only the odd-numbered pixel rows. Then the electron beam returns and scans the even-numbered pixel rows. Causes a flickering on the screen.
Degauss	In CRT monitors, removal of a magnetic field that can build up around the monitor, causing distortion on the display. The method used to degauss depends on the manufacturer, but common methods include (1) power cycling the monitor; (2) using a degauss button located on the front of the monitor; and (3) accessing the monitor menu, using a front panel button, and locating the degauss option (which may be an omega symbol (Ω)).

To set the resolution in Vista, access the *Personalization* control panel and click the *Display settings* link. Use the *Resolution* slide bar and the *Colors* drop-down menu to customize the display. To adjust the refresh rate, click the *Advanced Settings* button in this window. Select the *Monitor* tab and use the *Screen refresh rate* drop-down menu to customize.

Monitors frequently have a button that allows a menu to be accessed or have several buttons used to adjust the image quality. Common buttons include the following:

- Power—Powers the monitor on or off
- Input—Available when both analog and digital (VGA and DVI) input connectors are on the monitor and used to select between the two
- Auto adjust—Automatically refines the monitor settings, based on the incoming video signal
- Brightness—Controls the intensity of the image or the luminance of the backlight on an LCD
- Contrast—Adjusts the degree of difference between light and dark
- Position—Moves or adjusts the viewing area by using horizontal and vertical controls
- Reset—Resets the monitor to default settings

Tech Tip

The higher the resolution, the smaller the pixel appears on the screen

Selecting a higher resolution will make the icons in Windows appear smaller. Many users do not know or understand this concept and set their resolution too high relative to their monitor size.

Use a 75Hz or greater refresh rate

An improperly configured refresh rate can cause monitor flicker, which can lead to headaches or eye strain. Usually, a 75Hz or greater refresh rate produces less flicker.

LCD (Liquid Crystal Display)

LCD is a video technology used with laptops and flat screen monitors that are powered by a low-voltage DC power source. They are more reliable and have a longer life span than CRT monitors. There are two basic types of LCD: passive matrix and active matrix. The difference between the two lies in how the screen image is created. A video on the LCD creation process can be found at http://www.auo.com/auoDEV/content/technology/technology_tftprocess_popup_en.htm.

The cheaper of the two, passive matrix, is made up of rows and columns of conductors. Each pixel is located at the intersection of a row and a column. (This is a similar concept to a cell in a spreadsheet.) Current on the grid determines whether a pixel is turned on or off. Each pixel has three cells in a color monitor: one for red, one for green, and one for blue. Another name for passive matrix is STN (SuperTwist Nematic), which is a technology that twists light rays to improve the display's contrast. Passive matrix displays are not as bright as active matrix displays.

Active matrix displays have a transistor for each pixel. The number of transistors depends on the maximum resolution. A 1280×800 resolution requires 1,024,000 transistors (1280 times 800 and more are added for color). This technology provides a brighter display (more luminance). Active matrix monitors take more power than passive matrix, but both of them require less power than CRT-based displays. Another name for active matrix monitors is TFT (Thin Film Transistor). TFT displays use three transistors per pixel (one for each color). Table 2.44 lists some common LCD terms and explanations.

Table 2.44 LCD characteristics

LCD characteristic	Explanation
Viewable size	The diagonal length of the LCD screen surface.
Native resolution	The optimum setting for an LCD, shown as the number of pixels that go across the screen followed by the number of pixels that go down the screen. Examples include 1024×768 and 1280×800.
Response time or synchronization rate	The time it takes to draw one screen (lower is faster and better).
Pixel response rate	How fast a pixel can change colors in milliseconds (lower number is faster).
Viewing angle	At certain angles, the LCD becomes hard to read. The viewing angle is the maximum angle that you can view the LCD and still see the image properly. Some displays have different viewing angles for horizontal and vertical perspectives.
Aspect ratio	A ratio of monitor width to height. Common monitor aspect ratios are 4:3 or 5:4, but new widescreen formats such as 16:9 or 16:10 are available.
Contrast ratio	The difference in light intensity between the brightest white and darkest black, but measured in different ways by manufacturers. A higher contrast ratio such as 800:1 is better than 500:1.
Portrait/landscape mode	Some monitors can be physically turned so that the edge of the monitor that is on the left is turned to be the top or bottom of the monitor.
Luminance	How much light the monitor can produce expressed in cd/m^2 (candelas per square meter) or nits. An example of a computer display is 50 to 500 nits (200 to 250 is acceptable for most users, but 500 is better if video clips or movies are used).
Dead pixel	The number of pixels that do not light up on an LCD due to defective transistors. LCD panels with dead pixels can still be used and are common. Dead pixels can be (and usually are) present on LCDs—even new ones. Research the LCD manufacturing standard from a particular vendor for dead pixels before purchasing an LCD.

LCDs do not have multiple frequency settings like CRTs do, nor do they flicker (no beam tracing across and down the screen). The number of pixels on a screen is a fixed amount. Manufacturers use image scalers to change LCD resolution. Pixelation is the effect caused by sending a different resolution out to the LCD than the monitor was designed for. The LCD

Set the LCD resolution to the native resolution

You can change the resolution for an LCD monitor through the *Display* (XP) or *Personalization* (Vista) control panel, but it is best if left to the resolution for which it was designed. Otherwise, the output will not be as sharp as it can be.

monitor must rely on interpolation or scaling of the output rather than having things displayed in the LCD native resolution (the optimum choice).

LCDs are found in the desktop and laptop computer markets. The desktop monitors that use this technology are called flat panel displays. With flat panel displays, the viewing area is the same as the LCD measurements (so no trick advertisements). Popular sizes include 14-, 15-, 17-, 18-, and 21-inch.

Laptops use LCDs and have a video cable that connects the LCD to the motherboard. A backlight bulb is used on many models so images on the screen can be seen. The bulb connects to an inverter. The inverter converts low DC voltage to high AC voltage for the backlight bulb. Figure 2.114 demonstrates this concept.

Liquid crystals are poisonous

Be careful with cracked LCDs. If liquid crystals (which are not liquid) get on you, wash with soap and water and seek medical attention.

Is it worth fixing a laptop display?

Most laptop LCDs are expensive to repair, but if it is the inverter that is faulty, it might be cheaper to repair than replace.

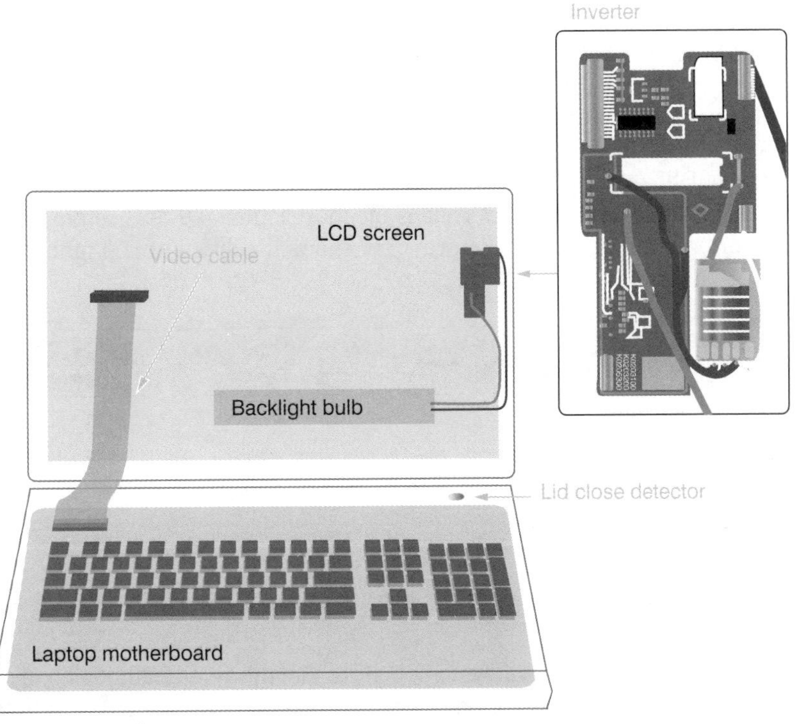

Figure 2.114 Laptop LCD video connectivity

The lid close detector can be a physical switch or magnetic switch located close to the back edge of the keyboard portion of a laptop. The laptop can be configured through power management configuration to go into hibernation or standby mode when the laptop is closed.

Video Ports

Flat panel monitors are digital, but some can work off an analog adapter (like the one most likely installed in your computer now). These digital monitors are more expensive, but offer better quality. The issue of colors with the old digital monitors is no longer relevant since the monitors use transistors to control colors. With the better flat panel monitors, you need an AGP or PCI-E adapter that has a **DVI** (Digital Video/Visual Interface). Figure 2.115 shows an adapter with VGA, DVI, and TV out ports. The DVI port is a 24-pin connector.

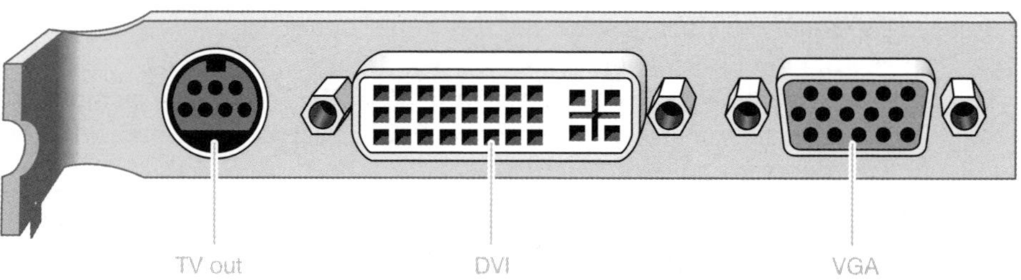

Figure 2.115 Video adapter with S-video (TV out), DVI, and VGA ports

Use a digital adapter for a flat panel monitor

Using an analog adapter is not recommended for connecting a flat panel display unless the flat panel accepts analog input. The computer uses digital signals. The digital signals get converted to analog at the video adapter, it is sent to the monitor as analog, and then the monitor has to convert it back to digital for the display output.

There are several types of DVI connectors and the one used depends on the type of monitor being connected. Two terms used with the connectors are dual link and single link. A **single link** connection allows video resolutions up to 1920×1080. With a **dual link** connection, more pins are available to send more signals, thus allowing higher resolutions for a monitor designed for it. The two major types of DVI are DVI-D and DVI-I. **DVI-D** is used for digital connectivity only. **DVI-I** is used for both digital and analog monitors and is the most common. A less common type is DVI-A, which is used for only analog output. Figure 2.116 shows the different DVI pinouts.

Figure 2.116 DVI connectors

Video adapter DVI connection must match the monitor DVI connection type

Be careful when installing a video subsystem. Ensure that the video card installed matches the DVI connection type for the monitor. Converters can be purchased to adapt to VGA.

Maximum DVI cable length is 5 meters

The specification for DVI states that the maximum cable length for DVI is 5 meters (approximately 16 feet) although there are longer ones available.

An upgrade to DVI is HDMI (High-Definition Multimedia Interface), which is a digital interface that can carry audio and video over the same cable. HDMI is already found on cable TV boxes and televisions, but is now appearing on video cards. Figure 2.117 shows a video adapter from XFX that has an S-video connector on the far left, an RCA jack, the HDMI connector, and a dual link DVI-I connector.

Figure 2.117 Video ports including an HDMI connector

The S-video connector shown in Figure 2.117 is called HDTV by the vendor for a connection to a TV, possibly a high-definition TV. The RCA jack is used for RGB connections (analog three color—red, green, blue) such as to a scanner or camera. Another type of connection you may see on a video card that is not very common is **component/RGB video**—three RCA jacks labeled YPrPb (Y is for the luminescence or brightness, Pr and Pb are for the color difference signals). This type of connection is of higher quality than the single RGB connection and is more commonly found on TVs, DVD players, and projectors.

Converting DVI to HDMI

A DVI to HDMI cable can be used to connect a PC with a DVI port to a device such as a home theater system or flat screen TV that has an HDMI port.

Some people like having two monitors connected to a single computer or two computers connected to a single monitor. To have two monitors connected to a single computer, you have several options.

- Use the two video ports on the motherboard (not common).
- Use the integrated motherboard port and buy a video card with one video port. (This is the cheapest solution, but the motherboard might disable the integrated video port automatically, and that setting has to be changed through BIOS.)
- Buy a video card that has two video ports (best option).
- Buy two video cards. (Usually the motherboard has one expansion slot for a video card, and that means using an older and slower technology expansion slot for the second video card.)

Once you install the monitor and Windows recognizes it (two monitors appear in Device Manager), right-click the Windows desktop and select *Properties* (XP) or the *Personalize and Display settings* link (Vista) followed by the *Settings* tab. Two displays are shown, with the numbers 1 and 2. An exercise at the end of the chapter demonstrates how to install two monitors.

Dual monitor modes of operation

You can have the same information shown in both monitors, extend your desktop across two monitors, or use dual view, where you can choose what items are on each desktop.

Another variation that some people or businesses want is the ability to use the same monitor (and sometimes mouse and keyboard) for two different computers. This is best done through a **KVM** (keyboard, video, mouse) **switch**, which allows one mouse, one keyboard, and one video output to be used by two or more computers. Many people would rather use software to do this function and remotely access the desktop of another computer. Windows calls this feature Remote Desktop.

A specialized use of video is with TV tuner cards and video capture cards. A **TV tuner card** allows TV signals to be brought into the computer and output to the monitor. Some TV tuner cards have the ability to record video. Figure 2.118 shows a photo of a TV tuner card.

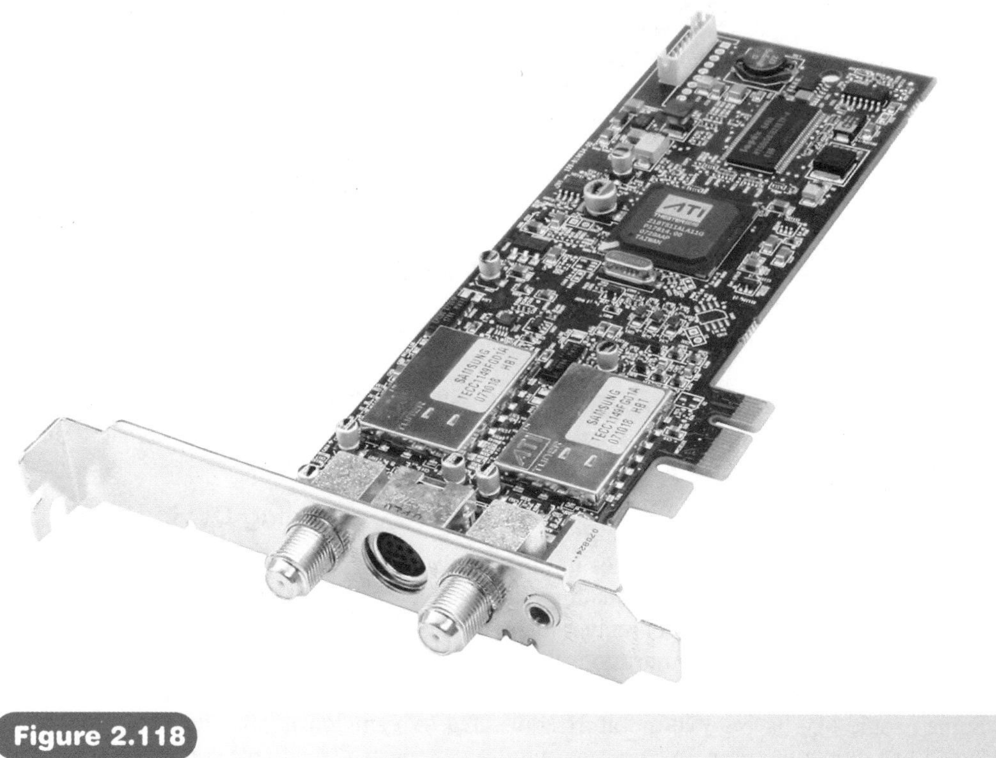

Figure 2.118

A **video capture card** usually has specialized software that allows video to be captured from a camera, tape, DVD, recorder, or live audio and video and manipulated into a presentation, an archived file, or a saved document or streamed onto the Internet. Not all video capture cards support audio. Video surveillance systems sometimes use video capture cards.

Another specialized use of video is SLI (scalale link interface) from Nvidia. SLI links two or more PCIe video cards to share processing on graphics-intensive operations.

Printers Overview

Printers are a difficult subject to cover because many different models exist (of course, that can be said about any peripheral); but the principles are the same for different categories of printers. The best way to begin is to look at what printers have in common. All printers have three subsystems: (1) the **paper transport** subsystem; (2) the **marking** subsystem; and (3) the **print engine** subsystem. Table 2.45 explains each of these subsystems.

Keep the three printer subsystems in mind when setting up a printer and troubleshooting it. Knowing how a specific type of printer places an image on the paper also helps when troubleshooting the printer.

Table 2.45 Printer subsystems

Subsystem	Explanation
Paper transport	Subsystem that pulls, pushes, or rolls paper through the printer. This can be done using a belt, tractor fee, or rollers. Some printers can even have a duplexer, which is an attachment option that allows printing on both sides of the paper.
Marking	Parts responsible for placing the image on the paper (also called the marking engine). This includes ribbons, ink (print) cartridges, toner cartridges, any moving part that is inside one of these, and anything else needed to print the image.
Print engine	The brains of the operation. It accepts data and commands from the computer and translates these commands into motion. It also redirects feedback to the computer.

Printer Ports

Printers connect to the parallel, serial, infrared, IEEE 1394 (FireWire), or USB ports. They can also connect through a wireless network. Most printers attach to a PC using the USB port. With USB printers, the USB host controller (built into the motherboard or on an adapter) powers up and queries all USB devices as to what type of data transfer they want to perform. Printers use bulk transfer on the USB, which means that data is sent in 64-byte sections. The USB host controller also assigns each USB a device so that the host controller can track them. Even though USB can provide power to smaller devices, a USB printer normally has its own power source.

USB is a good solution for printers because it is fast, and there are usually several ports available, or a hub can be added to provide more ports. USB uses only one interrupt for the devices connected to the bus.

Networked Printers

Many home users and almost all businesses use networked printers (printers that can be used by more than one computer). Printers can be networked using the following methods:

- A printer that is connected to a computer can be shared or made available to other computers through the Windows operating system. The other computers must be networked in some way.
- A printer can have a network card integrated into it or installed that allows it to participate as a network device. This includes wireless networks.
- A printer can attach to a device called an external **print server** (similar to attaching a printer to a computer) and the print server attaches to the network.

A networked printer can reduce costs. Laser printers can be expensive—especially ones that produce high speed, high volume, high quality, color output. Buying one printer and allowing users to access it from their individual desktops can be cost effective. It also reduces the amount of office or home space needed. Network printing is a viable alternative to using a computer's parallel or USB port.

Print servers are becoming quite common, even in homes. A print server connects to the network and allows any computer that is also connected to a network to print to it if the networks are the same or connected to one another. There are some print servers available that handle both wired and wireless connections. The print server attaches to a network switch and a network wireless router or wireless access point attaches to the same switch. Any PCs (wired or wireless) can print to the printer that attaches to the print server. Figure 2.119 illustrates this concept.

Wireless Printers

A PC can connect wirelessly to a printer using different methods: (1) the print server to which the printer connects can have wireless capabilities and wireless PCs can connect to the printer

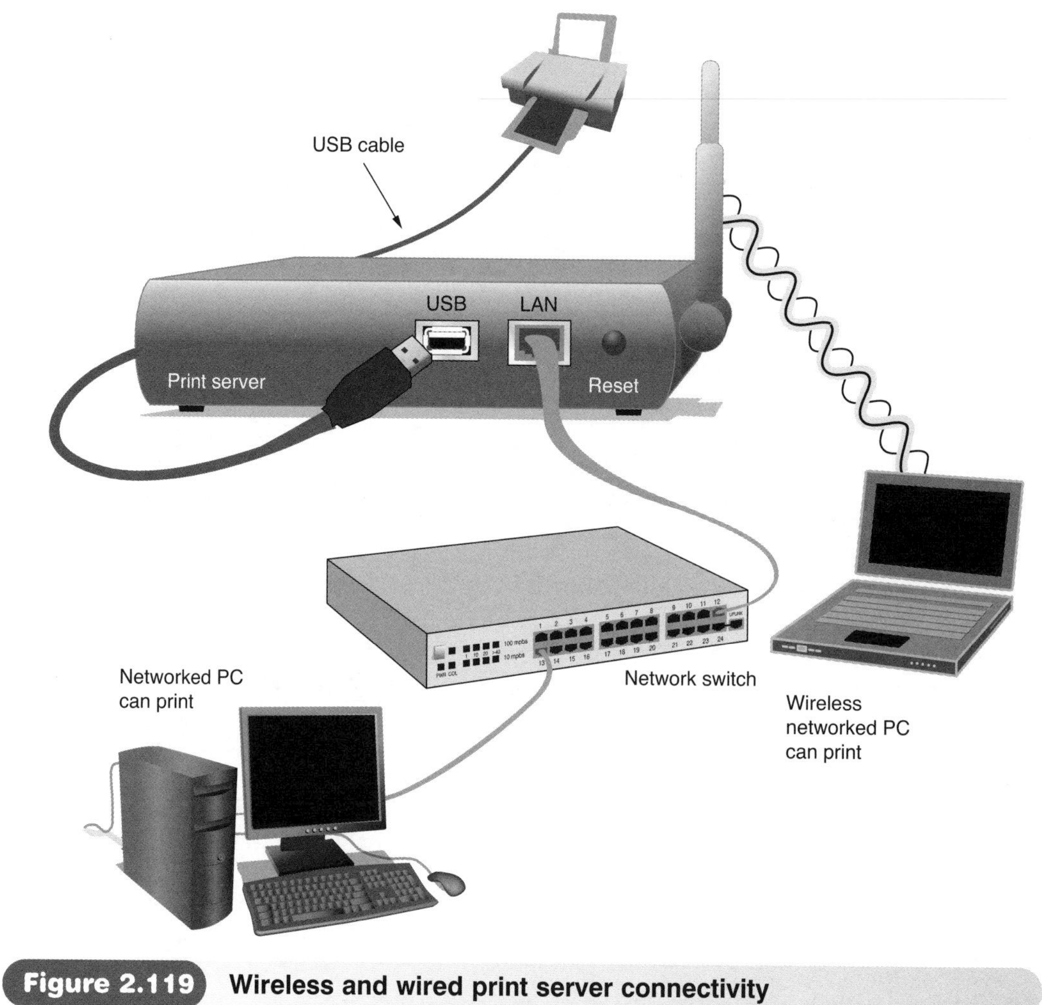

Figure 2.119 Wireless and wired print server connectivity

through the print server (as previously described and illustrated); (2) the printer can have a wireless NIC (network interface card) installed, attached via a USB port, or integrated and other devices on the wireless network can print to the printer; (3) the printer can have integrated Bluetooth capabilities or a Bluetooth adapter attached via a USB port. Printers with wireless capabilities are common, but the wireless adapter may have to be purchased separately.

Categories of Printers

Printers can be categorized according to how they put an image on paper. Printer categories are dot matrix, ink jet, and laser. There are more types, but these make up the majority of printers used in the workplace and home. Computer users normally choose a printer based on the type of printing they require. Table 2.46 describes the three major printer categories.

Each of the three basic printer types is discussed in greater detail in the next sections. The theory of operation for each printer type mainly concerns the marking subsystem.

Dot Matrix Printers

Dot matrix printers are called impact printers because of the way they create an image on the paper. They have a **printhead** that holds tiny wires called **printwires**. Figure 2.120 shows an Oki Data Americas, Inc. printhead. The printwires are shown on the front of the printhead. The printwires can get out of alignment and produce misformed characters.

Table 2.46 Printer categories

Type of printer	Description
Dot matrix	Good for text printing with multiple copies and can produce limited graphics. Uses ribbons, which keeps costs down. The only printer that can do multiple-part forms and supports the 132-column-wide paper needed by some industries.
Ink jet	Much quieter, weighs less, and produces higher-quality graphics than dot matrix. Uses a **print cartridge**, sometimes called an ink cartridge, that holds the ink used to produce the text and graphics; these cost $10 to $60 and last 100 to 200 pages, depending on manufacturer and print quality settings. Color can be done by dot matrix, but ink jet is best for color printing.
Laser	Produces the highest quality output at the fastest rate. Cartridges can cost $20 to $350. Common in the corporate network environment where users share peripherals. Used for graphic design and computer-generated art where high quality printing is a necessity. Some can produce color output, but at a much higher cost. Some even have stapling capabilities like copy machines.

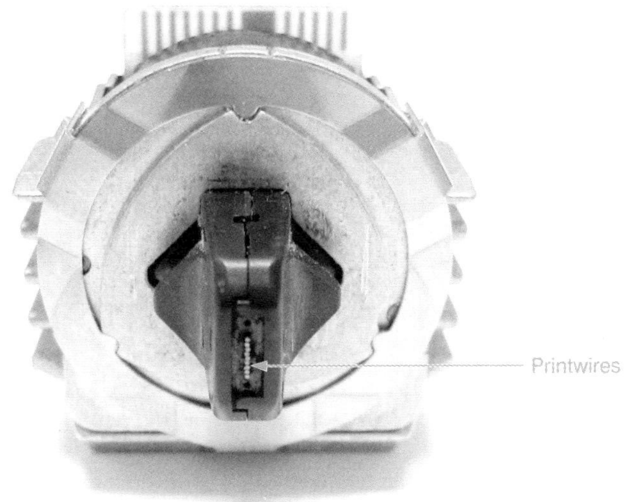

Figure 2.120 Dot matrix printhead

The wires individually strike a ribbon hard enough to create a dot on the paper. The dots collectively form letters or images. The speed that the printhead can place characters on the page is its **cps** (characters per second) rating. The number of printwires in the printhead determines the quality of print; the more printwires, the better the print quality. The most common printwires are 9, 18, and 24. The 24-pin printers can print NLQ (near letter quality) output.

Each printwire connects to a solenoid coil. When current flows to the printwire, a magnetic field causes the wire to move away from the printhead and out a tiny hole. The print wire impacts a ribbon to create a dot on the paper. Figure 2.121 shows a dot matrix printhead. To show the individual printwires, the casing that covers the printwires has been removed from the illustration.

Each wire connects to a spring that pulls the printwire back inside the printhead. The images created are nothing more than a series of dots on the page. Dot matrix printers are impact printers because the printwire springs out of the printhead. The act of the printwire coming out of the printhead is called pin firing. The impact of the printer physically striking the ribbon, which in turn touches the paper, causes dot matrix printers to be noisy.

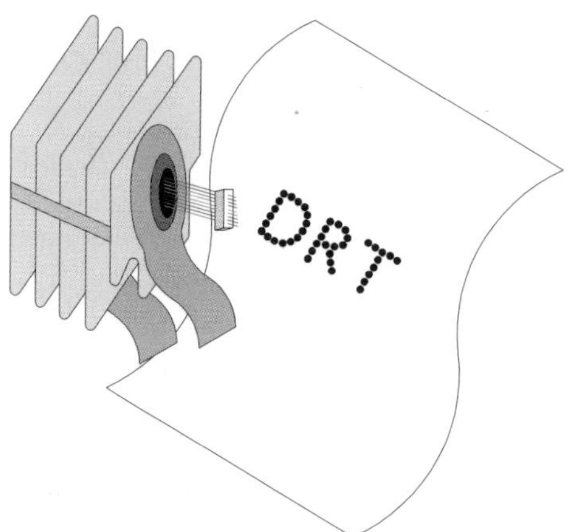

Figure 2.121 Dot matrix printhead operations

Because the printwire impacts the ribbon, one of the most common points of failure with dot matrix printers is the printhead. It can be expensive to replace printheads frequently in a high-usage situation; however, refurbished printheads work fine and they are available at a reduced price. The companies who refurbish them usually replace the faulty wires and test the printhead thoroughly.

Dot matrix printers are the workhorses of printers. One advantage to a dot matrix printer is that it will print multiple-part forms such as invoices, purchase orders, shipping documents, and wide forms. Multiple-part forms print easily on a dot matrix printer because the printer impacts the paper so very hard. The maximum number of multiple copies each dot matrix printer handles depends on the printer model. Laser and ink jet printers cannot produce multiple-part forms. They can only make multiple copies of the same document.

One direction is not a problem

Most dot matrix printers print bidirectionally. When the printhead gets too hot, the printer prints only in the left-to-right direction. This is normal.

Do not stack things on top of any printer, especially a dot matrix printer. The printhead gets hot and you should not add to the heat by stacking things on top of the printer. Keep the printer in a cool environment to avoid overheating. If the printer is used continuously, thus keeping the printhead hot, consider purchasing a second printer to handle the workload.

Ink Jet Printers

Ink jet printers are much quieter than dot matrix printers. They also have a printhead, but the ink jet's printhead does not have metal pins that fire out from the printhead. Instead, the ink jet's printhead has many tiny nozzles that squirt ink onto the paper. Each nozzle is smaller than a strand of human hair. Figure 2.122 shows a photo of a Hewlett Packard print cartridge.

Figure 2.122 Hewlett-Packard ink cartridge

One great thing about ink jet printers is that the printhead includes the nozzles and the reservoir for ink. When the ink runs out, you replace the entire printhead. The ink jet printer's printhead is known as the print cartridge. An ink cartridge has up to 6,000 nozzles instead of the 9-, 18-, or 24-metal pin configuration the dot matrix has. This is one reason why the ink jet quality is preferable to a dot matrix printer. Furthermore, with some manufacturers, the print cartridge is the printer printhead. Replacing the printhead, one of the most frequently used parts, keeps repair costs low but consumable costs are high. Two alternatives are for the manufacturers to use (1) a combination of a disposable printhead that is replaced as needed and a disposable ink tank, or (2) a replaceable printhead similar to the dot matrix printer. Figure 2.123 shows an expanded view of the front of the ink cartridge.

Run the calibration test when you install a new ink cartridge or as needed

Many ink jet printers have a calibration routine that automatically executes when a new cartridge is installed. Other manufacturers provide it as an option through the printer software or through the printer *Properties* window. If you find that the print output is not as clean and sharp as it should be, use this routine to adjust the print cartridge output.

Ink jet printers, also called bubble jet or thermal printers, use thermal (heat) technology to place the ink onto the paper. Each print nozzle attaches to a small ink chamber that attaches to a larger ink reservoir. A small amount of ink inside the chamber heats to a boiling temperature. Once the ink boils, a vapor bubble forms. As the bubble gets hotter, it expands and goes out through the print cartridge's nozzle onto the paper. The size of the ink droplet is approximately two ten-thousandths (.0002) of an inch, smaller than a human hair. As the small ink chamber cools down, suction occurs. The suction pulls more ink into the ink chamber for the production of the next ink droplet.

Figure 2.123 Ink jet cartridge nozzles

An alternative for producing the ink dots is to use piezo-electric technology, which uses pressure, not heat, to eject the ink onto the paper. Some companies use this technology to obtain 5760×1440 dpi and higher resolutions. **DPI** is the number of dots per inch a printer outputs. The higher the dpi, the better the quality of ink jet or laser printer output.

Be aware of optimized dpi

Many ink jet printers now show their dpi as optimized dpi. Optimized dpi is not describing how many drops of liquid are in an inch, but in a specific grid.

Most ink jet printers have different modes of printing. The draft mode uses the least amount of ink and the NLQ (near letter quality) mode uses the most ink. The quality produced by the ink jet printer is close to a laser printer, but in most high-end ink jet printers, the output is actually a higher dpi.

Color ink jet printers usually have a black cartridge for normal printing and a separate color cartridge for the colored ink or separate cartridges for each color. Buying an ink jet printer that uses a single cartridge for colors is cheaper on the initial printer purchase but more expensive in the long run. The black ink usually runs out much quicker than the colored ink. Users should buy an ink jet model with separate cartridges for black ink and colored ink.

There are some variations on the ink jet technology. Table 2.47 outlines three of them.

Table 2.47 Other printer technologies

Type of printer	Description
Solid ink	Sometimes called phase change or hot melt printers; uses colored wax sticks to create vivid color output. The wax stick is melted and sprayed through tiny nozzles onto the paper. The wax is smoothed and pressed as the paper is sent through rollers. The sticks can be installed one at a time as needed. The wax does not melt or bleed onto hands, clothing, or internal printer parts. It can print more colors, is faster, has fewer mechanical parts, and is cheaper than color laser printers, but is more expensive than normal ink jet printers.
Dye sublimation	Also known as dye diffusion thermal transfer printers; uses four film ribbons that contain color dyes. The ribbons are heated and applied to the paper. The quality is high, but the printers are expensive.
Thermal wax transfer	Uses wax-based inks like the solid ink printer, but prints in lower resolutions.
Large format ink jet	A wide printer to print large-scale media such as CAD drawings, posters, and artwork.

Inkjet printers are perfect for small businesses, home computer users, and individual computer office work. Some models of ink jet printers include faxing, scanning, copying, and printing capabilities. For higher output, the laser printer is more appropriate. A drawback to using ink is that sometimes the ink smears. Ink manufacturers vary greatly in how they respond to this problem. If the paper gets wet, some ink jet output becomes messy. The ink also smears if you touch the printed page before the ink dries. The ink can also soak into the paper and bleed down the paper. Using good quality paper and ink in the ink cartridge helps with this particular problem. Some manufacturers have a printer operation mode that slows down the printing to give the ink time to dry or a heating process to prevent smudges. See the section on printer supplies for more information on choosing the correct paper for different printers.

Laser Printers

The term *laser* stands for light amplification by stimulated emission of radiation. A laser printer operates similar to a copy machine's electrophotographic process. Before describing how a laser printer works, identifying the major parts inside the printer helps to understand how it works. Figure 2.124 shows a side view of a laser printer with a toner cartridge installed.

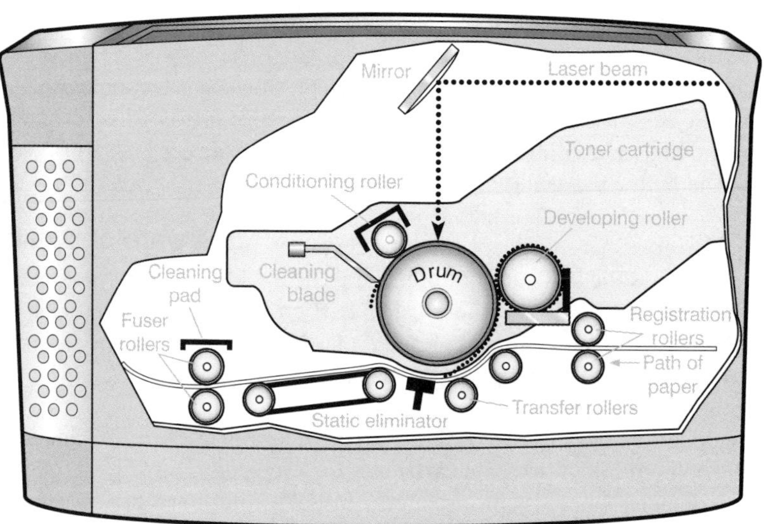

Figure 2.124 Laser printer parts

The computer sends 1s and 0s out the port and down the cable to the printer. Data transmits either through an array of LEDs or through a laser beam. The light beam strikes the photosensitive drum located inside the toner cartridge. Laser toner particles are attracted to the drum. The paper feeds through and the toner transfers to the paper. The toner is then fused or melted onto the paper.

Hewlett-Packard developed steps for the laser printing process. The six steps describe what happens when a laser printer prints a page. A computer technician must be familiar with the laser printing process to be certified and to troubleshoot laser printers. Table 2.48 lists the steps and explains them.

Tech Tip

Do not get burned when working inside a laser printer

Remember to allow a laser printer to cool down completely before working in the fusing roller area.

A **fuser cleaning pad** located above the top **fusing roller** lightly coats the roller with silicon oil to prevent the paper from sticking to the roller, which is often coated with Teflon. The cleaning pad also removes any residual toner from the roller. The cleaning pad is usually replaced when the toner cartridge is replaced. Figure 2.125 shows a fuser cleaning pad being removed.

Table 2.48 Laser printing process steps

Step	Description
Conditioning	Get the drum ready for use. Before any information goes onto the drum, the entire drum must have the same voltage level. The **primary corona** (main corona) is a thin wire located inside the toner cartridge. It has up to –6000vdc applied to it. A primary control grid is located behind the corona and it controls the amount of voltage applied to the drum's surface (approximately –600 to –1000 volts). Some manufacturers use a conditioning roller instead of a primary corona. No matter what method is used, the drum gets a uniform electrical charge.
Writing	Put 1s and 0s on the drum surface. Whether the printer uses a laser beam or an LED array, the light reflects to the drum surface in the form of 1s and 0s. Every place the beam touches, the drum's surface voltage reduces to approximately –100 volts (from the very high negative voltage level). The image on the drum is nothing more than dots of electrical charges and is invisible at this point.
Developing	Get toner on the drum (develop the image). A **developing cylinder** (or developing roller) is inside the toner cartridge (right next to the drum) and contains a magnet that runs the length of the cylinder. When the cylinder rotates, toner is attracted to the cylinder because the toner has iron particles in it. The toner receives a negative electrostatic charge. The magnetic charge is a voltage level between –200 and –500 volts. The magnetized toner particles are attracted to the places on the drum where the light beam strikes. A **density control blade** controls the amount of toner allowed through to the drum. The image is no longer transparent on the drum. The image is black on the drum surface.
Transferring	Transfer the image to the paper. A **transfer corona** (roller or pad) is located at the bottom of the printer. It places a positive charge on the back of the paper. The positive charge is strong enough to attract the negatively charged toner particles from the drum. The particles leave the drum and go onto the paper. At this point, the image is on the paper, but the particles are held only by their magnetic charge.
Fusing	Melt the toner onto the paper. Heat and pressure make the image permanent on the paper. The paper, with the toner particles clinging to it, immediately passes through fusing rollers or a belt that apply pressure to the toner. The top roller applies intense heat (350°F) to the toner and paper that literally squeezes and melts the toner into the paper fibers.
Cleaning	Wipe off any toner left on the drum. Some books list this as the first step, but the order does not matter because the process is a continuous cycle. During the cleaning stage a wiper blade or brush clears the photosensitive drum of any excess toner. Then an **erase lamp** neutralizes any charges left on the drum so the next printed page begins with a clean drum.

Laser printers *do* make weird noises

A laser printer frequently makes an unusual noise. The noise heard is the fusing rollers turning when the printer is not in use. Otherwise, the fusing rollers would have an indentation on one side. Users not familiar with laser printers sometimes complain about this noise but it is a normal function of the laser printer.

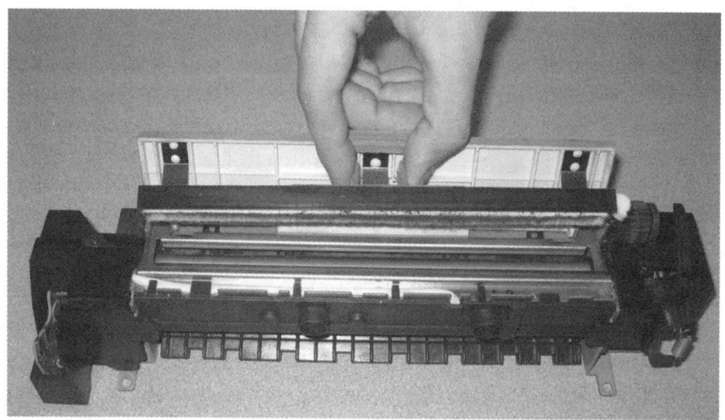

Figure 2.125 Fuser cleaning pad

Some books, manuals, and reference materials use the six phases of the electrophotographic process instead of Hewlett-Packard's (HP) terms. The six phases are listed in Table 2.49 with the equivalent HP terms. Keep in mind the same thing happens in each phase, only the terms differ.

Table 2.49 Laser printer process terms

Electrophotographic phase and term	Electrophotographic process	HP term
Phase 1 Charge	Charge the photoconductive drum	Conditioning
Phase 2 Expose	Expose the photoconductor	Writing
Phase 3 Develop	Develop the image	Developing
Phase 4 Transfer	Transfer the image onto the paper	Transferring
Phase 5 Fuse	Fuse the image to the paper	Fusing
Phase 6 Clean	Clean the photoconductor	Cleaning

Every laser printer that uses the six-phase process is known as a write-black laser printer. These laser printers produce a black dot every place the beam touches the drum. Most laser printers use the write-black technology. Write-white laser printers reverse the process and the toner attracts everywhere the light beam does *not* touch the drum surface. Write-black printers print finer details, but write-white laser printers can produce darker shades of black areas.

To help with the inundation of data, Table 2.50 lists the major parts of a printer with a short description of the purpose of each part.

Figure 2.126 shows a laser printer toner cartridge.

Table 2.50 Laser printer parts

Part	Purpose
AC power supply	The main power supply for the printer
Cleaning blade	Wipes away excess toner from the drum before printing the next page
Cleaning pad	Applies oil to the fusing roller to prevent sticking; also removes excess toner during the fusing stage
Conditioning roller	Used instead of a primary corona wire to apply a uniform negative charge to the drum's surface
Control panel assembly	The user interface on the printer
Density control blade	Controls the amount of toner allowed on the drum (usually user adjustable)
Developing cylinder	Rotates to magnetize the toner particles before they go on the drum (also called the developing roller)
Drum (photo-sensitive)	Accepts light beams (data) from LEDs or a laser; can be permanently damaged if exposed to light; humidity can adversely affect it
ECP (electronic control package)	The main board for the printer that usually holds most of the electronic circuitry, the CPU, and RAM
Erase lamp	Neutralizes any residual charges on the drum before printing the next page
Fusing assembly	Holds the fusing roller, conditioning pad, pressure roller, and heating unit
Fusing rollers	Applies pressure and heat to fuse the toner into the paper
High voltage power supply	Provides a charge to the primary corona or conditioning roller, which in turn puts a charge on the drum
Main motor	Provides the power to drive several smaller motors that drive the gears, rollers, and drum
Primary corona (main corona)	Applies a uniform negative charge to the drum's surface
Separation pad	A bar or pad in a laser printer that can have a rubber or cork surface that rubs against the paper as it is picked up
Scanner unit	Includes a laser or an LED array that is used to write the 1s and 0s onto the drum surface
Toner	Powder made of plastic resin particles and organic compounds bonded to iron oxide
Toner cartridge (EP cartridge)	Holds the conditioning roller, cleaning blade, drum, developing cylinder, and toner; always remove before shipping a laser printer
Transfer corona wire (transfer roller)	Applies a positive charge on the back of the paper to pull the toner from the drum onto the paper

Figure 2.126 Laser toner cartridge

Be careful working inside laser printers

Be very careful when working inside a laser printer. There are high voltages in various parts as well as high temperatures in the fusing area. Turn off the printer and let it cool down before servicing. Always remove power from the printer when possible.

A word about spilled toner

Toner melts when warmed; small toner spills outside the printer can be wiped using a cold, damp cloth. Toner spills in the printer require a special type of vacuum with special bags. Toner on clothing can normally be removed by washing in cold water. Do not put the clothing in a dryer if the toner is not yet removed.

Paper

The type of paper used in a printer can affect its performance and cause problems. Dot matrix printers are the most forgiving because a mechanism physically impacts the paper. On the other hand, ink jet printers spray ink onto the paper, so the quality of paper determines how well the ink adheres. If the paper absorbs too much of the ink, the printout appears faded. For the laser printer, how well the paper heats and absorbs the toner also affects the printed output. Paper is a big factor in the quality of how long color lasts and the quality of print produced.

Erasable bond paper also does not work well in laser printers because the paper does not allow the toner to fuse properly. Every type of paper imaginable is available for ink jet and laser printers: transparency paper for overhead projectors, high gloss, water resistant ink jet paper, fabric paper, greeting cards, labels, recycled paper, and so on. Recycled paper may cause printer jams and produce lower print quality.

The highest quality paper available does not work well if the surrounding area has too much humidity. Humidity is paper's worst enemy. It causes the paper to stick together and it reduces the paper's strength, which causes feed problems. Paper affected by humidity is sometimes noticeable because of the lumpy look it gives the paper. If you detect damaged paper, discard and recycle it immediately. For best printing results, keep paper stored in a non-humid storage area.

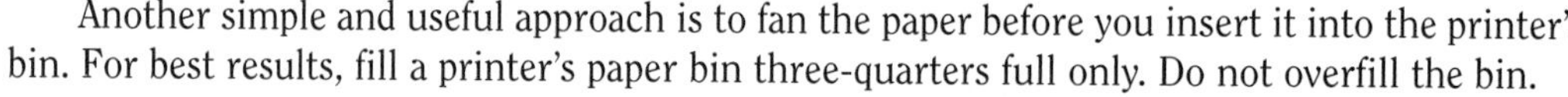

Another simple and useful approach is to fan the paper before you insert it into the printer's bin. For best results, fill a printer's paper bin three-quarters full only. Do not overfill the bin.

Paper options also relate to printers. Some dot matrix printers allow you to remove the normal paper feeder and attach a paper option that allows continuous paper to be fed through the printer. Both dot matrix and ink jet printers have special feeders or you move a slide bar to feed envelopes or unusual sized paper through. Laser printers sometimes ship with additional trays and must be configured for this option. Laser printers normally allow manual feeding and have a front cover that allows paper, labels, transparencies, and other unusual sizes and types of paper to be used.

How to control printer trays and manual feed options

The *Paper* tab on the printer *Properties* tab is commonly used to configure where you want the printer to look for paper to be used. Most printers also allow the default order in which the printer looks for paper to be configured through either the manufacturer-provider software, the printer *Properties* window.

Refilling Cartridges, Reinking Ribbons, and Recycling Cartridges

Much controversy exists when it comes to reinking dot matrix printer ribbons, refilling ink jet cartridges, or buying remanufactured laser cartridges. Many people who are concerned about the environment recycle their cartridges. Even if a company or an individual user decides not to purchase remanufactured products, some send their old empty cartridges to companies that do the remanufacturing. Refilling ink cartridges significantly lowers the printing costs.

If you refill the ink cartridges, add new ink before the old cartridge runs completely dry. If refilling ink cartridges, be sure the refill ink emulates the manufacturer's ink. Some ink refill companies use inferior ink that, over time, has a corrosive effect on the cartridge housing. A leaky cartridge or one that bursts causing ink to get into the printer is nothing but trouble.

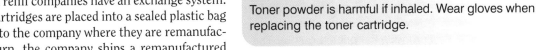

Beware of toner cartridges

Toner powder is harmful if inhaled. Wear gloves when replacing the toner cartridge.

Some ink refill companies have an exchange system. The old ink cartridges are placed into a sealed plastic bag and returned to the company where they are remanufactured. In return, the company ships a remanufactured cartridge filled with ink. If the empty ink cartridge sent to the company does not fit its standards criteria, the cartridge is thrown away. Some states have disposal requirements for ink jet cartridges.

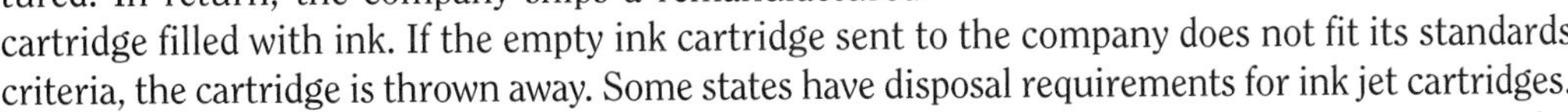

When it comes to laser cartridge remanufacturing, the most important components are the drum and the wiper blade that cleans the drum. Many laser cartridge remanufacturers use the same parts over and over again. A quality refill company will disassemble the cartridge and inspect each part. When the drum and wiper blade are worn, they are replaced with new parts. Some states have disposal requirements for laser printer cartridges.

Reinking a dot matrix printer ribbon is not a good idea. It can cause a mess and the ink is sometimes an inferior quality that causes deterioration of the printhead over time. Because dot matrix printer ribbons are so inexpensive, you should just replace them.

Print Drivers

How an application outputs to a printer is determined by the operating system used. A **print driver** is a small piece of software specifically written for a particular printer. The print driver enables the printer's specific features and allows an application to communicate with the printer. Windows applications use a single print driver—one written for the specific printer.

Use the latest driver from the printer manufacturer

Windows ships with various print drivers, all of which allow basic communication and access to the printer. For best results and performance, use the driver provided by the manufacturer or better yet, one downloaded from the Internet. Use the driver designed for the operating system installed.

Printers must accept as much data as possible from the computer, process that data, output it, communicate to the computer the need for more data, accept more data, and repeat the process. With Windows, a print spooler is used. A **print spooler**, or print manager, is a software program that intercepts the printer's request to print. Instead of going directly to the printer, the data goes to the hard drive. The spooler then controls the data from the hard drive going to the printer. Some printers come with their own print manager that replaces the one included with Windows.

The print spooler transmission retry option is the number of seconds the print manager waits before giving up on trying to send the printer more data. If the document contains multiple fonts, font sizes, or graphics, the transmission retry settings may need to be changed. For Windows, use the *Printers* control panel, right-click the specific printer, and select *Properties*. Note that the tab used to select options for transmission retry may vary between printer manufacturers.

Fonts

A font is a group of printable characters from a particular style such as Times New Roman, Script, Arial, and Courier. The font style refers to the appearance of the type such as bold or italic. The font size is in points such as 10pt or 12pt. The larger the point size, the larger the type appears on the paper. Point size is different from cpi (characters per inch). The larger the cpi, the smaller the font size. Table 2.51 explains the basic types of fonts.

Each printer has its own **PDL** (Page Description Language) that is a translator between the computer and the printer. The page description language handles the overall page look and has commands that treat the entire document as a single graphic. The two most popular page description languages are Adobe Systems Inc.'s **PostScript** and Hewlett-Packard's **PCL** (printer command language).

Table 2.51 Font types

Font type	Description
Raster	The most basic type and is nothing more than dots creating an image; dot matrix printers use raster fonts.
Vector	These are created from a mathematical formula. All characters are simply a series of lines between two points. Also known as outline fonts. The outline of each character is used to produce the printed output. The outline defines the shape of the character, but not the size. These are scalable, which means that the character can be created at any size.
TrueType	The most advanced type of outline (vector) font. Characters can be scaled (enlarged or shrunk) and rotated.

Watch out for PostScript drivers
If a document is created in a computer that has a PostScript printer driver loaded, and the document is taken to another computer without a PostScript printer driver, there is a good chance the document will not print properly.

GDI (graphics device interface) is the part of Windows that handles representing and transmitting graphical objects to output devices such as printers, monitors, and overhead projectors. In Windows XP, GDI+ is the improved model. It handles graphical images better as well as supports file formats such as JPEG and PNG. Windows Vista further upgrades GDI with **XPS** (XML paper specification) and documents sent to printers that support XPS will not have to be converted to a printer-specific language. XPS not only affects printing, but also document viewing. XPS is the replacement for **EMF** (enhanced metafile format), a graphics language for print drivers.

Printer Installation

A printer is one of the easiest devices to install. Always refer to the printer documentation for exact installation and configuration specifics. The following steps explain how to install a printer that attaches to a USB port:

1. Take the printer out of its box and remove the shipping materials. The number one cause of new printers not working properly is that all the shipping safeguards are not removed properly.
2. Connect the power cord from the printer to the wall outlet, surge protector, or UPS outlet. Note that most UPS units are not rated high enough for a laser printer to be connected to it.
3. Load paper and ribbon/ink/cartridge into the printer according to manufacturer's instructions. Most ink jet printers have a calibration routine that should be utilized as part of the installation routine.
4. Turn on the printer and verify that the power light is on.
5. Install the print driver by following the manufacturer's instructions for the particular operating system being used.
6. Attach the USB cable from the printer to the computer. Note that this cable might not be provided with the printer.
7. Configure options and default settings.
8. Perform a test print to verify communication between the computer and printer. Most ink jet printers have a calibration process that must be performed before normal printing. This calibration procedure is also performed when an ink cartridge is replaced.
9. Train the user on printer operation and leave all printer documentation with the customer.

Educate the user on printer functionality and print cartridges
As part of the installation process, ask the user to print something and show them any features with which they may not be familiar. Inform them that the cartridge that comes with the printer does not last long and that they should order a new one as soon as possible.

For a successful printer installation

The key to a successful printer installation is to read the printer documentation, use a good cable, load the latest printer drivers (from the manufacturer), and test. Many hours of frustration for the computer user and the technician can be avoided by doing the research during the install, not after a problem occurs.

Upgrading Printers

Printers can be upgraded in many ways, and the options available are vendor- and printer-dependent. The most common upgrades include memory and tray/paper feed options. The most commonly upgraded printers are ink jet and laser printers.

The most common upgrade for laser printers is memory. The amount of memory storage available for printers (especially those shared by multiple users) is very important because printing errors can occur with too little memory. It is also important to have some means of storage so that the documents can be sent and stored away from the computer that requested the print job. This frees up the computer's memory and hard drive space to do other tasks.

Printer memory upgrades

Many memory technologies are available for printers, but the common ones are RAM modules, flash memory, and PC Cards. These technologies are installed in the same manner they are installed into a computer. Always follow the manufacturer's installation instructions. Hard drives can also be attached to printers for additional storage.

The paper storage trays and feeders are another common upgrade. Laser printers frequently come with various paper storage tray options. When multiple people share a printer, a small capacity paper tray can be a nuisance. Ink jet printers often have different paper feed options relating to photograph printing. Paper designed for printing photographs is available in various sizes. Special paper feed options can be purchased that are mounted onto the printer for these rolls or different sizes of paper. With the increased popularity of digital photography, these printer options are quite popular.

Printer Preventive Maintenance

People sometimes forget to plug their printer into an uninterruptible surge protector (UPS). The printer can be damaged by electrical storms and power fluctuations just as a computer can. The laser printer AC power module and fuser assembly are especially susceptible to power problems. Protect any printer as well as the computer, but always make sure that the UPS has the ability to handle the higher power laser printer.

Dot matrix printers usually require cleaning more often than any other type of printer because they are frequently used for continuous fed paper or multiform paper and are often installed in industrial environments. Paper chafe, dust, and dirt cause an insulating layer of heat to the printer components, which causes them to fail faster. Vacuum dot matrix printers more often than other printers.

Ink jet printers require little preventive maintenance. Keep the interior and exterior clean of dust and particles. Use a soft brush or non-metallic vacuum nozzle to remove dust. Do not use any type of lubricants on the print cartridge bar. Use the printer's software or maintenance procedure for aligning the print cartridge each time it is replaced. Some printers have a "clean" maintenance procedure that can be done through the software that ships with the printer. Some of these processes do not clean the printhead well even when using this procedure and the printheads tend to clog during usage. Remove the printhead and clean with a lint-free cloth or with a dampened cotton swab. Allow the cartridge to dry thoroughly and reinstall.

Laser preventive maintenance is important

If any toner appears inside the printer, do *not* use a normal vacuum cleaner. The toner particles seep through the vacuum cleaner bag into the vacuum's motor (where the particles melt). Also, the toner can become electrically charged and ignite a fire. Special HEPA (high-efficiency particulate air) vacuum bags are available for some vacuum cleaners.

Laser printers, on the other hand, do require some periodic maintenance. Be careful using compressed air to clean a laser printer that has loose toner in it. The compressed air could push the toner in to hard-to-reach places or to parts that heat up and cause the part to fail. Vacuum the laser toner before using compressed air.

If the laser printer has a transfer corona instead of a transfer roller, clean it when you replace the toner cartridge. Some laser printers include a small cleaning brush to clean the corona wire. Some toner cartridges come with a cotton swab for cleaning the transfer corona. The transfer corona wire is normally in the bottom of the printer protected by monofilament wires. Be extremely careful not to break the wires or the transfer corona.

Ozone is a gas produced by larger business-type laser printers. The printer's ozone filter removes the gas as well as any toner and paper dust particles. The ozone filter needs replacing after a specific number of usage hours. Check the printer documentation for the filter replacement schedule. Simply vacuuming the ozone filter will not clean it. The ozone molecules are trapped and absorbed by the ozone filter. If you forget to replace the ozone filter, people in the immediate vicinity may develop headaches, nausea, irritability, and depression. Most home and small office laser printers do not have an ozone filter. When using these printers, the surrounding area must be well ventilated.

The fuser cleaning pad (sometimes known as the fuser wand) sits above the top fusing roller and is normally replaced at the same time as the toner cartridge. However, the cleaning pad sometimes becomes dirty before it is time to replace the cartridge. If so, remove the cleaning pad. Hold the pad over a trash can. Take a small flat-tipped screwdriver and use the shaft to rub along the felt pad. Replace the cleaning pad and wipe the screwdriver with a cloth.

The fusing roller sometimes has particles that cling to it. Once the assembly cools, *gently* scrape the particles from the roller. A small amount of alcohol on a soft, lint-free cloth can help with stubborn spots.

What if you just performed maintenance on a printer and now the print looks bad?

After performing preventive maintenance on a printer, the pages may appear smudged or slightly dirty. Run a couple of print jobs through the printer to allow the dust to settle (so to speak). Never do any kind of maintenance on any computer part or peripheral without testing the results of the maintenance or the repair.

If the laser printer uses a laser beam to write data to the photosensitive drum, the laser beam does not directly touch the drum. Instead, at least one mirror is used to redirect the laser beam onto the drum's surface. The mirror(s) need to be cleaned periodically with a lint-free cloth.

For some printers, preventive maintenance kits are available for purchase. Quality printer replacement parts and preventive maintenance kits are important to the technician. If a printer must be sent out for repair, warranty work, and so on, make sure to remove the toner cartridge, platen knobs, and power cords before packing the printer in a box. Check with the receiving company to see if you should send the toner cartridge separately.

CHAPTER 3

Employability and Professional Development

Unit 3: Employability and Professional Development

Unit code: M/601/1251
QCF Level 4: BTEC Higher National
Credit value: 15

Aim

To provide learners with the opportunity to acquire employability skills required for effective employment and to manage their own personal and professional development.

Unit abstract

All learners at all levels of education and experience require employability skills as a prerequisite to entering the job market. This unit gives learners an opportunity to assess and develop an understanding of their own responsibilities and performance in or when entering the workplace.

The unit considers the skills required for general employment such as interpersonal and transferable skills, and the dynamics of working with others in teams or groups including leadership and communication skills.

It also deals with the everyday working requirement of problem solving which includes the identification or specification of the 'problem', strategies for its solution and then evaluation of the results of the solution through reflective practices.

Learning outcomes

On successful completion of this unit a learner will:

1. Be able to take responsibility for own personal and professional development
2. Be able to demonstrate acquired interpersonal and transferable skills
3. Understand the dynamics of working with others
4. Be able to develop strategies for problem solving.

Unit content

1 Be able to take responsibility for own personal and professional development

Responsibilities: own responsibilities eg personal responsibility, direct and indirect relationships and adaptability, decision-making processes and skills, ability to learn and develop within the work role; other eg employment legislation, ethics, employment rights and responsibilities

Performance objectives: setting and monitoring performance objectives

Individual appraisal systems: uses of performance appraisals eg salary levels and bonus payments, promotion, strengths and weaknesses, training needs; communication; appraisal criteria eg production data, personnel data, judgemental data; rating methods eg ranking, paired comparison, checklist, management by objectives; skills audit (personal profile using appropriate self-assessment tools); evaluating self-management; personal and interpersonal skills; leadership skills

Motivation and performance: application and appraisal of motivational theories and techniques, rewards and incentives; manager's role; self-motivational factors.

Development plan: current performance; future needs; opportunities and threats to career progression; aims and objectives; achievement dates; review dates; learning programme/activities; action plans; personal development plan

Portfolio building: developing and maintaining a personal portfolio

Transcripts: maintaining and presenting transcripts including curriculum vitae

2 Be able to demonstrate acquired interpersonal and transferable skills

Effective communication: verbal and non-verbal eg awareness and use of body language, openness and responsiveness, formal and informal feedback to and from colleagues; IT as an effective communication medium; team meetings

Interpersonal skills: soft skills eg personal effectiveness, working with others, use of initiative, negotiating skills, assertiveness skills, social skills

Time management: prioritising workloads; setting work objectives; using time effectively; making and keeping appointments; reliable estimates of task time

3 Understand the dynamics of working with others

Working with others: nature and dynamics of team and group work; informal and formal settings; purpose of teams and groups eg long-term corporate objectives/strategy; problem solving and short-term development projects; flexibility/adaptability; team player

Teams and team building: selecting team members eg specialist roles, skill and style/approach mixes; identification of team/work group roles; stages in team development eg team building, identity, loyalty, commitment to shared beliefs, team health evaluation; action planning; monitoring and feedback; coaching skills; ethics; effective leadership skills, eg setting direction, setting standards, motivating, innovative, responsive, effective communicator, reliability, consistency

4 Be able to develop strategies for problem solving

Specification of the problem: definition of the problem; analysis and clarification

Identification of possible outcomes: identification and assessment of various alternative outcomes

Tools and methods: problem-solving methods and tools

Plan and implement: sources of information; solution methodologies; selection and implementation of the best corrective action eg timescale, stages, resources, critical path analysis

Evaluation: evaluation of whether the problem was solved or not; measurement of solution against specification and desired outcomes; sustainability

Learning outcomes and assessment criteria

Learning outcomes On successful completion of this unit a learner will:	Assessment criteria for pass The learner can:
LO1 Be able to take responsibility for own personal and professional development	1.1 reflect on own current skills and competencies against professional standards and organisational objectives 1.2 evaluate own development needs and the activities required to meet them 1.3 devise a personal and professional development plan based on identified needs 1.4 reflect on own development against original aims and objectives set in the personal and professional development plan
LO2 Be able to demonstrate acquired interpersonal and transferable skills	2.1 communicate in a variety of styles and appropriate manner at various levels 2.2 demonstrate effective time management strategies
LO3 Understand the dynamics of working with others	3.1 analyse team dynamics, discussing the roles people play in a team and how they can work together to achieve shared goals 3.2 discuss alternative ways to complete tasks and achieve team goals
LO4 Be able to develop strategies for problem solving	4.1 review tools and methods for developing solutions to problems 4.2 develop an appropriate strategy for resolving a particular problem 4.3 evaluate the potential impact on the business of implementing the strategy.

Guidance

Links to National Occupational Standards, other BTEC units, other BTEC qualifications and other relevant units and qualifications

The learning outcomes associated with this unit are closely linked with:

Level 3	Level 4	Level 5
Unit 1: Communication and Employability Skills for IT	Unit 3: Employability and Professional Development	Unit 4: Project Design, Implementation and Evaluation
		Unit 50: Work-based Experience

It also links with the following Asset Skills cross-sectoral Employability Matrix:

- Plan and manage time, money and other resources to achieve goals
- Find and suggest new ways to achieve goals and get the job done and achieve goals
- Plan for and achieve your learning goals
- Understand the roles people play in a group and how you can best work with them
- Lead or support and motivate a team to achieve high standards
- Find new and creative ways to solve a problem.

Essential requirements

Access to a range of work-related exemplars (for example appraisal and development systems, team health checks, job descriptions, action plans, communication strategies, etc) would be of assistance in delivering this unit. Case studies based on relevant sectors, workshops, career talks and work-based mentors would also be useful in the teaching and learning aspect of the unit.

Learners can generate assessment evidence through a range of possible activities including individual work placements, project management, research reports, development of case studies, the process of working with others (eg employee–supervisor roles, teamwork, group work) and everyday communication within the workplace.

Resources

Books

Thompson Leigh, L—*Making the Team: A Guide for Managers* (Pearson Education, 2008) ISBN: 9780136037767

NCCER—*Basic Employability Skills: Trainee Guide 00108-09* (Prentice Hall, 2009) ISBN 013609919X

Websites

http://www.stemnet.org.uk/resources/employability_skills_guide.cfm

http://www.prospects.ac.uk

Process analysis and modelling

INTRODUCTION

The purpose of this section is to illustrate the method to be adopted by the analyst in analysing and modelling the processes that handle the data and information within the organization. The approach taken is to move from a description and analysis of the existing physical system and to derive a logical model of the processes involved. Physical analysis is illustrated using manual systems flowcharts, which picture the formal document flows within departments and processes in an organization. The logical model is derived in the first instance using data flow diagrams, which show the relationships between logical data flows and processes. The content of each data flow together with other useful information on it is contained in a data dictionary. The logical content of the processes can be described using structured English, decision tables and logic flowcharts. These are all covered in this chapter. In order to be of use in systems design, the process model of the system must be supplemented with a data model. During this chapter, a case study will be introduced that is developed throughout the chapter and in Chapter 4.

The case study

Throughout this and the next chapter, it will be helpful in understanding the stages, tools and techniques if they are explained by way of a case study. The case study used here concerns a company called Kismet Ltd. Kismet purchases electrical goods from a range of suppliers and manufacturers and distributes these goods to retail trade outlets.

Case studies are a useful vehicle for understanding the process of systems analysis and design, but they will never be a substitute for learning through the actual *practice* of analysis and design. The most important respect in which any case study is limited is that it preselects information to be presented to the reader and presents this in a neatly summarized and organized way. In reality, the analyst would be subject to a large amount of (often unconnected) information collected from various interviews, existing works standards manuals, samples of transaction documents, auditors' reports, and so on.

Only a part of the Kismet organization is covered here. It is often convenient to view a business as being made up of several subsystems, each of which is determined by the function it fulfils. Examples are the sales, manufacturing, storage, purchasing, accounting, planning and control subsystems. This study provides a slice through three of these. It deals with the basic processing of orders from customers, the generation of invoices and the provision of some management information.

KISMET CASE STUDY 3.1

Kismet supplies a range of hi-fi, TV, radio and video goods to retail outlets throughout the country. The goods are supplied by manufacturers, who each supply a variety of types of equipment. Currently, Kismet has over 40 suppliers, who supply a total of over 500 different item types. The number of suppliers is expected to remain fairly constant during the foreseeable future, although the range of types of equipment may alter considerably. Kismet has approximately 1200 live customers and receives on average about 300 orders per day, each one averaging ten items requested.

Kismet employs about 150 people in a number of departments:

- *Sales order department*: Accepts and processes customer orders.
- *Credit control department*: Responsible for customer credit checks.
- *Stores department*: Responsible for stock control.
- *Invoicing department*: Responsible for customer invoicing.
- *Accounts department*: Handles general accounting requirements and the provision of reports.
- *Packing and dispatch department*: Responsible for goods inward and goods outward.
- *Purchasing department*: Responsible for placing orders with suppliers.

- *Sales and marketing department*: Deals with advertising and establishing new outlets.
- *Payroll department*: Prepares Kismet's payroll.
- *Maintenance department*: Responsible for general maintenance and also for maintenance of Kismet's fleet of vans.
- *General administration*: Handles administration not specifically covered elsewhere.

Kismet was started 30 years ago by Harold Kismet and has grown rapidly in the last five years with the increased consumer use of home media centres, digital music players and the whole range of modern electronic leisure equipment. Josephine Kismet (Harold's daughter) has pioneered this development, with a subsequent 300% increase in trade in the last three years. However, problems are beginning to emerge. Kismet's domination of the north-east of the country and its expansion into the north-west is being threatened by a serious rival, Hardy Ltd. This company was set up nine months previously with a large injection of capital. Hardy provides a website offering customers a range of electronic leisure equipment and the opportunity to place a credit card order. Also, and this is most serious for Kismet, Hardy is now moving into the area of supplying retail outlets, in direct competition with Kismet.

The management of Kismet has been conscious for some time of slowness in satisfying the orders received from retail outlets. These orders are taking an increasing time to process. This has been further exacerbated by the expansion of Kismet over the last three years. The entirely manual system that Kismet uses has not been able to cope adequately with the increase of trade, even though more staff have been employed. Hardy is able to offer a superior service because of its modern computerized data-processing and information systems, which give it a significant edge over Kismet.

Harold Kismet has long resisted his daughter's representations to computerize the business. This is partly because of loyalty to his older employees, who have been with Kismet since its foundation. He fears that they, like him, would be unable to make the transition to computerization. Also, he is conscious of the demise of his best friend's business, which rapidly moved from being a flourishing enterprise to bankruptcy as the result of a completely mismanaged and inappropriate introduction of a computer system.

The recent rise of Hardy and his own impending retirement have forced Harold Kismet to reconsider the possibility of computerization. He has subsequently given responsibility for the project to his daughter. Although knowing little about computers, the daughter realizes the potential and sees this as a necessary requirement if Kismet is to stave off the threat from Hardy and to expand further (possibly into satellite TV and personal computers).

SYSTEMS ANALYSIS

The purpose of systems analysis is to ascertain what must be done in order to carry out the functions of the system. This will involve a decomposition of the functions of the system into their logical constituents and the production of a logical model of the processes and of the data flows necessary to perform these. The logical model will be illustrated by data flow diagrams at the various levels of process decomposition. The algorithms will be revealed by structured process specification techniques such as structured English, decision tables and logic flowcharts. The importance of concentration on the logical features of a system (what logically needs to be done in order to carry out the functions) as distinct from the physical features (who does what, where, with which file, and so on) is to avoid making premature commitments to physical design.

Prior to production of the logical analysis, it is often helpful to carry out a physical analysis of the document flows between processes and departments within the existing system. As well as enabling the analyst to identify key tasks, these charts can be used to evaluate control and efficiency aspects of the current system.

The output of the stage of systems analysis will be a logical model of the functioning of the system. This will consist of diagrams, charts and dictionaries, which are the product of the techniques used in the analysis. An important feature of a structured approach to systems analysis and design is the generation of clear and helpful documentation that can assist communication not only between the programmer and analyst but also between management and users and the analyst. The fact that a logical model is produced in systems analysis removes complicating and distracting physical elements that would hamper communication. The movement from the physical to the logical model and the techniques used are illustrated in Figure 3.1.

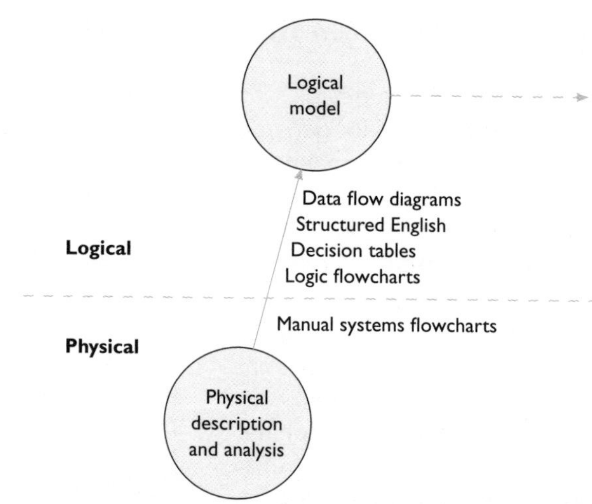

Figure 3.1 Tools used during the stage of systems analysis

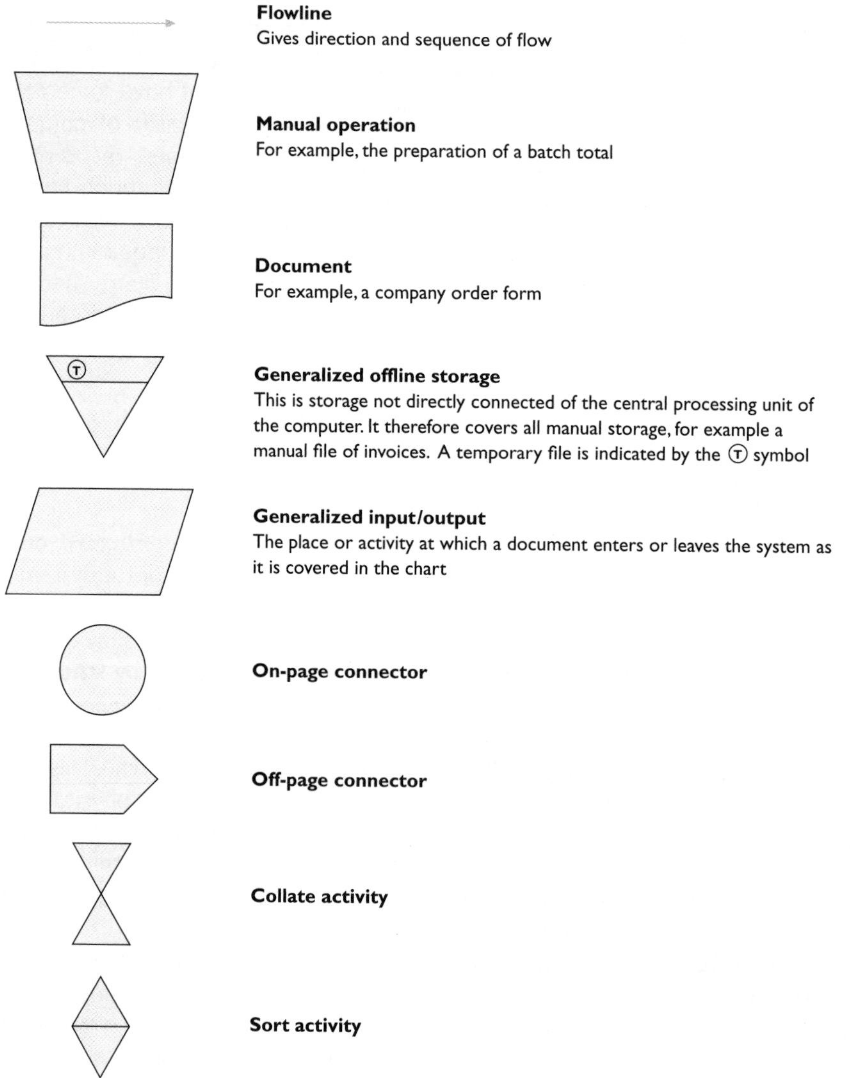

Flowline
Gives direction and sequence of flow
Manual operation
For example, the preparation of a batch total
Document
For example, a company order form
T
Generalized offline storage
This is storage not directly connected of the central processing unit of the computer. It therefore covers all manual storage, for example a manual file of invoices. A temporary file is indicated by the T symbol
Generalized input/output
The place or activity at which a document enters or leaves the system as it is covered in the chart
On-page connector
Off-page connector
Collate activity
Sort activity

Figure 3.2 Basic symbols used in the preparation of manual systems flowcharts

MANUAL SYSTEMS FLOWCHARTS

After investigation, the analyst may have collected an unwieldy batch of interview notes, details of observations, questionnaire responses and sundry documents. In the initial stages of analysis, it is important to arrive at a methodical description of the existing manual system and to carry out some analysis at a physical level prior to developing a logical model of the system. The flow of *formal* information within a system often occurs through documents that pass from one department to another. A traditional tool of systems analysis is the manual systems (document) flowchart.

The basic idea is that certain tasks performed on documents are common to many applications—filing, preparing multiple copies, collating, sorting. These are given specially agreed symbols (Figure 3.2). The life history of a document from origination (entry from outside the system or preparation within) to destination (exit from the system or filing) is recorded on the flowchart. The passage of the document from department to department is also shown.

KISMET CASE STUDY 3.2

The best way to understand a manual systems flowchart, sometimes called a document flowchart, is to study one. Here the Kismet case study is developed giving a detailed description of the processes occurring during order processing. A manual systems flowchart covering these is shown in Figure 3.3.

Order processing

Customers mail their orders to Kismet HQ. On receipt of an order in the sales order department, a five-part company order form is filled in giving (among other information) the ***order#***, ***order date***, ***customer#***, ***customer name***, ***item 1 code#***, ***item 1 quantity***, ***item 2 code#***, ***item 2 quantity***, and so on. The top copy of this form is filed temporarily in ***customer#*** sequence for customer enquiry purposes (rather than ***order#*** sequence, as when customers enquire about a recently placed order they will not be in possession of the ***order#***). Each item is provisionally priced on the remaining copies of the form from a sales catalogue held in the order department. The priced copies are sent to the credit control section.

The credit control section provisionally calculates the order value. Brief details of the customer account are then consulted to establish that the customer exists and is correctly named and that the total value of the order, when added to the current balance, does not exceed the credit limit of the customer. If all these conditions are met then the order copies are stamped 'approved', signed and returned to the sales order department, one copy of the order being retained in the credit control department filed by ***customer#***. If the above conditions are not met, the order copies are filed temporarily to be dealt with later by the credit control manager.

On receipt of the approved order copies in the sales order department, the top copy is extracted from the temporary file and sent to the customer as an acknowledgment. One of the 'approved' copies is filed in the order department in the 'approved order' file under ***order#*** to enable staff to retrieve details of the order in the event of further customer queries. The remaining two copies are sent to the stores department and the invoicing department. The invoicing department files the copy under ***order#***.

The stores department selects the goods as ordered and enters the quantities supplied on the order form. A two-part dispatch note is made out giving the goods supplied together with their quantities. One copy of this is sent to the invoicing department, and the other is sent with the goods to packing and dispatch. If the entire order is supplied then the order form is filed in the stores department under ***order#***, otherwise the goods supplied are noted on the form and it is filed in *date* sequence. Periodically, the stores department goes through the unsatisfied back orders and attempts to supply the goods ordered. The stores department also updates the inventory records.

On receipt of the dispatch note, the invoicing department prepares a three-part invoice using the sales price of the goods from the catalogue. The discount applicable to a customer is calculated. This is based on the customer's geographical location, total purchases during the last 12 months and the total value of the order. Sales tax is added and totals formed. One copy of the invoice is sent to the customer, and one is sent to accounts to update the customer accounts and other ledgers. The remaining copy is filed in the invoicing department with the order copy and dispatch note under ***order#***.

The flowchart for order processing and dispatch in Kismet is given in Figure 3.3. Note that the flow lines indicate flows of *documents*.

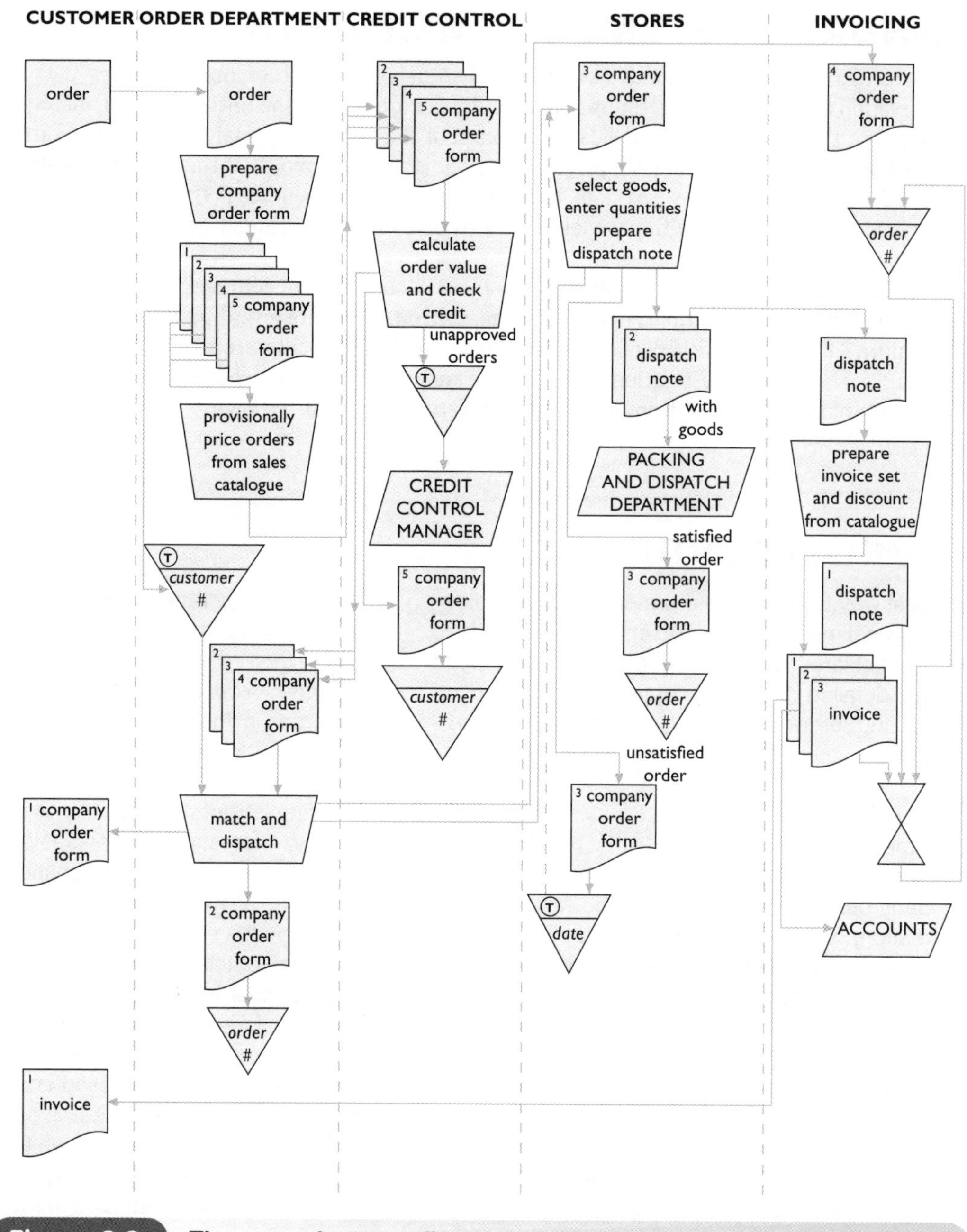

Figure 3.3 The manual system flowchart for order processing/dispatch in Kismet

The following practical points will assist in the drawing of flowcharts:

- The chart is divided into vertical sections representing different locations for operations.
- Although not shown, a far-left section may be used for additional (brief) narrative.
- The chart proceeds as far as possible from left to right and top to bottom.
- Documents are shown at origination, on entry into a section and then again only as required to avoid confusion with other documents.
- Ensure that all documents are accounted for by being permanently filed, being destroyed, leaving the system as charted (for example to the credit control manager in Kismet) or transferring to another flowchart.

There are a number of advantages and disadvantages in the use of manual systems flowcharts.

Advantages

- Flowcharts are easier to understand and assimilate than narrative. This becomes more pronounced with increasing complexity of the system.
- The preparation of a chart necessitates the full understanding by the analyst of the procedures and sequences of operations on documents.
- Incompleteness in tracing the destination of a document is easily discovered, indicating the need for further investigation on the part of the analyst (in Kismet, where does the customer's original order go?).
- Little technical knowledge is required to appreciate the document, so it can be used as a communication tool between the user of the system and the analyst in order to check and correct the latter's understanding.
- Weaknesses in the system, such as preparation of unnecessary documents, lack of control, unnecessary duplication of work and bottlenecks, are easily located.

Disadvantages

- With heavily integrated systems, flowcharts may become difficult to manage (large sheets of paper!). The use of off-page connectors and continuation is sometimes necessary but tends to reduce the visual impact and clarity of the chart.
- They are difficult to amend.
- It must be realized that when analysing an existing system informal information is an important part. The flowchart does not incorporate any recognition of this.

The systems flowchart is not only of use to the analyst when carrying out the stages of analysis and design of a computerized information system. Management may also use the flowchart to impose uniformity on groups of systems as the structure of the processes surrounding document handling are revealed. This may be necessary to ensure that, say, one branch of an organization handles order processing in the same way as another. The flowchart may be used as an aid in the preparation of internal audit and procedures manuals. In the former case, it is possible to ensure that essential information is provided to management at the correct stage. Auditors may use the flowchart in a review of internal control as a guide to determining auditing procedures in the annual audit.

The task of evaluation of the system is often considered as part of analysis. As has been pointed out, flowcharts assist in this task.

KISMET CASE STUDY 3.3

A typical approach to evaluation of the order and dispatch system of Kismet would use the chart to answer a number of questions. Note how easy it is to answer the following typical list of questions by using the flowchart:

1. Can goods be dispatched but not invoiced?
2. Can orders be received and not (completely) dealt with?
3. Can customers be invoiced for goods that are not dispatched because of low stocks?
4. Can goods be dispatched to customers who are not creditworthy?
5. Can invoicing errors occur?
6. Can sales be invoiced but not recorded?

DATA FLOW DIAGRAMS

Although systems flowcharts provide a useful tool for analysing a physical description, they may impede the design process. This is because they draw attention to physical detail. It is important to realize that the systems analyst will be designing a system to *do* something. This 'something' can be specified by describing its logic and the actions on data. To concentrate on existing physical detail will obscure the functions of the system, restrict the designer's creativity and cause premature commitments to physical design in the early stages of the project.

KISMET CASE STUDY 3.4

An example of the concentration on physical detail described above is given here. It is of little importance to a computer design that one copy of a Kismet company order form is filed temporarily in the order department while four copies go to credit control, where, after approval, one is filed, the remaining copies being returned to the order department, after which the first copy is sent to the customer.

If the whole procedure is to be computerized, including the order approval, the process will occur within the computer as an exchange of data between files or a database and programs. But again, to assume total computerization is to make a possibly premature physical design decision. It may be more effective to retain parts of the old manual system or design new manual procedures.

The point to realize is that the processes, the exchanges of data and the stores of data, are important, not their particular physical representation, whether it be, for instance, a sequential file on tape, an indexed file on disk or a composition of two manual files in two separate locations.

Data flow diagrams assist in building a logical model of the system independent of physical commitments. They show the various flows of data between the processes that transform it. Data stores and the points at which data enters and leaves a system are also shown. The basic symbols used in drawing data flow diagrams are shown in Figure 3.4.

- **Data source or data sink:** The square indicates a source or sink for data and is a reflection of the ignorance as to what happens to the data prior to its emergence from the source or after its disappearance into the sink.
- **Data process:** The circle or rounded rectangle indicates a data process. In this, a brief but meaningful identifier of the process is written. It is important to realize that only *data* processes occur in a data flow diagram. Physical processes are not mentioned. For instance, the fact that goods are selected from their stock locations to satisfy an order is not a data process but a material task. A data process is one that transforms only data. It may be that this process will be carried out by a computer program, a part of a computer program, a set of computer programs or manually. The data flow diagram is neutral on this point.

  The identifier used in the data process symbol should, ideally, be both meaningful and succinct. It is good practice to restrict identifiers to a concatenation of imperative

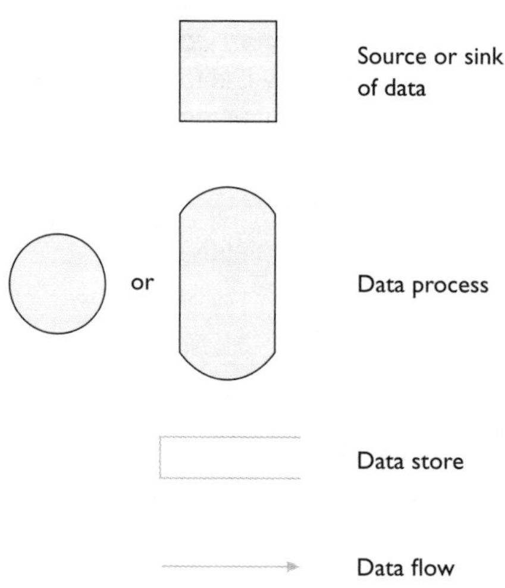

Figure 3.4 Symbols used in data flow diagrams

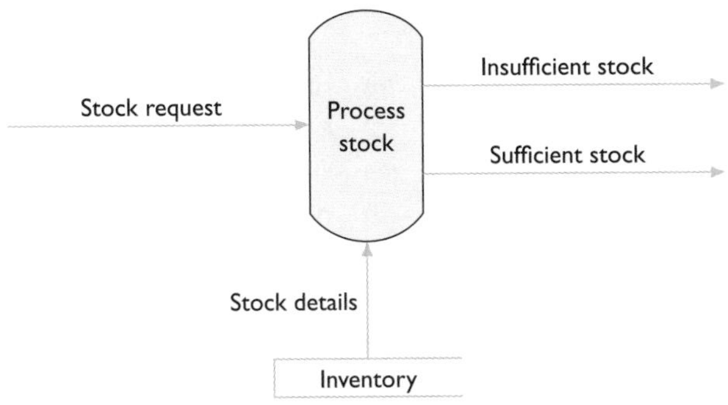

Figure 3.5 **Part of an erroneous data flow diagram**

verb and object. For example *process stock transaction* or *check credit status* are both acceptable. It is bad practice to try to describe the process. For example, it is a great temptation for the novice to 'name' a data process as *check the application for the account against the credit point list to establish the creditworthiness and the credit limit of the customer*. This is not acceptable.

- **Data store:** A data store is represented by an open-ended rectangle with a suitable identifier. This is distinguished from a data sink by the fact that the data is stored and it (or some part of it) will be retrieved. A sink indicates ignorance, as far as the diagram is concerned, of the fate of the data. No particular storage medium is implied by the data store symbol. It could be a magnetic tape or disk, a document or even some person's memory. Once again, it is a great temptation for the newcomer to represent material stores. This is a mistake.
- **Data flow:** The line represents a data flow. The nature of the data is indicated by a name (or names). Wherever that piece of data flows within the diagram it should be tagged with the same name. Once again, it is important to realize that these are flows of *data* and not material flows. If a data flow diagram is drawn representing part of a system in which goods accompanied by a dispatch note are moved, it is the dispatch note, or to be more exact the dispatch note details, that appear on the data flow diagram. There is no mention of the goods.

It is also a common error to confuse data flows with flows of control. This is illustrated in Figure 3.5. Obviously, what the designer of the diagram intended is that the exit data flow travels one way if there is sufficient stock and the other way if there is insufficient. It is not usual to indicate the conditions under which data flows on a data flow diagram. This would tempt the analyst into thinking of the system from the point of view of control rather than data flows.

The difference between a data store and a data flow often confuses the beginner. It is helpful to think of an analogy with water. Water flowing down a pipe is analogous to a data flow, whereas water in a reservoir is the analogy for a data store.

Data flow diagrams in detail

In systems investigation, the analyst will have collected a great deal of information on tasks performed on document flows within the system. These tasks will be involved in the processing of business transactions and the generation of management information. The document processing will probably have been charted in a manual systems flowchart. In drawing data flow diagrams a logical approach is taken. It is important to ignore the location of processes in the manual system, the documents involved and who is responsible for the tasks. The designer should concentrate on the functions that are carried out.

KISMET CASE STUDY 3.5

If Kismet is considered, as previously described, it can be seen that one very general course of action is taken. Orders from customers are processed to generate dispatch notes (which eventually accompany goods sent to the customer) and to make up invoices (sent to the customer and to the accounts department). In doing this, a price catalogue and customer account details are consulted and inventory records are updated.

This is indicated in Figure 3.6. In itself it is not very informative, although, even at this level, in a more comprehensive analysis of all Kismet's functions there would be other interfacing subsystems, such as purchasing, payroll and accounting. If the analyst had seriously misunderstood the structure of the system, this would be obvious at a glance.

Further progress can be made by decomposing this order-processing function into its component parts. Three different types of task occur when Kismet processes a customer order. First, the company order is generated and approved. Second, stock is selected, inventory updated and a dispatch note prepared. Finally, invoices are made up and sent to the customer and to accounts. Involved in this are various data flows, stores, processes, sources and sinks.

Read the case study and note where the sources, sinks, processes, stores and flows occur. These are:

1. Sources/sinks:
   (a) customer
   (b) credit control manager
   (c) packing and dispatch department
   (d) accounting.
2. Processes:
   (a) generate approved company order
   (b) process stock transaction
   (c) make up invoice.
3. Data stores:
   (a) inventory
   (b) catalogue
   (c) customer details
   (d) company order store
   (e) company order/invoice/dispatch note.
4. Data flows:
   (a) customer order
   (b) company order
   (c) price details
   (d) stock details
   (e) customer credit details
   (f) invoice
   (g) customer invoice details
   (h) dispatch note.

The data flow diagram at the first level can now be drawn (Figure 3.7). The following points should be noted:

1. The diagram can be thought of as starting at the top left and moving downwards and to the right. This gives some idea of the sequence of tasks performed, although it is not a rigid rule.
2. Each data flow, source/sink, process and store is labelled. It is a convention that where source/

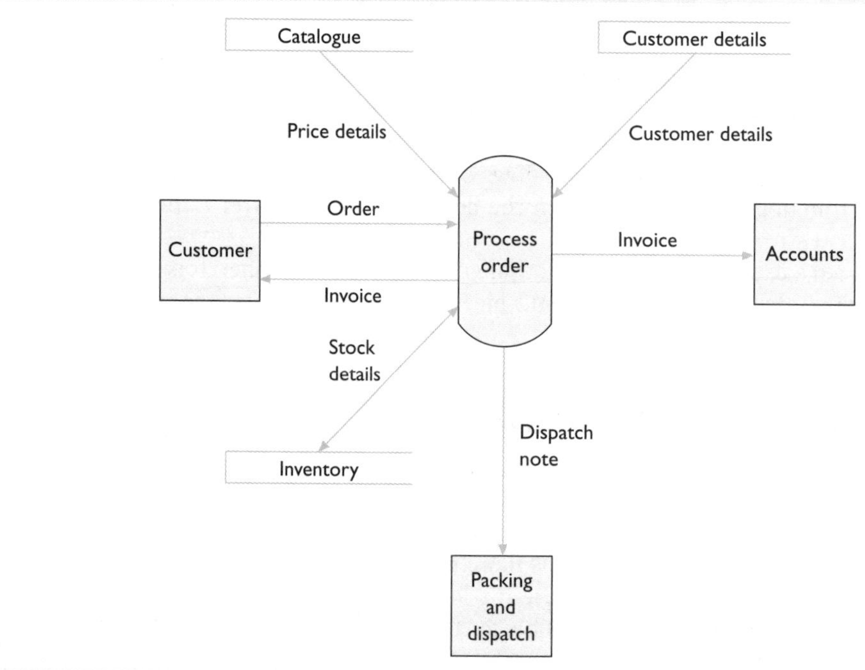

Figure 3.6 A high-level view of order processing for Kismet

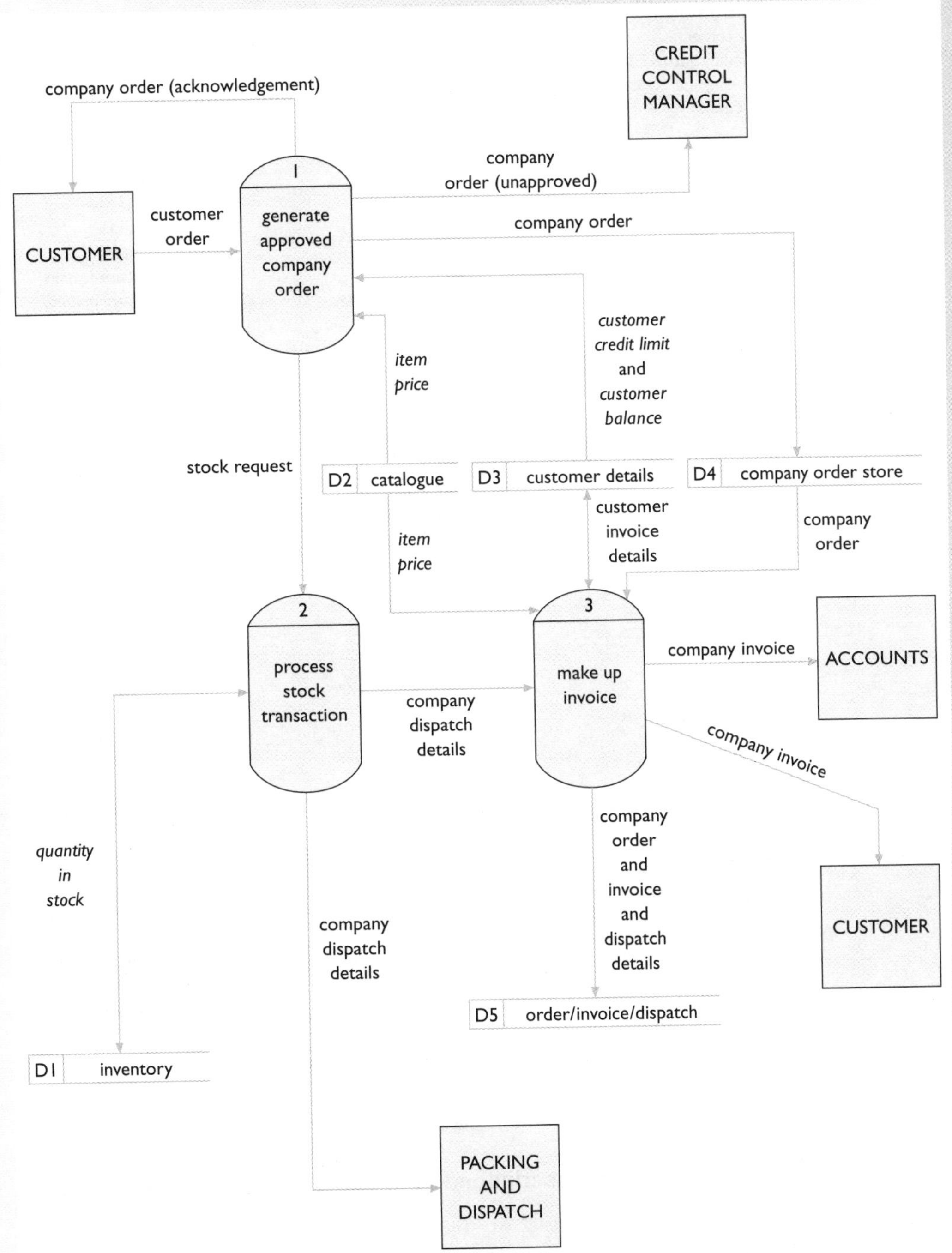

Figure 3.7 **A level 1 data flow diagram of the Kismet order-processing system**

sinks or stores are repeated they are given a diagonal line at the corner of the symbol (see the CUSTOMER source/sink). A data flow that is repeated is given the same name.

3. Certain tasks are left out of a data flow diagram. Any error-handling routine is usually omitted. For instance, although not stated, there would be a procedure for handling an incorrectly prepared company order form when the *customer name* and *customer#* were found not to correspond.

4. Departments and physical locations are ignored in the data flow diagram, except where they appear as sources or sinks. For instance, although the processing of the stock transaction occurs in the stores and the generation of the approved company order occurs in the order department, this information does not appear in the diagram.

5. Although the goods would accompany the dispatch note to PACKING AND DISPATCH, this is not shown on the data flow diagram as it is not a data flow.

Source/sink
Customer
Credit control manager
Packing and dispatch
Accounting

Process
(1) Generate approved company order
(2) Process stock transaction
(3) Make up invoice

Data flow

Customer order
customer#
customer name
[item#
*item quantity]**
delivery address

Company order
order#
order date
customer#
customer name
customer address
delivery address
[item#
item quantity
*item price]**
total

Company dispatch details
dispatch#
order#
customer#
customer name
delivery address
dispatch date
[item#
*item quantity]**

Company invoice
invoice#
invoice date
customer#
customer name
customer address
order#
[item#
item price
*item quantity]**
subtotal
sales tax
discount%
total payable

Stock request
order#
customer#
customer name
delivery address
[item#
*item quantity]**

Customer invoice details
customer#
customer name
customer address
turnover year to date

Data store

D1 Inventory
item#
quantity in stock
.
.
.
.
.
.

D2 Catalogue
item#
item price
.
.
.
.
.
.

D3 Customer details
customer#
customer name
customer address
[delivery address]
customer balance
customer credit limit
turnover year to date
registration date
.
.
.
.

D4 Company order store
see Company order

D5 Order/invoice/dispatch
see Company order
and invoice
and dispatch details

Figure 3.8 **Table of descriptions of the data flow diagram elements for Kismet**

The data flow diagram shows a great deal about the flows of data between processes. However, it is important that the contents of data flows and the data stores also be specified precisely. This will be of use when designing files or a database and when writing programs. A tabular representation of the contents of the various data elements appearing in the data flow diagram is shown in Figure 3.8.

The following points arising from this diagram should be noted:

- The description in the case study does not go into much detail on the contents of each document or file (except in the case of the company order form). These contents are either implied by the nature of the task (*customer address* must be present to dispatch the invoice) or should be found on the 'document description form' prepared by the analyst during investigation.

- Extra detail will be stored for other tasks that are not part of the case as documented. For instance, under inventory there would be reorder levels. This omission does not matter as it would be remedied when the procedures for purchase and reorder of goods were incorporated into a data flow diagram.
- The exact content of the data stores and flows will be recorded in a **data dictionary**. This is often described as a store of data about data. The dictionary is of considerable importance in analysis and design and is covered in the section on p. 224.
- The meaning of [. . . .]* is that the contents of the brackets may be repeated an indeterminate number of times.

Data flow diagrams for simple systems are relatively straightforward to design. However, for larger systems it is useful to follow a set of guidelines. These are:

1. Identify the major processes.
2. Identify the major data sources, sinks and stores.
3. Identify the major data flows.
4. Name the data flows, processes, sources, sinks and stores.
5. Draw the diagram.
6. Review the diagram, particularly checking that similar data flows, stores, sources and sinks have the same name and that different data flows and so on have different names.

Data flow diagrams at various levels

Two interconnected questions arise concerning data flow diagrams. These are:

1. What level of discrimination of processes should be shown on the data flow diagram? For instance, in Figure 3.7 the data process *generate approved company order* could be regarded as consisting of a number of subprocesses, such as *accept order, check credit limit* and *price order*. Should these be shown as processes?
2. What is the maximum number of processes that should be shown on a data flow diagram?

A major objective of a data flow diagram is its use in communication of the logical process model of the organization. It is difficult to understand a data flow diagram when it has more than seven to nine processes. This is the practical upper limit. If there is a tendency to overstep this then the data flow diagram should be redrawn, with processes that are logically grouped together being replaced by a single process that encompasses them all. The processes are not 'lost' from the model. They should appear on another data flow diagram that shows how this combined process can be exploded into its constituents. These constituents themselves may be complex and can be broken down into linked data processes shown on a data flow diagram at a lower level. This should be repeated until the processes are logically simple: that is, until they cannot be broken down any further. This is illustrated in Figure 3.9.

The generation of levels in data flow diagrams has two other advantages. First, it naturally falls into line with the analyst's approach to top-down decomposition. That is, the analyst considers the major functions and processes first. These are then decomposed into their constituents. The analyst can therefore concentrate on the higher-level data flow diagrams before designing the others. Second, the various levels correspond to the various degrees of detail by which the system is represented. This is useful for the analyst when discussing the results of the analysis with members of the organization. Senior managers are more likely to be interested in a global view as given in a high-level data flow diagram. Other personnel will be concerned with more localized areas but in greater detail.

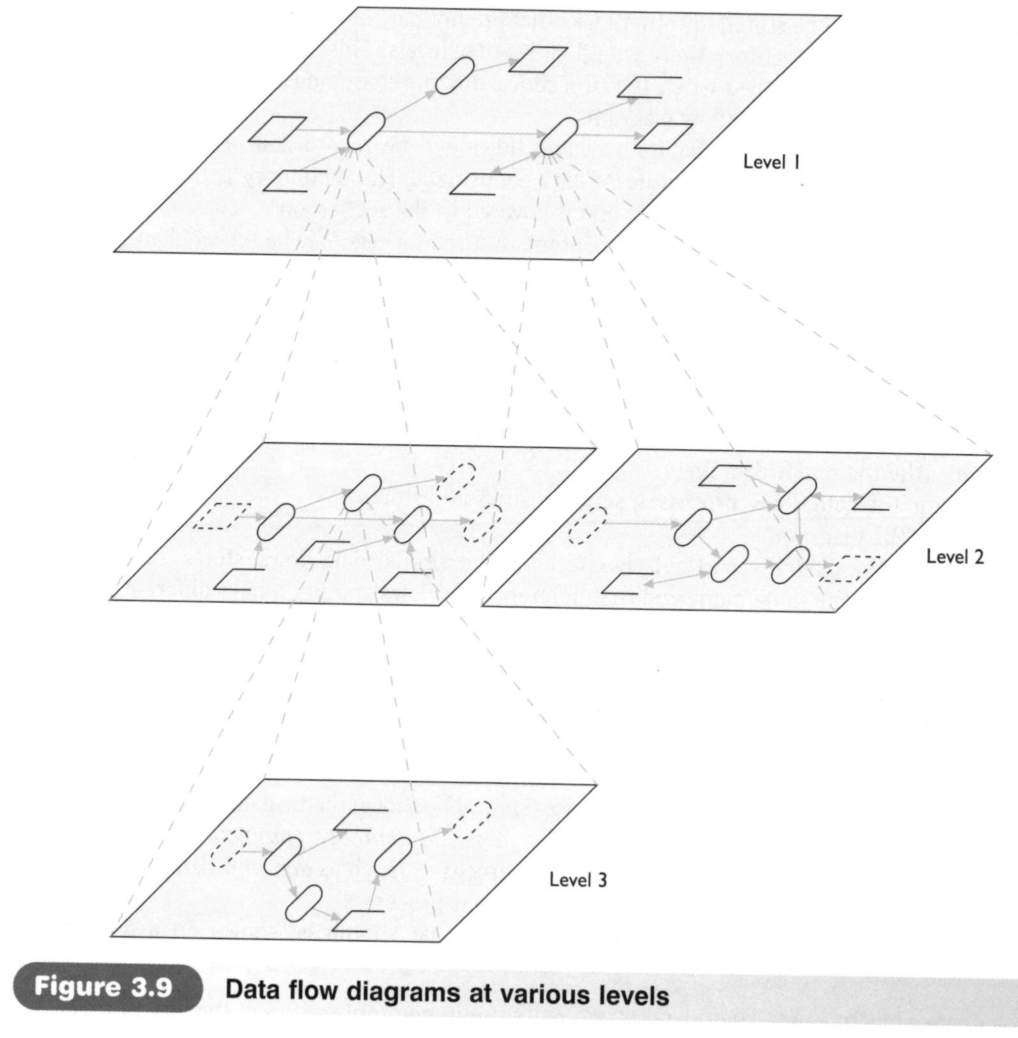

Figure 3.9 Data flow diagrams at various levels

KISMET CASE STUDY 3.6

The person responsible for supervising the generation of approved company orders in Kismet will be interested in a lower-level, more detailed explosion of the *generate approved company order* process.

The processes in the data flow diagram for Kismet (Figure 3.7) can be further decomposed. The generation of an approved company order is really a number of tasks:

1. Accept the order.
2. Prepare the company order form.
3. Price the goods.
4. Provisionally calculate the value of the order.
5. Check the creditworthiness of the customer.

This is shown on a level 2 data flow diagram (Figure 3.10). The number 1 task in level 1 is exploded into seven tasks, 1.1–1.7. The inputs and outputs of this exploded chart must match those of the *parent* for which it is the functional decomposition.

There are two exceptions to this. First, certain local files need not be shown on the parent. In Figure 3.10, the *unapproved orders* store is such a file. It is only used as a temporary repository for the unapproved orders and does not feature in the rest of the system. Second, for the sake of clarity it may be necessary to amalgamate a number of data flows at the parent level. If functional analysis were to be carried out on function number 2, *process stock transaction*, the input/output data flow would be composed of an input flow with *item#* and *quantity in stock* as the data elements and an output with *item#*, *transaction type* and *item quantity* as elements.

If necessary, further analysis of the level 2 diagram could be undertaken by exploding chosen processes to a level 3 diagram.

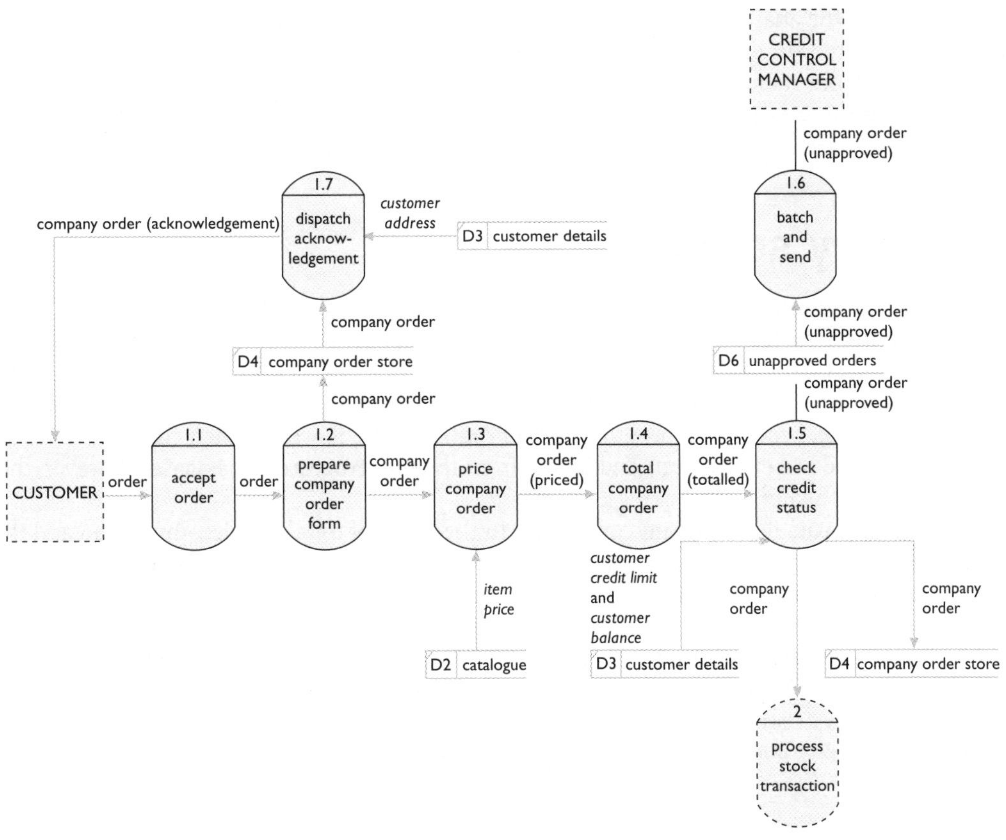

Figure 3.10 A level 2 data flow diagram of the Kismet *generate approved company order* process

Design commitments of the data flow diagram approach

It is important to separate the process of analysis from that of design. This may be difficult. The process of analysis goes beyond description, as every case of model building is partly a process of design. Another aspect of design is that the choice of data flows, stores, processes, sources and sinks is just one way of characterizing what is important in an organization's information system. To use these to build a model already commits the analyst to a certain design strategy: that of top-down, reductionist design.

However, within the design implications inherited through the use of structured techniques such as data flow diagrams, there is some separation of analysis from design.

KISMET CASE STUDY 3.7

In the case of Kismet, the generation of an approved company order follows a certain (unnecessarily repetitive) procedure, which is illustrated in the data flow diagram (Figure 3.10). In an ideal design, it is unlikely that the company order emanating from task 1.2 would be stored in the company order file awaiting the trigger from the successful order vetting (task 1.5) before dispatch of the acknowledgement. Rather, a copy of the approved company order form would be sent to the customer as part of the output of task 1.5.

In analysis, the analyst considers what, logically, *is* done in order to carry out the functions of the organization. In design, the analyst states what, logically, *should* be done for the organization to carry out its functions efficiently and effectively. The data flow diagram, by stripping away the physical aspects of a system and revealing its logic at the appropriate level of detail, makes it easy to see improvements that can be made.

Summary so far

The data flow diagram is an important tool of structured analysis and design. It ensures that a top-down approach is taken. This promotes a logical, as opposed to physical, view of data stores, flows and processes. In this way, no premature commitment to physical aspects of design is made. Eventually, the data stores *may* form part of the file structure or database of the system, and the data processes *may* become the programs or subroutines. The flows will then correspond to the data passed in and out of programs and to and from the file structure or database. However, this can be decided at a later stage.

The levels of data flow diagram correspond to the levels of top-down decomposition and the various levels of detail that management and users will need in order to discuss sensibly the analyst's understanding of processes.

The diagram may also be part of the agreed document provided at the end of analysis. Its non-technical nature means that it can be easily understood by users and agreed upon as a correct analysis of the system. This makes it a powerful communication tool, bridging the gap between analysts and users.

Finally, it makes it easy to sketch out different design alternatives for a future computerized system.

DATA DICTIONARIES

A data dictionary is a store of data about data. It provides information on the structure and use of data in an organization. It is therefore closely connected to the data flow diagram and to the data model. The contents of a typical entry in a data dictionary are given in Figure 3.11.

The data dictionary provides a precise and unambiguous specification of the data elements within the system. It is normally stored on a computer to facilitate cross-referencing between data elements. The data element *order#* referred to in the entry under invoice can easily be cross-referenced to discover that its structure is, for instance, followed by five digits.

It is important that data descriptions held in a data dictionary not be duplicated in several places. This is done so that if a change is made to some aspect of a data element the alteration is made in only one place in the dictionary, thus ensuring the maintenance of consistency.

The data dictionary is used right through the process of analysis to detailed design and into programming as the reference point to which any questions on the structure of data can be directed. Nowadays, computerized data dictionaries, sometimes called **data encyclopedias**, enable a considerable amount of extra information to be held on data, thus increasing the reliance of analysis and design on an adequate data dictionary.

If a table is made out when a data flow diagram is first drawn (as in Figure 3.8), this will provide much of the information for the data dictionary. Along with the data flow diagrams and process specifications (covered in the next three sections) the data dictionary constitutes the logical model of the system.

DECISION TABLES

The data flow diagram demonstrates the decomposition of the functions performed in an organization into simpler data processes and flows. Some of these processes may be complex in themselves but are not suitable for further decomposition in the data flow diagram.

Name:
Included here are all the names by which this data element is known. If there is more than one then these are termed 'aliases'.

Type of data
For example: data flow, data store, data item.

Structure
In the case of a data flow or data store this gives the list of data items, including repeats. If the type of data is a data item its 'picture' may be given—for example. 'AA9999'—together with the range of permissible values.

Usage characteristics:
This details the list of processes that the data flows/data stores interact with. In the case of a data item this list will give the data aggregates which use the item. Information on the data such as the frequency, volume and security issues surrounding the data is often given, as this will aid the designer in deciding on the physical characteristics of the proposed system.

Name:
Invoice

Type:
Data flow

aliases:
customer invoice
client invoice

Structure:
Aggregate: (*invoice#, invoice date, customer#, customer name, order#, [item#, item price, item quantity]*, subtotal, sales tax, discount%, total payable*)

Usage characteristics:
Output process 3 – *make up invoice*
input to sink – *accounts*
input to sink – *customer*

Figure 3.11 Typical contents of a data dictionary entry

KISMET CASE STUDY 3.8

An example of the use of decision tables might be Kismet's procedure for calculating discounts. Although not given previously in the case study, the firm's policy was summarized by the invoice manager to the systems analyst as follows:

> Three factors determine the percentage of discount. The first is the total value of the order (we like to encourage our customers to place large single orders rather than smaller multiple orders as it makes delivery and van scheduling easier). The discount is 3% for orders over £4000. If the delivery is within 50 miles of the warehouse, delivery costs are lower and a 2% discount is given, except if the 3% discount for large orders has been granted. In this latter case, only a 1% discount is given if the delivery is within 50 miles. Customers who have made purchases of more than £100,000 over the past 12 months are granted a further 2% discount. These measures are designed to encourage large purchases from local high-turnover retailers. We would like to offer a more targeted discount policy, although this would be more difficult to administer. We hope that one aspect of computerization is that automated discount calculation will help us to give more personalized encouragement to our customers.

The decision table for this policy is shown in Figure 3.12. The conditions that are important for determining the discount are shown in the top left-hand quadrant. In the top right-hand quadrant are the range of entries for these conditions. In this case, a condition applies (Y = yes) or does not (N = no). Note the pattern of the entries. It makes it easy to

Order > £4,000	Y	Y	Y	Y	N	N	N	N
Delivery < 50 miles	Y	Y	N	N	Y	Y	N	N
Turnover > £100,000	Y	N	Y	N	Y	N	Y	N
Discount 0%								X
1%								
2%						X	X	
3%				X				
4%		X			X			
5%			X					
6%	X							

Figure 3.12 A decision table for Kismet's discount policy

see that all eight entries have been included. Each column can be thought of as representing a type of order. For instance, column 3 represents a large order (>£4000), not delivered within 50 miles, from a customer with a turnover of more than £100,000. The action to be taken can be found by following the column down to discover that a discount of 5% (X = action) is to be allowed. This is an example of the general format for decision tables. This format is given in Figure 3.13.

Conditions being tested	Condition stub	Condition entries
Range of possible actions to be taken	Action stub	Action entries

Figure 3.13 The format of a decision table

Figure 3.12 is a simple decision table. There are only two possible entries for each condition, Y or N. This is called a **limited-entry decision table.** With three conditions there are $2^3 = 8$ columns; with four conditions there are $2^4 = 16$ columns. If there are n conditions there will be 2^n columns. With a large number of conditions, the decision table becomes very wide: for example, seven conditions leads to $2^7 = 128$ columns. Fortunately, it is often possible to collapse the columns. Wherever two columns differ only to the extent of one entry and the action(s) associated with each column are identical, the effect of the Y or N entry is nil. The two columns can be replaced by one column, which has the Y and the N replaced by a single '–' but is otherwise identical to the columns it replaces. The decision table can be collapsed until no two columns satisfy the pairwise condition stated.

As well as limited-entry tables there are **mixed** or **extended-entry tables.** These are used when there is not a simple value yes or no (true or false) associated with a condition. For instance, there might have been three possible ways of differentiating the size of the order as far as discounting was concerned: <£2000, ≥£2000 but >£5000 and ≥£5000. These three entries would appear in the condition entry, and the condition 'order size' would appear in the condition stub.

Finally, there are a range of special actions that may be present in the decision table. These concern the way that the user of the decision table moves around the table or to another table. Perhaps the most useful is the **GOTO** action, which causes the execution of another decision table. This is used when the types of action and conditions applicable to a case divide neatly into exclusive classes depending on the value of some condition. Care should be taken when using this action, as a number of tables interconnected by **GOTO**s can give the appearance of logical spaghetti.

KISMET CASE STUDY 3.9

The variations on the basic table are illustrated in Figure 3.14. This is the revealed discount policy of Kismet's competitor, Hardy Ltd.

In the case of an order from a retail electrical store chain a discount of 4% is allowed if the order is less than £2000, 6% if the order is between £2000 and £5000 and 10% if the order is £5000 or more. There is a further discount of 5% if there is only one delivery address. A note of the invoice is sent to the manager if the total amount invoiced is greater than £10,000. With all other types of customer, a 4% discount is given if the order is more than £3000. A 5% discount is also allowed if the delivery is within 50 miles, 3% is allowed if no other discounts have been made and the customer has an annual turnover with Hardy of more than £100,000. A note of any invoice in excess of £5000 is sent to the manager.

Table A

Retail store chain	Y	Y	Y	Y	Y	Y	Y	Y	N
Order size	<£2,000	<£2,000	£2,000 to less than £5,000	£2,000 to less than £5,000	£5,000 to less than £10,000	£5,000 to less than £10,000	>£10,000	>£10,000	–
One delivery	Y	N	Y	N	Y	N	Y	N	–
Discount 4%		X							
6%				X					
9%	X								
10%						X		X	
11%			X						
15%					X		X		
Note to manager							X	X	
GO TO table B									X

Table B

Order > £3,000	Y	Y	Y	Y	N	N	N
Order > £5,000	Y	Y	N	N	N	N	N
Delivery < 50 miles	Y	N	Y	N	Y	N	N
Turnover > £100,000	–	–	–	–	–	Y	N
Discount 0%							X
3%						X	
4%					X		
5%		X		X			
9%	X		X				
Send note to manager	X	X					

Figure 3.14 **Decision tables illustrating Hardy's discount policy**

Decision tables are a valuable tool in analysis. Within the general format of the table conditions are specified unambiguously and separated from actions, which are clearly stated. The declarative style of the table accords well with the way that certain processes are considered as the implementation of a set of conditions.

The straightforward, non-technical character of the tables makes them a valuable communication tool between analysts and users in checking the analyst's understanding of a process. In design, the tables can be used to specify the requirements of a program. They facilitate analyst–programmer communication.

Although it takes intelligence to construct a decision table, it requires a very limited repertoire of mental abilities to use one. They are therefore in a form suitable for incorporation into a computer program. There are programs that accept a decision table as input and produce program code to implement the table as output. The program runs interactively with users by requiring answers to basic questions. These questions correspond to the conditions.

Finally, decision tables cover in a methodical way the totality of possible combinations of conditions that might apply in a particular case and so can be used to check on the completeness and consistency of a policy that involves the taking of different actions when different conditions are satisfied.

KISMET CASE STUDY 3.10

In order to appreciate the completeness and consistency of a policy, consider the following example:

> Kismet's management has decided that computerization offers it the opportunity to offer a more complex and targeted discount policy. It has decided to offer its customers a differential discount depending on whether the order is large (over £5000), whether the year-to-date turnover of the customer is large (over £100,000), whether the order is to be delivered to one address only and whether the delivery, or deliveries, is within 50 miles. After many hours of discussion, the management has arrived at the following policy:
>
> 1. A high-priority order is defined to be one from a high-turnover customer who requires a large order or who is using only one delivery address.
> 2. A low-priority order is defined to be one that is neither large nor from a customer with a high turnover.
> 3. If the order is large and to be delivered to only one address a discount of 10% is allowed, with an additional discount of 5% if that address is within 50 miles.
> 4. No order that is to be delivered to multiple addresses may receive more than 5% discount.
> 5. However, an order that is not large from a customer with a turnover of more than £100,000 should receive a 10% discount except in as far as this conflicts with rule 4, in which case they will obtain the maximum discount applicable under that rule.
> 6. High-priority orders are to be given at least 5% discount.
> 7. Low-priority orders are to be given a 3% discount if there is only one delivery address.
> 8. Orders from customers with a turnover of less than £100,000 to be delivered to multiple addresses shall receive a discount of 5% if the order is large, irrespective of whether the delivery is within 50 miles or not.
> 9. All large orders that are to be delivered within a 50-mile radius are to receive at least 10% discount.
> 10. All applicable discounts are to be totalled.

This policy has been analysed in Figure 3.15. Although this does not exactly follow the format of Figure 3.13, it is, in principle, a decision table separating conditions and actions. The effects of each of the rules on each of the types of order (each type of order corresponds to one column in the condition entry quadrant) are shown in the action entry quadrant. The total effect of all rules on a type of order is shown, where possible, in the TOTAL row. For example, column 2 corresponds to a large order from a customer with a turnover in excess of £100,000. The order has one delivery address, which is not within the 50-mile zone surrounding the Kismet warehouse. It is judged to be a high-priority order (rule 1) and so is to be accorded at least 5% discount (rule 6). The order satisfies rule 2 and so is given a 10% discount.

It is clear that the policy is inconsistent. Notes (a) and (b) of Figure 3.15 indicate where the inconsistency arises. This could be eliminated by removing rule 9. It would be the analyst's responsibility to point out to management the inconsistency and advise on possible ways of eliminating it. An inconsistent policy cannot be incorporated into a program. It is ultimately the responsibility of Kismet to decide on the policy. It is a business decision. Normally, all the analyst would do is to comment on the formal properties of the policy.

		1	2	3	4	5	6	7	8	9	10	11	12	13	14	15	16
		H	H	H	H					H	H			L	L	L	L
Large order		Y	Y	Y	Y	Y	Y	Y	Y	N	N	N	N	N	N	N	N
Large turnover		Y	Y	Y	Y	N	N	N	N	Y	Y	Y	Y	N	N	N	N
One address		Y	Y	N	N	Y	Y	N	N	Y	Y	N	N	Y	Y	N	N
Within 50 miles		Y	N	Y	N	Y	N	Y	N	Y	N	Y	N	Y	N	Y	N
Actions																	
Give percent discount	Rule 3	15	10			15	10										
	Rule 4			≤5	≤5			≤5	≤5			≤5	≤5			≤5	≤5
	Rule 5									10	10	5	5				
	Rule 6	≥5	≥5	≥5	≥5					≥5	≥5						
	Rule 7													3	3		
	Rule 8							5	5								
	Rule 9	≥10		≥10		≥10		≥10									
TOTAL		15	10	(a)	5	15	10	(b)	5	10	10	5	5	3	3	(c)	(c)

Notes

H = High-priority order (Rule 1)
L = Low-priority order (Rule 2)

(a) Rules 4, 6 and 9 are inconsistent
(b) Rules 4, 8 and 9 are inconsistent
(c) There is insufficient information to assign a discount.

Figure 3.15 **The use of a decision table to illustrate inconsistency**

In summary, there are a number of advantages and disadvantages in the use of decision tables to represent the links between conditions and actions.

Advantages

- They provide a clear tabular representation linking conditions with actions and so act as a communication tool.
- The declarative style corresponds to the way that many processes are understood as conditions that determine actions.
- They ensure an exhaustive coverage of all possible cases.
- They can be used to investigate inconsistency and redundancy in a set of rules.
- They are easy to follow in operation.
- They can be incorporated into program specifications.

Disadvantages

- They can become very large and unwieldy with large numbers of conditions.
- They are only suitable for representing processes where there is little interleaving between the evaluation of conditions and the execution of actions.

LOGIC FLOWCHARTS

Decision tables are one way of clearly representing the logic of a process and are most suitable when only few actions need to be undertaken as a result of the evaluation of a (possibly complex) set of conditions. If, though, the process is one that involves intermingling the evaluation of conditions with the execution of various actions, then the proliferation of **GOTO** statements to subsidiary decision tables makes it difficult to follow the logic of the process. Logic flowcharts overcome this difficulty. The symbols used in logic flowcharts are shown in Figure 3.16.

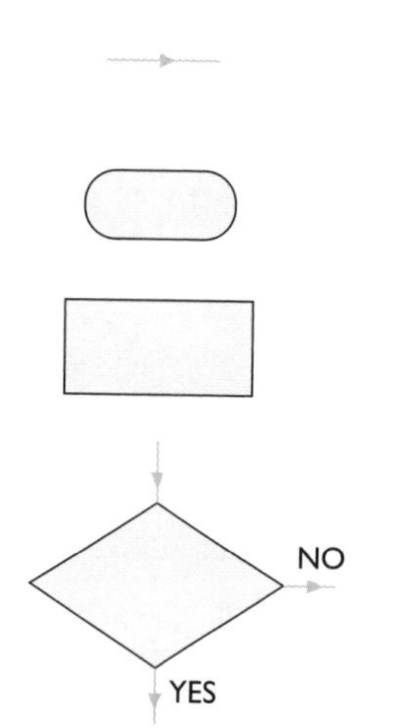

Flowline
Used to indicate the direction of movement between other symbols: that is, control

Terminator
Used to indicate the start and finish of the flowchart

Process or **Action**
Used to illustrate the occurrence of any process: for example, add 1 to the running total

Decision or **Question**
Used to distinguish between two states of affairs: as a consequence the flow of control is directed one way or another. There are only two possible exits to a decision box, YES and NO

Figure 3.16 **Basic symbols used in the preparation of logic flowcharts**

KISMET CASE STUDY 3.11

The use of logic flowcharts can be illustrated by the representation of the following example. It concerns the approval of orders in the credit control section of Kismet. The procedure, stated here, can be regarded as a fuller version of the summary that appeared previously in Case study 3.1. The additions mainly concern the procedure to be followed in the case of error discovery and the maintenance of a running total of the value of approved orders. The order set has been priced and valued. Now is the time for credit approval.

The credit control clerk processes a stack of order sets for which provisional values have been calculated and inserted. The presence of the *customer#* and *customer name* are first checked. If either is absent then the customer file is consulted and the missing entry inserted. If there is no reference to the customer in the file the order set is sent to the credit control manager. If the number and name are found not to match then the order 4 set is sent back to the order-processing section together with an internal company P22 form for investigation. In all other cases, the *order value* is added to the *current balance* and compared with the *credit limit*. If this has been exceeded, the order set is sent to the credit control manager along with the customer records. If the order has passed these tests, the order set is stamped 'OK approved' and put in the out tray. At the end of the stack, the contents of the out tray are returned to the order-processing section, and the total value of all approved orders is entered on the daily totals sheet.

The flowchart is shown in Figure 3.17. The flow lines indicate flows of control, *not* flows of data or documents. When it is said that there is a flow of control between points A and B, all this means is that after the operation at A has been carried out the operation at B is carried out. Nothing passes between points A and B.

The following conditions apply to flowcharts:

- Each question or decision box has exactly two exits: one corresponding to 'yes' or 'true' and the other to 'no' or 'false'.
- All flows of control must end in a decision box, action box or terminator and must always ensure that the process eventually stops.
- Generally, the flowchart is designed so that the flow of control goes from the top of the page downwards.

The flowchart in Figure 3.17 follows these principles. The repetitious nature of the processing of one order after another is accomplished by directing the flow of control from the end of the approval process, as applied to one order, back to the top of the chart. There, a test is performed

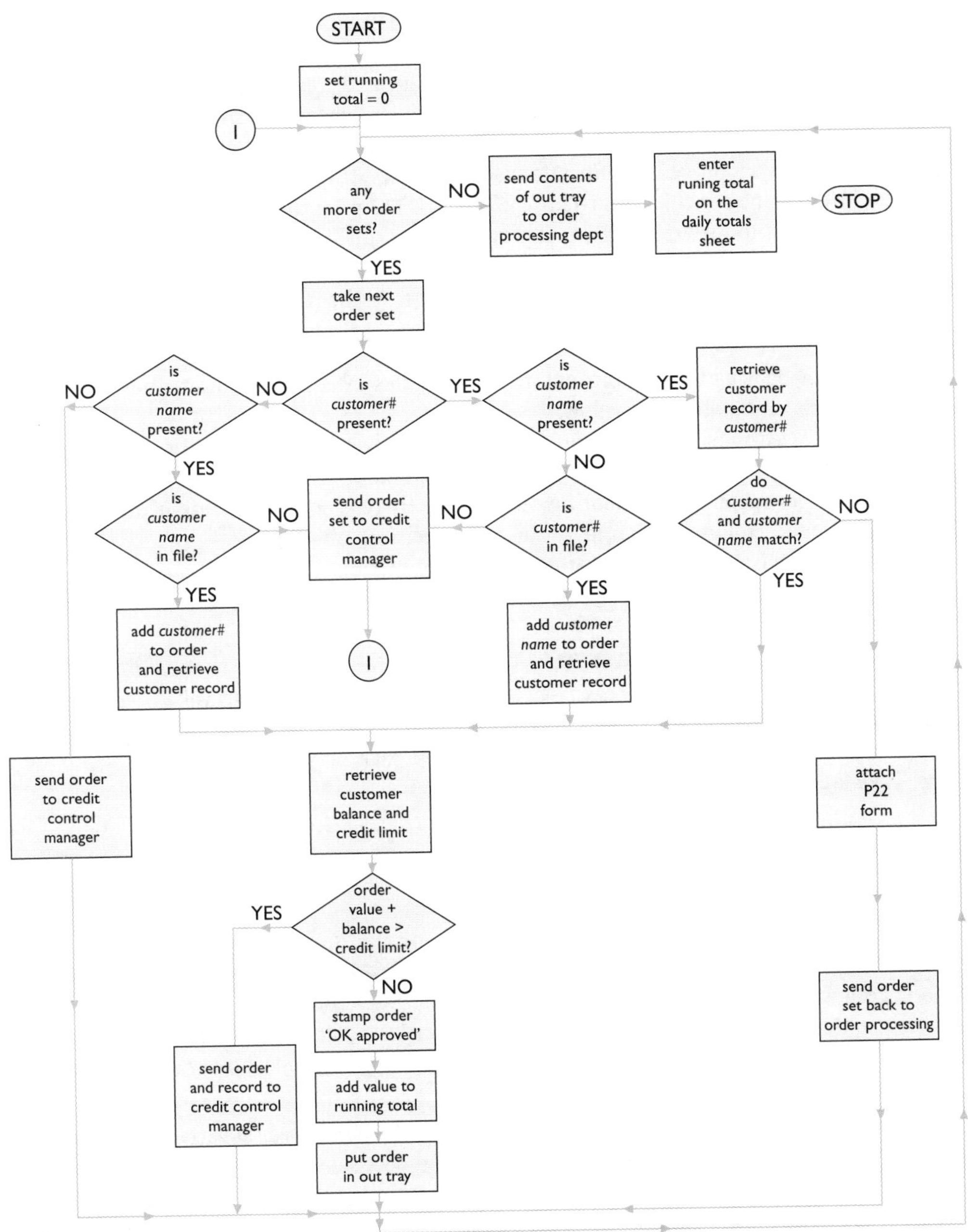

Figure 3.17 The logic flowchart for credit approval in Kismet

to establish whether there are any more orders in the stack before proceeding. A running total is maintained.

Flowcharts have several advantages. Their pictorial representation makes them easy to follow and understand—the different paths through the process are obvious at a glance. They can therefore be used as a basis for agreement between the analyst and the user on the correctness of the analyst's understanding. They may also form part of the firm's procedures manual.

Flowcharts can be given for high or low levels of analysis. For instance, to answer the simple question 'is the customer name in the file?' requires the execution of a number of actions and the consideration of further questions. If the records in the file are ordered by *customer#*, it implies the following type of procedure for the clerk. Go to the filing cabinet, start at the first record, compare the *customer name* with the target *name*, if identical, stop—the *customer name* is in the file, otherwise carry out the procedure on the next record, and so on. The level of the chart is generally high at the analysis stage, and such low-level specifications are ignored.

Logic flowcharts can also be used in the design stage as a way of specifying a procedure precisely. If it is intended that a program be written from this specification, it is called a **program logic flowchart**. The flowchart will be presented generally at a much more detailed level. Variable names will be included, procedures for establishing counts will be outlined, and so on. The presence of the decision box encourages the use of the **GOTO** programming structure, so program flowcharts may lead to programming techniques that result in non-structured programs. This may be a reason to discourage their use at the design stage.

In summary, the main advantages and disadvantages in the use of logic flowcharts are:

Advantages

- They provide a pictorial representation of a series of actions and are therefore easy to understand and natural to follow.
- They are used in procedures manuals to indicate the sequences of actions that are to be followed in carrying out a task—for example, an audit.
- They are very good at representing cases where there is an interleaving of actions and the evaluation of conditions (compare this with decision tables).
- They may be used to specify programs to programmers.

Disadvantages

- They encourage the use of **GOTO** statements if used in program specifications in design. This may lead to programs that have a logic that is difficult to unravel.
- They force the developer to work at a very low level of detail at an early stage of the project, therefore losing the benefit of the top-down approach previously advocated.
- They are difficult and time-consuming to alter once drawn.

STRUCTURED ENGLISH

As well as using decision tables or logic flowcharts, procedures can be represented through the use of structured English. This also has the effect of imposing a structure on the specification, which encourages the use of structured programming. Structured English is a precise, highly restricted subset of the natural English language. There is no accepted standard for structured English, but all usages have a number of features in common. The vocabulary of the language is restricted to:

- Precise verbs phrased in the imperative mood. All adjectives, adverbs and words with vague or ambiguous meanings are avoided. Complex sentence structures involving subordinate clauses are broken down into their atomic constituents. Irrelevant phrases are dropped. For instance, the sentence 'The large document containing the particular details on the customer should now be edited carefully by the clerk making sure that all entries are made clearly with an indelible pen' would probably be reduced to 'edit document containing customer details'.
- References to items of data should use the same terms as applied in the data flow diagram and the data dictionary.
- Certain reserved words are used for revealing the logical structure of processes.

The logic of any process can be described by using three structures (Figure 3.18):

1. **A sequential block of statements:** The statements should be concise and contain a verb and object. For example:

   (a) Compute total
   (b) Set sales tax equal to total multiplied by sales tax rate
   (c) Set total equal to total plus sales tax
   (d) Compute discount
   (e) Set net total equal to total minus discount
   (f) Write net total on invoice.

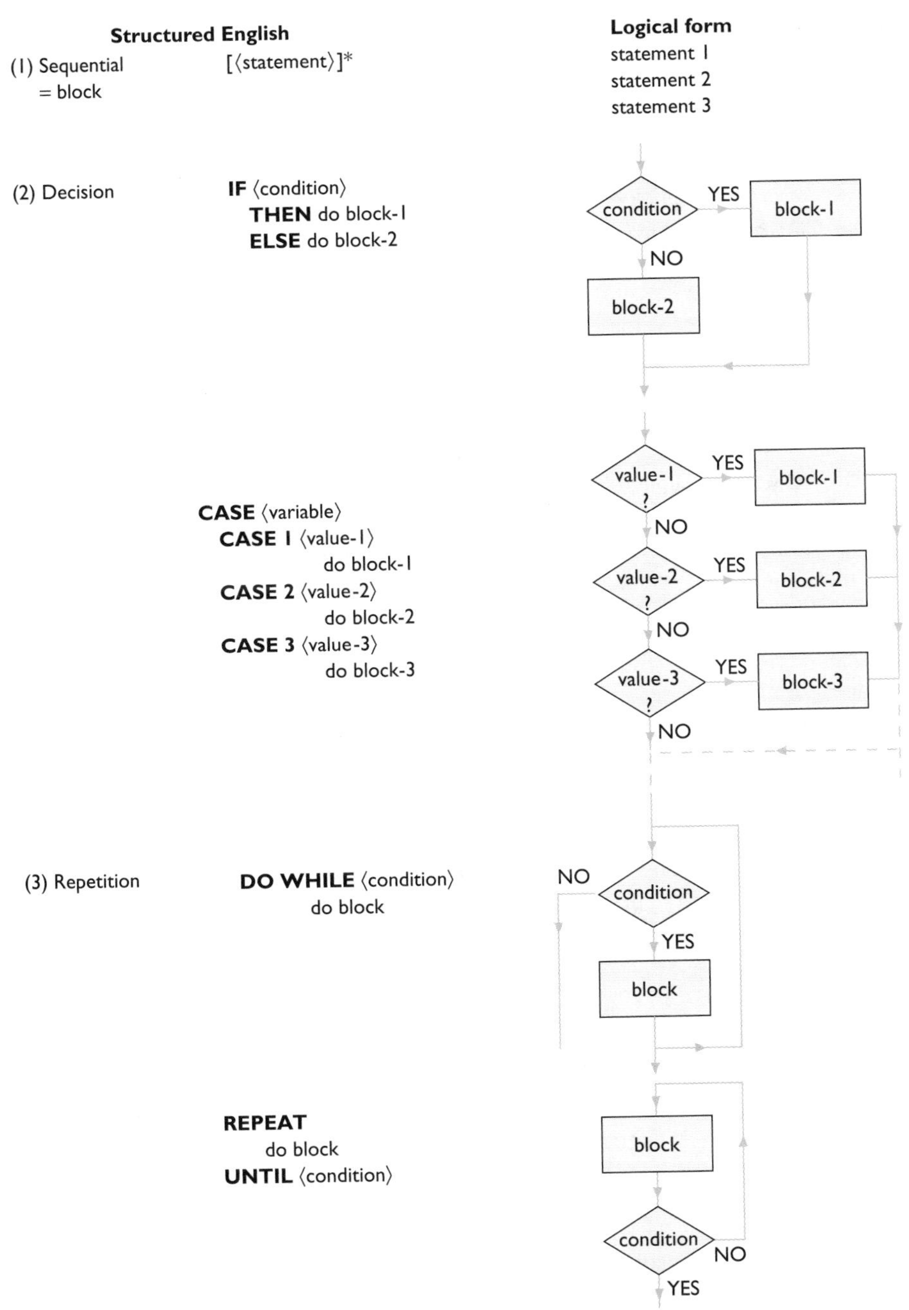

Figure 3.18 The logical form of structured English

2. **Decision structures:** These are used when it is required that one sequence of operations be carried out if a condition is satisfied and another set if it is not satisfied. The structure takes two forms:

   (a) The two-way decision:

   IF ⟨condition⟩
   THEN ⟨block-1⟩
   ELSE ⟨block-2⟩

   where the **ELSE** is not compulsory. For example:

   IF total > credit limit **THEN** refer to credit control manager
   ELSE stamp 'OK approved'

(b) The multi-way decision:

```
CASE ⟨variable⟩
CASE 1 ⟨value-1⟩
        do block-1
CASE 2 ⟨value-2⟩
        do block-2
CASE 3 ⟨value-3⟩
        do block-3
```

For example:

```
CASE invoice value
  CASE 1 invoice value <£2000
              add 1% to discount percent
  CASE 2 £2000 ≤ invoice value <£5000
              add 3% to discount percent
  CASE 3 invoice value ≥£5000
              add 6% to discount percent
```

3. **Repetition structures:** These are used where a process is repeated until some condition is met. There are two forms of repetition statement:

```
DO WHILE ⟨condition⟩
  do block
```

and

```
REPEAT
  do block
UNTIL ⟨condition⟩
```

In the former, the test as to whether the condition is satisfied occurs before the loop is entered (so the loop will not be traversed at all if the condition fails first time). In the latter, the test occurs after the loop has been traversed, implying that the loop is traversed at least once. For example:

```
DO WHILE stack of invoices is not empty
  get next invoice
  add invoice total to running total
```

Structured English representations of processes may be a little difficult to follow for the uninitiated, particularly if there is a high degree of internal nesting. However, as mentioned at the beginning of this section they do have the attraction of encouraging structured coding of programs.

Whether decision tables, a logic flowchart or structured English is chosen as the representation of a process depends on its nature. Complex sets of conditions determining few actions with little iteration suggest a decision table representation. Otherwise a logic flowchart or structured English representation will be suitable, the choice being the result of the trade-off between diagrammatic clarity and the wish to encourage structured code in the design stage.

KISMET CASE STUDY 3.12

The example now discussed illustrates the use of structured English to specify a process. It concerns the task of pricing the Kismet company order sets and is taken from a statement supplied by the clerk responsible for pricing the orders. It covers error cases not given in the case study.

> I get the stack of orders to price from the supervisor. I first of all tidy the pile and then go through the orders one by one until I have finished. After this I put the stack of priced orders in the credit control section's in tray. I carefully price each item in turn by consulting the sales catalogue. Sometimes I cannot find the item because it is a new product and I then have to look at the supplement. If I have no luck there I just put a big query mark by it on the form. After I have finished I put the order in the out tray.

```
(a) get stack of orders
    DO WHILE there are more orders in the stack
        get the top order
        DO WHILE there are more unpriced items on the order
            get next unpriced item#
            IF item# is in the catalogue
              THEN write item price on the order
              ELSE IF item price is in the supplement
                   THEN write item price on the order
                   ELSE write? on the order
      put the order in the out tray
    get the stack of orders from the out tray
    put the stack of orders in the credit control section's in tray

(b) get stack of orders
    DO WHILE there are more orders in the stack
        get the top order
        DO WHILE there are more unpriced items on the order
            get next unpriced item#
            IF item# is in the catalogue
              THEN write item price on the order
              ELSE IF item price is in the supplement
                   THEN write item price on the order
                   ELSE write ? on the order
                ENDIF
            ENDIF
        ENDDO
        put the order in the out tray
    ENDDO
    get the stack of orders from the out tray
    put the stack of orders in the credit control section's in tray
```

Figure 3.19 **The structured English representation of the pricing process for Kismet: (a) structured English without ENDIF and ENDDO; (b) structured English with ENDIF and ENDDO**

The structured English version is given in Figure 3.19(a). Note how the rambling description of the process, as given by the order pricing clerk, is transformed into a set of precise statements.

The indenting is important as it gives a clear indication of the structure of the logic governing the process. Statements may also be nested, as shown in the example.

To illustrate the scope of an **IF** statement or a **DO** statement it is sometimes clearer to use **ENDDO**, **ENDIF** and **ENDCASE** statements. These fill a role analogous to brackets in elementary arithmetic. The expression $6 - 3 \times 7 + 3$ can be made much clearer by the insertion of brackets: $(6 - (3 \times (7 + 3)))$. In fact, in many cases the brackets are necessary to indicate the precise meaning of the formula. Similarly, **ENDDO**, **ENDIF** and **ENDCASE** fulfil the role analogous to the right-hand bracket.

The structured English version of the Kismet pricing clerk's routine using **ENDDO** and **ENDIF** statements is shown in Figure 3.19(b).

Summary

The purpose of systems analysis is to arrive at an understanding of a system that is sufficient to design a computerized replacement. This replacement may involve substantial redesign and the integration of physically disparate manual systems. In order to achieve this, a structured approach is taken to systems analysis. This chapter was concerned with structured process analysis and modelling. Its main features are:

- a commitment to a 'top-down' decomposition in which data and processes are analysed into their constituent parts;

- an emphasis on the development of a model of the system as a prerequisite for successful design; and
- an assumption that developing an information system is largely a technical exercise.

The main tool used is the data flow diagram, which models the data flows between data processes, stores and sinks. This diagram reveals the logical model at various levels of detail, depending on the degree of decomposition and the intended recipient of the diagram. The nature of the processes is specified via decision tables, logic flowcharts or structured English, all of which have their relative strengths and limitations. The data dictionary maintains information on the nature of the data itself. The entire repertoire of techniques is aimed at deriving a logical model, independent of physical commitments, and at producing documentation that is precise, thus facilitating communication between users, management, programmers and the analyst.

Much attention has been given to the analysis of the organization into its functional components, the further breakdown of these into individual processes, the charting of the data flows between them and their representation by various tools. What has been missing from the analysis is the treatment of the data stores and the nature of the data itself. Some would regard this as perhaps the most important feature of analysis, and it is to this that the next chapter is devoted.

REVIEW QUESTIONS

1. What are the scope and objectives of systems analysis?

2. When considering a complex integrated system, why is it important to use a methodical approach to systems analysis and design?

3. What benefits are to be obtained in analysis by initially focusing on processes and functions at a general rather than a detailed level?

4. What are the advantages and limitations of:

(a) decision tables
(b) logic flowcharts
(c) structured English

as representation tools for processes?

5. What are the advantages and limitations of manual systems flowcharts?

6. Explain the purpose of a data dictionary.

EXERCISES

1. Can a situation represented by a logic flowchart, decision table or structured English always be represented without loss of information by all three? What determines the choice of method of process specification?

2. 'There is little difference between data flow diagrams and document flowcharts—they both represent the flow of data between processes.' Do you agree?

3. 'At the stage of analysis an understanding of the existing system is more important than technical computer expertise, and as the tools of analysis are relatively easy to understand, it is more effective if existing users carry out the analysis and computer experts are brought in only at the design stage.' Do you agree?

4. 'By concentrating on formal data and processes, the analyst ignores the fact that much useful information in an organization is of an informal nature—opinions, hunches and qualitative approximations. The analyst is therefore bound to produce an inadequate analysis and design of a computerized information system.' What is to be said for and against this view?

5. A large lending library handles book issues, returns and enquiries and sends out notices regarding overdue books to borrowers. All procedures are currently manual. The library deals with a large number of postal and telephone transactions. The majority of its books are stored in underground stacks. The library thus needs a fast response information system and to this end has purchased a database management system.

Initial analysis indicates that the following information has been stored on books, borrowers and loans in the current manual system:

- For each book: book number, author, title.
- For each borrower: ID number, name, address.
- For each loan of a book to a borrower: date due for return.
- A record of books reserved for potential borrowers is also maintained.

The database is to be designed to support the following functions currently carried out manually:

- *Book issue processing*: On receipt of a request for a loan the librarian makes an enquiry to establish whether the book is held by the library and is available (that is, not on loan). If the book is not held, then that information is given to the potential borrower by a note.

  If the book is held but is on loan the potential borrower is also informed, a note that the book is to be reserved on return is made, and it is established by enquiry whether the book is overdue or not. If it is overdue, a note is sent to the current borrower pointing out the overdue status of the loan and that a request for the book has been made. If the book is directly available then it is issued to the potential borrower and details of this loan, including the date due for return, are stored.
- *Book return processing*: On receipt of a returned book, the librarian cancels the loan and makes an enquiry to establish whether the book is reserved. If it is reserved, then it is issued to the reserver and the reserve note is cancelled. Otherwise, the book is returned to the stack.
- *Enquiry processing*: There are two types of enquiry:
  (a) Given the name of the borrower, establish what books he/she has on loan and when they are due for return.
  (b) Given the name of the book, establish which borrower, if any, has the book and the date due for return.
- *Overdue processing*: When books become two weeks overdue, a notice is sent out requesting their return. A similar note is sent every two weeks until return.
  (a) Draw a high-level combined data flow diagram for the processes.
  (b) Draw an exploded data flow diagram for each of the processes.

6. The daily invoicing routine for an invoice clerk is as follows. At the beginning of the day the stack of sales orders with their associated dispatch notes is taken from the in tray and processed. The details of each order are checked against the details of the relevant customer account and a discount is calculated. A customer in the trade is allowed 15% off the list price. There is also a special 5% discount for any customer who has been ordering regularly for two years, provided that the customer has not received the trade discount. Any order over £1000 is allowed a bulk discount of 10% off the list price in addition to any other discounts. If the total to be invoiced exceeds the customer's credit limit, a note is sent to the manager prior to dispatch of the invoice. When all invoices have been dispatched, a note of the total invoiced is sent to the manager.
   (a) Draw a logic flowchart illustrating the day's procedure.
   (b) Represent the above by using structured English.

7. Design a manual systems flowchart to illustrate a procedure that Kismet might use to handle return of goods. This flowchart should be compatible with Figure 3.3.

8. The following is an account of the manual operations that occur at the head office of a chain of supermarkets:

   Each supermarket submits a daily cash report plus supporting documentation to the head office by post. This is passed from the mail room to the area manager. The area manager's staff carry out checks on the arithmetic of the cash reports and on submitted bank deposit slips and petty cash vouchers. All of these documents are then passed to the cashier's department after any queries have been reconciled.

   Each day's cash report is summarized and entered into a cash analysis book in the cashier's department. This cash analysis book forms part of the main cash book into which weekly totals are entered. At the end of each week, the cashier's department reconciles the cash book with the bank pass sheets. The cash reports are then sent to the accounts department.

   Every week, each supermarket also submits, by post, records of deliveries made by suppliers together with other stock movement details. These are sent to the area manager's office, where the unit costs and sales prices are entered on the document and delivery records. The complete set of documents is then passed to the accounts department. The area manager's office also receives delivery sheets sent from the company's own warehouses. These are for goods supplied to the supermarkets.

These sheets are priced at cost and at selling prices before being submitted to the accounts department.

The accounts department receives the stock movement forms, the direct and internal delivery sheets and the cash reports. The department then prepares a monthly report for each supermarket at cost and selling prices.

Draw a document systems flowchart with any necessary narrative showing the various document flows. (Note that many temporary and permanent files are implied in the description without being explicitly stated.)

9. When a library first receives a book from a publisher it is sent, together with the accompanying delivery note, to the library desk. Here the delivery note is checked against a file of books ordered. If no order can be found to match the note, a letter of enquiry is sent to the publishers. If a matching order is found, a catalogue note is prepared from the details on the validated delivery note. The catalogue note, together with the book, is sent to the registration department. The validated delivery note is sent to the accounts department, where it is stored. On receipt of an invoice from the publisher, the accounts department checks its store of delivery notes. If the corresponding delivery note is found then an instruction to pay the publisher is made, and subsequently a cheque is sent. If no corresponding delivery note is found, the invoice is stored in a pending file.

Draw a data flow diagram for this information.

10. As a systems analyst, you have been commissioned by the ABC Company to computerize its sales order processing. It is believed by the board of ABC that the attractiveness of its product to customers can be increased by ensuring that all customers receive a discount off the list price of ABC's products. It is further intended that a maximum discount of 25% on any transaction should not be exceeded. To this end, it has isolated the following customer/transaction features:

- regular customers
- cash transactions
- bulk order
- trade customers.

The board suggests the following policy, where (all discounts are off the list price and are to be added together):

(a) Those customers who are trade receive 15% discount, provided that the transaction is a bulk order; otherwise, the discount is 12%.

(b) Non-trade customers are allowed 5% discount, provided that the order is bulk.

(c) Cash transactions receive 13% discount if trade; if not a 10% discount.

(d) All regular customers are allowed 10% discount unless the total discount allowable under rules (a), (b) and (c) is greater than 10%, in which case the greater discount will apply.

By means of a decision table, advise the board as to the suitability of its discount policy in the light of its stated aims.

11. A stack of student records, ordered by *student#*, contains up to five records on each student covering the student's exam results in one or more of the following—accounting, economics, law, maths, systems analysis. A clerk is required to process these records and must produce an average for each student, which is then entered on a summary sheet. Not all students take all five subjects. The clerk also computes an average mark for each exam for each of the five subjects and enters it on the summary sheet.

(a) Produce a structured English specification of a suitable process to achieve these aims.

(b) Represent this process by a logic flowchart.

12. A firm pursues the following discount policy on its products (all discounts being offered as a percentage of advertised price).

(a) Those customers ordering more than ten items receive at least a 1% discount.

(b) Those customers who are not regular customers receive at most a 2% discount.

(c) All those regular customers who order more than ten items receive a 2% discount plus an additional 1% discount if they pay cash.

(d) Any person paying cash and who is either a regular customer or orders more than ten items (but not both) is to receive a 2% discount.

(e) All customers who satisfy just one of the following conditions—ordering more than ten items, paying cash or being a regular customer—receive a 1% discount in as far as this does not conflict with rules (a)–(d).

(f) Any customer not covered by the preceding rules receives no discount.

Using decision tables, evaluate the above rules as to their consistency, comprehensiveness and redundancy. Can the rules be replaced by a simpler set?

MINI CASE 3.1

KEMSING THEATRE

The Kemsing Theatre is a small regionally based theatre in south-east England. For most of the year the theatre stages plays, but it also screens cinema films, hosts visiting speakers and stages musical events. The theatre accepts postal and telephone bookings for its forthcoming performances up to six months in advance. About half of the bookings are directly from the public, the remainder being from agencies. The theatre employs 25 people, whose functions range from set design and special effects through to marketing, box office and accounting functions.

When a member of the public makes a booking by telephone either a credit card number is taken and the booking is firmly made, or a reservation for the seat is taken. In the latter case, the member of the public must collect and pay for the ticket at least half an hour before the performance.

In the case of agencies, on receipt of a block booking request by phone or mail, the theatre runs a credit check on the agency account and makes out a confirmation note for those requested seats that are still available.

This is sent to the agency as both a confirmation of booking and an invoice. At the end of each month, the theatre sends a statement of account to each agency.

Half an hour before the performance starts, all those seats that have been reserved by the public but have not been collected are released for general sale. The theatre also receives enquiries on seat availability from both agencies and the public.

QUESTIONS

1. Draw a data flow diagram illustrating the data flows, processes and stores necessary to carry out the invoicing, enquiry and booking facilities of the theatre.
2. For each data flow and data store, illustrate the structure of the data concerned.

Recommended reading

Avison D., Wood-Harper A.T., Vidgen R. and Wood R. (2000). *Multiview*, reissued 2nd edn. McGraw-Hill

This book applies the structured techniques covered in this section to a case study. The approach is integrated with other approaches, particularly data analysis.

Bowman K. (2003). *Systems Analysis: A Beginner's Guide*. Palgrave Macmillan

This provides a helpful introduction to the topic of systems analysis. Concepts are illustrated by case studies that run through the book.

Cutts J. (1997). *Structured Systems Analysis and Design Methodology*, 3rd edn. Blackwell Scientific Publications

This is a standard text on structured systems analysis and design. It is comprehensive, clear and suitable for a detailed understanding of structured methods.

Deeks D. (2002). *An Introduction to System Analysis Techniques*, 2nd edn. Addison-Wesley

A good all-round introduction to the analysis of data and processes in both structured and object-oriented paradigms.

Kendall K. and Kendall J. (2007). *Systems Analysis and Design*, 7th rev edn. Prentice Hall

An accessible and well-illustrated book that covers the topics of data flow diagrams and data dictionaries particularly well.

Langer A.M. (2007) *Analysis and Design of Information Systems*, 3rd edn. Springer-Verlag London Ltd

This is design for professionals and information systems students who need an in-depth view of the process and tools of systems development (particularly documentation) in the analysis stage.

Yeates D. (ed.) (2006). *Business Analysis*. British Computer Society

An interesting and informative coverage of systems analysis from a business perspective. The section on business process modelling is particularly relevant to the topics covered in this section.

Systems development: further tools, techniques and alternative approaches

INTRODUCTION

This section introduces and examines some additional tools and techniques and approaches that have attracted significant interest and gained importance with the developers of information systems. In some cases they are complementary to the approach described in the previous section, in others they are alternatives. First the concept of project management is introduced. A number of approaches, including the popular PRINCE2™ approach, are described and their applicability to information systems development is discussed.

Next, the increasingly important use of computers themselves as tools in the process of analysis and design is described. The power of modern hardware and software has brought about an increasing reliance upon computer-aided software engineering (CASE) to address the complexity of managing large systems development projects.

Next, rapid applications development (RAD) is considered as a framework for employing the chosen systems development methodology. Like CASE, the interest in RAD also reflects concerns over the management of large projects and the failure in some cases of traditional methodologies. RAD is not necessarily an alternative to these methodologies, as it does not claim to be a complete methodology itself. However, it does provide a framework of techniques that proponents claim allows the chosen methodology to be implemented more effectively.

Different approaches to the analysis and design of computerized information systems have differing strengths and weaknesses, differing areas of applicability and differing objectives. It is the purpose of this chapter to outline some alternatives and highlight their points of difference. Those already introduced are in the category of 'hard' approaches to systems development. By way of contrast, two 'soft' approaches will then be introduced: the first is due to Peter Checkland and generally known by his name; the second is a socio-technical approach stressing the participation of users in analysis and design. Here, both of these will be termed 'soft' approaches, compared with the 'hard' approaches, of which the structured and object-oriented methodologies considered so far are exemplars.

This section will also provide a general comparison between hard and soft methodologies. The underlying philosophies of each will be explained and contrasted. It is not intended to treat these additional approaches in detail but rather to give the reader a flavour of the debate that occurs between the proponents of hard and soft methodologies. This is a fruitful topic for discussion. It not only reveals deep and important divergences in attitudes to the analysis and design of information systems, particularly those in which people as social beings are heavily involved, but also sets the framework for a debate that is likely to persist for several years and may mark an important turning point in the development of attitudes to systems analysis and design.

PROJECT MANAGEMENT

The success rate of IT projects over time makes for mixed reading. Estimates have been made that as much as 30% of the money spent on software development is used rescuing failed projects and reworking software that does not satisfy the initial requirements. Many explanations have been provided for project failure, for example:

- the project scope was not fully appreciated;
- the user needs were not completely understood;
- lack of management continuity;
- over-optimistic estimates of the benefits that can be attained;
- high user expectations;

- poor alignment between IT departments and business users.

The classic benchmarks are that a project is considered successful if:

- it meets the specification;
- it is delivered on time;
- it comes in within budget.

The history of IT project management is littered with projects that have failed in one or more, even all, of the above criteria. The adoption of standard, recognized methods in developing information systems, such as structured methodologies or object oriented approaches, has been cited as a factor in improving in project success rate. Other factors that can improve project success include the adoption of a standard project management approach, and paying due attention to the human factors in team management.

Project management approaches

A number of authors have commented on project management techniques. Fowler (2004) states that it is not possible to have a single process for software development. He believes that the multitude of factors associated with software development lead to different processes. This might include the type of software being produced (such as real-time systems, information systems etc.) the size of the project (single developer, small team, large team—100 plus) and so on. Figure 3.20 shows his high-level view of the process.

Under this model the process of systems development is intended to be iterative and incremental. During the inception phase the business case for the project and its scope are established. The elaboration phase sees detailed requirements gathering and high-level analysis. The construction phases consist of iterations of software construction, testing and integration. The transition phase involves final handover, performance tuning and user training.

Larman (2004) defines a model comprising three macro-level steps: Plan and elaborate—Build—Deploy. He then subdivides these three steps to further describe the development process.

He describes a model of stages but one that is very iterative in deployment. The Plan and elaborate step, shown in Figure 3.21, is analogous to the Analysis phase in more traditional approaches. It includes the initial project conception, investigation of alternatives, planning, requirements specification etc. It focuses on producing the higher-level use cases that capture the business processes.

The Build step, shown in Figure 3.22, is analogous to the design stage in more traditional approaches. An iterative rolling out of development cycles takes place, each progressively extending the system. Within each development cycle a series of stages is identified: Refine plan, Synchronize artefacts, Analyse, Design, Construct, Test. The development cycle made up of this series of stages is usually subject to **time-boxing**, i.e. a rigid time frame is applied within which all work must be completed. A range of two weeks to two months is typical for time-boxing a development cycle.

Some steps are identified as being optional, for example prototype implementation (step 5) in the *Plan and evaluate step* and the state diagram production (step 7) in the *Build step*.

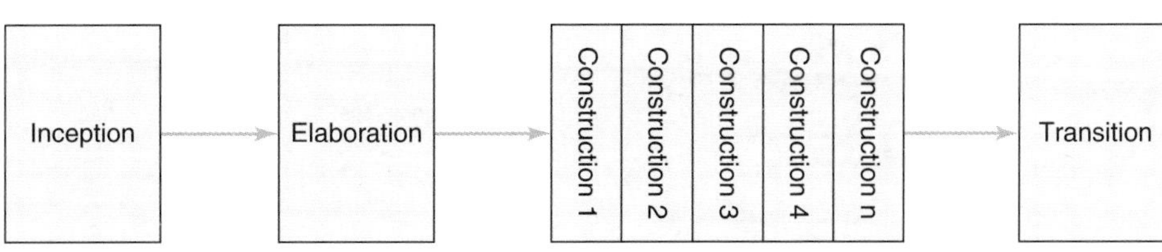

(Adapted from Fowler, 2004)

Figure 3.20 **High-level model of systems development**

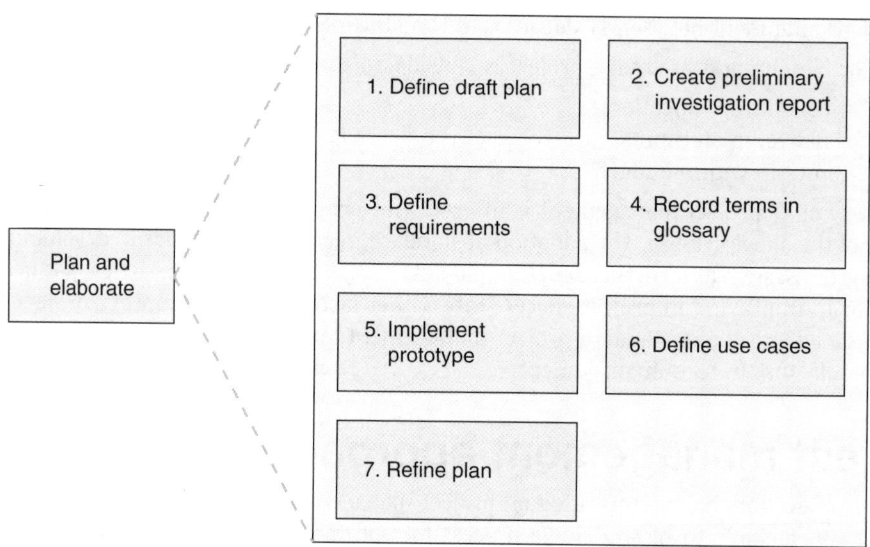

(Adapted from Larman, 2004. Larman, Craig, *Applying UML and Patterns: An Introduction to Object-Oriented Analysis and Design and Iterative Development*, 3rd, © 2005. Reproduced by permission of Pearson Education, Inc., Upper Saddle River, New Jersey.)

Figure 3.21 **The *Plan and Elaborate* step**

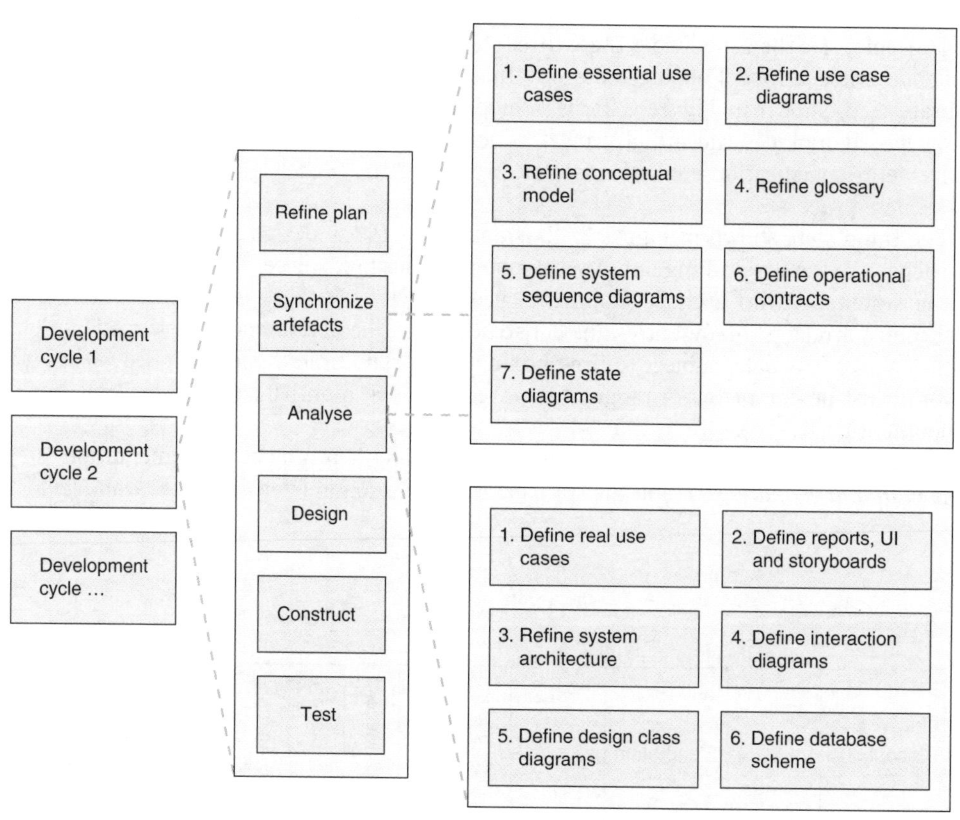

(Adapted from Larman, 2004. Larman, Craig, *Applying UML and Patterns: An Introduction to Object-Oriented Analysis and Design and Iterative Development*, 3rd, © 2005. Reproduced by permission of Pearson Education, Inc., Upper Saddle River, New Jersey.)

Figure 3.22 **The *Build* step**

PRINCE2™

PRINCE® is an acronym standing for **PRojects IN Controlled Environments**. It is an approach to project management that includes the organization, management and control of projects.

PRINCE has become widely used in both the public and private sectors since its introduction, and is becoming a de facto standard for project management. Although PRINCE was originally intended for information systems development, it has also been used on a number of non-IT projects.

The most recent release, PRINCE2™, incorporates the requirements of existing users and has been designed to enhance the method towards a generic, best practice approach for the management of all types of projects. PRINCE2 has become a UK Government standard for IT project management.

PRINCE2 offers a project management approach that is process-based. Each process is framed in terms of the key inputs and outputs together with the deliverables and activities anticipated. The processes indicate the management activities that will steer the project. Figure 3.23 shows the PRINCE2 process model and the various constituent management activities. For any particular project it will be essential to establish the importance of each of these processes and therefore the attention that should be given to each.

Under PRINCE2 a project is divided into well-defined stages; at each stage it is intended that resources will be controlled efficiently and progress will be monitored regularly. The project management team members' roles and responsibilities are fully described. Project planning using PRINCE2 is product-based, which means the project plans are focused on delivering results and are not simply about planning when the various activities on the project will be done.

The UK Office of Government Commerce cites the benefits of PRINCE2 to be:

- a controlled and organized start, middle and end;
- regular reviews of progress against plan and against the business case;
- flexible decision points;
- automatic management control of any deviations from the plan;
- the involvement of management and stakeholders at the right time and place during the project;
- good communication channels between the project, project management, and the rest of the organization.

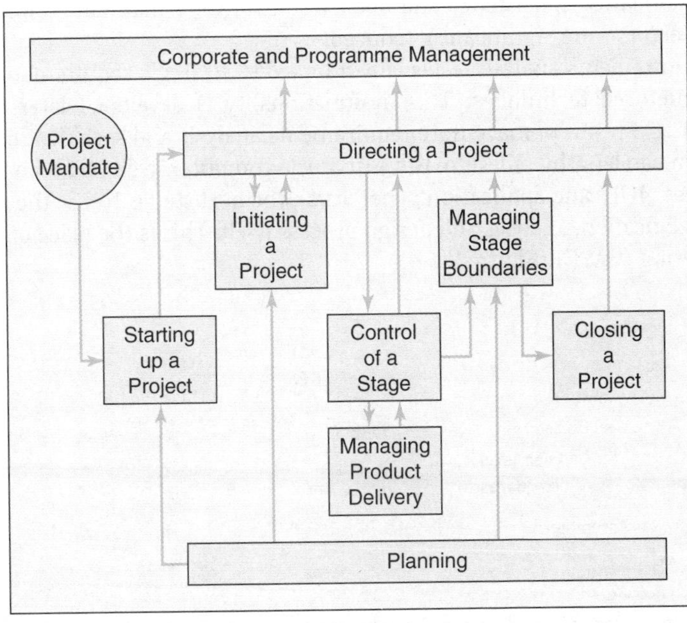

Figure 3.23 The PRINCE2 Process Model

PRINCE2 focuses on the business benefits that can be obtained from a project. These often take the form of financial benefits but can also be strategic (e.g. the fulfilment of an overarching organizational strategic aim) or legislative (e.g. fulfilling a requirement of a government body or of the organization's head office).

To account for the changing environment in which projects are carried out, PRINCE2 includes a system of version control which is termed **configuration management**. This allows for tracking of the products being delivered, knowing their current status and which version is the latest.

Although PRINCE2 is very popular for projects concerned with the development of information systems it is in fact applicable to any project type, regardless of its environment. However, although the set of concepts and processes are laid down, the way they are applied to each particular project will vary and a successful implementation will inevitably entail some tailoring of the method.

COMPUTER-AIDED SOFTWARE ENGINEERING

Computer-aided software engineering (CASE) provides new tools for the rapid development of reliable computer systems. The traditional cost curve for the design and development of a business information system locates most of the cost as falling within the area of implementation, particularly coding. Fourth-generation languages (4GLs) and other applications-generation tools are an attempt to cut the cost in this area by enabling speedy development of systems through the automation of the production of code.

The success of this can be measured by the fact that it is now possible to build a system and, if it fails to meet user needs, to redevelop it quickly and cheaply. This, in essence, is the philosophy behind prototyping. A problem with the approach is that it diminishes the role of formal requirements specification and systems design. This may be acceptable or even desirable for small systems, particularly for decision support, but the approach cannot cope with larger projects unless considerable design effort has been undertaken.

Structured methodologies, developed in the late 1970s and early 1980s and covered elsewhere in this book, were a significant improvement in approaches to systems analysis and design compared with previous methods. By clearly identifying stages, tools and techniques, and documentation standards, consistency and quality control were maintained for systems design projects. Design errors were significantly reduced.

However, requirements analysis, especially if linked to strategic requirements, is not readily accessible to structured techniques. This dysfunctionality is developed later in this chapter. Errors still occur as a result of inaccurate requirements analysis and specifications, and changes in requirements mean lengthy redesign. But just as the computer itself has been utilized to assist the coding process (4GLs and application generators), the next step is to use the computer in the requirements specification, analysis and design process itself. This is the place of computer-aided software engineering (CASE) (Figure 3.24).

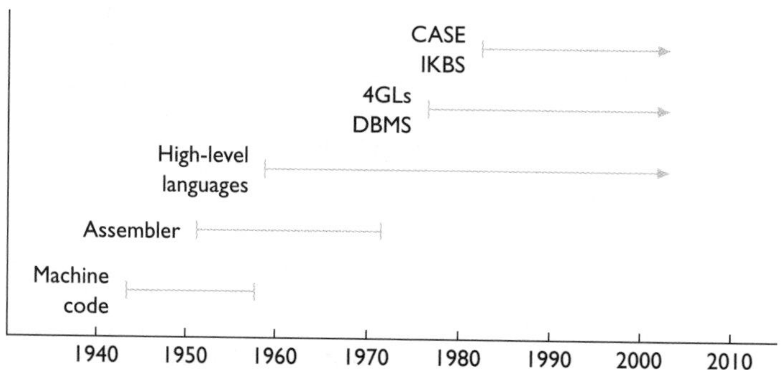

Figure 3.24 **The place of CASE tools in software development**

CASE automates various stages of the analysis and design process with the assistance of software tools. The CASE philosophy involves the use of these software tools working together with a methodology of systems analysis and design to:

- develop models that describe the business;
- aid in corporate planning;
- provide support for systems specification, documentation and design; and
- aid in the implementation process.

CASE tools are used by computer professionals to carry out some part of the systems analysis/design process. They are not end-user oriented, although they may be used in conjunction with end users. The tools are normally run on high-performance development workstations.

CASE support

CASE tools provide assistance in the following ways (see Figure 3.25):

1. **Corporate planning of information systems:** Software is used to describe the organization, its goals, resources, responsibilities and structure. These descriptions may be used to create strategic plans. The software will be used to indicate and track relationships between the various components of the plan. The planning specifications will identify activities for incorporation into information systems developments. Many CASE tools also include facilities for cost estimation calculations. Outline design parameters are fed in, and an indication of the expected cost and duration of the project is generated.
2. **Creating specifications of requirements:** This corresponds to the non-strategic stages of systems analysis. At this stage, an information system is analysed into its component activities and data requirements. Many diagrammatic tools familiar to the reader from the stages of structured process and data analysis are used—for example, data flow diagrams and entity models.
3. **Creating design specifications:** CASE tools can be used to specify a design for a new system. These tools include software for producing HIPO (Hierarchy, Input, Process, Output) charts, structured module specifications and decision tables.
4. **Code-generation tools:** CASE support in this area will accept the outputs of the design specification and produce computer-generated code for direct execution.
5. **An information repository:** Central to any CASE assistance in systems analysis, design and implementation is the information repository. This stores information on entities, processes, data structures, business rules, source code and project management data. It is important, as at any one stage of development consistency and completeness must be maintained in descriptions of data, processes, rules, and so on. Throughout the various stages of analysis and design it is vital that as each component develops, for example from an item in a high-level plan through to a record type in a database, it can be

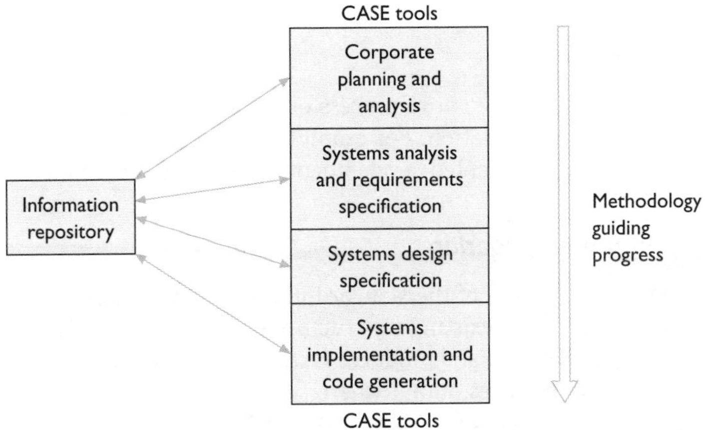

Figure 3.25 CASE assistance in the systems development process

tracked. In short, the information repository does for the CASE process what the data dictionary, in a more limited way, does for structured process analysis and design.

6. **A development methodology:** Underlying any CASE approach is a development methodology. The CASE tool provides the developer with support for the various development stages identified by that methodology. Automated facilities allow for the production of the particular style of diagrams expected of the methodology. The cost estimation routines will similarly reflect the philosophy of the methodology.

CASE terminology

There are no agreed international or de facto standards on CASE. This is a problem not least because the terminology can be used in widely varying ways. However, the following are in common use.

Front-end CASE/upper CASE/analyst workbench

This refers to a set of tools that aid productivity in the analysis, design and documentation of systems. These tools are used to define the systems requirements and the systems properties. Typically, the outputs of front-end CASE are:

- process and data structure specifications: data flow diagrams, state transition diagrams, flowcharts, entity–relationship diagrams, data dictionaries, pseudo-code, structured English, decision tables, decision trees, structure charts, module specifications, Warnier–Orr diagrams;
- screen definitions;
- report definitions.

In order to achieve this, there will be a wide variety of highly interactive screen-based prototyping facilities, including:

- diagram editors;
- screen painters;
- dialogue prototyping aids.

Back-end CASE/lower CASE/code generator/4GL generator

This refers to tools that automate the latter stages of the implementation process. As input, back-end CASE tools may take the output specifications of front-end CASE tools. The outputs of back-end CASE might be:

- source and object program code;
- database and file definitions;
- job control language.

Life cycle CASE/I-CASE

This encapsulates tools covering the entire process of corporate analysis and planning, systems analysis and design, and implementation. For example, the unified modelling language (UML), proposed as a standard for object oriented development, is incorporated into several I-CASE tools.

Reverse engineering/re-engineering

Reverse engineering is the opposite of the standard implementation process for the production of code. Reverse engineering takes existing unstructured code as input (often COBOL programs that can be found in legacy systems) and produces restructured code as output. In particular, the reverse engineering process produces output where:

- Common subroutines and modules are identified.
- Conditional branches and loops are simplified in structure.
- Blocks of code are collapsed into single-line statements for ease of reference and use.

- Subroutines are called in hierarchies.
- New source code is generated fitting the above conditions.

The need for reverse engineering is generated by the recognition that most software used in an organization needs enhancement from time to time. Unless this was produced using a rigorous methodology (and many systems still in use based on COBOL code were not), the task facing the programmer is immense. Complex spaghetti logic structures are impossible or, at best, time-consuming to disentangle and alter. If the software has undergone amendment, the side effects of code alteration are not easily identifiable. The software tends to be bug-ridden and difficult to validate. Reverse engineering creates code that is structured and easily amendable. It thus enables existing software to be enhanced rather than abandoned when update is necessary.

CASE benefits

CASE has grown rapidly in use over the last decade and is predicted to continue to increase in importance over the next decade. Some of the benefits of CASE are as follows:

1. **Enhancement of existing applications:** This can occur in two ways. First, systems produced using CASE tools can be rejuvenated when required by altering the systems specifications, already incorporated into the previous use of CASE, to take account of new needs. These can then be fed into back-end CASE tools to produce new code. The process is considerably quicker than attempting alterations via manually held systems specifications. Second, using reverse engineering tools, existing applications can be recast in a way that makes them suitable for amendment.
2. **Complete, accurate and consistent design specifications:** Most errors in the development of a new system occur in the systems specification stage. Most of these are not picked up until acceptance testing by users has taken place. CASE, by the use of computer specification tools and a central information repository, forces certain aspects of consistency and completeness on the design process.
3. **Reducing human effort:** CASE tools reduce human effort in analysis and design by offloading development work on to computers.

   Diagramming and charting tools cut the development time, especially when it is considered that each diagram may have to undergo several versions before completion.

   By keeping track of the development process, CASE tools can relieve the human of considerable project management burdens. These tools keep note of authors, versions of models and a calendar. CASE tools also provide for consistency and completeness checking across various stages of the development process. They do this by tracking entities, processes, data definitions, diagrams and other things that would otherwise take up much human effort.

   Back-end CASE tools significantly reduce the human programming requirement by generating source and object code, and database definitions.
4. **Integration of development:** CASE tools, particularly I-CASE tools, encourage integration of the development process from the early stages of corporate analysis through information systems specification to code implementation. This is a trend that has been emerging in paper-based methodologies and is now mirrored in CASE tools and methodologies. It is based on a recognition that the design of an information system is not merely a technical issue deriving from a clear understanding of where we are now and where we want to go, but rather an activity that has to link and translate corporate information systems requirements into deliverable systems.
5. **Speed:** CASE tools speed up the development process for a project. The tools also allow considerable interactive input from systems developers during the process. This is compatible with a prototyping approach to systems development.
6. **Links to object oriented analysis:** Object oriented analysis and design are rapidly gaining support. Object oriented methods are particularly suited to incorporation into CASE tools as the terminology and diagrammatical requirements are similar throughout the stages of development. The emphasis in object oriented methodologies on team development, reuse of code and message passing between objects are all facilitated by the central repository, libraries and group support found in CASE tools.

RAPID APPLICATIONS DEVELOPMENT

Rapid applications development (RAD) grew out of the recognition that businesses need to respond quickly to a changing and often uncertain environment in the development of their information systems. RAD is directly opposed to the traditional life-cycle approach, which is characterized by a completely linear development of a system and a concentration on technical perspectives. In traditional approaches, the *requirements* of a project are fixed at an early stage, but the *resources* and *time* tend to vary to fulfil those requirements. In RAD, the opposite view is taken. *Time* is fixed and *resources* are fixed as much as possible, but *requirements* are allowed to change as the project develops to meet the real business objectives.

RAD borrows from other approaches and uses prototyping, participation and CASE tools as well as other formal techniques. It recognizes the importance of gaining user participation, particularly senior management involvement, in its evolutionary approach to information systems development. RAD was first separately identified and introduced by James Martin (1991). His exposition was set clearly within his information engineering approach to the development of business information systems. Now, however, the term 'rapid applications development' is used much more loosely to encompass any approach which emphasizes fast development of systems. Rather than being a methodology itself, RAD is a framework for systems development that can be applied to a range of methodologies. In the UK, a consortium of systems developers have defined a set of standards for RAD called the dynamic systems development method (DSDM).

RAD concepts

Central to the concept of RAD is the role of clearly defined workshops. These should:

- involve business and information systems personnel;
- be of a defined length of time (typically between one and five days);
- be in 'clean rooms'—i.e. rooms set aside for the purpose, removed from everyday operations, provided with technical support, and without interruption;
- involve a facilitator who will be independent, control the meeting, set agendas and be responsible for steering the meeting to deliverables;
- involve a scribe to record.

RAD has four phases:

1. **Requirements planning:** The role of joint requirements planning (JRP) is to establish high-level management and strategic objectives for the organization. The workshop will contain senior managers, often cooperating in a cross-functional way. They will have the authority to take decisions over the strategic direction of the business. The assumption behind RAD is that JRP will drive the process from a high-level business perspective rather than a technical one.
2. **Applications development:** Joint applications development (JAD) follows JRP and involves users in participation in the workshops. JAD follows a top-down approach and may use prototyping tools. Any techniques that can aid user design, especially data flow diagrams and entity modelling, will be employed. I-CASE (see the section on computer-aided software engineering, p. 244) will be used at this stage. The important feature of applications development is that the JAD workshops short-circuit the traditional life-cycle approach, which involves lengthy interviews with users and the collection of documentation, often over considerable time periods. In JAD, the momentum is not lost and several focused workshops may be called quite quickly.
3. **Systems construction:** The designs specifications output by JAD are used to develop detailed designs and generate code. In this phase, graphical user interface building tools, database management system development tools, 4GLs and back-end CASE tools are used (see the section on computer-aided software engineering, p. 244). A series of prototypes are created, which are then assessed by end users, which may result in further iterations and modifications. The various parts of the system are developed by small teams, known as SWAT teams (*s*killed *w*ith *a*dvanced *t*ools). The central system can

be built quickly using this approach. The focus of RAD is on the development of core functionality, rather than the 'bells and whistles' of the system—it is often claimed that 80% (the core) of the system can be built in 20% of the time.

4. **Cutover:** During cutover, users are trained and the system is tested comprehensively. The objective is to have the core functioning effectively. The remainder of the system can be built later. By concentration on the core and the need to develop systems rapidly within a 'time box', the development process can concentrate on the most important aspects of the information system from a business perspective. If the process looks as though it is slipping behind schedule, out of its time box, it is likely that the requirements will be reduced rather than the deadline extended.

Rapid applications developments make the assumptions that:

- Businesses face continuous change and uncertainty.
- Information requirements and therefore information systems must change to meet this challenge.
- Information systems development should be driven by business requirements.
- It is important that information systems be developed quickly.
- Prototyping and development tools are necessary to ensure quick responses.
- Users should participate in development.
- The 'final system' does not exist.

RAD and e-commerce

The growth in web-based technologies has led in many businesses to a review of their approaches to information systems development. With its focus on fast development, prototyping and user involvement, RAD appears to be an attractive candidate as a framework for developing e-commerce activities. Proponents of RAD, who believe that it is ideally suited to electronic business activities, give the following reasons for its adoption:

- **Time to market:** The fast-changing technology of e-commerce requires a rapid development cycle to preserve competitive advantage. Business needs must often be met within weeks rather than months.
- **Whole system solutions:** A move into electronic business requires significant changes in work practices. As a consequence the system needs to be developed and introduced collaboratively in order to be successful.
- **Fast-changing requirements:** The constant change in the electronic economy means that it is almost impossible to establish the business requirements at the outset of the project. RAD, unlike the traditional methodologies previously discussed, does not insist on a complete understanding of the requirements at the outset of the initiative.
- **Decision taking:** Many hard decisions have to be taken as the requirements of the project change. RAD provides effective frameworks for taking and implementing these difficult decisions.

AN EVALUATION OF 'HARD' APPROACHES TO SYSTEMS ANALYSIS AND DESIGN

Several approaches to the analysis and design of information systems have been termed 'hard' approaches. What do they have in common? In answering this, it is useful to take a look at three central examples of hard systems approaches as applied to the analysis and design of computerized information systems. The common features of these will then be more apparent. The three examples chosen here are structured functional/process analysis and design, data analysis and the object oriented approach to the development of computer systems. The focus of the remainder of this section is the underlying assumptions, philosophies and typical areas of application of each approach. The aim is to compare and assess them rather than explain how to undertake practical projects.

Structured functional/process analysis and design

This has spawned many commercial methodologies. These are highly detailed, giving precise instructions as to the tools to be used at each stage and the documentation to be completed. Although each of these methodologies will differ, they all share most of the following characteristics:

- **Function/process oriented:** The attention of the analyst is concentrated on analysing and designing what are seen as the most important elements in systems analysis and design. These are the functions and processes that are carried out in the existing system and are designed to be present in the new system. Once these are clearly specified, the remainder of analysis and design is seen to follow naturally.
- **Top-down:** In analysis and design, the approach taken is to concentrate on the most general processes and functions in the initial stages. Only then are these decomposed again and again until a fine-grained representation of the systems processes is obtained.
- **Logical has priority over physical:** Compatible with a top-down approach is the emphasis on a logical analysis of the functions/processes of the existing system and on the design of a logical model of the desired system. Physical aspects of design—file, program and hardware specifications—are postponed for as long as possible. This lack of early commitment to the physical aspects of design is seen as preventing premature physical decisions that would constrain design alternatives. In the early stages, physical analysis is seen as a necessary stepping stone to deriving a logical model of what the existing system does. It then plays little role in the remainder of the project.
- **Stages and exit criteria:** In common with other hard approaches to systems analysis and design, the process is seen as a linear development from the initial systems investigation and feasibility study, through analysis and design, to implementation and review. Each of these has its own exit criteria. For instance, the feasibility study is completed by the production and agreement of a feasibility report. This staged approach with objective deliverables is a characteristic of approaches that place a high emphasis on project control.
- **Tools and techniques:** Structured tools and techniques emphasize the general philosophy of the approach. Processes, top-down analysis and design, and the development of logical models are encouraged by use of the techniques. Data flow diagrams illustrate the logical flow of information and data between processes, structured English represents the logic of a process, and data dictionaries specify the logical content of data flows and data stores. The emphasis is always on the logical rather than on the physical aspects of information systems, so these paper representations are clear communication devices between users, analysts and programmers. Repeated use of these structured tools ensures a program specification suitable for structured programming techniques and the use of structured programming languages. Hierarchical input/process/output charts ensure that complete modular specifications are developed. Different programmers can work independently on different parts of the system.

The movement to develop structured methods arose from severe problems in software engineering. It was not uncommon for computer projects to run considerably over budget on both time and costs. This often arose out of the difficulty of coordinating large teams of programmers. By concentrating on a top-down approach leading to modular specifications, structured approaches make possible a more accurate estimation of costs and schedules.

Another area in which structured approaches attempt to overcome difficulties is in the design of complex, highly integrated systems. Traditional methods are unsuitable for these. By concentrating on the overall logic of an information system it is possible for the analyst to transcend the barriers imposed by physical departmental divisions.

Structured techniques in analysis and design, backed up by structured programming, ensure that the final software is modular in nature. This means that not only individual programs but also parts of programs are testable separately and can be amended easily. The modular nature of the program specifications also allows more adequate project control. The scope of the programmer for ingenuity and creativity is significantly reduced. Quality control techniques are more easily applicable to the programmer's end product. This changes the nature of the programmer's task. The 'art' of programming has been deskilled to meet the needs of 'scientific' management.

Data analysis

All approaches to systems analysis and design require attention to be paid at some stage to the data store aspects of the information system. What distinguishes approaches that are said to be based on data analysis is the importance and priority attached to the analysis and design of a logical *data* model of the organization in the design of an information system.

Up to now, an entity–relationship approach to data modelling has been taken. This is the most common, although there are now alternatives that attempt to overcome some of the limitations imposed by the oversimplicity of the entity–relationship structure. The various methodologies based on data analysis share the following features:

- **Data model oriented:** The emphasis is on deriving a data model of the entities and relationships within the organization rather than attempting to analyse or model the functions and processes. The thinking behind this is that the overall structure of an organization changes little over time. Once an accurate data model of this has been established and incorporated into a computer-based data store, it will be the foundation on which applications programs can be written. These programs will carry out the various data processes required by the organization. Applications change over time. It is therefore sensible to analyse and design around a common database rather than on the shifting sands of changing functions.
- **Logical has priority over physical:** The emphasis is on building a logical data model of the organization prior to taking any physical decisions on how this is to be incorporated into a physical database, how many records there are, what file sizes will be, and so on. The logical model is later translated into a form suitable for implementation, using one of the commercial database systems.
- **Top-down:** Data analysis approaches stress the need to concentrate on an overall analysis prior to detail. For example, in entity–relationship modelling the important entities and their relationships are identified first. The structure of the model is then specified. Only at a later stage will attention be directed to attributes. This is to be contrasted with a bottom-up strategy, in which the concentration would be on the attributes at an earlier stage.
- **Documentation:** All approaches based on data analysis emphasize the importance of structure. The clearest way of revealing structure is pictorially. Diagrammatic representations play an important role in data analysis at the early stages.

The impetus to develop methodologies based on data analysis came from a number of areas. Modern commercial databases allow the sharing of common data by different applications and users within an organization. They also allow for considerable complexity in storage structures and retrieval. It is crucial to ensure that the best use is made of these facilities. Entity–relationship modelling and other data analysis modelling approaches assist the design of the complex models suitable for modern database management systems.

Another reason for the emphasis on data analysis is the recognition that data structures, if they are to be enduring, should mirror the real world of the organization. Organizations have complex structures. It requires more than a piecemeal approach to deal adequately with the modelling task.

Object oriented approaches

The characteristics of object oriented approaches are:

- **Logical has priority over physical:** The emphasis is placed on building a logical object model of the organization and establishing the necessary associations and communications between the logical objects prior to taking any physical decisions on how the objects are to be implemented.
- **Top-down/bottom-up:** The modelling of the system usually starts with a top-down partitioning into related groups of classes. The terminology for these groups differs; Bertrand

Meyer (1995) calls them **clusters**, whereas Coad and Yourdon (1991) describe them as **subjects**. This initial partitioning is then followed by a combination of top-down and bottom-up development activities. The top-down development can be illustrated by the inheritance mechanism, whereby abstract classes are created and then refined into more specialized classes that implement specific activities in the system. The bottom-up development is evidenced by the use of primitive (building block) classes, which are aggregated together into larger so-called container classes to implement increasingly complex levels of the solution.

- **Transition between stages:** A major attraction of object oriented approaches is the uniformity of terminology and concepts throughout the development process. The analyst searches for candidate classes and considers the data (attributes) and functions (methods) that each class must implement. The designer puts detail into the implementation of the methods and considers the associations and the message passing between classes. The programmer implements the classes, their attributes and methods. Because of the uniformity, it is said that transition from one stage to the next is **seamless**.
- **Documentation:** At each stage of analysis and design detailed documentation is produced. This is often generated by a CASE tool. The seamless nature of the transition between stages described above means that the same diagrams produced at the analysis stage can be enhanced at the design stage. Many CASE tools can then generate skeleton code from those diagrams, extending the seamless feel throughout the development process. The documentation, automatically generated by a CASE tool, is particularly beneficial in recording the libraries of classes, both newly created and reused.

Characteristics of 'hard' approaches

The examples of 'hard' systems approaches covered in the previous sections of this chapter may seem to have little in common. Why, then, are they characterized together as 'hard' approaches?

1. They all assume that there is a clearly identifiable existing system in some state or other. To make this discovery is essential to the process of systems analysis and design. No major problem is presented by this task; it is a matter of investigation and documentation.
2. There can be a clear and agreed statement of the objective of systems analysis and design. Generally, this is established in conjunction with the 'owners' of the system. It is the role of the systems analyst/designer and programmer to provide this system on time and within cost.
3. It is assumed that the end result of the process of analysis will be a design that will incorporate a technological system. In other words, the problem—that is, the disparity between the existing system and the desired system—is seen to be soluble by technical means. In most cases, this means a computer.
4. Just as it is clearly possible to describe the existing system objectively, it is possible to determine whether the designed system, once implemented, meets the objectives set of it. Thus there is a measure of performance.
5. The process of analysis and design needs to be carried out by experts. This follows from the general assumption that the solution to the problem will be technical. The client/expert dichotomy is essential to 'hard' systems approaches.

As a summary, it can be said that 'where we are now' and 'where we want to go' can be clearly established. The problem facing the analyst is 'how to get there'. The solution is in terms of a prescribed progression from the current state to the desired state through several stages. Four distinct phases can be identified:

1. Investigating the existing system—information gathering, problem identification, feasibility study.
2. Analysis of the existing system and the provision of a solution to the problem by designing a new system on paper or using a CASE tool.
3. Implementing the solution.
4. Evaluating its effectiveness.

Although 'hard' approaches have been presented as applying to the analysis and design of information systems, their scope is much larger. They are similar to a general engineering approach to problem solving. The assumptions and overall strategy are similar whether one is designing a transport network, building a bridge, running a project to put someone on the Moon or designing a computer system.

Hard systems approaches have their antecedents in engineering and military applications. They emphasize a scientific approach towards problem solving rather than intuition or experience. A high premium is placed on logic and rationality. Philosophically, they assume a realist view—the world is 'out there' independent of us; all that has to be done is to discover it and alter it to meet our desires. In so far as people enter analysis and design considerations, they are either sources of information about the current system or operators of the new system. In the latter case, their importance is taken into account in the design of the human–computer interface.

Criticisms of 'hard' systems approaches

Hard systems approaches have vastly predominated in the development of computer systems. Project control failures, difficulties in designing highly integrated systems and the increasing importance of data model design for databases have led to the evolution of hard methodologies, which have superseded the more traditional approaches. Hard systems analysis and design has been hugely successful. However, there have been some notable failures. Systems that have been designed, implemented and are technically perfect but nobody uses them, systems that seem to be built to solve a problem that does not exist—these are two such examples. These failures may be located not in the poor application of systems analysis and design techniques but rather in the (mis)application of these techniques in the first place. Hard approaches make certain assumptions that limit their applicability. They do not provide fix-all methodologies that are universally applicable to all situations.

1. Hard systems approaches assume that an engineering perspective is applicable in all cases. This is unlikely to be true in situations that are unstructured. This may occur when there is no common agreement about the cause of the current problem. There may not even be a clearly identifiable problem. Once again, there may be no agreement about a desired solution. In these circumstances, hard approaches find it difficult to get off the ground. They assume that there is no difficulty in defining the existing and desired states of the system. When this assumption fails, they provide no help in further analysis.
2. Hard systems approaches are mathematically/logically based. This limits the range of problems that can be tackled. Moreover, they assume that factors and models to be used in remedying problems also have this orientation. Decision tables, entity–relationship models and logic flowcharts are all cases in point from the area of systems analysis and design. However, it goes further than this. As one might expect from their antecedents in engineering, operational research techniques play an important part in suggested aids to decision making. Linear programming, queuing theory, Monte Carlo simulation and statistical sampling theory are used. These all presuppose that a mathematical model is useful in the decision process. However, problems in an organization may not be amenable to this type of approach. For example, a failure to coordinate production schedules may not be the result of poor information flows and scheduling, which can be solved by the use of a computerized system with computer-based operational research-scheduling techniques. It may be caused by disagreement about the role of production and sales in the organization, personality conflicts, individual interests not coinciding with company objectives, or any number of things. To use a hard approach is already to straitjacket the problem as one soluble by mathematical/logical techniques when it may not be.
3. The emphasis on mathematics and logic presupposes the importance of quantitative information as compared with qualitative or vague information, intuition and psychological models of decision making. This may be acceptable when there is clear agreement on problems and solutions and the task is seen as one of moving from the given

undesirable state to a new desired state. In other cases, however, the range of useful types of information is broader. Closely connected to this is the assumption that quantitative information equals objectivity, whereas qualitative information equals subjectivity. From the scientific outlook, the latter is to be avoided. Whether subjectivity is to be avoided is a moot point. However, the proponents of a hard approach often ignore the fact that the requirement to provide quantitative information where none is accurately known often leads to unjustified assumptions being made. Claims to objectivity can then be seen to be spurious.

4. Closely allied to the previous points is the lack of recognition given to the organizational context in which a problem lies. Hard approaches tend to concentrate on data, processes, functions, tasks, decisions, data stores, flows, entities and relationships. They do not pay any attention to the social or organizational aspects of the system.
5. The emphasis is always on linear problem solving: there is a problem, it is solved, the next problem arises, it is solved, and so on. This leads to a reactive approach to management. An alternative is an ongoing developmental approach that stresses proactive attitudes.
6. The dichotomy between the client and the expert can act as a barrier to successful systems analysis and development. This may happen in a number of ways. There may be communication problems. The client is an expert in the area for which systems analysis is being carried out. The expert is probably from a technical background, so they do not share the same language. Tools used in structured approaches help to overcome this limitation. By stressing the logical aspects of the system and using diagrammatic tools that illustrate this, technicalities that may confuse the clients are removed. However, there is a more subtle effect of this dichotomy. The expert is seen to be outside the problem area. He or she observes it objectively. Not so! Once involved, the analyst interacts with the system—particularly the people operating within it. The analyst brings his or her own set of experiences, knowledge, prejudices and background to bear on the problem area.

These comments on hard approaches to systems analysis and design are not meant to be damning. Rather, they illustrate the need for caution before adopting a hard methodology. In particular, the applicability of the chosen methodology should first be established. Areas that are unstructured, with a lack of agreement on problems and what would count as a solution, are just those areas that are not suited to a technical approach to systems analysis and design.

'SOFT' APPROACHES TO SYSTEMS ANALYSIS AND DESIGN

Hard approaches to systems analysis and design have been very successful in developing computer systems that, viewed from a technical perspective, are efficient and effective information providers. However, there have been cases when new information systems have not had user acceptance or have seemed to be misplaced as a solution to a spurious problem. These difficulties have led to developments that challenge the assumptions made by approaches deriving from a 'hard' view of systems.

Two approaches are outlined in this section. Each perceives different weaknesses in the approaches considered so far, so each has a different remedy. They both identify the presence of people in a system as leading to complications not acknowledged by proponents of hard approaches.

Checkland's (1999) approach recognizes that different people have different perceptions of problems and of the systems in which they lie. It is therefore a mistake to assume automatically that there is agreement on 'where we are now' or even on 'where we want to go'. Rather, problems are much less structured, much fuzzier than supporters of hard approaches would have us believe.

The socio-technical approach stresses the recognition that computerized information systems are part of interacting social and technical systems. If one part is changed, for example the technical system, by means of computerization, then the other will be affected. It is important to realize that the social and technical systems (the socio-technical system) cannot be designed independently of each other. One way to ensure that sufficient weight is given to the social aspects of the system is to involve users in the process of analysis and design. This undercuts the assumption of 'hard' approaches that the end product of design is a purely technical system. It also challenges the assumption of the necessity or desirability of the expert/user division.

Checkland's approach

In order to understand the rationale for Checkland's approach, it is helpful to look at some of the underlying philosophical assumptions made.

First, the assumption is that problems are not regarded as being 'out there' in a realist sense. There are no objectively given problems. Different people may see different problems in the 'same' situation.

It is, perhaps, misleading to talk of the 'situation' as though it were objectively given. A situation is a combination of the external world together with the way that it seems to the observer. This will be influenced by the background and beliefs of that observer. For example, an experienced doctor will unconsciously interpret an X-ray photograph and see shapes of importance in it. However, to the untrained observer there is very little of substance. Or again, different cultural backgrounds interpret voice inflections in different ways. So the same sentence uttered by two different people may be variously interpreted as being hostile or friendly.

Not only will different people disagree over the 'neutral' description of a situation but they will also disagree as to its problematic nature. For example, the student may regard end-of-course failure rates in professional exams as a problem—another hurdle to cross on the way to a career. However, a qualified professional may regard them as a non-problematic essential for the maintenance of small numbers of qualified professionals. This guarantees high incomes for those who are qualified. The professional institute setting the exams has a third view—the failure rates are taken as evidence that standards are being maintained.

It should be clear not only that different people may see the same situation as problematic in different ways but also that some may not see any problem at all. One man's meat is another man's poison. What determines an individual's view of a situation is the nexus of beliefs, desires and interests that the individual has. It is the combination of beliefs about 'what is' and 'what ought to be' that is so important in determining a situation as 'problematic' for an individual.

Second, just as problems are intellectual constructs, so are solutions. Two people may agree on a problem and yet disagree as to what constitutes a solution. Take an examination for example. Very high failure rates on a course may be regarded as problematic by both students and the course director. Students see the solution in terms of easier examinations and more effective teaching. The course director sees the need to raise entry qualifications.

The third assumption states that problems very rarely come singly, neatly packaged and ready for a solution. It is more likely that there are several interlocking problems. Moreover, if one problem is solved, this may generate a problem elsewhere. Problems are often messy and not amenable to simple solutions such as the installation of a computerized information system. This is another reason why the term 'problem situation' rather than 'problem' is used to describe what confronts the analyst.

Fourth, it is obvious from these points that it is important that the problem area be investigated and analysed prior to any decisions on the desirability of computer systems. The role of the systems analyst is seen, at least initially, as much more akin to a therapist than to a technical computer expert. The analyst encourages participants in the existing system to examine their own perceptions of the system and its interconnections with others, its objectives, their role in it and the role of others. This learning process is an essential prerequisite for development. It is recognized at the outset that a computer system may not be suitable for the organization, or at least not a total solution.

The final assumption implies that the analyst cannot be divorced from the system and the participants involved in it owing to the early therapeutic role of the analyst.

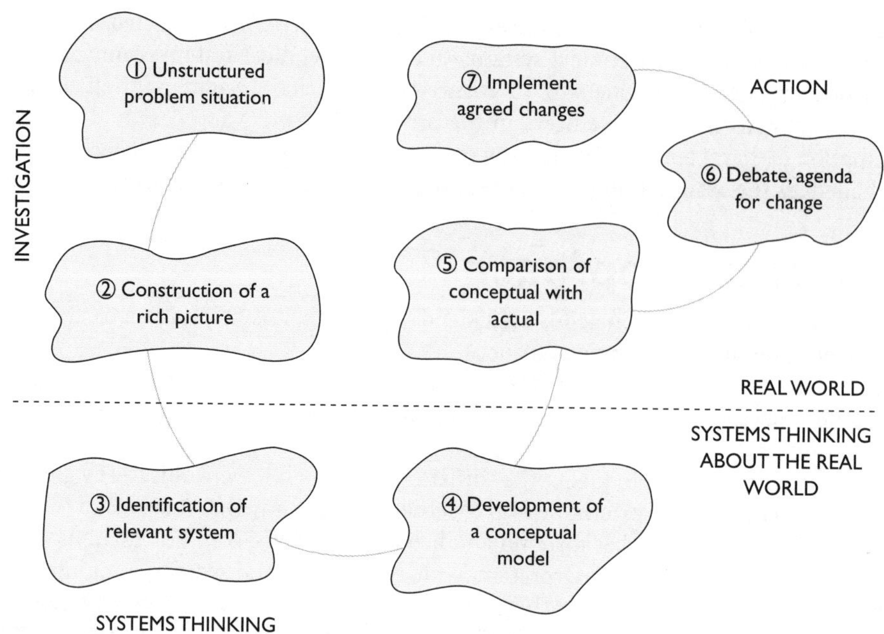

Figure 3.26 The stages in Checkland's methodology

The methodology

Checkland's methodology (Figure 3.26) evolved out of the area of management consultancy. The analyst is not an expert in any particular area so is therefore not employed to give technical advice. Rather, the analyst should be thought of as a change agent or therapist who is able to stimulate others to new perceptions of the problem situation. The approach is particularly effective compared with other methodologies in cases where there are messy problems. The stages are now outlined. Although progression is from one stage to the next, there is not the same rigidity and control over stage exits as in the structured life-cycle approach. Stages may be re-entered once left. The process is iterative rather than linear.

Stage 1 The development of rich pictures

The first task of the analyst is to become acquainted with the problem situation, and an attempt is made to build up a **rich picture** of the problem situation. This is a cartoon of the important influences and constituents of the problem situation. The analyst collects information to incorporate into this picture. Not only is hard information collected, such as facts and other quantitative data, but soft information is also obtained. Here are included the participants in the problem situation, any worries, fears and aspirations they have that are thought by the analyst to be relevant, conflicts and alliances between departments or individuals, and hunches and guesses. In particular, the analyst is looking for structure, key processes, and the interaction between process and structure.

It is important that the analyst does not impose a systems structure on the problem situation at this stage. The analyst will be interested in determining meaningful roles that individuals fulfil, such as boss or counsellor. In drawing the rich picture, the analyst will identify primary tasks and issues and will attempt to see varying perspectives. At this stage, the analyst should take particular care not to pigeonhole the problem, say as a marketing problem or a communications problem. This will limit the types of change that may ultimately be suggested.

Three important roles in the problem situation are identified. The **client** is the individual who is paying the analyst. The **problem owner** will be the individual who is responsible, or the area within which the problem situation arises. It may not be clear initially who the owner is. Different perceptions of the situation will assume different problem owners (we are all familiar with the conversation 'that's your problem', 'no it's yours'). The analyst may need to experiment with several individuals in order to establish a realistic problem owner. The **problem solver** is normally the analyst. These three roles may be held by three different people, or they may coincide in two individuals. It is common for the client and problem owner to be the same person.

The purpose of a rich picture is:

- To help to visualize a complex mess of interacting people, roles, threats, facts, observations, and so on. Its purpose is to facilitate understanding of the problem situation.
- To avoid imposing a rigid structure on the appreciation of the problem situation. A systems perspective is to be avoided at this early stage. It would tend to force perception of the problem through systems concepts such as inputs/outputs, systems objectives, feedback and the like. This may not be appropriate for the situation.
- To aid an investigative approach by the analyst towards the problem situation.
- To act as a communication tool between participants. This will aid a consensus perception of the problem situation. It is all too easy for the fact that different participants have importantly divergent views of the situation to go unnoticed.

It should already be clear that there is considerable divergence between this approach and the structured approach taken in the previous section. There, the initial stages were restricted to the identification of key functions and processes, key entities in the organization and their formal relationships.

Stage 2 Identification of the relevant system and the root definition

The rich picture is a pictorial representation of the problem situation. In order to progress, it is necessary to view the problem from a systemic point of view. This is where the idea of a **relevant system** comes in. This is the most appropriate way of viewing the problem situation as a system. It is not always clear what the relevant system is. The relevant system is extracted from the rich picture. There is no one correct answer to the question 'what is the relevant system?' Several suggestions may be made. The one that is accepted is agreed by negotiation, often between the problem owner and the problem solver. This relevant system should be the one that provides most insight into the problem situation and is most appropriate for stimulating understanding and change in the organization—the ultimate goal of the methodology.

Other cases where things are less structured may require consideration of several 'relevant' systems before one that fits becomes apparent. For instance, a local technical college might be regarded alternatively as 'a system for educating pupils in order to meet the labour need of the local area' or 'a system for removing local unemployed adolescents at their potentially most disruptive and destructive age from the streets'. Or again, the owner/manager of a small business may regard it as 'a system for maintaining a stable financial income', 'a system for maintaining a stable and interesting employment for himself and his employees' or 'a system for providing a valued community service'.

Generally, relevant systems are issue-based or primary-task-based. When agreed on, they may come as quite a revelation to some of those participating in the problem situation. Identification of the relevant system may help to cast light on the otherwise seemingly non-understandable behaviour of their colleagues.

Just to name the relevant system gives a highly generalized specification of the area associated with the problem situation. It is important to be more precise. This is done by developing a **root definition** of the relevant system. The root definition gives a precise description of the *essence* of the relevant system.

Producing a root definition is not a mechanical task. It can only be achieved through trial and error. However, there is a checklist, called by its mnemonic CATWOE, which every adequate root definition should satisfy. All the CATWOE components should be present (or at least their absence needs to be justified and acknowledged).

1. **Customers:** These are the group of people or body who are served by or who benefit from the system. In the Kismet case, it is not only the customers of Kismet but also the stores and accounts functions.
2. **Actors:** These are the people, or rather types of people, who carry out the essential activities in the relevant system.

3. **Transformation process:** This is what the system does—that is, the process that converts inputs into outputs.
4. **Weltanschauung:** The *Weltanschauung* or 'world view' that is relevant to the system is specified somewhere in the root definition. In the case of Kismet, this is indicated by the assumption of performance according to cost and time constraints.
5. **Owners:** The owners of the system are those to whom the system is answerable. They have power to change the system or make it cease to exist. In the case of Kismet, this will probably be the management of the company.
6. **Environment:** This is the environment in which the relevant system is located.

KISMET CASE STUDY 3.13

The CATWOE components for Kismet are now discussed. The following summary is produced:

- Customers: For Kismet, it is not only the customers but also the stores and accounts functions that must be considered.
- Actors: The task of identifying actors can be assisted by the work done on the creation of rich pictures.
- Transformation process: The processing of inputs and outputs can be summarized as transforming the orders placed by customers into requests for stock and notifications to accounts.
- The 'world view': In the case of Kismet, this is indicated by the assumption of performance according to cost and time constraints.
- The owners of the system: For Kismet, this will probably be the management of the company.
- The environment in which the relevant system is located must be established.

This leads to a root definition of the Kismet sales order processing as follows:

A business function within Kismet operated by sales and credit control staff to accept and process orders provided by customers, transforming them into validated requests to stock and notifications into accounts, within speed and cost constraints set by Kismet management.

The purpose of identifying the relevant system and deriving a root definition is to concentrate on the *essence* of the system covering the problem situation. It is then easier to proceed to develop a logical model of a system that meets this description.

Stage 3 Building a conceptual model

Given that the relevant system has been identified and a root definition has been provided, the next stage of the methodology is to develop a conceptual model. This is a logical model of the key activities or processes that must be carried out in order to satisfy the root definition of the system. It is not a model of the real world. It may bear no resemblance to what occurs in the problem situation and is not derived by observing it. Rather, it consists of what is logically required by the root definition. The distinction between what *must* be done in order to satisfy the root definition and what *is* actually done in the system is of fundamental importance. Its recognition is at the heart of the usefulness of the methodology in stimulating organizational learning and change.

The key activities are shown in the conceptual model in Figure 3.27. Each of these key activities themselves represents a subsystem that would carry the activity out—for example, the subsystem to monitor and control performance. These high-level activities give rise to second-level activities that must be performed in order that the high-level activities can be executed. For instance, monitoring and control require collection of the standard, collection of the sensed data, comparison between the two and taking the necessary action. This gives rise to second-level conceptual models that can replace the relevant part of the first-level model.

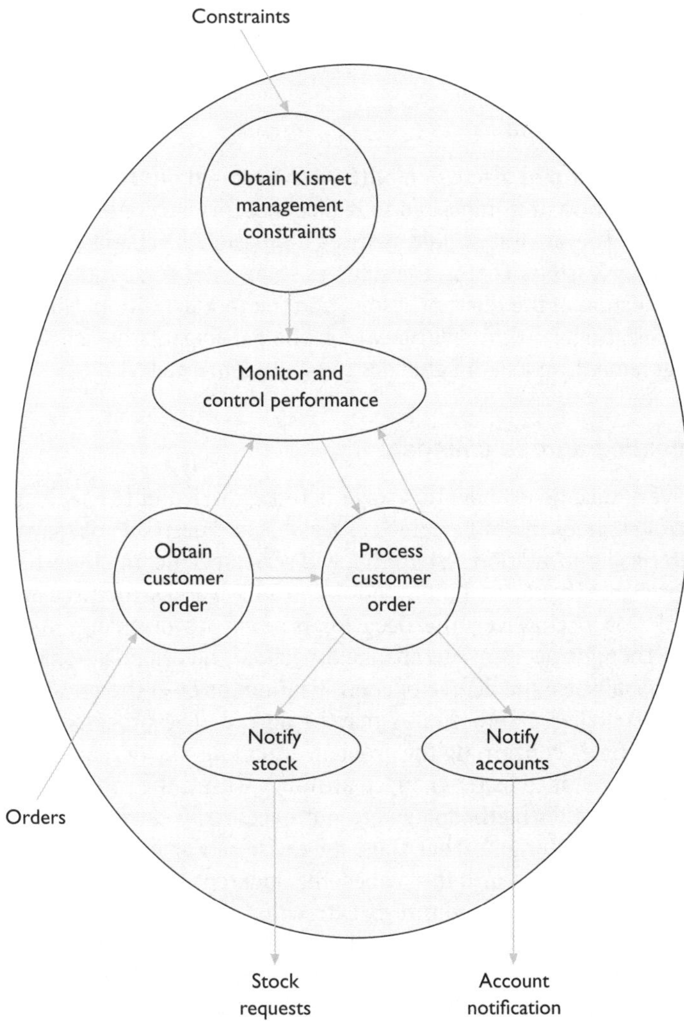

Figure 3.27 **A conceptual model**

When completed, the conceptual model is tested against the formal requirement of a general systems model. Examples of typical questions that need to be asked are:

- Does the model illustrate an activity that has a continuous purpose?
- Is there a measure of performance?
- Is there some kind of decision-making process or role?
- Are there subsystems that are connected?
- Is there a boundary?
- Is there some guarantee of long-term stability?

Stage 4 Comparing the conceptual model with the real world

The previous two stages have attempted to build up some ideal model of what should happen in a system that carries out the essential activities required by the agreed root definition of the relevant system. Now is the time to see what actually happens.

The rich picture provides a good representation of the real situation, and it is against this that the conceptual model must be compared. Alternatively, the conceptual model may be compared directly with the problem situation. Differences should be highlighted as possible points for discussion. Typical of the questions considered by the analyst at this stage are 'Why is there a discrepancy between the conceptual model and the real world at this point?' and 'Does this activity in the conceptual model really occur?' The point of this investigation is not to criticize the way that things are actually done but rather to derive a list of topics—an **agenda for change**—that can be discussed with the actors in the problem situation.

Stage 5 Debating the agenda

This stage involves a structured discussion of the points raised on the agenda with the participants in the problem situation. It is important to realize that this is a consciousness-raising exercise as much as anything. The analyst should restrict discussion to changes that are systemically desirable and culturally feasible. That is, the changes should not run counter to the thinking that has gone into the selection of the relevant system and the root definition. Nor should they ignore the particular organizational culture within which the participants have lived and worked. The aim is to obtain agreement on a list of changes to be implemented.

Stage 6 Implementing agreed changes

Checkland is not very specific on how this stage is to be carried out. This is understandable in that a large range of changes might be agreed as feasible and desirable. It may be the case that a need for a computerized information system that will serve specific functions has been identified. In this case, it is probable that formal information modelling and structured analysis and design techniques will take over. However, the need for other types of change may be agreed. For instance, it may be thought necessary to change aspects of the organizational structure such as departmental responsibilities, the degree of centralization, or even the physical layout. Changes in overall policies, strategies or procedures may be agreed. The process of analysis may have revealed divergent attitudes concerning the problem situation. The outcome of the debate on the agenda may be an agreement to foster changed attitudes within the problem situation.

The stages in Checkland's methodology are not necessarily carried out in a linear fashion. It is often necessary to re-enter an earlier stage for revision. For instance, when comparing the conceptual model with the real world it may become apparent that the relevant system has not been identified correctly. This will require backtracking. There is another important way in which Checkland's methodology is not linear. It would be a mistake to assume that once the stages have been executed the problem in the problem situation has been resolved. It is not a problem-solving methodology but rather aims at *improvement* of situations through organizational understanding, learning and change.

Participation in socio-technical analysis and design

The socio-technical approach grew out of work started in the Tavistock Institute for Behavioural Research in the 1950s. This derived from the introduction of new technology in the coal mines. The approach recognized that successful introduction of new technology required the identification of social needs and goals as well as technical/economic objectives. The underlying assumption was that a system will only function effectively if human needs such as job satisfaction are acknowledged.

In the 1970s, the socio-technical approach began to be adopted in various guises for the development of computer systems in organizational environments. The common element in these approaches is the recognition of the interdependence of four factors—technology, tasks, people and the organization (Figure 3.28). If one of these is altered, for example the introduction of new computerized technology, it will have an impact on all the others. It therefore makes sense to take account of all aspects of the socio-technical system in computerization so that harmony can be maintained.

One socio-technical approach, due to Mumford (2003, and colleagues) (Land and Hirscheim, 1983), sees the best way of obtaining this harmony as involving users participatively in the process of analysis and design. This idea meshes neatly with the general trend towards industrial democracy experienced over the last 20 years, together with the increasing acceptance of humanistic values as applied to the workplace.

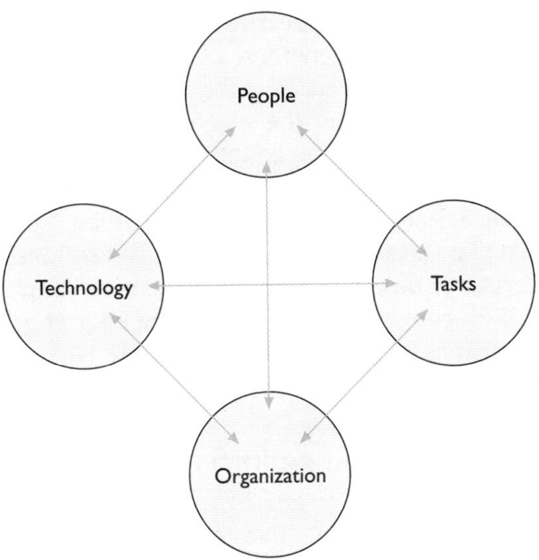

Figure 3.28 Socio-technical connections

Benefits of participation

From the management point of view, participation in analysis and design enables the valuable knowledge and skills of the workforce to be incorporated into the final system. The analyst may be a technical expert in the area of computers but is unlikely to be familiar with the organization, tasks and people within which the final system must fit. Participation is seen as a more effective way of obtaining this experience than the 'classical' approaches such as the formal interview or questionnaire.

Also, from the management perspective, it is more likely that users will show commitment to and confidence in the final installed system if they have had a hand in its development. This stems from two sources. First, it is difficult for an individual to participate in the design of a system and not establish a psychological investment in and therefore commitment to it. Second, the continued presence of the participants in the process of analysis and design educates them in an appreciation of the final system and also allays their fears of its likely effects. Users may fear job deskilling, removal of job satisfaction or their ability to cope with the new system. Even if groundless, these fears lead to resistance to the implementation of the new system and ultimately to its ineffective use or failure. Participation allays these fears by providing information as the system is developed.

From a 'worker' point of view, participation can be seen as a way of maintaining control over the introduction of new technology. By being involved at all stages of the process participants can ensure that jobs and job satisfaction are maintained. It also serves as a public recognition of the importance of participants' knowledge and skills in the workplace.

Issues involved in participation

Several issues are involved in participation:

1. What role do participants play in the design process?
2. At which stage in the life cycle are participants involved?
3. Which groups should participate in the design process?
4. How are participants to be selected?

These questions are dealt with below:

1. **What role do participants play in the design process?** Three different levels of involvement can be identified for participants. These correspond to deepening degrees of commitment to the participative approach.

   (a) **Consultative:** The participants are consulted for their views and understanding by an expert. The expert analysts note these responses and take account of them at their discretion. This is little different from the 'traditional' approach towards interview as a source of information about the system. Where this differs in a socio-technical approach is that the analyst will be interested not only in the technical aspects of analysis and design but also in a complete socio-technical design.
   (b) **Representative:** Selected users from relevant interest groups join the design teams. Their views are taken into account, although it is still recognized that the analysts are the 'experts' and ultimately they are responsible for design.
   (c) **Consensus:** With consensus participation, the interest groups take over responsibility for the analysis and design. Analysts are now regarded as just another interest group whose responsibility it is to provide technical knowledge and to ensure that the design is technically sound.

2. **At which stage in the life cycle are participants involved?** This may happen at any or all stages of the project. Major stages are as follows:
   (a) Project initiation—it is unlikely that management will allow participation at this stage. It is traditionally regarded as the province of strategic decision making.
   (b) Definition of systems objectives.
   (c) Description and analysis of the existing system.
   (d) Identification of problem areas within the existing system.
   (e) Suggestion, design and evaluation of alternative solutions to the problems identified in (d).
   (f) Detailed design of the human work (social) and computer (technical) systems.
   (g) Preparation of systems specification.
   (h) Implementation of the human work and computer systems.
   (i) Evaluation and monitoring of the working system.
3. **Which groups should participate in the design process?** The answer to this is 'any group that will be significantly affected by the computer system'. This may include outside groups in the early stages (such as watchdog committees for the nationalized industries) as well as groups from within the organization. Examples of the latter are trade unions, clerical and shopfloor workers, middle management, and programmers and analysts.
4. **How are participants to be selected?** Interest groups may elect their own members, or participants may be chosen by management. Both approaches may be politically sensitive. With the former method, it may be the case that only those with the most strongly militant anti-technology views are put forward, whereas with the latter, management's buddies may be chosen.

The presupposition so far has been that participation is to be thought of as being limited to analysis and design. There is no reason why participants should not be involved in the decision-making process. However, this is unlikely to be agreed by management at the major decision points—when global terms of reference are being established for the project or when stop/go decisions are needed. At other points—fixing of local terms of reference or choice between alternative solutions—the decision-making process is almost invariably interwoven with analysis and design. Then participation in decision making goes hand in hand with analysis and design.

Methodology

In order to gain the benefits promised by participation it is necessary to have an effective methodology. Without this those involved in participation will be directionless. The methodology outlined here is due to Enid Mumford. It involves various procedures such as variance analysis, job satisfaction analysis and future analysis to aid the participative approach: these procedures are briefly described. However, it does not preclude the use of other tools or techniques, such as data flow diagrams or entity–relationship modelling, particularly in the latter stages of systems design. Mumford has given her approach to IS development the acronym ETHICS (*e*ffective, *t*echnical and *h*uman *i*mplementation of *c*omputer *s*ystems). The important components in the approach advocated by Mumford are now discussed.

The diagnosis of needs and problems

Three diagnostic tools are used here, variance analysis, job satisfaction analysis and future analysis:

1. **Variance analysis:** This involves identifying weak parts of the existing system that produce operational problems. The design group will identify key operations within a department and note those areas where there is a systematic deviation of the results of those operations from the standards set. This may often occur on the boundaries of a system, where there are coordination problems. Variances may affect one another; therefore it is important to reveal connections and dependencies. A variance matrix may be of assistance here. In systems design, the aim is to control these variances where they originate rather than by control at a later stage.
2. **Job satisfaction analysis:** The amount of job satisfaction obtained in a work situation may be explained in terms of the fit between what participants expect from their jobs and what they are obtaining. Three important needs should be considered. These are connected with the personality of the individual, the personal values held by that individual and the need for competence and efficiency. If systems are designed with these in mind, job satisfaction will be improved. This is a necessary condition to ensure that the socio-technical system will function effectively.
3. **Future analysis:** Large systems take a long time to design. If a large project is undertaken, it may be three or four years or even longer from initiation to the start of the successful operation of the new system. The life of the new system will need to be more than three or four years in order to recover the costs of the project. This implies that in analysis and design the time horizon with which the project is concerned is many years. In order to achieve a system that will meet the needs of the future, then the future has to be predicted. This becomes more difficult and uncertain the greater the forecasting period. Future changes may not be just in volumes of transactions processed or types of information required of the information system. Changes in the economic climate, new technology and changes in organizational structure such as decentralization or merging of companies will all have a significant impact on the satisfaction of future needs by the system currently being designed.

Many traditional approaches do not take the need to design for the future seriously and have consequently produced systems suffering from the 'dinosaur syndrome'. The requirement of a system to meet future demands can be achieved by:

(a) **Predicting the future by modelling and simulation:** The predictions are then catered for in current design.

(b) **Designing a system that is robust:** This means that the system has built-in redundancy and flexibility to deal with uncertain future requirements. The system is also designed to be modular for easy adaptation.

(c) **A structured approach to future analysis:** This involves the design team(s) drawing up a list of factors of relevance to the system that may be the subject of change. The likelihood of each of the factors changing over the lifetime of the system is then evaluated. The impact of these changes on the system is then assessed. The components of the system that are subject to these effects should be identified so that the stage of design can take account of them.

The consideration of the groups affected by the system

The groups that will be affected by the system are identified. The goals of these are then established by consultation with company policy and the diagnosis of user needs and job satisfaction analysis. An attempt is made to establish the weightings to be associated with each goal. Ideally, this would be by consensus between the various groups as a result of negotiation.

Socio-technical approach to the analysis and design of the system

The purpose of socio-technical analysis and design is to produce an end system consisting of social and technical structures that satisfies both technical and social goals. This proceeds by using a general stage, which is followed by a detailed one.

Initially, alternative systems strategies are suggested. The effects of each of these are forecast for the period of the planning horizon. The impact of each strategy is then compared against both the goals of the system and the predicted performance of the existing socio-technical system up to the planning horizon. Optimistic and pessimistic estimations are made for each strategy by changing the values of uncertain parameters. The strategy with the best fit to the social and technical goals is selected.

Detailed design progresses through social and technical analysis. In technical analysis, logically integrated sets of tasks, called **unit operations**, are identified. These unit operations consist of tasks that are logically cohesive in transforming an input into an output in preparation for the next unit operation or stage. For example, a unit operation would be the batching, error checking and input of sales data into a daybook preparatory to updating the sales ledger. Each design group receives one or more operation within its scope. In the analysis of the social aspects of the work system the relationships between individuals and the roles they play are investigated. The results of job satisfaction analysis would be used at this point. Each work group has the responsibility for eliminating variances that have been discovered in variance analysis. Within the work group, the existing and future users of the system are of particular importance in the development of the social system and the earlier stages of technical analysis. The impact of the computer analysts is felt most during the latter stages of technical design.

Implementation

Once designed, the system can be implemented. This may occur as a linear process or may take the form of prototyping. In prototyping, an experimental smaller version of the system is built. This will not have the full functionality of the final system and will probably not be technically efficient in a computing sense. However, it does enable an evaluation to be made of the extent to which it meets some of the social and technical goals of the design. This will provide a direction for improvement of the final system before any major expenditure has gone into its weaknesses. Indeed, several prototypes may be built before a satisfactory version on which the final design can be based is reached.

Post-implementation evaluation

After the system has been installed and is running, some assessment of its performance in the light of its social and technical goals is made. This allows correction as part of normal ongoing maintenance or provides valuable knowledge that is relevant in the design of a future system.

In summary, the participative approach differs from 'hard' approaches in a number of ways:

1. There is a recognition that technical systems cannot be treated independently of the social systems with which they interact.
2. Following from point 1, in the design of computer-based information systems the social system within which the work occurs must be the subject of analysis and design as much as the technical system itself. Without this harmonious design, any resultant technical system is subject to a high risk of failure on the grounds of its inadequacy from a social point of view.
3. The current and future users of the system possess a knowledge of existing work practices and deficiencies that makes their experience valuable in the process of analysis and design. In order to utilize this experience, it is necessary to use a set of diagnostic procedures (job satisfaction analysis, variance analysis, and so on). The traditional role of the expert systems analyst is restricted to technical aspects of analysis and design.
4. Participation in analysis and design is a prerequisite for a successful implementation of technical systems as it reduces users' fears over the introduction of new technology.
5. There is an ethical commitment to the belief that users of technology and those affected by it have a right to have some say on the design and operation of these systems.

Checkland's methodology and the participative approach: reservations

Both Checkland's methodology and the participative socio-technical approach offer alternatives to the 'hard' approaches covered in previous chapters. How realistic are they? Although they both have their supporters, there are serious questions that need to be addressed.

Checkland

The main criticism levelled at Checkland's methodology is its lack of comprehensiveness, particularly in the later stages of analysis and design. This has led critics to argue that it is not a methodology that takes the analyst through the life cycle. The idea of a 'life cycle' is not one that fits well with Checkland's approach, although it is undeniable that the methodology is strongest in the early stages of problem identification and analysis. At the very least, proponents would argue that it explores possibilities for organizational learning and progress in problem situations that are neglected by 'hard' approaches. The methodology from this viewpoint is regarded more as a front-end approach to carrying out the necessary problem analysis prior to the technical analysis that would imply a computerized system.

Another comment made on the methodology is that the analyst is not only in the position of attempting to understand an existing system but is also required by the methodology, via root definitions and conceptual models, to be an originator of systems. Although this remark has some foundation, it is not clear that it does not also apply to structured methods if properly carried out. In these, during the transition from analysis to systems design, there is always an element of assessing what needs to be done logically in order to perform a function, as well as analysing what actually is done.

Although Checkland's methodology has been used commercially, it does not have the same extensive track record as is associated with the structured methods covered in the previous section of this chapter. This is not to say that there have been significant failures using the methodology but rather that the number of times it has been employed provide an insufficiently large sample from which to draw conclusions. It remains to be seen whether the methodology will have a lasting impact on approaches to analysis and design.

Participative socio-technical approaches

The participative element of this has been criticized from the point of view of its heavy cost. To involve users participatively in analysis and design places a great burden on the personnel in an organization. Proponents of the approach would not argue with this but would point out that the extra cost is more than justified by the production of systems that are accepted by and meet user needs—it produces effective and not merely technically efficient systems.

The emphasis on participation and the omission of specific tools is seen as a shortcoming by critics. However, the approach should be seen as setting a framework within which successful analysis and design can be carried out. It does not preclude the use of data flow diagrams, entity modelling or any other technique that aids analysis and design. Participation is seen as a recognition of the importance of implementing a system that meets socio-technical as well as purely technical goals.

There may be resistance to the use of participation in its fullest forms. From one quarter, management can see it as a way of losing managerial control; from another, analysts can view it as diminishing the importance of their status and roles. This is not an objection to the approach, but resistance to its use will weaken its effectiveness, so it is important that a commitment to participation be obtained from all parties involved.

Finally, in common with Checkland's methodology, there are too few cases in which the approach has been applied to judge its success from an empirical standpoint.

Both Checkland and those who have developed the participative approach have undoubtedly identified weaknesses in the universal applicability of 'hard' approaches. It remains to be seen whether their solutions will fulfil the promises they intend to keep.

Summary

This section has expanded on the material covered previously by introducing and examining additional systems development tools, techniques and approaches.

Project management is an essential element to the successful implementation of a project. Indeed in many system developments, particularly state-funded projects, the use of a specific project management approach is a contractual requirement without which sponsorship is not made available. The PRINCE2 method, a well-established approach, was described.

CASE tools are an essential aid for the analyst/designer. Initially they offered a tool for the generation of the diagrams that model the logical system. As they have matured CASE tools now provide an entire environment for the capture of the required aspects of the physical system, for the modelling of the logical system and often the generation of code that will comprise the physical solution.

Approaches to systems analysis and design have been divided into two categories—'hard' and 'soft'. Although this is a useful division, it must always be remembered that there are many differences in the underlying assumptions and practices between different methodologies within each category.

'Hard' approaches seek to develop a technical solution to problems through the implementation of a computer system (Table 3.1—structured, data analysis, object oriented). They assume the possibility of a clear and agreed statement both of the current situation and its problems and of the desired state of affairs to be achieved. The problem for systems analysis and design is then seen as designing a solution that will take us from where we are now to where we want to go. The assumptions underlying this approach are akin to those in engineering. Users of the existing system are seen as providers of useful information about it. Users of the proposed system are seen in terms of their information requirements and as devices for input of data. The role of the analyst is as *the* expert brought in on a client–consultant basis to design the system.

Traditional methodologies concentrate on the automation of existing business processes. They do this by recommending procedures and documentation to describe the current system and turn this into a set of program and file specifications. Structured process analysis and design grew out of the failure of traditional methods when designing complex integrated systems or when providing systems that involve substantial redesign of functions or procedures. The emphasis is on transcending the physical limitations of the current system by developing a logical model of data flows, functions and processes prior to design. The perspective of approaches based on data analysis acknowledges that databases are a corporate resource and consequently need careful design. This is achieved by deriving a logical data model of the organization from which a database structure can be defined.

'Soft' approaches recognize the impact of human beings in the area of systems analysis and design (Table 3.1—Checkland, socio-technical participation). First, these methodologies deny the premise that it is easy to specify current and desired systems—problem situations are messy, and the solutions are intellectual constructs as perceived by actors within the system (Checkland). Second, the role of the analyst is not one of an expert to give definitive knowledge on systems analysis and design but rather that of a therapist (Checkland) or as just one of a design team involving users (participative approach). Third, the role of participants in the existing system is integral to successful system development. Checkland's approach concentrates on enriching the systems participants' perceptions of the current system. This is aimed at stimulation of change and improvement of the problem situation in the fuzzy system within which it occurs. The participative approach emphasizes the need to obtain a harmonious design of interacting social and technical systems by involving users in the process of analysis and design. Both deny that a computer system is the *only* solution: the former by recognizing that not all problems require computer-based solutions; the latter by asserting that designing a technical computer system independently of people's needs will lead to failure.

Approaches to development are not static. The influence of CASE tools on the process of analysis and design is becoming increasingly significant. These are likely to be centred on object oriented approaches, which concentrate on a perspective of the world as being composed of objects, relationships between objects and operations using those objects. CASE may cover the entire spectrum of systems analysis and design from the strategic planning of information systems to the automatic generation of executable code.

Table 3.1 Comparison of approaches

Approach	Reasons for development	Aim	Area	Method	Key words/concepts examples
Structured	Failures at developing large integrated systems and inability to coordinate programmer teams	To develop a technically efficient, modular, integrated system	Functions, total systems	Development of a logical model of a system emphasizing functions, data processes and data flows	Data flow diagrams, data dictionaries, structured HIPO charts
Data analysis	Development and increasing importance of database technology	To develop a database structure suitable for supporting the organization's changing applications	Organizational data structures	Development of a logical data model of an organization emphasizing entities, relationships and structures	Entity–relationships models
Object oriented	Failures of structured methodologies to produce systems on time, within budget and future-proofed	To develop and maintain applications with greater ease and higher quality	Objects, total systems	Development of static and dynamic object models emphasizing associations, inheritance structures and message passing	Class/object model, object interaction diagram, state transition, inheritance, reuse of previous designs and code
Checkland	Failure to take account of fuzzy problems in organizational contexts	To achieve user understanding of organizational problem situations, thereby leading to learning and improvement	Fuzzy systems, problem situations	Development of a conceptual model of an ideal system through which participants can identify weaknesses and stimulate change	Rich pictures, conceptual models, root definitions, CATWOE, agenda for change
Socio-technical participation	Failures of systems as a result of user non-acceptance	To develop a fit between social and technical systems by participation, thereby ensuring systems acceptance	Socio-technical system	Involvement of the user in the process of analysis and design	Participation, consensus, job satisfaction, variance analysis, autonomous work groups
Rapid applications development	The need to develop systems quickly to respond to changing business needs	To develop an effective core system quickly to meet user needs	Functions, end-user needs	Involvement of management and users in an iterative development process, which may involve a variety of tools, including CASE	Joint requirements planning, workshops, joint applications development, prototyping

The recent development of rapid applications development (RAD) has emphasized the need for fast core systems development to meet rapidly changing business needs. RAD is gaining popularity, particularly in the development of e-commerce solutions.

REVIEW QUESTIONS

1. Explain the difference in the meanings of the terms *hard* and *soft* as applied to approaches to systems analysis.
2. State *four* main features of:
   (a) structured process analysis and design
   (b) structured data analysis and design
   (c) object oriented systems analysis and design.
3. What are the limitations of 'hard' approaches to systems analysis and design?
4. Outline the stages in Checkland's methodology.
5. What is the purpose of drawing rich pictures?
6. What is a CASE tool? What benefits can be gained from using a CASE tool? What are the drawbacks?
7. Describe the PRINCE2 approach to Project Management.

EXERCISES

1. What is meant by 'a participative approach to socio-technical design'?
2. Explain and distinguish the different possible levels of involvement of participants in the analysis and design stages of a project.
3. What benefits are claimed for user participation in analysis and design?
4. What roles do variance analysis, job satisfaction analysis and future analysis play in socio-technical analysis and design?
5. The hard approaches to analysis and design are often criticized for assuming that by using a technical solution it is possible to solve, or at least alleviate, problems in an organization. But if a technical solution is what the organization wants, why should this be a criticism?
6. 'User participation is an advantage in analysis and design, but the real benefits for the workforce and ultimately management would occur if users also participated in the decision process involving new technology and information systems.' Do you agree?
7. What are the key features of a RAD approach? Why has RAD been described as being 'well suited' to e-commerce systems developments?
8. This chapter, in common with many texts, uses the term *methodology* frequently. Provide and justify a definition of a methodology.
9. Why is PRINCE2 project management well suited to information systems projects?

MINI CASE 3.2

RAPID APPLICATIONS DEVELOPMENT

Post Office IT (POiT) supplies technology solutions to the Post Office and its businesses and as such is one of the largest IT suppliers in the UK. POiT had investigated ways of improving productivity and understood that rapid application development (RAD) could deliver benefits such as:

- reducing time to market for new applications by cutting development times;
- getting more for less by improving productivity;
- building greater user buy-in by including end users from the word go.

But the challenge facing POiT staff was how to put RAD into practice and realize these benefits.

POiT had an ideal opportunity to use RAD as it needed to demonstrate reduced lead times and costs for one of its main clients, SSL. SSL (Subscription Services Ltd) is a customer management and telemarketing specialist and is particularly well known as the organization that collects the TV licence fee on behalf of the BBC under the brand TV Licensing. POiT had been retained to develop a system to automate a small specialist licensing section, which it had not previously been cost-effective to automate; SSL and POiT jointly chose this as the pilot RAD project. When they had investigated RAD in the past, POiT had chosen the dynamic systems development method (DSDM)—the industry-standard, public domain methodology for RAD. POiT was already an active member of the DSDM Consortium, the body that promotes the method, and decided that DSDM would underpin the approach that it adopted for the pilot project.

When it started out on the pilot, POiT was given a rigorous set of targets. This included doubling productivity against traditional methods and developing the new system to a very tight development budget. In fact, the entire project took seven and a half months—for an application that would have taken 13 months to develop by normal methods, thus halving the labour costs of the project. As everyone becomes more and more price-conscious, the need to deliver to fixed cost is becoming an ever more important driver, and users are beginning to expect this for IT as well as other services and products they purchase. The POiT pilot was no exception. Once the functional model had been defined, the project was supplied to a fixed price, yet it delivered almost 50% more function than was planned.

To outsource or mentor?

To implement a new way of working and deliver significant quantifiable benefits in one project is a very tall order. If POiT was to be successful, it had to get up to speed fast. It felt that, while it could have hired expertise to deliver the project in double-quick time, when the 'hired guns' left, it would have found itself back at square one. POiT wanted to retain RAD knowledge at the end of the project.

Mentoring is an excellent way of investing in in-house staff so that they retain knowledge and experience gained from the real world in real projects. To this end, POiT looked around for a partner who could not only transfer expertise and knowledge but also support it as it worked through the pilot. Like POiT, IBM is an active member of the DSDM Consortium, and as a founder member has worked with the method since its inception. This, combined with its willingness to work in true partnership with customers, made IBM the natural choice.

Shortening the learning curve

In order to get everyone 'singing from the same hymn sheet', the IBM consultants implemented an intensive programme of training and education. Equally important as education is building team spirit and motivation, which is vital to a successful RAD project. These intensive education sessions, which included users and IT staff, provided the ideal catalyst.

POiT was well aware that the best way to learn is not necessarily in the classroom. Indeed, its experience was that learning 'on the job' was often more useful, so it was delighted with IBM's approach.

IBM followed up the initial education sessions with regular health checks. These sessions reviewed the entire project, including the people, the development environment and the technology. These reviews formed the basis of a positive feedback loop, which meant that lessons learned throughout the life of the pilot were acted on as it progressed. This positive feedback loop enabled vital fine-tuning of the development process, helping to ensure that all members of the team were able get the most from the learning experience that the pilot project provided.

Building assets for the future

It is one thing to retain the knowledge and experience once the consultants have left, but what about the process? POiT was keen to build a repeatable process so that when the next project came along it would not have to 'reinvent the wheel'. With this in mind, IBM set up a DSDM workbench, comprising techniques and guidelines based on its wealth of experience in traditional and RAD projects. This meant that through the pilot, although the first using RAD and DSDM, POiT was already building work practices and an environment that could be expected to be found in companies with far more experience.

The way forward

The project was successful as a pilot and pioneered many new tools and techniques that POiT can use in the future. One of the benefits of combining IBM's mentoring with DSDM is that POiT is now in a position to pick and choose from the DSDM elements available without being tied to the entire structure. It can do this safe in the knowledge that it knows what it is doing.

Both POiT and SSL are keen to use RAD again and to continue developing and refining their processes and standards. In fact, a senior SSL manager was heard to ask 'When are we doing the next project?'

QUESTIONS

1. In what ways did the RAD approach followed in the PoiT project differ from the traditional structured analysis and design approaches introduced in earlier chapters?
2. Identify the features of the PoiT project that made it particularly successful.
3. Were there any aspects of the PoiT project that made it particularly suited to an RAD approach? Can RAD deliver better-quality solutions in all situations?

References and recommended reading

Avgerou C. and Cornford T. (1998). *Developing Information Systems: Concepts, Issues and Practice*, 2nd edn. Palgrave (formerly Macmillan)

This provides an interesting introduction to approaches and issues in information systems development. The book adopts a conceptual and critical perspective. It is suitable as a supplementary to a detailed explanatory text.

Avison D. and Fitzgerald G. (2003). *Information Systems Development: Methodologies, Techniques and Tools*, 3rd edn. McGraw-Hill

This well-established text covers a range of techniques and methodologies for systems analysis and design. The book provides a comprehensive coverage of data, process, rapid, blended, and people-oriented methodologies. This edition contains new material on ERP and the development of e-commerce applications. The book is suitable for those covering an information systems course at undergraduate level.

Bennet S., McRobb S. and Farmer R. (2002). *Object Oriented Systems Analysis and Design using UML*. McGraw-Hill

This text for undergraduate courses presents various life cycle models and develops object oriented approaches using UML. The book contains two extensive case studies with end of chapter summaries, questions and case reviews.

Bittner K. and Spence I. (2006). *Managing Iterative Software Development Projects*. Addison-Wesley

This book acknowledges the environment of change within which projects are usually developed and provides strategies of dynamic planning and iterative development including extreme programming.

Checkland P.B. (1999). *Systems Thinking, Systems Practice*. John Wiley & Sons.

This book develops the thinking behind the Checkland methodology.

Coad P. and Yourdon E. (1991). *Object-oriented Analysis*, 2nd edn. Prentice Hall

A straightforward introductory text covering the major tasks associated with object-oriented analysis.

Cobham D., Harston J., Kretsis M. and Kyte J. (1999). *The Uptake and Usage of Object Technology*, Proceedings of BIT Conference

Fettke P. and Loos P *et al.* (2007). *Reference Modelling for Business Systems Analysis*. IGI Global

The starting point of referencing modelling is to identify various conceptual modules for different types of industry and use these as a guide to commonality in systems development. This text provides insights into languages and models for reference modelling. There are a large number of contributors. It is suitable for advanced readers.

Fowler M. (2004). *UML Distilled: A Brief Guide to the Standard Modelling Language*. Addison-Wesley, Pearson

This is a short practical book enabling readers to become up to speed with UML 2.0 and learn the essentials of the UML language. The book gives a clear coverage of UML diagramming tools and a useful introduction to OO techniques in software development.

Land F. and Hirscheim R. (1983). Participative systems design: rationale, tools and techniques. *Journal of Applied Systems Analysis*, **10**

Larman C. (2004). *Applying UML and Patterns: An Introduction to Object-Oriented Analysis and Design and Iterative Development*, 3rd edn. Prentice Hall

An excellent step-by-step guide to UML and object oriented development.

Martin J. (1989). *Information Engineering*. Prentice Hall

A clear and comprehensive statement of the main ideas behind the influential methodology of information engineering.

Martin J. (1991). *Rapid Applications Development*. Prentice Hall

This is an important text as the first identifiable approach with the underlying theme of rapid applications development. Other texts on RAD have diverged from Martin's original approach, and the term 'RAD' is now more loosely defined.

Meyer B. (1995). *Object Success*. Prentice Hall

A very clear exposition of Meyer's view of object oriented approaches, illustrated with many real case studies and some amusing anecdotes. The book contains a useful section on managing projects in an object oriented environment.

Mumford E. (2003). *Redesigning Human Systems*. IGI Publishing

A fascinating view on systems design and the management of change. The author emphasizes the need for an ethical approach in implementing changes to systems.

Newman W.M. and Lamming M.J. (2004). *Interactive Systems Design*. Addison-Wesley

This text provides a coherent framework for user oriented design covering all stages of analysis, design, implementation and evaluation. It illustrates points with examples from air traffic control, police detective work and medical practice. Prototyping and evaluation play a major role in this approach, and this is fully explained.

Office of Government Commerce (2005). *Managing Successful Projects with PRINCE2*. Her Majesty's Stationery Office

This well-illustrated official guide lays out the PRINCE2 method in its entirety. It is a manual for successful adoption and usage of PRINCE2.

Career management practices

Question

Think what your organization can do for you, not (just) what you can do for your organization.

How well would you like to be treated by your organization? What kind of career planning and management activities would you expect? What may your organization plan for you without your knowing about it?

In this chapter we dwell on the third 'P', the practical level: the activities, actions and operations that form the practice of career planning and management.

EXHIBIT 3.1

CREATING THE FUNCTION

Here is a question I used to give my HRM students in their final exam:

You have just been recruited by a company which employs some 1000 employees, a company that previously did not have an HRM/Personnel department, for historic reasons and because the former CEO believed that HR issues should be dealt with directly by line managers. However, a new CEO is now in charge, and she believes that there should be a specific professional unit within the organization to deal with HRM/personnel issues. You have been recruited to create the new department and head it. The HR manager will be one of the board level team (you would not have accepted the offer had this not been the case).

On your first day you set yourself the task of building a comprehensive system to include all the necessary HR practices. In particular, you need to decide which practices to apply and how these will be integrated.

QUESTIONS

If the situation in the company was satisfactory under the old system, and since we believe in delegation, why not continue letting the line managers be the HR managers?

What impact will the type of organization and its characteristics have on your answer? The above scenario may vary, depending on such factors as: whether it is a production or service based firm; whether it is an established or new enterprise; which sector it is in—high or low technology; what form of control—centralized or decentralized, and others.

Question

As a consultant, the scenario depicted above may face you with a challenge: If you are asked to advise an HR director about how to rebuild their HR department from scratch, what would you be doing in terms of the constituencies of the department?

Introduction

This section takes on the more pragmatic task of focusing on career practices, a sub-section of overall HR practices. The section outlines a comprehensive portfolio of HRM practices, which can be conducted by organizations to plan and manage employees' careers. It develops and expands upon earlier work of the author.[1] The chapter provides a systematic presentation and critical examination, rooted in both theory and practice, of a range of career management practices, techniques, activities and programmes. For each career practice referred to, an explanation is given of how it may be utilized by organizations in the 2000s. The chapter also integrates these practices into a comprehensive organizational framework.

The importance and prominence of organizational Career Planning and Management (CPM) as part of HRM has been widely recognized.[2] From the early writing on modern career systems to recent inputs, academic scholars have emphasized that organizational career systems should ensure the fit between individual needs and aspirations and organizational requirements.[3] However, much of the literature on careers has focused on the individual whereas there is an acute lack of conceptual and theoretical formulation of organizational practices. An exception is the Baruch and Peiperl model presented in this section a model developed as a result of empirical investigation, and integrating a variety of organizational career practices.

A good starting point for establishing a comprehensive updated organizational career system is to examine what was available in the 1980s and 1990s. The section goes on to project which career practices will remain valid and relevant, which will need significant change and adaptation, which might become obsolete, and which new ones may emerge. The first part of the section critically examines a traditional portfolio for career practices.

There have been several attempts to establish what comprises a conventional set of organizational career practices. Several sources in the literature suggest specific lists of career practices.[4] Walker and Gutteridge (1979)[5] identified 10 career activities, although some of these were closer to other constituencies of HRM than to career management. A different problem occurs with the work of Gutteridge and Otte (1983),[6] which focused on some aspects of career practices, limiting the discussion to 10 practices and evaluating only three of them. Perhaps the most comprehensive list was that provided by Gutteridge, Leibowitz and Shore in their study of careers in the United States.[7] However, their study concentrated on large business organizations only (the top 1000 US corporations), and might thus have been non-representative of broader practice.

EXHIBIT 3.2

ANALYSIS

In the USA, the 1000th largest company (PC Connection, in the *Fortune 1000* list) employs some 1500 people. Number 200 in the *Fortune 500*, Entergy Corporation, with annual revenues of nearly $10 billion, has more than 15 000 employees. The size in terms of employee numbers varies, with some companies employing more than 100 000 people. However, the US labour market consists of about 126 million people. Thus, the majority of people work in small or medium-sized companies. While all have career, whether they all need a formal career system is another matter.

Question

At what stage in terms of size of the organization should an HR function be introduced into an organization? At what stage in terms of size should a career management function be introduced into the HR unit? What organizational and environmental characteristics will influence your answer?

The use of career practices: empirical evidence

The list of practices presented and discussed in this section evolved from several earlier works on CPM practices. Most practices were covered in many sources, but some new ones were added to the list, including induction, special programmes for unique populations, and secondments

Table 3.2 Use of career practices in 1990s studies

Career practices	Scale of 1–7		Per cent use by the organizations		
	A mean	sd	B1 %	B2 %	C %
Job postings	5.62	1.65	55	89	68
Formal education/tuition reimbursement	5.08	1.48	100	100	78
PA for career planning	4.80	1.63	82	89	
Counselling by manager	4.52	1.62	59	89	97
Lateral moves (job rotations in USA)	4.33	1.6			60
Counselling by HR	4.16	1.78	41	56	67
Pre-retirement programmes	4.15	2.15	90	78	5
Succession planning	3.6	1.75	63	33	69
Formal mentoring	2.95	1.79	43	44	44
Common career paths	2.73	1.8	67	56	
Dual ladder	2.42	1.77	75	44	34
Career booklets/pamphlets	2.41	1.6	22	33	19
Written individual career plans	2.38	1.82	14	33	
Assessment centre	2.34	1.79	69	67	23
Peer appraisal	2.26	1.73			
Career workshops	2.15	1.6	14	44	24
Upward appraisal	2.04	1.7			
Appraisal committees			37	11	30
Training programmes for managers			75	44	30
Orientation programme					78
Special needs (dual-career couples)					13

A—Baruch and Peiperl 1997: use in 194 UK organizations. Scale of 1–7: 1 = not applied at all; 7 = applied extensively.

B1—Baruch 1996b: use in 51 high-tech firms in Israel.

B2—Baruch 1996b: use in 9 high-tech firms in the UK.

C—Gutteridge, Leibowitz and Shore (1993): use in 256 large firms in the USA.

Sources: Derived from Y. Baruch and M.A. Peiperl (1997) 'High flyers: glorious past, gloomy present, any future?', *Career Development International*, 2(7), 354–8; Y. Baruch (1996) 'Organizational career planning and management techniques and activities in use in high-tech organizations', *Career Development International*, 1(1), 40–9; T.G. Gutteridge, Z.B. Leibowitz and J.E. Shore (1993) *Organizational Career Development*, San Francisco: Jossey-Bass.

(temporary assignments to another area/organization). Table 3.2 summarizes findings from studies in the 1990s, all of which tested the use of career management and planning practices in organizations. The sources for the data in these studies are responses from HR managers, as they are considered most likely to be best acquainted with career practices, both as professionals and as representatives of the organization.

The rest of the chapter is devoted, first to an elaboration of each practice, and then brings them together in an integrated framework. The presentation of the practices is in line with the classification offered by Baruch and Peiperl's (2000a) model,[8] which comprises five clusters of career practices (see Figure 3.29). It is a descriptive model (see Exhibit 3.3), i.e. based on field-research data, gathered from almost 200 organizations, and was constructed using the statistical procedure of factor analysis, a procedure utilized to measure interrelationships among variables. The classification is configured along two dimensions: degree of practice sophistication and level of organizational involvement.

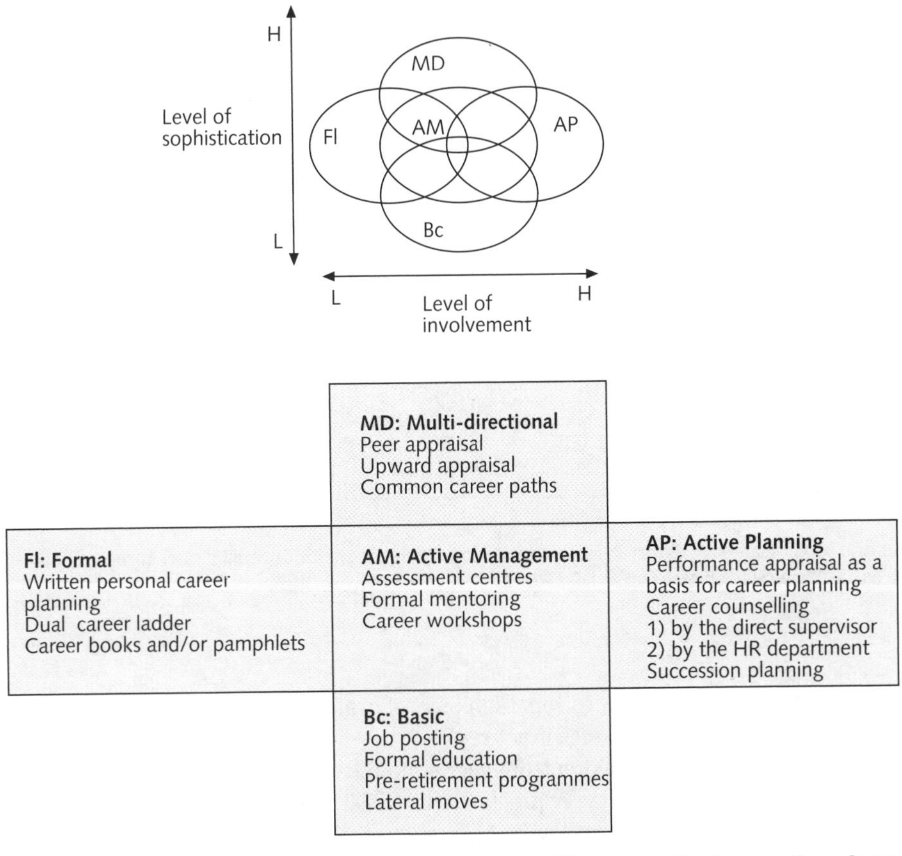

Source: Y. Baruch and M.A. Peiperl (2000) 'Career management practices: An empirical survey and implications', *Human Resource Management*, 39(4), 347–66 © John Wiley & Sons, Inc., reproduced with permission.

Figure 3.29 **Two-dimensional model of career management practices**

EXHIBIT 3.3

NORMATIVE VERSUS DESCRIPTIVE MODELS

A normative model is one that tries to establish what *should be* the right way to do something—to conduct a process, to develop a product, to form a relationship, etc. In this case, it is to develop a comprehensive set of organizational career practices and to find out how they may be associated with each other.

A descriptive model is one based on factual reality, i.e. how things *are* in real life. It is based on data collected and assembled, and is subjected to analysis that checks the relationships among constructs or variables.

While the majority of clusters in the model appear to be logical, and clearly based on factual evidence (i.e. a descriptive model, based on actual organizational cases), it is not necessarily the best model for developing a career system. Another way to look at clusters of career practices would be to develop a normative model—a model which tries to establish what career practices *should* be applied, and when establishing connections, to point to the right way to classify the clusters. In this sense, a normative model may add to our understanding and to the development of organizational career systems. The following set of dimensions may provide insights into the nature of each career practice (the first two were used in the Baruch and Peiperl (2000) model, the rest were introduced by Baruch, 2003).[9]

Table 3.3 Descriptive statistics and inter-correlation between the six dimensions

	Mean	SD	1	2	3	4	5
1. Developmental oriented	3.64	0.52					
2. Decision making oriented	2.82	0.59	0.48 (0.02)				
3. Innovative oriented	2.81	0.53	0.62 (0.00)	0.53 (0.01)			
4. Organizational involvement level	3.57	0.51	0.33 (0.12)	0.82 (0.00)	0.61 (0.00)		
5. Sophistication and complexity of practices	2.94	0.67	0.67 (0.00)	0.75 (0.00)	0.90 (0.00)	0.76 (0.00)	
6. Strategic oriented	3.05	0.63	0.56 (0.00)	0.85 (0.00)	0.65 (0.00)	0.75 (0.00)	0.82 (0.00)

Note: Coefficient/(cases)/two-tailed significance

Source: Reprinted from Y. Baruch (2003) 'Career systems in transition: A normative model for organizational career practices', Personnel Review, 32(2), 231–51, with permission from MCB UP Ltd.

- **Involvement:** from very low to very high level of organizational involvement needed while dealing with the specific career practice.
- **Sophistication and complexity:** from very simple to highly sophisticated and complex.
- **Strategic orientation:** from very practical, 'tactical', to very strategic.
- **Developmental focused:** from low to high relevance for developing individuals.
- **Organizational decision making focused:** from low to high relevance for organizational decision-making processes.
- **Innovative:** from very traditional or conventional, to innovative and unorthodox.

Using a Delphi approach, a normative model was generated from the views of 16 leading scholars from the Career division of the Academy of Management. The career practices presented were rated on the six dimensions. In view of the variety of practices and the complexity of working life, the advantage of this analytical approach appears to be that it utilizes the wide base of knowledge and depth of understanding of the participants.

Table 3.3 presents the evaluation of the practices along the six dimensions.

The relatively low standard deviations in Table 3.3 indicate considerable agreement amongst the respondents about the rating of the practices across the dimensions. The developmental-oriented dimension ratings were the highest, indicating that present career practices are highly directed towards individual development, as suggested by much of the writing on contemporary career systems. However, the application of career practices is still associated with a high level of organizational involvement. At the lower end of the scale we find the decision-making element and innovation, indicating the need for HR professionals to develop further the practices used to manage people's career in organizations.

CPM practices: clusters

Basic

The practices below were grouped under the title Basic (low on sophistication, medium on involvement) by the Baruch and Peiperl model:

- Postings regarding internal job openings
- Formal education as part of career development
- Lateral moves to create cross-functional experience
- Retirement preparation programmes

Formal

The practices below were grouped under the title Formal (medium on sophistication, low on involvement) by the Baruch and Peiperl model:

- Booklets and/or pamphlets on career issues
- Dual ladder (parallel hierarchy for professional staff)
- Written personal career planning

Active management

The practices below were grouped under the title Active Management (medium on sophistication, medium on involvement) by the Baruch and Peiperl model:

- Induction
- Assessment centres
- Mentoring
- Career workshops

Active planning

The practices below were grouped under the title Active Planning (medium on sophistication, high on involvement) by the Baruch and Peiperl model:

- Performance appraisal as a basis for career planning
- Career counselling by direct supervisor
- Career counselling by HR Department
- Succession planning

Multi-directional

The practices below were grouped under the title Multi-directional (high on sophistication, medium on involvement) by the Baruch and Peiperl model:

- 360-degree performance appraisal systems
- Common career paths
- Special programmes for ethnic minorities, women, disabled, dual career couples, etc., expatriates and repatriates, high-flyers

New CPM practices

The following additional practices listed by managers are not classified under any cluster in the Baruch and Peiperl model:

- Building psychological contracts
- Secondments
- Intrapreneurship

Another general career practice is:

- Training programmes for managers to enable them to handle careers issues

This practice is needed to provide managers with the skills required for handling their employees' careers. It is not one specific practice but combines several of the above-mentioned practices and activities, and is part of a training programme for managers.

Career practices for whom?

Each person, be they the porter or the CEO, has a career. Many develop their career outside the boundaries of large organizations. Among these are the self-employed, people who run small businesses, free-lancers, the unemployed. However, most working people are in organizations, usually as employees. Career practices are carried out by organizations to meet employees' needs.

They exist to support employees at all organizational levels, but in particular those in the higher echelons. Managerial and professional careers are more complex than those of some of the rank and file personnel. Consequently certain career practices are conducted only for managers. Throughout this section a distinction is made between practices directed mainly or exclusively at the managerial population and those aimed at employees at various hierarchy levels.

In considering career practices it may be advisable to review the above-mentioned practices to ascertain which are still valid and necessary, and which might be deemed unnecessary in the context of the twenty-first century. Even those expected to be essential in the future may need to be revised and adapted, e.g. in the light of contemporary organizational and environment turbulence.

The reader should bear in mind that the practices vary in their applicability and relevance to different kinds of organizations: small companies usually need fewer official bureaucratic and regulated systems, since informal procedures can be applied successfully. Organizations operating in different industrial sectors and countries may apply different sets of practices, or apply the same practice differently. Centralization versus de-centralization will also influence the application and structure of the CPM system. A special case is large multinational companies operating in diverse cultures. For such companies a variety of approaches in their different subsidiaries may be appropriate.

The final consideration is the impact that future innovations in information technology (IT) systems are expected to have on how careers are managed. The implications of the ever-increasing use of the Internet is just one example. However, the pace of technological breakthroughs in IT means that any attempt at forecasting long-term future practices may prove risky.

Career practices: detailed discussion

Advertising internal job openings

Whenever a vacancy occurs, the organization can look to fill it with either internal or external people. The choice depends on the level and type of position and the norms of the organization's career management practices.

For vacant rank and file positions, people may be hired from outside, even though there may be internal personnel who wish to apply for the new post, so creating another vacancy. When the search focus is internal, the vacancy can be advertised within the organization. Many organizations have a policy that jobs are advertised internally before any external search is conducted. The growing importance of internal job advertising as part of a comprehensive organizational career system was demonstrated by Douglas Tim Hall and others. Extensive use of internal job

Our people make the difference

We need good people for great jobs.

- Departments
- College Recruiting
- Search Careers
- Submit Resume
- Hourly Employment
- Application for Employment
- Benefits
- Diversity
- Life in Northwest Arkansas
- Success Stories

Note that for such a complex organization, there are several streams of applications (plus a separate one for Walmart.com, a subsidiary of some 250 employees which deals with their e-business only).

Source: www.walmart.com

Figure 3.30 **Web job openings for Wal-Mart stores**

advertising indicates to employees that the organization prefers internal promotion to recruiting managers from outside (i.e. a focus on the internal labour market).

Traditionally, jobs were advertised internally either on notice-boards or in the company newsletter. During the 1990s we witnessed a shift to advertising via internal e-mail and e-notice-boards, advertisements which may subsequently be distributed outside on external networks via the Internet.

Formal education as part of career development

Organizations may select people of managerial or technical potential and send them on a formal training or study programme as part of their career development path. The formal education may be a first degree in engineering, an MBA, or other graduate or postgraduate studies for managerial personnel, or professional and vocational qualification courses for non-managerial employees. Once an organization has identified an immediate future appointment need, such education can provide a solution. Even if there is no acute need, the organization may identify people who are worth the investment and justify the trust associated with such investment. Alternatively individuals can propose themselves for such a programme. As the timespan for HR planning gets shorter, and with widespread redundancies, many organizations have been less prepared to offer such long-term investment in people. This is due not just to the short-term nature of modern job contracts, but also to the lower level of mutual commitment organizations might expect. This tendency is expected to continue, and organizations will prefer to acquire people who already possess the necessary qualifications rather than those who need to be sent on study programmes. As a consequence, short-term specific training may replace academic studies sponsored by organizations.

The qualification most frequently utilized to develop managerial competence is the Master in Business Administration (MBA) degree. Several studies have indicated the importance of the MBA, and the reputation of certain business schools.[10] An MBA degree from a leading business school can make a difference for its holder in terms of managerial competence, career progress and remuneration[11] but the problem organizations face is the insecurity and instability of investment in people. Employees are not the property of the employer; they can move on to different jobs and organizations, with the new employer (who may be a competitor) benefiting from the former employer's investment.

All in all, organizations need to be very careful in their long-term investment in training and development. If employees are promised that they will gain 'employability', investment in terms of training is the most visible manifestation of the commitment on the part of the organization to fulfil its role in this respect.

EXHIBIT 3.4

IS IT GOOD FOR YOUR COMPANY TO HAVE MANAGERS WITH AN MBA QUALIFICATION?

Here are two stories of leading global companies which place a high value on an MBA.

VERIZON

Some 10–15 per cent of **Verizon**'s managerial workforce has an MBA. For **Verizon**, an MBA is a valuable asset, and it expects the holder of an MBA to have a better strategic perspective and orientation, more sophisticated knowledge and awareness of its application and a more balanced set of skills than a person without an MBA or one who is a specialist in a particular business discipline. However, in terms of who gains the most from an MBA, the perception is that the individual gets more upfront benefits. The benefits to the organization are harder to quantify and observe. When organizations are filling management positions, an MBA can be a tie-breaker and evidence of achievement, focus, skills and commitment.

Still, when on looks at what has happened in the past to **Verizon** employees who earn an MBA, one sees that they have not done especially well. For a number of reasons **Verizon** generally does not attract MBA graduates (perhaps because it is a mature business or because it has a 'sales culture').

EDS

At **EDS**, with more than 1500 MBA graduates, the contribution of MBA studies stems from the knowledge and skills associated with an MBA curriculum which, according to **EDS**, benefits the company in all aspects of their business, but primarily in finance and accounting, strategic planning and management development. However, since **EDS** does not impose a requirement to obtain an MBA for any particular job, there is no company policy on MBAs. Still, in terms of who gains the most from an MBA, the MBA graduate or **EDS** as their employing organization, the answer is clearly both. Thus, in hiring for management positions, an MBA tends to generally be more of an advantage. In practice, the MBA tends to give an advantage to the MBA graduate, which propels the individual forward in his or her career. All in all, while a benefit to start with, it is the knowledge and the performance that matters. MBAs from the 'Top' schools do tend to produce very distinguished graduates. However, even among the graduates from a nearby state university evening programme, **EDS** finds good talent.

Lateral moves to create cross-functional experience

Lateral moves to create cross-functional experience are increasing, and it seems this trend will continue. These may be seen as elementary career planning and management practices which most organizations with HRM systems need to apply. The flattening of organization was one of the flagships of the 1990s. When there are fewer hierarchy levels and horizontal communication is the key to success, people will no longer move up the ladder so fast. A slow climb to the top, perhaps in the Japanese style, became quite typical in Western organizations.[12] Organizations need to indicate clearly that such a route reflects career success rather than failure; this is a shift from the past practice, which perceived only 'climbing up' as evidence of career success. People should be advised that career advancement is not necessarily along the traditional upward path.

Some of these lateral movements may take the form of developing new ventures, secondments and cross-functional moves. In 1978, Edgar Schein presented the spiral cross-functional move, but that too was part of upward progress (see Figure 3.31).[13] Lateral moves (see Figure 3.32) will characterize the career path of the future manager, while job rotations and role changes will be frequent for the rank-and-file workforce. Relevant examples of this trend include the moving of insurance agents and bank clerks to direct marketing jobs.[14]

Retirement preparation programmes

This practice is directed at the target population of employees—those approaching retirement and about to leave the organization. These programmes can be short, e.g. a three-day workshop, taking place a couple of months before retirement. In addition to the 'standard' programme, large corporations may have a diversity programme, such as pre-retirement planning for women or minorities. They can also be longer, in terms of both programme time and its spread over a wider timespan. An investment in this practice is evidence of high commitment on the part of the organization to its employees, an essential part of developing mutual trust and commitment.[15] In these programmes the employee is prepared for retirement in several ways. Much time is devoted to financial considerations and ensuring that participants understand pension conditions and learn tax regulations. However, the better programmes take into account also the psychological need to adjust to life without work, a transformation that, if not managed, might end in deterioration of the health and well-being of people used to full-time hard work. Information on leisure activities and other fulfilling tasks forms a significant part of the better programmes, and in some of them the spouse is invited to take part too.

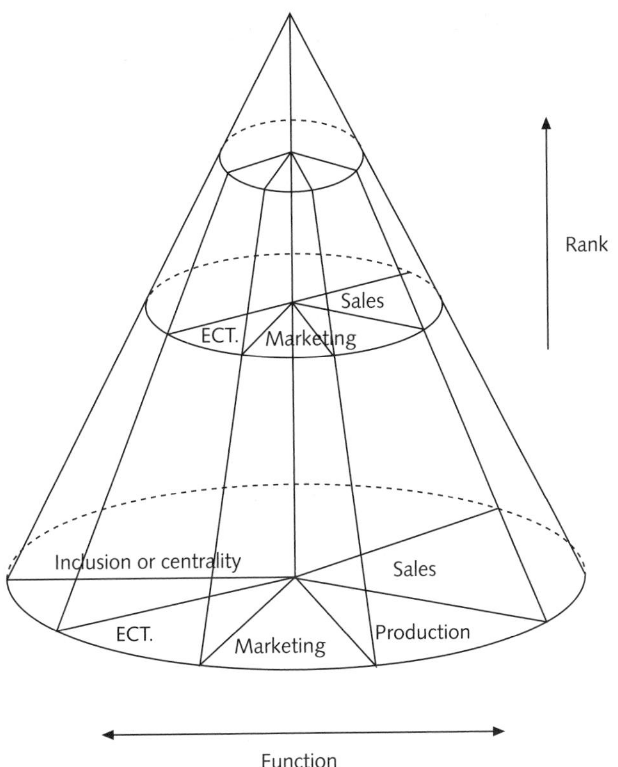

Source: Schein (1978). Taken from http://152.30.22.232/kirk/CDTheories/schein_organ_cone.html

Figure 3.31 Schein's organizational cone

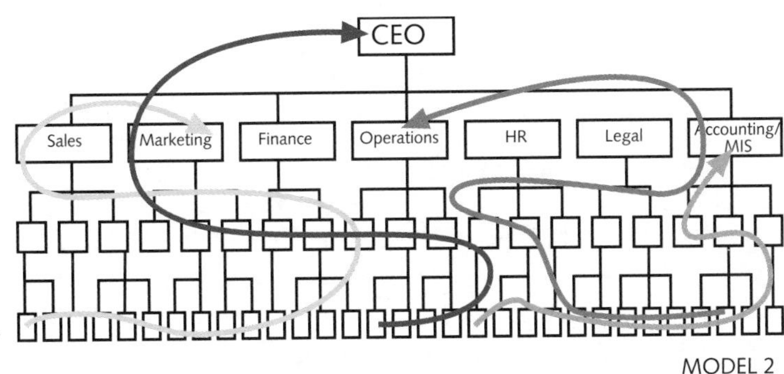

Source: Reprinted from M.A. Peiperl and Y. Baruch (1997) 'Models of careers: back to square zero', *Organizational Dynamics*, 25(4), 7–22, copyright 1997, with permission from Elsevier Science.

Figure 3.32 Lateral moves

EXHIBIT 3.5

PRE-RETIREMENT PROGRAMMES

Companies may run their own programmes or acquire one from an external consultancy.

Career Management Consultants is one of many consultancies who offer companies to manage their retirement programmes to assist employees to plan for the transition to retirement. The preparation includes emotional adjustments and lifestyle preparation. Their specific programme takes into consideration:

- Financial realities
- Geographic preferences
- Physical and emotional services
- Planning for positive change
- Decision making
- Career change
- Volunteering
- Dealing with family reactions and adjustments
- Aiming towards happiness

An internal programme is offered by the Wisconsin Department of Employee Trust Funds. Their motto is 'Retirement—A New Beginning'. The pre-retirement planning programme takes the form of a 12-hour course held in the evening for two hours a week for six weeks. The content of the course will typically include:

- Financial planning
  - Social security
  - Retirement benefits
- Insurance
  - Life insurance
  - Health insurance/Medicare
- Legal tips (e.g. taxes, wills and lawyers)
- Consumerism, housing, employment and retirement, wellness in retirement, and leisure.

The heavy redundancies of recent years mean that fewer people are remaining at the workplace until the legal retirement age (70 in the USA and 65 in most EU countries). Thus traditional pre-retirement programmes might become quite rare in the future. The need for this practice obviously depends also on the age of the organization and the maturity of its employees. For organizations that have been in existence for about 20–30 years, with most founders being aged about 30 at the time of the start-up, there is no real need for formal institutionalized pre-retirement programmes. If there are only a very few due to retire, the issue may best be dealt with by a private consultancy that will conduct an internal organizational programme of preparation for retirement, in line with the present-day approach of outsourcing HR functions.

If large-scale redundancy programmes are likely to prevail in the near future, pre-retirement programmes may be transformed into pre-redundancy programmes. In this kind of programme, the organization will first prepare the employees for the possibility that 'it could happen to you, too'. Subsequently the focus will move to what can be done, how an employee whose career has reached a plateau stage can be trained to look successfully for a new job in declining industrial sectors. In addition to such a pre-redundancy programme, the same organization will need an after-redundancy programme, to deal with the 'survivor syndrome' which might affect those who have stayed. Professional use of best practice may combat survivor syndrome successfully.[16]

Booklets and/or pamphlets on career issues

Booklets, pamphlets or leaflets are part of an organization's formal stock of career-related information. They introduce what career opportunities the organization offers and provide an introduction to all available CPM practices. Information that may be covered includes career paths, the competencies required for each position on the path, time scales (e.g. the minimum time to be spent in a certain position before promotion), conditions for certain developments. The aim of such booklets is to provide everyone in the organization with relevant information, releasing the direct manager from the job of presenting that information to subordinates.

Such information is directed at all employees, but is important especially for newcomers, either those recently recruited to the organization, or those recently promoted to the managerial ranks. In the 2000s we expect fewer of these booklets to exist. Complex company re-structurings, mergers and acquisitions will make most written forms obsolete very quickly. Booklets may be made available in electronic form as part of the company website, with access either limited to the employees of the company who have the password, or open to all.

With companies facing an increasing number of lawsuits due to a failure to satisfy employees' expectations, employers do not like to present what might later be seen as unfulfilled promises. This factor, coupled with the lower potential for long-term planning, means that the importance of such booklets is declining, and they are being replaced by different forms, such as electronic boards and directories which can incorporate structural change fed into the system, resulting in an updated version of an electronic booklet.

Dual ladder

The dual ladder is a parallel hierarchy, created for non-managerial staff, such as professional or technical employees. The major role of such a 'ladder' is to provide 'upward mobility' and recognition for those who cannot or do not wish to hold a managerial role. The dual ladder emerged in response to the need to provide professionals in non-managerial roles a different promotion path. A typical case is that of the excellent, promising engineer who is promoted to a managerial role (because there is no alternative means of recognizing or remunerating them within the professional roles). Such promotions often end with an accomplished professional transformed into a poor manager.

The dual ladder is very important, but is suitable only for the particular group (professionals without managerial skills or with no aspiration to become managers). Many large firms use this technique (Feuer, 1986), and its use is continually growing (Badway, 1988).[17] The reason for creating the dual ladder will still be valid in the 2000s, and perhaps even more so, as a new sector of professionals will be involved—professional experts, counsellors, etc.—not managers, but people working in crucial roles, with a responsibility and remuneration level similar to that of managers. The CPM system will need to identify the population eligible for this status, and ensure that only a small proportion enter the stream. Otherwise it will lose its power as an alternative system of recognition for those few who deserve it.

Induction

The process of introducing people to their new organization is the first CPM practice a new employee experiences (it will be entitled induction or socialization). This is a process whereby all newcomers learn the behaviours and attitudes necessary for assuming roles in an organization (Van Mannen, 1976).[18] Part of it is formal, led by organizational officials, whereas other aspects are learned in an informal manner, not necessarily in line with organizational formal norms and policies (see, for example, Ashford, 1986).[19] Newcomers are not always passive in their search for information (Morrison, 1993).[20] The set of mutual expectations in the boundaryless organization will be different from the one most people have experienced in the past (for further elaboration see the discussion of psychological contracts later in this chapter). Nevertheless, it remains essential that employers should introduce newcomers to the varied aspects of their organizational life and their role within it. These can be related to ideology or philosophy, culture, policies, rules and regulations, norms, expected behaviours and performance, and any other information, including social, which will help them to master their jobs and become integrated into the new workplace. One of the main changes witnessed in the 1990s is the much wider age span of newcomers. Whereas in the old type of careers people joined organizations at an early age, and in many cases stayed for their whole working life in the same workplace, people now tend to have a multiple career path, and frequent changes of employers are common. An induction process for the experienced professional or manager is very different from that directed at young school leavers or new graduates. The long-lasting impact of this early experience for newcomers on their later life in the organization should not be underestimated (Bauer and Green, 1994).[21]

Assessment and development centres

Assessment centres have attracted much interest in academia and from organizational practitioners. They have been found as a reliable and valid tool for career development (c.f. Tziner,

Ronen and Hacohen, 1993; Thornton, Tziner, Dahan, Clevenger and Meir, 1997; Iles, 1999) and are expected to continue to play an important role in the twenty-first century (Howard, 1997).[22] In the recent past, assessment centres were used for two main purposes: as a selection tool for managerial recruitment, and as an indicator of managerial potential; now they are also being used for developmental purposes (Spychalski, Quinones, Gaugler and Pohley, 1997).[23] Development centres evolved from assessment centres, and share many features with them, but are directed not necessarily towards selection but rather to general development and enhancement of the manager, preparing him/her for future roles. There is widespread discussion of assessment centres in the literature and most studies provide strong support for their effectiveness (e.g. Bray, 1985; Portwood and Granrose, 1986; Laser, 1990).[24] Large organizations may have their own assessment centres whereas small firms generally use external institutions. The use of assessment centres for selection is expected to decline, as fewer positions will be available following the trend towards downsizing (Cameron, 1996).[25] Thus we may witness more use of assessment centres for developmental purposes and identification of managerial potential (Iles, 1999).[26]

Mentoring

The principal aim of mentoring is to bring together a person with managerial potential and an experienced manager, who is not necessarily that person's direct manager. The senior manager can provide advice and tutoring, serving as a kind of 'uncle' or 'godfather' in the workplace. Thus mentoring is directed mostly at managerial personnel, and is used frequently in graduate recruitment programmes. The potential of this practice has been suggested in many studies (e.g. Baird and Kram, 1983; Clawson, 1980; Kram, 1985; Scandura, 1992; Baugh, Lankau and Scandura, 1996, and others).[27] In particular Kram (1986)[28] argues that both mentors and protégés benefit from this practice, and that the organization can shape the kind of mentoring relationships it wants. Such a win-win situation, when achievable, will be needed in the future too. Moreover, the organization is a clear beneficiary from having mentoring practice (Scandura and Viator, 1994),[29] in terms of protégés' attitudes and performance.

Mentoring, though acclaimed as a novel and esteemed approach for managerial development, also has pitfalls. Scandura (1998)[30] analysed the main dysfunctions of mentoring, which she saw as negative relations, sabotage, difficulty and spoiling. Another significant problem associated with mentoring is the possible collision of interests between the direct manager and the mentor. Cross-gender mentoring can also give rise to questions of possible sexual harassment on the one side and creating or encouraging unintended types of relationships on the other. Problems of this sort can be prevented by same-gender mentoring, which will be more feasible when more females enter managerial positions. The availability of mentors may also be a problem: with fewer hierarchical layers in the 2000s organization it will be more difficult to find enough people to serve as mentors—a factor which might reduce the present considerable use of this practice. To overcome these problems novel ideas are offered, for example the introduction of peer mentoring. A different approach to encourage senior managers to take on protégés would be to emphasize that being a mentor is a sign of seniority and recognition. Thus mentoring may replace position in the formal hierarchy as a status symbol for mature and loyal managers, those who wish to contribute to the success of the organization and at the same time to be recognized as a senior member of the organization.

Career workshops

Career workshops are short-term workshops focusing on specific aspect(s) of career management, and aiming to provide managers with relevant knowledge, skills and experience (see Figure 3.33). Participating in career workshops can contribute to the effectiveness of the employee (Sweeney, Haller and Sale, 1989).[31] Career workshops usually focus on specific aspects such as identifying future opportunities, rather than just general development (e.g. interviewing skills). With frequent structural changes in organizations people certainly need adaptation mechanisms, and workshops of this kind will help in this. Career workshops can improve the employability of the participants, enhancing their career resilience (Waterman, Waterman and Collard,

Career workshops		
Career resilience workshop		
Altman and Baruch (2002)[35] developed a workshop to help individuals identify their resilience and coherence with their employing organization. An extract from the workshop is presented below (participants are asked, among other activities, to evaluate several statements about themselves and their workplace).		
Evaluation scales: 1 low; 2 moderately low; 3 neither low nor high; 4 moderately high; 5 high; 6 very high; 7 extremely high		
	Actual presence	Valence – how important this is for you
1. Individuals are encouraged to take responsibility for their own development	1 2 3 4 5 6 7	1 2 3 4 5 6 7
2. Employees are encouraged to take initiatives to enhance their own employability	1 2 3 4 5 6 7	1 2 3 4 5 6 7
Etc.		
Intelligent career workshop		
Parker and Arthur (2002)[36] developed a workshop based on sort cards to identify and analyse individual 'components' of career intelligence. Further information can be found in Parker and Arthur (2002).		

Figure 3.33 **Career workshops**

1994).[32] The impetus for sending people to workshops can come from their manager or mentor or the HR counselling system as well as self nomination. With an increasing number of organizations making redundancies or undergoing restructuring, future career workshops may concentrate on inter- and intra-organizational opportunities. Among the many ideas on which workshops can focus are how to increase employability, how to create new satellite companies or joint ventures, the concept and practice of the management buy-out. These and other ideas can help participants to develop new insights into the future of their career—within the organization or elsewhere.

Performance appraisal as a basis for career planning

Numerous works emphasize the need for a close connection between the performance appraisal (PA) system and career development (e.g. Jacobson and Kaye, 1986; Weitzel, 1987; Murphy and Cleveland, 1995).[33] Hall, Posner and Harder (1989)[34] demonstrated the gap between the theory behind PA systems and their implementation, suggesting the need to combine CPM with the PA system. PA systems were found to operate in most of the organizations studied.

Of all the CPM practices, PA is perhaps the most fundamental. It can be utilized in HRM in a very similar way to that by which accountancy reports (such as the profit and loss account or the balance sheet) cater for the finance and accountancy systems. Valid and reliable PA would identify who should be promoted, who should be made redundant at a time of downsizing, and identify training and development needs. In terms of choosing people for future development, e.g. the selection of high potential employees for assessment centres, can be done on the basis of their PA results. A variety of CPM practices, such as appointing mentors or building succession planning, depend on the PA system. If the system is valid and reliable it may serve as the foundation stone for an integrated CPM system.

Career counselling

Career counselling is a two-way communication with the employee and two main sources are available for conducting this. The first is the direct manager (or another higher manager) who has a good knowledge of the employee's attitudes, behaviours, skills, etc.; the second is an HRM manager. Depending on the complexity of an organization, and its financial resources, external counselling can also be provided. This practice can be closely associated with the core of the Herriot and Pemberton (1996) model,[35] which shows the need to match organizational requirements and possibilities with individual career aspirations and abilities. Many agencies now provide career counselling services to both individuals and organizations.

Career counselling by direct manager and by the HRM unit

In many organizations the direct manager is in the best position to conduct career counselling, because he or she has perhaps the most accurate and up-to-date knowledge of the person. On the other hand, for such counselling to be fruitful, the person conducting it needs to have good standing in the organization, and to know the career options available and the direction of future organizational developments. In addition serving as a counsellor can conflict with other roles of the manager, such as loyalty (i.e. whether his/her loyalty resides with the organization or with the subordinate). Career counselling can be conducted also by the HRM unit staff. The advantages of their doing the counselling include knowledge of organizational goals and development; familiarity with HRM planning for the whole enterprise and knowledge, skills and experience of counselling in general. The obstacle that frequently prevents HRM from carrying out this task is its detachment from the professional life of the organization.

One of the long-standing problems relating to this practice is the fact that direct managers frequently see it as a bureaucratic burden, as Walker and Gutteridge (1979) found.[36] They also found that most of the supervisors in their survey (87 per cent) were not trained for counselling. A new problem is that there may be major changes of which the direct manager may have no prior knowledge. For example, in mergers and acquisitions, many layers of management become aware of a significant organizational structural change only after its announcement. In the 2000s we expect HRM to be more closely aligned with the general business strategy, so that the HR manager will be more aware of future plans, and consequently will be better equipped to deal with individual career counselling.

One solution could be to make two or three counsellors available—the direct manager and an HRM manager, with the option also of external counselling. Sometimes counselling can touch on sensitive issues, and individual employees may prefer the latter option. For personal matters which may require confidentiality, integration is not recommended (e.g. certain issues should not be reported to the formal PA system), but on the other hand, individual interest in secondments (see the discussion later in this chapter) could be expressed and identified through counselling.

EXHIBIT 3.6

EXTERNAL COUNSELLING

A worldwide downturn in the sales of machine tools caused an engineering company located in Birmingham to review its capacity, resulting in the loss of more than 100 jobs. The job losses included labourers, warehousing, operators, clerical, supervision, management, engineers and apprentices.

They selected an outside consultancy (the Quo Group) due to their extensive knowledge and experience of the Midlands job market. They were able to provide counsellors with relevant sector expertise along with the empathy to work with the varying levels of skills and attributes in the company.

The programme consisted of a series of two-day workshops for all non-managerial staff* to attend. These workshops concentrated on: identifying life and career goals, developing the appropriate action plan (including CV and interview preparation), mapping routes to the job market (including advertisement analysis, job and government agencies and networking), and dealing with offer negotiations.

Clients were seen in the consulting firm's premises and/or in individual sessions depending on their needs.

Major elements in the success of the programme were a mailshot to more than 500 companies within a 5-mile radius of the site, coupled with contacting local job agencies. These resulted in hundreds of enquiries. The Quo Group provided a job researcher who matched enquiries to skills and arranged interviews for all concerned. In addition a helpline was in place for those individuals who required support after the programme was completed.

Six weeks after the end of the programme only 4 per cent of those wanting jobs were still unemployed.

*Managers were provided with the Quo Group's one-to-one Executive Programme.

Source: This case was kindly provided by the Quo Group Ltd.

Succession planning

Miner and Miner (1985)[37] suggested a framework of organizational planning in which the organization decides on the possible replacement of every manager within the organization, and evaluates the potential for promotion of each manager. By its nature, this programme is primarily directed towards the managerial workforce. Succession planning (also termed a management inventory) can be valuable in the context of long-term planning. It will be different, but not less important, in a flattened organization where lateral movements occur. In the latter, succession planning will be more complicated but will still show who should first be considered when a new vacancy arises or job rotation is planned.

It should be noted that succession planning builds on the internal labour market, and looks mostly within the organizational boundary (Rothwell, 1994; Sessa and Campbell, 1997).[38] With less loyalty and a higher turnover of employees, and managers in particular (Baruch, 1998), succession planning may possess less predictive power in the 2000s.[39]

A different approach was advised by Leibman, Bruer and Maki (1996),[40] who suggested a new concept, entitled 'succession management', should replace succession planning. They emphasized the gap between the traditional and the contemporary approaches, the former prone to be rigid in form, based on skills and experience, whereas the latter is dynamic and flexible. The gap could be bridged if HR focuses on the competencies and leadership qualities of managers. Inputs for the creation and updating of succession planning will come from several sources—primarily the PA system, and then mentors' perceptions, assessment centre results and career counselling. Special attention is needed in responding to equal employment opportunities (EEO) and particular groups that may have specific requirements. Careful analysis of any succession planning programme will look at its implications for other CPM practices such as formal education training programmes, or appropriate and relevant secondments.

Figure 3.34 presents an example of a succession planning form.

360-degree performance appraisal systems

The late 1990s saw a growth in unorthodox methods of PA, mainly 360-degree feedback (see the special issue of the journal *HRM* in 1993) with a variety of PA methods applied (Tziner, Kopelman and Joanis, 1997).[41] 360-degree feedback can take the form of peer appraisal, upward appraisal, committee appraisal, or a combination of several sources in addition to appraisal by the direct manager (Baruch and Harel, 1993; Bernardin, Kane, Ross, Spina and Johnson, 1995).[42] Self- and upward appraisal (Baruch, 1996a and Bernardin, 1986, respectively)[43] are also valuable sources of PA, increasing the reliability and validity of the process. All signs indicate that this trend will continue, with PA being used more as a feedback tool and for development purposes rather than being used in gathering information for organizational decision making. The latter use will persist where individual performance-related PA is practised (cf. Kessler and Purcell, 1992; Kessler, 1994).[44] While the literature supports the use of 360-degree feedback (cf. Tornow, London, *et al.*, 1998),[45] it should be noted that this practice is very demanding in terms of time invested and analysis required, so it may not be easy to apply it routinely in organizations.

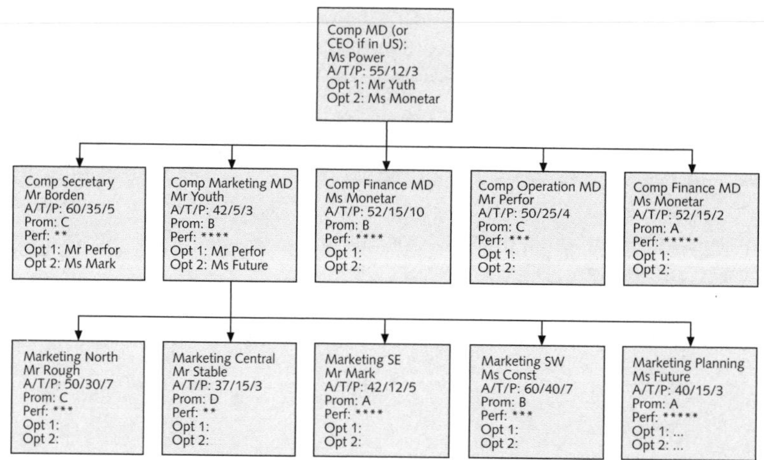

Key:

A/T/P: Age in years (clear indication of time before retirement) / Tenure (and within the company it can be decided whether it is tenure in the company, in the sector, or in a managerial position in general / Time in present position (indication of readiness for a new move).

Prom: Promotability, with different letters indicating whether the person is:

A: top performer, ready for next career upward move;
B: good performer; maybe move to a similar level job;
C: reasonable, all round performer;
D: unsatisfactory performance level;
F: a failure, must be replaced ASAP;
&: not enough time in job to be evaluated.

A different sign may be added to indicate readiness for promotability in the short or long term (or that the person has reached the highest possible level).

For example, Ms Monetar may be excellent in her job, but having been there only 2 years means she should not yet be moved.

Perf: Performance level, from 1 to 5 stars (*) according to whatever PA system is used at Comp.

Opt 1, 2. . .: Who is a prospective successor—can be from the same hierarchy level or from one level below—either in the same department or from another department; lack of options means a need to recruit from outside (as no viable option exists within). The company may decide to add a line of 'crisis replacement': who can step in if the manager leaves with short notice or suffers health problems or death.

Figure 3.34 **Succession planning form**

Special programmes for ethnic minorities, women, people with disabilities, dual-career couples, etc.

Organizations should develop special programmes to tackle all possible kinds of discrimination, such as the 'glass ceiling' effect for women, i.e. not being promoted above certain managerial level (Morrison, White and Van Velsor, 1987).[46] Many programmes are intended to support the population discriminated against, sometimes even to apply 'positive discrimination'. It is important, though, that such 'positive discrimination' does not imply the abandonment of a policy of selection according to skills, competencies and suitability for the job. Problems of discrimination exist for many groups, not just women. Discrimination on the basis of ethnic background, disability, age and religion can prevent appropriate people from making a full contribution. For example, mass early retirements accepted by or imposed on people in their 50s might deprive organizations of a pool of talented and experienced people. Disabled people can be highly committed and productive when that disability is irrelevant to the requirements of the role under consideration. Organizations which recognize these issues will benefit from pursuing different career management practices with respect to particular populations with specific needs.

Special programmes are not necessarily concerned with discrimination. The case of dual-career couples raises another matter, i.e. how to enable two people to develop side by side when both have a career. With the continuing growth in education and equality in employment we will see even more dual-career couples in the 2000s. The HR system must recognize this, especially where international relocations become necessary as part of career progress (Baruch, 1995; Harvey, 1997).[47] The trend of globalization is expected to continue and managing expatriates will be a crucial issue in the twenty-first century (see Punnett, Crocker and Stevens, 1992, and also the next section).[48]

Special programmes for expatriates and repatriates

International HRM is a fast-developing issue in the management of people (Kopp, 1994).[49] For multinational/global enterprises, the management of expatriates is a crucial part of their CPM agenda (Black, Gregersen and Mendenhall, 1992; Borg and Harzing, 1995).[50] In addition, there are growing concerns about the special attention needed for the management of repatriation: Rodrigues (1996)[51] referred especially to the 'reverse culture shock' effect. Evidence indicates a high rate of failure in the management of expatriates (Marquardt and Engel, 1993; Zetlin, 1994).[52] The most important aspect of this management is rigorous preparation for the assignment, with emphasis on cultural induction, maintaining communication with expatriates and paying attention to the repatriation period. The expatriate population is likely to expand in the future, as globalization spreads. Career paths in multinational corporations will include overseas posts as a crucial part of the developmental process for the managerial workforce.

Special programmes for high-flyers

All employees, as the prime asset of the organization, deserve investment in their career by their organization. However, the so-called high-flyers are perceived as a special asset, with the potential to make a unique contribution to the future of the organization, and thus worthy of having greater attention and resources dedicated specifically to them. Derr, Jones and Toomey (1988) look at high-flyers as a scarce resource, and because of the reduction in workforce numbers, including managerial layers, suggest that organizations will look for more ways of developing future leaders.[53] In contrast with the variety of separate practices discussed in this section, 'Special programmes for high-flyers' could form a group of practices and activities from those mentioned in the list, applied extensively to the high-flyers.

London and Stumpf (1982) suggested a two-part model for organizational CPM, especially designed for high-flyers.[54] The first part relates to the identification of the high-flyers at the beginning of their careers while the second refers to the accelerated path set for them. Such a development programme provides the high-flyer with a unique opportunity and wider options for fast development, but might also create pressure and stress for the individual. Recent developments, however, question the necessity for specifically designated high-flyer programmes, due to the unpredictable nature of the present-day workplace, and constant structural changes (Baruch and Peiperl, 2000a).[55] Trends already under way in the 1990s indicate that what will be required from the twenty-first century high-flyer is entrepreneurship competencies rather than the ability to exercise control and power in a bureaucratic system. In a boundaryless organization, a boundaryless career is called for (Ashkenas, Ulrich, Jick and Kerr, 1995; Arthur, 1994).[56]

New CPM practices for the 2000s

Building psychological contracts

The concept that a psychological contract exists between the employee and the workplace was discussed earlier in this book, and is acknowledged as a crucial aspect of the relationship between both sides. Recent works examine the results of breaking these contracts (cf. Rousseau, 1996; Morrison and Robinson, 1997).[57] The beginning of the 1990s saw a significant change in the nature and notion of the psychological contract. In future employers will have to clarify this concept—as a set of mutual expectations which need to be agreed upon, explicitly or implicitly—to their employees (see also Herriot and Pemberton, 1995).[58] These expectations are, first, what the organization perceives as a fair contribution from the employee, and second, what the organization will provide in return. Employees will be persuaded and required then to 'sign' this unwritten contract. This is in line with Wanous' (1992) ideas of the realistic job preview, taking it in the broader sense of the realistic career preview (see also Semmer and Schallberger, 1996).[59] The cycle of career planning and development for each person joining the workforce will start with the establishment of a mutual agreement, a psychological contract, which sets the type and style of future relationships. Two different populations will be involved here: existing employees, for some of whom the old psychological contract will be altered (for many this process occurred in the 1990s), and the newly hired, for whom the essential part will be delivered during the induction period, with reinforcement to follow later.

Secondments

Secondment is the temporary assignment of a person to another area within the organization, or sometimes to another associated organization (such as a customer or supplier). In a recent study, Baruch and Peiperl (2000a)[60] asked HR managers to refer to a list of career practices and also to indicate whether they used additional practices. Several of the 194 respondents suggested 'secondments' as an additional practice. Secondment is a period in which the manager acquires a different perspective within the company boundaries or from the outside; and a period of time spent in marketing, HRM or finance can improve a production manager's knowledge of organizational processes, help build interrelations with colleagues and increase communication thereafter. At a more advanced level, secondments can be taken outside the organization. Exchange programmes under which managers and executives serve a period of time in another company, sharing knowledge and gaining some insight in return, can provide a win-win situation for both companies involved.

As in the other practices described, the impetus to offer people secondments can come from their manager or mentor, or from HR counselling and PA systems. A possible problem with secondment programmes is the need for long-term HR planning and for mutuality, thus making it feasible mostly for large or well-established corporations. There is a risk of losing successful managers to the company they are seconded to, and there is also the usual risk of benchmarking, where it might be that only one side benefits from the deal. If the practice of creating satellite firms develops in the West, as in Japan for example, the use of secondments will expand and it is possible that the 2000s may see more of this practice in a wider range of organizations.

Intrapreneurship

Different people have different approaches to their life and career. Employers should identify those who possess the qualities needed to generate new business within the organization. Organizations should encourage organizational learning, and provide employees with options for inner sources of growth, via intrapreneurship. Instead of outsourcing activities and operations, organizations can use people from within who desire to develop something new, but still remain within the organization.

EXHIBIT 3.7

COMPANY CASE: INTRAPRENEURSHIP AT THE TIMES OF INDIA GROUP

The Times of India Group is the largest media and entertainment company in India with an annual turnover exceeding US$320 billion or £210 million. It employs some 7000 people in the company directly, and about 1000 on contractual appointment, a ratio typical in this business sector, and publishes 4 Newspapers, 2 Magazines, 1 Tabloid, has 12 Radio stations, 10 Retail stores and divisions in Music (Times Music, the largest music company in India), the Internet, Multimedia and News Syndication.

A fast-growing group, with a heritage of 164 years, it is perceived as a highly vibrant and creative media company.

The Times of India Group has long recognized that the company can grow only when entrepreneurship thrives within the organization. Thus, the Board of Directors have always encouraged employees to start new brands, sub-brands and new ventures which augment the organization's mission to grow as the largest information and entertainment company in Asia. The company's 26 main brands and 116 sub-brands are largely accounted for by such encouragement of intrapreneurship.

In addition, the company has ventured into the Internet (www.indiatimes.com), with some eight hundred million page views per month. For most professionals one of the most exciting reasons to work with the group has been the constant pace of growth of the company and the freedom offered to do one's job and to play with ideas and give birth to new ventures and for those who have latent entrepreneurship talent . . . this has been a constant source of encouragement.

Many health surveys conducted in different companies show that most people at some stage in life want to do something new, fresh, relevant in a field that they are passionate about. Organizations like the Times Group offer this opportunity to harness the creative potential of each individual to benefit the company. In such a scenario, both the organization and the individual win.

Thanks to Ashoke K. Maitra, HR Director of The Times of India Group for providing this case.

CPM practices which require reassessment for the 2000s

Common career paths

A career path is the most preferred and recommended route for the career advancement of a manager in an organization. Such career paths can lead people through various departments and units within the organization and, in multinational companies, in overseas subsidiaries. The use of career paths spread rapidly in the 1970s and 1980s in many organizations (Portwood and Granrose, 1986)[61] and its significance was demonstrated by Carulli, Noroian and Levine (1989) and Boyle and Leibovitz (1990).[62] The use of career paths is more widespread in larger organizations, whereas one may find more informal paths or a complete lack of paths in smaller organizations. The base for career path planning is stability and a wide range of layers and positions. With traditional hierarchical structures flattening and diminishing (see Cameron, 1996)[63] and with the creation of boundaryless and virtual organizations, it is likely that career paths will not develop much in future. The consequences for career paths are that there are fewer fast tracks in organizations, including large ones. As Peiperl and Baruch (1997)[64] argued, it is now the norm, rather than the exception, for organizations to have no fixed career paths and for individuals in them to see no further than one or two years ahead.

Written personal career planning for employees

Written documents generate commitment, at least on the organization's part. Long-term commitment (e.g. life-time employment) became virtually extinct as a feature of organizational life in the 1990s and this trend seems sure to continue in the 2000s. Written personal career plans are problematic also because they create expectations. Past experience of such plans provides examples of frustration as where a plan suggests the same job for several people, which only one can attain. Few organizations use this technique (Baruch, 1996b),[65] and it could be that this practice will die out in the 2000s, for reasons similar to those suggested for the common career path.

EXHIBIT 3.8

COMPANY CASE: HIGH-FLYERS AND CAREER PATHS AT THE TIMES OF INDIA GROUP

The Times of India Group has a long history of capacity building and talent development. Let us look at their Management Trainee scheme. Over the last 30 years, the company has inducted bright young professionals at entry levels in Marketing, Manufacturing, Finance and HRD. In 2002, their Directors in Marketing, Production, Modernization, Sales, and all the heads of publishing centres have come from the several Management Trainee schemes in the company.

In marketing, the recruitment team goes every year to the best management schools and selects management trainees in marketing. The new entrants are put in the sales job for about 2 years. After that they are put in charge of a group, where they have 6–8 people reporting to them. Once they effectively supervise the group, they are then appointed as category head to be in charge of a total category. Categories in the newspaper industry are sections like appointments or displays, etc. The category head of appointments is in charge of generating revenues through recruitment advertisements. Similarly, displays are large advertisements for products. Once a person has successfully been a category head for 2–3 years, the person is then given charge of an entire branch, where s/he not only has to head the advertising function, but also look after all the other areas like corporate communication, human resources, industrial relations, material management and finance. After the person has been a successful branch head for 2–3 years, s/he is then put either in charge of a region, say the southern part of India or given a Brand to develop. If a person performs effectively and demonstrates greater potential, the person could perhaps become Director of the company or could be given an opportunity to start new brands.

In the production function, the company selects two kinds of trainees. The first are those with a diploma in printing, who start on the shop floor and later are put in charge of specific areas as unit heads. The selected people later advance to the level of Works Manager. The company also recruits Graduate Engineer Trainees from professional engineering colleges with Bachelors in Engineering in the area of production, manufacturing, mechanical and electronics. These students initially work on the shop floor for about 2 years, later they are put in charge of a section for about 4–5 years and then offered complete responsibility for one of the smaller production factories. Once they have successfully run a factory, they are put in a large printing establishment in charge either of the printing operation or processing or of colour. Later, they are promoted to head the total factory.

Thus we see that common career paths are still valid in large organizations that benefit from relative stability and growth.

Thanks to Ashoke K. Maitra, HR Director of The Times of India Group for providing this case.

From a collection to a collective: integrating practices into a system

Throughout this section, career practices have been discussed mostly in isolation, almost as if they are unrelated, albeit grouped in several clusters. However, careers in organizations are meant to be planned and managed in a joint manner. A system should be designed to answer the needs and requirements of both the individual and the organization. Professional, effective HR management will make sure that the career system operates in a well-integrated, comprehensive way.

Applying a two-fold level of integration is necessary to achieve a fit and to make the optimal use of career practices. These levels are the 'internal', amongst the variety of practices, and the 'external'—integration between the career system and the organizational culture and strategy.

Both internal and external integration should be strategy led: an HRM strategy that is part of and aligned with the whole organizational strategy, including the career area.[66] Day-to-day management of career practices is derived from the strategy. Strategy, for example, will determine whether an organization should go international or stay within its national borders. The derived implementation of career practices following this strategy will deal with expatriation and repatriation policies and practices. HRM strategy will determine which is the preferred labour market (i.e. internal or external) and career practices will determine which type of job advertising will be implemented. Similarly, organizations will develop career practices according to the organization's wider HRM strategy.

Internal integration

Internal integration relates to the level of harmony between the various career practices; a fit for which there is a dire need. This has been demonstrated throughout the section in discussions of the relationships between specific practices: how the PA system is associated with other practices, how inputs from one practice (mentoring, for example) influence the use of others (e.g. workshops, secondments).

As indicated and presented above, career practices may appear in clusters, where groups of practices are interrelated. The wide range of career management practices may naturally be clustered in groups according to their common use and interrelations among them. Further, these clusters are associated with certain organizational characteristics such as size, age or culture and the clusters vary according to the sophistication and extent of involvement of the organization in the career management process.[67] The future seems to promise more managerial complexity, resulting in a need for more sophisticated career systems. The involvement of the organization will vary too, according to the target population (e.g. characteristics such as employees' level of education, lifestyle, etc.), the culture of the organization and the business sector.

The integration may follow the 'cafeteria method'. Cafeteria-style career management programmes are among the newer approaches to career pluralism in organizations.[68] Fundamentally, cafeteria plans provide an array of career-track options, training opportunities, performance evaluation schemes and reward systems to enable employees to have career experiences that are most in line with their own career concepts and motives and with the strategy of the organization.

One of the most important ingredients of internal integration is the use of advanced IT systems. Internal e-mail systems can be used for the distribution of information not only on job vacancies but also on career workshops, booklets, training and the development opportunities and other features. Having a website has become the norm for organizations. Part of the information available on organizations' websites relates to career options in the organization, the type of people who work there and their roles (such data are available now for most universities or at least those of the industrial world). One may also find information on how to apply for jobs, and more and more data will be accessible as organizational information continues to grow and expand. This is subject to the stability of the Internet, which is not guaranteed: the Internet might collapse as a result of misuse, abuse, or even terrorist action (including the spread of computer viruses).

Support systems, increasingly the IT-based ones, have an important role to play in the management of career systems. The results of PA are likely to be processed by IT, particularly in view of the complexity of 360-degree PA systems. These systems require much integration and comparative analysis for the understanding and utilization of the data. Similarly, creating reliable and valid succession planning depends on the use of IT systems to gather and analyse information from many sources. We are seeing an increase in the number of organizations utilizing performance related payment (PRP), with remuneration depending partially on individual and/or group performance. This seems to be the direction for the near future, in particular for knowledge workers. For complex PRP systems, IT may combine the career and payment systems to generate an integrated output, which will consider the variety of inputs into an accepted two-fold output. Internal integration will not be limited to the tangible element of payment. It will also enable flexibility and reflect the new type of psychological contracts between the employer (or employers, when individuals work in more than one workplace) and the employee.

External integration

As far as external integration is concerned, we observed that the career system that best fits the organization depends on the operational strategy of the whole enterprise. The Sonnenfeld and Peiperl (1988) career system model,[69] was based on the Miles and Snow organizational strategic model.[70] This is in line with the theoretical works of the early 1980s, introducing the concept of strategic HRM.[71] The career system should be developed in line with business objectives and needs.[72] The types of practices carried out will depend on the culture of the organization. In a bureaucratic system, which is relatively stable (e.g. the civil service, traditional manufacturing), common career paths can still be applied for long-term career progress. In a dynamic, turbulent sector (e.g. IT companies), career paths will have to be revised every year or two. In this latter type of work environment career practices such as mentoring become even more important, although it becomes increasingly difficult to identify enough senior managers suitable and ready to serve as mentors. In terms of the continuum from individualism to collectivism, another recognized dimension in organizational culture studies, succession planning or secondment will appeal to individualistic cultures whereas group-oriented cultures will probably focus on developing induction programmes, workshops and special practices for supposedly disadvantaged groups. The organizational culture will help in shaping the career practices and their use, but in a complementary way, career management can help in the reshaping of organizational culture.

Impact factors

Several factors are expected to influence the way career practices will be integrated. The most prominent are size, age, globalization, workforce diversity and the chosen labour market. These factors will determine whether certain practices are applied and the importance of their implementation.

Size is crucial, as small organizations neither have nor need the resources required to implement practices such as succession planning or a dual ladder. In terms of age, new organizations will not need retirement-preparation programmes and will be less inclined to encourage secondments. The level of globalization of the company will determine the need for special expatriation programmes and the type of mentoring imperative for overseas appointments. Workforce diversity will influence not only special career programmes but also the tone of career counselling, booklets, workshops and other practices, and focus on either the internal or the external labour market will have to be taken into consideration in any induction programme, mentoring, succession planning and psychological contracts.

Implications for organizations

Organizations will find it increasingly difficult to rely upon textbook prescriptions. Solutions developed to fit the latter part of the twentieth century are not expected to match the needs of the twenty-first century organization. As a general rule, more responsibility will lie with the individual. It will be very much up to the individual to look for information and to learn of opportunities inside and outside their present workplace. The role of the employer is changing similarly. As Peiperl and Baruch argued: 'The successful organizations of the next century will be those whose people have control of their own work and who make decisions to align that work with the goals of the organization'.[73]

As suggested here and elsewhere, a new type of psychological contract emerged in the 1990s and it may be the sort that we will have to live with in the coming decades. Employers will need to offer employees a psychological contract that they will appreciate and believe in and employers must ensure that they are able to fulfil their side of the new contracts. Sometimes the content of these contracts is demonstrated by the use of buzz-words such as Empowerment or Employability. Career management needs to create the right balance between empowering people to seek their own destiny and creating essential organizational support mechanisms to maintain and direct people's careers.

Outsourcing is another option—for non-core roles and activities. It should be used wisely, and not as a first resort. It seems better for an organization to use its own people when feasible, but outsourcing increases flexibility. Sometimes outsourcing works best with external providers of a temporary workforce. Whereas once such agencies mostly dealt with low-skilled workers, more professional roles and even managerial-level roles (i.e. the interim manager) can be filled by external agencies. To increase flexibility it may be useful for organizations not only to provide information on job opportunities within company boundaries, but to create a network of suppliers, customers, even competitors, which will generate a labour market of benefit not only to the organization's own staff but to all participants.

The general advice for organizations is—support your staff. Employees do not wish to be managed in an old-style paternalistic manner, but they need support mechanisms to enable them to fulfil their aims and ambitions. In a turbulent era people need more assistance. Organizations should ensure that their managers and HR people have both the capacities, not only to make tough decisions and confront the consequences, but also to provide emotional support. Some will be incapable of managing these seemingly two contradictory requirements—but the options should be made available anyway. Even those who appear tough may need support systems, not necessarily the same systems as for those who are made redundant—and for these, and especially for the survivors, individual counselling will be needed more then ever.

Summary

This section has outlined a comprehensive portfolio of HRM career-related practices, i.e. practices which can be used by organizations to plan and manage employees' careers. The practices have been discussed in no specific order of importance, but an attempt has been made to group them according to their role in a comprehensive organizational career system. Most of the career practices in use are expected to be developed and cultivated in the future, although some may disappear, as there is no apparent managerial need for them. This will be mainly due to structural developments within organizations, coupled with the new type of psychological contract. This characterizes a relationship between employees and employers which will be continued and developed in the organization of the future.

The portfolio has included a separate discussion of each practice, and an analysis of its fit for the future. The whole set of career practices have been combined into a broad integrated package which organizations may apply when implementing career systems. While I hope that the list is comprehensive and covers the whole area of organizational career planning and management, I make no pretensions to having provided a full or precise prescription, either for the present or for the future. First, with so many changes affecting individuals, organizations and nations, it is very difficult to make forecasts. Second, there is huge variety within organizations, even within the boundaries of one nation or one sector of industry. Based on the outlines presented in this section, it is left to HR managers in each organization to determine and decide what practices are needed to answer their specific situation, using sense, sensibility and professionalism.

References

1 Baruch, Y. (1996b) 'Organizational career planning and management techniques and activities in use in high-tech organizations', *Career Development International*, 1(1), 40–9; Baruch, Y. (1999) 'Integrated Career systems for the 2000s', *International Journal of Manpower*, 20(7), 432–57; Baruch, Y. and Peiperl, M.A. (2000a) 'Career Management Practices: An Empirical Survey and Implications', *Human Resource Management*, 39(4), 347–66.

2 Van Mannen, J. and Schein, E.H. (1977) 'Career Development', in J.R. Hackman and J.L. Suttle (eds) *Improving Life at Work: Behavioral Science Approaches to Organizational Change*, Santa Monica, CA: Goodyear, pp. 30–95; Schein, E.H. (1978) *Career Dynamics: Matching Individual and Organizational Needs*, Reading, MA: Addison-Wesley; Gutteridge, T.G. (1986) 'Organizational Career Development Systems: The State of the Practice', in D.T. Hall, *Career Development in Organizations*, San Francisco: Jossey-Bass, pp. 50–94; Hall, D.T. (1986) *Career Development in Organizations*, San Francisco: Jossey-Bass, pp. 50–94; Gutteridge, T.G., Leibowitz, Z.B. and Shore, J.E. (1993) *Organizational Career Development*, San Francisco: Jossey-Bass; Herriot, P., Gibbons, P., Pemberton, C. and Jackson, R. (1994) 'An empirical model of managerial careers in organizations', *British Journal of Management*, 5(2), 113–21; Leach, J. (1977) 'The notion and nature of careers', *The Personnel Administrator*, 22(7), 53–63.

3 Schein, E.H. (1978) *Career Dynamics: Matching Individual and Organizational Needs*, Reading, MA: Addison-Wesley; Herriot, P. and Pemberton, C. (1996) 'Contracting Careers', *Human Relations*, 49(6), 757–90.

4 A comprehensive list of such sources is: Baruch, Y. (1996b) 'Organizational career planning and management techniques and activities in use in high-tech organizations', *Career Development International*, 1(1), 40–9; Baruch, Y. and Peiperl, M.A. (2000a) 'Career Management Practices: An Empirical Survey and Implications', *Human Resource Management*, 39(4), 347–66; Bowen, D. and Hall, D.T. (1977) 'Career planning for employee development: a primer for managers', *California Management Review*, 20(2), 33–5; Herriot, P., Gibbons, P., Pemberton, C. and Jackson, R. (1994) 'An empirical model of managerial careers in organizations', *British Journal of Management*, 5(2), 113–21; London, M. and Stumpf, S.A. (1982) *Managing Careers*, Reading, MA: Addison-Wesley; Louchheim, F. and Lord, V. (1988) 'Who is taking care of your career?' *Personnel Administrator*, 33(4), 46–51; Walker, J.W. and Gutteridge, J.G. (1979) *Career Planning Practices: An AMA Survey Report*, NY: AMACOM.

5 See note 4 above.

6 Gutteridge, T.G. and Otte, F.L. (1983) 'Organizational career development: what's going on out there?' *Training and Development Journal*, 37(2), 22–6.

7 See note 2 above.

8 See note 1 above.

9 Baruch, Y. and Peiperl, M.A. (2000a) 'Career Management Practices: An Empirical Survey and Implications', *Human Resource Management*, 39(4), 347–66; Baruch, Y. (2003) 'Career systems in transition: A normative model for organizational career practices', *Personnel Review*, 32(2), 231–51.

10 Lorinc, J. (1989) 'Class action', *Canadian Business*, 62(9), 68–76.

11 Baruch, Y. and Peiperl, M.A. (2000b) 'The Impact of an MBA on Graduates' Career', *Human Resource Management Journal*, 10(2), 69–90; Baruch, Y. and Leeming, A. (2001) 'The Added Value of MBA Studies—Graduates' Perceptions', *Personnel Review*, 30(5), 589–601.

12 Bailyn, L. (1980) 'The slow burn to the top: Some thoughts on the early years of organization careers', in C.B. Derr (ed.) *Work, Family and Careers: New Frontiers in Theory and Research,* NY: Praeger, pp. 94–106.

13 Schein (1978), see note 2 above.

14 Peiperl, M.A. and Baruch, Y. (1997) 'Models of careers: back to square zero', *Organizational Dynamics*, 25(4), 7–22.

15 Eisenberger, R., Fasolo, P. and Davis-LaMastro, V. (1990) 'Perceived organizational support and employee diligence, commitment, and innovation', *Journal of Applied Psychology*, 75(1), 51–9.

16 Brockner, J., Tyler, T.R. and Cooper-Schieder, R. (1992) 'The influence of prior commitment to institution on reactions to perceived unfairness: The higher they are, the harder they fall', *Administrative Science Quarterly*, 37, 241–61; Baruch, Y. and Hind, P. (1999) 'Perpetual Motion in Organizations: Effective Management and the impact of the new psychological contracts on "Survivor Syndrome"', *European Journal of Work and Organizational Psychology*, 8(2), 295–306.

17 Feuer, D. (1986) 'Two ways to the top?', *Training*, 23(2), 26–34; Badway, M.K. (1988) 'What we've learned managing Human Resources', *Research-Technology Management*, 31(5), 19–35.

18 Van Mannen, J. (1976) 'Breaking in: Socialization to work', in R. Dubin (ed.) *Handbook of Work, Organization and Society*, Chicago: Rand McNally, pp. 7–130.

19 Ashford, S.J. (1986) 'The role of feedback seeking in individual adaptation: A perspective', *Academy of Management Journal*, 29, 465–87.

20 Morrison, E.W. (1993) 'Newcomer information seeking: Exploring types, modes, sources, and outcomes', *Academy of Management Journal*, 36(3), 557–89.

21 Bauer, T. and Green, S. (1994) 'Effects of newcomers' involvement in work-related activities: A longitudinal study of socialization', *Journal of Applied Psychology*, 79, 211–23.

22 Tziner, A., Ronen, S. and Hacohen, D. (1993) 'A four-year validation study of an assessment center in a financial corporation', *Journal of Organizational Behavior*, 14(3), 225–37; Thornton III, G.C., Tziner, A., Dahan, M., Clevenger, J.P. and Meir, E. (1997) 'Construct validity of assessment center judgements: analysis of behavioral reporting method', *Journal of Social Behavior and Personality*, 12(5), 109–28; Iles, P. (1999) *Managing Staff Selection and Assessment*, Buckingham: Open University; Howard, A. (1997) 'A reassessment of assessment centers: challenges for the 21st century', *Journal of Social Behavior and Personality*, 12(5), 13–52.

23 Spychalski, A.C., Quinones, M.A., Gaugler, B.B. and Pohley, K. (1997) 'A survey of assessment center practices in organizations in the United States', *Personnel Review*, 50(1), 71–90.

24 Bray, D.W. (1985) 'Fifty years of Assessment Centres: A retrospective and perspective view', *Journal of Management Development*, 4(4), 4–12; Portwood, J.D. and Granrose, C.S. (1986) 'Organizational career management programmes: what's available? What's effective?', *Human Resource Planning*, 19(3), 107–19; Laser, S.A. (1990) 'Management Development in a Changing Environment', in R.J. Niehaus and K.F. Price, *Human Resource Strategies for Organizations in Transition*, NY: Plenum Press, pp. 255–63.

25 Cameron, K.S. (1996) Downsizing, an entry in M. Warner (ed.) *International Encyclopaedia of Business and Management* (Thompson Int.), V2, 1050–6.

26 See note 22 above.

27 Baird, L. and Kram, K.E. (1983) 'Career dynamics: Managing the supervisor-subordinate relationship', *Organizational Dynamics*, Summer, 46–64; Clawson, J.G. (1980) 'Mentoring in Managerial Careers', in C.B. Derr (ed.) *Work, Family, and the Career*, NY: Praeger; Kram, K.E. (1985) *Mentoring in the Work*, Glenview, IL: Scott, Foresman; Scandura, T.A. (1992) 'Mentorship and career mobility: An empirical investigation', *Journal of Organizational Behavior*, 13, 169–74; Baugh, S.G., Lankau, M.J. and Scandura, T.A. (1996) 'An investigation of the effects of protégé gender on responses to mentoring', *Journal of Vocational Behavior*, 49, 309–23.

28 Kram, K.E. (1986) 'Mentoring in the Workplace', in D.T. Hall, *Career Development in Organizations*, San Francisco: Jossey-Bass, pp. 50–94.

29 Scandura, T.A. and Viator, R.E. (1994) 'Mentoring in public accounting firms: An analysis of mentor-protégé relationships', *Accounting Organizations & Society*, 19(8), 717–34.

30 Scandura, T.A. (1998) 'Dysfunctional mentoring relationships and outcomes', *Journal of Management*, 24(3), 449–67.

31 Sweeney, D.S., Haller, D. and Sale, F. (1989) 'Individually controlled career counselling', *Training and Development Journal*, Aug., 58–61.

32 Waterman, R.H. Jr, Waterman, J.A. and Collard, B.A. (1994) 'Toward a career-resilient workforce', *Harvard Business Review*, 72(4), 87–95.

33 Jacobson, B. and Kaye, B.L. (1986) 'Career development and the performance appraisal: it takes two to tango', *Personnel*, 63(1), 26–32; Weitzel, W. (1987) 'How to improve performance through successful appraisals', *Personnel*, 64(10), 18–23; Murphy, K.R. and Cleveland, J.N. (1995) *Understanding Performance Appraisal*, Thousand Oaks, CA: Sage.

34 Hall, J.L., Posner, B.Z. and Harder, J.W. (1989) 'Performance appraisal systems', *Group & Organizational Studies*, 14(1), 51–9.

35 Herriot, P. and Pemberton, C. (1996) 'Contracting Careers', *Human Relations*, 49(6), 757–90.

36 Walker and Gutteridge (1979), see note 4 above.

37 Miner, J.B. and Miner, M.G. (1979) *Personnel and Industrial Relations: A Managerial Approach*, NY: MacMillan, pp. 208–31.

38 Rothwell, W.J. (1994) *Effective Succession Planning: Ensuring Leadership Continuity and Building Talent from Within*, Saranac Lake, NY: AMACOM; Sessa, V.I. and Campbell, R.J. (1997) *Selection at the Top: An Annotated Bibliography*, Greensboro, NC: Center for Creative Leadership.

39 Baruch, Y. (1998) 'The Rise and Fall of Organizational Commitment', *Human System Management*, 17(2), 135–43.

40 Leibman, M., Bruer, B.A. and Maki, B.R. (1996) 'Succession management: the next generation of succession planning', *Human Resource Planning*, 19(3), 16–29.

41 Tziner, A., Kopelman, R. and Joanis, C. (1997) 'Investigation of raters' and ratees' reactions to three methods of performance appraisal: BOS, BARS, and GRS', *Canadian Journal of Administrative Sciences*, 14(4), 396–404.

42 Baruch, Y. and Harel, G. (1993) 'Combining multi-source performance appraisal: An empirical and methodological note', *Pubic Administration Quarterly*, 17(1), 96–111; Bernardin, H.J., Kane, J.S., Ross, S., Spina, J.D. and Johnson, D.L. (1995) 'Performance appraisal design, development and implementation', in G.R. Ferris, S.D. Rosen and D.T. Barnum (eds) *Handbook of Human Resource Management*, Cambridge, MA: Blackwell, pp. 462–93.

43 Baruch, Y. (1996a) 'Self performance appraisal vs. direct manager appraisal: A case of congruence', *Journal of Managerial Psychology*, 11(6), 50–65; Bernardin, H.J. (1986) 'Subordinate appraisal: A valuable source of information about managers', *Human Resource Management*, 25, 421–39.

44 Kessler, I. And Purcell, J. (1992) 'Performance related pay: objectives and application', *Human Resource Management*, 2(3), 16–33; Kessler, I. (1994) 'Performance related pay: contrasting approaches', *Industrial Relations Journal*, 25(2), 122–35.

45 Tornow, W.W., London, M. *et al.* (1998) *Maximizing the Value of 360-Degree Feedback*, San Francisco: Jossey-Bass.

46 Morrison, A.M., White, R.P. and Van Velsor, E. (1987) 'Executive women: Substance plus style', *Psychology Today*, 21, 18–26.

47 Baruch, Y. (1995) 'Business globalization—the Human Resource Management aspect', *Human Systems Management*, 14(4), 313–33; Harvey, M. (1997) 'Dual-career expatriates: expectations, adjustment and satisfaction with international relocation', *Journal of International Business Studies*, 28(3), 627–58.

48 Punnett, B.J., Crocker, O. and Stevens, M.A. (1992) 'The challenge for women expatriates and spouses: some empirical evidence', *International Journal of Human Resource Management*, 3(3), 585–92.

49 Kopp, R. (1994) 'International human resource policies and practices in Japanese, European, and United States multinationals', *Human Resource Management*, 33(4), 581–99.

50 Black, J.S., Gregersen, H.B. and Mendenhall, M.E. (1992) *Global Assignments*, San Francisco: Jossey-Bass; Borg, M. and Harzing, A.W. (1995) 'Composing an International Staff', in A.W. Harzing and J.V. Ruysseveldt (eds) *International Human Resource Management*, London: Sage, pp. 179–204.

51 Rodrigues, C. (1996) *International Management*, Minneapolis/St. Paul: West Publication.

52 Marquardt, M.J. and Engel, D.W. (1993) 'HRD competencies for a shrinking world', *Training & Development*, 47(5), 59–65; Zetlin, M. (1994) 'Making tracks', *Journal of European Business*, 5(5), 40–7.

53 Derr, C.B., Jones, C. and Toomey, E.L. (1988) 'Managing high-potential employees: current practices in 33 US corporations', *Human Resource Management*, 27(3), 273–90.

54 See note 4 above.

55 See note 1 above.

56 Ashkenas, R., Ulrich, D., Jick, T. and Kerr, S. (1995) *The Boundaryless Organization*, San Francisco: Jossey-Bass; Arthur, M.B. (1994) 'The boundaryless career: A new perspective for organizational inquiry', *Journal of Organizational Behavior*, 15(4), 295–306.

57 Rousseau, D.M. (1996) 'Changing the deal while keeping the people', *Academy of Management Executive*, 10(1), 50–9; Morrison, E.W. and Robinson, S.L. (1997) 'When employees feel betrayed: A model of how psychological contract violation develops', *Academy of Management Review*, 22(1), 226–56.

58 Herriot, P. and Pemberton, C. (1995) *New Deals*, Chichester: John Wiley.

59 Wanous, J.P. (1992) *Organizational Entry: Recruitment, Selection, Orientation, and Socialization of Newcomers*, 2nd edn, Reading, MA: Addison-Wesley; Semmer, N. and Schallberger, U. (1996) 'Selection, socialisation, and mutual adaptation: Resolving discrepancies between people and work', *Applied Psychology: An International Review*, 45(3), 263–88.

60 See note 1 above.

61 See note 24 above.

62 Carulli, L.M., Noroian, C.L. and Levine, C. (1989) 'Employee-driven career development', *Personnel Administrator*, 34(3), 66–70; Boyle, T.J. and Leibovitz, S.J. (1990) 'Hiring thoroughbreds: Pitfalls to avoid and the rules to follow', *Business Horizons*, Nov–Dec, 28–33.

63 See note 25 above.

64 See note 14 above.

65 See note 1 above.

66 Gunz, H.P. and Jalland, R.M. (1996) 'Managerial careers and business strategies', *Academy of Management Review*, 21(3), 718–56.

67 Baruch and Peiperl (2000a), see note 1 above.

68 Brousseau, K.R., Driver, M.J., Eneroth, K. and Larsson, R. (1996) 'Career pandemonium: Realigning organizations and individuals', *Academy of Management Executive*, 10(4), 52–66.

69 Sonnenfeld, J.A. and Peiperl, M.A. (1988) 'Staffing policy as a strategic response: a typology of career systems', *Academy of Management Review*, 13(4), 568–600.

70 Miles, R.E. and Snow, C.C. (1978) *Organizational Strategy, Structure, and Process*, NY: McGraw-Hill.

71 Devanna, M.A., Fombrun, C.J. and Tichy, N.M. (1981) 'Human Resource Management: Strategic Perspective', *Organizational Dynamics*, 9(3), 51–67; Fombrun, C.J., Tichy, N.M. and Devanna, M.A. (1984) *Strategic Human Resource Management*, NY: John Wiley & Sons, pp. 19–31.

72 Holbeche, L. (1999) *Aligning Human Resource and Business Strategy*, Oxford: Butterworth-Heinemann; Purcell, J. (1995) 'Corporate Strategy and human resource management', in J. Storey (ed.) *Human Resource Management—A Critical Text*, London: Routledge, pp. 63–86; Tyson, S. (1997) 'Human Resource Management comes of age: Strategic integration', in S. Tyson (ed.) *Human Resource Strategy*, London: Pitman, pp. 1–15.

73 Peiperl and Baruch (1997), see note 14 above.

CHAPTER 4

Project Design, Implementation and Evaluation

Unit 4: Project Design Implementation and Evaluation

Unit code: L/601/0995
QCF level 5: BTEC Higher National
Credit value: 20

Aim

To develop learners' skills of independent enquiry by undertaking a sustained investigation of direct relevance to their vocational, academic and professional development.

Unit abstract

This unit provides opportunities to develop skills in decision making, problem solving and communication integrated with the skills and knowledge developed in many of the other units within the programme to complete a realistic project.

It requires the learner to select, plan, implement and evaluate a project and finally present the outcomes, in terms of the process and the product of the project. It also allows learners to develop the ability to work individually and/or with others, within a defined timescale and given constraints, to produce an acceptable and viable solution to an agreed brief.

If this is a group project, each member of the team must be clear about their responsibilities at the start of the project and supervisors must ensure that everyone is accountable for each aspect of the work and makes a contribution to the end result.

Learners must work under the supervision of programme tutors or work-based managers.

Learning outcomes

On successful completion of this unit a learner will:

1. Be able to formulate a project
2. Be able to implement the project within agreed procedures and to specification
3. Be able to evaluate the project outcomes
4. Be able to present the project outcomes.

Unit content

1 Be able to formulate a project

Project selection: researching and reviewing areas of interest; literature review; methods of evaluating feasibility of projects, initial critical analysis of the outline specification, selection of project option, initiating a project logbook/diary, estimating costs and resource implications, identifying goals and limitations; value of project, rationale for selection, agree roles and allocate responsibilities (individually with tutor/supervisor and within project group if appropriate)

Project specifications: developing and structuring a list of requirements relevant to project specifications eg costs, timescales, scale of operation, standards, legislation, ethics, sustainability, quality, fitness-for-purpose, business data, resource implications

Procedures: planning and monitoring methods; operating methods; lines of communication; risk analysis; structure of groups and collaborative working eg learner groups or roles and responsibilities within a work-based project; targets and aims

Project plan: production of a plan for the project including timescales, deliverables, milestones, quality assurance systems and quality plans; monitoring progress

2 Be able to implement the project within agreed procedures and to specification

Implement: proper use of resources, working within agreed timescale, use of appropriate techniques for generating solutions, monitoring development against the agreed project plan, maintaining and adapting project plan where appropriate

Record: systematic recording of relevant outcomes of all aspects and stages of the project to agreed standards

3 Be able to evaluate the project outcomes

Evaluation techniques: detailed analysis of results, conclusions and recommendations; critical analysis against the project specification and planned procedures; use of appropriate evaluation techniques; application of project evaluation and review techniques (PERT); opportunities for further studies and development

Interpretation: use of appropriate techniques to justify project progress and outcomes in terms of the original agreed project specification

Further consideration: significance of project; application of project results; implications; limitations of the project; improvements; recommendations for further consideration

4 Be able to present the project outcomes

Record of procedures and results: relevant documentation of all aspects and stages of the project

Format: professional delivery format appropriate to the audience; appropriate media

Learning outcomes and assessment criteria

Learning outcomes **On successful completion of this unit a learner will:**	**Assessment criteria for pass** **The learner can:**
LO1 Be able to formulate a project	1.1 formulate and record possible outline project specifications 1.2 identify the factors that contribute to the process of project selection 1.3 produce a specification for the agreed project 1.4 produce an appropriate project plan for the agreed project
LO2 Be able to implement the project within agreed procedures and to specification	2.1 match resources efficiently to the project 2.2 undertake the proposed project in accordance with the agreed specification 2.3 organise, analyse and interpret relevant outcomes
LO3 Be able to evaluate the project outcomes	3.1 use appropriate project evaluation techniques 3.2 interpret and analyse the results in terms of the original project specification 3.3 make recommendations and justify areas for further consideration
LO4 Be able to present the project outcomes	4.1 produce a record of all project procedures used 4.2 use an agreed format and appropriate media to present the outcomes of the project to an audience

Guidance

Links to National Occupational Standards, other BTEC units, other BTEC qualifications and other relevant units and qualifications

This unit is suitable for use in all sectors and should utilise the full range of skills developed through study of other units in the programme. These include planning, practical work, data handling and processing, analysis and presentation skills. The knowledge applied may link to one particular unit or to a number of other units.

Essential requirements

The required resources will vary significantly with the nature of the project. The identification of the equipment and materials required, and the establishment of their availability, is a vital part of the planning phase. Learners should therefore have access to a wide variety of physical resources and data sources relevant to the project. Tutors should ensure that learners do not embark on work that cannot succeed because of lack of access to the required resources.

Employer engagement and vocational contexts

Centres must establish relationships with appropriate organisations in order to bring realism and relevance to the project.

The systems project: early stages

INTRODUCTION

This section deals with the early stages in the development of a computerized information system. The main channels of information open to the analyst for information gathering during systems investigation are explained, together with their weaknesses in the accurate provision of information. It is important that the analyst has a frame of reference through which to conduct the systems investigation. Here the systems model is used. During investigation the feasibility of a proposed system is assessed. The central ideas behind the economic, technical and operational feasibility of a system are explained, together with the difficulties encountered in arriving at an overall economic assessment of the project. The feasibility report and its role in project control and decision making are covered.

INITIAL STAGES

The impetus to develop a computerized information system arises because someone somewhere has perceived a need or opportunity that can be satisfied by the introduction of modern information technology. Ideas for developments and enhancements to information systems might originate from many sources, but in a large organization with an information systems strategy and existing technology the focus is through the information systems steering committee. In a smaller organization, the idea will be introduced by, or at least channelled through, a senior member of management.

The reason for initiation of a computer systems project is likely to be a combination of a number of the following reasons:

- The current information system, whether manual or computer-based, cannot cope with the demands placed upon it.
- Significant cost savings are realizable by the cheap processing power of a computer.
- Management perceive a need for better internal information for decision making.
- Computerization will provide better services for the organization's customers.
- The advent of new types of technology opens up a range of available facilities that the organization wishes to exploit.
- The organization wishes to promote a high-technology image, possibly as part of a much wider-ranging marketing strategy or a venture into e-commerce.
- Changes in legislation require systems redesign.

STATEMENT OF SCOPE AND OBJECTIVES

It is important to 'get the project off the ground' in the right way. It would be a mistake to call in the systems analyst, provide a verbal indication of what is needed and let the analyst 'get on with it'. Very often it is not clear at the outset what the task of the analyst is to be—it is clear neither to the analyst nor to the steering committee nor to management.

A common approach that avoids this pitfall is that the analyst is required to provide a written statement of the scope and objectives of the project. It works like this. The analyst is given a rough indication, often verbally, of the problem or opportunity as perceived by the project initiator. The analyst then looks into the problem and the system within which it is located. The purpose is to come up with a written statement of what the analyst perceives to be the problems to which the systems project is addressed, its scope and objectives and some very rough estimate of the costs. This document will act as a starting point from which the analyst will investigate further and eventually produce a feasibility report.

The statement will not be the result of much investigation on the part of the analyst. Indeed, it is important that only a small amount of time, and therefore cost, is incurred before the analyst and management have an agreed understanding, however broadly specified, of the project. The investigation may take only a day or two.

KISMET CASE STUDY 4.1

Harold Kismet has called in a systems analyst with whom he wishes to discuss the problems and opportunities presented by computerizing his business. The analyst spends some time with the new managing director Josephine Kismet and then tours the company for the remainder of the day, where he talks to a number of personnel. After this, the analyst produces the statement of scope and objectives (see Figure 4.1). This is to be taken as the initially agreed scope of the project. At this stage, the analyst will not feel tied to any of the figures except the requirement to provide a feasibility report within two weeks at a cost of around £5000.

Statement of scope and objectives

Project name: Sales order processing—Kismet Ltd date: dd/mm/yy

Current problems:

The following problems have been identified:

1. The sales catalogue of prices and products used to price customer orders is often out of date. In particular, new items are not catalogued immediately and items that are now no longer stocked still appear. The problem is located in the time-consuming nature of the manual preparation of the catalogue from the inventory records.
2. Customer enquiries are sometimes difficult to deal with as records of orders are not stored in a form that is easily accessible.
3. Orders that cannot be immediately satisfied from current stock—that is, back orders—are not processed consistently.
4. Owing to the large number of documents flowing through the system, the time taken to process an order may be days, even if all the goods are held in the warehouse.
5. Data in the system is generally stored in a way that makes it difficult for management to retrieve useful information. For instance, regular reports are time-consuming to produce and are often late, rendering them ineffective for control purposes or to aid medium-term strategies.

Objectives:

To investigate initially the feasibility for computerization of the sales order processing, invoicing and stock systems.

Constraints:

The entire project is to be budgeted for completion within six months at a cost of approximately £500,000.

Plan of action:

Investigate fully the existing sales order processing, stock and invoicing systems. Investigate the feasibility of a computerized system as a solution to the current problems.
Outline in general terms the recommended system(s) with costs.
Produce a report on this feasibility within two weeks with a budget of £5,000.

Figure 4.1 A statement of scope and objectives

SYSTEMS INVESTIGATION

The analyst must now become thoroughly familiar with the existing system. In particular, the analyst has to determine:

- the objectives of the existing system;
- how the existing system works;
- any legal, government or other regulations that might affect the operation of the system—for example, the Data Protection Act in the UK;
- the economic and organizational environment within which the system lies and in particular any changes that are likely to occur.

Why should the analyst pay much attention to the workings of the existing system, because, after all, is this system not deficient or else why would there be a need to replace it? There are a number of observations to make. First, although it is assumed that the problem is one that is amenable to a computerized solution, this has not yet been established. It may turn out that a change in existing manual procedures or organizational structure is the best way of solving the problem. This will only come to light after investigation of the existing system. Of course, analysts may be blind to such alternatives. Analysts are trained to look for technical solutions. They may also have a vested commercial interest in a computerized solution, so it is easy for them to miss alternative solutions. There is, though, a second reason for extensively studying the existing system. This will give the analyst a thorough understanding of the nature of the activities to be incorporated into the final computerized system. No matter how weak the existing system is, it must function at some level of effectiveness. This will provide a rich source of information from which the analyst can work.

The analyst's channels of information

The analyst needs to obtain information about the existing system and its environment. There are five main sources that the analyst can use:

1. interviews;
2. documentation;
3. observation;
4. questionnaires;
5. measuring.

Interviews

This is the most important way in which an analyst will obtain information. Setting up interviews with key personnel at all levels in the organization ensures a rich and complete view of what is happening. Interviewing is more of an art than a mechanical technique. It improves with experience. There are, however, several guidelines that are recognized as being essential to successful interviewing.

First, the analyst must have a clear purpose for each interview undertaken. This should be specified by the analyst as part of the preparation for the interview. It is not enough to define the purpose as 'attempting to find out more about such-and-such an area'. This will lead to a rambling interview. Rather, the analyst should establish the missing information that the interview is meant to supply. The analyst should prepare thoroughly for the interview by becoming familiar with technical terms that are likely to be used by the interviewees and with their positions and general responsibilities. The analyst should also outline a list of questions to be asked during the interview.

During the interview, the analyst should:

- Explain at the beginning the purpose of the interview. This gives the interviewee a framework of reference for answering questions.
- Attempt to put the interviewee at ease.
- Go through the questions that were prepared. General questions should be asked first, followed by more specific questions on each topic area. The analyst should always listen

carefully to replies and be able to follow up answers with questions that were not in the original list. The analyst must always bear in mind the purpose of the interview and discourage time-wasting digressions.
- Never criticize the interviewee. The analyst is merely seeking information.
- Not enter into a discussion of the various merits or weaknesses of other personnel in the organization.
- Summarize points made by the interviewee at suitable stages in the interview.
- Explain the purpose of note taking or a tape recorder if used.
- Keep the interview short; generally 20 minutes or half an hour is sufficient.
- Summarize the main points of the interview at the end.
- Book a following interview, if required, with the interviewee at the end of the interview.

No checklist of guidelines is adequate to become a good interviewer, but the list given should enable any serious pitfalls to be avoided.

Problems with the interview as a channel of information

The interview, although the most valuable tool for information gathering for the analyst, is limited in that:

- The interviewee may refuse to cooperate with the interviewer through fear of job deskilling, redundancy or the inability to cope with the new technology as a result of computerization. This may take the form of a direct refusal to take part (unlikely), being vague in replies, or, by omission, continuing to let the analyst believe what the interviewee knows to be false.
- The interviewee may feel that they should tell the analyst how the tasks that they carry out *should* be performed rather than how they actually *are* performed. It is common for people to cut corners, not follow works procedures, adopt alternative practices. All of these may be more efficient than the officially recommended practice, but it is difficult for the interviewee to be honest in this area.
- Clerical workers do tasks. They generally do not have to describe them and may not be articulate in doing so. Indeed, many managers might have some difficulty in articulating their decision-making processes.
- The analyst cannot avoid filtering all that the interviewee says through the analyst's model of the world. The analyst's background and preconceptions may interfere with the process of communication. One of the distinguishing marks of good interviewers is the ability to think themselves quickly into the interviewee's frame of mind. This almost therapeutic skill is not one that is usually developed through training in computing.

Documentation

Most business organizations, particularly large ones, have documentation that is of help to the analyst in understanding the way they work:

- Instruction manuals and procedures manuals provide a statement of the way that tasks are to be performed.
- Document blanks that are filled in by personnel in the organization and then passed between departments or stored for reference give the analyst an indication of the formal data flows and data stores.
- Job descriptions define the responsibilities of personnel.
- Statements of company policy provide information on overall objectives and likely changes.
- Publicity and information booklets for external bodies provide a useful overview of the way that a company works.

The problem with using documentation is that there is often a great deal of it, particularly in large organizations. The analyst has to read extensively in order to gather a small amount of useful information. Unlike interviews, where the analyst can direct the information that is provided by targeted questions, documents cannot be so easily probed. Finally, documentation may be out of date, and the analyst has little way of knowing this. The last thing to be changed when a clerical procedure is altered is usually the documentation governing it. Despite these weaknesses, documentation is a useful channel for information gathering.

Observation

Observation of employees performing activities in the area of investigation is another source of information for the analyst. Observation has the edge over the other methods of information gathering in that it is direct. The analyst wishes to understand the way that the existing system functions. Interviews provide reports from people of what they do, subject to all the distorting influences stated. Documents are an indication of what employees should be doing, which is not necessarily what they are doing. Only by observation does the analyst see directly how activities are performed.

However, there are some notable drawbacks:

- It is extremely time-consuming for the analyst.
- When observed, people tend to behave differently from when their behaviour is unobserved—the 'Hawthorn effect'—thus devaluing the information obtained.
- Observation, unlike interviewing, does not reveal the beliefs and attitudes of the people involved.

However, observation is an important source for the analyst on informal information flows between individuals. These are often essential for the efficient execution of activities. They may not be obvious from interviews and would not appear in documentation.

Questionnaires

Questionnaires are of only limited use in obtaining information for the purposes of investigating an existing system (as opposed to market research, where they are essential). This is because:

- It is difficult to avoid misunderstandings on the part of respondents as they cannot gain clarification of a question on the questionnaire if it is judged to be vague or confusing.
- Questionnaires that are simple provide little information; questionnaires that are more ambitious are likely to be misunderstood.
- Response rates to questionnaires are often low.
- To set a good questionnaire, the analyst often has to have more information about the system under investigation than the questionnaire could hope to provide in the first place.

Certain limited situations may make a questionnaire suitable. These usually occur when the number of people involved makes interviewing prohibitively expensive, the questions are generally simple, a low response rate is satisfactory, and the questionnaire is used to confirm evidence collected elsewhere.

In designing questionnaires, it is important to:

- Keep questions simple, unambiguous and unbiased.
- Use multiple-choice questions rather than ask for comments. This makes the questionnaire both easier to answer and easier to analyse.
- Have a clear idea of the information that is required from the questionnaire.
- Make sure that the questions are aimed at the level of intellect and particular interests of the respondents.
- Avoid branching: for example, 'if your answer to question 8 was "yes" then go to question 23 otherwise go to question 19'.
- Make clear the deadline date by which the questionnaire is to be returned and enclose an addressed and prepaid envelope.

Measuring

Sometimes it is important to have statistical information about the workings of the existing system. The total number of sales ledger accounts and the activity of each will be of interest to the analyst who is looking at the possible computerization of an accounting system. The statistical spread as well as the gross figures may be relevant. For instance, with a sales order-processing system not only may the average number of sales orders processed in a day be of use to the analyst but the pattern of these orders throughout the day and throughout the week may also be of significance. Are there peaks and troughs, or is it a constant flow?

Approaching the investigation

Although the foregoing channels provide the analyst with information, it is necessary to have some plan or some framework within which to study the existing system.

Flow block diagrams

A flow block diagram may be developed at an early stage in the investigation to represent the system. Flow block diagrams show the important subsystems in an organization and the flows between them. They provide a good overview of a system, within which more detailed investigation can occur. It is common for flow block diagrams to be based around the traditional functions of a business—sales, purchasing, manufacturing, stores, accounting, planning, control, and so on.

KISMET CASE STUDY 4.2

A flow block diagram of Kismet is given in Figure 4.2.

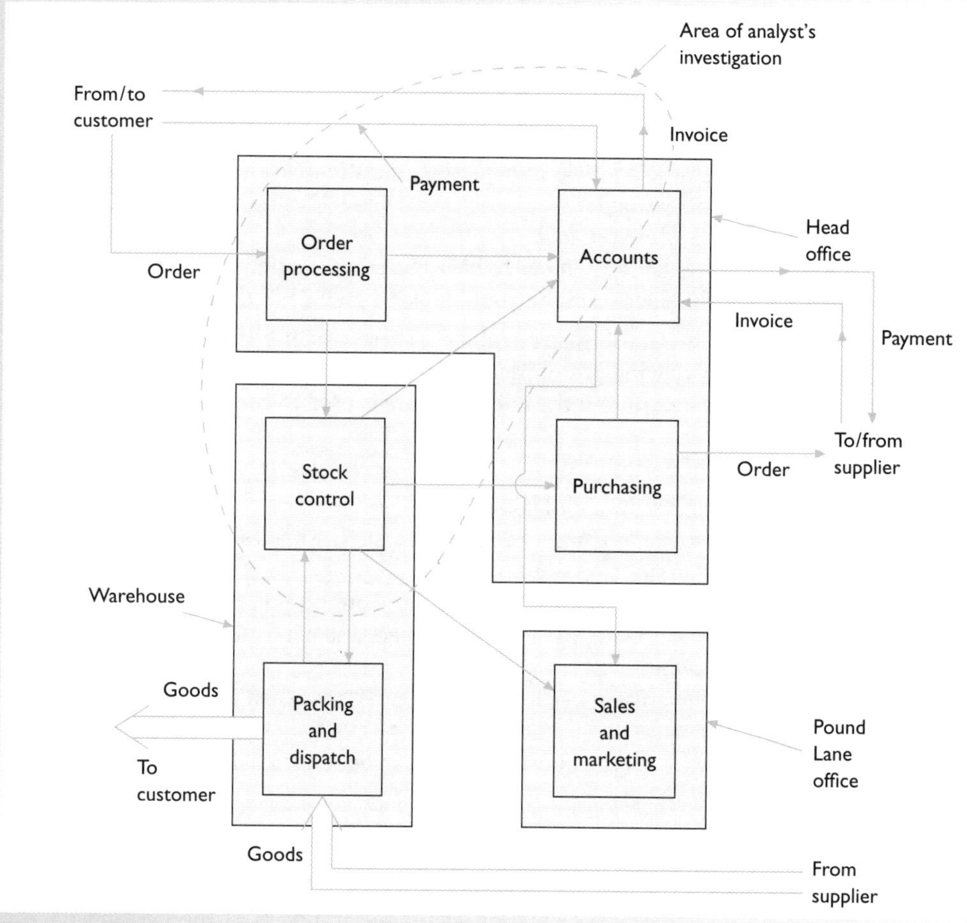

Figure 4.2 A flow block diagram of Kismet

Organization charts

Organization charts show the various roles and their relationships within an organization. They are usually hierarchical in nature, reflecting relationships of control, decision flow and levels of managerial activity between the various elements of the hierarchy. The chart enables the analyst to establish key personnel for interview.

KISMET CASE STUDY 4.3

An organization chart for Kismet is given in Figure 4.3.

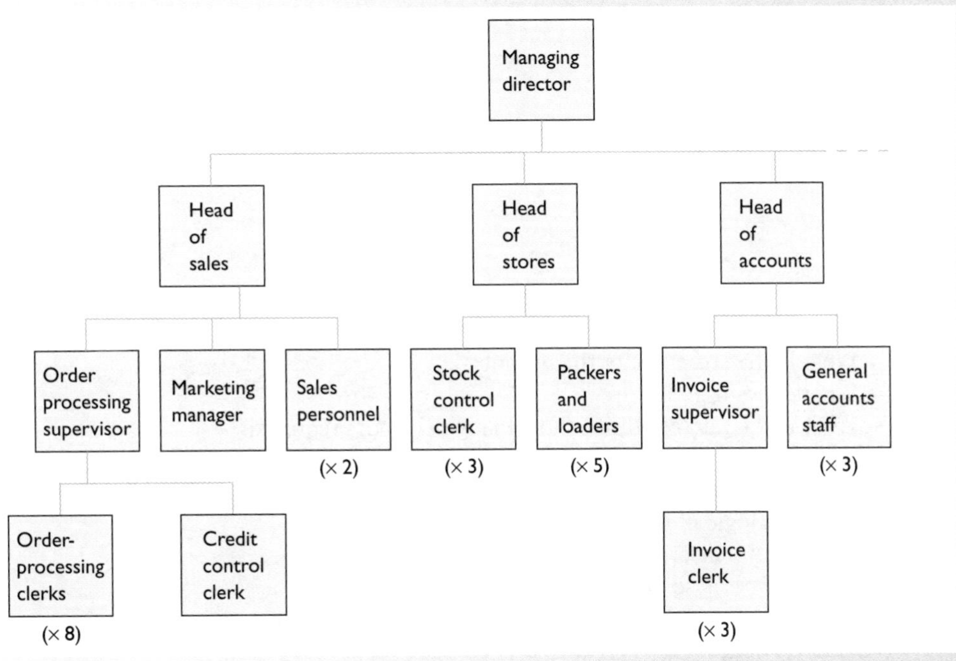

Figure 4.3 An organization chart for Kismet

Task identification

The analyst will identify key tasks within each subsystem. A useful model to adopt is the system model (see Figure 4.4), where the task is regarded as a process for converting an input into an output. There may be intermediate storage requirements, and there will be some control over the operation of the task. This gives the analyst a template by which a task can be investigated. Key questions that should be satisfied are:

- What different types of input are there into the task?
- And for each input:
  - What is the structure of the input?
  - Where does it come from?
  - What is the rate of input (how many per hour)?
  - Is it regular, or are there peaks and troughs?
- What different types of output are there to the task?

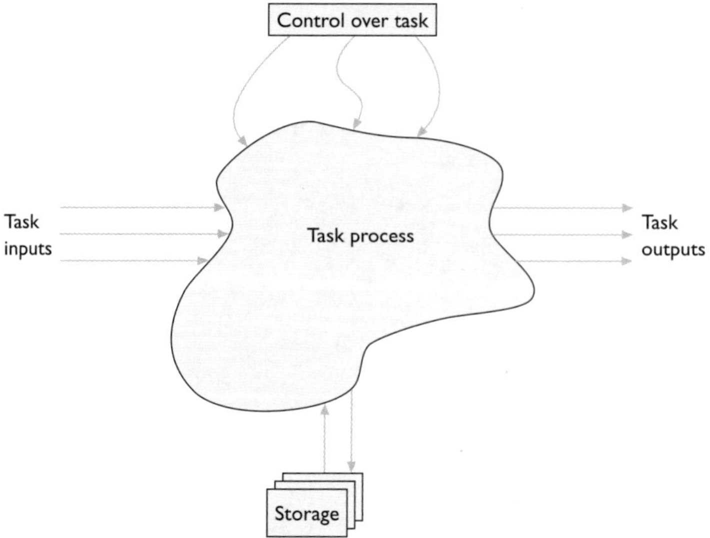

Figure 4.4 **A systems model of a task (task template)**

- And for each output:
  - What is the structure of the output?
  - Where does it go to?
  - What is the rate of output (how many per hour) required?
  - Is it regular, or are there peaks and troughs?
  - What is the purpose of the output?
- What is the logic of the process?
- Does it require discretion, or is it rule-governed?
- What is the purpose of the process?
- What experience or training is necessary to become competent at it?
- What level of accuracy is required?
- What stores, files or records are consulted in performing the task?
- How often are these consulted?
- What indexes or keys are used for selecting the correct record?
- How many records are in the available record store?
- What types of control are exerted over the task?
- Who is responsible for each control?

After investigation, the analyst should have a good understanding of:

- Who does what.
- Where it is done.
- Why it is done.
- When it is done.
- How it is done.

This framework provides a useful outline on which the analyst can base questions during an interview.

KISMET CASE STUDY 4.4

Figure 4.5 gives an example of some of the questions to be asked of the sales order processing supervisor at Kismet. These are based on the framework outlined above.

Inputs

What is the content of a customer sales order?
Does the company transcribe customer orders to company documentation?
How many sales orders are received per day?
Are there heavy/light times of the week/year?
What do you do if a sales order is incomplete in its specification?

Process

What is done with the sales orders?
How are they divided among the sales order processing personnel?
At what stage is it established that stock exists?
What is done if stock is not currently held?
How are the orders priced?
What happens to an order for an item of stock not held by the company?

Outputs

What is produced by the process?
Where does it go?
Are reports, summaries or totals provided?
How quickly are the priced sales orders produced from the customer orders?

Control

What accuracy controls operate over the transcription of the orders to company documentation?
What controls operate to ensure that all customer orders received are processed?
How is it established that customers have not exceeded credit limits?

Storage

What catalogues, records, files are consulted?
What information is obtained from them?
Whose responsibility is it for ensuring the accuracy of the information?

Staffing

How many staff are involved?
What are their roles?
How do the controls operate over staff?

Costs

What is the budgeted cost for processing an order?
What is the actual cost of processing an order?
How are costs split between variable and fixed costs?

Growth

Is it envisaged that there will be growth in demand for sales order processing?

Figure 4.5 **Examples of questions to be asked of the Kismet sales order processing supervisor during a systems investigation**

THE FEASIBILITY STUDY AND REPORT

One of the purposes of carrying out a systems investigation, perhaps *the* main purpose, is to establish the feasibility of introducing a computer system. Among other things, this will provide some estimate of the likely costs and benefits of a proposed system. The reason for the study is to establish at as early a stage as possible whether the project is realistic. This must be determined with the minimum of expenditure. If the project turns out not to be feasible then all the time and money spent on the systems investigation will be 'down the drain'.

There is a conflict here. On the one hand, the earlier the feasibility study is done the less money will have been sunk, but the less likely it will be that the feasibility study gives an accurate estimate of costs and benefits. On the other hand, a more accurate assessment can only be made if more money is spent on the feasibility survey.

There is no completely satisfactory way of resolving this dilemma. In practice, the analyst is more likely to recommend an extensive feasibility study in more unusual and innovative projects. This is because the degree of uncertainty in success, costs and benefits is greater. However, many analysts become familiar with certain types of project, such as the computerization of a standard accounting system. In these cases, it will be possible to make reasonably accurate feasibility assessments quickly.

There is inevitably an element of guesswork at the feasibility stage (despite what some analysts might claim). The long history of notable failures of computerization is testimony to this fact, as they can, in part, be put down to unrealistic feasibility studies. The more effort put into the study, the less the guesswork. Sometimes, parts of the stages of systems analysis and systems (high-level) design may be undertaken using the structured tools such as data flow diagrams and entity relationship models explained in Chapter 3, prior to producing a feasibility report.

KISMET CASE STUDY 4.5

It is assumed here, in the case of Kismet, that the analyst has established enough information after investigation and initial interviews to have a thorough understanding of the present physical system and is able to recommend the feasibility of a computer system. The suggestion will be based on an understanding of the tasks to be performed, the volume of transactions processed and the types of information to be produced.

In looking at feasibility, the analyst considers three main areas—economic, technical and organizational feasibility.

Economic feasibility

As with any project that an organization undertakes, there will be economic costs and economic benefits. These have to be compared and a view taken as to whether the benefits justify the costs. If not, then the project is unlikely to be undertaken.

Economic costs

There are a number of different types of cost associated with a computer project. These are:

1. **Systems analysis and design:** The cost of the analyst must be taken into the calculation of the total cost of the project. Of course, the analyst's costs in carrying out the stages up to and including the feasibility study will not be included in this calculation. These are already a sunk cost of the project.
2. **Purchase of hardware:** Alternatives to purchase, such as leasing or renting, may be considered here.
3. **Software costs:** These are often the hardest to estimate. Software may be written from scratch, developed using fourth-generation tools or purchased, in the form of an applications package.
4. **Training costs:** Staff need to be trained to use the new system.
5. **Installation costs:** This may be a significant cost if new rooms have to be built, cables laid and work environments altered.
6. **Conversion and changeover costs:** These concern the loading of data from the existing system into the new system in a secure manner. There are also costs associated with the resulting changeover from the old to the new system.
7. **Redundancy costs:** If the purpose of computerization is to replace people with machines then redundancy money may have to be paid.

8. **Operating costs:**
   (a) maintenance costs for hardware and software;
   (b) costs of power, paper, and so on;
   (c) costs associated with personnel to operate the new system—for example, computer centre staff, data input clerks, and so on.

Economic benefits

These are often very varied. Some may be estimable with a high degree of accuracy, others may be uncertain. Many benefits will be completely non-measurable. Examples of benefits are:

1. **Savings in labour costs:** These may be predictable, allowing for uncertainties in future wage rates, and so on.
2. **Benefits due to faster processing:** Examples of these might be a reduced debtor period as a result of speedier debtor processing, or reduced buffer stock due to better stock control. These may be estimable.
3. **Better decision making:** Computerized information systems provide more targeted and accurate information more quickly and cheaply than manual systems. This leads to better managerial decisions. It is generally not possible to put a figure on the value of better managerial decisions. Even if it were, it would be impossible to assign what percentage of this improvement was the result of better information and what was the result of other factors.
4. **Better customer service:** Once again, it will generally not be possible to estimate the economic benefits of either better customer service or more competitive services. This will be only one factor affecting customer choice.
5. **Error reduction:** The benefits of this may be estimable if current losses associated with erroneous processing are known.

Comparison of costs and benefits

Both costs and benefits occur in the future, although not usually in the same future periods (see Figure 4.6). The costs occur largely during the initial stages of the systems' development, whereas the benefits occur later in the useful life of the system. These must be compared.

One method is to discount the future streams of costs and benefits back to the present by means of an assumed rate. This will be near to the prevailing rate of interest in the financial markets, although its exact determination will depend on the project, the company undertaking

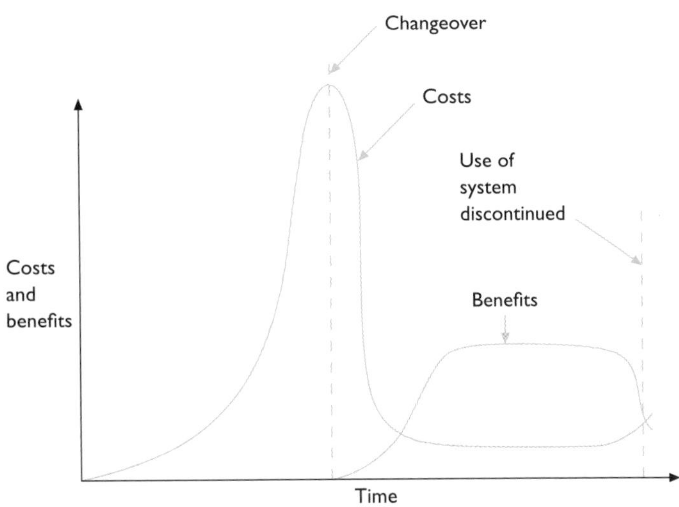

Figure 4.6 **The time profile of costs and benefits for a typical systems life cycle**

the project and the sector within which the company functions. This discount rate is arbitrary within certain limits.

All of the following factors:

- the non-measurable nature of some of the costs and benefits;
- the fact that many of the benefits occur far into the uncertain future; and
- the degree of arbitrariness associated with the choice of the cost–benefit comparison calculation

mean that the estimation of economic feasibility must be made with much reservation. It is tempting to regard the figure in the net present value calculation of the economic feasibility of the project as the 'hard' piece of data on which a decision to continue the project can be made. This would be a mistake. It ignores not only the non-measurable nature of certain costs and benefits but also other aspects of feasibility covered in the following sections.

Technical feasibility

This is concerned with the technical possibility and desirability of a computer solution in the problem area. Some of the issues will overlap with points brought out in the discussion on costs and benefits in the previous section. Many suggestions are not technically impossible per se. Rather, it is a question of how much money an organization is prepared to invest in order to achieve a technical solution. The following categories are important in determining the technical feasibility of a project.

1. **Rule-governed tasks:** If the tasks undertaken in the area of investigation are not governed by rules but require discretion and judgement then it is unlikely that computerization will be feasible. For example, the processing of a sales order, the production of a summary of aged debtors report or the calculation of creditworthiness on a points basis are all rule-governed. The selection of candidates for jobs is not. This could not be incorporated into a computer system (although new developments in expert systems raise the possibility that this might not always be so).
2. **Repetitive tasks:** If a task is performed only rarely then it may not be feasible to invest the time, effort and money in developing a program to carry it out. The tasks that are most suitable for computerization are those that are repetitive.
3. **Complex tasks:** If a complex task can be broken down into simple constituent tasks then it is generally easy and desirable to computerize.
4. **High degree of accuracy:** Humans are quite good at making quick estimates based on 'rule of thumb' assumptions in flexible circumstances. Computers are not. However, if a high degree of numerical accuracy is required then computers outstrip humans by both speed and low error rates.
5. **Speed of response:** Computer systems give fast responses if required and are designed to do so.
6. **Data used for many tasks:** Once data is inside a computer it is generally easy and cheap to use it repeatedly for different tasks.

Organizational feasibility

Organizational feasibility, or as it is sometimes called, 'operational feasibility', concerns the viability of the proposed system within the operational and organizational environment. The issues to consider vary from organization to organization, but the analyst is wise to address at least the following questions:

1. Does the organization for which the information system is to be supplied have a history of acceptance of information technology, or has past introduction led to conflict? Some sectors are notorious for their opposition to computerization. For instance, in the UK the print industry unions fought an extended battle opposing the introduction of computer technology. Other sectors, such as banking, have a history of acceptance of and

adaptation to information technology. A previous history of opposition to the introduction of computer systems may have taken the form of a formalized union opposition, or it may have been revealed in the attitude of users. High levels of absenteeism and high turnover rates subsequent to a previous introduction of new technology are good indicators of future poor acceptance.

2. Will the personnel in the organization be able to cope with operating the new technology? It is unrealistic, for instance, to expect staff with long-established working practices to adapt readily to new technology no matter how much training is given.
3. Is the organizational structure compatible with the proposed information system? For example, a highly centralized autocratic management structure is generally not compatible with a distributed computer system. Decentralized systems inevitably lead to local autonomy and local management of computer resources. Similarly, if departments or divisions in an organization have a history of competing with one another rather than cooperating, it is unlikely that it will be easy to develop a successful integrated system.

These are all issues in the area of organizational behaviour and 'people problems'. Analysts often have a training in programming or other technical areas, and it is easy for them to ignore this vital component of feasibility.

Feasibility report

A feasibility report will be written by the analyst and considered by management prior to allowing the project to continue further. It will go to the steering committee in the case of a large organization. In a smaller organization without a steering committee structure, the report will be assessed by senior managers as part of their normal activities.

As well as providing information on the feasibility of the project, the systems investigation will have provided much information that will also be incorporated into the feasibility report. In particular:

- The principal work areas for the project will have been identified.
- Any needs for specialist staff to be involved in the later stages of the project will have been noted.
- Possible improvement or potential for savings may have become apparent during the investigation.

Outline headings for a typical feasibility report are given in Figure 4.7. Once the feasibility report has been accepted, the project can proceed to the next stage. This is to provide an analysis from which a new system can be designed and implemented. Chapter 3 covered the two main aspects of analysis—analysis of processes and analysis of data. Various tools and techniques will be explained; although these are normally used in analysis, there is nothing to stop the analyst using them in the stages of systems investigation. The various charts and diagrams can then be included in the feasibility report. This is tantamount to carrying out broad aspects of *systems* analysis and *systems* design (as opposed to *detailed* design) prior to the provision of the feasibility report. This makes possible a more comprehensive development of a proposal or range of proposals. It also allows better communication of these proposals within the feasibility report as the techniques used are designed to facilitate communication.

Summary

After senior management or the steering committee has recognized the need for the development of an information system, it is necessary to carry out a formal feasibility study. This will involve an analyst. The analyst will need to have an understanding of the scope and objectives of the proposed systems project. It is customary for a written statement in this area to be agreed between the analyst and those who are commissioning the project. Although this will only give the broadest indication of the scope of the intended system, it will provide the analyst with a direction in which to proceed in systems investigation. Also, importantly, it will give the analyst a budget and schedule within which to provide a feasibility report.

Title page: Name of project, report name, version number, author, date.

Terms of reference: These will be taken from the statement of scope and objectives.

Summary: This gives a clear, concise statement of the feasibility study and its recommendations.

Background: Statement of the reasons for initiation of the project, the background of the current system, how it features in the organization, how it figures in the organization's development plans, what problems it encounters.

Method of study: Detailed description of the systems investigation including personnel interviewed and documents searched, together with any other channels of information. Assumptions made and limitations imposed.

Present system: Statement of the main features of the current system, including its major tasks, its staffing, its storage, its equipment, its control procedures, and the way it relates to other systems in the organization.

Proposed system(s): Each proposed system, if there is more than one, is outlined. This will include a statement of the facilities provided. (Data flow diagrams, explained in Chapter 3, and other charting techniques may be used as a pictorial representation of the proposal.) For each proposal, its economic, technical and organizational feasibility will be assessed. Major control features will be included.

Recommendation: The recommended system will be clearly indicated with reasons why it is preferred.

Development plan: A development plan for the recommended system is given in some detail; this will include projected costs for future stages in the life cycle with estimates of the time schedule for each.

Appendix: This will provide supporting material to the main report. It will include references to documents, summaries of interviews, charts and graphs showing details of transaction processing, estimates of hardware costs and so on. In fact, anything that is likely to be of use to those reading the report that will enable them to make a more informed decision will be included.

Figure 4.7 The contents of a typical feasibility report

During systems investigation, the analyst will obtain information by interviewing key personnel, searching current documentation and reports, observing the existing system, measuring various key variables such as the number of transactions processed and the time taken for each transaction, and possibly using questionnaires for response from large groups. All of these channels of information suffer from distorting influences that devalue the accuracy and use of the information gathered through them.

In order to organize the way that the information is obtained, it is helpful for the analyst to have a framework of reference. This is provided by the systems model. At the highest level, flow block diagrams will aid the analyst in representing the major components within the organization and the flows between them. At the more detailed level, when key tasks are considered, it is appropriate to view them as processes for converting inputs into outputs using storage while being subject to control. Organization charts give the relationships between the various roles in the organization.

A feasibility report is provided by the analyst for the systems project. As well as giving a description of the present and proposed systems it contains an assessment of the feasibility of the proposal(s). This will not only take account of the economic feasibility—the economic costs and benefits—but will also look at the technical and organizational feasibility. The feasibility study and report is essential for proper project control. It enables senior management, which is responsible for major resource decisions, to take a decision on the continuation of the project with a minimum of sunk cost. The more unusual the requirements of the proposed system or the greater the sums involved in its development, the more extensive will be the systems investigation prior to the feasibility report. Various charting and diagrammatically based techniques such as data flow diagrams and entity–relationship models, explained in Chapter 3, may also be used. After acceptance of the feasibility study the analyst, together with a project group in the case of larger systems, will proceed to full-scale analysis and design.

REVIEW QUESTIONS

1. What is the purpose of a statement of scope and objectives?
2. During systems investigation, what channels are open to the analyst in gathering information about a system? What are the strengths and weaknesses of each?
3. What is the purpose of a feasibility study?
4. Explain the terms *economic feasibility*, *technical feasibility* and *organizational feasibility*.

EXERCISES

1. Why is it difficult to undertake an economic assessment of a project at an early stage in its development?
2. What features of a task (or group of tasks) are likely to make it technically non-feasible?
3. 'In the feasibility report, it is common for the analyst to outline more than one proposal and recommend just one of these.' Surely the analyst should either give only the recommended option or, alternatively, outline several proposals with their implications and let management decide the most suitable?
4. What benefits are likely to result from:
   (a) computerizing the records system in a library?
   (b) computerizing a sales order and invoicing system (as in Kismet)?
   (c) providing a computerized point of sales system in a supermarket?

MINI CASE 4.1

SHARED SERVICES FEASIBILITY

The feasibility study is finished. Suppliers and customers have agreed as to what shared services can achieve. A deal has been signed. So what comes between that happy moment and actually making it happen? If clarity was the watchword for the start-up phase, engagement could be the one for getting the project going.

In short, it requires a governance strategy that coordinates and manages all the streams of the work being undertaken. Suppliers and customers must engage via what might be called a project management ecosystem. From assessing progress weekly and managing issues, to steering the project at the highest level and assessing the realization of benefits, this is a mutually reinforcing system of reporting committees and managers that bear responsibility for the programme in every aspect.

'Most shared services implementation involves a mix of partners', says Alan Richell, head of transformation leadership at Capgemini. 'It is, therefore, essential to establish a collaborative working environment for success. Making shared services happen is not a one-off event. Continual innovation and collaboration needs to be built into the delivery model.'

Capgemini advises breaking the management down into four streams: business transformation; IT; applications; and service provision. 'You need the business transformation partner to support organisational and process changes, whether dealing with internal shared services or BPO', continues Tony Kelly, BPO director, Capgemini. 'The IT transformation partner is needed to manage technology changes, working with the applications partner. Finally, if the decision is to outsource, then you need a BPO or service provision partner to deliver the services. The key point to remember is: do not assume one delivery partner. All of these are very important streams and must be managed appropriately. If any one of these is not given the right attention, the project can easily fail.'

It is the transformational element that lies at the heart of this. It is so important because it seems somewhat counterintuitive. The assumption of management might be that to opt for shared services is to take a load off their mind. This is not so. It is rather to change the responsibility they must bear.

Outsourcing adds another layer of complexity to the management of shared services. The point about these relationships is that they are both deep and long term. Even if it is 'only' administration and back-office management that is outsourced, they are still functions that are crucial to the success of the business. They will also change over time. So, it is vital that the provider is open with the customer as to what they require for commercial success: they must avoid foisting any unpleasant surprises upon the customer farther down the line, and ending up squeezing the client in order to make their own ends meet.

Even when an in-house department is set up, it should be treated as an external supplier to ensure that the best processes are set in place and strict service-level agreements are adhered to. In short, contracts should be put in place whether the supplier is internal or external to ensure that the service meets the required criteria and that if it doesn't, action can be taken to rectify the failure.

Adapted from: **Partners**
Mark Vernon, FT.com, 7 September 2006

QUESTION

1. Taking a step back from the starting point of this case study, construct a skeleton feasibility report evaluating the introduction of a shared service for IT provision.

Recommended reading

Avison D. and Fitzgerald G. (2007). *Information Systems Development: Methodologies, Techniques and Tools*, 4th revised edn. McGraw Hill

A leading textbook that provdes extensive coverage of the area. Practical examples are provided and contextualized through consideration of social and business factors.

Harris D. (2003). *Systems Analysis and Design for the Small Enterprise*, 3rd edn. Dryden Press

This is a business-focused book that uses mini case studies and running case studies throughout. It is very readable and well illustrated.

Wiley W. (2000). *Essential Business Requirements*. Addison-Wesley

This well-illustrated and easy-to-read book covers business events and system developments, looking at system data processes and behaviour. The book considers the estimation of project costs and has a business focus.

Managing Projects

THE IMPORTANCE OF PROJECT MANAGEMENT

There is a very high failure rate among information systems projects. In nearly every organization, information systems projects take much more time and money to implement than originally anticipated or the completed system does not work properly. When an information system fails to work properly or costs too much to develop, companies may not realize any benefit from their information system investment, and the system may not be able to solve the problems for which it was intended. The development of a new system must be carefully managed and orchestrated, and the way a project is executed is likely to be the most important factor influencing its outcome. That's why it's essential to have some knowledge about managing information systems projects and the reasons why they succeed or fail.

Runaway Projects and System Failure

How badly are projects managed? On average, private sector projects are underestimated by one-half in terms of budget and time required to deliver the complete system promised in the system plan. A very large number of projects are delivered with missing functionality (promised for delivery in later versions). The Standish Group consultancy, which monitors IT project success rates, found that only 29 percent of all technology investments were completed on time, on budget, and with all features and functions originally specified (Levinson, 2006). Between 30 and 40 percent of all software projects are "runaway" projects that far exceed the original schedule and budget projections and fail to perform as originally specified.

As illustrated in Figure 4.8, a systems development project without proper management will most likely suffer these consequences:

- Costs that vastly exceed budgets
- Unexpected time slippage
- Technical performance that is less than expected
- Failure to obtain anticipated benefits

The systems produced by failed information projects are often not used in the way they were intended, or they are not used at all. Users often have to develop parallel manual systems to make these systems work.

The actual design of the system may fail to capture essential business requirements or improve organizational performance. Information may not be provided quickly enough to be helpful; it may be in a format that is impossible to digest and use; or it may represent the wrong pieces of data.

The way in which nontechnical business users must interact with the system may be excessively complicated and discouraging. A system may be designed with a poor user interface. The **user interface** is the part of the system with which end users interact. For example, an online input form or data entry screen may be so poorly arranged that no one wants to submit data or request information. System outputs may be displayed in a format that is too difficult to comprehend (Spier and Morris, 2003).

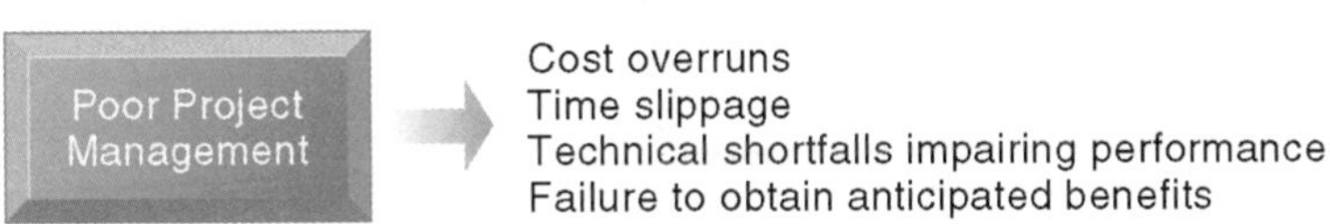

Without proper management, a systems development project takes longer to complete and most often exceeds the allocated budget. The resulting information system most likely is technically inferior and may not be able to demonstrate any benefits to the organization.

Figure 4.8 **Consequences of poor project management**

Web sites may discourage visitors from exploring further if the Web pages are cluttered and poorly arranged, if users cannot easily find the information they are seeking, or if it takes too long to access and display the Web page on the user's computer.

Additionally, the data in the system may have a high level of inaccuracy or inconsistency. The information in certain fields may be erroneous or ambiguous, or it may not be organized properly for business purposes. Information required for a specific business function may be inaccessible because the data are incomplete.

The Interactive Session on Management provides an example of a failed project. Kaiser Permanente, one of the largest health management organizations in the United States, was unable to establish its own center for handling kidney transplants. Kaiser opened its transplant center in 2004 but had to shut down the facility less than two years after it opened. A major factor was the company's mismanagement of information and information systems.

Project Management Objectives

A **project** is a planned series of related activities for achieving a specific business objective. Information systems projects include the development of new information systems, enhancement of existing systems, or upgrade or replacement of the firm's information technology (IT) infrastructure.

Project management refers to the application of knowledge, skills, tools, and techniques to achieve specific targets within specified budget and time constraints. Project management activities include planning the work, assessing risk, estimating resources required to accomplish the work, organizing the work, acquiring human and material resources, assigning tasks, directing activities, controlling project execution, reporting progress, and analyzing the results. As in other areas of business, project management for information systems must deal with five major variables: scope, time, cost, quality, and risk.

Scope defines what work is or is not included in a project. For example, the scope of project for a new order processing system might be to include new modules for inputting orders and transmitting them to production and accounting but not any changes to related accounts receivable, manufacturing, distribution, or inventory control systems. Project management defines all the work required to complete a project successfully, and should ensure that the scope of a project not expand beyond what was originally intended.

Time is the amount of time required to complete the project. Project management typically establishes the amount of time required to complete major components of a project. Each of these components is further broken down into activities and tasks. Project management tries to determine the time required to complete each task and establish a schedule for completing the work.

Cost is based on the time to complete a project multiplied by the cost of human resources required to complete the project. Information systems project costs also include the cost of hardware, software, and work space. Project management develops a budget for the project and monitors ongoing project expenses.

INTERACTIVE SESSION: MANAGEMENT

KAISER PERMANENTE BOTCHES ITS KIDNEY TRANSPLANT CENTER PROJECT

Kaiser Permanente is one of the country's foremost health maintenance organizations (HMOs), also referred to as integrated managed care organizations. HMOs provide health care that is fulfilled by hospitals, doctors, and other providers with which the HMO has a contract. While Kaiser is a non-profit organization, the company earned $34.4 billion in revenues in 2007. Kaiser has approximately 170,000 employees, over 13,000 doctors, and serves 8.7 million members in 9 states. The company is headquartered in Oakland, California.

Kaiser is known for pioneering electronic medical records and currently boasts the world's largest electronic medical record storage system.

The company also consistently ranks among the top HMOs in customer satisfaction. However, a 2004 attempt by Kaiser to handle kidney transplants on its own by setting up a transplant center was a public relations and information technology disaster. The company forced its members to transfer to its kidney transplant program without having adequately prepared to treat those patients.

In 2004, Kaiser implemented a kidney transplant program in Northern California under which transplants would be performed in-house at a transplant center owned and managed by Kaiser. Previously, the HMO had contracted with nearby university-affiliated California hospitals, such as UC San Francisco and UC Davis. The fledgling transplant center was shut down just two years later because of a litany of mistakes pertaining to paperwork, technology, and procedural planning. Through the duration of the doomed project, twice as many people died waiting for a transplant as received successful transplants. Patients now receive care from local hospitals once again.

Kaiser did very little correctly in its attempt to create its own kidney transplant program. The company lost track of records when transferring them to the new transplant center. More than 1,000 of the 1,500 patient records had incomplete or incorrect data, such as erroneous Social Security numbers and missing test results. Despite Kaiser's longtime experience with electronic medical records, the new center's records were stored primarily on paper. Kaiser had no comprehensive transplant patient master list or database. Many other transplant programs have multiple IT professionals assigned to maintain the complicated databases required for a transplant program. Kaiser attempted to run such a program without similar resources. Kaiser employees dedicated to processing information on prospective transplant recipients were overworked, logging 10-to 16-hour days as they tried to keep up with the avalanche of information. The company did not accurately anticipate the personnel requirements of their undertaking.

These were by no means the company's only mistakes, however. There were no specific procedures for transferring data on the initial patients to the United Network for Organ Sharing (UNOS), which oversees national transplant waiting lists. There were no systematic processes for tracking or responding to patient complaints or requests. The Kaiser staff lacked guidance and training regarding their job requirements and uniformly lacked prior experience with transplant programs. And there was no executive governance to identify and correct any of these procedural problems that arose almost immediately after the beginning of the project. Kaiser had seemingly made no attempt to identify and define the processes required to ensure a smooth transition from external transplant programs to an in-house program.

Kaiser also failed to give patients credit for time spent on waiting lists at the other hospitals, sometimes dropping patients who had waited the longest down to the bottom of the list. Unlike other companies, IT mismanagement in health care companies can cost individuals their lives, and in Kaiser's case many plaintiffs seeking damages against the company believe the errors surrounding their transplant center have done just that.

At the outset of the transition, Kaiser mailed potential kidney recipients consent forms, but did not offer specific directions about what to do with the forms. Many patients failed to respond to the letter, unsure of how to handle it, and others returned the forms to the wrong entity. Other patients were unable to correct inaccurate information, and as a result UNOS was not able to approve those patients for inclusion on Kaiser's repopulated kidney wait list.

Despite all of the IT mishaps, the medical aspect of the transplant program was quite successful. All 56 transplant recipients in the first full year of business were still living one year later, which is considered to be strong evidence of high quality. But as the organizational woes continued to mount, Kaiser was forced to shut the program down in 2006, absorbing heavy losses and incurring what figures to be considerable legal expenses.

Kaiser paid a $2 million fine levied by the California Department of Managed Health Care (DMHC) for the various state and federal regulations it failed to adhere to in its attempt to set up a transplant program. Kaiser was also forced to make a $3 million charitable donation.

Many families of people who died waiting for kidneys from Kaiser are suing the company for medical negligence and wrongful death. Other patients, such as Bernard Burks, are going after Kaiser themselves for the same reasons. In March 2008, Burks won the right to have his case heard by a jury in a public courtroom, rather than a private judge or lawyer in arbitration. Most patient disputes with Kaiser are traditionally settled behind closed doors, presumably to minimize the damage to the company's reputation and increasing the likelihood of winning their cases. Burks was the first of over 100 patients on Kaiser's kidney transplant waiting list to win the right to a jury trial.

Sources: Marie-Anne Hogarth, "Kidney Patient Beats Kaiser Arbitration Rule," *East Bay Business Times*, March 21, 2008 and Kim S. Nash, "We Really Did Screw Up," *Baseline Magazine*, May 2007.

CASE STUDY QUESTIONS

1. Classify and describe the problems Kaiser faced in setting up the transplant center. What was the role of information systems and information management in these problems?
2. What were the management, organization, and technology factors responsible for those problems?
3. What steps would you have taken to increase the project's chances for success?
4. Were there any ethical problems created by this failed project? Explain your answer.

MIS IN ACTION

Explore the Web site for TeleResults, a provider of state-of-the-art electronic medical record (EMR) solutions and transplant software (www.teleresults.com), then answer the following question:

1. How could this company's products have helped Kaiser Permanente manage transplant information?

Quality is an indicator of how well the end result of a project satisfies the objectives specified by management. The quality of information systems projects usually boils down to improved organizational performance and decision making. Quality also considers the accuracy and timeliness of information produced by the new system and ease of use.

Risk refers to potential problems that would threaten the success of a project. These potential problems might prevent a project from achieving its objectives by increasing time and cost, lowering the quality of project outputs, or preventing the project from being completed altogether. The section entitled Establishing the Business Value of Information Systems (p. 327) describes the most important risk factors for information systems.

SELECTING PROJECTS

Companies typically are presented with many different projects for solving problems and improving performance. There are far more ideas for systems projects than there are resources. Firms will need to select from this group the projects that promise the greatest benefit to the business. Obviously the firm's overall business strategy should drive project selection.

Management Structure for Information Systems Projects

Figure 4.9 shows the elements of a management structure for information systems projects in a large corporation. It helps ensure that the most important systems projects are given priority.

At the apex of this structure is the corporate strategic planning group and the information system steering committee. The corporate strategic planning group is responsible for developing the firm's strategic plan, which may require the development of new systems.

The information systems steering committee is the senior management group with responsibility for systems development and operation. It is composed of department heads from both end-user and information systems areas. The steering committee reviews and approves plans for systems in all divisions, seeks to coordinate and integrate systems, and occasionally becomes involved in selecting specific information systems projects.

The project team is supervised by a project management group composed of information systems managers and end-user managers responsible for overseeing several specific information systems projects. The project team is directly responsible for the individual systems project. It consists of systems analysts, specialists from the relevant end-user business areas, application programmers, and perhaps database specialists. The mix of skills and the size of the project team depend on the specific nature of the system solution.

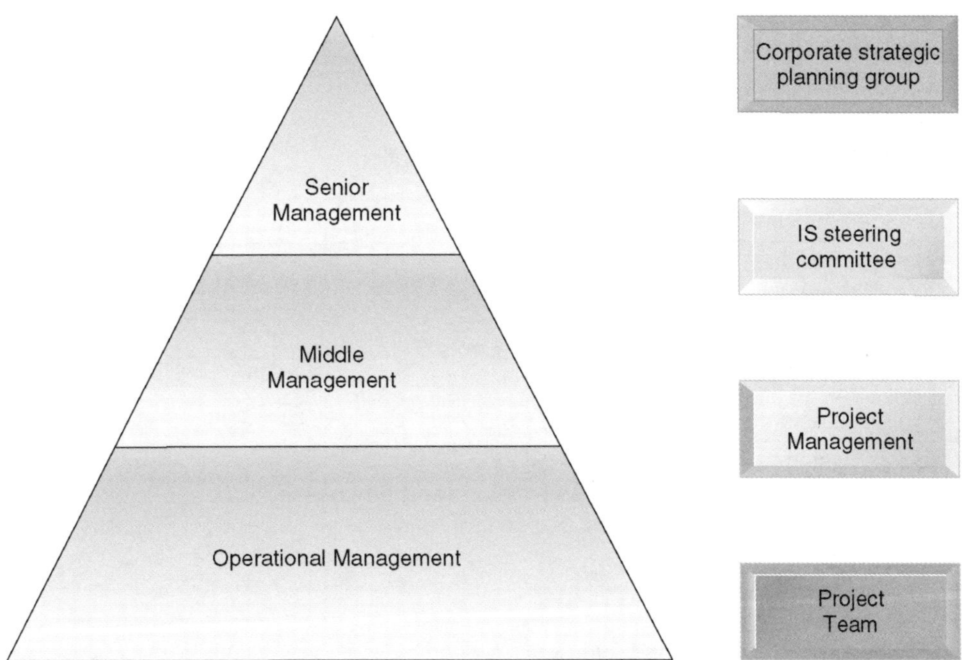

Each level of management in the hierarchy is responsible for specific aspects of systems projects, and this structure helps give priority to the most important systems projects for the organization.

Figure 4.9 **Management control of systems projects**

Linking Systems Projects to the Business Plan

In order to identify the information systems projects that will deliver the most business value, organizations need to develop an **information systems plan** that supports their overall business plan and in which strategic systems are incorporated into top-level planning. The plan serves as a road map indicating the direction of systems development (the purpose of the plan), the rationale, the current systems/situation, new developments to consider, the management strategy, the implementation plan, and the budget (see Table 4.1).

The plan contains a statement of corporate goals and specifies how information technology will support the attainment of those goals. The report shows how general goals will be achieved by specific systems projects. It identifies specific target dates and milestones that can be used later to evaluate the plan's progress in terms of how many objectives were actually attained in the time frame specified in the plan. The plan indicates the key management decisions concerning hardware acquisition; telecommunications; centralization/decentralization of authority, data, and hardware; and required organizational change. Organizational changes are also usually described, including management and employee training requirements; recruiting efforts; changes in business processes; and changes in authority, structure, or management practice.

In order to plan effectively, firms will need to inventory and document all of their information system applications and IT infrastructure components. For projects in which benefits involve improved decision making, managers should try to identify the decision improvements that would provide the greatest additional value to the firm. They should then develop a set of metrics to quantify the value of more timely and precise information on the outcome of the decision.

Table 4.1 Information Systems Plan

1.	Purpose of the Plan Overview of plan contents Current business organization and future organization Key business processes Management strategy
2.	Strategic Business Plan Rationale Current situation Current business organization Changing environments Major goals of the business plan Firm's strategic plan

3.	Current Systems
	Major systems supporting business functions and processes
	Current infrastructure capabilities
	    Hardware
	    Software
	    Database
	    Telecommunications and Internet
	Difficulties meeting business requirements
	Anticipated future demands

4.	New Developments
	New system projects
	    Project descriptions
	    Business rationale
	    Applications' role in strategy
	New infrastructure capabilities required
	    Hardware
	    Software
	    Database
	    Telecommunications and Internet

5.	Management Strategy Acquisition plans Milestones and timing Organizational realignment Internal reorganization Management controls Major training initiatives Personnel strategy
6.	Implementation Plan Anticipated difficulties in implementation Progress reports
7.	Budget Requirements Requirements Potential savings Financing Acquisition cycle

Critical Success Factors

To develop an effective information systems plan, the organization must have a clear understanding of both its long- and short-term information requirements. The strategic analysis, or critical success factors, approach argues that an organization's information requirements are determined by a small number of **critical success factors (CSFs)** of managers. If these goals can be attained, success of the firm or organization is assured (Rockart, 1979; Rockart and Treacy, 1982). CSFs are shaped by the industry, the firm, the manager, and the broader environment. For example, CSFs for the automobile industry might include styling, quality, and cost to meet the goals of increasing market share and raising profits. New information systems should focus on providing information that helps the firm meet these goals.

The principal method used in CSF analysis is personal interviews—three or four—with a number of top managers identifying their goals and the resulting CSFs. These personal CSFs are aggregated to develop a picture of the firm's CSFs. Then systems are built to deliver information on these CSFs. (For the method of developing CSFs in an organization, see Figure 4.10.)

Only top managers are interviewed, and the questions focus on a small number of CSFs rather than requiring a broad inquiry into what information is used in the organization. It is especially suitable for top management and for the development of decision-support systems (DSS) and executive support systems (ESS). The CSF method focuses organizational attention on how information should be handled.

The method's primary weakness is that there is no particularly rigorous way in which individual CSFs can be aggregated into a clear company pattern. In addition, interviewees (and interviewers) often become confused when distinguishing between *individual* and *organizational* CSFs. These types of CSFs are not necessarily the same. What may be considered critical to a manager may not be important for the organization as a whole. This method is clearly biased toward top managers, although it could be extended to elicit ideas for promising new systems from lower-level members of the organization (Peffers and Gengler, 2003).

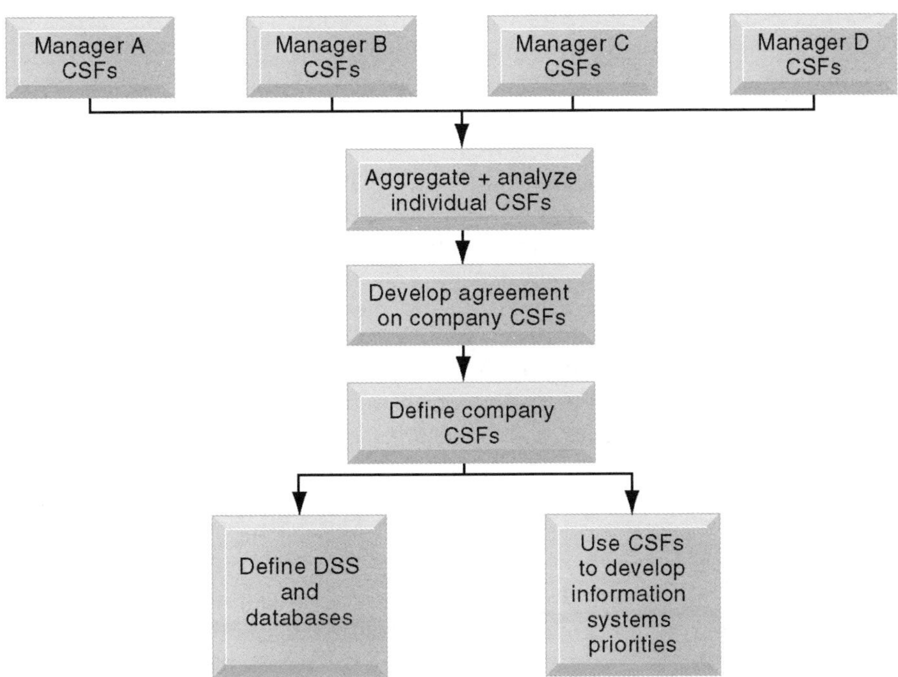

The CSF approach relies on interviews with key managers to identify their CSFs. Individual CSFs are aggregated to develop CSFs for the entire firm. Systems can then be built to deliver information on these CSFs.

Figure 4.10 **Using CSFs to develop systems**

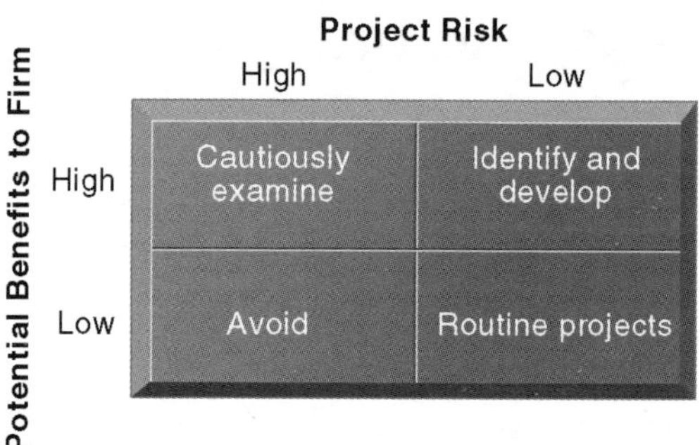

Companies should examine their portfolio of projects in terms of potential benefits and likely risks. Certain kinds of projects should be avoided altogether and others developed rapidly. There is no ideal mix. Companies in different industries have different profiles.

Figure 4.11 **A system portfolio**

Portfolio Analysis

Once strategic analyses have determined the overall direction of systems development, **portfolio analysis** can be used to evaluate alternative system projects. Portfolio analysis inventories all of the organization's information systems projects and assets, including infrastructure, outsourcing contracts, and licenses. This portfolio of information systems investments can be described as having a certain profile of risk and benefit to the firm (see Figure 4.11) similar to a financial portfolio.

Each information systems project carries its own set of risks and benefits. (The section entitled Managing Project Risk, p. 330 describes the factors that increase the risks of systems projects.) Firms would try to improve the return on their portfolios of IT assets by balancing the risk and return from their systems investments. Although there is no ideal profile for all firms, information-intensive industries (e.g., finance) should have a few high-risk, high-benefit projects to ensure that they stay current with technology. Firms in non-information-intensive industries should focus on high-benefit, low-risk projects.

Most desirable, of course, are systems with high benefit and low risk. These promise early returns and low risks. Second, high-benefit, high-risk systems should be examined; low-benefit, high-risk systems should be totally avoided; and low-benefit, low-risk systems should be reexamined for the possibility of rebuilding and replacing them with more desirable systems having higher benefits. By using portfolio analysis, management can determine the optimal mix of investment risk and reward for their firms, balancing riskier high-reward projects with safer lower-reward ones. Firms where portfolio analysis is aligned with business strategy have been found to have a superior return on their IT assets, better alignment of information technology investments with business objectives, and better organization-wide coordination of IT investments (Jeffrey and Leliveld, 2004).

Scoring Models

A **scoring model** is useful for selecting projects where many criteria must be considered. It assigns weights to various features of a system and then calculates the weighted totals. Using Table 4.2, the firm must decide among two alternative enterprise resource planning (ERP) systems. The first column lists the criteria that decision makers will use to evaluate the systems. These criteria are usually the result of lengthy discussions among the decision-making group. Often the most important outcome of a scoring model is not the score but agreement on the criteria used to judge a system.

Table 4.2 shows that this particular company attaches the most importance to capabilities for sales order processing, inventory management, and warehousing. The second column in

Table 4.2 Example of a Scoring Model for an ERP System

Criteria	Weight	ERP System A %	ERP System A Score	ERP System B %	ERP System B Score
1.0 Order Processing					
1.1 Online order entry	4	67	268	73	292
1.2 Online pricing	4	81	324	87	348
1.3 Inventory check	4	72	288	81	324
1.4 Customer credit check	3	66	198	59	177
1.5 Invoicing	4	73	292	82	328
Total Order Processing			1,370		1,469
2.0 Inventory Management					
2.1 Production forecasting	3	72	216	76	228
2.2 Production planning	4	79	316	81	324
2.3 Inventory control	4	68	272	80	320
2.4 Reports	3	71	213	69	207
Total Inventory Management			1,017		1,079
3.0 Warehousing					
3.1 Receiving	2	71	142	75	150
3.2 Picking/packing	3	77	231	82	246
3.3 Shipping	4	92	368	89	356
Total Warehousing			741		752
Grand Total			3,128		3,300

Table 4.2 lists the weights that decision makers attached to the decision criteria. Columns 3 and 5 show the percentage of requirements for each function that each alternative ERP system can provide. Each vendor's score can be calculated by multiplying the percentage of requirements met for each function by the weight attached to that function. ERP System B has the highest total score.

As with all "objective" techniques, there are many qualitative judgments involved in using the scoring model. This model requires experts who understand the issues and the technology. It is appropriate to cycle through the scoring model several times, changing the criteria and weights, to see how sensitive the outcome is to reasonable changes in criteria. Scoring models are used most commonly to confirm, to rationalize, and to support decisions, rather than as the final arbiters of system selection.

ESTABLISHING THE BUSINESS VALUE OF INFORMATION SYSTEMS

Even if a system project supports a firm's strategic goals and meets user information requirements, it needs to be a good investment for the firm. The value of systems from a financial perspective essentially revolves around the issue of return on invested capital. Does a particular information system investment produce sufficient returns to justify its costs?

Information System Costs and Benefits

Table 4.3 lists some of the more common costs and benefits of systems. **Tangible benefits** can be quantified and assigned a monetary value. **Intangible benefits**, such as more efficient customer service or enhanced decision making, cannot be immediately quantified but may lead to quantifiable gains in the long run. Transaction and clerical systems that displace labor and save space always produce more measurable, tangible benefits than management information systems, decision-support systems, and computer-supported collaborative work systems.

Total cost of ownership (TCO) is a concept designed to identify and measure the components of information technology expenditures beyond the initial cost of purchasing and installing hardware and software. However, TCO analysis provides only part of the information needed to evaluate an information technology investment because it does not typically deal with benefits, cost categories such as complexity costs, and "soft" and strategic factors discussed later in this section.

Table 4.3 Costs and Benefits of Information Systems

COSTS
Hardware
Telecommunications
Software
Services
Personnel
TANGIBLE BENEFITS (COST SAVINGS)
Increased productivity
Lower operational costs
Reduced workforce
Lower computer expenses
Lower outside vendor costs
Lower clerical and professional costs
Reduced rate of growth in expenses
Reduced facility costs
INTANGIBLE BENEFITS
Improved asset utilization
Improved resource control
Improved organizational planning
Increased organizational flexibility
More timely information
More information
Increased organizational learning
Legal requirements attained
Enhanced employee goodwill
Increased job satisfaction
Improved decision making
Improved operations
Higher client satisfaction
Better corporate image

Capital Budgeting for Information Systems

To determine the benefits of a particular project, you'll need to calculate all of its costs and all of its benefits. Obviously, a project where costs exceed benefits should be rejected. But even if the benefits outweigh the costs, additional financial analysis is required to determine whether the project represents a good return on the firm's invested capital. **Capital budgeting** models are one of several techniques used to measure the value of investing in long-term capital investment projects.

Capital budgeting methods rely on measures of cash flows into and out of the firm; capital projects generate those cash flows. The investment cost for information systems projects is an immediate cash outflow caused by expenditures for hardware, software, and labor. In subsequent years, the investment may cause additional cash outflows that will be balanced by cash inflows resulting from the investment. Cash inflows take the form of increased sales of more products (for reasons such as new products, higher quality, or increasing market share) or reduced costs in production and operations. The difference between cash outflows and cash inflows is used for calculating the financial worth of an investment. Once the cash flows have been established, several alternative methods are available for comparing different projects and deciding about the investment.

The principal capital budgeting models for evaluating IT projects are: the payback method, the accounting rate of return on investment (ROI), net present value, and the internal rate of return (IRR). You can find out more about how these capital budgeting models are used to justify information system investments in the Learning Tracks for this chapter.

Real Options Pricing Models

Some information systems projects are highly uncertain, especially investments in IT infrastructure. Their future revenue streams are unclear and their up-front costs are high. Suppose, for instance, that a firm is considering a $20 million investment to upgrade its IT infrastructure—its hardware, software, data management tools, and networking technology. If this upgraded infrastructure were available, the organization would have the technology capabilities to respond more easily to future problems and opportunities. Although the costs of this investment can be calculated, not all of the benefits of making this investment can be established in advance. But if the firm waits a few years until the revenue potential becomes more obvious, it might be too late to make the infrastructure investment. In such cases, managers might benefit from using real options pricing models to evaluate information technology investments.

Real options pricing models (ROPMs) use the concept of options valuation borrowed from the financial industry. An *option* is essentially the right, but not the obligation, to act at some future date. A typical *call option*, for instance, is a financial option in which a person buys the right (but not the obligation) to purchase an underlying asset (usually a stock) at a fixed price (strike price) on or before a given date.

For instance, on October 28, 2008, for $11.30 you could purchase the right (a call option) maturing in January 2009 to buy a share of P&G common stock for $50 per share. If, by the end of January 2009, the price of P&G stock did not rise above $50 per share, you would not exercise the option, and the value of the option would fall to zero on the strike date. If, however, the price of Procter & Gamble common stock rose to, say, $100 per share, you could purchase the stock for the strike price of $50 and retain the profit of $50 per share minus the cost of the option. (Because the option is sold as a 100-share contract, the cost of the contract would be 100 × $11.30 before commissions, or $1,130, and you would be purchasing and obtaining a profit from 100 shares of Procter & Gamble.) The stock option enables the owner to benefit from the upside potential of an opportunity while limiting the downside risk.

ROPMs value information systems projects similar to stock options, where an initial expenditure on technology creates the right, but not the obligation, to obtain the benefits associated with further development and deployment of the technology as long as management has the freedom to cancel, defer, restart, or expand the project. ROPMs give managers the flexibility to stage their IT investment or test the waters with small pilot projects or prototypes to gain more knowledge about the risks of a project before investing in the entire implementation. The disadvantages of this model are primarily in estimating all the key variables affecting option value, including anticipated cash flows from the underlying asset and changes in the cost of implementation. Models for determining option value of information technology platforms are being developed (Fichman, 2004; McGrath and MacMillan, 2000).

Limitations of Financial Models

The traditional focus on the financial and technical aspects of an information system tends to overlook the social and organizational dimensions of information systems that may affect the true costs and benefits of the investment. Many companies' information systems investment decisions do not adequately consider costs from organizational disruptions created by a new system, such as the cost to train end users, the impact that users' learning curves for a new system have on productivity, or the time managers need to spend overseeing new system-related changes. Benefits, such as more timely decisions from a new system or enhanced employee learning and expertise, may also be overlooked in a traditional financial analysis (Ryan, Harrison, and Schkade, 2002).

MANAGING PROJECT RISK

We have already introduced the topic of information system risks and risk assessment in Chapter 1. In this section we describe the specific risks to information systems projects and show what can be done to manage them effectively.

Dimensions of Project Risk

Systems differ dramatically in their size, scope, level of complexity, and organizational and technical components. Some systems development projects are more likely to create the problems we have described earlier or to suffer delays because they carry a much higher level of risk than others. The level of project risk is influenced by project size, project structure, and the level of technical expertise of the information systems staff and project team.

- **Project size:** The larger the project—as indicated by the dollars spent, the size of the implementation staff, the time allocated for implementation, and the number of organizational units affected—the greater the risk. Very large-scale systems projects have a failure rate that is 50 to 75 percent higher than that for other projects because such projects are complex and difficult to control. The organizational complexity of the system—how many units and groups use it and how much it influences business processes—contribute to the complexity of large-scale systems projects just as much as technical characteristics, such as the number of lines of program code, length of project, and budget (Xia and Lee, 2004; Concours Group, 2000; Laudon, 1989). In addition, there are few reliable techniques for estimating the time and cost to develop large-scale information systems.
- **Project structure:** Some projects are more highly structured than others. Their requirements are clear and straightforward so outputs and processes can be easily defined. Users know exactly what they want and what the system should do; there is almost no possibility of the users changing their minds. Such projects run a much lower risk than those with relatively undefined, fluid, and constantly changing requirements; with outputs that cannot be fixed easily because they are subject to users' changing ideas; or with users who cannot agree on what they want.
- **Experience with technology:** The project risk rises if the project team and the information system staff lack the required technical expertise. If the team is unfamiliar with the hardware, system software, application software, or database management system proposed for the project, it is highly likely that the project will experience technical problems or take more time to complete because of the need to master new skills.

Although the difficulty of the technology is one risk factor in information systems projects, the other factors are primarily organizational, dealing with the complexity of information requirements, the scope of the project, and how many parts of the organization will be affected by a new information system.

Change Management and the Concept of Implementation

The introduction or alteration of an information system has a powerful behavioral and organizational impact. Changes in the way that information is defined, accessed, and used to manage the organization's resources often lead to new distributions of authority and power. This internal organizational change breeds resistance and opposition and can lead to the demise of an otherwise good system.

A very large percentage of information systems projects stumble because the process of organizational change surrounding system building was not properly addressed. Successful system building requires careful **change management**.

The Concept of Implementation

To manage the organizational change surrounding the introduction of a new information system effectively, you must examine the process of implementation. **Implementation** refers to all organizational activities working toward the adoption, management, and routinization of an innovation, such as a new information system. In the implementation process, the systems analyst is a **change agent**. The analyst not only develops technical solutions but also redefines the configurations, interactions, job activities, and power relationships of various organizational groups. The analyst is the catalyst for the entire change process and is responsible for ensuring that all parties involved accept the changes created by a new system. The change agent communicates with users, mediates between competing interest groups, and ensures that the organizational adjustment to such changes is complete.

The Role of End Users

System implementation generally benefits from high levels of user involvement and management support. User participation in the design and operation of information systems has several positive results. First, if users are heavily involved in systems design, they have more opportunities to mold the system according to their priorities and business requirements, and more opportunities to control the outcome. Second, they are more likely to react positively to the completed system because they have been active participants in the change process. Incorporating user knowledge and expertise leads to better solutions.

The relationship between users and information systems specialists has traditionally been a problem area for information systems implementation efforts. Users and information systems specialists tend to have different backgrounds, interests, and priorities. This is referred to as the **user-designer communications gap**. These differences lead to divergent organizational loyalties, approaches to problem solving, and vocabularies.

Information systems specialists, for example, often have a highly technical, or machine, orientation to problem solving. They look for elegant and sophisticated technical solutions in which hardware and software efficiency is optimized at the expense of ease of use or organizational effectiveness. Users prefer systems that are oriented toward solving business problems or facilitating organizational tasks. Often the orientations of both groups are so at odds that they appear to speak in different tongues.

These differences are illustrated in Table 4.4, which depicts the typical concerns of end users and technical specialists (information systems designers) regarding the development of a new information system. Communication problems between end users and designers are a major reason why user requirements are not properly incorporated into information systems and why users are driven out of the implementation process.

Systems development projects run a very high risk of failure when there is a pronounced gap between users and technical specialists and when these groups continue to pursue different goals. Under such conditions, users are often driven away from the project. Because they cannot comprehend what the technicians are saying, users conclude that the entire project is best left in the hands of the information specialists alone.

Table 4.4 **The User-Designer Communications Gap**

User Concerns	Designer Concerns
Will the system deliver the information I need for my work?	How much disk storage space will the master file consume?
How quickly can I access the data?	How many lines of program code will it take to perform this function?
How easily can I retrieve the data?	How can we cut down on CPU time when we run the system?
How much clerical support will I need to enter data into the system?	What is the most efficient way of storing these data?
How will the operation of the system fit into my daily business schedule?	What database management system should we use?

Management Support and Commitment

If an information systems project has the backing and commitment of management at various levels, it is more likely to be perceived positively by both users and the technical information services staff. Both groups will believe that their participation in the development process will receive higher-level attention and priority. They will be recognized and rewarded for the time and effort they devote to implementation. Management backing also ensures that a systems project receives sufficient funding and resources to be successful. Furthermore, to be enforced effectively, all the changes in work habits and procedures and any organizational realignments associated with a new system depend on management backing. If a manager considers a new system a priority, the system will more likely be treated that way by his or her subordinates.

Change Management Challenges for Business Process Reengineering, Enterprise Applications, and Mergers and Acquisitions

Given the challenges of innovation and implementation, it is not surprising to find a very high failure rate among enterprise application and business process reengineering (BPR) projects, which typically require extensive organizational change and which may require replacing old technologies and legacy systems that are deeply rooted in many interrelated business processes. A number of studies have indicated that 70 percent of all business process reengineering projects fail to deliver promised benefits. Likewise, a high percentage of enterprise applications fail to be fully implemented or to meet the goals of their users even after three years of work.

Many enterprise application and reengineering projects have been undermined by poor implementation and change management practices that failed to address employees' concerns about change. Dealing with fear and anxiety throughout the organization; overcoming resistance by key managers; changing job functions, career paths, and recruitment practices; and training have posed greater threats to reengineering than the difficulties companies faced visualizing and designing breakthrough changes to business processes. All of the enterprise applications require tighter coordination among different functional groups as well as extensive business process change.

Projects related to mergers and acquisitions have a similar failure rate. Mergers and acquisitions are deeply affected by the organizational characteristics of the merging companies as well as by their IT infrastructures. Combining the information systems of two different companies usually requires considerable organizational change and complex systems projects to manage. If the integration is not properly managed, firms can emerge with a tangled hodgepodge of inherited legacy systems built by aggregating the systems of one firm after another. Without a successful systems integration, the benefits anticipated from the merger cannot be realized, or, worse, the merged entity cannot execute its business processes effectively.

Controlling Risk Factors

Various project management, requirements gathering, and planning methodologies have been developed for specific categories of implementation problems. Strategies have also been devised for ensuring that users play appropriate roles throughout the implementation period and for managing the organizational change process. Not all aspects of the implementation process can be easily controlled or planned. However, anticipating potential implementation problems and applying appropriate corrective strategies can increase the chances for system success.

The first step in managing project risk involves identifying the nature and level of risk confronting the project (Schmidt et al., 2001). Implementers can then handle each project with the tools and risk-management approaches geared to its level of risk (Iversen, Mathiassen, and Nielsen, 2004; Barki, Rivard, and Talbot, 2001; McFarlan, 1981).

Managing Technical Complexity

Projects with challenging and complex technology for users to master benefit from **internal integration tools**. The success of such projects depends on how well their technical complexity can be managed. Project leaders need both heavy technical and administrative experience. They must be able to anticipate problems and develop smooth working relationships among a predominantly technical team. The team should be under the leadership of a manager with a strong technical and project management background, and team members should be highly experienced. Team meetings should take place frequently. Essential technical skills or expertise not available internally should be secured from outside the organization.

Formal Planning and Control Tools

Large projects benefit from appropriate use of **formal planning tools** and **formal control tools** for documenting and monitoring project plans. The two most commonly used methods for documenting project plans are Gantt charts and PERT charts. A **Gantt chart** lists project activities and their corresponding start and completion dates. The Gantt chart visually represents the timing and duration of different tasks in a development project as well as their human resource requirements (see Figure 4.12). It shows each task as a horizontal bar whose length is proportional to the time required to complete it.

Although Gantt charts show when project activities begin and end, they don't depict task dependencies, how one task is affected if another is behind schedule, or how tasks should be ordered. That is where **PERT charts** are useful. PERT stands for Program Evaluation and Review Technique, a methodology developed by the U.S. Navy during the 1950s to manage the Polaris submarine missile program. A PERT chart graphically depicts project tasks and their interrelationships. The PERT chart lists the specific activities that make up a project and the activities that must be completed before a specific activity can start, as illustrated in Figure 4.13.

The PERT chart portrays a project as a network diagram consisting of numbered nodes (either circles or rectangles) representing project tasks. Each node is numbered and shows the task, its duration, the starting date, and the completion date. The direction of the arrows on the lines indicates the sequence of tasks and shows which activities must be completed before the commencement of another activity. In Figure 4.13, the tasks in nodes 2, 3, and 4 are not dependent on each other and can be undertaken simultaneously, but each is dependent on completion of the first task. PERT charts for complex projects can be difficult to interpret, and project managers often use both techniques.

These project management techniques can help managers identify bottlenecks and determine the impact that problems will have on project completion times. They can also help systems developers partition projects into smaller, more manageable segments with defined, measurable business results. Standard control techniques can successfully chart the progress of the project against budgets and target dates, so deviations from the plan can be spotted.

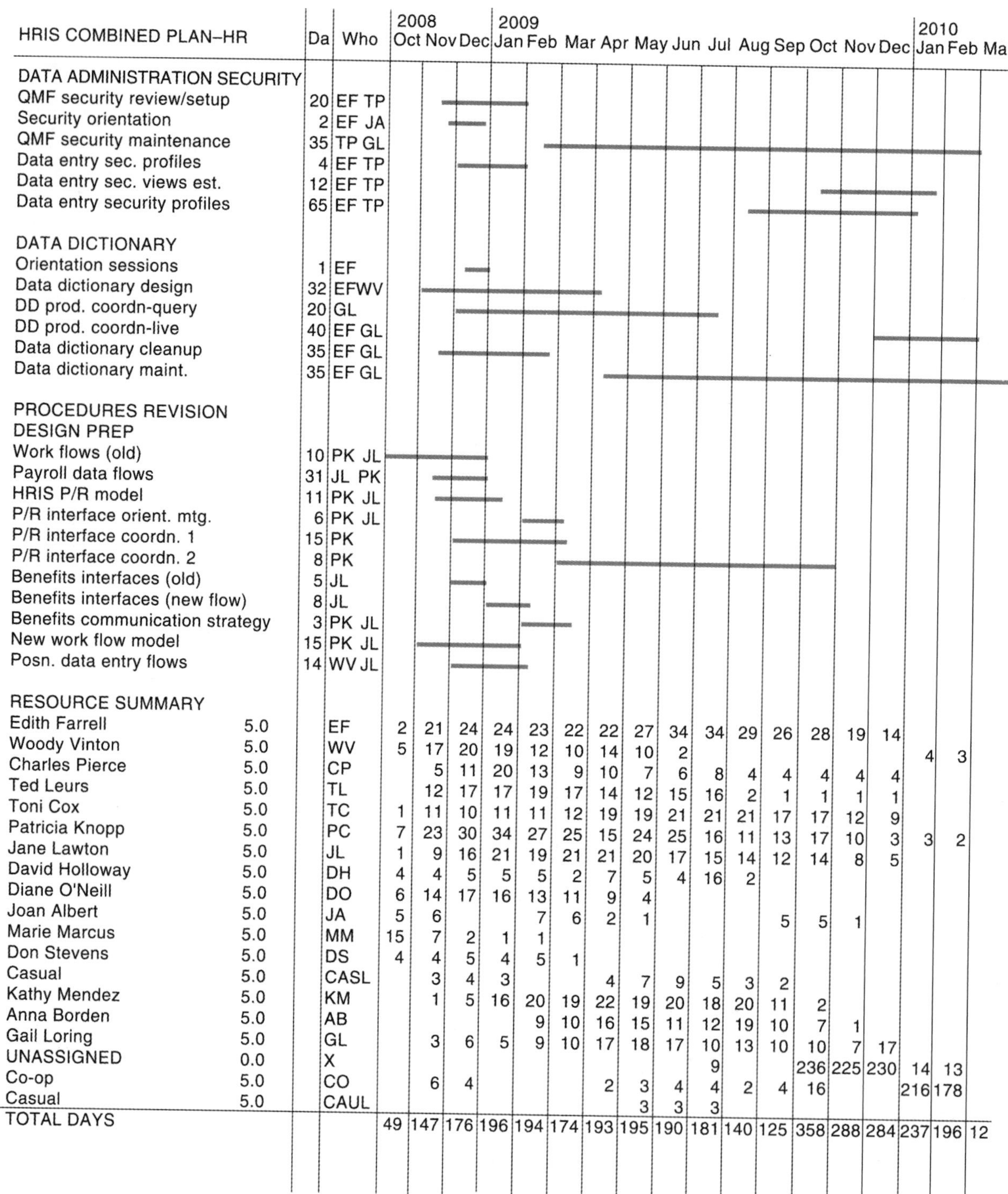

HRIS COMBINED PLAN–HR
Da Who
2008 Oct Nov Dec
2009 Jan Feb Mar Apr May Jun Jul Aug Sep Oct Nov Dec
2010 Jan Feb Mar
DATA ADMINISTRATION SECURITY
QMF security review/setup 20 EF TP
Security orientation 2 EF JA
QMF security maintenance 35 TP GL
Data entry sec. profiles 4 EF TP
Data entry sec. views est. 12 EF TP
Data entry security profiles 65 EF TP
DATA DICTIONARY
Orientation sessions 1 EF
Data dictionary design 32 EFWV
DD prod. coordn-query 20 GL
DD prod. coordn-live 40 EF GL
Data dictionary cleanup 35 EF GL
Data dictionary maint. 35 EF GL
PROCEDURES REVISION DESIGN PREP
Work flows (old) 10 PK JL
Payroll data flows 31 JL PK
HRIS P/R model 11 PK JL
P/R interface orient. mtg. 6 PK JL
P/R interface coordn. 1 15 PK
P/R interface coordn. 2 8 PK
Benefits interfaces (old) 5 JL
Benefits interfaces (new flow) 8 JL
Benefits communication strategy 3 PK JL
New work flow model 15 PK JL
Posn. data entry flows 14 WV JL
RESOURCE SUMMARY
Edith Farrell 5.0 EF 2 21 24 24 23 22 22 27 34 34 29 26 28 19 14
Woody Vinton 5.0 WV 5 17 20 19 12 10 14 10 2 4 3
Charles Pierce 5.0 CP 5 11 20 13 9 10 7 6 8 4 4 4 4 4
Ted Leurs 5.0 TL 12 17 17 19 17 14 12 15 16 2 1 1 1 1
Toni Cox 5.0 TC 1 11 10 11 11 12 19 19 21 21 21 17 17 12 9
Patricia Knopp 5.0 PC 7 23 30 34 27 25 15 24 25 16 11 13 17 10 3 3 2
Jane Lawton 5.0 JL 1 9 16 21 19 21 21 20 17 15 14 12 14 8 5
David Holloway 5.0 DH 4 4 5 5 5 2 7 5 4 16 2
Diane O'Neill 5.0 DO 6 14 17 16 13 11 9 4
Joan Albert 5.0 JA 5 6 7 6 2 1 5 5 1
Marie Marcus 5.0 MM 15 7 2 1 1
Don Stevens 5.0 DS 4 4 5 4 5 1
Casual 5.0 CASL 3 4 3 4 7 9 5 3 2
Kathy Mendez 5.0 KM 1 5 16 20 19 22 19 20 18 20 11 2
Anna Borden 5.0 AB 9 10 16 15 11 12 19 10 7 1
Gail Loring 5.0 GL 3 6 5 9 10 17 18 17 10 13 10 10 7 17
UNASSIGNED 0.0 X 9 236 225 230 14 13
Co-op 5.0 CO 6 4 2 3 4 4 2 4 16 216 178
Casual 5.0 CAUL 3 3 3
TOTAL DAYS 49 147 176 196 194 174 193 195 190 181 140 125 358 288 284 237 196 12

The Gantt chart in this figure shows the task, person-days, and initials of each responsible person, as well as the start and finish dates for each task. The resource summary provides a good manager with the total person-days for each month and for each person working on the project to manage the project successfully. The project described here is a data administration project.

Figure 4.12 **A Gantt chart**

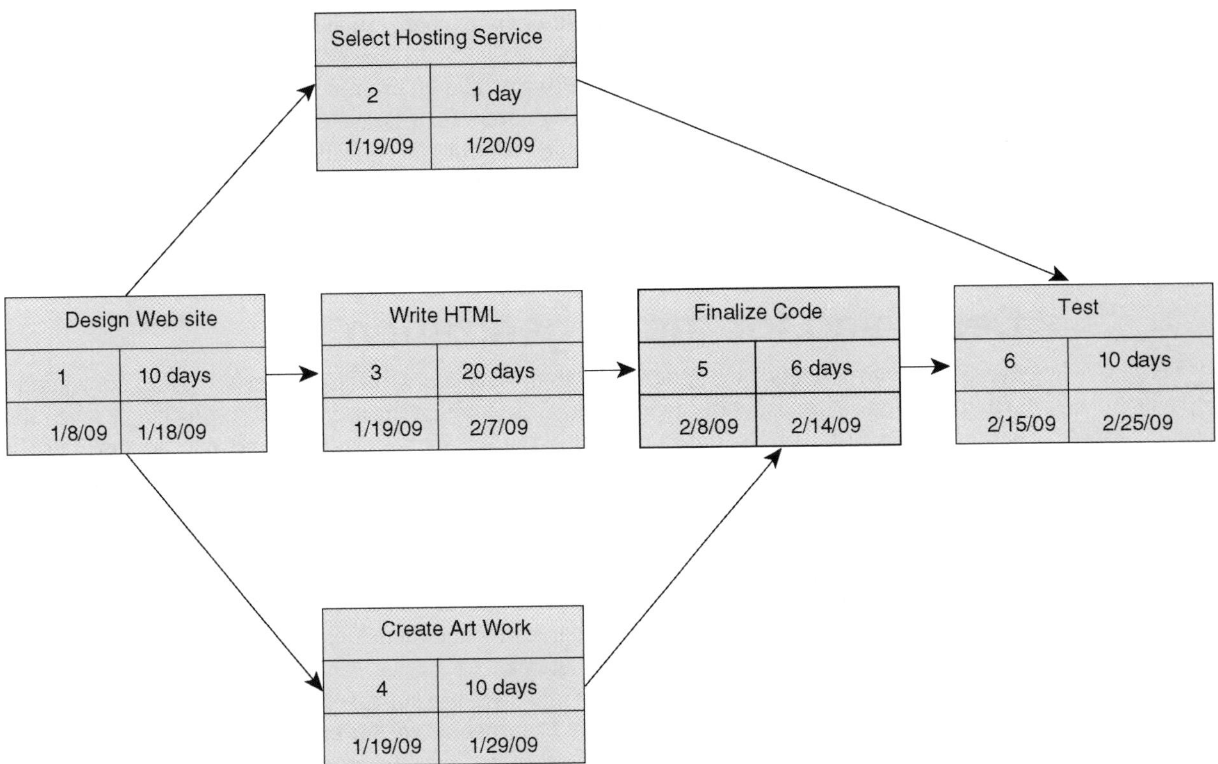

This is a simplified PERT chart for creating a small Web site. It shows the ordering of project tasks and the relationship of a task with preceding and succeeding tasks.

Figure 4.13 **A PERT chart**

Increasing User Involvement and Overcoming User Resistance

Projects with relatively little structure and many undefined requirements must involve users fully at all stages. Users must be mobilized to support one of many possible design options and to remain committed to a single design. **External integration tools** consist of ways to link the work of the implementation team to users at all organizational levels. For instance, users can become active members of the project team, take on leadership roles, and take charge of installation and training. The implementation team can demonstrate its responsiveness to users, promptly answering questions, incorporating user feedback, and showing their willingness to help (Gefen and Ridings, 2002).

Participation in implementation activities may not be enough to overcome the problem of user resistance to organizational change. Different users may be affected by the system in different ways. Whereas some users may welcome a new system because it brings changes they perceive as beneficial to them, others may resist these changes because they believe the shifts are detrimental to their interests.

If the use of a system is voluntary, users may choose to avoid it; if use is mandatory, resistance will take the form of increased error rates, disruptions, turnover, and even sabotage. Therefore, the implementation strategy must not only encourage user participation and involvement, but it must also address the issue of counterimplementation (Keen, 1981). **Counterimplementation** is a deliberate strategy to thwart the implementation of an information system or an innovation in an organization.

Strategies to overcome user resistance include user participation (to elicit commitment as well as to improve design), user education and training, management edicts and policies, and better incentives for users who cooperate. The new system can be made more user friendly by improving the end-user interface. Users will be more cooperative if organizational problems are solved prior to introducing the new system.

The Interactive Session on Organizations provides an example of a large-scale project where many of these issues are at work. The U.S. Centers for Disease Control and Prevention (CDC) have had trouble implementing a nationwide system to alert health care providers and agencies to potential health crises such as flu pandemics or bioterrorist attacks. As you read this case, try to identify the risks of this project and whether the appropriate strategies were used for dealing with these risks.

Designing for the Organization

Because the purpose of a new system is to improve the organization's performance, information systems projects must explicitly address the ways in which the organization will change when the new system is installed, including installation of intranets, extranets, and Web applications. In addition to procedural changes, transformations in job functions, organizational structure, power relationships, and the work environment should be carefully planned.

Areas where users interface with the system require special attention, with sensitivity to ergonomics issues. **Ergonomics** refers to the interaction of people and machines in the work environment. It considers the design of jobs, health issues, and the end-user interface of information systems. Table 4.5 lists the organizational dimensions that must be addressed when planning and implementing information systems.

Although systems analysis and design activities are supposed to include an organizational impact analysis, this area has traditionally been neglected. An **organizational impact analysis** explains how a proposed system will affect organizational structure, attitudes, decision making, and operations. To integrate information systems successfully with the organization, thorough and fully documented organizational impact assessments must be given more attention in the development effort.

Table 4.5 Organizational Factors in Systems Planning and Implementation

Organizational Factors in Systems Planning and Implementation
Employee participation and involvement
Job design
Standards and performance monitoring
Ergonomics (including equipment, user interfaces, and the work environment)
Employee grievance resolution procedures
Health and safety
Government regulatory compliance

INTERACTIVE SESSION: ORGANIZATIONS

WHY CAN'T BIOSENSE TAKE OFF?

If you turn on the television, read a newspaper, or surf the Web, you're bound to find many dire predictions about large-scale loss of life from biological or chemical attacks or an avian influenza pandemic. Computer models estimate that between 2 and 100 million people could die in the event of a flu pandemic.

On May 3, 2006, the United States government issued an Implementation Plan for its National Strategy for Pandemic Influenza to improve coordination among federal, state, and local authorities and the private sector for pandemics and other public health emergencies. The implementation plan called for improving mechanisms for "real-time" clinical surveillance of hospital emergency rooms, intensive care units, and laboratories to inform local, state, and federal public health officials about rapidly spreading illness.

The centerpiece of this plan is the BioSense Real-Time Clinical Connections Program developed by the U.S. CDC. BioSense sits atop a hospital's existing information systems, continually gathering and analyzing their data as they are generated. Custom software developed by CDC monitors the facility's network traffic and captures relevant patient records, diagnoses, and prescription information. The data include patient age, sex, ZIP code of residence, ZIP code of the medical facility handling the patient, the principal medical complaint, symptoms, onset of illness, diagnoses, medical procedures, medications prescribed, and laboratory results. The software converts these data to the HL7 data messaging format, which is the standard for the health care industry, encrypts the data, and transmits them every 15 minutes over the Web to the CDC where they are maintained in a large data repository.

The system summarizes and presents analytical results by source, day, and syndrome for each ZIP code, state, and metropolitan area using maps, graphs, and tables. Registered state and local public health agencies as well as hospitals and health care providers are allowed to access data that pertain to their jurisdiction using a Web-based application over a secure data network. Information from BioSense could show early signs of a pandemic or biologic attack and alert local hospitals, health workers, and federal and state agencies to take preventive measures.

The traditional process for public health surveillance is manual and much slower. Hospitals, physicians, and laboratories would mail or fax paper reports to public health agencies, who would then call health care providers for more detailed information. This slow chain of person-to-person communication is not well-suited to a major public health emergency.

BioSense first became operational in 2004, when it began gathering daily data from U.S. Defense Department and Veterans Affairs (VA) hospitals and Laboratory Corporation of America (LabCorp) orders for medical tests. (LabCorp operates a large nationwide network of testing locations and service centers and is one of the largest clinical lab service providers in the United States.) Approximately 700 Defense Department and 1110 VA facilities report data to BioSense. In late 2005, CDC started to expand the BioSense network to civilian hospitals in major metropolitan areas.

However, in 2006 and 2007 Biosence encountered significant resistance from hospital administrators and physicians around the country. As of May, 2008, only 563 hospitals and state health organizations were participating. To transmit data to BioSense, each hospital must standardize its patient and other medical data. Most hospitals use their own coding systems for symptoms, diseases, and medications. CDC's contractors would have to work with each hospital to translate its data codes into the standards used by CDC's software. This is a massive task, given hospitals' limited IT staffs and resources.

Some in the medical community question whether the BioSense network is worth the effort. According to Dr. John Rosenberg, director of the Infectious Disease Laboratory at the State of California's Department of Health Services in Richmond, California, if an epidemic broke out, "You'd know it before the data rolled in. When your emergency rooms fill up you make a phone call; this is probably a better measure."

Although participation in BioSense is voluntary, physicians and health officials might resent the system because it enables the federal government to encroach on what has traditionally been the domain of local health care providers and organizations. They note that they and not the CDC have the responsibility for responding to and managing a pandemic. Additionally, hospitals are reluctant to sign up because of concerns about maintaining privacy and security of patient information. BioSense would let the CDC "listen in" on their treatment of patients on a real-time basis. The CDC does not use any data that would identify individual patients.

After investing an estimated $100 million on hospital recruitment and technology for BioSense in 2005 and 2006, the CDC decided in 2007 to work with state and local public health care systems instead of competing with them. It will continue to use BioSense in its limited form while simultaneously pursuing information-sharing measures with state health departments. CDC will not require states to move their detailed data into a national repository but instead encourage them to link their databases with that of BioSense into some sort nationwide bio-surveillance system. The final design of the system is still unclear. CDC is piloting different strategies to determine the best approach. One effort, for example, focuses on building an alert system to notify state and regional public health care officials electronically about pandemic outbreaks instead of relying on e-mail or the telephone.

Sources: Doug Bartholomew and Chris Gonsalves, "CDC Issues Pandemic Systems Plan," *Baseline Magazine*, April 2008; Doug Bartholomew, "Second Opinions," *Baseline Magazine*, March 2006; and Wilson P. Dizard III, "CDC Weaving National Information Web," *Government Computer News*, April 3, 2006.

CASE STUDY QUESTIONS

1. Identify the risks in the BioSense project.
2. What management, organization, and technology factors explain why this project has been difficult to implement?
3. Is the CDC's new approach to improving pandemic warnings a viable solution? Why or why not?

MIS IN ACTION

Explore the BioSense Web site (www.cdc.gov/biosense/) and then answer the following question:

1. What information technologies do you see mentioned in the description of BioSense? Why would they be especially useful for this type of application?

Sociotechnical Design

One way of addressing human and organizational issues is to incorporate **sociotechnical design** practices into information systems projects. Designers set forth separate sets of technical and social design solutions. The social design plans explore different workgroup structures, allocation of tasks, and the design of individual jobs. The proposed technical solutions are compared with the proposed social solutions. The solution that best meets both social and technical objectives is selected for the final design. The resulting sociotechnical design is expected to produce an information system that blends technical efficiency with sensitivity to organizational and human needs, leading to higher job satisfaction and productivity.

Project Management Software Tools

Commercial software tools that automate many aspects of project management facilitate the project management process. Project management software typically features capabilities for defining and ordering tasks, assigning resources to tasks, establishing starting and ending dates to tasks, tracking progress, and facilitating modifications to tasks and resources. Many automate the creation of Gantt and PERT charts.

Some of these tools are large sophisticated programs for managing very large projects, dispersed work groups, and enterprise functions. These high-end tools can manage very large numbers of tasks and activities and complex relationships.

Microsoft Office Project 2007 has become the most widely used project management software today. It is PC-based, with capabilities for producing PERT and Gantt charts and for supporting critical path analysis, resource allocation, project tracking, and status reporting. Project also tracks the way changes in one aspect of a project affect others. Project Professional 2007 provides collaborative project management capabilities when used with Microsoft Office Project Server 2007. Project Server stores project data in a central SQL Server database, enabling authorized users to access and update the data over the Internet. Project Server 2007 is tightly integrated with the Microsoft Windows SharePoint Services collaborative workspace platform. These features help large enterprises manage projects in many different locations. Products such as EasyProjects.NET and Vertabase are also useful for firms that want Web-based project management tools.